St. Louis Community College

Forest Park
Florissant Valley
Meramec

Instructional Resources
St. Louis, Missouri

Fortune-tellers and Philosophers
Divination in Traditional Chinese Society

Fortune-tellers and Philosophers

Divination in Traditional Chinese Society

Richard J. Smith

Westview Press

BOULDER • SAN FRANCISCO • OXFORD

Published in 1991 in the United States of America by Westview Press, Inc., 5500 Central Avenue, Boulder, Colorado 80301, and in the United Kingdom by Westview Press, 36 Lonsdale Road, Summertown, Oxford OX2 7EW

Library of Congress Cataloging-in-Publication Data
Smith, Richard J. (Richard Joseph), 1944–
  Fortune-tellers and philosophers : divination in traditional
Chinese society / Richard J. Smith.
    p. cm.
  Includes bibliographical references and index.
  ISBN 0-8133-7753-6
  1. Divination—China—History. 2. Fortune-telling—China—
History. 3. Divination—Social aspects—China. 4. Fortune-
telling—Social aspects—China. 5. China—Social life and
customs—1644-1912. I. Title.
BF1773.2.C5S64   1991
133.3′0951—dc20   91-16100
                                                                            CIP

Printed and bound in the United States of America

    The paper used in this publication meets the requirements
       of the American National Standard for Permanence of Paper
       for Printed Library Materials Z39.48-1984.

10   9   8   7 . 6   5   4   3   2   1

Do you believe then that the sciences would ever have arisen and become great if there had not beforehand been magicians, alchemists, astrologers, and wizards, who thirsted and hungered after abscondite and forbidden powers?

—Friedrich Nietzsche, 1886

Contents

Dream Divination, 245

Figures

Preface

The *Oxford English Dictionary* (1989) defines divination as "the foretelling of future events or discovery of what is hidden or obscure by supernatural or magical means." The techniques, limited only by the human imagination, include casting lots, spinning coconuts, consulting sacred texts, reading almanacs, gazing into crystal balls, listening to shells, watching spiders, reflecting on dreams, charting the stars, interpreting entrails, and analyzing footprints in ashes. Fortune-telling has existed in all societies, past and present, but its different manifestations and social purposes naturally reflect distinctive cultural characteristics and preoccupations. My assumption is therefore that an analysis of divination—particularly in societies where it is widely practiced—will shed light not only on conceptions of cosmology and causality but also on values, logic, symbols, structures, and styles of discourse. It should also illumine questions of personal and political power, class and gender, social order and social conflict, orthodoxy and heterodoxy. The more pervasive the phenomenon of divination, the more revealing it will be as a window to culture.

My own interest is in what fortune-telling says about traditional China—the Qing dynasty (1644–1912) in particular. Surprisingly, very little scholarly attention has been devoted to this important subject. One reason is undoubtedly the attitude of Chinese intellectuals, who have long regarded most forms of divination as nothing more than popular "superstition" (*mixin*), unworthy of serious study. Another factor is more recent and less culture specific: the widespread belief that traditional practices such as fortune-telling are incompatible with the principles of modern science and therefore to be actively discouraged. This viewpoint can be found today in Chinese textbooks on both sides of the Taiwan Straits. A third problem is that those closest to the subject—professional fortune-tellers, amateur practitioners, and their clients—tend to be either unwilling or unable to bring sufficient detachment to the subject of divination; most true believers have difficulty seeing themselves clearly. As a result, much of the best work on Chinese divination has been done by Western-trained anthropologists who have mastered one or more Chinese dialects and have spent significant amounts of field time in Taiwan or Hong Kong. But even their pioneering research, although solid and stimulating, has seldom been historically grounded and is often limited to one or two major fortune-telling systems or techniques. To my knowledge there is as yet no comprehensive interdisciplinary study of Chinese divination in late imperial times.

This book attempts to fill the void. Although I do not believe in divination personally, I certainly take it seriously. As a historian of the Qing period I am concerned with questions of institutional and intellectual development, including the perennial problem of evaluating continuity and change. But I am also fascinated by the anthropological and psychological significance of Chinese divination. Like drama and ritual, with which it shows remarkable affinities, divination can often be "read" as a social performance as well as evaluated on the basis of its own written materials—whether esoteric manuals or simply worded oracles. Like the practice of medicine, it is both diagnostic and prescriptive and invites a wide range of reactions, from wholehearted acceptance to skepticism and outright denial. It is for some a game and for others an important, perhaps even vital, means of gaining psychological insights. In short, divination is a device for constructing social meaning. As history orders the past, and ritual the present, so divination orders the future. Naturally, it reflects different social perspectives, different ways of world-making.

I have tried in this book to approach Chinese fortune-telling from all of these viewpoints and to develop an interpretation that does justice to the diversity and sophistication of traditional Chinese society without sacrificing either analytical rigor or conceptual clarity. Although much more work remains to be done on the subject, a preliminary study of the sort that I have attempted seems long overdue.

Many scholars have assisted me in this interdisciplinary project. Carole Morgan—whom I have never met, but whose stimulating work in French helped spark my interest in divination—has read the entire manuscript and offered invaluable advice and encouragement. Wang Ming-hsiung, an amateur fortune-teller in Taibei, generously shared his thoughts on divination and traditional Chinese culture on many occasions and opened all kinds of opportunities for me to do my research in Taiwan. My longtime friend James Hayes did the same in Hong Kong. A great number of other friends and colleagues around the world have read various parts of the book, or papers related to it, and have kindly shared with me their comments and criticisms. Among them, the following deserve special mention (in alphabetical order): Chen Chuanchang, Lilly Chen, Kai-wing Chow, Benjamin Elman, John Fairbank, Judith Farquhar, Charlotte Furth, John Henderson, Huang Yi-long, David Jordan, Marc Kalinowski, David Keightley, Anne Klein, Li Jing, Kwang-Ching Liu, Michael Loewe, Allen Matusow, Joseph Needham, Vivien Ng, Jonathan Ocko, Daniel Overmyer, Donald Price, Joseph B. Smith, Kidder Smith, Jonathan Spence, Donald Sutton, Frederic Wakeman, Jr., and Mi Chu Wiens. I usually heeded their well-considered advice but not invariably. Naturally, then, I alone bear responsibility for any errors of fact or interpretation that remain.

I would like to thank the Pacific Cultural Foundation, the American Philosophical Society, and Rice University for generous financial support and thank the librarians and staff of several major research facilities—most especially the Beijing National Library, the Bibliotheque Nationale, the British Library, the Library of Congress, the Taibei Central Library, and the East Asiatic libraries of the University of California (Berkeley, Davis, and Los Angeles), the University of Chicago, Columbia University, Harvard University, the University of Hong Kong, the University of London (School of Oriental and African

Studies), Princeton University, and the University of Washington at Seattle—for their patient assistance in locating rare documents for me. Thanks also to Susan McEachern and Libby Barstow for their outstanding editorial efforts.

Finally, I take great pleasure in once again expressing the most profound appreciation to my wife, Lisa, and my son, Tyler, for their unfailing support, for their heroic understanding, and above all, for making me laugh. To them this book is affectionately dedicated.

Richard J. Smith

Introduction

The god's name is Huang Daxian. He is a minor figure in a vast Chinese pantheon, unworthy of even the briefest mention in most standard reference works, and virtually unknown outside of Hong Kong. But he is considered particularly efficacious by his local constituents, who flock daily and in large numbers to his temple in Kowloon, both to pay their respects and to ask for his advice and assistance. The temple is large and ornate, built in the Qing imperial style, with yellow-tiled roofing, brightly-colored upper panels of red, blue and gold, and conventional Chinese symbols of cosmic power and good fortune, including depictions of dragons, paired protective lions at the front entrance, and auspicious calligraphic inscriptions on its large red pillars. The temple also has two prominently displayed donation boxes, which indicate explicitly that blessings come to those who give.

Huang Daxian is ensconced in the dark recesses of the main building, but the action is all outside. Dozens of worshippers, most of them women, are kneeling in prayer, bowing, burning incense, and offering oranges, bananas and other gifts of food. Some of the offerings are presented on long tables in front of the major gateways known as *pailou;* others are brought directly to the central courtyard. The air is thick with fragrant smoke that rises from dark metal incense burners and wafts gently throughout the temple complex. Within the courtyard, and on the periphery opposite the main hall, a number of worshippers kneel next to small, tube-shaped bamboo containers about ten inches tall and seven inches around. These containers are supplied by the temple, and each holds a hundred individually-numbered bamboo sticks, called *qian.* After offering devotions to Huang Daxian, each supplicant asks for his help in solving a particular problem. The worshipper then shakes the bamboo container in a downward motion until a single stick falls away from the rest. He or she then removes it, and casts a pair of crescent-shaped bamboo or wooden blocks called *jiao* to see if the stick selected was the "correct" one. These *jiao* are rounded on one side and flat on the other. If both blocks land flat side down on the ground, the answer is no; if one flat side is up and the other down, the answer is yes; if both flat sides land facing upward, it means that the god is laughing—try again.

Eventually the process yields a "yes," and the temple provides a handy printed message corresponding to the number written on the bamboo stick.

This message consists of a simple, classical-style poem of four lines written in red ink on a small pink slip of paper. Each poem is identified with a famous culture hero of the past, such as the "creator" Pan Gu, who "opened up Heaven and Earth" (stick number 52), the philosopher Zhuang Zhou (Zhuangzi), who "dreamt he was a butterfly" (stick number 54), or the military strategist Zhuge Liang, who "planned the defeat of Cao Cao" (stick number 33). A booklet entitled *Huang Daxian lingqian* (The Spiritual Sticks of Huang Daxian) can also be purchased, which provides poetic texts for all one hundred possibilities. The main commentary of this booklet explains the symbolism and meaning of each poem, while shorter commentaries provide appropriate answers to general questions regarding wealth, illness, marriage, travel, and so forth. Individuals in need of further guidance can consult a stable of fortune-tellers located down a series of stone steps in a wood-frame structure adjacent to the temple complex.

Dozens of fortune-telling stalls line the dark passageway leading down the stairway. Many bear exotic names: Five Elements Hall (Wuxing tang); The Dragon Gate (Longmen); Green Spring Pavilion (Qingchun ge); Dark Mystery of the North (Beixuan); Sun-Moon Brightness (Riyue ming); The Retired Scholar of Emei Mountain (Emei jushi). Some stalls are bare except for a table, some chairs, and a few books. Others are much more elaborate, with portraits, testimonials and credentials, charts and illustrations, calligraphic scrolls, auspicious inscriptions, and religious icons in various combinations and arrangements. All fortune-tellers possess at least one version of the annual almanac, and the majority have at least a small collection of reference works such as the *Sanming tonghui* (Compendium of the Three Fates) and the *Fuzhou quanshu* (Complete Book of Charms and Spells). Most advertise their particular area or areas of specialization: the selection of auspicious days, palm-reading, geomancy, word analysis, divination by hexagrams, and so on. Most of the several dozen fortune-tellers are male, ranging in age from about thirty to eighty. Sometimes their clients are individuals; sometimes families; and sometimes groups of people. The mood of the clients ranges from frivolous to deadly earnest.

Consultation in each stall is a more or less public affair, accessible to individuals waiting their turn as well as curious passers-by who may speak the dialect of choice. Some fortune-tellers are active and energetic, with loud voices and rapid-fire delivery; others are more measured, and appear more pensive. They are all self-confident, and seldom at a loss for words. The dialogue between fortune-teller and client has a decidedly dramatic quality, regardless of whether it is animated or subdued, and the diviner's pronouncements are laced with homilies, historical allusions, and various esoteric terms drawn from an ancient and elaborate cosmology. The client asks the basic questions, but the fortune-teller defines the terms of discourse, treating the encounter like a medical diagnosis. For nearly all fortune-tellers, the most crucial variables are a client's "four pillars"—that is, the year, month, day and hour of that person's birth—but many other cosmological factors have to be taken into account for a complete reading. And even those diviners who are not specialists in physiognomy seem to devote inordinate attention to the facial expressions and body movements of their clients.

Quite naturally, the fortune-tellers find it necessary to discuss the background of their clients in order to establish credibility for their predictions, since the past, present and future are all considered parts of an interconnected web of significance to which they enjoy special access. Their statements come as self-confident assertions, usually intoned as if from social superiors to inferiors. Ge Tianmin, a septuagenarian specialist in palm-reading from Guangdong province, tells a middle-aged client: "The economic circumstances of your family were undistinguished; you therefore could not rely on your parents for financial protection. . . . Looking from your left ear to your right [for clues to your early life, I see that] you were seriously ill when you were eight to fourteen years old. . . . You had good fortune from twenty to twenty-five, and made considerable progress despite your lack of book-learning."

Such remarks—at times vague, at times more specific—lead naturally to similar comments about the present and future. "You are," Mr. Ge asserts to the same client, "by nature serious and reserved, unflappable, and objective." He goes on to break down the client's future into a number of discrete blocks of time, each several years in duration. He observes, for example: "From age fifty-one to fifty-three all will be well with you; but from fifty-four to fifty-five you will become sick, and a family member will die. . . . Your own lifespan will be more than eighty years, perhaps ninety." During the course of the discussion, Mr. Ge gives practical advice as well as general guidance: "During the two years from age forty-nine to fifty, don't act as a guarantee for anyone or lend them money, otherwise you will suffer financial loss."

Some fortune-tellers have elaborate birth charts, which they fill out and annotate according to information supplied by their clients. Men are designated *Qian* and women *Kun*—both terms derived from the two main hexagrams of the hallowed Chinese classic known as the *Yijing* (Classic of Changes). Each "horoscope" divides the client's life into ten-year segments, which fall under various influences described by esoteric symbolic terms such as the Courier Horse, Peach Blossom, and Great Literary Star. Clients are free to ask questions about particular features of the chart, and even to challenge assertions made about their backgrounds or personal characteristics; but in the end the fortune-teller always has the last word—the obvious prerogative of his experience and esoteric expertise. The Retired Scholar of the Enlightened Way condescendingly tells a client, "It is very difficult for you non-specialists [*waimen han;* lit., those outside the gate] to understand my methods of fate calculation."

Not far away, on a hillside in the New Territories, is the so-called Monkey Temple, a nondescript and relatively cramped religious complex without any external pretense whatsoever. Here, the action is all inside. A group of about twenty people, at least half of them men, have gathered to hear their fortunes told by the temple's principal deity, Li Daoming. Like Huang Daxian, Li is a relatively obscure god. He speaks through the medium of a youthful-looking man named Chen Xitai, who claims that he has been practicing "spirit-writing" for some forty years. After questions to Li Daoming have been reverently written down, the session begins with prayerful chanting by the petitioners, each of whom is tapped lightly on the head by Mr. Chen with a short horsehair brush as part of a preliminary ritual of purification. They all bow reverently and repeatedly toward a bright yellow octagonal kiosk in the ornately decorated main room of the temple—the spot where the spirit of Li Daoming will eventually descend. The roof of the kiosk is predominantly red, and each side displays one of the eight primary trigrams of the *Yijing* painted in gold. At the base of the kiosk, and also attached to the green eaves of the roof, are several round, black-and-white "diagrams of the Supreme Ultimate," which symbolize the creative cosmic forces of *yin* and *yang*. Inside, on a small flat table, rests a smooth and shiny Y-shaped branch—vaguely reminiscent of a water dowser's stick—about an inch and a half in diameter and cut to an arm's length or so.

Mr. Chen enters the kiosk together with his more elderly assistant. Each man grabs a prong of the stick and Chen, eyes closed, summons the spirit of Li Daoming. The stick suddenly begins to move wildly, writing words which Mr. Chen shouts in cadence to a third man sitting at a nearby yellow desk. This man, in turn, rapidly transcribes the words with a brush onto large pink sheets of paper. One by one, the god answers the questions posed to him. These questions have been written down on a standard form—also pink—with a place for the person's name and the day's date, together with a pre-printed preface asking the spirit of Li Daoming to elucidate the problem and provide guidance. The language is flowery and deferential: The petitioner, "steeped in bounty" and with a "sincere heart," "prayerfully seeks assistance" and is "eternally grateful" to Li Daoming for his "vast kindness."

The spirit's replies are often highly metaphorical and reflect a blend of Buddhist, Daoist and Confucian influences. Confucian morality looms especially large in the narratives: Li Daoming often refers to conventional Chinese culture-heros, and speaks of traditional values such as "filial piety" (*xiao*), "loyalty and right behavior" (*zhongyi*), and "womanly virtue" (*shude*). One woman is told that she has the character of Meng Guang, a famous Han dynasty figure known for her physical strength as well as her obedience and moderation as a wife. (The reference is not entirely flattering, the client feels, as Meng Guang was rather unattractive.) Li Daoming also dispenses concrete advice. One young woman is admonished to avoid rash action with the hoary maxim: "Think three times before acting." A middle-aged man is informed that he should change the last character of his given name to *mei* (plum blossom) in order to bring good fortune. A number of individuals receive charms to be displayed or burned, and some are advised to seek additional assistance from other deities. The frenetic session lasts about two hours, during which time Mr. Chen works virtually non-stop. At the end of the ritual, grateful participants give donations to the temple, and their names are dutifully recorded in a prominently-displayed red book.

Such scenes, drawn directly from the notes, recordings and photographs of my own field work, can be seen today in Chinese environments throughout the world—not only in Hong Kong, but also in Taiwan, overseas Chinese communities from Southeast Asia to Western Europe and the Americas, and even to a limited extent in the People's Republic of China, where divination and other so-called "feudal superstitions" have been officially discouraged and sometimes harshly suppressed for more than three decades. That modern science and modern politics have taken their inevitable toll on ancient beliefs and customs everywhere cannot be denied; yet as with much of the rest of traditional Chinese culture, divination methods have proven remarkably resistant to change. Most contemporary theories and practices date back hundreds and sometimes thousands of years, and concessions to modernity, although evident, have been minimal. It is difficult to know how widespread divination remains in various Chinese communities around the world, but in Hong Kong and Taiwan at least, it is still a deeply entrenched social phenomenon—despite the growing influence of modern Western culture.

Divination was even more powerful and pervasive in late imperial China— the Qing dynasty (1644–1912) in particular. One indication of its importance, at least as a category of cultural concern, is the massive Qing encyclopedia *Qinding gujin tushu jicheng* (Imperially Approved Complete Collection of Writings and Illustrations, Past and Present; 1726; hereafter *Tushu jicheng*), which devotes well over two thousand pages to fortune-tellers and mantic techniques. Another index is Yuan Shushan's monumental *Zhongguo lidai buren zhuan* (Biographies of Diviners in China by Period; 1948), which consists largely of excerpts from local Chinese gazetteers, official histories, and other such sources. Of the more than 3,000 biographical entries in Yuan's book, about a third are from the Qing period. Yuan, born in 1881 and himself a fortune-teller of some renown, was a rare specimen: a Chinese scholar who gave serious attention to divination as a social phenomenon, and who chronicled out of his own personal interest both the techniques and the lives of its major exponents.[1] Although some other Qing intellectuals wrote about fortune-telling, often critically or equivocally, most Chinese in traditional times simply took it for granted. As with weather forecasting in the present day, people generally acted on the advice of seers and almanacs without bothering to acknowledge the fact in their daily discourse.[2]

Western sojourners, on the other hand—from the Jesuits in the sixteenth, seventeenth and eighteenth centuries, to diplomats, Protestant missionaries and free-lance foreign employees of the Qing government in the nineteenth and early twentieth centuries—constantly commented on the prevalence of divination in China. The remarks of S.W. Williams, a long-time resident in the nineteenth century, are typical in tone and substance: "No people are more enslaved by fear of the unknown than the Chinese, and none resort more frequently to sortilege to ascertain whether an enterprise will be successful or a proposed remedy avail to a cure. This desire actuates all classes, and thousands and myriads of persons take advantage of it to their own profit." Similarly, Henrietta Shuck asserted that "There is probably no country in the present age of the world, in which divination is carried on to so great an extent as in China." William Milne observed in 1820 that "Astrology, divination, geomancy and necromancy every where prevail [in China];" and several decades later, A. P. Parker stated that fortune-telling in China was "universally believed in." At the end of the century, Arthur Smith remarked that "the number of Chinese who make a living out of . . . [divination] is past all estimation."[3]

But how accurate were such observations? Many Westerners, after all, had a deep-seated hostility to practices such as geomancy, which they viewed as an impediment to modern "progress." Could they possibly evaluate Chinese divination objectively? Missionaries, as attuned to "superstition" as to sin, might well have exaggerated the situation in China to justify their own "civilizing" enterprise. Yet where evidence exists from the Chinese side, whether in the form of official documents, letters, anecdotes, proverbs, popular fiction, or scholarly indictments of fortune-telling, it almost invariably confirms the accuracy of Western accounts. Taken together, Chinese and Western sources indicate that divination was an extraordinarily significant social phenomenon in Qing times and thereafter.

What does divination tell us about Chinese culture—its language, its logic, its cosmology, and its values? As indicated in the preface, the primary focus of this book is the Qing dynasty, a crucial bridge between "traditional" and "modern" China. My special interest is in the relationship between cultural unity and cultural diversity in late imperial China; that is, the degree of "fit" between the perceptions, values, attitudes and activities of different levels and sectors of Qing society. At first glance, the most striking feature of premodern China seems to be its cultural unity, especially when compared with other "peasant societies." James Watson writes, for example, "one need only read Eugen Weber's account of nineteenth century France to appreciate just how integrated Chinese society was during the late imperial era. . . . In China most villagers already identified themselves with an overarching 'Chinese culture,' an abstraction they had no difficulty understanding. The general peasantry did not need urban leaders to remind them that they shared a grand cultural tradition [as was necessary in the case of France]."[4] Other Western scholars have expressed similar views, echoing the chorus of Chinese authors, past and present, who have stressed the remarkable "unifying" and "absorptive" capacities of traditional Chinese civilization.[5]

The major reasons for China's cultural unity are comparatively well known. One factor was certainly the ideographic nature of the Chinese written script, which became standardized in the third century B.C. From that point onward, Chinese characters could be read by any literate person, regardless of how they might have been pronounced, thus providing extraordinary continuity across space as well as over time (some two thousand years). Despite the long-standing existence of several mutually unintelligible dialects in various parts of China, there was no development comparable to the decline of Latin and the rise of national vernaculars in Europe.

Among other factors that unified China was the civil service examination system, established in a rudimentary form during the second century B.C. and extended nationwide in the sixth and seventh centuries A.D. During the Ming and Qing dynasties, this system produced a highly literate, culturally homogenous social and bureaucratic elite—one that served as a conscious model to be emulated by all levels of Chinese society. Elite cultural influences proved to be especially strong in rural market areas where peasants gathered periodically to sell their produce, and because the examination system drew candidates from nearly every part of the empire and every major social class (including the peasantry) in late imperial times, it encouraged a relatively high degree of both geographical and social mobility.[6]

Furthermore, China's government leaders had long recognized the need for centrally-supervised political and social control mechanisms that transcended kinship ties and helped to overcome local loyalties—devices such as the frequent transfer of officials, the rule of avoidance (which prohibited officials from serving in their home areas), and various systems of mutual responsibility in matters such as tax collection and the maintenance of order. All the while, the imperial Chinese state, with its enormous authority and substantial coercive power, attempted to standardize conduct, regulate customs, maintain status distinctions, and promote ideological orthodoxy by means of carefully crafted systems of law, education, ritual, religion and propaganda. During the Qing period in particular, China's alien Manchu rulers—outnumbered perhaps 100-1 by the Han Chinese majority—saw the practical value in patronizing and enhancing inherited forms of political, social, and ideological control. As a result of their vigorous and self-conscious promotion of Ming dynasty institutions and culture, together with the dramatic growth of agriculture, industry, commerce and literacy during the sixteenth and early seventeenth centuries, the Qing dynasty witnessed the fullest development of traditional political, economic and social institutions up to that time, as well as the greatest degree of regional integration within China Proper.[7]

Yet cultural integration in the Qing period was far from complete. As the largest consolidated empire in Chinese history, Qing dynasty China remained a sprawling patchwork of more or less discrete physiographic regions of varying sizes—all with different landforms, soils, climates, natural resources, marketing systems, communication networks, population densities, local dialects, non-Chinese ethnic minorities, and so forth. Feelings of local affinity ran deep, and regional peculiarities were expressed in the common saying: "Customs differ every ten *li*" [i.e. several miles] (*shili butong feng*). Qing propaganda efforts, such as the Yongzheng emperor's *Shengyu guangxun* (Amplified Instructions on the Sacred Edict)—first promulgated in 1724 and designed to be read aloud to commoners by local officials or scholars throughout the empire on the first and fifteenth days of each month—openly acknowledged China's regional variety. One version states, for example: "In some places people are kindly, in others, reserved; in some places they are extravagant and pompous, in others, frugal and simple. Because the customs of each place differed, the ancient sages created ceremonial practices [*li*] to standardize conduct."[8]

Regional stereotypes, which were deeply rooted in the consciousness of all Chinese, remained remarkably consistent throughout the Ming and Qing dynasties, and many persist to this day. Some focused on fundamental differences between the North and South; others were based on a few large geographical areas defined primarily by prominent river drainage systems; and still others had a provincial foundation. Thus, for instance, the people of north China were generally considered stronger, more diligent, honest, and conservative than their southern counterparts; the people of Yue (part of the Xi River drainage system in the far south of China) were described as "the most susceptible to a belief in ghosts and spirits" (*zui xin guishen*); and the Kangxi emperor reflected widely prevailing attitudes in describing the people of Jiangsu province as "prosperous but immoral."[9] Not only did such stereotypes affect the way people from one area perceived (and treated) people from another; they also affected the self-image of residents within each particular subculture. Moreover, because Chinese localism was so powerful and ubiquitous a force, sojourners and even long-time residents in urban centers continued to identify strongly with their "home" areas—hence the popularity of native-place guild halls (*huiguan*) and other associations based on common geographical origins. Natives, for their part, categorized "outsiders" hierarchically according to different gradations of "Chineseness."[10]

As might be expected, urban and rural dwellers in China had different viewpoints and lifestyles; but the cultural gap between them was perhaps not as great as in many other "peasant" societies because only about twenty-five percent of the traditional elite in Qing times had permanent urban residences, and many of them played an active role in rural affairs within the structure of the so-called standard marketing system. Nonetheless, Robert Redfield's famous distinction between the "great tradition" of literate urban elites and the "little tradition" of essentially non-literate peasants has been highly influential as a conceptual paradigm, especially for studies of Chinese religion. Arthur Wolf, for example, contends that "There has always been a vast gulf between the religion of the [Chinese] elite and that of the peasantry."[11]

Of course many scholars maintain that this dichotomy is too stark, that it does not do justice to "complex historical and spatial patterns of cultural interaction." Majorie Topley, for one, emphasizes the way "the scholar's tradition acted on that of the ordinary man . . . [and] the latter's tradition reflected back on him." In the same spirit, Maurice Freedman castigates those who distinguish too sharply between elite "rationality" and peasant "superstition." G. William Skinner's pioneering research on marketing communities shows that China has always been a multi-tiered society, not simply a two-leveled one; that instead of a single "little tradition" there were in fact many "little traditions." And Wolf himself argues that the most significant point to be made about Chinese religion is that "it mirrors the social landscape of its adherents. There are as many meanings as there are vantage points."[12]

David Johnson, co-editor of *Popular Culture in Late Imperial China* (1985), identifies at least nine different vantage points. In an effort to do justice to the complexity of traditional Chinese society, and to illustrate the ways in which consciousness is influenced by "relations of dominance and subordination," Johnson proposes a model of late imperial China based on three crucial variables: education, legal privilege, and economic position (either self-sufficiency or dependence). In his conceptual framework, the Chinese social spectrum ranges from the classically-educated, legally privileged, and economically self-sufficient elite (the most dominant group) to illiterate and dependent commoners (the least influential). Intermediate groups reflect different combinations of these three variables—for instance, self-sufficient and literate but neither legally privileged nor classically educated; legally privileged and self-sufficient but not literate.[13]

The virtue of this scheme is that it provides a way to identify with greater precision the relationship between any given social or political strategy and any given system of thought—whether conveyed through symbols and myths, religious visions, or other products of the human "verbal imagination"—and China's hierarchy of dominance. At the same time, it alerts us to the various ways ideas and strategies may have moved from one social group to another—a process which Johnson hypothesizes "must almost always have involved the mediation of some of the groups lying in between." On the other hand, Johnson's model is not particularly helpful in identifying differences in outlook and activity within any one of the nine groupings. After all, dominance in traditional China involved more than literacy, legal protection, and economic well-being. An elite woman could enjoy all three of these advantages and still be subordinated, not to say oppressed. What about the problem of gender?

The many ways in which women suffered at the hands of men (and other women) in late imperial China need not be recounted at length here. We know that their subordinate status was reflected in law and social customs, elite and popular literature, proverbs, handbooks on household ritual, and even medical texts. Yet despite these forms of prejudice and discrimination, there were ways for women to establish a positive identity and to protect their interests in a male-dominated world. One was to cultivate what Margery Wolf has described as a "uterine family"—that is, a personal, non-institutionalized domestic system built upon the emotional bonds established between mother and child within the larger patriarchal, patronymic and patrilinear kinship structure. Another was to use religion as a means for protecting themselves and their families. Thus, just as among Chinese males there were class differences between elite and popular conceptions of religion, so gender distinctions in China produced differing attitudes toward religion within any given social stratum—and probably for many of the same social and psychological reasons.[14]

We may now leave the theme of diversity. Taken to extremes, this kind of sociological "deconstruction"—like its counterpart in literary criticism—leads to the discomfitting conclusion that ultimately there can be no cultural meaning beyond individual experience and idiosyncratic interpretation. This will not do, for the term "culture" itself implies *shared* meaning, and I hold as an article of interpretive faith the assumption that cultural meanings can in fact be derived from a careful "reading" of various forms of social discourse and symbolic action, whether expressed in written texts, simple conversation, art, architecture, music, the production and exchange of artifacts and commodities, rituals, dramas and performances, or predictive activities such as science, economic speculation, medicine, and divination. The question then becomes, how do we measure the degree of shared discourse in traditional Chinese culture?

Divination provides us with a valuable tool. Although its particular manifestations and social significance may have varied from time to time, place to place, and group to group, divination touched every sector of Chinese society, from emperor to peasant. Everyone in China believed that certain cosmological factors affected human destiny, and all used a similar symbolic vocabulary to express these cosmic variables. Although the notion of "fate" may have been differently conceived, and despite the fact that certain cosmological symbols could be interpreted in different ways, there nonetheless existed a shared "grammar" in the discourse of divination, a common ground of cultural understanding. In other words, fortune-telling, like religion and culture itself, was capable of generating an infinite number of statements, but it was nonetheless constrained by its own internal "logic." Furthermore, like magic, divination had the potential of empowering everyone in Chinese society—a notion particularly appealing to the traditionally disadvantaged. Knowledge of the future could be in some respects more efficacious than conventional knowledge, at least if one could do something about it.

Among the questions I have attempted to address in this book are: What were the primary forms of divination in late imperial China, and what sorts of cosmologies and other conceptual systems did they reflect? How does the vocabulary of divination shed light on the way the Chinese organized their experience and interpreted "reality"? Did divining techniques differ over time and space, and if so, why and in what particular ways? How was fortune-telling viewed by the various sectors of traditional Chinese society in the Qing period? What social and cultural factors affected the popularity of divination? Who were its main practitioners? What were their backgrounds and where were they located? What special knowledge did they possess, how did they acquire it, and how did they use it? What social or political power did they enjoy? Who were the clients of diviners? What in particular did they want to know? How were the messages of divination conveyed? What rituals, symbols, and modes of discourse were employed, what specific values were expressed, and how did various fortune-telling techniques relate to one another? What did people do with the knowledge they acquired through divination? How, in other words, did they try to deal with the future, and how did the imperial Chinese state and society at large react to their activities? Finally, what is the place of traditional-style divination in modern China?

I have used a wide variety of primary sources in an effort to answer these questions. Among the most valuable, in addition to Yuan Shushan's indispensable collection of diviner biographies, have been: (1) Compendia such as the *Tushu jicheng*; (2) the imperially-sponsored review of literature entitled *Siku quanshu zongmu* (Annotated Catalogue of the Complete Collection of the Four Treasuries; 1782); (3) a number of comprehensive and widely-read collections of essays by Qing authors, including the *Huangchao jingshi wenbian* (Qing Dynasty Writings on Statecraft; 1826) and its several supplements; and (4) informal accounts of Chinese life contained in compilations such as the *Qingbai leichao* (Classified Anecdotes from the Qing Period; 1916). I have also drawn on the Qing dynasty's *Shilu* (Veritable Records, organized by reign), various official and unofficial histories, local gazetteers, legal documents, official memorials, diaries and other private writings, state calendars and popular almanacs, diviners manuals, ritual handbooks, medical tracts, collections of proverbs, and vernacular literature, including novels, short stories and plays. And, as indicated above, I have supplemented these and other written materials—including a vast secondary literature in Chinese, Japanese, and Western languages—with my own fieldwork based on a number of extended visits to Hong Kong, Taiwan, and the People's Republic of China.

ONE

Viewing the Flowers from Horseback

From neolithic times into the twentieth century, divination occupied a prominent place in Chinese culture, embedded in ritual, enshrined in myth and solidly entrenched in social and political life. Among the legendary achievements of China's earliest culture hero, Fu Xi, was the invention of the famous three-line symbols known as trigrams, which were devised, we are told, to aid in prognostication, to promote invention, and to facilitate communication and classification. According to one well-known version of the myth:

> When Fu Xi ruled the world in early antiquity, he looked up and contemplated the images [xiang] in Heaven, and looked downward to contemplate the patterns [fa] on Earth. He contemplated the markings of birds and beasts and their adaptations to the various areas. He proceeded directly from himself and indirectly from objects. Thus he invented the eight trigrams in order to enter into communication with the virtuous power of the spiritual intelligence [shenming] and to classify the conditions of all things.[1]

Other myths credit either Fu Xi, his successor, Shen Nong, or the fully historical King Wen with developing a system of sixty-four hexagrams based on the eight trigrams. These hexagrams, like the trigrams, were used to classify and explain phenomena as well as to promote inventiveness and to serve as oracular symbols.[2]

The Fu Xi myth suggests several distinctive features of Chinese divination that persisted for at least three thousand years. The first is that the practice had a distinguished pedigree and enjoyed abundant classical sanction. The second is that the symbols used in divining—whether abstract, naturalistic or numerical—were assumed to represent the heavenly images and earthly patterns that reflected, in turn, a unified and harmonious cosmic order. Man, the ancient Chinese assumed, was not only an integral part of this order, but in fact a microcosm of it, although the Fu Xi myth makes this central point only indirectly. A third distinctive feature of traditional Chinese divination is the belief that the cosmos contained an active spiritual presence or intelligence (shen or shenming) that could assist human beings in discerning patterns of change and in elucidating meaning. The exact nature of the spirit world was, however, a matter of much debate (see also chapters 2, 3, and 6).[3]

So was the question of whether fate was fixed or mutable. Throughout Chinese history we can see a profound ambivalence regarding human destiny. On the one hand, nearly every Chinese believed that certain aspects of life were fixed at birth, and that certain times and situations were either auspicious or inauspicious. On the other hand, most Chinese, and virtually all representatives of the scholarly elite, maintained for at least two millennia that a person could not only "know fate" (*zhiming*) but also "establish fate" (*liming*); that through self-cultivation and self-assertion an individual could help shape the course of destiny.[4] Yet the question remained: What was predestined and what was subject to human control? No one knew for sure, and nearly everyone tried to find out, if only in the process of "resolving doubts" (*jueyi*).[5]

This chapter traces the general development of Chinese divining practices and cosmological assumptions from early antiquity to the seventeenth century A.D., with emphasis on a few individuals whose contributions were acknowledged by later practitioners as particularly significant. The striking feature of these practices and assumptions, most of which will be discussed in greater detail in subsequent chapters, is their tenacity over time. Virtually all major systems of divination, including the earliest techniques on record, continued into the Qing dynasty, and most persist to this day. This overview is necessarily brief and highly selective—no more, as the Chinese might say, than "a glance at the flowers from horseback" (*zouma kanhua*). But it may, at least, highlight a few themes of importance to an understanding of divination in the Qing period.[6]

Divination in Ancient China

By the third millennium B.C. at the latest, specialists in reading stress cracks in the bones of deer, sheep, pigs, and cattle had already emerged as a distinct occupational group in north China's neolithic cultures. During the Shang dynasty (c. 1500–c. 1100 B.C.), the use of oracle bones reached a high degree of sophistication, since this form of divination became the principal means by which the Shang kings were able to establish communication, through the medium of their ancestors, with their supreme deity, Shangdi ("God on High"). By applying intense heat to the dried plastrons of turtles and to the scapulae of cattle—a technique sometimes known as pyromancy—the Shang kings and their priestly diviners were able to produce cracks in the bone, which yielded answers to questions both trivial and weighty. Such "questions," which modern Chinese scholars describe as "charges" (*mingci*), were normally phrased as declarations.

David Keightley provides a vivid reconstruction of the process as it might have appeared when King Wu Ding of the Shang (c. 1200 B.C.) suffered a toothache:

Five turtle shells lie on the rammed-earth altar. The plastrons have been polished like jade, but are scarred on their inner side with rows of oval hollows, some already blackened by fire. Into one of the unburned hollows, on the right side of the shell, the diviner Chui is thrusting a brand of flaming thorn. As he does so, he cries aloud, "The sick tooth is not due to Father Jia [Wu Ding's uncle, a former king]!" Fanned by an assistant to keep the glowing tip intensely hot, the stick flames against the surface of the shell. Smoke rises. The seconds slowly pass. The stench of scorched bone mingles with the aroma of millet wine scattered in libation. And then, with a sharp, clear, *puk*like sound, the turtle, most silent of creatures, speaks. A . . . crack has formed in the hollow where the plastron was scorched. Once again the brand is thrust, now into a matching hollow on the left side of the shell: "It is due to Father Jia!" More time passes . . . [and] another crack forms in response.

The process is repeated for each of the five turtle shells. The diviners consult, and after several more divinations they reach a verdict. A blood sacrifice is made, after which scribes carve into the shells a record of the charges proposed and the results obtained (see Fig. 1.1).[7]

Shang divination bore on a wide range of topics, from the stars, weather, agriculture, hunting, construction, warfare and travel, to administrative problems and sacrifices, personal health, dreams, childbearing, and so forth. In the eyes of some Chinese scholars, this use of oracle bones was nothing more than base "superstition"—evidence that the Shang people did not dare make up their own minds, even about trivial matters. But Shang pyromancy was anything but trivial. In fact, it expressed "the very ethos and world view of the Shang elite," albeit incompletely.[8] Furthermore, since the Shang dynasty serves as a baseline for our understanding of China's subsequent historical development, its early artifacts—particularly oracle bones and bronzes—assume added importance. For instance, the physical and conceptual symmetry of Shang art and divinatory inscriptions suggests the beginnings of a *yinyang* metaphysics in China, just as their symbolism and vocabulary indicate enduring Chinese cultural attitudes—not least the power of nature and a strong preference for male children (referred to as "good," *jia*) over females (*bujia*, "not good").[9]

Shang oracle bones and bronze inscriptions also reveal patterns of conceptualization and categorization that lasted for several millennia in China. They document, for example, the early use of sexegenary cyclical characters ("stems" and "branches;" *ganzhi*) for marking time—a practice that continued in all subsequent dynasties and can still be seen today in traditional Chinese almanacs.[10] They also demonstrate an interest in astronomical observation, at least for astrological purposes.[11] A number of Shang rituals, spiritual agencies, and terrestrial organizations were categorized according to groupings of five, indicating a possible affinity with later pentadic correlations in China; and there is growing evidence to support the view that the Shang Chinese developed a numerical system capable of producing linear hexagrams even prior to the invention of trigrams. This numerical system seems also to have been related to the practice of divination by milfoil stalks, also know as yarrow sticks (*shi*; see below).[12]

During the Shang period, all political questions (and most matters relating to the personal affairs of the king) were by definition religious questions, since the realms of secular and sacred were not at all distinct. The Shang rulers were, we must remember, theocrats, whose legitimacy rested upon their ability to communicate with Shangdi through the medium of their own ancestors. The Shang religious world was fundamentally hierarchical and increasingly

Figure 1.1 Late Qing representation of turtle shell and
milfoil divination for the sage emperor Shun and his
minister Yu. *Source:* Joseph Needham et al., *Science and
Civilisation in China* (Cambridge, England, Cambridge
University Press, 1969), 2: 348. Reprinted by permission.

bureaucratic, a reflection of the existing terrestrial political and social order.
The Shang kings worshipped a host of naturalistic deities in addition to the
spirits of their departed ancestors, and offered both human and animal sacrifices
on appropriate ritual occasions. Over time these ritual occasions grew ever
more numerous and more highly regularized. According to some authorities,
Shang religious practice also involved some sort of spirit possession by shamans
(*wu*), but the exact nature of early Chinese shamanism remains a matter of
considerable debate. Later on, shamans came to play a significant role in Chinese
medicine and popular religion as well as divination.[13]

Whatever the place of shamans at court and in society at large, pyromancy
was by far a more important feature of Shang religious life. It was not, however,

simply a means by which the kings sought to find out about the future. It also became a device for manipulating both gods and men. David Nivison argues, for example, that the "questions" inscribed on oracle bones were phrased as statements because the diviner may well have been doing more than simply seeking information about the past, present or future. He may also have been trying to attract spiritual attention to a sacrificial ritual that was being undertaken concurrently with the "divination;" or validating a policy that had already been decided upon; or ritually "guaranteeing" a desired outcome for the future; or seeking a favorable response to an entreaty to a spirit.[14] These and like purposes can be seen in the divination practices of many cultures worldwide.[15]

Early Shang oracle bone inscriptions indicate an interest in dream interpretation that persisted throughout Chinese history. Shang diviners sought to determine not only the symbolic significance of the king's dreams but also their cause. Often the ruler's dreams were ascribed to the spirits of deceased ancestors who demanded sacrificial offerings. King Wu Ding is especially well known for dreaming about his family members, consorts, and courtiers, and wondering whether their oneric appearance portended disaster. Dream interpretation can also be found in a number of anecdotes about early Chinese culture heros, including not only Tang, the founder of the Shang dynasty, but also his illustrious mythical predecessors such as the Yellow Emperor, Yao, Shun, and Yu.[16] The *Huangdi changliu zhanmeng* (Long Willow Dream Prognostication Book of the Yellow Emperor)—listed in the section on literature in the *Hanshu* (History of the Former Han)—is only one early example of the many Chinese dreamworks that circulated throughout the imperial era and into the twentieth century.[17]

Shang divination did not, of course, remain static during the seven centuries of Shang rule. Although neither bronzes nor oracle bones provide us with enough information to generalize about specific methods of pyromantic interpretation, we can identify certain basic changes in subject matter. During the early Shang, for instance, oracle bone inscriptions relating to dreams, ancestral curses, sacrifices to non-ancestral powers of nature, sickness, and so on were common. By the end of the dynasty, however, such inscriptions were either rare or absent altogether. Late Shang divinations focused instead on a fixed sacrificial schedule and ritualized affairs such as the hunt (*tian*; lit. "[taking] the field"). Furthermore, whereas the earliest prognostications (*zhanci*) were often elaborate and could be either auspicious or inauspicious, by the end of the Shang period such prognostications tended to be brief, formalized, and invariably auspicious. Similarly, verifications (*yanci*), that is, records of what actually happened after a prognostication had been made, were often detailed in the early Shang and far more terse by the end of the dynasty.[18] This and other evidence suggests that in the twilight of Shang rule pyromancy lost much of its mystique, and became more accessible to non-royalty.[19] Meanwhile, other forms of divination, including the use of milfoil stalks to divine, seem to have gained in popularity.[20]

Shang theocratic rule eventually surrendered to a more secular feudalism in the Zhou dynasty (c. 1100–256 B.C.). But divination along Shang lines continued to be practiced by the conquerors, who apparently employed Shang-style oracle bones even prior to the conquest.[21] New archaeological evidence now confirms traditional accounts of the divination(s) performed by (or on behalf of) King Wu that encouraged him to launch his eventually successful attack on the Shang.[22] The Zhou kings, like their Shang dynasty predecessors, worshipped a supreme deity—generally known as Tian or "Heaven" rather than Shangdi—and employed professional diviners, who, according to the *Zhouli* (Rites of Zhou), assumed bureaucratic titles such as Grand Diviner (*dabu*), Diviner (*zhanren* or *bujen*) and Interpreter of Dreams (*zhanmeng*)—all official positions within the Ministry of Rites (Chunguan). There were also officials responsible for astrological and calendrical calculations, and even a court exorcist.[23] In addition, we know from the *Zuozhuan* (Commentary of Zuo) that the Zhou rulers, in administering at least some of their fiefs, apportioned not only land, priests, superintendents of ancestral temples, historians and officials, but also diviners, who assumed important local roles.[24]

As is well known, the Zhou justified its conquest of the Shang by reference to the so-called Mandate of Heaven (*Tianming*). This explicitly moral concept gave Heaven responsibility for determining if earthly government was benevolent and just. If so, there would be harmony in nature and peace on earth; if not, then Heaven's displeasure would be expressed through anomolies, and natural disasters. Rebellions would arise, and the existing government's mandate would be withdrawn. Oppressed people, it came to be believed, had the right to rebel, and heavenly signs pointed the way. For this reason, the Zhou state, and all subsequent Chinese regimes, made every effort to divine Heaven's will with the milfoil and turtle shell, to predict the movements of the sun, moon, stars and planets, and to interpret portents correctly. Chinese astrology, astronomy, divination and calendrical science coalesced into a single administratively-grounded science.[25]

Classical sources such as the *Shijing* (Classic of Poetry), the *Shujing* (Classic of History), the *Chunqiu* (Spring and Autumn Annals), the *Zuozhuan* (Commentary of Zuo), the *Liji* (Record of Ritual), and the *Zhouli*, together with recently excavated inscribed bronzes and writings on both silk and bamboo, attest to the importance of divination in China throughout the Zhou period. During the early Zhou, as had been the case in Shang times, divination remained primarily a royal prerogative. By the Spring and Autumn era (722–481 B.C.), however, it had become more diversified and widespread, practiced by private individuals as well as the court, women as well as men. Among the most famous and long-remembered exponents of divination in the Spring and Autumn era were Bei Zao, Guo Yan (also known as Bu Yan), Shi Su and Shi Kuang, the latter a specialist in the interpretation of sounds.[26]

Classical accounts of divination reveal not only the many occasions of their use, but also the various ways that oracles could be used to gain or consolidate political support. One instance is the Duke of Zhou's "Grand Announcement" of the *Shujing*, in which he informs his allies and subordinates that repeated divinations by the turtle shell indicate a punitive expedition he has been planning will be successful. He remarks: "I tell you, the princes of my friendly

states, and you, the directors of departments, my officers, and the managers of my affairs, that I have obtained an auspicious reply to my divinations. I will now go forward . . . and punish the vagabond ministers of Yin."[27] Here, divination may have performed the psychological function of helping the Duke of Zhou to resolve his own personal doubts, but it also had an unmistakable political purpose: to convince his allies of the correctness of his course of action.

The *Shijing* reveals a more intimate side to royal divination. In one poem, for example, the king asks his chief diviner to interpret the meaning of dreams involving bears and snakes. The bears, he discovers, are "auspicious intimations of sons," and the snakes, "auspicious intimations of daughters."[28] Another poem in the same collection refers to the use of divination by non-royalty. In it, the wife of a Zhou military officer awaits the return of her husband, noting:

The time [for his return] is past, and he is not here;
My sorrows are multiplied.
[But] I have divined with both the turtle shell and the milfoil,
And they unite in saying he is near;
My soldier is at hand.[29]

Milfoil divination, traditionally believed to have been invented by Wu Xian in the Shang period, involved the manipulation of milfoil stalks (and perhaps bamboo) rather than reading cracks. Although both pyromancy and milfoil divination could yield either the equivalent of yes/no answers or more complicated numerical sets, suitable for producing hexagrams, the milfoil proved to be far more convenient. We cannot be certain how the stalks were manipulated during the Shang and early Zhou periods, but late Zhou sources and works written in subsequent dynasties—notably the "Treatise on Turtle and Milfoil Divination" of the early Han—suggest several possibilities.[30] By the second century B.C., and probably earlier, this process had become more or less standardized. It involved the random division of 49 milfoil stalks into two groups, and then the reduction of each group by the successive removal of four stalks at a time until only four stalks or less remained. These stalks were then assigned a numerical value that determined the structure and nature of a line (*yao*): solid (____) or broken (__ __), firm or yielding, in movement or at rest. By repeating this process several times a full hexagram could be created.[31]

The most common use of the milfoil during the late Zhou period, and indeed throughout the entire imperial era (221 B.C. to 1912 A.D.), was in conjunction with the legendary *Zhouyi* (Zhou Changes). This fascinating work, "an assorted and jumbled compilation of omens, rhymed proverbs, riddles and paradoxes, snatches of song and story, drawn from popular lore and archaic traditions of divination," provided prognostication statements for the hexagrams produced by milfoil manipulation. The basic text of the *Zhouyi*, which evolved gradually over a millennium or so, consisted of all sixty-four possible hexagrams, each with a name that referred to a physical object, an activity, a state, a situation, a quality, an emotion or a relationship. Thus we find Ding, "The Cauldron;" Dun, "Retreat;" Meng, "Youthful Ignorance;" Yu, "Enthusiasm;"

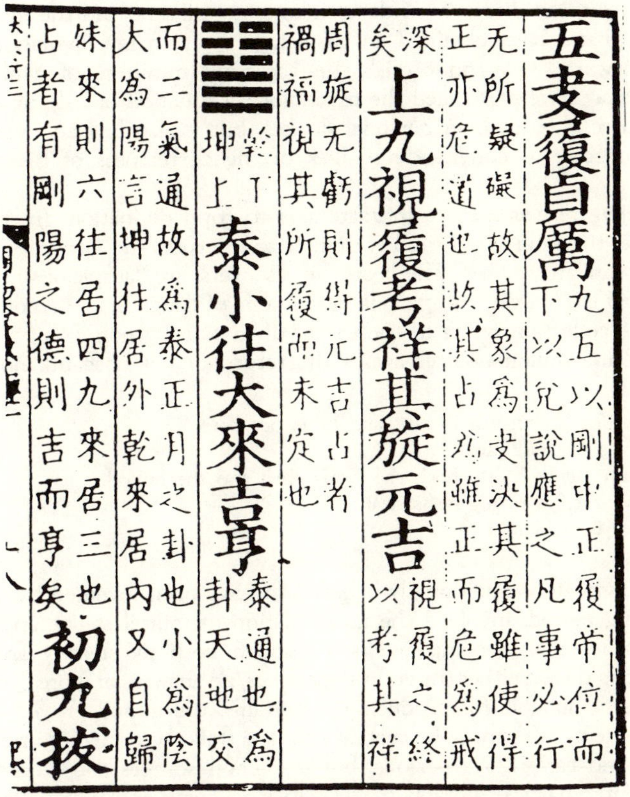
五夬履貞厲九五以剛中正履帝位而下以兌說應之凡事必行
无所疑礙故其象爲夬決其履雖使得正亦危道也故其占爲雖正而危爲戒
深矣上九視履考祥其旋元吉視履之終以考其祥
周旋无虧則得元吉占者禍福視其所履而未定也
乾下坤上泰小往大來吉亨泰通也爲卦天地交
而二氣通故爲泰正月之卦也小爲陰大爲陽言坤往居外乾來居內又自歸
妹來則六往居四九來居三也占者有剛陽之德則吉而亨矣初九拔

Figure 1.2 Excerpt from a Song dynasty edition of the *Zhouyi*, illustrating at mid-page a hexagram, the names of its constituent trigrams (Qian below, Kun above), the hexagram name (Tai; lit. "penetration" or "communication"), the judgment (lit. "the small departs, the great arrives, auspicious divination"), and part of the initial line reading. The text in small characters is Zhu Xi's commentary on the judgment. *Source*: Zhu Xi, *Zhouyi benyi* (Taibei, 1979 reprint), 1: 18a.

Song, "Conflict;" Tongren, "Human Fellowship;" and so forth. In addition each hexagram possessed a short, cryptic description of several characters called a "judgment" (*tuan* or *guaci*), and a brief, one-sentence reading for each line (*yaoci*). The hexagrams also contained a pair of trigrams which, like the hexagrams themselves, had individual names and various symbolic associations (see Fig. 1.2).[32] According to the theory of the *Zhouyi*, which will be discussed at greater length below and in chapters 2 and 3, the hexagrams represented symbolically the images or structures of change in the universe; and as such, they had explanatory value, if correctly interpreted.

Interpretation required an appreciation not only of the relationship between the individual lines and trigrams within each hexagram, but also an understanding of the various relationships between different hexagrams. Let us take a relatively simple example from the *Zuozhuan*:

> Bi Wan divined by the milfoil about becoming an officer of Jin, and obtained the hexagram Zhun, which changed [by virtue of a line transformation] to the hexagram Bi. Xin Liao interpreted it to be auspicious. Zhun, he said, indicates firmness [*gu*] while Bi indicates entering [*ru*]. What could be more fortunate? . . . The [lower] trigram Zhen becomes Kun. Carriages and horses follow one another; the feet stand firm; the elder brother grows; the mother protects; the masses return. These six indications [of the lines] will not change. United, they indicate firmness; at rest, they indicate awesomeness. The divination is that of a duke or marquis.[33]

The remarks on both the hexagrams and the individual lines of the *Zhouyi* provide an illuminating inventory of early and enduring Chinese cultural concerns. Prominent and recurrent themes include the need to use language properly; the importance of family, ancestors, ritual, music, beauty, antiquity, and the refinement of one's nature; the inevitability of change; the regulation of time and physical space; the proper conduct of a "superior man" (*junzi*); and an acute awareness of status. Virtually all sectors and strata of society are represented in the line readings: men, women and children; royalty and other elites, merchants, servants, robbers, priests and magicians. Primary social values include loyalty, sincerity, and truthfulness. Military affairs and the administration of justice receive substantial attention as matters of both political and social significance.[34]

At first glance, the symbolism of the *Changes* seems simple and straightforward. Much of it is related to nature: celestial objects; thunder and lightning, wind and rain, earth and fire; mountains, lakes, rocks, and trees; and animals of every description, from supernatural beasts such as dragons to both wild and domestic animals, even hamsters. Color and directional symbolism is prevalent, and many lines refer to various parts of the human body. Other common symbolic referents include precious objects such as gold, silk and jade; food of various sorts; eating utensils; sacrificial vessels; vehicles such as wagons and carts; weapons; and mundane household items. Among the more esoteric references in the basic text are those that refer to "a husband and wife rolling their eyes (*fuqi fanmu*)," "dried gristly meat (*ganzi*)," the "tusk of a gelded boar" (*fenshi zhi ya*) and the "big toe" (*mu*)—which is only one of at least half a dozen toe references in the line readings.[35]

But the specific significance of many of these symbols, as well as the meaning of certain basic words in the text itself, has been (and continues to be) a matter of dispute.[36] The reasons are not difficult to find. In the first place, the cryptic nature of the early hexagram and line references makes it extremely difficult to fill in ellipses. Many details of actual divinations, myths, anecdotes, "omen songs" (*tongyao* or *geyao*) and other sources that obviously helped to explain and amplify the original text of the *Zhouyi* came to be lost or distorted. Moreover, the meanings of some characters and concepts changed over time, and a few varied from region to region.[37] A great number of commentaries were written by successive generations of scholars in an effort to clarify the text—and no less than two hundred of them were incorporated into the Kangxi emperor's officially sanctioned edition of 1715. But the *Zhouyi* resisted any sort of exegetical consensus. The late Ming scholar Ni Yuanlu expressed a common opinion in stating that after more than "ten thousand generations" of written commentaries there was still no standard interpretation of the *Changes*.[38] On the other hand, many terms and phrases from the *Zhouyi* became clichés, such as the term *qianlong* ("hidden dragon"), which conventionally referred to the idea of "retreating and waiting for the right opportunity."[39]

Like oracle bones, dream interpretation, astrology, and other early forms of Chinese divination, the *Zhouyi* served a wide variety of political and personal purposes. References in the classics, as well as sources such as the *Shiji* (Historical Records), testify to its employment in matters of state ranging from the establishment and naming of towns and cities to the conduct of war.[40] Private individuals used the *Changes* to find out about their own destiny or that of their children,[41] and physicians even referred to it in their medical diagnoses. The *Zuozhuan* tells us of a doctor by the name of He, who was summoned from Qin to treat the marquis of Jin. The doctor pronounced the marquis incurably insane, equating the latter's excessive sexual indulgence with poison (*gu*). In explaining the matter to Zhao Meng, chief minister of Jin, the doctor said:

> "Look at the word *gu*; it is formed by the characters for a vessel (*min*) and for insects (*chong*). It is also used to refer to [spoiled] grain [that seems to be] flying away. In the *Zhouyi*, the constituent trigrams of the hexagram Gu are Gen above, signifying a woman deluding a young man, and Sun below, indicating the wind blowing down a mountain. These all refer to the same thing." Zhao Meng pronounced He an excellent doctor, rewarded him abundantly, and sent him back to Qin.[42]

This diagnostic application of the *Zhouyi* illustrates two common and persistent forms of rhetorical usage in traditional China, etymological analysis and analogy.[43] It also underscores the growing importance of the *Changes* as a source of textual authority—even when not actually employed in divination. Increasingly, late Zhou philosophers, including Confucius (c. 551–479 B.C.) and Xunzi (310–c. 230 B.C.), cited hexagram texts to illustrate their arguments; and, as with the example cited above, these arguments generally had a moral point to make.[44] For Confucians, at least, the acquisition of knowledge was only the beginning of *Zhouyi* consultation. Proper behavior had to follow. The sage himself, referring to the Heng ("Constancy") hexagram (and perhaps also punning on the name of an ancient shamanistic ritual), tells us in the *Lunyu* (Analects): "The people of the south have a saying that a person without constancy cannot be a shaman or a doctor. Well said! He who is inconstant in his virtue will invite disgrace. . . . Prognostication is not the end of things."[45]

Parallel to the growing popularity of the Zhouyi as a device for knowing the future in the late Zhou era was a burst of interest in other divination systems—astrology (*zhanxing*), geomancy (*dixing* or *xingfa*), physiognomy (*xiang-ren*), and various computational arts (*shushu*). This development had its origins in the dramatic series of political and social events that occurred in China following the capture of the Western Zhou capital by "barbarian" invaders in 770 B.C. With the subsequent breakdown of the old feudal order came the emergence of warring states, expanded opportunities for social and geographical mobility, the exchange of new ideas, increased professional specialization, and the introduction of new technologies, including advanced techniques of astronomical and calendrical calculation.[46] Not surprisingly, many of the most illustrious diviners of the late Zhou period were astronomers—Zi Shen, Shi Shen and Gan De—although other practitioners, notably the woman physiognomer Tang Ju, were also widely known and admired both by contemporaries and later generations.[47]

Another factor contributing to the popularity of divination during the Warring States period (453–221 B.C.) was the chaos and uncertainty of the times. People wanted to know how to cope more effectively with the future, and fortune-tellers were able to provide some measure of guidance and assurance—not least by providing almanacs or "day books" (*rishu*) that specified propitious and impropitious times for a wide range of activities, from marriage and milfoil divination, to bathing, washing one's hair, or beginning a construction project. Meanwhile, the widespread late Zhou belief in demons (*gui*) as an increasingly harmful influence on man fostered a surge of interest in all kinds of occult arts, including the use of exorcisms and magical spells. As the occult manuscripts uncovered at Shuihudi in Hubei during the mid-1970s reveal, the line between individuals who claimed to know about the future (diviners) and those who claimed to be able to do something about it (magicians, sorcerors and shamans) was often impossible to draw.[48]

For our purposes, the single most important intellectual development of the Warring States period—aside from the well-known contributions of philosophers such as Confucius, Laozi (6th century?), Mozi (c. 470–c. 391), Mencius (c. 372–c. 289), Zhuangzi (c. 389–286), and Xunzi to ethical and epistemological discourse in China—was the growing influence of correlative cosmology, championed, according to tradition, by the "naturalist" philosopher Zou Yan (c. 305–240 B.C.).[49] At the heart of this cosmology lay the concepts of *yinyang* and *wuxing*. Yin and *yang* originally referred respectively to the shady and bright sides of a hill; but by the mid- or late Zhou period they had come to denote primal cosmic forces. *Yin* was considered negative, passive and weak; *yang*, positive, active and strong. *Wuxing* originally denoted five primary elements—earth, wood, fire, water and metal—but, like *yin* and *yang*, these elements became identified with the processes of cosmic creativity and change; hence, they are often translated, and best understood, as "agents," "activities," or "phases" (see Glossary A). Implicit in both sets of concepts is the idea of mutual interaction and cyclical movement: bipolar alternation in the case of *yin* and *yang*, and periodicity or successive recurrence in the case of *wuxing* (see also Chapter 2).[50]

Late Zhou texts, influenced by Daoist naturalism as well as Confucian social categories and concerns, identify *yinyang* and *wuxing* with a wide range of phenomena. *Yang*, for instance, is associated not only with light and activity, but also with Heaven, males, the sun, fire, heat, the color red, and roundness. *Yin*, on the other hand, is correlated with the Earth, females, the moon, water, coldness, the color black and squareness, as well as darkness and passivity. In a similar fashion and for similar reasons, the *wuxing* are linked with various colors, directions, flavors, musical notes, senses, grains, sacrifices, punishments and so forth. From this point onward, the concepts of *yinyang* and *wuxing* become virtually indispensible as evaluative and explanatory terms in the realms of Chinese philosophy, science, divination, and medicine (see below), and treatises on the *wuxing* are included in every dynastic history from the Han to the Ming. Significantly, the Confucian classics that best represent *yinyang/wuxing* correlative cosmology in the Warring States period—the "Duke of Zhao" section of the *Zuozhuan*, the "Great Commentary" of the *Zhouyi*, the "Great Plan" chapter of the *Shujing*, and the "Evolution of Rites" chapter of the *Liji* (Record of Ritual)—are all concerned in fundamental ways with divination.[51]

The Han Legacy

Correlative cosmology reached maturity in the Han dynasty (206 B.C.–222 A.D.). The intervening Qin regime (221–206 B.C.) left an enduring imprint on many areas of Chinese life for the next two thousand years, but its significance in the history of divination lies primarily in the Qin emperor's pragmatic decision to preserve the *Zhouyi* from harm during the notorious "Burning of the Books and the Burying of the Scholars." At this point the emperor clearly considered the *Changes* to be more valuable as a divination manual than it was threatening as a Confucian text.[52] By the reign of Han Wudi (141–89 B.C.), the *Zhouyi*—now amplified by a number of commentaries known collectively as the "Ten Wings"—had become a bona fide Confucian classic, often referred to as the *Yijing* (Classic of Changes).[53] The "Ten Wings," as will be discussed more fully below and in chapter 3, clarified and amplified the symbolism of the hexagrams and their constituent trigrams, helped to explain the cryptic *tuan* and line readings of the basic text, suffused the *Yijing* with Confucian ethical judgments, and articulated its fundamental principles, including the idea of *yinyang* complementarity and the unity and interaction of the "three cosmic powers" (*sancai*): Heaven, Earth and Man.[54]

The single individual most responsible for incorporating the *Yijing* into the classical canon and for systematizing and popularizing Han correlative cosmology was the redoubtable scholar Dong Zhongshu (c. 179–c. 104 B.C.). Dong's *Chunqiu fanlu* (Luxuriant Gems of the Spring and Autumn Annals) sets forth a comprehensive world view based on the assumption that human beings are microcosms of the universe. He wrote

Man receives his mandate [*ming*; also translated "destiny"] from Heaven and is therefore superior to all creatures. Other creatures suffer troubles and defects and cannot practice humanity and righteousness; man alone can practice them. Other creatures suffer troubles and defects and cannot match Heaven and Earth; man alone can match them. Man has 360 joints which match the number of Heaven.

. . . He has ears and eyes above, with their keen sense of hearing and seeing, which resemble the sun and the moon. His body has its orifices, which resemble rivers and valleys. His heart has feelings of sorrow, joy, pleasure, and anger, which are analogous to the spiritual feelings [of Heaven]. As we look at man's body, how much superior it is to that of other creatures and how similar to Heaven! . . . Man is distinct from other creatures and forms a trinity with Heaven and Earth.

Dong went on to assert:

The agreement of Heaven and Earth and the correspondence between *yin* and *yang* are ever found complete in the human body. The body is like Heaven. Its numerical categories and those of Heaven are mutually interlocked. . . . Internally the body has five viscera, which correspond to the five agents. Externally there are the four limbs, which correspond to the four seasons. The alternating of opening and closing the eyes corresponds to day and night . . . [and] the alternating of sorrow and joy corresponds to *yin* and *yang*. . . . In what may be numbered, there is correspondence in number. In what may not be numbered, there is correspondence in kind.[55]

Dong and most other Confucian scholars of the Han believed that Confucian ethics were inherent in the cosmic order and that human relationships and institutions were reflections of that order. The Han dynasty "Treatise on Astrology" of the *Shiji* (Historical Records) established an explicit analogy between the realm of Heaven and the realm of Man: Asterisms and stars had their counterparts in government bureaus and official positions, just as divisions of the heavens had their analogues on earth. According to this correspondence theory, which displayed remarkable tenacity in China, proper behavior, proper government and proper rituals contributed to cosmic harmony, while immoral actions and improper relationships disrupted the balance of *yin* and *yang* and *wuxing* forces in the universe, striking a discordant and therefore disruptive note in the cosmic symphony.

For this reason, among others, Han Confucians, following the lead of Dong Zhongshu, placed special emphasis on preserving and strengthening the "Three Bonds" (*sangang*) that united rulers and subjects, husbands and wives, and parents and children. These bonds expressed, in Dong's view, a natural hierarchy based on the assumed superiority of *yang* over *yin*: Rulers were superior to their subjects, husbands to their wives, and children to their parents. For the next two thousand years these relationships were considered sacrosanct in Chinese society. Inferiors owed their superiors loyalty and devotion, while subordinates received kindness from their superiors—just as "wood receives from water, fire from wood, earth from fire, metal from earth, and water from metal."[56]

Although on the whole Han correlative cosmology preserved status distinctions and emphasized submissiveness to authority, it also provided a tool for limiting despotic power. The idea of a spiritual resonance (*ganying*) between the emperor, the state and the cosmos gave Han officials greater scope for using natural disasters and the appearance of inauspicious portents as a way of admonishing

against maladministration, and thus influencing policy. This approach to re-
monstrance, fully consistent with the hoary notion of the Mandate of Heaven,
acquired greater force from the authority of a fully elaborated cosmology. Dong
himself encouraged Emperor Wu to follow the path of Confucian virtue rather
than Legalist punishments by linking the former with *yang*, summer, life and
growth, and the latter with *yin*, winter, emptiness, and uselessness.[57] But while
Heaven could express its moral will by means of portents, its power was basically
limited to "sustaining life" (*shengsheng*, in the captivating words of the *Yijing*),
and maintaining the regular rhythms of nature.

Han cosmological assumptions and analogies can be found in medical texts
of the period, including two of the most famous and influential books on
medicine in all of Chinese history: the *Huangdi neijing* (Inner Classic of the
Yellow Emperor) and the *Nanjing* (Classic of Difficult [Questions]). These works
are solidly grounded in *yinyang* and *wuxing* correspondences, which apply to
parts and functions of the body as well as to illnesses, diagnoses, and remedies.
In the most general terms, the skin is *yang*, the interior is *yin*; the upper half
of the body is *yang*, the lower half is *yin*; the left side is *yang*, the right side
is *yin*; the back is *yang*; the front is *yin*; the heart and liver (corresponding to
"fire" and "wood," respectively) are considered *yang* organs; the spleen ("earth"),
lungs ("metal") and kidneys ("water"), *yin*. Because the back is *yang* and the
lung is *yin*, *yin* may be within *yang* and so forth. Generally speaking, an
affliction is *yang* when it arises from external causes and *yin* when it arises
from internal causes, although pathological influences are also identified by
wuxing associations. Stimulants, resolvents, expectorants, pungent substances
and hot decoctations are classified as *yang* drugs; astrigents, purgatives, haemetics,
bitter substances, and cold infusions are *yin* drugs.[58]

Han medical texts also employ bureaucratic metaphors drawn from the world
of Chinese civil and military administration to explain bodily functions and
afflictions. Thus the *Huangdi neijing* equates the heart with the ruler ("spirit
and enlightment have their origin here"); the lung with the minister ("the
order of life's rhythm has its origin here"); the liver with the general ("planning
and deliberation have their origin here"); and so on. The body could be
"attacked" (*chong*) by outside invaders and therefore required protection from
"guards" (*wei*) and "army camps" (*ying*). By Han times, however, the specifically
demonological explanations of disease that prevailed in the late Zhou had given
way, at least temporarily, to new concepts of etiology. Texts now referred to
the effect of evil influences or emanations (*xieqi*; lit. "evil vapors") rather than
to evil demons (*xiegui*), and a far greater emphasis came to be placed on
harmonizing not only food, drink, climate and other external variables, but
also music, emotions and morals—all related to the *wuxing*. On the other hand,
the Chinese did not abandon recourse to shamanistic healers or the use of
magical charms and spells for protection and treatment, and demonology would
later reassert itself.[59]

A striking and enduring feature of early Chinese medical and scientific
thought is that *yinyang/wuxing* correlations and bureaucratic analogies often
counted for more than empirical observation—even when, as often proved to

be the case, the correspondences and analogies were internally inconsistent or incompatible with one another.[60] The result was that for some two thousand years Chinese physicians chose freely from various diagnostic options which, although all related in some way to the dominant system of *yinyang/wuxing* cosmological correspondence, could not, in most cases, be reconciled with each other. The same was true of Chinese divination—for many of the same reasons.[61] Paul Unschuld has observed that in traditional Chinese medicine "the 'either/ or' question that might be posed by a scientist used to deductive reasoning obviously did not concern a Chinese theoretician or practitioner who thought in terms of systematic correspondence." He goes on to say that this phenomenon is one of the basic characteristics distinguishing traditional Chinese thought from modern Western science, and that we should regard as both questionable and misleading any effort "to eliminate this feature of traditional Chinese thought by artificially isolating a coherent and—in a Western sense—consistent set of ideas and patterns from ancient Chinese sources."[62]

Not surprisingly, the *Yijing* occupied a central position in the development of Han correlative thinking—not to mention the later evolution of science and medicine in China (see chapter 3). As indicated above, the "Ten Wings" of the classic affirmed man's fundamental unity with the cosmos, underscoring the identity between Heaven, Earth and Man by reference to both numbers and physical correspondences. The "Great Commentary" linked heavenly images (*xiang*) with earthly forms (*xing*), while the "Discussion of the Trigrams" enhanced the value of the trigrams and hexagrams as explanatory symbols by investing them with a range of meanings well beyond their original significations. Trigrams, for example, came to be known not only by their primary attributes (Qian, "The Creative;" Kun, "The Receptive;" Dui, "The Arousing;" etc.) but also by new associations involving different family relationships, animals, elements, directions of the compass, seasons, parts of the day, parts of the body, social roles, and colors. Hexagrams, comprised of trigrams and representative of actual situations in nature, implied cosmic powers similar to, and often correlated directly with, *yinyang* and *wuxing*.[63] Thus, the symbols of the *Yijing* came to be used to explain natural processes as well as to identify specific relationships between things and phenomena. Wei Boyang's *Zhouyi cantong qi* (Accordance of the Zhou Changes with Composite Phenomena), written about 140 A.D., provides an excellent if somewhat obscure example of *Yijing* symbolism in the service of Daoist alchemy.[64]

The *Yijing*—like Han medical texts, the writings of Dong Zhongshu, and even some early alchemical tracts—emphasized morality as the key to both cosmic harmony and individual well-being. Laozi could claim that Heaven was not benevolent, that it treated all things like straw dogs, but most Han scholars held that the mind of Heaven was a moral mind. Thus, although Daoist influences found their way into the "Ten Wings" of the *Changes*, as they did many other works of the Han period, Confucian values predominated. In the ethical language of the "Great Commentary," by using the *Yijing* man "comes to resemble Heaven and Earth, and is not in conflict with them. His wisdom embraces all things, and his way (*dao*) brings order into the world; therefore he does not err. He is active everywhere, but does not allow himself to be carried away. He rejoices in Heaven and has knowledge of fate; therefore he is free from care. He is content with his circumstances and genuine in his benevolence. Therefore he can practice love."[65]

Scholarly approaches to the *Yijing* varied substantially in the Han—in part, no doubt, because different versions of the work existed. For instance, we know that the Mawangdui silk manuscript of the *Yijing*, sealed in the second century B.C. and unearthed in 1973, departs in several significant respects from later "standard" editions of the classic, not least in its ordering of the trigrams and hexagrams. So, it seems, did the ordering scheme of the Han scholar Meng Xi (flourished first century B.C.), whose student, Jiao Yanshou (flourished c. 50 B.C.), supposedly compiled the *Yilin* (Forest of the Changes) following Meng's system.[66] The circulation of these and other versions of the *Changes* in the early Han presumably made it easier for scholars to devise variant systems of grouping hexagrams, even after the text was "standardized" later in the Han period.[67]

According to the "Biographies of Confucian Scholars" in the *Hanshu* (History of the [Former] Han), Meng Xi and his fellow *Yijing* specialists in the Imperial Academy were part of a long line of orthodox transmission of the text leading from Confucius and his disciples down to Tian He (c. 200-143 B.C.). Meng's widely influential interpretation of the *Changes*, which drew inspiration from early Han correlative cosmology and numerology, established relationships between various hexagrams and divisions of the year. In his system, called *guaqi* (lit. "breaths of the hexagrams"), each of the lines of four separate hexagrams govern one of twenty-four solar periods (*qi*; lit. "breaths") of the year, while the sixty remaining hexagrams match successive periods of about six days each. This sort of analysis, based upon hexagram and trigram images as well as the numerical values associated with *yang* and *yin* lines and various divisions of the year, came to be known as "images and numbers" (*xiangshu*).[68] Jing Fang (79-37 B.C.), the renowned disciple of Jiao Yanshou, extended *Yijing* correlations to the realm of music, developed the idea of a mutual response between the "breaths" of Heaven and Earth (*shiying*), and articulated the notion of manifest and latent (*feifu*; lit. "flying and hiding") hexagrams. He is also often credited with introducing a system of relating the hexagrams to the heavenly stems and earthly branches called *najia*. All of these conceptions were closely connected with court astronomy, astrology, calendrical calculations and numerology.[69]

Near the end of the Former Han period (206 B.C.-25 A.D.) alternative versions of the Confucian classics began to appear. Written in a more archaic script than prevailing editions, and therefore purporting to be older than the "New Texts" that had been reconstructed from memory after the Qin dynasty's "Burning of the Books," they became known as the "Old Texts." An Old Text arrangement of the *Yijing* even appeared, although the work had been spared the Qin emperor's torch and was thus presumably less likely to be corrupt. Most Han scholars believed the Old Texts to be forgeries, but several late Han intellectuals—notably Xun Shuang (128-190), Zheng Xuan (127-200) and Yu

Fan (170–239)—embraced them enthusiastically, and all three individuals wrote extensive commentaries on Old Text versions of the *Yijing*.[70] As we shall see (chapter 3), their interpretations proved to be of great interest to Qing dynasty scholars about fourteen hundred years later.

Xun Shuang is best known for employing the lines and hexagrams of the *Yijing* to illustrate fundamental patterns of "rise and decline" (*shengjiang*). These patterns, correlated with the movement of *yin* and *yang*, carried explicitly political connotations. In Xun's eyes, the structural tension within certain hexagrams reflected the political tensions inherent in any bureaucratic organization that was ripe for change. Zheng Xuan, by contrast, emphasized the idea of stability and permanence. His approach to the classic placed special stress on the fixed positions of Heaven and Earth (represented by the hexagrams Qian and Kun, respectively), and on the established, immutable institutional and ritual responsibilities of individuals within society. Zheng developed a correlative system known as *xiaochen*, which related the twelve months of the year to the twelve combined lines of Qian and Kun, but he believed that changes in the structure of hexagrams had significance only in divination— which he viewed as distinctly subordinate to moral and ritual instruction. Yu Fan, for his part, reaffirmed Xun Shuang's emphasis on change, and accepted his general theory of "rise and fall;" but he moved Xun's analysis to a much more abstract level and replaced the straightforward notion of *shengjiang* with a more sophisticated idea of sequential movement of the component lines in neighboring hexagrams. He also modified the *najia* system of Jing Fang.[71]

At the same time that the *Yijing* provided grist for different commentarial traditions, it also inspired various derivative works. Some were simple prognostication texts (*chanwei* or *tuchan*), designed primarily for "determining good or bad fortune."[72] Others, in the tradition of Han apocrypha, sought to explain and amplify the numerology and trigram correspondences of the *Yijing* and to link them with popular astrology. The *Yiwei Qianzuodu* (Apocryphal Treatise on the Changes: A Penetration of the Laws of Qian), to which Zheng Xuan added his own commentary, is a good example of such a work.[73] Still others were elaborate "imitations" of the *Yijing*—the most interesting and influential example of which is the *Taixuan jing* (Classic of Supreme Mystery) of Yang Xiong (53 B.C.–18 A.D.).[74]

Based on linear figures and an elaborate numerology, Yang's eclectic book of divination reflects Han dynasty cosmological assumptions and intellectual fashions, including *yinyang/wuxing* correspondence theory. There is, however, some evidence suggesting Shang dynasty origins for its numerical system.[75] Instead of sixty-four hexagrams and 384 lines it has eighty-one tetragrams (*shou*) and a total of 729 lines, each with an "appraisal" (*zan*) loosely patterned on the line texts of the *Changes*. Yang invented a method of milfoil divination for the work in which the manipulation of thirty-three stalks provided three possibilities for each line, rather than the *Yijing*'s two possibilities. In Yang's scheme, an unbroken line represented Heaven; a line broken once (like a *yin* line in the *Yi*) represented Earth; and a line broken twice represented Man. Four repetitions of the divination procedure yielded the eighty-one possibilities.

The text of the *Taixuan jing* was more coherent and internally consistent than the *Yijing*'s, and it employed a rather different vocabulary. But like all of the Yi scholars mentioned above, and many others as well, Yang could not resist the impulse to correlate his linear symbols with periods of the year as well as a wide range of both "natural" and social phenomena.[76] Furthermore, despite the heavy imprint of Daoist naturalism in the *Taixuan jing*, Yang's companion work, *Fayan* (Model Sayings) indicates clearly that he remained solidly wed to Confucian values. The *Taixuan jing* inspired a number of scholarly commentaries over the next two millennia, but it never seriously challenged the predominance of the *Yijing* as either a divination manual or a book of wisdom. Even one of Yang's most ardent admirers of a later era had to admit that "the *Changes* is Heaven, and the *Mystery* provides what is needed to build a staircase up to it."[77]

The wide circulation of Han divination texts—from the *Yijing* and the *Taixuan jing* to various prognostication books and recently-excavated astrology manuals—testifies to the growing appeal of fortune-telling at all levels of Chinese society.[78] In part, as I have argued, the expansion and sophistication of divining techniques was a product of late Zhou technological, social, and intellectual factors. The Han dynasty's contribution to the process was to provide an unprecedented degree of cultural unity, a cosmology predicated on the assumption that human beings could comprehend the subtle patterns of change in the universe, and official support for occult specialists (*fangshi*), who found themselves in a position to obtain wealth, eminence and power by virtue of their ability to tell the future, heal illnesses, or restore cosmic harmony by magical means.[79] So influential were these specialists that from Han times onward, every official dynastic history, as well as many local gazetteers and other sources, contained special sections devoted to biographies of *fangshi*, usually called "technicians" (*fangji*).[80]

Experts in divination and numerology were especially valuable to the throne, since imperial legitimacy depended to such a significant degree on the correct interpretation of portents and on the proper regulation of human affairs. From an administrative standpoint alone the vast and highly centralized Han empire required a standardized calendar so that officials at all levels could operate on the same schedule, and know whether months were long (thirty days) or short (twenty-nine days), and when an intercalary month had to be inserted. An additional factor, inextricably linked to Han cosmology, was the need to determine, on the basis of astrological and numerical calculations, auspicious days and times for royal ceremonies as well as for empire-wide rituals, festivals, and other activities.[81] From the government's standpoint, the more predictable life was, the better. The throne thus had a vital interest in knowing all it could about the future.[82] At the popular level, too, predictability was a virtue. For this reason, the use of almanacs that indicated days which were auspicious or inauspicious for various ritual and more mundane activities became ever more widespread.

Among the many divination techniques employed by *fangshi* in the Han were various forms of astrology, "fate calculation" and numerology—including consultation of the *Hetu* (Yellow River Chart) and *Luoshu* (Luo River Writing) diagrams associated with the *Yijing* (see chapters 2 and 3), the use of divining boards, milfoil stalks, oracle bones, and prognostication texts; the geomantic analysis of landforms; the selection of lucky days; the analysis of heavenly stems and earthly branches; communication with spirits; crack-making with bamboo; the interpretation of winds and vapors, birdcalls, and dreams; physiognomy; and the evaluation of written characters.[83] Most of these techniques existed in the late Zhou period or earlier, and virtually all continued to be used in some form throughout the imperial era.[84]

Ironically, the high point of political influence for occult specialists in the Han was during the reign of Emperor Wu (140–87 B.C.), a time when Confucian scholars—the avowed enemies of *fangshi*—were also heavily patronized by the throne. The hostility and suspicion of these scholars is evident in the official histories of the Han and Six Dynasties period (222–589). The *Hou Hanshu* (History of the later Han) states, for instance:

> During the [Former] Han dynasty, especially from the time of Emperor Wu, there was great favor shown the esoteric techniques and arts. . . . Later, Wang Mang was given to manipulative use of the portents of fate, and Emperor Guangwu held an abiding belief in the art of prophecy. The time was right for the *fangshi* to rush forward. . . . Strange writings were venerated and unusual calculations were prized. It was the pervasive trend of the times. . . . Given this situation, the Confucian scholars became outraged at the treachery and heterodoxy of the *fangshi*. . . . The Grand Historian even said, "Looking at the manuals of *yin* and *yang* divination makes the people feel imprisoned and burdened with fears."[85]

Of course many Confucian scholars, whose official duties included divination and calendrical calculations, felt threatened by the presence and influence of *fangshi* who were, by definition, outsiders—many from the far reaches of the empire. Class prejudices also came into play. One indication can be found in the biography of Sima Jizhu in the section on "Diviners of Lucky Days" in the *Shiji*. Two of Emperor Wu's high-ranking courtiers, curious about the activities of fortune-tellers in the Han capital of Chang'an, decided to visit the diviners' stalls in the city marketplace. Encountering Sima Jizhu, they listened to him lecture on the cycles of Heaven and Earth, and of the movements of the sun, moon, stars, and constellations. Marvelling at his intelligence and erudition, they asked why he occupied such a humble abode and pursued such an ignoble occupation. They went on to remark: "People all say, 'Oh, the diviners—all they do is talk in exaggerated ways, impose nonsense to play on people's feelings, make absurdly glorious predictions about people's fates to delight them, invent stories about disasters to fill their hearts with fear, and babble lies about the spirits to get all their money away from them, demanding generous rewards so they can line their own pockets.' "

Sima Jizhu defended his profession eloquently against such criticisms, emphasizing his concern with morality and with proper ritual. He cited classical precedents for use of the milfoil and the turtle, and noted that as a result of pronouncements by diviners, "offerings are made to the spirits of the dead [*guishen*], loyal ministers serve their lords, filial sons look after their parents, and affectionate fathers take care of their sons. . . . As a result of their instructions the sick are sometimes made well, those in mortal danger are saved from death, and those in distress are freed from their worries. Undertakings are brought to a successful conclusion, sons and daughters are happily married off, and people live to a ripe old age." The Han officials, both famous scholars, came away overawed and envious.[86] Another Han period diviner, Yan Junping, reportedly the teacher of Yang Xiong, also established a reputation for encouraging right behavior. As a professional fortune-teller he became famous throughout the imperial era for "closing up shop and drawing the blinds" (*bisi xialian*) as soon as he had earned enough to meet his minimal daily needs.[87]

On the whole, Han literati tended to be critical of diviners rather than divination itself. Few scholars, if any, condemned the practice categorically. Critics quarreled more with the improper or inconsistent use of divining techniques than with the cosmological assumptions that underlay them. To be sure, certain techniques or practitioners might be branded as heterodox— particularly if they ran counter to the perceived interests of the state. But for most Confucians, the only danger aside from misuse was the possibility that an excessive reliance on fortune-tellers and other occult specialists would encourage fatalism rather than self-assertion, thus undermining the impulse toward moral improvement.[88] It is true that the notorious Han skeptic Wang Chong (27-c. 100 A.D.) assailed much of the prevailing cosmology, including the idea of a cosmic resonance between Heaven and Man and the notion that Heaven rewarded good behavior and punished evil. He also denied that by means of divination individuals could either communicate with or influence Heaven. Further, he expressed special scorn for the misguided interpretations of those who designated certain days as auspicious or inauspicious for burials, sacrifices, house-building, bathing, clothes-cutting, studying, and so forth— activities which, as I have indicated, were specified in popular almanacs of the time. Yet even Wang accepted many basic principles of *yinyang/wuxing* interaction; he believed in portents, and felt that astral influences played an important role in human destiny.[89]

Divination in Medieval China

The fall of the Han dynasty, like the fall of Rome, brought an extended period of division to a once-unified empire; but these were not China's Dark Ages. In fact, art, literature, and intellectual life all flourished under the Six Dynasties (222–589)—despite the turmoil occasioned by repeated "barbarian" invasions in the north and a succession of Chinese regimes in the south. This cultural fluorescence grew out of several significant changes that originated in the late Han period, including the rise of both Buddhism and "Religious" Daoism, and the triumph of Old Text scholarship over the once-orthodox New Text School. After unity was restored to China under the Sui dynasty (581–618) and its successor, the Tang (618–907), Chinese culture continued to blossom spectacularly. Through it all, *fangshi* and other divination specialists retained their place in Chinese society, serving the throne and the public, debating old enemies, confronting new rivals, and at once contributing to and reflecting the dramatically changing times.[90]

Above all, the Six Dynasties period is known for its freewheeling intellectual atmosphere, reflected not only in formal philosophical and religious tracts but also in colorful semi-historical works such as the *Shishuo xinyu* (New Account of Worldly Tales) and "records of strange events," such as *Soushen ji* (In Search of Spirits) and *Bowu zhi* (On Diverse Things).[91] Liberated from Han imperial orthodoxy, and invigorated by new currents of Buddhism and Daoism, Chinese thought wandered at will. Reclusive scholars engaged in "pure conversations" (*qingtan*), unfettered by the requirements of office or ideology. Buddhism, Confucianism and Daoism competed freely in the marketplace of ideas, and at different times all found favor in competing regimes. The Jin dynasty (286–316), for example, used Confucianism in briefly reuniting the empire, while the alien Toba Wei dynasty (386–543) heavily patronized Daoism. The growth and influence of Buddhism was particularly dramatic. Although only a vaguely understood foreign import in the late Han, by the end of the Six Dynasties period Buddhism had become solidly entrenched at all levels of Chinese society, and enjoyed great political favor despite its world-denying impulses.[92]

Daoism, meanwhile, had acquired ever more sophistication, appropriating religious ideas not only from alien Buddhism, but also from long-standing indigenous beliefs and practices—including the worship of popular deities and the use of alchemy and magic. At the same time, however, Daoist priests took pains to distinguish their religion from the unregenerate cults of the masses. During the Later Han period, sectarian Daoism, in the political form of millennarian rebellion, helped to topple the dynasty, while more purely philosophical forms of Daoism subverted Confucian orthodoxy in equally effective but less dramatic ways. Building on foundations established by Han scholars such as Yang Xiong, Liu An, and Ma Rong, Daoist thought of the Six Dynasties period found its most brilliant expression in the *Yijing*-inspired philosophy of Wang Bi (226–249). Wang's influential school of thought, known as "the study of mysteries" (*xuanxue*), represented a compromise between Daoist themes of naturalism and individual liberation, and Confucian preoccupations with the "teachings of status" (*mingjiao*) and service to society. His emphasis was on non-exertion (*wuwei*) and merging with the cosmos, but he did not deny, and in fact embraced, Confucian values. His sage-hero was Confucius, not Laozi or Zhuangzi. And although Wang felt that "good and bad fortune" were predestined, he did not accept the Daoist notion of "resting with fate" (*anming*) and condemned vulgar prophesying.[93]

Wang's approach to the *Yijing*, expounded in the first systematic treatise on the classic, the *Zhouyi lueli* (Introduction to the Zhou Changes), was to strip away the astrological and numerical symbolism the work had acquired from Jing Fang and other Han commentators, and to invest it with a new metaphysics, heavily influenced by the vocabulary and concerns of Daoism. This metaphysics centered on the idea of a primal state of nothingness (*wu*) from which everything that is (*you*) arises. *Wu* is the quiescent foundation (*ti*) that gives rise to all active functions (*yong*). The sage, who is a model of Heaven's virtue, takes his

inspiration from *wu* in acting within *you*. He knows intuitively when the way
of Heaven is about to change. This knowledge of the incipient moment or
"trigger" of change (*ji*) is a central concept of the *Yijing*.[94] Wang's metaphysical
interpretation of the *Yijing* exerted a powerful influence on other medieval
commentators, such as Kong Yingda (587–684), whose *Zhouyi zhengyi* (The
Correct Meaning of the Zhou Changes) was in effect a sub-commentary to
Wang's pioneering text.[95] Wang also provided philosophical grist for the neo-
Confucian revival of the Song (see next section).

Cosmological speculation was rife in the Six Dynasties period. Influenced
by pre-existing concepts as well as new notions introduced from without by
Indian Buddhism and developed indigenously by sectarian Daoists, Chinese
scholars argued incessantly about the shape, scope, constitution and ultimate
meaning of the cosmos. Indian astrology books began to be translated into
Chinese along with Buddhist sutras; and by the sixth century the Western
zodiac had been introduced to the Middle Kingdom. This astrological concept
did not survive beyond medieval times, however—presumably because the
Chinese had long before developed a comparable system of twelve divisions of
the ecliptic known as the stations (*ci*) of Jupiter. Every one of these stations,
in turn, contained two or three "lodges" (*xiu*), which divided the sky like the
slices of an orange into a total of twenty-eight unequal parts—each marked
by an asterism and known by that asterism's name.[96]

Prevailing Chinese conceptions of the universe in the Six Dynasties period
included the *gaitian* ("covered sky") theory, which likened the heavens to a
covering umbrella and the earth to an upturned bowl; the *huntian* ("enveloped
sky") theory, which posited a spherical heaven surrounding the earth; and the
xuanye ("expansive night") theory, in which space was empty and infinite. From
the sixth century onward, the late Zhou *huntian* theory prevailed in the official
dynastic histories, complemented by an equally long-standing idea known as
fenye ("allocated fields"), which presumed an astrological correspondence between
various sectors of the heavens and territories on earth. During the Han, the
fenye concept developed into a complex system of prognostication, "linking the
earthly regions not only with heavenly fields and lunar lodges, but also with
the ten heavenly stems, the twelve earthly branches, the eight trigrams, the
five phases, and so forth."[97] Subsequently, it became, in various forms, a staple
feature of official Chinese astrology throughout the imperial era.

These ideas also influenced the cosmologies of both sectarian Daoism and
Buddhism. Although the defining metaphors of Daoist cosmogony remained
the egg-gourd and the womb ("pregnant with beings and events"), the cosmology
of Daoism incorporated *yinyang* and *wuxing* correlations, as well as Buddhist
elements, into its world view. It also became ever more intertwined with popular
practices such as geomancy, astrology, and other forms of divination. Daoist
worship of personified forces of nature, which included not only heavenly
bodies such as stars and asterisms but also deified individuals such as Laozi,
was designed primarily to tap the vast energy of the cosmos, and to direct it
toward the eradication of sickness and disaster and the achievement of longevity
and immortality. In pursuit of these goals, Daoist priests summoned spirits,

issued charms, and both practiced and instructed others in the mystical arts of internal and external alchemy.[98]

The Buddhists, for their part, held a number of different views of the universe, ranging from the idea of a "single world" consisting of a flat disk with the heavens and meditative realms above and hells below, to the notion of innumerable world systems existing in infinite space and time. One of the most common Buddhist metaphysical systems introduced from India into China was known as the "three worlds" (*sanjie*). It posited three distinct realms divided into a total of thirty-two heavens.[99] Such realms were not, however, "real" worlds. From a Buddhist standpoint, all sensory phenomena were illusions created by the false idea that ego exists. The point of Buddhist mental and moral discipline was therefore to penetrate the "veil of illusion" that bound individuals to the "wheel of life and death" and caused them to be born again and again into a world of pain and suffering. Rebirth revealed "the retribution of karma" (*yeyin* or *yebao*)—that is, the consequences of one's deeds and thoughts in a previous incarnation. According to Buddhist doctrine, the net accumulation of "good" and "bad" karma determined the rebirth of each sentient being on one or another existential plane (divine, human, animal, insect, etc.). This, the Buddhists termed "fate according to actions in a previous existence" (*suming*). The only way to break the "chain of causation" was to attain Enlightenment, which brought oneness with Ultimate Reality. This indescribable state (or, more aptly, non-state) was termed Nirvana, which literally means "extinction."[100]

Mutual borrowing was common among Buddhism, Daoism and Confucianism in the Six Dynasties period, despite their different orientations. Confucianism, for example, contributed ethical values to both Buddhism and sectarian Daoism, helping, in turn, to keep itself alive at a time of temporary intellectual eclipse. Buddhism borrowed *Yijing* symbolism and Han-style astrological and numerical correlations, in addition to developing a huge pantheon of recognizably Chinese gods—some of whom they shared with Daoism. The Daoists took most freely. They not only drew heavily upon *Yijing* symbolism and appropriated Buddhist metaphysical concepts such as the idea of multiple heavens, but they also imitated Buddhist monasteries and temples, Buddhist forms of clerical organization, and Buddhist-style images, ceremonies, and canonical literature. And although sectarian Daoism lacked the concept of reincarnation, it recast Buddhist karma in terms of merits and demerits, which either added to, or subtracted from, one's lifespan. Ultimately, Buddhism aimed at the elimination of consciousness and "self" in order to attain Nirvana, while Daoist priests sought to manipulate the supernatural environment in the interest of longevity or immortality; but both belief systems gave their adherents a substantial role to play in determining their own fate.[101]

Buddhist and Daoist concepts of causality, based largely on Confucian standards of good and evil, must be seen against the backdrop of three prevailing Chinese conceptions of fate, all dating from at least the Han. These were "regular fate" (*zhengming*)—also known as "great fate" (*daming*), "received fate" (*shouming*), or "longevity fate" (*shouming*)—"fate following behavior" (*suiming*), and encountered fate (*zaoming*). According to the Han commentator Zhao Qi

(108–201), "regular fate" referred to "doing good and getting good;" "fate following behavior" referred to "doing evil and getting evil;" and "encountered fate" referred to "doing good and getting evil."[102] Wang Chong, in an effort to refute the idea of moral requital or retribution (*bao*), also pointed out that it was possible to do evil and yet reap rewards. He wrote:

> [Man's] nature and destiny are distinct from one another, for there are persons whose natures are good and yet who meet an unlucky fate, whereas there are others whose natures are bad and yet who meet a lucky fate. The doing of good or bad depends on one's nature, but calamity or good fortune and good or bad luck depend on fate. Some people perform good deeds and yet reap calamity; this is a case where the nature is good but fate is unlucky. Others perform bad deeds and yet gain good fortune; this is a case where the nature is bad but fate is good.[103]

Confucians acknowledged that rewards did not always come to the virtuous nor was evil always punished, but they relentlessly stressed the need for moral behavior regardless of the circumstances. Matters such as sickness and health, life and death, poverty and prosperity, seemed ordained by Heaven and beyond human control, but other things were not.[104] To Confucians, the important point was to know what could be known and to do what could be done. Mencius said: "There is a fate for everything. One must submissively embrace that which is correct."[105] "Knowing fate" (*zhiming*) in the standard Confucian view meant simply making the best of a situation by devising the appropriate moral strategy for dealing with it.[106] Laozi, Zhuangzi and their followers advocated a more complete submission to fate, but they, too, tried to discover their destiny, if only to find their proper niche in the cosmic scheme.[107]

And even Buddhists and sectarian Daoists, who went furthest in trying to influence the future through personal behavior, and whose communions were sometimes quite outspoken in their condemnation of Chinese-style mantic arts, used the *Yijing* and other forms of divination in order to know fate.[108] Thus we find a number of monks, priests and lay adherents from the Six Dynasties era who were experts in techniques such as the use of the tortoise shell and milfoil, physiognomy, and various occult computations—despite specific religious injunctions dating from at least the fourth century that forbade them from interpreting portents, making calendrical or astronomical calculations, selecting lucky and unlucky days, engaging in spirit healing and magic, and divining good or bad fortune.[109] Some Buddhist and Daoist clerics also compiled mantic texts (*bujing*), such as the mid-fifth century work entitled *Guanding jing* (Sutra of Consecration), which included elements of traditional Chinese cosmology, and became the precursors of the "spiritual stick" (*lingqian*) divination books that proved to be so popular in late imperial China.[110]

Meanwhile, geomancy or "siting" (*dili, kanyu*) became firmly established as a popular preoccupation during the Six Dynasties period, practiced with particular skill by two famous diviners: Guan Lu (210–256) and Guo Pu (276–324). Of the two, only Guo has a biographical entry in the *kanyu* section of the *Tushu jicheng*; but we know from the *Weizhi* (Record of Wei) and other sources that

Guan was fully conversant with the subject and may even have written a tract about it.[111] In the Han dynasty, *kanyu* calculations had been concerned largely with matters of auspicious timing for various domestic activities, including the construction of houses and graves; but during the Six Dynasties period these calculations increasingly took into account topographical factors, and assumed special importance in the location of gravesites. The earliest book on grave location, entitled the *Zangjing* (Burial Classic), is generally ascribed to a Mr. Qingwu ("Green Raven") of the Qin-Han period, whose pseudonym became a common term for geomancy in late imperial times.[112] Concern with divination as a device to assure a proper burial for one's parents had been mandated by the *Xiaojing* (Classic of Filial Piety), also of Han provenance, but the Chinese increasingly came to believe that an auspicious burial site would also bring good fortune to subsequent generations of the family.[113] Geomancy, then, became a means to influence the future, not just to know it.

Guan Lu gained greatest and most enduring fame for his influential theories of "fate extrapolation" (*tuiming;* also known as *luming,* "the fate of emoluments"). His accomplishments as a diviner merited long biographies in the *Sanguo zhi* (Record of the Three Kingdoms) and the *Weizhi,* as well as a "Separate Biography" written by his younger brother. Later encyclopedias and compendia such as the *Tushu jicheng* devote considerable space to his exploits. Although described in official sources as coarse, ugly and a poor judge of character (the last, a common criticism leveled against *fangshi* by Confucians, who congratulated themselves on their superior ability to assess character), Guan excelled in the use of the tortoise shell and milfoil stalks, astrology, physiognomy, and the interpretation of both "wind angles" (*fengjiao*) and bird calls. He was also an accomplished practitioner of the popular guessing game known as "shoot the cover" (*shefou*)—a skill for which the Han dynasty *fangshi* Dongfang Shuo (fl. c. 100 B.C.) was also admired.[114]

Considering the mantic techniques Guan used and the books he is known to have studied, it is evident that his contemporaries were correct in identifying him with the tradition of the great astrologer, numerologist and prognosticator of the Han dynasty, Jing Fang.[115] But Guan's astrologically based system of fate calculation, unlike Jing's *guaqi* system of calendrical correspondences, placed special emphasis on the year, month and day of one's birth. He is said to have remarked: "By the contained note [*nayin*] one's fate may be judged;" and again: "My fate is with the [earthly branch] *yin;* I was born at night during a lunar eclipse. Heaven has a fixed number, which can be known; but the common people don't know it." By these statements Guan Lu meant that one's life span was determined by the "agents" (*xing*) and astrological configurations associated with the time of that person's birth. Musical phraseology came to be used because, in keeping with Han-style correlative thinking, the notes on the standard Chinese bamboo pitchpipes were each associated with a particular element.[116]

Most of the stories told about Guan Lu revolve around his use of the *Yijing;* but the dynastic record also provides information concerning other types of fortune-telling, including Guan's creative combination of different but related techniques. His *Sanguo zhi* biography, for instance, tells us how he employed hexagrams, *nayin* calculations, and wind interpretation to predict the impending demise of an official's son. While visiting the official, Guan noticed a small whirlwind arising from the east. Mr. Wang, the official, asked his guest what this occurrence meant and Guan replied: "A mounted messenger is about to arrive from the east. I fear a father will be weeping for his son." The next day a clerk on horseback arrived with the news that Wang's own son had died. When asked to explain his prognostication, Guan responded:

> That day was the fifty-second day in the sexagenary cycle, a day that corresponds to the eldest son. Now wood declines in the ninth branch [*shen*], and the tail of the dipper sets up *shen*. *Shen* counteracts the third branch, *yin*, so this corresponds to death and mourning. The sun had entered the sector of the sixth branch [*si*], as it was midday, and a wind arose, which corresponds to a horse. The hexagram Li means writing, and is therefore clearly the sign of a clerk-messenger. The junction of the hours of *shen* and *wei* [3 P.M.], is the time of the tiger. The tiger stands for the master. This was therefore an indication of the father.[117]

The individuals Guan Lu most admired, and those with whom he later came to be compared, provide a litany of some of the most prestigious and influential diviners in Chinese history. The former category includes such ancient notables as Zi Shen, Bei Zao, Bu Yan, and Zi Wei, as well as the renowned Han dynasty fortune-teller Sima Jizhu; the latter group includes the illustrious Zhou diviners Gan De, Shi Shen, and Tang Ju, as well as the Han specialists Xu Fu and Jing Fang, and Guan's successor, Guo Pu.[118] Of particular significance is Guan Lu's admiration for, and effort to emulate, Sima Jizhu, who exemplified Confucian concern with the virtues of humaneness and right behavior, and who gained the admiration of high officials despite his lowly position. On the other hand, as critics of professional diviners pointed out, Guan—like Jing Fang before him and Guo Pu after him—failed to achieve a significant official position, and suffered an untimely death, despite his mantic skills.[119]

By the end of the Six Dynasties era, fate calculation techniques had spread throughout China, promoted by the writings as well as the practices of a number of talented diviners—notably Xiao Ji (d. c. 610)—whose book, *Wuxing dayi* (The Great Meaning of the "Five Agents"), is the sole surviving example of its genre from the period. Grounded solidly in *yinyang/wuxing* correspondence theory, and expressing the idea of an intimate relationship between Heaven, Earth and Man, Xiao's work explores images and numbers as they apply to human affairs. He attempts to show how the activities of the heavens (such as thunder, wind and rain) and groupings of heavenly bodies (such as the twenty-eight lunar lodges) reflect celestial images and numbers; how terrestrial configurations (such as mountains and rivers) and geographical groupings (the three rivers, four seas, five lakes, nine continents, etc.) exemplify earthly images and numbers; and how human activities (such as ritual and music) and groups of people and values (the hundred officials, the four teachings, the seven virtues, etc.) illustrate the images and numbers of human beings. By understanding such images and numbers, Xiao asserts, the workings of the *wuxing* can be understood.[120]

Xiao Ji served a number of rulers, including Emperor Wen, founder of the Sui dynasty. Sui Wendi's short-lived regime, like the Qin before it, brought strong centralized rule to China, but it engendered widespread enmity, and fell to popular rebellion. The Tang, like the Han, became great, glorious, and long-lasting, despite its ill-advised expansionism. In both instances the centralization of Chinese administration and the development of commerce and communications brought greater cultural unity to the Middle Kingdom. But history was not simply repeating itself. The Qin-Han and Sui-Tang periods were different in a number of ways—not least in their approach to ritual, religion, and divination. It is true that during both eras the reigning emperors continued to promote the ancestral cult and state religion, paid close attention to portents (with an eye toward using them to enhance their own power and legitimacy), and tried to maintain official orthodoxy, however defined. They selected auspicious days on which to undertake important events, and employed both *fangshi* and regular officials to undertake astrological and calendrical calculations on behalf of the dynasty.[121] But Buddhism and Religious Daoism played a far more important role in the daily life of Tang China than they did during the Han, and Tang state ritual had a more explicitly public function than it did in Han times.[122]

Calendrical science, undertaken during the Tang with the help of foreign (especially Indian) astronomers and foreign astronomical texts, became ever more precise, and ever more carefully guarded as a sphere of imperial responsibility. As a result, the dynasty made especially stringent efforts to control popular mantic practices—particularly those bearing on astrological and calendrical matters. The dynasty's legal code, for instance, stipulated that with only a few trivial exceptions, no private household could possess books, implements and other objects pertaining to "occult images" (*xuanxiang*); nor could its members keep astrological charts and prognostication texts.[123] Periodically, individual emperors attempted to make the state's prohibitions even more stringent. Thus, the Xuanzong emperor decreed in 739 that "All *yinyang* extrapolative numerology, unless it be for choosing [auspicious] days for weddings and funerals by divination, is forbidden."[124] Clearly the state worried incessantly about the political potential of divination in the hands of individuals operating outside the official state structure. This concern was not unwarranted. In the founding of the Tang, for example, millenarian prophecies by Buddhist and Daoist diviners helped Li Yuan (Gaozu, reigned 618–626) gain and consolidate popular support. Fortune-telling, the Tang rulers perceived, could be self-fulfilling.[125]

Attempts to constrain divination did not, of course, diminish interest in it, and the state was powerless in any case to control most mantic practices at the local level. In the first place, omen books circulated freely, and Han-style non-official almanacs, designating auspicious and inauspicious days for various activities, became increasingly popular.[126] Furthermore, the invention and spread of printing allowed enterprising entrepreneurs to begin producing illegal versions of the official state calendar itself, much to the dismay of Tang officials. By the tenth century at the latest the state itself began issuing special editions of the calendar for public consumption.[127] Popular astrology, meanwhile, was encouraged by the growth and sophistication of Religious Daoist star lore, as well as by the introduction and translation of Indian, Iranian and Tantric Buddhist texts. Concepts such as the twelve asterisms (*chen*) that marked the "stations" (*ci*) of the Jupiter ecliptic—analogous to the twelve signs of the Western zodiac—and the twenty-eight lodges gained widespread currency during the Tang. So did various new theories of "allocated fields" that correlated occurrences in a certain part of the sky with human affairs in a corresponding section of the earth.[128] The poetry of the period contains numerous references to "omen-taking from the stars" (*zhanxing*) as a device for determining individual fate. Liu Yuxi, writes, for example:

A merchant's daughter from the market of Yangzhou
Comes to take omens from the moonlit sky west of the Jiang.[129]

Fate extrapolation enjoyed unprecedented popularity during the Tang, despite periodic attacks by individual scholars such as Lü Cai (600–665), whose historical essay entitled "On Emolument Fate," included in the *Tushu jicheng*, became a model for later critics of unorthodox divination.[130] Li Xuzhong (fl. c. 790–835) built on the theoretical foundations laid by Guan Lu and Xiao Ji to become the most illustrious exponent of fate extrapolation in the Tang. Li, whose highly influential *Mingshu* (Book of Fate) is still extant, emphasized the day of birth as the most important single factor in determining one's destiny. He was later eulogized by the great Tang scholar Han Yu (768–824) for his deep knowledge of *yinyang/wuxing* transformations and for his infallability as a diviner. To this day he is considered one of the most important figures in the history of Chinese fate calculation.[131]

As in the Six Dynasties period, members of the Tang Buddhist and Daoist clergy, both men and women, continued to practice various forms of divination— including the use of the tortoise shell and the milfoil, astrology, physiognomy, geomancy, and various computational arts.[132] The most famous cleric of the Tang era was Yixing (d. c. 740), a Buddhist monk and official court astronomer during the reign of emperor Xuanzong. Renowned for his sagacity, perspicacity, and mantic skill, Yixing excelled in fate extrapolation, physiognomy and geomancy as well as mathematics, calendrical science and classical studies. He studied Han scholarship on the *Yijing*, authored or edited several books on astrology and other forms of divination, built a sophisticated armillary sphere for the emperor in order to make more accurate predictions of eclipses, and served as a trusted adviser and interpreter of portents for his imperial patron. At the same time, in self-conscious testimony to Buddhism's adoption of Confucian values, he promoted the idea that adherence to, or departure from, loyalty, filial piety, humaneness and right behavior influenced one's fortunes. Yixing is reputed to have been the teacher of one Li Mi, who later transmitted Yixing's methods of fate extrapolation to Li Xuzhong.[133]

The Late Imperial Era

Sui-Tang inventions such as printing, gunpowder and the compass, together with the dramatic social and economic changes that followed in the wake of An Lushan's rebellion (755–763), paved the way for a fundamental transformation of Chinese society in the Song dynasty (960–1279) and thereafter. This transformation was marked by, among other things, a revival of Confucian philosophy, the spread of literacy, and the introduction and maintenance of a rigid orthodoxy in the empire-wide civil service examination system from 1313 to 1904. For our purposes, the most important point is that the advent and expansion of printing facilitated the penetration of divination even further into Chinese popular culture, accentuating the inherent tension between official orthodoxy and less conventional modes of thought and behavior.[134]

The Song dynasty is perhaps best known for the rise of neo-Confucian philosophy. Among the most influential thinkers of the Song period were such well-known names as Fan Zhongyan (989–1052), Shao Yong (1011–1077), Zhou Dunyi (1017–1073), Sima Guang (1019–1086), Zhang Zai (1020–1077), Wang Anshi (1021–1086), Cheng Hao (1032–1085) and his brother, Cheng Yi (1033–1107), Su Shi (1037–1101), Zhu Xi (1130–1200) and Lu Zuqian (1137–1181). Despite the many differences separating these outstanding minds, all were concerned with reestablishing the reputation of Confucianism after centuries of eclipse. The process had begun in the Tang, but it accelerated rapidly in the eleventh and twelfth centuries. And although these thinkers were intent on renewing the luster of all the Confucian classics, they gave special attention to the *Yijing*.[135]

The reasons are not difficult to find. One was, of course, that the *Changes* proved to be such a rich repository of indigenous concepts—concepts that could be used to provide an appropriate and compelling Confucian response to the metaphysical challenge of Buddhism and Daoism. The classic offered, in the neo-Confucian view, a vision of pre-Qin rationalism and a celebration of life that contrasted starkly with the negative, world-denying philosophical tendencies of Buddhism and Daoism. Furthermore, since the Daoists had long claimed the *Yijing* as a classic, and because for nearly a thousand years it had been associated with occult practices and mysticism, neo-Confucian thinkers proved anxious to reestablish the work as a statement of rational principle (*li*). Some Song thinkers, notably Zhou Dunyi, continued to interpret the *Changes* in terms of Daoist "images and numbers," but most resisted interpretations that smacked of either Jing Fang's numerology or Wang Bi's "mysterious learning."[136]

The orthodox neo-Confucian view of the *Yijing* is perhaps best expressed in the well-known and highly influential compilation entitled *Jinsi lu* (Reflections on Things at Hand), edited by Zhu Xi and Lu Zuqian in the twelfth century. In it, Cheng Yi remarks that the classic is "comprehensive, great, and perfect. It is intended to bring about accord with the principle of the nature and destiny, to penetrate the causes of the hidden and the manifest, to reveal completely the nature of things and affairs, and to show the way to open resources and to accomplish great undertakings."[137] Yet despite the universal esteem Song scholars had for the *Changes*, they approached the book from several different angles, and with several different emphases. Shao Yong, for example, believed that its images and numbers "ordered the processes of an integrated universe." Cheng Yi took the book to be an explanation of principle, and as such, an essential device for teaching correct behavior in a world threatened by selfishness and corruption. Su Shi saw the *Changes* as evidence that an integrated human order "ultimately depended on individual creativity," while Zhu Xi felt that the *Yijing* was primarily a book of divination, to be used for realizing "the mind of the sages."[138]

Although Zhu was responsible for including in his *Zhouyi benyi* (The Basic Meaning of the Zhou Changes) Daoist-inspired numerological charts which had not been part of the original text of the *Yijing*, he was harshly critical of the sort of *Yijing* numerology espoused by Shao Yong. Zhu Xi also criticized Shao for his rigidly deterministic theory of cyclical change called "rhythms of fate" (*yunhui*), based on *yinyang* alternation and four primary variables: the sun (*yuan*), the moon (*hui*), the stars (*xing*), and divisions of time (*chen*). His quarrel was not so much with Shao's notions of cosmological chronology, however, as it was with his implication of inevitability.[139] Like all proper Confucians, Zhu viewed "fate" as something to be realized through moral exertion, not simply accepted passively as a "given."[140]

While Song scholars contemplated patterns of cosmic change with the help of the *Yijing*, geomancers investigated the cosmos with the aid of a new device, the compass (*luopan*, *luojing*, etc.). This south-pointing invention, derived in part from Han dynasty divining boards (*shi*) and designed explicitly for geomantic purposes, revealed celestial and terrestrial relationships by means of a series of concentric circles marked with standard symbols of time and space. Among the symbols regularly employed were the eight trigrams, the ten "heavenly stems" and twelve "earthly branches" of the sexegenary cycle, the twenty-eight "lodges," and so forth. A Song dynasty poem, written by the founder of the so-called Fujian school of geomancy (Wang Ji), and reproduced in the *Tushu jicheng*, attests to the importance of the compass to the geomancer's craft. It contains the following lines:

> Between the lodges Xu and Wei points clearly the needle's path
> But to the south the lodge Zhang "rides upon all three;"
> The trigrams Kan and Li stand due north and south, though people
>   cannot recognize [their subtleties],
> And if there is the slightest mistake there will be no correct
>   predictions.[141]

A Song prose text, also preserved in the *Tushu jicheng*, provides another indication of the way the compass linked heavenly patterns and earthly forms: "Nowadays geomancers use the *zhengzhen* [astronomical north and south points] and the *tianpan* [heaven-plate] system to find out where the dragon is; and they use the *fengzhen* [magnetic north and south points] to perform other divinations. Naturally the round plate follows Heaven and the square plate follows Earth."[142] Over time, the geomancer's compass became increasingly sophisticated, with up to forty concentric rings and symbolic variables that applied to several different divination systems (see chapter 4).

Similarly, fate extrapolation grew more complex. Whereas the techniques of Li Xuzhong and his predecessors in the Tang involved at most a consideration of the year, month and day of birth, later diviners—notably the tenth-century hermit Xu Ziping and his many followers—took into account the hour as well. These "four pillars" (*sizhu*) of destiny, each designated by two characters, came to be known as one's "eight characters" (*bazi*), a common term in Chinese divination today. This refinement, together with the addition of certain variables derived from popular astrology and the notion of decennial periods of fate (*yun*), produced a system, still in widespread use today, that found its most complete expression in a Ming dynasty work entitled *Sanming tonghui* (Compendium of the Three Fates).[143]

The spread of printing in the Song dynasty contributed to the rise of Chinese popular literature, and to the gradual growth of literacy. Books of all kinds, including calendars, almanacs, and divining manuals, became ever more accessible to the general public. Divination no longer required a direct line of transmission from master to pupil, and fortune-tellers seem to have been increasingly self-taught from this period onward. Although the greater availability of information on mantic techniques made them appear somewhat less "occult," it certainly did not diminish demand for the services of fortune-tellers. Divination became a common literary theme, reflected not only in poetry, but also in narrative works such as short stories, and later, during the Yuan and Ming dynasties, in plays and novels. Though often the butt of scholarly jokes, fortune-tellers were ubiquitous.[144]

A heightened awareness of the written language through the printed word seems to have been at least partially responsible for the popularity of "dissecting" characters (*chaizi*) as a form of divination during the Song period and thereafter. The acknowledged progenitor of this art in late imperial times was the eleventh century savant Xie Shi.[145] Printing also contributed to the mass appeal of divination by "spiritual sticks" (*lingqian*), which, like many fortune-telling techniques in the late imperial era, came to be practiced in or near Buddhist and Daoist religious temples. The *lingqian* system grew out of several preexisting Chinese mantic practices, all related at least tangentially to the *Yijing*. These included the selection of lots and the use of prophetic verses. Although the techniques varied from region to region and time to time, all *lingqian* divination involved the selection of versified mantic messages by means of numbered bamboo slips. It promoted Confucian values and drew heavily upon Buddhist and Daoist religious inspiration as well. Two of the most famous books in the *lingqian* tradition are the *Lingqi jing* (Classic of the Spiritual Chessman), which boasted a poetic core dating from the fifth century at the latest, and the *Tianzhu lingqian* (Heavenly Bamboo [Indian] Spiritual Sticks), produced in the early or mid-thirteenth century. These works, and others modeled after them, exerted a profound influence on mantic practices in China, as well as in other areas that fell under China's powerful cultural influence—Tibet, Japan, Korea and Annam.[146]

One of the most interesting and enduring innovations in Chinese divination during the Tang-Song period was "spirit-writing" (*fuji* or *fuluan*), in which "possessed" images, objects, and individuals conveyed messages about the present and future. Early shamanistic spirit possession in China did not generally involve literacy, but by the eleventh century A.D. it had come to be associated closely with the scholarly elite. Over time, the *fuji* tradition merged with the "morality book" (*shanshu*) and "precious scroll" (*baojuan*) tradition of popular literature, with the result that entire volumes came to be written by deities on ethical themes.[147] Meanwhile, Song dynasty sectarian Buddhism had begun to promote the messianic idea of a world-wide "Heavenly destiny" (*Tianyun*), predicated on the assumption that a new utopian age would be inaugurated by the advent of the Buddha of the Future. Naturally enough, the subsections on divination in the *Tushu jicheng* and other officially-compiled sources ignore such threatening notions, but they do indicate that a large number of Buddhist (and Daoist) clerics continued to indulge in more orthodox mantic techniques, and that many wrote books on geomancy and other related subjects.[148]

During the Yuan dynasty (1279–1368), few fundamental changes took place in either the theory or practice of divination. Tang-Song techniques of fate calculation, geomancy and physiognomy, Daoist prayers and rituals, Buddhist incantations and spells and the activities of shamans and witches all proved to be fully compatible with syncretic Mongol beliefs. Yelü Chucai (1189–1243), a sinicized Khitan adviser to Chinggis Khan, employed Chinese-style divination on behalf of the khan before the latter headed into battle, and thereafter the Mongols almost always divined to determine the most auspicious time to embark on military expeditions. Later emperors built on this precedent. Thus, for example, Liu Bingzhong (1216–1274), a trusted adviser to Qubilai Khan, came to be particularly valued for his expertise with the *Yijing*, and Zhang Liusun, a disciple of the Religious Daoist Celestial Master, Zhang Zongyan, won favor at the court of emperor Wuzong (1307–1311) for his divining skills.[149]

The more sinicized the Mongols became, the more their divining practices approximated those of the Tang-Song era. But the Yuan dynasty continued to draw upon Mongol and other non-Chinese traditions in its divinatory and calendrical affairs, as it had in many realms of civil and military administration. The Yuan established, for example, a Muslim Astronomy Bureau (Huihui sitian jian) which employed Islamic astronomers, and used an Arabic calendar from 1267 to 1281.[150] It also patronized Tibetan lamaism, which provided a rich store of divining lore. Although influenced heavily by Chinese ideas and practices since the Tang dynasty, divination in Tibet had its own unique cast.[151]

The establishment of the Ming dynasty in 1368 brought a reassertion of native Chinese rule, but the syncretic spirit of the Yuan remained, and in fact intensified. The first emperor, Zhu Yuanzhang (Ming Taizu, reigned 1368–1398), a former Buddhist novice, vigorously promoted the idea of the "unity of the three teachings [Confucianism, Daoism and Buddhism]" (*sanjiao heyi*). He believed in ghosts and spirits, and placed special faith in divination as a means of receiving spiritual guidance (see also chapter 5).[152] Most of his successors held similar views, and some were even more entranced by "sorcery and superstitious practices." These included not only Daoist magic and rituals but also divination techniques such as astrology, geomancy, *fengjiao*, and even spirit-writing.[153] As a result of imperial patronage, Ming syncretism had an unprecedented impact on the Chinese religious imagination at all levels. Liu Ts'un-yan asserts, for instance, that the occult arts and beliefs of Religious Daoism were "never more powerful or pervasive among all social strata" in China than during the Ming.[154]

Ming syncretism also had institutional manifestations. Zhu Yuanzhang permitted the Yuan dynasty's Muslim Astronomy Bureau to function alongside its more traditional Chinese counterpart, and he employed a number of Islamic experts to translate Muslim texts on astronomy, astrology and the calendar. The Ming emperors even allowed an unofficial Muslim calendar (*Huihui li*) to exist together with the official Ming calendar (*Datong li*).[155] When the Jesuits reached Peking in the early seventeenth century, their astronomical and calendrical skills immediately caught the attention of the Chinese. Their predictions of eclipses were more precise, and they brought with them marvelous new technologies from the West, including, of course, the telescope. Thus, they, like their Islamic predecessors and contemporaries, found official employment in the Imperial Board of Astronomy (Qintian jian), established in 1380.[156]

Western missionary accounts of the late Ming period attest to the nearly universal prevalence of astrology and other forms of divination in China. Matteo Ricci, the pioneering Jesuit scientist and official Ming court astronomer, wrote, for example, of the deeply-held conviction among his colleagues in the Board of Astronomy that "everything happening on this terrestrial globe of ours depends on the stars."[157] He also remarked disparagingly on the common practice of choosing auspicious and inauspicious days (*zeri*) for various activities and events. According to the *Da Ming huidian* (Collected Statutes of the Ming Dynasty), the Board of Astronomy held responsibility for determining appropriate and inappropriate times for literally dozens of undertakings, from imperial and official rituals to mundane matters such as bathing and receiving medical care. In both the official calendar and in popular almanacs these activities were indicated by individual columns for each day of the year.[158] Ricci observed of the practice: "No superstition is so common in the entire kingdom. . . . [and] the imposture has assumed such a semblance of truth among the people that two calendars are edited each year, . . . [and] are said to be sold in such great quantities that every house has a supply of them."[159] Ironically, one of the accusations later leveled against the Jesuits by jealous and hostile Chinese scholars was the improper selection of a burial date and site for a deceased Manchu prince (see chapter 2).

Despite the mysticism and metaphysical speculation that prevailed in Ming times—particularly toward the end of the dynasty—there were at least a few individuals in addition to the Jesuits who attempted to steer China toward a different intellectual course. Lai Zhide (1525–1604), for example, devised new interpretations of the *Yijing* in order to remedy what he saw as the deficiencies of both Han and Song scholarship (see chapter 3); and Wang Tingxiang (1474–1544) launched a vigorous attack on various systems of correlative cosmology, including the analogies of Dong Zhongshu, the numerology of Shao Yong, the *fenye* system, and efforts to coordinate the *Yijing* with astronomy and the calendar. Lü Kun (1536–1618) called special attention to the many irregularities in nature that defied arbitrary correlative schemes, and he criticized in particular the neatness of *yinyang* categorization.[160]

These early voices of dissent were joined by a rising chorus of cosmological criticism that followed the Manchu conquest of 1644. This traumatic event, which impelled many Chinese scholars to retire from public life and at least a few to take up divination as either a vocation or a full-time job, encouraged a growing number of individuals to repudiate Ming dynasty patterns of thought and scholarship. The Jesuits of the late seventeenth and early eighteenth century became enthusiastic allies in this intellectual enterprise, motivated by evangelical concerns and possessed of a growing arsenal of scientific, mathematical, and technological weapons. But critics of the inherited cosmology faced a formidable enemy. In the first place, the traditional civil service examination system powerfully reinforced traditional attitudes. Since 1313, Zhu Xi's commentaries had provided the orthodox neo-Confucian interpretation of the classics; and only a complete mastery of these sacred texts and Zhu's comprehensive interpretations brought the assurance of social mobility and bureaucratic success to aspiring Chinese scholars. Secondly, the Qing state, like all of its imperial predecessors, rested on explicitly cosmological assumptions that were not only reflected in official ideology but also institutionalized in the bureaucracy, state worship, secular rituals and the annual calendar. A comprehensive assault on the cosmology was nothing less than an attack on the imperial system itself. Third, as related systems of "applied cosmology," practices such as divination and medicine were an integral part of Chinese society at all levels.

In short, well over three thousand years of development had produced a colorful patchwork of mantic beliefs and practices that were neither internally consistent nor universally admired, but which nonetheless had become essential to the conduct of Chinese daily life. Although the pattern of their evolution remains to be more fully delineated, it is clear that from earliest times Chinese divination followed the general contours of Chinese social and political thought, both reflecting it and in turn affecting it. As a ritualized procedure, royal divination conformed to the trend of growing secularization from Shang to Zhou times, and, symptomatic of the intellectual changes occurring in the late Zhou, divining techniques became ever more diverse and widespread. In the Han, divination blended smoothly with the correlative cosmology of Dong Zhongshu, and began to reflect orthodox Confucian values in a self-conscious way—although it also suffered the stigma of its association with a new breed of occult specialists, the *fangshi*.

Throughout the imperial era, new divining techniques grew out of new historical circumstances, but old practices were seldom abandoned entirely. After some initial reluctance, Buddhism and Religious Daoism embraced divination and contributed to its popularity. Reunification of the empire, together with dramatic new intellectual and technological developments in the Tang-Song era, brought a knowledge of divination to virtually everyone in Chinese society, high and low, and to many people outside of China as well. The new print culture of the late imperial era, which included story books, dramas, and eventually novels, reflected the pervasiveness of divination as a social phenomenon. So did the orthodox dynastic histories of every era, not to mention local gazetteers, encyclopedias, and other reference works. The editors of the *Tushu jicheng* in the Qing period thus had a vast store of material to draw upon in putting together their several large subsections on divination. The important point to keep in mind is that the techniques and works included in this monumental work were part of a living and still vital tradition.

TWO

Orthodox Cosmology in the Qing

The Qing was the largest consolidated empire in Chinese history and by far the most successful dynasty of conquest. No regime was more "Confucian" in outlook and emphasis or more self-consciously antiquarian. The reasons were essentially pragmatic: As alien invaders, the Manchus had to legitimize the position they had won solely by force of arms. They did so by claiming to be the high-minded and upright protectors of China's cultural heritage against the "barbarism" of the domestic rebel, Li Zicheng (1605-1645), who had toppled the Ming dynasty in 1644. In a self-conscious (and self-interested) effort to demonstrate their devotion to traditional Chinese values, the Manchus not only adopted the cosmology, calendar, political institutions, rituals and religious practices of the fallen dynasty, but they also supported the Ming civil service examination system and its official orthodoxy. They ardently patronized traditional Chinese art, music and literature, and, on the whole, preserved existing patterns of social and economic life. Thanks largely to this systematic policy of sinicization, and to the phenomenal peace and prosperity enjoyed by most Chinese during the reigns of the Kangxi (1662-1722), Yongzheng (1723-1735) and Qianlong (1736-1795) emperors, the Qing was a period of enrichment and "leisurely fulfillment" in material culture and the arts.[1]

The Qing inheritance included elements of transformation as well as tradition. Beginning in the latter part of the Ming, a series of important changes began to take place in China: urbanization of the lower Yangzi River valley, the commutation of labor services into money payments, the growth of regional trade, the emergence of a national market in bulk commodities, increased geographical mobility, the explosion of popular literacy, an increase in the size of the gentry class, the professionalization of local managerial activities, and so forth.[2] These social and economic changes, together with the dramatic political events of the Ming-Qing transition, led to transformations in the style of local politics, in patterns of personal and intellectual affiliation, and ultimately in modes of thought. It was no accident that the major scholarly development of the early Qing—the rise of the iconoclastic school of "evidential research" (*kaozheng xue*)—emerged in the prosperous lower Yangzi delta, where initially the Manchu rulers had taken pains to gain the support of Chinese scholars through semi-official patronage, and where both wealth and lineage connections brought to local literati a large measure of intellectual independence from the state's official orthodoxy.[3]

Ironically, the individuals who attacked Qing orthodoxy most vigorously in the eighteenth century were themselves the products of a civil service examination system based on orthodox principles. From the early years of Manchu rule until 1905, Zhu Xi's neo-Confucian interpretations of the classics, known generally as Song learning, remained the key to success in the examinations. Most *kaozheng* scholars possessed the advanced degrees necessary for bureaucratic advancement, but they had little interest in official careers themselves. Liberated from careerism and armed with sophisticated philological techniques as well as a passionate desire for "seeking truth from facts" (*shishi qiu shi*), they attacked the hitherto sacred texts of neo-Confucianism as transmitted and annotated by Zhu Xi; and with their assault came vigorous criticisms of the inherited cosmology.[4] During the next century, dynastic decline and the invasion of the Western powers brought new challenges to both the throne and Qing intellectuals that undermined the socio-economic foundations of the *kaozheng* movement on the one hand, while generating intense interest in "practical statecraft" (*jingshi zhi xue*) and radical "New Text" (*jinwen*) Confucianism on the other.[5]

The question of interest here is the relationship between changing intellectual currents and inherited notions of cosmology and cosmography that underlay Qing theories of divination. John Henderson, in his broad-ranging and highly influential study entitled *The Rise and Decline of Chinese Cosmology*, has written that one of the most significant trends in Chinese intellectual history during the late imperial era was the "assimilation of cosmologically subversive technical and empirical studies such as classical philology, mathematical astronomy, and historical and physical geography into the mainstream of Confucian scholarship."[6] Assaults by Qing scholars on the inherited cosmology were so effective, he claims, that the radical intellectual leaders of the New Culture Movement (c. 1915–1925) "did not think it necessary to compose a comprehensive [cosmological] critique."[7] Henderson asserts, moreover, that along with the decline of the traditional cosmology, came "more or less popular criticism" of at least a few of the more prevalent forms of Chinese divination, notably geomancy.[8] There can be no doubt that a fundamental epistemological shift took place in Chinese thinking during the seventeenth and eighteenth centuries, and that this shift had important intellectual implications. Yet it is possible that Henderson has overemphasized the subversive impact of *kaozheng* scholarship. How pervasive in fact were Qing criticisms of cosmology and divination, and how effective were these critiques in transforming Chinese attitudes toward fate and fortune? Let us begin with a general picture of what was under attack.

State-sponsored Cosmology

The Qing government's view of the cosmos was extraordinarily complex. As the possessors of the Heavenly Mandate and inheritors of a long tradition of celestial observation and earthly administrative responsibility, the Manchus— like all of their dynastic predecessors—found it necessary to develop a cosmology that took into account every relevant variable and penetrated every meaningful realm of Chinese life. Their interest was essentially pragmatic, for, as Mencius had emphasized, Heaven's desire was that those who had foreknowledge (*qianzhi*) should instruct those who were slower to apprehend.[9] And who should know first, or most, about the universe than the Son of Heaven himself? Viewed from another perspective, the emperor had to understand the processes of cosmic change so as to assure that the social order and nature's *dao* would be fully congruent. "Failure of the official system to predict [cosmic events] was necessarily a sign of moral imperfection, a warning that the monarch's virtue was not adequate to keep him in touch with the celestial rhythms."[10] Above all, knowledge of the patterns of cosmic change made possible attainment of the Chinese ritual ideal: doing the right thing, at the right time, in the right place, facing the right direction.[11]

The following discussion of Qing cosmology is based primarily on the *Xingli kaoyuan* (An Investigation into Astrological Calendrics), the *Xieji bianfang shu* (Book of Harmonizing the Times and Distinguishing the Directions), and other imperially-authorized sources that were used in divinatory calculations by the state. It makes no claim to comprehensiveness, and in fact merely hints at the complexities of time, space and causality expounded upon in these documents. My purpose is simply to introduce certain cosmological concepts that will recur throughout this book, and to show the many ways in which they are interrelated and interdependent.[12]

One of the most striking features of the inherited cosmology is its ability to tolerate a high degree of apparent inconsistency, despite continual efforts on the part of the state to eliminate "contradictions" (*maodun*) in its various official cosmological works.[13] One reason for this toleration was undoubtedly the harmonizing, syncretic nature of traditional Chinese thought, which resisted the idea of mutual exclusiveness even while recognizing the principle, and esteemed "unitary meaning" (*yiyi*) more than "mere logic." As Paul Unschuld has observed in his study of Chinese medicine: "Somehow a way was always found in China to reconcile opposing views and to build bridges—fragile as they may appear to the outside observer—permitting thinkers and practitioners to employ liberally all the concepts available, as long as they were not regarded as destructive to society."[14]

The Qianlong emperor's preface to the *Xieji bianfang shu* suggests another reason for tolerating inconsistency—a pragmatic concern for the preservation of popular customs that bolstered, or at least did not threaten, imperial authority. Pointing out that terrestrial harmony could only be achieved by faithfully following the patterns and principles of Heaven, the emperor's preface emphasized that errors in previous Qing publications, including the *Xingli kaoyuan*, necessitated revisions in the form of the *Xieji bianfang shu*. Significantly, however, he admitted that not all of the mistakes in previous works could be corrected, since a number of popular practices based on admittedly flawed principles were so well established that "to eradicate them completely would be inconvenient to the people."[15]

The *Xingli kaoyuan* and *Xieji bianfang shu* both begin with discussions of "the basics" (*benyao* or *benyuan*)—the fundamental powers that interacted to produce change in the universe. The most important of these were, of course, the primal forces of *yin* and *yang*. The "Great Commentary" of the *Yijing* states simply: "One *yin* and one *yang* constitute the Way [*dao*]."[16] The interaction between *yin* and *yang* was, however, anything but simple. In some situations they harmonized and in others they clashed—though balanced harmony was always the natural (cultural) ideal. As generative forces *yin* and *yang* produced all things, including each other; and at the same time they were inseparable from one another. Zhu Xi once remarked: "In the things produced by Heaven, there cannot be *yin* alone; there must also be *yang*. And there cannot be *yang* alone; there must always be *yin*." This statement recalls Zhang Zai's idea of "one thing in dual form" (*yiwu liangti*).[17] It would be misleading, however, to think of *yin* and *yang* only as things, for although they had a concrete manifestation when expressed in *qi* (material force), they also represented *aspects* of things, and above all, aspects of natural process: growth and decline, activity and tranquility, rise and fall, condensation and dispersion, influence and response.[18]

According to orthodox cosmology, *yin* and *yang* animated the processes of cosmic change. From their interaction and alternation all other transformations became possible; and with the creation of the *Yijing*, these processes could be depicted symbolically.[19] The *Xingli kaoyuan* begins with a quotation from the classic: "[In making the *Changes*, the ancient sages] determined the Way of Heaven and called it *yin* and *yang*; they determined the way of Earth and called it the yielding and the firm."[20] One of the several illuminating charts in Zhu Xi's *Zhouyi benyi* (Basic Meaning of the Changes) shows how *yin* and *yang*—themselves generated by a "Supreme Ultimate" (*Taiji*)—produced the "four images" of greater *yang* and lesser *yang*, greater *yin* and lesser *yin*. These, in turn, became the eight trigrams, which by the same process of doubling eventually yielded the sixty-four hexagrams. Each of these hexagrams, like the primary trigrams, had a *yin* or *yang* identification and each possessed cosmic power.[21] In Qing popular art, the eight trigrams often surrounded Zhou Dunyi's depiction of *yin* and *yang* as two balanced forces of dark and light within a circle, known as the "Diagram of the Supreme Ultimate" (*Taiji tu*; see Fig. 2.1).[22]

The "Great Commentary" of the *Yijing* tells us: "The unfathomable aspect of *yin* and *yang* is called spirit [*shen*]."[23] The term *shen* appears often in the "Ten Wings" of the *Changes*, but in many different contexts, and with a number of possible meanings. Sometimes *shen* refers to an actual spiritual presence or deity, while at others it denotes the more abstract quality of "essential spirit" (*jingshen*) or "spiritual intelligence" (*shenming*).[24] In the "Great Commentary" this quality applies to things as seemingly diverse as human beings and milfoil stalks, suggesting a common ground of spirituality in all natural phenomena. *Shen*, in the orthodox view, provided the means by which the superior man could gain access to, and identify with, the mind of Heaven (see chapter 3). Zhu Xi, who once described *shen* as "the character of the sage, mysterious and unfathomable," wrote in the preface of his *Zhouyi benyi*: "Take [the *Yijing*] into the circulation of your spirit [*jingshen*] and the movement of

Taiji 太極

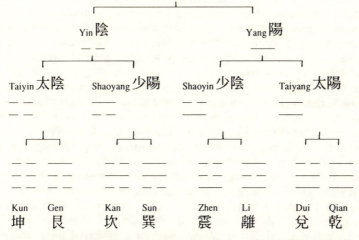

Yin 陰   Yang 陽

Taiyin 太陰   Shaoyang 少陽   Shaoyin 少陰   Taiyang 太陽

| Kun | Gen | Kan | Sun | Zhen | Li | Dui | Qian |
| 坤 | 艮 | 坎 | 巽 | 震 | 離 | 兌 | 乾 |

Figure 2.1 *Top:* The *Taiji tu* (*yinyang*) symbol surrounded by the eight trigrams in the Former Heaven order. *Bottom:* Origins of the eight trigrams, adapted from Zhu Xi, *Zhouyi benyi* (Taibei, 1979 reprint), *yitu*, p. 3a.

your mind. Join your virtue with Heaven and Earth, your brightness with the sun and the moon, your orderliness with the four seasons, and your fortune and misfortune with the ghosts and spirits [*guishen*]. After this is done, you can speak of knowing the *Changes.*"[25]

The term *guishen* appears often in the *Yijing* and other classical sources, as well as the writings of later scholars. From a popular standpoint, *gui* instantly conjures up the idea of evil spirits or "ghosts," while *shen* evokes notions of benevolent spirits or "gods." But Qing intellectuals, following the lead of Zhu Xi and his disciples, tended to interpret the explicitly spiritual vocabulary of the classics in rather abstract terms; thus, good and evil spirits became equated with *yang* and *yin*—even though both sets of terms might be found together in the same classical passage.[26] Chen Chun (1159–1223), one of Zhu's most capable students, discussed *gui* and *shen* at length in his influential *Beixi ziyi*

(My Explanation of [neo-Confucian] Terms), reprinted several times in the early Qing and republished in 1882 as the *Xingli ziyi* (Explanation of Terms Concerning Nature and Principle). So extensive is his discussion of these terms that it occupies about one sixth of the entire text.[27]

By Chen's account, *gui* and *shen* represent the contraction and expansion, or advance and retreat, of the two material forces (*qi*) of *yin* and *yang*. "In terms of material force as two," he tells us, "the positive spiritual force [*shen*] is the spirit [*ling*] of *yang* and the negative spiritual force [*gui*] is the spirit of *yin*. By spirit is meant simply the liveliness of spontaneous expansion and contraction or coming and going. In terms of material force as one, the material force that is in the process of expanding and coming belongs to *yang* and constitutes the positive spiritual force, while the material force that has already contracted and gone belongs to *yin* and constitutes the negative spiritual force."[28] Thus, for example, he says: "spring and summer are material force that is in the process of growing; they belong to *yang* and constitute the positive spiritual force. Autumn and winter are material force that has already receded; they belong to *yin* and constitute the negative spiritual force. In reality, the two material forces are only one."[29]

Qing scholars expressed similar views, using much the same language. Zhou Yuanding, for example, wrote a widely circulated tract in the nineteenth century, entitled "Essay on Ghosts and Spirits," which seems in several places to be lifted almost verbatim from Chen Chun.[30] Likewise, the compilers of the imperial edition of the *Liji* during the Qianlong period—in glossing a passage that reads: "Man is a product of the powers of Heaven and Earth, the interaction of *yin* and *yang*, the union of *gui* and *shen*, and the refined essence of the five agents [*wuxing*]—explain that the characteristic attributes of Heaven and Earth are contained in the two primal forces, which, when spoken of in their fundamental character, are called *yin* and *yang*, and when spoken of in their developing power are called *gui* and *shen*. When manifest in material force, the editors go on to say, they are called the *wuxing*.[31]

Although orthodox neo-Confucians (and virtually all other Chinese) understood the creation of the so-called five agents or activities—identified with the "elements" of wood, metal, fire, water, and earth (see chapter 1)—as arising from the spontaneous interaction of *yin* and *yang*, few Qing intellectuals showed an interest in how this process actually took place, from the standpoint of either science or metaphysics.[32] Zhu Xi's time-worn explanation (which was no real answer at all) centered on the idea of a Supreme Ultimate that generated the forces of *yin* and *yang* and served as the source and sum of the ideal forms or principles (*li*) around which material force coalesced to comprise all things. He likened the process to a millwheel grinding out *qi* like cosmic flour; according to different times and thus different combinations of *yinyang* and *wuxing* influences, "material force could be coarse or refined, and therefore men and things might be balanced or unbalanced, refined or coarse."[33]

The five agents had *yinyang* identifications that were designated either "greater" or "lesser;" and, like *yin* and *yang*, each of the five had tangible cosmic power embodied in, or at least exerting an influence on, "material force."[34] The

important point, then, is that both *yinyang* and the *wuxing*, whether conceived
as external forces or intrinsic qualities, constantly fluctuated and interacted as
part of the eternal, cyclical rhythms of nature. In discerning patterns of change,
everything depended on timing and the relative strength of the variables
involved. By taking into account these factors, one could predict whether
movement would be progressive or retrogressive, fast or slow, auspicious or
inauspicious.[35]

As cosmic forces, the *wuxing* operated in sequential patterns, dominating
situations according to the principle that things of the same kind (*tonglei*)
activate each other. And just as the balance of *yin* and *yang* determined the
physical makeup of material things, so it influenced cosmic process. At the
most basic level, it dictated whether the sequential operation of the *wuxing*
would be one of "mutual production" (*xiangsheng*) or "mutual conquest"
(*xiangke*).[36] In the former sequence, wood produced fire, fire produced earth,
earth produced metal, metal produced water, and water produced wood. In
the latter, wood conquered earth, metal conquered wood, fire conquered metal,
water conquered fire, and earth conquered water (see Glossary A). From these
two fundamental sequences, two others arose: "mutual transformation" (*xianghua*)
and "mutual control" (*xiangzhi*). According to the theory of mutual transformation, conquest could be undermined by the process of production; thus,
although wood conquered earth, fire transformed the process (by producing
earth faster than wood conquered it). Similarly, in mutual control, wood
conquered earth but metal controlled the process by overcoming the destroyer.
Yet another conception of *wuxing* activity involved twelve phases of change,
roughly analogous to stages in the human life-cycle, from the womb (*tai*) to
extinction (*jue*). From this standpoint, if fire were in an ascending phase and
water were in a descending phase, the two would neutralize each other rather
than allowing the latter to dominate the former (see chapter 5).[37]

Like the *wuxing*, with which they were usually associated, the eight trigrams
worked their power in predictable sequences or patterns (see Glossary A). They
were symbols with substance. The two most common depictions of their
relationship appear in the *Xingli kaoyuan* and the *Xieji bianfang shu* as octagonal
forms, each constructed according to the "Discussion of the Trigrams" commentary to the *Yijing*. The Former Heaven (*xiantian*) arrangement, attributed
to Fu Xi, displays the eight trigrams in four sets, each set corresponding to
one of the four seasons (depicted in clockwise order, with summer located in
the south, at the top of the diagram). The juxtapositions are: Qian (heaven)
and Kun (earth); Sun (wind) and Zhen (thunder); Kan (water) and Li (fire); and
Gen (mountain) and Dui (lake). In this conception, the forces represented by
the trigrams take effect as pairs of complementary opposites, although their
wuxing correlations do not not reflect these pairings. Qian and Dui are associated
with metal; Sun and Zhen with wood; Kan with water; Gen and Kun with
earth; and Li with fire.[38]

The Later Heaven (*houtian*) arrangement, attributed to King Wen, presents
the trigrams in a temporal order that depicts developmentally the course of
the year, and by analogy, the course of the day. In this scheme, Zhen ("the

arousing," in the east) marks the beginning of the year/day, followed by Sun ("the gentle," in the southeast), Li ("the clinging," in the south), Kun ("the receptive," in the southwest), Dui ("the joyous," in the west), Qian ("the creative," northwest), Kan ("the abysmal," in the north), and Gen ("keeping still," in the northeast). In terms of *wuxing* correlations, Kun and Gen are linked with earth, Dui and Qian with metal, Kan with water, Zhen and Sun with wood, and Li with fire (see Fig. 2.2).

The Qing physician Li Yanshi (1628–1697) provides an excellent illustration of how the trigrams, representing not only developmental processes but also positions in space, exert influence—in this case on specific parts of the body. He is discussing the evaluation of pulse sites (*xue*) on the hands:

> North is Kan, the site of water. South is Li, the site of fire. East is Zhen, the site of wood. West is Dui, the site of metal. The center is Kun, the site of earth. Try facing south and looking at the sites in the two hands. The heart belongs to fire and resides in the *cun* [inch] site. This also is in the south. The kidneys belong to water. They reside in the *chi* [foot] site. This also is in the north. The liver belongs to wood. It resides in the left. This is also in the east. The lungs belong to metal. They reside in the right. This also is in the west. The spleen belongs to earth. It resides in the *guan* [pass] site. This is also in the center.

Li's assumption, an article of cosmological faith, is that each location in the universe, and—according to correspondence theory—each site on the body, is enmeshed in a specific network of responsiveness dictated solely by position.[39]

As first conceived in the *najia* system of Jing Fang and his successors (see chapter 1), the ten stems and the twelve branches of the sexegenary cycle were correlated with yin and yang, the *wuxing*, and the eight trigrams; so naturally they acquired cosmic power (see Glossary A).[40] Of the stems, *jia, bing, wu, geng,* and *ren* were considered yang, while *yi, ding, ji, xin,* and *gui* were considered yin. Of the branches, *yin, wu, chen, shen, zi,* and *xu* were considered yang, while *mao, si, chou, you, hai,* and *wei* were considered yin. From the standpoint of *wuxing* correlations (and therefore also trigram configurations), *jia* and *yi* were linked with wood and the east; *bing* and *ding,* with fire and the south; *wu* and *ji,* with earth and the center; *geng* and *xin,* with metal and the west; and *ren* and *gui,* with water and the north. The branches followed the same basic pattern, except that earth accomodated four of them instead of two: *chen, xu, chou* and *wei.*[41] Of course, as indicated above, trigram affiliations varied according to the configuration or sequence, whether Former Heaven or Later Heaven[42] (see Fig. 2.3).

When brought together to make a complete cycle of sixty in the *nayin* ("contained note") system of calendars, almanacs and personal horoscopes (see next section and chapter 5), the stem-branch combinations fell into five groups of twelve, each group associated with an "element," and each combination paired with another combination under an appropriate name. Thus, the first two stem-branch combinations, *jiazi* and *yichou,* were identified with metal and called "gold in the sea" (*haizhong jin*). The third and fourth, *bingyin* and *dingmao,* were identified with fire; the fifth and sixth, *wuchen* and *jisi,* with

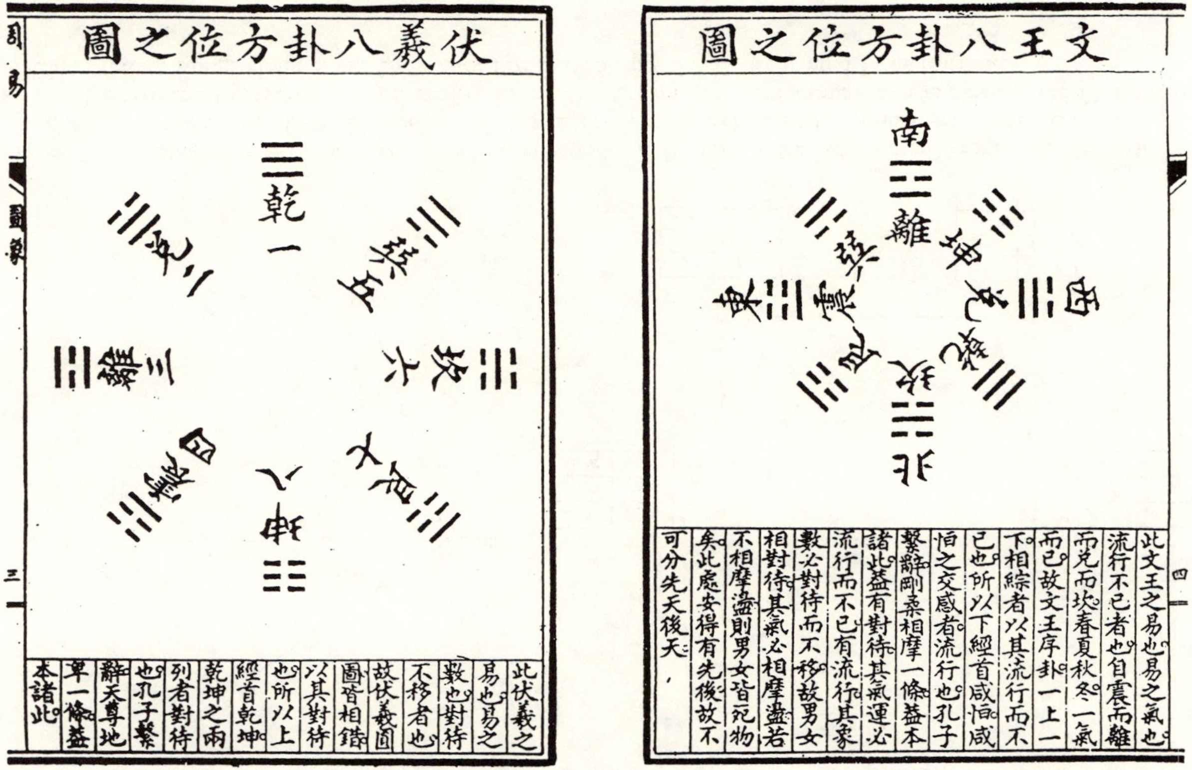

Figure 2.2 *Left*: The eight trigrams in Fu Xi's Former Heaven sequence. *Right*: The eight trigrams in King Wen's Later Heaven sequence. *Source*: Lai Zhide, *Yijing Laizhu tujie* (Taibei, 1971 reprint), *tuxiang*, pp. 3 and 4.

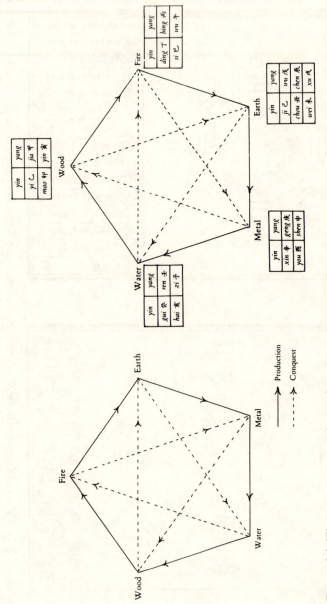

Figure 2.3 *Wuxing activities and stem-branch correlations. Left:* The orders of Mutual Production and Mutual Conquest of the five *xing. Right:* The orders of Mutual Production and Mutual Conquest of the ten celestial stems and twelve terrestrial branches. *Source:* Peng-Yoke Ho, Li, Qi, and Shu: *An Introduction to Science and Civilization in China* (Hong Kong, Hong Kong University Press, 1985), pp. 32–33. Reprinted by permission.

wood, and so on through the *wuxing* in either the production or the conquest order. After each sequence of five, the pattern repeated itself, so that the eleventh and twelfth stem-branch combinations, *renshen* and *guiyou* ("metal in the sword tip;" *jianfeng jin*) were followed by *jiaxu* and *yihai* ("fire on the mountain top;" *shantou huo*), and so forth. Cycles of sixty and their various sub-cycles were considered part of larger rhythmic cycles, culminating ultimately in Shao Yong's notion of recurrent and eternal periods of 129,600 years.[43]

By virtue of their correlations with the *wuxing*, the stems and branches operated in both production and conquest sequences. Thus, for example, the stem *jia* (wood) produced the stem *bing* (fire), just as the branch *si* (fire) conquered the branch *shen* (metal). On the other hand, certain opposing signs had affinities with their opposites. Thus, the stem *jia* (identified with wood and *yang*) harmonized with the stem *ji* (earth and *yin*), just as the stem *bing* (identified with fire and *yang*) harmonized with *xin* (metal and *yin*). The character of the stems and branches could also change in combination, for when a *yin* stem became linked to a *yin* branch, it acted like *yang*. Thus a pairing of any of the stems *yi, ding, ji, xing* or *gui* with any of the branches *chou, mao, si, wei, you* and *hai*, produced a *yang* effect.[44]

The *wuxing* and trigrams (and therefore the stems and branches) were correlated with the *Hetu* (Yellow River Chart) and the *Luoshu* (Luo River Writing)—both of which, as the *Yijing* informs us, served as conceptual models for the sages[45] (see Fig. 2.4). The compilers of the *Xieji bianfang shu* assert: "The *Hetu* and the *Luoshu* are the source of the production and conquest sequences of the *wuxing*; the trigram numbers are the foundation for the changes and transformations [*bianhua*] of good and bad fortune."[46] Cryptic references to these diagrams can be found in late Zhou sources, and by the Han period they had become a part of the accepted cosmology. Their numerical genesis is suggested in the "Great Commentary" of the *Yijing*, which states:

> Heaven is one, Earth is two, Heaven is three, Earth is four, Heaven is five, Earth is six, Heaven is seven, Earth is eight, Heaven is nine, Earth is ten. There are thus five heavenly numbers and five earthly numbers. When these numbers are distributed among the five places, each finds its complement. The sum of the heavenly numbers is twenty-five and that of the earthly numbers is thirty. The sum total of heavenly numbers and earthly numbers is fifty-five. It is this which completes the changes and transformations and sets the spirits [*guishen*] in motion.[47]

By the Song period, Daoist-inspired diagrams of the *Hetu* and *Luoshu*, using "knotted cord" configurations for numbers, had been appended to the text of the *Yijing*—each diagram representing a numerical interpretation of the natural order. The standard *Hetu*, for instance, arranged the numbers 1 to 10 in such a way as to pair odd (*yang*) numbers with even (*yin*) ones. These numbers were then correlated with the five directions (and hence, elements): 2 and 7 to the south (fire), 1 and 6 to the north (water), 3 and 8 to the east (wood), 4 and 9 in the west (metal), and 5 and 10 at the center (earth).[48] In this scheme, which reflected the mutual production sequence of the *wuxing*, all the odd numbers added up to 25, and all the even numbers added up to 30. In the

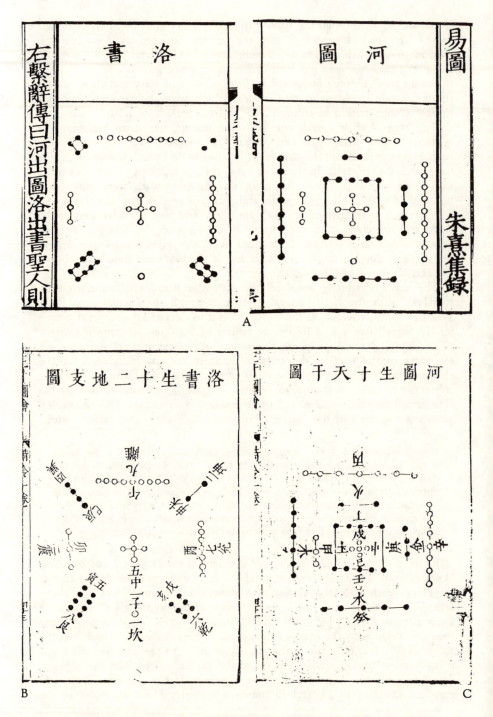

易圖

洛書 河圖

右繫辭傳曰河出圖洛出書聖人則 朱熹集錄

A

洛書生十二地支圖

B

河圖生十天干圖

C

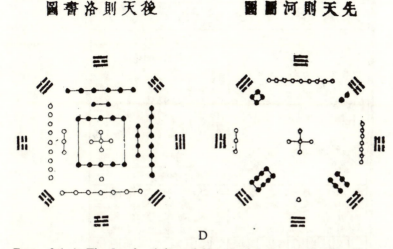

後天則洛書圖   先天則河圖

D

Figure 2.4 A: The *Luoshu* (left) and *Hetu* (right). *Source*: Zhu Xi, *Zhouyi benyi* (Taibei, 1979 reprint), *yitu*, pp. 1a-1b. B: Generation of the twelve earthly branches from the *Luoshu*. *Source*: Wang Qi, *Sancai tuhui* (1609), *shiling*, 1: 42b. C: Generation of the ten heavenly stems from the *Hetu*. *Source*: Wang Qi, *Sancai tuhui* (1609), *shiling*, 1: 42b. D: Two of many different correlational systems involving the *Hetu*, *Luoshu*, and eight trigrams. *Source*: Jiang Tingxi, ed., *Qinding gujin tushu jicheng* (Taibei, 1977 reprint), 55: 572.

Luoshu, linked by the compilers of the *Xieji bianfang shu* with the nine divisions outlined in the "Great Plan" chapter of the *Shujing*, we find a "magic square" of three, in which all the numbers in any row, whether perpendicular, horizontal, or diagonal, added up to fifteen. Even (*yin*) numbers occupied all the corners, and the sequence was one of mutual conquest. Thus, for example, the wood of three and eight conquered the earth of five and ten (in the center); the earth conquered the water of two and six; and so on.[49]

This was, of course, just the beginning of *Yijing*-inspired numerology.[50] The possibilities for interpreting the trigrams, hexagrams, *Hetu* and *Luoshu* by means of numbers were endless, as the schemes of Jiao Yanshou, Shao Yong, Lai Zhide and others (see chapters 1 and 3) indicate.[51] Lai, for instance, viewed the *wuxing* operations expressed in the *Hetu* as a function of ascending values of odd and even digits. According to him, odd numbers began in the north (the origin of all *yang* tendencies) with one, and passed clockwise through three, seven, and nine, thereby describing one circuit of accumulation (*xi*) and dispersal (*xiao*). Even numbers began in the south and followed a similar clockwise path from two through four, six, and eight. With variations, the same process could be used with the *Luotu*[52] (see Fig. 2.5). The *Xingli kaoyuan* and *Xieji bianfang shu* are full of this sort of numerology as it pertains to the four seasons, the

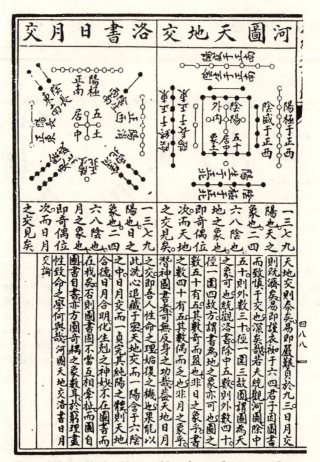

Figure 2.5 Lai Zhide's *Hetu* and *Luoshu* configurations. *Source:*
Lai Zhide, *Yijing Laizhu tujie* (Taibei, 1971 reprint), p. 488.

twelve musical notes, the twenty-four points of the compass, and so forth.[53]
What must be kept in mind is that any and all such systems were based on
the assumption of the *Changes* that by exploring numbers to the fullest (*jishu*)
the past could be understood and the future could be known.[54]

Observation of the sky yielded similar insights. Thus, complementary to,
and often linked with, the powers of *yinyang*, *wuxing*, the eight trigrams and
the stems and branches, were a wide variety of astrological influences in Chinese
cosmology.[55] Among these celestial bodies or forces, which received ritual
validation in the Qing system of official sacrifice, the most important were the
"seven regulators" (*qizheng*): the sun, the moon, and the five visible planets—
Jupiter, Mars, Saturn, Venus, and Mercury. The sun and moon represented,
respectively, the emperor and his empress (as well as other royalty and senior
officials); changes in the appearance of either of these celestial bodies generally

portended potential problems in imperial administration, including the possibility of usurpation of power. Jupiter, associated with the east, spring, wood, and humaneness (*ren*), could exert positive or negative influence on terrestrial affairs, depending on its color, position, and movement (see below). The same was true of Mars (associated with the south, summer, fire and ritual [*li*]), Saturn (center, late summer, earth, faithfulness [*xin*]), Venus (west, autumn, metal and right behavior [*yi*]), and Mercury (north, winter, water, and wisdom [*zhi*]).[56]

Other celestial influences of major significance included the twelve zodiacal "stations" (*ci*), the twenty-eight lunar "lodges" (*xiu*), and a vast number of asterisms and individual stars—some of which were actual heavenly bodies and others of which existed only in the Chinese cultural imagination as "star spirits" or "empty" stars.[57] All interacted with the "seven regulators" in predictable ways. Thus, for example, the asterisms that dominated the lodges known as Jiao (The "Horn"), Dou ("Dipper"), Kui ("Strider"), and Jing ("Well") formed an auspicious conjunction with Jupiter. Similarly, Kang ("Parched Throat"), Niu ("Ox"), Lou ("Gatherer"), and Jing ("Well") were considered lucky together with Venus; Di ("Base"), Nü ("Woman"), Wei ("Stomach") and Liu ("Willow") with Saturn; Wei ("Tail"), Shi ("Abode"), Can ("Triad"), and Yi ("Wing") with Mars; Ji ("Winnower"), Bi ("Wall"), Zi ("Beak"), and Zhen ("Carriage") with Mercury; Fang ("Room"), Xu ("Void"), Mao ("Mane"), and Xing ("Star") with the sun; and Xin ("Heart"), Wei ("Roof"), Bi ("Net") and Zhang ("Displayer") with the moon (see Glossary A and Fig. 2.6).[58] Specialists in astrological prediction (known variously as *xingming, xingbu, guan xingdou, xingsuan*, etc.) played the principal role in interpreting the movement and relationship between such heavenly bodies, but other diviners made related predictions based on their observations of the sky, water, wind, clouds, rain, rainbows, and so forth—a type of prognostication known generically as "meteorological divination" or *zhanhou* (see chapter 5).[59]

In Qing cosmology, heavenly spirits, designated either baneful (*sha*) or beneficial (*shen*), were particularly important, for ultimately they determined whether activities would be auspicious (*ji*) or inauspicious (*xiong*) at any given moment and in any given place. The simplest and most straightforward rationalist interpretation of this spiritual presence can be found in a review of the *Xingli kaoyuan*, published in the *Siku quanshu zongmu tiyao* (Essentials of the Catalogue of the Four Treasuries) of the Qianlong period. It states simply that when the *yang* phase of material force predominates in the process of mutual production, the spirits are auspicious; and when the *yin* phase prevails in the process of mutual conquest, they are inauspicious. This, in the opinion of the reviewers of the *Xingli kaoyuan*, was all in accordance with natural principle (*ziran zhi li*).[60]

The *Xieji bianfang shu*, following in the footsteps of the *Xingli kaoyuan*, provides an inventory of about 250 star-spirits—the majority of which were negative—together with background information on each, including the year, month, hour and position or direction in which they were presumed to be dominant.[61] Among these, only the spirits associated with the sun, moon, five planets, asterisms of the twenty-eight lodges, and the Big Dipper (Northern

64

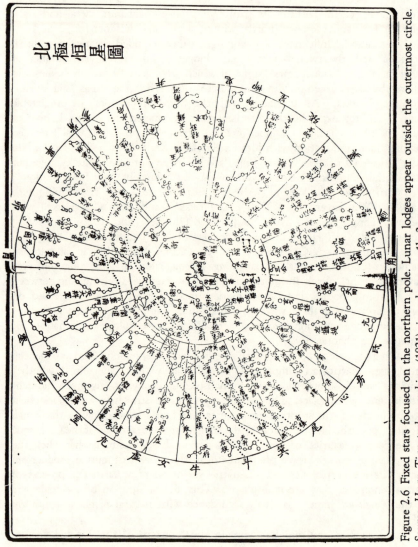

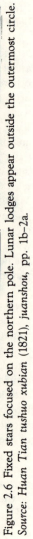

Figure 2.6 Fixed stars focused on the northern pole. Lunar lodges appear outside the outermost circle.
Source: Huan Tian tushuo xubian (1821), *juanshou*, pp. 1b–2a.

Ladle, or Beidou) seem to be linked to observable celestial bodies.[62] From an orthodox standpoint, concern with selecting the proper time and direction to undertake various ritual as well as more mundane affairs was, in the words of the *Xieji bianfang shu*, a matter of "reverence for Heaven and the celestial spirits;" but there was much more to it than this. In practical terms, nothing could be so dangerous for individuals or the state as to pick an inappropriate time or place for the conduct of important matters. The Confucian classics are full of advice on this score.[63]

In Chinese astrology, star-spirits with suffixes such as *de* (virtue), *he* (conjunction), *xi* (happiness), *cai* (wealth) and *gui* (nobility) were generally considered auspicious, while those involving names such as *sha* (evil or death), *bai* (defeat), *po* (ruin), *ye* (repression), *hai* (harm), *huo* (fire), *xue* (blood), and *dao* (knife) were, predictably, inauspicious.[64] But the actual influence of a given star at any moment involved other cosmic factors, including its relationship to other stars (whether in harmony or opposition), its phase (ascendant or descendant), the time of its apogee, and its relationship to the "five elements" and cyclical characters of the year in question.[65] Among the most influential of the positive spirits were the Great One (Taiyi), the Heavenly Virtue Star (Tiande), the Year Virtue Star (Suide), and the Monthly Conjunction Star (Yuehe); among the most potentially negative were the Great Year Star (Taisui, associated with Jupiter), the Monthly Repression Star (Yueye) and the Monthly Evil Star (Yuesha).[66]

Since precautions had to be taken against malevolent spirits, Chinese beliefs regarding *sha* were more highly developed than those pertaining to *shen*.[67] This was particularly true of the Great Year Star, the *yin* counterpart to Jupiter, to whose spirit the Qing emperors offered sacrifices before every military expedition.[68] Prohibitions relating to the compass points occupied by Taisui existed as early as the Warring States period, and by Qing times concern with Jupiter's regular twelve-year rotation through the twenty-eight lodges was reflected not only in state rituals and official calendrical calculations, but also in popular manuals of divination, Daoist ritual books, and exorcisms.[69] Jupiter played a leading but ambiguous role in all celestial affairs. When situated in conjunction with auspicious star-spirits it brought good fortune; and in conjunction with baleful stars, misfortune. According to the *Xiangji beiyao* (Essentials Concerning Auspicious Images), compiled by Wei Jian in the early Qing period, Jupiter operated like an emperor: If its "ministers" were good, peace and prosperity prevailed on earth; if not, calamities ensued.[70]

As I have already indicated, the idea of a "spiritual" resonance between celestial and earthly phenomena had deep roots in Chinese thought for well over two thousand years. Things and events were not so much "caused" as connected. The primary manifestation of this relationship between the "Heavenly way" (*Tiandao*) and human affairs (*renshi*) was, of course, omens and portents (see also chapter 6). The Qing dynasty, like all of its imperial predecessors, dutifully recorded all unusual signs from Heaven, and the Qing emperors took them very seriously.[71] About a third of the imperial amnesties granted from the early seventeenth century to the late nineteenth were justified as a means of restoring harmony to the natural order after portents indicated that it had been disrupted by human excesses.[72]

To be sure, the illustrious Kangxi emperor—arguably the most "scientific" and skeptical of all the Manchu rulers—might assert that while the dynastic histories were full of accounts of omens, they were of no help in governing the country; that "the best omens were good harvests and contented people."[73] But the "Respecting Heaven" sections of the *Da Qing shichao shengxun* (Sacred Instructions for Ten Reigns of the Great Qing) provide numerous instances in which he, like both his predecessors and successors, registers great concern over portents, is moved to self-examination because of them, and admonishes his officials to rectify their administration as a result.[74] Scholars might disagree over whether the sovereign's self-cultivation could actually prevent anomalous events from occurring, as Zhu Xi seems to have believed, but few doubted that a relationship existed between portents and the need for an immediate imperial response to the messages they conveyed.

Kangxi insisted that the Board of Astronomy report all portents, good or bad, and admonished his officials not to distort their findings. In 1710, for instance, he discovered that the diviners in the Board had misleadingly reported a benevolent southeast wind (identified with the trigram Sun in the Later Heaven sequence of the *Yijing*) to be blowing at the time of the beginning of summer (May 6), when in fact it was an inauspicious northeast wind. In an edict dated May 9, he chastized his diviners for "shunning bad omens," pointing out that the purpose of Confucius in recording calamities (*zai*) in the *Chunqiu* (Spring and Autumn Annals) was precisely to convey such warnings.[75] On another occasion he remarked: "Human affairs are involved in the phenomenon of eclipses, and it makes no difference that we can calculate them with absolute precision; we must still make the reforms necessary to avoid trouble and obtain peace."[76]

In the provinces, too, celestial signs and natural disasters were matters of grave concern, not least because they reflected the quality of imperial rule at the local level. Compilers of county, prefectural, and provincial gazetteers, like court astrologers, almost invariably provided a section on auspicious omens and anomolies (*xiangyi*), for although they might disagree on how these signs should be interpreted, none doubted the principle of a resonance between Heaven and Man.[77] This awareness had a geographical as well as a metaphysical aspect. Since at least the late Zhou period, Chinese observers accepted as an article of faith that meteors, eclipses, planetary movements, or changes in the appearance of stars in any given section of the heavens had meaning for the corresponding area on earth. The influential Han astronomer, Zhang Heng (78–139 A.D.), put the matter this way: "The stars are scattered in a confused arrangement, but every one of them has its own distant connections. In the countryside these stars denote articles and objects; at court they denote the officials; among the people they denote human action. . . . The movements of the sun and the moon reveal signs of good and evil, while the five planets and the lunar lodges forebode fortune and misfortune."[78]

During the Qing period, the inventory of identifiable stars increased substantially over earlier dynasties, thanks largely to the new astronomical methods and modern technology of the Jesuits. In 1674, for example, Ferdinand Verbiest (see next section) added hundreds of new stars to the traditional Chinese list.[79] Meanwhile, the pioneering work of Chinese scholars such as Gu Zuyu (1631–1692) indicated that important geographical changes had taken place in China since ancient times, requiring a reconsideration of traditional cosmographic conceptions.[80] Yet none of these discoveries, nor even knowledge of the Copernican notion of the earth as a planet and the discovery of Uranus, significantly changed the state's cosmological outlook. Although Chinese astronomical science progressed rapidly during the Qing, it had no impact on state-sponsored astrology. *Wuxing* correlative thinking, after all, required no more than five planets, and the influence of invisible star-spirits quite obviously could not be determined by mere observation.[81]

The general term used to describe the temporal and spatial relationship between heavenly patterns and earthly phenomena was *fenye* ("allocated fields").[82] In Qing times, as in earlier periods, several *fenye* systems existed side by side (see Fig. 2.7). The imperially-commissioned *Rixia jiuwen kao* (Examination of the Antiquities of Beijing), published in 1774, provides an excellent illustration of how various *fenye* correlations could be applied to the Qing capital. In the opening chapter, entitled "Stars and Earth," the *Rixia jiuwen kao* discusses three different *fenye* systems, without attempting to reconcile them. One system was the ancient *Zhouli* scheme linking the nine major geographical regions of China with the nine divisions of the heavens. Another was based on the twelve "stations" of the Jupiter cycle and their earthly analogues. These corresponded to twelve of the more prominent states of the late Zhou period—including, of course, Yen, the area of modern-day Beijing, associated with the Jupiter station known as Ximu ("Split Wood"). A third and related system identified the twenty-eight lunar lodges with twenty-eight analogous sectors of China.[83] As the *Rixia jiuwen kao* points out, by Tang times the idea of heavenly counterparts (*tianxiang*) came to be extended not only to administrative areas but also to topographical configurations. For this reason, the renowned Buddhist monk and court astrologer of the Tang period, Yixing, included mountains and rivers in his *fenye* scheme.[84]

The confusion of *fenye* alternatives mounts when the *Rixia jiuwen kao* considers potentially influential stars and asterisms. Again, the editors are interested primarily in listing the possibilities as they appear in a wide variety of historical sources. Accordingly, when Beijing was correlated with the Jupiter station Ximu, its major asterisms appeared to be Wei and Ji; and because Ximu was also part of a group of seven asterisms called the Green Dragon (Qinglong, one of four such groupings for the twenty-eight lodges), the city became identified with *yang*, wood, the east and spring.[85] But when Beijing was viewed in isolation from this system of stations, it fell under the primary influence of the asterism known as Tianshi yuan ("Heavenly Market Enclosure"). In these circumstances, the city's primary identification was with *yin*, water, the west, and fall.[86]

One of the stars of the Tianshi yuan asterism was called Yen. Because of its classical name and location, it was generally considered to be the primary

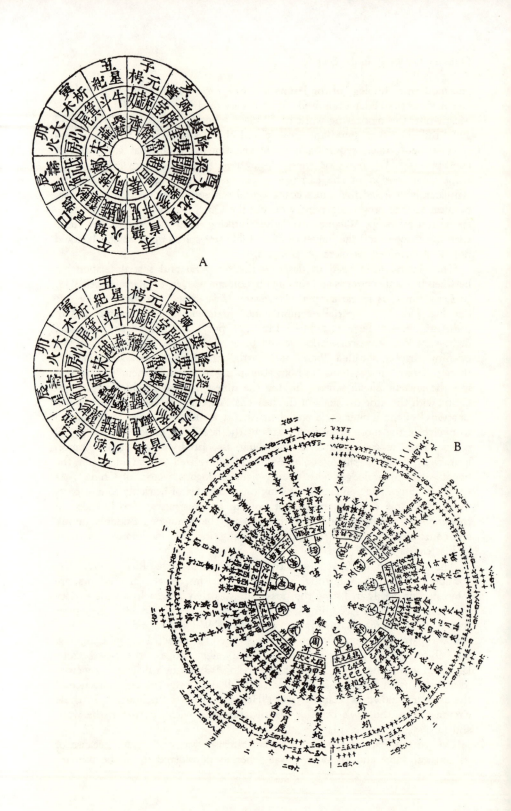

A

B

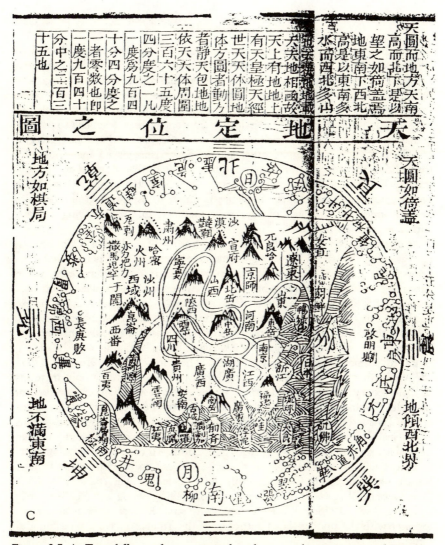

Figure 2.7 A: Two different *fenye* systems based on overlapping ancient locations. Yan (the area of modern day Beijing), for example, falls under the lodges "Winnower" and "Dipper" in the upper scheme and under "Ox" and "Dipper" in the lower. *Source*: He Changling, ed., *Huangchao jingshi wenbian* (1826), 69: 22b. B: A more complex *fenye* system based on the overlapping locations noted in A. Here, the locations are correlated not only with lunar lodges but also with trigrams, stems and branches, Jupiter "stations" (*ci*), animals, the five activities, and so forth. *Source*: Lai Zhide, *Yijing Laizhu tujie* (Taibei, 1971 reprint), pp. 546 and 547. C: A *fenye*-influenced map of "the world" (i.e., China, surrounded by tributary states and various "barbarous" regions). In this depiction, Heaven is round like a canopy, and Earth is square like a chessboard. The heavens are divided into four groupings of seven lodges each and also oriented toward the Later Heaven sequence of the eight trigrams. *Source*: *Zengbu jixiang beiyao tongshu* (1721), 1: 4b–5a.

star for Beijing in late imperial times—whether or not the city happened to be the capital of China. By contrast, the heavenly counterpart to the imperial palace (The Purple Forbidden City) remained the Pole Star (Tianhuang dadi; lit. the Great Emperor of Heaven), regardless of where the capital was located. In the general area of the Pole Star, the astrological nomenclature reflected imperial administration; thus, the names of stars and asterisms applied to palaces, granaries, and ritual fields, as well as to members of royalty and various categories of officials.[87] *Mutatis mutandis,* other stars and asterisms played analogous roles throughout the rest of the empire. Thus we find that a number of local gazetteers (but not all) contain discussions of *fenye* systems appropriate to the area in question. Here, too, the tendency is simply to list astrological references as they appear in a variety of sources, sometimes, in the late Qing at least, with a note of skepticism.[88]

A distinctive, though hardly surprising, feature of traditional Chinese cosmology—*fenye* in particular—is its inveterate Sinocentrism. It is true that even prior to the Jesuits there were at least a few thinkers in China, notably Wang Tingxiang (1474–1544), who pointed out the cultural bias in considering unusual celestial phenomena to be directed as a warning only against the Chinese emperor. But the arrival of Westerners on China's shores, especially during the late eighteenth and nineteenth centuries, imposed a global consciousness on a number of Qing scholar-officials, who began applying aspects of the inherited cosmology to the new situation. Thus, for example, Xu Jiyu (1795–1873) explained the technological superiority of Europeans not only in terms of their geographical position (*qianxu,* in the northwest), which endowed them with the domineering spirit of metal, but also to the fact that the "rhythms of fate" (Shao Yong's concept of *yunhui;* see chapter 1) had moved the auspicious *qi* of Heaven and Earth in a position to favor the Westerners, and to make inevitable an encounter between them and China. Xu took these developments to be the will of Heaven, but his response was not to bend passively to fate. Rather, like many other Chinese of his time—including Wei Yuan (1794–1856), Zeng Guofan (1811–1872), Li Hongzhang (1823–1901), Wang Tao (1828–c. 1890) and even Yan Fu (1883–1921)—he used this strained cosmological argument, together with the unquestioned authority of the *Yijing,* to advocate meaningful reform.[89]

Of course the glaring inconsistencies of the orthodox cosmology, not to mention the rigid, numerically-grounded determinism of Shao Yong, invited heavy criticism from Qing scholars well before the nineteenth century. Individuals such as Huang Zongxi (1610–1695), Fang Yizhi (1611–1671), Gu Yanwu (1613–1682), Wang Fuzhi (1619–1692), Mei Wending (1633–1721), Hu Wei (1633–1714), Yan Yuan (1635–1704), Yan Ruoju (1636–1704), Li Gong (1659–1733), Hui Dong (1697–1758), Dai Zhen (1724–1777), and Zhang Huiyan (1761–1802) were among the many illustrious figures in early Qing intellectual history who, inspired in part by newly-introduced Western scientific concepts, assailed various aspects of traditional Chinese correlative thought, numerology, and cosmography.[90] Wang and Li, for instance, vigorously criticized the artificiality of *wuxing* correspondences—particularly those involving numerically uneven trigram affiliations such as those of the *najia* and *nayin* systems—while Fang railed against the incommensurability of *fenye* correlations.[91] Many other *kaozheng* scholars pointed out the unorthodox origins of the *Hetu* and *Luoshu;* and most condemned the *Yijing*-based numerological schemes of Jing Fang, Shao Yong and others.[92] The editors of the *Siku quanshu* also got into the act, criticizing, among other things, the gratuitous precision of certain *fenye* systems, and noting in their review of an anonymous Ming work on astrology that correlations between the *wuxing* and the five segments of each lunar lodge were impossible because the lodges varied so much in length.[93]

Yet such critiques remained focused narrowly on the faults of one or another schema, rather than on the inherited cosmology as a whole. Most Qing savants felt that the problem rested primarily with misguided efforts to "force a [cosmological] fit" (*qiangpei*)—not with basic assumptions about the workings of the universe itself. Although, as John Henderson has shown, a new recognition of anomaly as "constitutive of the fundamental order, or disorder, of the cosmos" undoubtedly caused at least some Qing intellectuals to doubt that traditional numerological and other correlative systems (and even Western science) could adequately describe the nature of the universe, few abandoned the *Yijing* as a device for discovering basic patterns of cosmic change, including those of the future.[94]

No prominent Confucian scholar denied the idea of a spiritual link between man and the cosmos, and none proved willing to abandon correlative thinking altogether.[95] For every critic of Jing Fang or Shao Yong there were dozens, perhaps hundreds, of Qing scholars who held closely to their views.[96] In fact, the eclectic nature of Chinese thought made it possible for an individual such as Li Keqi to embrace Shao's "unorthodox" numerology personally, and yet teach Zhu Xi's standard works to his students.[97] Moreover, the seventeenth and eighteenth century emphasis on "Han Learning" in China led paradoxically to a revival of interest in ancient cosmology.[98] Pi Xirui (1850-1908) might declare that by late Qing times no one believed in the *Hetu* and *Luoshu* anymore, but this was assuredly not the case—particularly in the realm of divination.[99]

Even the rejection by Huang, Gu, Wang, Li, Dai, and others of Zhu Xi's dualistic assumption of the ontological primacy of *li* (principle) over *qi* (material force), in favor of an emphasis on the concrete reality of *qi*, did not entail abandonment of the metaphysical concept of *li*. And although the idea of an immutable *dao* or Way of ultimate truth gave way to the notion of a relativized *dao* embodying only transient and finite truths, no major thinker of the Qing period denied the *Yijing's* basic premise that this *dao*, however conceived, united Heaven, Earth, and Man. Nor, as I have indicated, did anyone doubt that the basic patterns of nature were discernable in the *Changes*. Thus, we find that Hu Wei's attempt to redefine the terms *xiang* and *shu* in the *Yi* did not lead to the abandonment of efforts to understand the patterns and principles of cosmic change using images and numbers.[100] In fact, most Chinese intellectuals continued to view trigrams and hexagrams as essential to an understanding of the subtle ways of the universe. For all the iconoclastic work done in the Qing period, no one offered a comprehensive attack on the foundations of orthodox cosmology, much less offer a radically different alternative.[101]

The criticisms of divination by Qing *kaozheng* scholars were even more narrow than those directed against cosmology. In fact, they followed closely the lines of attack crafted centuries before by individuals such as Xunzi in the late Zhou, Wang Chong in the Han, and Lü Cai in the Tang (see chapter 1), all of whom are excerpted in the *Tushu jicheng*. Like their ancient predecessors, not to mention their more orthodox neo-Confucian contemporaries, *kaozheng* scholars had no quarrel with the idea of divination itself, for the practice had far too long and illustrious a pedigree in China's classical tradition to ignore.[102] Rather, their hostility was directed toward specific misapplications of the practice—especially by professional fortune-tellers who selfishly deluded and exploited their "ignorant" clients. As in the case of religion, the Qing elite made a sharp (though somewhat artificial) distinction between their own "enlightened" beliefs and the "crude" customs of the popular masses.[103] The bias against divination was in large measure a class prejudice, often masked by the rhetoric of Confucian morality.

In the eyes of many Chinese intellectuals, fortune-telling—like medicine, husbandry, gardening, and a number of other other non-scholarly pursuits—was a "minor employment" (*xiaodao*), unworthy of serious attention. Introductions to the biographical sections on "technicians" (*fangji*) in local gazetteers often refer to a remark by Zixia in the Confucian *Analects*, which states: "Although there is something to be considered in minor employments, if extended too far, I fear they won't work. Thus, the superior man does not become involved in them."[104] The idea behind this somewhat contradictory statement was that if technical skills were indeed useful, they should be learned by Confucian gentlemen for the benefit of their own families, not left to mean people (*xiaoren*) who were concerned only with profit.[105] This elitist view of divination was also reflected in a well-known adage in Qing China attributed to the Song scholar Zhang Zai: "The *Changes* are for the planning of the superior man, not the mean man" (*Yi wei junzi mou buwei xiaoren mou*).[106]

The several essays on fate and fortune-telling by scholars such as Gu Yanwu, Lu Shiyi (1611–1672), Feng Jing (1652–1715) and Quan Zuwang (1705–1755) that are reprinted in the "Rectifying Customs" section of the *Huangchao jingshi wenbian* (Qing Dynasty Essays on Statecraft), evince the major concerns of the Qing elite. One common complaint was simply that fortune-tellers were unreliable. Gu, Lu, Feng and Quan all used examples from history to show the limitations of fate extrapolation, geomancy, portent interpretation and other forms of divination. Quan, citing the opinions of Huang Zongxi and others, demonstrated that calculations based on the time of one's birth could not possibly yield a satisfactory discussion of destiny, since "many people are born on the same day, yet some are fortunate and some are not; some will enjoy longevity and others will die young." Gu underscored the divergent and often misleading interpretations of diviners, while Lu questioned the validity of astrological predictions and portent interpretations because they were unscientific. ("Western studies," he reports, "say absolutely nothing about divination.") Feng, in "Refuting the Theories of Yinyang Soothsayers," argued along with the Tang scholar Lü Cai that skill with esoteric numerical calculations was "not equal to an understanding of the principles of things."[107]

Another widely shared concern was that blind acceptance of "fate" on the part of commoners would diminish their impulse toward moral improvement and self-reliance.[108] Quan, like Gu, took the position that although Heaven endowed Man with his nature, it had no control over his actions. Surely, he argued, the will of Heaven was that every man should be a sage, and that virtuous government by sage-rulers would bring peace to the world. Heaven also undoubtedly wanted all people on earth to be healthy, strong, and properly provided for. Yet not everyone was a sage; villains often ruled as hegemons; and the virtuous might well suffer from cold, hunger and premature death, while villains lived long and comfortable lives. "These things," he claimed, "Heaven can do nothing about." His point was that what appeared to petty men as "blessings" (*fu*) and "calamities" (*huo*) were nothing more than ephemeral phenomena, "like morning dew and melting icebergs." History, he argued, ultimately reveals good and evil, and human beings are therefore bound to strive relentlessly for sagehood. Superior men, he asserted, referred to fate only in unavoidable situations—such as Confucius did in the face of Boniu's fatal illness (*Lunyu*, VI. 8), or in the case of Gongbo Liao's slander of Zilu (*Lunyu*, XIV. 38). This was not at all the same, he emphasized, as passively accepting the predictions of fortune-tellers.[109]

There were also political problems associated with fortune-telling, for, as Lu emphasized, false prophecy could easily "delude people into creating disorder" (*huoren zuoluan*), that is, instigating rebellion.[110] The Kangxi emperor provides us with an illustration. On the one hand, he wrote that "When a man casts a horoscope as well as blindman Luo, then even the most senior generals should be sent to consult with him." On the other, he recognized that "When a soothsayer is crazy and heterodox like Zhu Fangdan, and able to mislead the governor of a province or the senior military commanders with his wild remarks and seditious books, then he must be beheaded."[111] In order to minimize the political dangers—particularly since, as we shall see, the use of fortune-tellers by officials and the throne was quite widespread—the Qing legal code explicitly prohibited "practitioners of *yinyang* prognostication" (*yinyang shushu*) from entering the houses of civil and military officials and "falsely prophesying" (*wangyan*) fortune or misfortune, just as it forbade magicians, shamans and other ritual specialists from writing charms, carrying idols, summoning "heretical spirits" (*xieshen*), performing heretical arts (*xieshu*), writing books on sorcery (*yaoshu*) or promoting "heretical formulas" (*xieyan*).[112] Yet here, too, we find class bias, for Gu Yanwu indicates in one of his three essays on divination reprinted in the *Huangchao jingshi wenbian* that strictures against prognostication were intended primarily for commoners, not for scholar-officials.[113]

As it developed, Qing intellectuals were no more successful in eradicating popular mantic practices than their predecessors. This was not only because scholarly critiques carried little weight in village culture. It was also because most divination systems, like the cosmology on which they were based, had a high degree of complexity. This complexity provided conceptual flexibility, and contributed to the self-confirming character of Chinese popular beliefs. Wrong predictions did not invalidate the idea that fate could be known; they merely indicated that someone had misinterpreted the huge number of cosmic variables involved, or that either the diviner or his client was insufficiently "sincere" (cheng).[114] Members of the elite, for their part, also believed that the use of the Yijing required sincerity above all (see chapter 3). Another factor, to be discussed at greater length in subsequent chapters, is that mantic practices were deeply woven into the fabric of Qing society at all levels, from the Forbidden City to local villages. Even scholarly critics of divination often had profoundly ambivalent feelings about it, as the writings of several scholars I have cited above reveal.[115] A popular fortune-telling book by Wang Weide, published in 1709 and entitled Bushi zhengzong (Orthodox Divination), indicates that many members of the Chinese elite affected disdain for divination, only to use it surreptitiously through the agency of friends or servants.[116]

Like Qing scholars, the imperial government periodically denounced the very mantic practices it employed.[117] But here again, the problem was not with the theory of divination; only with the practice. On the whole, the state reaffirmed and reinforced the inherited cosmology at every turn, in every way possible. Perhaps the single most significant way was in publishing the state calendar (Shixian li or Shixian shu).

The State Calendar and Its Derivatives

The Qing calendar embodied official cosmology and reflected the state's unmistakable concern with divination. No single document did more to symbolize the legitimacy of the regime, and none was taken more seriously by the throne. Traditionally, one of the most important acts of any new dynasty was to "fix the time" (shoushi) and to regulate the lunar calendar. So it was with the Qing dynasty. Thus, for example, newly-recruited ritual specialists delayed the official ascension of the Shunzhi emperor in 1644 until the first day (jiazi) of a new sexagenary cycle in order to assure an auspicious start for the alien dynasty.[118]

The Manchus, like all of their imperial predecessors, jealously guarded the emperor's astronomical and calendrical prerogatives. The Qing legal code, for example, forbade the keeping of astronomical instruments and charts at home, and the Collected Statutes of the dynasty outlawed all unauthorized versions of Shixian li and Shixian shu. Other prohibitions, stipulated in the administrative regulations of the Six Boards (Liubu), applied to astrological or calendrical books that might be used "to predict order and disorder" in the empire.[119] Most, if not all, official editions of the Qing calendar carried an explicit warning on the cover or the back to the effect that those who forged copies were subject to decapitation, and that those who informed on such persons would receive an imperial reward of 50 ounces of silver (liang; or taels).[120] Calendars that did not carry an official seal were considered to be private, and therefore, strictly speaking, illegal.

The cosmic sanctity of the state calendar can be seen in the solemn rituals that attended its annual presentation to the emperor, and its official promulgation after months of preparation. According to the Collected Statutes of the late Qing, the presentation of the calendar took place at dawn each year at the new moon of the eleventh month (the first month of winter). At that time, the Director of the Board of Astronomy and a number of his subordinates presented the calendar to the Emperor, his Empress, and the principal concubines and other court women, as well as to princes of the blood and representatives of the lower nobility. These ceremonies were marked by kowtowing, musical processions, and elaborate displays of the calendar at certain points in the Imperial City complex—including the Meridian Gate (Wumen) and the Hall of Supreme Harmony (Taihe dian). Later rituals involved the presentation of the calendar to eunuchs in the inner court of the Forbidden City at the Gate of Heavenly Purity (Qianqing men).[121]

Similar ceremonies marked the formal publication and promulgation of the calendar, which was distributed at a specified time not only to the various members of the Imperial Household, but also to representatives of the Board of Civil Appointments and the Board of War, for redistribution to civil and military officials, respectively. The official proclamation announcing the promulgation of the new calendar was made at the Meridian Gate before a huge array of nobles and officials, including representatives of the Censorate and the Board of Ritual. After this awe-inspiring ceremony, each of the nobles, as well as all of the civil and military officials involved, received individual copies of the calendar in rank order. Additional copies were sent in specified numbers to prefectural and county yamens in the metropolitan province of Zhili.[122]

Eventually, versions of the Qing calendar found their way to every corner of the empire. In all, about 2,340,000 of them were officially printed each year. Manchu functionaries received Manchu-language copies of the document; Mongol functionaries, Mongol-language copies; and Han functionaries, Chinese-language copies. Chinese-language copies were also provided to tributary states, notably Korea and Annam, as a tangible symbol of imperial sway over these areas. At the provincial level in China Proper, under the supervision of governors and/ or governors-general, official copies of the calendar were printed in specified numbers and then sent by the provincial treasurer to appropriate civil and military officials. Upon receipt, these officials, like their superiors within the provincial hierarchy, kowtowed to the north in homage to the emperor. Excess copies became available for sale to an eager public.[123]

The agency formally in charge of the Qing state calendar was the Imperial Board of Astronomy (Qintian jian)—an institution closely connected to the exalted Board of Ritual (Libu). Its basic calendrical responsibilities, as in Yuan and Ming times, were to make astronomical and meteorological observations and predictions—particularly regarding eclipses—to select auspicious days for conducting state rituals and other important matters, to determine auspicious and inauspicious times for more mundane affairs, and to provide information on concerns relating directly to agriculture. Europeans dominated the Imperial Board of Astronomy almost continuously from the Qing succession in 1644 to 1826, by which time Western calendrical methods had been fully assimilated by the Chinese. During these 182 years, at least fourteen Europeans served as Directors of the Board.[124]

As the "Calendrical Treatise" of the *Qingshi* (History of the Qing) and other sources indicate, a number of significant changes took place in the technical side of Chinese calendrical science over the 268 years of Manchu rule.[125] Many of these changes were inspired by the scientific and mathematical knowledge provided by Jesuits employed in the Board of Astronomy during the seventeenth century—notably Adam Schall von Bell and Ferdinand Verbiest. Schall, who had served the Ming court as a calendrical specialist, produced the first official Qing calendar according to new Western methods. Unfortunately for Schall, his calculations, especially his predictions of eclipses, were invariably more accurate than those of the other Qing court astronomers, creating much jealousy and resentment on the part of obscurantist Chinese scholars such as Yang Guangxian (1597-1669). Yang, in his ceaseless campaign to discredit Schall, went so far as to accuse him of choosing an inauspicious date for the burial of an infant prince (Prince Rong); and although Schall was eventually exonerated, five of his Chinese colleagues were executed for this alleged crime. Verbiest won the confidence of the Qing throne by virtue of his scientific skills, and managed after Schall's death in 1666 to have Schall's titles and ranks restored, along with those of his executed colleagues. Verbiest's good service, in turn, encouraged the Kangxi emperor to pursue Western science and mathematics, and laid the foundation for further high-level Jesuit involvement in Chinese calendar-making during the eighteenth and nineteenth centuries.[126]

Calculations by the Board of Astronomy were made not only on the basis of direct observation and mathematical calculation, but also according to the stipulations of several traditional-style works on calendar-making: the *Wannian li* or *Wannian shu* (Perpetual Calendar)—which covered the period from 1624 to 2020—the *Xuanze tongshu* (Almanac for the Selection [of Days and Times]), the *Xingli kaoyuan*, and the *Xieji bianfang shu*. Errors in each of these publications necessitated substantial revisions, but even so, egregious mistakes in the calendar continued to be made. The periodic insertion of intercalary months in order to reconcile the lunar calendar with the solar year proved to be a particularly troublesome problem for Qing calendar-makers.[127]

Of the hundred or so Qing calendars I have seen, all range in size from small versions of about four and a half inches by six and a half inches, to larger versions about six inches by twelve, thirteen, or fourteen inches. These works conform closely to an organizational format based on the Ming dynasty's *Datong li*, and most are graced by an imperial yellow silk cover. The quality of print and paper varies substantially, however, as does the specific content— including not only the presence or absence of various charts and diagrams, but also the use of red, black and blue ink. Most such works bear "official" seals, but here again we find considerable variation in size and type, even for calendars bearing the same date.[128]

In part, these variations can be explained by different target audiences. According to the *Qingbai leichao*, there were three principal versions of the calendar presented to the emperor in the early Qing period: one called the Superior Position Calendar (*Shangwei li*); another designated the Calendar of the Sun, Moon and Five Planets (*Qizheng li*); and another, the Monthly-

Ordinance Calendar (*Yueling li*). Of the three, the *Qizheng li* remained the standard version throughout the remainder of the Qing era. The calendar distributed to nobles was generally known as the Middle Calendar (*Zhong li*), while the calendar designed for civil and military officials was identified simply as one promulgated by the Board of Ritual and bearing the seal of the Board of Astronomy (*Qintian jian yinzao li*). Versions of this work available for sale to the public were referred to as People's Calendars (*Min li*).[129]

Certain variations in calendars, then, reflected distinctions in the ethnicity, status, administrative responsibilities, and personal concerns of the respective recipients within the Qing social and political hierarchy.[130] Other differences, however, may be attributable to factors that remained beyond imperial control. Sources such as the *Huangchao zhengdian leizuan* (Classified Compendium of Qing Government Statutes) indicate that although the Qing emperors tried steadfastly to maintain an imperial monopoly over production of the state calendar, they were clearly not able to do so. Pirated editions (*sili*, lit. "private calendars") that did not conform to official standards circulated widely during the eighteenth and nineteenth centuries, despite dire warnings printed on the covers of authorized prototypes and repeated efforts on the part of the throne to punish offenders. An edict issued by the Yongzheng emperor in 1729, for instance, acknowledged the widespread publication of illegal private calendars in southern provinces such as Jiangsu, Zhejiang and Fujian; and nearly a century later, the Jiaqing emperor all but conceded defeat in the war against premature circulation of the calendar and publication of pirated editions.[131]

Carole Morgan, in an illuminating article entitled "De l'authenticité des calendriers Qing," argues that since popular demand for the calendar in China consistently outstripped the supply available from official printing shops at the provincial level, private printshops increasingly assumed responsibility for providing the public with "official" calendars as the dynasty weakened—perhaps as part of a sub-contracting system that can be found in other realms of Qing administration as well. After government production quotas for each area had been met, the private firms could produce and sell to the public modified versions of the calendar that satisfied local tastes, but still appeared to be in some sense "official." These modified publications, although strictly speaking illegal, occupied a position in Chinese society roughly analogous to the several different published versions of the Kangxi emperor's Sacred Edict.[132] On the other hand, some pirated calendars were clearly dangerous to possess. Some, for example, contain an elliptical but still ominous handwritten warning on the front cover to the effect that the work in hand might best be consulted at night (*yeguan wuji*; lit. "night viewing is not prohibited").[133]

All Qing calendars, official as well as non-official and quasi-official, set forth the number of days in each month and the total number of days in the year. In addition, they inserted intercalary months when necessary (and occasionally by mistake), and provided precise information concerning phases of the moon, the onset of each of the year's twenty-four solar divisions (*jie*), and times for sunrise and sunset. Days—identified successively by the names of lunar lodges as well as by the sexegenary system of cyclical characters—were reckoned from

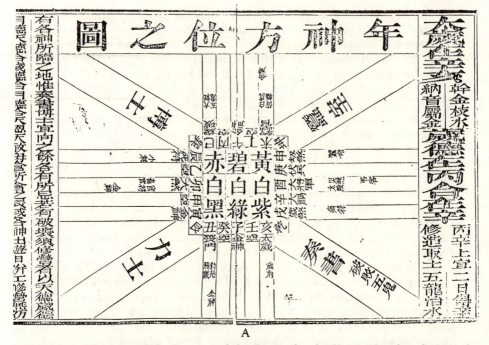

A

Figure 2.8 A: "Diagram of the Position of the Spirits for the Year" (*Nianshen fangwei zhi tu*) from a late Qing calendar, showing the Silkworm Room located in the Kun (southwest) direction, the Memorialist in the Qian (northwest) direction, the Strongman in the Gen (northwest) direction, and the Erudite in the Sun (southeast) direction. *Source: Shixian shu* (1911), no pagination. B: A Qing calendar from the early Guangxu reign, with columns showing appropriate and inappropriate activities for the first thirteen days of the second month of the third year (March 15–28, 1877). The prohibitions on this page (detached in most cases from auspicious activities) have to do with planting, traveling, beginning construction, sewing, and moving. *Source: Shixian shu* (1877), no pagination.

midnight to midnight and divided into twelve equal parts (*shi*), each denoted by one of the twelve branches. These two-hour periods, in turn, were subdivided into single hours marked by the characters *chu* and *zheng*, respectively. Thus eleven P.M. was designated *zichu*; midnight, *zizheng*; one A.M., *chouchu*; and so on. One Chinese *shi* equalled eight *ke*; and one *ke* equalled 15 *fen*. Some calendars included information pertaining only to a single locality, such as Beijing (Shuntian prefecture), while others contained times for different provinces. Some also covered outlying areas such as Manchuria and Mongolia, and even tributary states. At least a few devoted more space to these temporal concerns than to the individual days of the year. One way of determining the target audience of any given calendar is to consider the geographical range of its time charts.[134]

B

Each official calendar displayed a square, color-coded "diagram of the position of the spirits for the year" (*nianshen fangwei zhi tu*) near the front of the book, and a smaller version for the beginning of each month. This diagram, based on the "nine palaces" (*jiugong*) system reportedly devised by Zhang Heng, indicated the relationship of various stars to nine primary compass points: center, north, south, east, west and four intermediate directions. Similar in appearance to the "magic square" of the *Luoshu*, the *nianshen fangwei zhi tu* consisted of nine individual squares, each representing a directional "palace." Each palace, in turn, contained a number indicated by a specific color and corresponding to a given trigram, although there were only seven colors in all. In this scheme, red was divided into "true red" (*chi*) and "purple" (*zi*), while green was divided into "true green" (*lü*) and "azure" (*bi*). The numbers

1, 6, and 8, all associated with the color white, represented good fortune for the direction in question, while the rest (2/black; 3/azure; 4/true green; 5/ yellow; 7/true red and 9/purple) indicated bad fortune. Each year the numbers rotated in a pattern corresponding to the "Later Heaven" sequence of the trigrams.[135]

The exterior of the main *nianshen fangwei zhi tu* was subdivided into 24 directional units. Each corner of the square had a character representing one of four primary trigrams (Qian at the northwest, Kun at the southwest, Sun at the southeast and Gen at the northeast); and each side had five characters representing various stems and branches. From year to year, four main stars (The Silkworm Room [Canshi]; The Erudite [Boshi]; The Strongman [Lishi]; and the Memorialist [Zoushu]) appeared in one or another of the four corners, while lesser stars (a majority of them harmful to greater or lesser degrees) appeared in various locations on each side. Usually one or more of these twenty side spaces would be designated "empty" (*kong*) in any given year, free from stellar influences. Columns of characters on the right side of the main diagram established the location of the Great Year Star (Taisui), the Year Virtue Star (Suide) and the Conjunction Star (He). They also identified the relevant *nayin*, *wuxing* and stem/branch correlations for the year, and indicated the best time and location for undertaking repairs and construction. Columns on the left contained a standard admonition to the effect that of the four major star-spirits located on the corners, only Boshi and Zoushu were auspicious; and that if building repairs had to be made in any other direction, proper precautions would have to be made to assure the presence of a lucky star spirit or at least the absence of an unlucky one in order to avoid calamity[136] (see Fig. 2.8).

Many calendars included a section listing the death dates of emperors and empresses, since these days, like the specified times for sacrificial abstinence, were taboo for certain activities.[137] Most calendars also presented general information in tabular form concerning undertakings that should (*yi*) or should not (*ji*) be carried out under the influence of designated lucky and unlucky "star-spirits" (*xingshen*). In these tabulations, the occasional appearance of the term *bujiang* (lit. "not taken in hand") gave notice that an unlucky star would not be able to exert its normal malevolent influence.[138] A number of calendars contained supplementary information, which, although not specified by statute, might be useful to recipients. One such addition was a list of the "birthdays" of various popular deities that were commonly celebrated in Chinese society. Another was a chart which contained columns counting backward from the present—year to year by reigns, for several decades—in order to show prevailing *wuxing* influences and "nine palaces" locations for men and women born in each of the years marked by cycles of the twelve zodiacal animals. One purpose of this chart was to convey information regarding auspicious and inauspicious marriage relationships.[139]

At the core of all state calendars in late imperial times was a month-by-month, day-by-day breakdown of the entire year, designed to coordinate or control all aspects of Chinese political, social, ritual, and economic life.[140] For each month the calendar included basic agricultural and meteorological information, the direction of the handle of the Northern Dipper (Beidou) at nightfall as a point of reference; the exact time for the onset of solar periods; and the location of major positive and negative celestial influences—such as the Heavenly Virtue Star (Tiande; positive) and the Lunar Repression Star (Yueye; negative). One literally "followed directions" for the month. Thus, for example, if the Way of Heaven (Tiandao) moved eastward, journeys should begin in an easterly direction; sedan chairs sent to bring a bride home should likewise go eastward initially; and buildings and repairs ought to be undertaken on the east side, if possible.[141]

The days, like the months, fell under the influence of various positive and negative spirits, which might or might not be specified.[142] If indicated in the text, the positive spiritual influences (*shen*) for each day appeared at the top of each daily column, and the negative spirits (*sha*) at the bottom—a symbolic depiction of their celestial struggle for ascendancy in earthly affairs.[143] Each day was identified with one of the five "agents" and assigned to one of the twenty-eight lunar lodges in succession. In Chinese popular lore, every lodge represented an animal with distinctive characteristics, and each one came to be associated with specific lucky and unlucky activities.[144] For every day—with only a few exceptions in any given year—there were a certain number of activities designated appropriate (*yi*; i.e., auspicious) or inappropriate (*buyi*; inauspicious), some with specific indications of the proper time during the day or night for undertaking this or that affair.[145] As with the tabular chart mentioned above, the term *bujiang* in a column denoted a "neutralized" star spirit.

This concern with selecting lucky and unlucky days and times can be found in many classical Chinese texts, including the *Shijing*, the *Shujing*, and the *Liji*, which are often cited in Qing official documents as well as popular publications.[146] In view of the cultural importance of day-selection in Chinese society, the Qing government did not hesitate to seek private diviners with this particular specialty to serve in the Board of Astronomy. Some even helped put together and revise the *Xieji bianfang shu*.[147] Day-selection involved a myriad of cosmic variables; but one fundamental assumption, dating from at least the Han dynasty, was that different qualities or powers were linked to successive periods of time marked by cycles of twelve days and twelve years. These cycles came to be distinguished by a series of twelve terms, beginning with *jian* (to establish) and *chu* (to remove) and ending with *kai* (to open) and *bi* (to close). This so-called *jianchu* system, which can be found in Han almanacs, is discussed at length in the *Xieji bianfang shu*. Generally speaking, times marked by the characters *chu*, *ding* (to settle), and *zhi* (to hold) were considered to be most auspicious; *jian*, *man* (to fill), *ping* (to level), *shou* (to receive), *cheng* (to complete) and *kai*, somewhat less auspicious; and *po* (to destroy) and *bi*, most unfortunate. Although *wei* (to be endangered) generally signified misfortune, it occasionally denoted extremely good fortune, just as *shou*, although generally auspicious, was sometimes considered unlucky.[148]

Activities subject to designation as auspicious or inauspicious in the state calendar were categorized and included in the Collected Statutes of both the

Ming and Qing dynasties. During the Qing, sixty-seven matters fell under the rubric "imperial use" (*yuyong*), thirty-seven under "people's use" (*minyong*), and sixty under "almanac selection" (*tongshu xuanze*).[149] Of the sixty-seven categories of imperial concern, a great number naturally dealt with general administrative and ritual matters, such as various forms of sacrifice and prayer, the submission of documents, the promulgation of edicts, the bestowal of favors and awards (including amnesties, compensation, and titles), personnel matters (such as official appointments and the search for virtue and talent), diplomatic and military affairs, and events such as banquets. On a more personal level, the calendar provided guidance in choosing days for educational activities, domestic rituals (birth, capping, marriage, etc.), health, business decisions, and the solicitation and adoption of suggestions and advice. Among mundane activities regulated by the calendar we find bathing and grooming, cutting out clothes, household cleaning and decoration, establishing a new bed, discarding things, moving things, travelling, breaking ground, well-digging, construction and repair (of furniture and roof beams, rooms, buildings, roads, dams, canals, walls, and so forth), hunting, fishing, trapping, planting, cutting wood, and herding animals.[150]

The thirty-seven activities designated "for the people" encompassed virtually all of the major personal and mundane matters indicated above. This category also included a few additional mundane items, such as visiting and receiving relatives and friends, as well as important ritual and administrative acts such as carrying out sacrifices, submitting a memorial to the throne, assuming an official post, and arranging for burials (the last not expressly specified in the imperial list).

The almanac category, although listed last, stood midway between the two previously-mentioned sets of concerns. It included most of the major categories of activity noted above, but omitted those that were obviously the exclusive prerogatives of the emperor. At the same time, it was especially specific about certain personal and mundane affairs. It indicated, for example, particular stages of marriage ritual (such as *nacai* and *wenming*), the treatment of particular afflictions (such as eye diseases), and the use of specific medical remedies (such as acupuncture). It also mentioned a few activities not included in either of the preceding categories, such as constructing, opening, and repairing storehouses and granaries, fermenting liquor, smelting metals, and crossing the water by boat or other means.[151]

Relatively few activities were designated "inappropriate" in the Qing calendars I have seen. By far the most common categories were travelling (*chuxing*); moving one's residence (*yixi*); beginning construction (*dongtu*; lit. "stirring the earth"); planting or sowing (*zaizhong*); and sewing (*zhenci*). Particularly striking are the number of days that calendar-makers considered inauspicious for travel— as many as eighty-two in a year of 354 days, for instance.[152] In this same year (1886), forty-two days were designated inappropriate for planting; thirty-seven for beginning construction; thirty-five for sewing; and thirty-three for moving. As a rule, when the evil star Lunar Repression dominated a day, both travelling and moving one's residence became inadvisable, and often planting as well.

Despite such limits on common activities, the Chinese found ways to get around the problem. One was, of course, to consult a fortune-teller, whose presumed knowledge of directional influences and other variables enabled him or her to give advice on how to avoid or overcome negative spirits at a particular place or time. Thus, for example, when a man in Zhejiang wanted to begin the construction of waterworks under inauspicious circumstances, a local diviner informed him that the time of his birth, reckoned according to the system of "eight characters" (see chapter 5), was in fact auspicious enough to offset the evil star affecting his enterprise. He could thus proceed without risk.[153] In another case, a man who had the misfortune to encounter an evil spirit (xiongsha) on his wedding day, presumably because he did not take the proper precautions, received from an Yijing specialist directional advice that enabled him to overcome the negative power of this malevolent spectre.[154]

Individuals might also consult divining manuals on their own. The Xuanze tianjing (Heavenly Mirror of [Day and Time] Selection), written in 1748 by a scholar named Ren Duanshu, was one of many such popular reference works. It provided concrete information on how to use cosmic variables such as the stem and branch correlations of the nayin system to "control" (zhi) and "cultivate" (xiu) certain situations or spirits.[155] The Xieji bianfang shu offered similar counsel to an exclusively elite audience. It suggested, for instance, that if construction had to be undertaken in an unlucky direction, the person concerned might temporarily move to another location which, in relation to the place to be repaired or built, would then be auspicious.[156]

In addition to official and unofficial versions of the state calendar, privately published almanacs (lishu, tongshu, tongsheng, etc.) circulated freely throughout the Qing period and throughout the empire. These works were quite possibly the best-selling books in all of China—not only because they were extremely cheap, but also because they were extremely useful. The vast majority of almanacs seem to have been produced in South China—especially Guangdong, Fujian, and Jiangsu—and then distributed to the north and west. The forty or fifty Qing almanacs I have consulted come mainly from the Canton area, Ningpo, or Shanghai.[157] Although little concrete information exists on distribution patterns, we know that certain almanacs were extremely popular over large areas. For instance, a late Qing gazetteer for Tongan county in Fujian indicates that an astrologer by the name of Hong Chaohe produced a work that was not only used widely within south and central China but was also purchased overseas. "Everyone bought it [wu bu gou zhi]," states the gazetteer.[158]

The introductions to many almanacs refer specifically to works such as the Shixian shu and Xieji bianfang shu either as prototypes or as sources of additional calendrical information.[159] A number of almanacs also include prefaces by Qing civil or military officials, designed to indicate a measure of administrative approval and support.[160] Fei Chun (c. 1739–1811), governor of Jiangsu province in the late eighteenth century, was one such official. His elegantly written preface to an almanac entitled Zouji bianlan (A Handy Reference for Selecting Good Fortune) can be found on editions of the work dating from at least 1797 to 1865 or later. In his preface, Fei begins by emphasizing that the theories of day-selection specialists are undeniably "contrary and confusing" (fenfen buyi). Nonetheless, decisions regarding auspicious and inauspicious dates and times have to be made, and it is clearly impractical for most people to buy, much less carry around, a voluminous work like the *Xieji bianfang shu.* He goes on to say that during his tenure as provincial treasurer of Yunnan, one of his subordinates—a *yinyang* specialist named Yu Rongkuan—presented him with an almanac that he (Yu) had compiled using the *Xieji bianfang shu* as a model. This work, Fei tells us, was simple, easy to use, and as clear, in the Confucian cliché, as the back of your hand (*liao ru zhizhang*). It became the *Zouji bianlan.*[161]

Since most almanacs took as their model imperially-authorized sources such as the *Wannian shu* and *Xieji bianfang shu,* they tended to approximate state calendars in the designation of auspicious and inauspicious days. One can see, however, a number of discrepancies for any given year. If, for example, we compare one version of the official calendar for 1857 with a work such as the *Bianmin tongshu* (Almanac for the Convenience of the People) for the same year, we find that whereas the calendar designates the fourth day of the first month as inappropriate for travel, the almanac lists the third as inauspicious for this purpose and not the fourth. And although both works indicate that the ninth day of the first month is auspicious for sacrifices, only the calendar specifies that it is not a good day to travel.[162]

Other differences existed between almanacs and official calendars. In the first place, almanacs were easily attainable, and their production and distribution, as with quasi-official calendars, involved none of the ceremonial fanfare connected with formal state publications.[163] Secondly, almanacs were not normally designated *Shixian li* or *Shixian shu.*[164] Rather, they went by a bewildering variety of names. Some were colorful and auspicious, such as the *Jixiang ruyi tongshu* (Almanac for All the Good Luck You Could Want); others were more down to earth: *Guanshang kuailan* (A Quick Reference for Officials and Merchants); *Riyong bianlan* (A Handy Reference for Daily Use); *Xuanze tongshu* (Almanac for Choosing [Lucky Days]), and so forth. A number were preceded by the name of an auspicious-sounding place, such as "The Hall of Riches and Honor" (*Fugui tang*), and many contained terms designed to indicate comprehensiveness (*daquan*).[165]

Almanacs generally had auspicious red covers rather than imperial yellow ones, and some were decorated with Buddhist or Daoist symbols drawn from Chinese popular culture.[166] They also possessed a number of pages of written text in addition to the stark columns, charts and diagrams of their official counterparts. Although the information almanacs provided on auspicious and inauspicious activities for each month and day of the year was similar to that of state calendars, they were far more likely to include material in day-columns not expressly stipulated in the Collected Statutes. For example, some *tongshu* identified the daily location of "womb spirits" so that pregnant women and members of their households could avoid miscarriages and birth defects by staying away from those parts of the house (front gate, pestle, mill, chicken coop, kitchen, stove, bed, storage area, toilet, etc.) where such spirits might be present at a certain time.[167]

Many almanacs were illustrated with woodblock prints not to be found in state calendars. They also contained a layered (*ceng*) geometrical chart designated

"Important Affairs of the Year" (*Liunian shikuan*) which, by symbolic devices similar to those of the *nianshen fangwei zhi tu* (see above), conveyed the same kinds of information.[168] Virtually all Qing almanacs from the late eighteenth century onward contained illustrations of, or at least written information about, the "spring ox" (*chunniu*) and its "herdsman" (*shentong* or *mangshen*), whose rich and evocative symbolism was universal in traditional China (see Fig. 2.9). This symbolism was never depicted in official calendars, however. Rather, it found more orthodox expression in seasonal rituals.[169] Every year, both at the capital and in the provinces, Qing officials "welcomed spring" (*yingchun*) in elaborate state-sponsored ceremonies that involved presentation of the ox and its herdsman as effigies. The dynasty's Collected Statutes and the *Xieji bianfang shu* contain elaborate descriptions of these rituals, together with specific instructions for the manufacture of each effigy.[170]

According to popular belief, the colors of the spring ox and the clothes of the herdsman—as displayed both in official ceremonies and on the pages of local almanacs—indicated agricultural and other prospects for the coming year. By one account, a predominance of white portended floods and rain; red suggested fire and heat; green, strong winds and storms; black, disease; and yellow, a bountiful harvest. Another similar version invested the color green with the meaning of conflict. Yet another tells us that if the head of the ox is yellow, then there will be great summer heat; and if, green, there will be much sickness in the spring. If red, there will be a drought; if black, much rain; and if white, high winds and storms.[171]

In fact, however, this symbolism of color and attire had nothing to do with actual meteorological observations. Rather, it was based arbitrarily on traditional cosmological calculations involving yin and yang, *wuxing* correlations, and stem-branch considerations. If, for example, yang governed a certain year, the mouth of the ox would be open; if yin, it would be closed. For those years marked by the stems *jia* and *yi*, the head of the ox would be green; for those marked by the branches *yin* and *mao*, the body would be green; for years corresponding to wood (according to the *nayin* system), the abdomen would be green, and so forth. The same kinds of calculations dictated the color of horns, hooves, neck and tail, as well as the specific features of the herdsman.[172] Although this symbolism yielded different interpretations, and was of no practical value to farmers, its periodic expression in Qing ritual, as well as its ubiquitous presence in popular almanacs, reaffirmed the importance of agriculture in Chinese society and contributed to a shared sense of culture at all levels.[173]

As cultural documents, almanacs provide an illuminating inventory of Chinese popular concerns. Relatively few early Qing almanacs are extant, and the ones I have seen tend to be rather straightforward, like calendars, without much cultural embellishment.[174] By the late eighteenth and early nineteenth centuries, however, almanacs begin to display more and more popular elements. We commonly find, for example, discussions of the life of Confucius and other morality tales—notably the "Twenty-four Examples of Filial Piety" (*Ershisi xiao*). Other frequently-seen illustrations include annotated (and often personalized) pictures of the sun, moon, five planets and other "stars," as well as the dominant

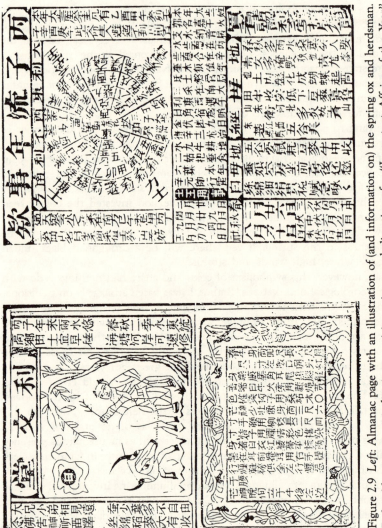

Figure 2.9 *Left:* Almanac page with an illustration of (and information on) the spring ox and herdsman. *Right:* Almanac page indicating auspicious times and directions for "Important Affairs of the Year" (*Liunian shikuan*). During this particular year, we are told, east and west are the most favorable directions, whereas south is unlucky. *Source: Liwen tang zouji tongshu* (1876), no pagination.

asterisms of the twenty-eight lunar lodges and their general influence on life situations. One also finds depictions of the twenty-six or more difficult or dangerous "passes" (guan) encountered by Chinese children as they grow to adulthood, along with concrete advice on how to avoid harm (see also chapter 5). These hazardous situations, which differ slightly from almanac to almanac, range from relatively common dangers (deep water, burning broth, falling into a well, etc.) to more frightening encounters with generals, demons, tigers, snakes, and even the King of Hell.[175]

Almanacs also included advice on matters relating to agriculture, business, health, family life, food, etiquette, travel, and, of course, divination. Among the most common forms of portent interpretation discussed in such works were those concerned with dreams, body sensations and animal sounds (see chapter 6). Popular mantic techniques included a rudimentary system of counting on finger joints, as well as materials relating to "spiritual sticks," physiognomy and geomancy (chapters 4 and 5). Most almanacs provided lists of anniversary dates for deceased emperors and empresses, the birthdays of positive spirits, and charms for protection against evil spirits. Some even had a section entitled "Methods for Producing Children" (Zhongzi fangfa), which contained surprisingly explicit information for women (and men) concerning menstruation, times for (and frequency of) sexual intercourse, preparations for pregnancy, and so forth. These sections—which included medical prescriptions for regulating menstruation, strengthening vital essence (jing), and consolidating pregnancy—indicated that while the birth of sons or daughters was fundamentally a matter of Heaven-conferred fate (Tianming), human action (renshi) could, after all, influence events.[176]

By the late nineteenth and early twentieth centuries, tongshu had become conduits for new information on recent educational and political changes, modern science and technology, and news regarding foreign nations. One late Qing almanac, for example, prefaced by a military taotai in Jiangsu surnamed Liang, provided—in addition to the usual wealth of cosmological and divinatory detail—a map of China, photographs of Chinese political leaders such as Prince Gong and Prince Qing, pictures of Chinese and foreign national and commercial flags, postal and telegraphic information, and lists of new institutions, offices, and titles.[177] Such works at once expressed and contributed to an evolving awareness of China's new international and domestic circumstances.

As long as almanacs reflected orthodox views and reinforced imperial legitimacy, they could be tolerated; but if not, the state suppressed them with a vengeance. This was naturally true of calendars produced by contenders for political power, such as the Yongli emperor of the southern Ming during the latter half of the seventeenth century, or the Taiping rebels of the mid-nineteenth century (see below).[178] But it was also true of certain privately printed "heretical" (xie) almanacs such as the early nineteenth century handbook entitled San Fo yingjie tongguan tongshu (Comprehensive Almanac for Responding to the Kalpas of the Three Buddhas [Past, Present and Future])—used by the rebel Lin Qing of the Eight Trigrams sect to, in the Jiaqing emperor's words, "deceive the people" and "violate the authority of Heaven." After discovery of this document, the emperor ordered all copies destroyed and engaged in a relentless search for the authors and publishers.[179]

From the standpoint of the Chinese government, to surrender calendrical authority of any sort to non-orthodox elements of society was to compromise the very foundations of imperial rule. Thus, when official sources on calendar-making such as the *Xieji bianfang shu* criticized fortune-tellers who "talk of good luck and bad luck (*jixiong*), and of calamities and blessings (*huofu*)," their criticisms were directed more toward the political purposes to which occult skills might be put than to the cosmological principles that informed such skills.[180] Put another way, state astrologers (*baozhang zheng*, *wuguan zheng*, etc.), almanac-makers, and most private divination specialists (aside from those connected directly with millenarian cults and other clandestine organizations) shared a cosmological outlook that was remarkably uniform and philosophically unexceptionable. "Heresy" in the Qing period was defined largely in political rather than religious or philosophical terms.[181]

Of course calendars and almanacs did not have to be heretical to be criticized. The well-known Qing astronomer and mathematician Mei Wending, for example, argued that the practice of designating specific days of the year as appropriate or inappropriate for certain activities lacked classical calendrical precedent and was at best a cumbersome superfluity. Like the courageous Ming scholar-official Jie Dashen, whose views he forcefully reiterated, Mei saw no value in the *jianchu* system, nor any reason for officials of the Board of Astronomy to concern themselves with benevolent spirits and "evil stars" such as The Orphan (Gu) and The Void (Xu). He did acknowledge the legitimate use of divination by the ancient sages; but like the Tang scholar Lü Cai, whom he cited for additional authority, Mei distinguished classical forms of divination from the misleading and pernicious predictions of more modern *yinyang* soothsayers.[182] His critique of lucky and unlucky days, one might add, coincided with the views of Jesuit court astronomers such as Verbiest, who wrote two tracts in Chinese, both published in 1669, refuting prevailing notions of good and bad fortune (*jixiong*), as well as specific divining practices such as day-selection.[183] But Mei did not bother to cite the Jesuits in making his argument—perhaps because he knew that as officials in the Board of Astronomy they engaged in the practices they decried.[184]

The leaders of the Christian-inspired Taiping Rebellion (1850–1864) took an explicitly religious tack in denouncing the "superstitious" elements of the Qing calendar, even as they secretly sought out fortune-tellers to serve their cause.[185] Their "new calendar" (*xinli*)—promulgated at Nanjing in 1853 and preserved now in the British Library—utilized the conventional sexegenary system for marking years, months and days (with only a few modifications), assigned lunar lodges to each month and day, and included the twenty-four solar terms of the traditional Chinese calendar. But it contained no references whatsoever to auspicious or inauspicious days. Indeed, the preface indicates that the express purpose of this new document was to eradicate the heretical doctrines (*xieshuo*) of previous calendars, including the Qing dynasty's *Shixian shu*. Since the Taipings claimed that the years, months, hours and days were all determined by God, how could any of them be particularly lucky or unlucky? Those who worshipped the Heavenly Father, they reasoned, would enjoy good fortune all of the time.[186]

Criticisms of day-selection can also be found in popular literature of the Qing period. *Honglou meng* (Dream of the Red Chamber), arguably China's greatest and most influential novel, provides a particularly apt illustration. Early in the book, Zhen Shiyin, a retired scholar from Suzhou, devoted to the pleasures of wine and poetry, urges the careerist Jia Yucun to hasten to the capital to order to participate in the triennial examinations. "The almanac gives the nineteenth as a good day for travelling," he observes, after arranging to provide Jia with a parcel of fifty taels and two suits of winter clothes. The next day, the seemingly ungrateful Jia departs abruptly for the capital, leaving a curt message for his generous benefactor: "A scholar should not concern himself with almanacs, but should act as the situation demands."[187] This theme of intellectual autonomy occupies a central place in most elite discussions of divination.

Scholarly criticisms of day-selection seem to have made no dent in the popularity of either almanacs or official calendars. A report of the Society for the Diffusion of Useful Knowledge in China (November 21, 1838) refers to "the almost universal demand . . . [for calendars and almanacs] among all classes of Chinese," echoing the views of many other informed contemporary observers.[188] Most Qing fortune-tellers kept almanacs close at hand for reference (as they do to this day), and people from many other walks of life relied heavily upon them as well. One late Qing ritual handbook asserts that "no household is complete without an almanac;" and according to a knowledgeable Westerner writing in the 1870s, "The great use of an Almanac, it might perhaps be said the only purpose for which Chinese buy it, is to choose lucky days, to divine on what days undertakings may be begun, and when they had better be left alone."[189] During the Taiping Rebellion, even in areas under rebel control, most Chinese resisted using the new-style calendar—primarily, it appears, because the document failed to provide information on lucky and unlucky days.[190]

The popularity of calendars and almanacs in Qing China had little if anything to do with entertainment, for the former offered only the most stark form of practical guidance, and the latter had none of the humorous content of their Western counterparts.[191] In China, calendars and almanacs were taken seriously because they contained culturally essential advice and information for all levels of society, from emperor to peasant. Furthermore, many commoners believed calendars to possess magical power by virtue of their association with imperial authority—an effect achieved in almanacs by devices such as official prefaces and the inclusion of written charms. In Anhui province, residents of certain prefectures would suspend a copy of the calendar on the bedstead of a sick person in order to bring cosmic power to bear on the situation, since the document contained the names of all auspicious stars, the twenty-eight lodges, and the name of the reigning emperor "whose power over the hosts of spirits is unbounded."[192]

According to at least some contemporary accounts, "the better-informed Chinese" were ashamed of "the farrago of odds and ends" contained in almanacs.[193] Yet it appears that most members of the Qing elite took the stipulations of calendars, if not also almanacs, quite seriously. Qing documents often refer to imperial activities that take place only at times designated auspicious; and the writings of foreigners in the Chinese service—from Matteo Ricci in the early seventeenth century to Robert Hart in the late nineteenth— testify to a firm belief in lucky and unlucky days on the part of many Ming and Qing officials.[194] W. A. P. Martin, who, like Hart, had extensive contact with Chinese bureaucrats as head of the Interpreter's College (Tongwen guan), once remarked that "No man [in China] thinks of beginning a journey, laying a corner-stone, planting a tree, marrying a wife, burying a parent, or any of a thousand functions in public or private life, without consulting this convenient oracle." Further, he noted: "The late archimandrite Palladius told me that he found . . . [the Qing] calendar useful, as it enabled him to select an unlucky day for his visits to the Russian legation, four miles distant, when he was sure to find the streets unobstructed by marriages or funerals."[195]

A. P. Parker, another well-informed Westerner, tells us:

> The astrological part [of the Chinese calendar] is universally believed in, though there seems to be considerable difference in the practice of the details by different persons—some considering it necessary to be careful about the times and places of carrying out the most important affairs of life, such as marriage, burial, house-building, &c., while others believe it necessary to be careful as to the time and place for the most commonplace details of everyday life, such as opening a shop, entering school, going on a journey, giving an entertainment, sweeping the floor, shaving the head, taking a bath, &c.[196]

According to S. W. Williams, "No one ventures to be without an almanac [or calendar], lest he be liable to the greatest misfortunes, and run the imminent hazard of undertaking the important events on black-balled days."[197]

Williams goes on to assert that by "perpetuating folly and ignorance among the people, when they know that the whole system is false and absurd," the Chinese authorities were engaging in a deliberate effort to mystify and thus overawe the common people. "Such governments as that of China," he maintains, "deem it necessary to uphold ancient superstitions, if they can thereby influence their security, or strengthen the reverence due to them." The Taipings said essentially the same thing when they declared that the Qing calendar was an attempt by the "impish" Manchus "to deceive and misguide mankind."[198] These remarks are not without point, for much of imperial authority indeed rested upon the mystifying effect of official rituals and the aura of imperial omnipotence that they created.[199]

Yet it would be a mistake, I think, to view calendars and almanacs as nothing more than manipulative devices—just as it would be wrong to see state sacrifices only in this narrow light. If the "ignorant masses" were fooled into believing in lucky and unlucky days, so were many, if not most, Chinese scholar-officials, and the Qing emperors themselves. Works on day-selection by intellectuals such as Ren Duanshu, a 1737 *jinshi*, were clearly written out of genuine conviction, and, like almanacs, suggest the possibility of a comfortable fit between

Confucian ethics and popular mantic practices. The *Xuanze tianshu jing* casts divination explicitly in terms of orthodox social values such as filial piety (*xiao*) and humaneness (*ren*), and assails "stupid people who do not distinguish between right and wrong." At the same time, the author warns that without a cosmic awareness of proper time and place, earthly disorder (*luan*) will surely ensue.[200]

In short, calendars, almanacs and related works expressed cosmological assumptions and/or moral values that were widely shared by elites and commoners alike in late imperial China. The fact that these assumptions and values were communicated by somewhat different media, and interpreted in somewhat different ways, did not diminish their significance as cultural common denominators in the Middle Kingdom across space and time. Late Qing and early Republican almanacs might incorporate new knowledge from the West, but they continued to promote traditional ethics as well as inherited cosmological concepts.[201] And although radical proposals for calendrical reform began to surface by the end of the dynasty—in part, presumably, as a political weapon against the Manchus—the last official Qing calendar, for the year 1912, was in every meaningful way a carbon copy not only of its immediate predecessors, but of its Ming prototype as well.[202]

When the Qing dynasty was finally overthrown in 1911-1912, state-sponsored cosmology suffered a mortal blow. But, as we shall see in the concluding chapter of this book, the downfall of the Qing and the destruction of the imperial system had far less to do with the decline of cosmology than with the rise of modern Chinese nationalism. Put another way, the production of a new state calendar for the Republic in 1912, with its vigorous denunciations of the old Qing calendar's "superstitions," does not warrant the conclusion that the inherited cosmology had already died. In fact, the revolutionary government's self-conscious repudiation of the inherited cosmology may be viewed precisely as an effort to eradicate a still dangerous potential source of imperial authority.[203]

THREE

The *Yijing* in Qing Society

As should already be apparent, few aspects of traditional Chinese history and culture can be discussed without reference to the *Yijing*. During the Qing period the cryptic classic touched every sector of Chinese society in some way, whether through its philosophy, its symbolism or its use as a fortune-telling tool. The "Great Commentary" tells us: "The *Changes* contains the fourfold Way of the sages: In speaking, we value its judgments; in action, we value its changes; in making objects, we value its images; and in divination, we value its prognostications [*zhan*]."[1] For well over two thousand years the *Yijing* provided concrete guidance in all of these realms, shaping Chinese discourse, influencing behavior, inspiring invention, and serving various mantic functions. No other classical work served so many practical and philosophical purposes. Small wonder, then, as Qing scholars repeatedly observed, Confucius wore out the bindings of his copy three times in assiduous study.[2]

A fundamental assumption of the *Changes* is that all things in the universe are interrelated, and that eternal, inexhaustible processes of cosmic change will naturally alter the context in which everything becomes defined and positioned. By duplicating these processes through its use of symbolic images, the *Yijing* allows human beings to understand their place in the present structure of the universe as well as to determine their future position. In the words of the "Great Commentary," "The *Book of Changes* contains the measure of Heaven and Earth; therefore it enables us to comprehend completely the *dao* of Heaven and Earth."[3] The sixty-four hexagrams, their written judgments (*tuan*), and their line readings (*yaoci*) illumine the way, while self-cultivation instills the creative capacity and provides the motive force. The *Zhongyong* (Doctrine of the Mean) states, "one who is possessed of the most complete sincerity can fully develop his nature, and in so doing, both assist the transforming and nourishing powers of Heaven and Earth and join together with them."[4]

Most Chinese of the Qing period considered the *Changes* to be "the consummation of all wisdom," and many believed that it possessed magical power as well. Commoners used it as a charm to ward off evil, and scholars gave it pride of place as "first among the [Confucian] classics" in both of the dynasty's major literary compilations, the *Tushu jicheng* and the *Siku quanshu*. Even the most skeptical thinkers of the Qing era had unrestrained admiration for the document. Wang Fuzhi wrote, for example: "The *Yijing* is the manifestation of the Heavenly Way, the unexpressed form of nature, and the showcase for sagely achievement. Yin and yang, movement and stillness, darkness and brightness, withdrawing and extending are all inherent in it. Spirit operates within it; the refined subtlety of ritual and music is stored in it; the transformative capacity of ghosts and gods [guishen] emerges from it; the great utility of humaneness and uprightness issues forth from it; and the calculation of order and disorder, good and bad fortune, life and death is in accordance with it."[5]

Yet despite such universal esteem, Qing scholars, like their predecessors for some two millennia, could not agree on how to interpret it. Of the literally thousands of diverse commentaries written on the Changes during the imperial era, over two hundred are cited in the Kangxi emperor's officially-sanctioned edition of 1715, known as the Zhouyi zhezhong (A Balanced [Version of the] Zhou Changes). The Siku quanshu project, which contains reprints of nearly 170 works on the Yijing and supplies reviews for over three hundred more—about half of which date from the Qing period—also attests to the wide variety of opinions and approaches stimulated by the classic.[6] Toda Toyosaburo has identified nearly twenty different schools of Yijing interpretation during the seventeenth and eighteenth centuries alone.[7]

Approaches to the Changes

A fundamental issue confronting all Qing scholars was whether to emphasize the ethical principles of the Yijing or its utility as a book of divination and numerology. As indicated briefly in chapter 1, the debate between those who emphasized "morality and principle" (yili) and those who favored "images and numbers" (xiangshu) in approaching the classic arose out of Wang Bi's influential critique of Han dynasty scholarship in the third century A.D. Among Song devotees of the Changes, Cheng Yi represented Wang's ethical emphasis, while Shao Yong reflected the Han tradition of numerological speculation and divination. In the Qing period, debate over the proper use of the Yijing became hopelessly entangled with the fierce textual controversies dividing advocates of "Han Learning" and "Song Learning." As one late Qing scholar, Zheng Xianfu, remarked in his Duyi lu (Record of Reading the Changes): "When people of the Han period spoke of the Yi it was all in terms of illuminating images; while in the Song period it was all in terms of illuminating principle."[8]

This was, of course, an oversimplification. Zhu Xi, the towering Song intellectual whose Zhouyi benyi (Basic Meaning of the Zhou Changes) provided the point of departure for most Yijing scholarship in the early Qing period, had long before recognized the need to reconcile these two approaches, feeling that "Confucians who talk about images and number give strained interpretations and draw far-fetched analogies, while those who preach [only] morality and principle stray far from the subject."[9] Zhu's intent was to negotiate a path to understanding the Changes that would avoid the moralistic extremes of Cheng Yi as well as the numerological excesses of Shao Yong.

In some respects Zhu's approach was closer to Shao's than to Cheng's, since he maintained that the Yijing was originally a book of divination, and that "what is described in it is simply images and numbers by which to foretell one's good or evil fortune."[10] This did not mean, however, that he failed to appreciate the moral dimension of the document, or that he thought Cheng's ethics were somehow "wrong." On the contrary, Zhu's morally-grounded view was precisely that the ultimate purpose of the *Changes* was to contribute to self-cultivation, and that without sincerity and the rectification of character it would be of no use in divination. Like most Confucians, he drew a sharp distinction between superficial techniques of fortune-telling, which involved numerical calculations but remained "far from the *dao*," and proper use of the *Yijing*, which brought a person closer to a true understanding of the Way.[11]

From a Confucian standpoint, moral cultivation and a knowledge of the future went hand in hand. The *Zhongyong* said as much: "Complete sincerity entails the capacity to foreknow. When calamity or good fortune is about to occur, one can be aware of it in advance. Therefore, the individual possessed of complete sincerity is like a spirit [*shen*]."[12] The *Yijing*, as a medium linking man and the cosmos, thus enabled sage-like individuals to "know fate" (*zhiming*). Although the term *ming* sometimes refers to Heaven's mandate, nature as a whole, or man's natural endowment, we may best think of it as a series or set of predestined situations evolving out of the natural processes of eternal cosmic change. By using the *Yijing* and establishing a spirtual link with Heaven, one could not only "know fate" but also "establish fate" (*liming*)—that is, devise an appropriate moral strategy for dealing with any causal matrix, any encountered circumstances.[13] In the words of the famous Qing dynasty scholar, Tang Jian (1778-1861), "He who knows fate will cultivate the Way; he who [merely] relies on fate will do harm to the Way."[14]

The idea of knowing fate proved appealing not only to Confucians, but also to Buddhists and Daoists. For this reason we find among both clerics and lay believers in the Qing period numerous *Yijing* practitioners and at least a few prominent scholarly commentators.[15] Mainstream Confucians, however, tried mightily to dissociate the *Changes* from such "unorthodox teachings." Thus, although the editors of the *Siku quanshu* felt obliged to acknowledge that the classic served as inspiration for a number of popular divination systems, they made unprecedented efforts to distinguish the orthodox tradition of Yi scholarship from what they considered to be the Daoist tradition of magical practices.[16] Similarly, the compilers of the *Tushu jicheng* relegated popular divinatory works based on the *Changes* to the "Arts and Occupations" section of the encyclopedia, rather than to the section on the "Classics."[17]

During the Qing, as in earlier periods, the *Yijing* attracted more scholarly attention than any other Confucian text. This was not simply because of its unparalleled utility as a divinatory manual, a book of wisdom and a repository of information about the natural world. It was also because of its enormous structural complexity, which proved endlessly fascinating to creative Chinese minds. Yet another reason the classic absorbed so much intellectual energy was, of course, its cryptic character, which begged for exegesis.[18] Scholars pored obsessively over the *Yijing*, analyzing it phrase by phrase, concept by concept, word by word.[19] Some wrote systematic tracts, while others employed a question-

and-answer format.[20] Several scholars produced works that explained, modified, or supplemented pre-existing compendia, notably Li Dingzuo's invaluable *Zhouyi jijie* (Collected Explanations of the Zhou Changes), compiled in the Tang dynasty.[21]

Qing scholarship on the *Changes* revolved around four distinct but related concerns. One was the ever-elusive meaning of the basic text—that is, the sixty-four hexagrams, their judgments, and their line readings. Another was the authenticity of charts such as the *Hetu* and *Luoshu*, which Zhu Xi had appended to his *Zhouyi benyi* as an integral part of the text. A third was the reliability of various commentaries on the *Yijing*, beginning with the original Ten Wings; and a fourth was the utility of various interpretive schemes of Han, Tang, Song, and Ming provenance.[22]

The many ambiguous terms and obscure passages of the *Yi*, all of which reflect its mantic origins and "word magic,"[23] provided much room for discussion and debate in the Qing period. Scholars argued endlessly over how to understand hexagram names (*guaming*), how to interpret various images and symbols, how to gloss individual words and phrases, and even how to punctuate the text.[24] Virtually no passage of the *Changes* was so clear as to preclude debate. Consider the judgment and line texts of Gou (44), which are quite typical of the *Yijing* in both language and tone.

[Gou, Coming to Meet] shows a woman who is bold and strong. It will not be good to marry (such) a woman. The first line shows how the subject (of the hexagram) should be kept (like a carriage) tied and fastened to a metal drag, in which case with firm correctness [*zhen*] there will be good fortune. (But) if he moves in any direction, evil will appear. He will be (like) a lean pig in captivity which is sure to keep jumping about. The second line shows its subject with a container of fish. There will be no error, but it will not be well to let (the subject of the first line) go forward to the guests. The third line shows one from whose buttocks the skin has been stripped so that he walks with difficulty. The position is perilous, but there will be no great error. The fourth line shows its subject with a container, but no fish in it. This will give rise to evil. The fifth line (shows its subject as) a melon gourd covered by a willow. If he keeps his brilliant qualities [lit. jade talisman (*zhang*)] concealed, (something good) will descend from Heaven. The sixth line shows its subject locking horns with others. There will be occasion for regret, but no error.[25]

Virtually every substantive word in this passage is susceptible to multiple readings. This ambiguity unquestionably contributes to the overall richness and subtlety of the text, but it also complicates the search for meaning—not to mention the problem of adequate translation.[26] Take the phrase: "He will be (like) a lean pig in captivity which is sure to keep jumping about" (*leishi fu zhizhu*). Putting aside the animal symbolism, which is itself quite problematic,[27] we are still left with a sense of uncertainty about what is actually going on. *Zhi* ("to walk"), when pronounced *di*, refers to the hoof of a pig, while *zhu* can mean both to limp and to amble, as a horse might. In Qing dynasty usage, *zhizhu* connotates embarrassment, or doubt over what to do. The term *lei* ("lean" or "emaciated") may be a loan word for *lei* ("to tie with a rope"), which would, of course, reinforce the notion of captivity; but, as the late Qing scholar-official Yu Yue (1821–1907) pointed out, *fu* (captive) may well be a loan word for *ru* ("to suckle")—in which case the meaning of the passage (a pig suckling its young) would change considerably, even if *lei* were still understood as a loan word.[28]

Certain passages of the *Yijing* attracted inordinate attention, such as the four characters *xi, ti, ruo* and *li* in line three of Qian (1)—conventionally translated "At nightfall the mind [of the superior man] is beset with cares. Danger."[29] Controversies also raged over historical questions, such as the identification and significance of Jizi ("The Winnower"), who appears in line five of the hexagram Mingyi (36).[30] In attempting to resolve these and other textual questions, Qing intellectuals mined every available resource, from the earliest commentaries on the *Changes* to reference works such as Xu Shen's *Shuowen jiezi* (Explanation of Characters for the Discussion of Writing) and Lu Deming's *Jingdian shiwen* (Explication of Terms from the Classics).

At another level of scholarly discourse, Zhu Xi's inclusion in his *Zhouyi benyi* of diagrams purporting to represent the original *Hetu* and *Luoshu* gave rise to a bitter controversy between individuals such as Mao Qiling (1623–1716) and Hu Wei (1633–1714), who claimed that the diagrams were forgeries of Daoist inspiration, and others, including Dai Zhen and Fang Dongshu (1772–1851), who defended Zhu on the grounds that his inclusion of the diagrams preserved a rich and valuable traditional understanding of the text. In the end, Mao and Hu prevailed, dealing what Liang Qichao describes as a "fatal blow" to Song scholarship in the Qing. Nonetheless, interest in the *Hetu* and *Luoshu* remained high, judging not only from the large section devoted to such illustrations in the "Classics" section of the *Tushu jicheng*, but also by the biographies of scholar-diviners in local gazetteers.[31] Moreover, the reputation of the *Yijing* itself remained unimpaired, even in the eyes of the most radical *kaozheng* scholars.

The commentaries known as the Ten Wings also held up well under close scrutiny, despite their comparatively late appearance in the history of the *Changes* and their obviously heterogeneous content. According to convention, the first and second "wings" are together called the "Commentary on the Judgment." The third and fourth—collectively styled the "Commentary on the Images"—are divided into a "Big Image Commentary," which discusses the images associated with the two primary trigrams of each hexagram (see below), and a "Small Image Commentary," which refers to the images of individual lines. The "Great Commentary" or "Appended Verbalizations" comprises the fifth and sixth wings; the "Commentary on the Words," the seventh; the "Discussion of the Trigrams," the eighth; the "Orderly Sequence of the Hexagrams," the ninth; and "Miscellaneous Notes on the Hexagrams," the tenth. Different editions of the *Changes* organize this material in different ways.[32]

A few Qing intellectuals questioned the provenance, or at least the explanatory value, of certain "wings." Wang Fuzhi, for example, believed that the "Orderly Sequence of the Hexagrams" represented such an arbitrary and unreasonable scheme that it could not possibly be the work of the ancient sages. He also felt that the "Big Image Commentary" and the "Discussion of the Trigrams" should be grouped together since they both elucidated the principles of the diagrams that had been originally "drawn" by Fu Xi.[33] On the whole, however, Qing scholars accepted the traditional organization of the Ten Wings, and believed that they represented the authentic words and thoughts of Confucius himself.

Han and Song commentaries to the *Yijing* naturally underwent intense scrutiny during the Qing period—especially since Han Learning remained in fashion for so long and Song scholarship was so often the target of its attacks. Most of the hundred or so Qing works on the *Changes* that I have consulted draw primarily on Han sources for exegetical support. A few *kaozheng* scholars, including Huang Zongxi and Hu Wei, were content to seek inspiration from Cheng Yi's highly-regarded Song dynasty commentary to the *Yi*, but most others, notably Mao Qiling and Hui Dong (1697–1758), viewed all Song learning with contempt, and argued passionately for the revival of Han scholarship. Of the seven books written by Mao on the *Changes*, four are reviewed in the *Siku quanshu zongmu*—more works than any other early Qing commentator. Hui Dong proved to be less prolific than Mao, but he is generally regarded as a more profound thinker. Hui, who spent about thirty years of his life on the *Yi*, is best known for his *Yi Hanxue* (Han Scholarship on the Changes), which evaluates five major schools of interpretation: those of Meng Xi, Yu Fan, Jing Fang, Zheng Xuan, and Xun Shuang. Hui "clarified and illuminated" the ideas of these pioneering individuals, while at the same time developing his own etymologically-grounded (although sometimes contradictory) theories of *Yijing* interpretation. Of the five Han scholars, Hui most admired Yu Fan, whom he considered to have synthesized the best ideas of Meng, Jing, and Xun.[34]

Zhang Huiyan (1761–1802), following Hui Dong's lead, brought textual analysis of the *Changes* in the Qing to new heights with two major works. His *Zhouyi Yushi yi* (The Meaning of the Zhou Changes Based on [the Interpretations of] Yu Fan) refined Hui's explanation of Yu's significance as an interpreter of the *Yijing*, while his *Yiyi bielu* (Supplement to the Meaning of the Changes) offered a comprehensive analysis of fifteen schools of Han and Jin scholarship that went well beyond Hui's *Yi Hanxue* in both scope and sophistication. But the work of Zhang did not go unchallenged. Jiao Xun, for one, attacked Yu Fan's scholarship as strained and fragmented, even though he, like Hui, Zhang and many other advocates of Han Learning, also had harsh words for Wang Bi and his Daoist leanings.[35]

Despite attacks by advocates of Han Learning, Song scholarship on the *Yijing* retained a considerable measure of popularity throughout the Qing period. Dai Zhen (1724–1777), for example, cited Zhu Xi and Cheng Yi freely in his *Zhouyi kao* (Analysis of the Zhou Changes), and Gu Yanwu followed Zhu's basic interpretations of the *Changes*, even as he denied the authenticity of the *Hetu* and *Luoshu*.[36] Even Shao Yong enjoyed a certain vogue—at least among low-ranking literati. In addition, there were always a number of illustrious defenders of neo-Confucian orthodoxy who devoted themselves to the *Yi* from Tang Bin (1627–1687) and Li Guangdi (1642–1718) to Hu Xu (1655–1736), and

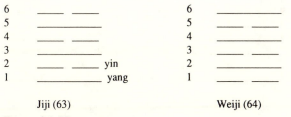

Figure 3.1 Hexagrams.

Zhang Xuecheng (1738–1801).[37] Furthermore, Song commentaries continued to feature prominently in the official version of the *Changes* first promulgated during the Kangxi period. In fact, each hexagram judgment and each line reading of the *Zhouyi zhezhong* contains three main categories of commentary: one for the remarks of Zhu Xi; one for those of Cheng Yi; and one for "others" (*jishuo*).

The Kangxi emperor once admonished his court lecturers not to make the *Yijing* appear simple, for it contained meanings that "lie beyond words."[38] His advice was sound, for the very structure of the classic, with its obscure but colorful language, multivalent symbols, and elaborate patterns of relationship among lines, trigrams, and hexagrams, militated against facile explanations— except by the simple-minded. We may begin to appreciate some of this complexity by taking a closer look at the composition of the hexagrams and by considering a few fundamental rules followed by most traditional interpreters of the *Changes* in Qing times.[39]

Each hexagram line is designated either *yin* (yielding, *rou*) or *yang* (firm, *gang*). Divided lines represent *yin*; solid lines, *yang*. *Yin* lines are even-numbered and inferior; *yang* lines are odd-numbered and superior. According to the "Great Commentary," these lines, by virtue of both their position and their movement in the hexagrams, imitate the changes of the universe and thus provide a model of it.[40] Lines are considered "correct" or "appropriate" if they correspond to the number of their position in the hexagram—that is, if *yang* lines are in odd-numbered places (1, 3 and 5), and *yin* lines are in even-numbered places (2, 4, and 6). From this standpoint, the most "correct" hexagram is Jiji (63); the most "incorrect," Weiji (64) (Fig. 3.1). Usually a central location is favorable for a line, whether associated with correctness or not. From a developmental standpoint, the first line of a hexagram denotes the beginning of a situation, and the sixth, the end; but the first and last lines are generally considered to be relatively unimportant compared to the middle lines. In any case the overall meaning of the hexagram must be taken into account. Furthermore, if one or more of the lines in a hexagram changes in the process of divination (see below), the derivative hexagram (*zhigua*) naturally has to be taken into account.

The places occupied by hexagram lines are differentiated as superior and inferior, according to their relative elevation. The sixth place is generally occupied by the sage; the fifth, by the ruler; the fourth, by a minister close to the king; the third by a middle-ranking official; the second, a lower official;

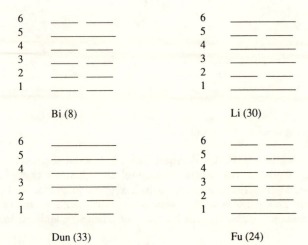

Figure 3.2 Hexagrams.

and the first or bottom, a commoner. By analogy, the fifth line may represent the husband; the fourth, the wife; the second the son, and so forth. The lines are also sometimes correlated with the body parts of both humans and animals.[41] Under some circumstances, as when the situation indicated by a hexagram has no prince, the fifth place is not that of the king. Thus, for example, the Kangxi emperor used Dun (33) to illustrate the point that in his time a ruler could not really rule by "non-action" (wuwei) as the ancient emperor Shun had done. In Kangxi's words: "In the hexagram 'Retreat' [Dun], not one of the six lines deals with a ruler's concerns; from this we can see that there is no place for rulers to rest, and no resting place to which they can retreat."[42] There are also occasions when a yang line in the fifth place is not necessarily optimal. A "yielding" king, for example, may occupy a very favorable position if supported by a strong, firm official in the second place.

A relationship described as "holding together" (bi) may exist between any two adjacent lines of different character in the top three places of a given hexagram. Under these conditions, the upper line is said to "rest upon" the lower line, while the lower line "receives" the upper. If this occurs between the fourth and fifth line, the relationship is generally viewed as auspicious, as when the yielding fourth line of Bi (8) complements the firm fifth line. On the other hand, the firm fourth line of Li (30) does not complement the weak fifth line. When "holding together" occurs between the fifth and the sixth lines, it may be advantageous if the king is humble (a yielding line in the fifth place) and the sage is strong (a firm line in the sixth place) (Fig. 3.2).

Hexagrams have two kinds of "rulers" (zhu)—those that "govern" by virtue of their position (usually the fifth place), known as zhugua zhi zhu; and those that give the hexagram its overall meaning (chenggua zhi zhu), such as the weak top line in Guai (43)—which, as the only yin line in the hexagram, indicates a "breakthrough." The ruler(s) of a hexagram can be determined by consulting the "Commentary on the Judgment." When two kinds of ruling lines are identical, the hexagram has only one ruler, as is the case with Jian (39); otherwise it has two and sometimes three rulers. Thus, the yielding second line of Pi (12) gives the hexagram its overall meaning ("standstill"), while the firm fifth line rules by virtue of its position. And in the case of Dun (33), the solid fifth line rules by virtue of its position, while the first two yielding lines rule jointly because they are pushing back four strong lines in their "retreat." In considering lines that are the rulers of their hexagrams, relationships of correspondence and holding together must be taken into account regardless of the positions occupied by the lines. Thus, in the hexagram for "return," Fu (24), *yang* in the first place, as the only firm line, is the ruler, the second holds together with it, and the fourth corresponds with it. Both of these latter relationships are favorable (see Fig. 3.2).[43]

Each hexagram has two basic trigram configurations. One involves the relationship between the primary inner trigram (*neigua*, lines 1, 2 and 3) and the primary outer trigram (*waigua*, lines 4, 5 and 6); the other involves two overlapping lower and upper "nuclear" trigrams (*hugua*)— lines 2, 3 and 4 and lines 3, 4 and 5, respectively (also known as "middle lines," *zhongyao*). The first and last lines of any hexagram are thus part of only one trigram, while the second and fifth line each belong to two trigrams, and the third and fourth belong to three. In considering the relationship between primary trigrams, the inner, which refers to the party consulting the *Yijing*, is below, within, and behind; while the outer, which refers to the opposite party, is above, without and in front. The inner usually indicates "substance" (*ti*) while the outer is "function" (*yong*). The lines emphasized in the outer trigram are characterized as "going," and those of the inner as "coming."[44]

Each trigram, whether primary or nuclear, is designated either *yin* (inferior) or *yang* (superior), depending upon the total numerical value of its constituent lines (broken lines are either six or eight; solid lines are either seven or nine). The trigrams also convey concrete visual images based on their respective line configurations. In the *Zhouyi benyi* these images are expressed in a folk rhyme: "Qian is three [lines] connected; Kun is six broken. Zhen is a bowl turned upward; Gen is a bowl overturned. Li is empty in the middle; Kan is full in the middle. Dui has a space on top; Sun is broken on the bottom."[45] Viewed another way, the eight trigrams are "blood-related," since each line of the "parent" trigrams Qian (father) and Kun (mother) is associated with one of the remaining six trigrams—three of which, reading from bottom to top, denote the eldest, middle and youngest sons (for Qian), and three of which represent the eldest, middle and youngest daughter (for Kun).[46]

In addition, each of the eight symbols possesses a wide range of other correlations or characteristics known as "trigram virtues" (*guade*), most of which are indicated in the "Discussion of Trigrams." These refer not only to intrinsic qualities or "powers" (see chapter 2), but also to natural phenomena, colors, times, seasons, directions, types of people, parts of the body, animals, and so forth. Thus Qian, in addition to being strong and active, can also be viewed as representing Heaven, deep red, metal, early night, late autumn, south or

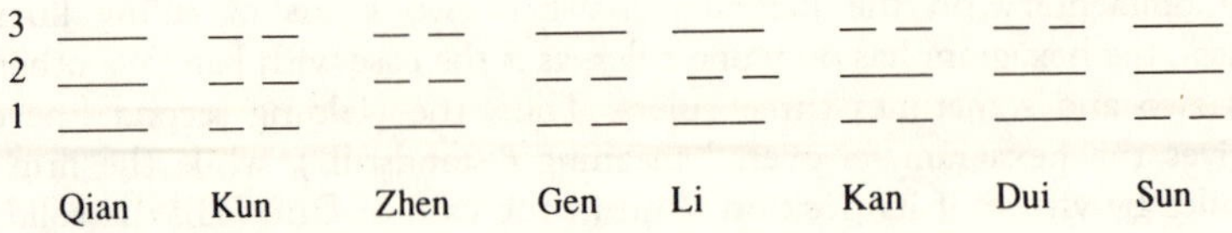

Figure 3.3 Trigrams.

northwest (depending on the trigram sequence), the sovereign, the head, a horse or dragon, etc. Kun, in addition to possessing the attributes of docility and receptiveness, can also represent Earth, the mother, black, earth, afternoon, late summer/early autumn, north or southwest, the people, the abdomen, a mare or ox, etc. Zhen not only connotes movement and speed (as with a chariot), but also thunder, yellow, wood, morning, spring, northeast or east, a young man, the foot, a galloping horse or flying dragon, etc. Although these and other such correlations are not always consistently applied in hexagram analysis, they vastly increase the interpretive possibilities of any given trigram configuration (see Fig. 3.3).[47]

As indicated above, the "Big Image Commentary" of every hexagram indicates the symbolism of its primary trigram configurations. In general, these symbols are naturalistic: Qian represents "creative" Heaven; Kun, "receptive" Earth or "nourishing" earth; Zhen, "arousing" thunder; Kan, "lowly" water; Gen, a "stationary" mountain; Sun, "gentle" wind; Li, "clinging" fire; and Dui, a "joyous" lake.[48] The commentary for Shi (7) reads: "In the midst of earth [Kun, above] there is water [Kan, below]. The image is of the army. Thus the superior man increases the masses under him by generosity toward the people." The orthodox explanation of this symbolism is that the military power of a people is invisibly present in the masses, just as ground water is invisibly present in the earth; but that in order to tap this potential and achieve victory in war, the government must shelter its people, in the way that ground water is sheltered by the earth.[49]

When two opposite trigrams harmonize, as in the case of Qian moving upward from below and Kun moving downward from above in Tai (11), they can have favorable connotations ("peace"); but in the reverse relationship, when Qian is above and Kun is below in Pi (12), the connotation may be negative ("stagnation"). Other seemingly similar oppositional configurations do not always yield the same interpretations, however. In the case of Weiji (64), for example, Li (fire) over Kan (water) denotes "separation," while the reverse trigram configuration in Jiji (63) can indicate either an equilibrium or a collapse, as when either water extinguishes fire or fire evaporates water.[50]

Opposite lines that occupy analogous positions in the inner and outer primary trigrams of any given hexagram (i.e. 1-4, 2-5, 3-6) may sometimes enjoy a particularly close relationship or "correspondence." Thus, for example, a yang line in the first place corresponds (zhengying, lit. "correctly resonates") with a yin line in the fourth place; a yin line in the second place corresponds with a yang line in the fifth place, and a yin line in the third place corresponds with a yang line in the sixth place. Of these three types of relationship, the most important occurs when two middle lines occupy the second and fifth places. As indicated above, they symbolize the "correct" relationship of official to ruler, son to father, wife to husband. Occasionally there may be a corre-. spondence between the first and fourth line, but rarely between the third and the sixth. And, of course, when a particular line rules a hexagram, relationships of correspondence exist that are determined more by the nature of the hexagram as a whole than by virtue of analogous line positions in the inner and outer trigrams.[51]

Another common way of viewing the relationship between the lines in a hexagram is to see them as representing spatially the "three powers" of Heaven, Earth and Man. That is, the first two lines symbolize Earth; the next two, Man; and the top two, Heaven. This tripartite structure, emphasized in the "Great Commentary," has its counterpart in the individual lines of each individual trigram. According to the "Discussion of Trigrams," the principles of Heaven are *yin* and *yang*; those of Earth are yielding and firmness; and those of Man, humaneness and right behavior.[52] Heaven provides the predestined time, Earth the place, and Man the action of any given situation or event.[53]

Relationships may also exist between the individual lines of different hexagrams in which the same or similar line readings occur—such as the phrase "don't act" (*wuyong*; lit. "don't use [the divinatory information under consideration]), which is shared by Qian (1), Shi (7), Yi (27), Kan (29), and Jiji (63). Some scholars, such as the philologist Wang Yinzhi (1766–1834), explored these line relationships primarily for insights into language, while others, such as the textual critic Feng Dengfu (1783–1841) treated them rather more like sophisticated riddles.[54] A typical question might be: Why in the hexagram Tongren (13) does the subject of the fifth line first cry out and then laugh, while in the sixth line of Lü (56) the subject first laughs and then cries out? A similar "riddle" might be: Why is the expression "dense clouds do not rain" (*miyun buyu*) shared in the judgment of Xiaochu (9) and one of the line readings of Xiaoguo (62)? When Jiao Xun was only fourteen years old his father posed this latter question to him and Jiao could not answer it. In apparent reaction, he spent the remainder of his scholarly life devising a sophisticated mathematical theory of analogues (*bili*) to explain hexagram relationships.[55]

Yet another factor to be taken into account in interpreting hexagrams is the time (*shi*). This term varies in meaning according to the characteristics of the hexagram in question. Thus, for example, with hexagrams that deal with movement, such as Bo (23), "splitting apart," or Fu (24), "return," the "time" means increase or decrease, fullness or emptiness. "Time" can also refer to a process, such as "conflict" (Song, 6); a characteristic, such as "modesty" (Qian, 15); or a symbolic situation, such as "the well" (Jing, 48). In each case, the "time" affects the meaning of each individual line, so that the meaning can be either favorable or unfavorable, depending on the situation as a whole. That is, if a time calls for firmness, firm lines are favorable, and vice-versa. And when the time requires yielding, a firm line in the third place, although normally correct in itself, is harmful because it is too firm for the situation.

Throughout the imperial era devotees of the *Changes* sought ways of integrating the sixty-four hexagrams into coherent systems of meaning based

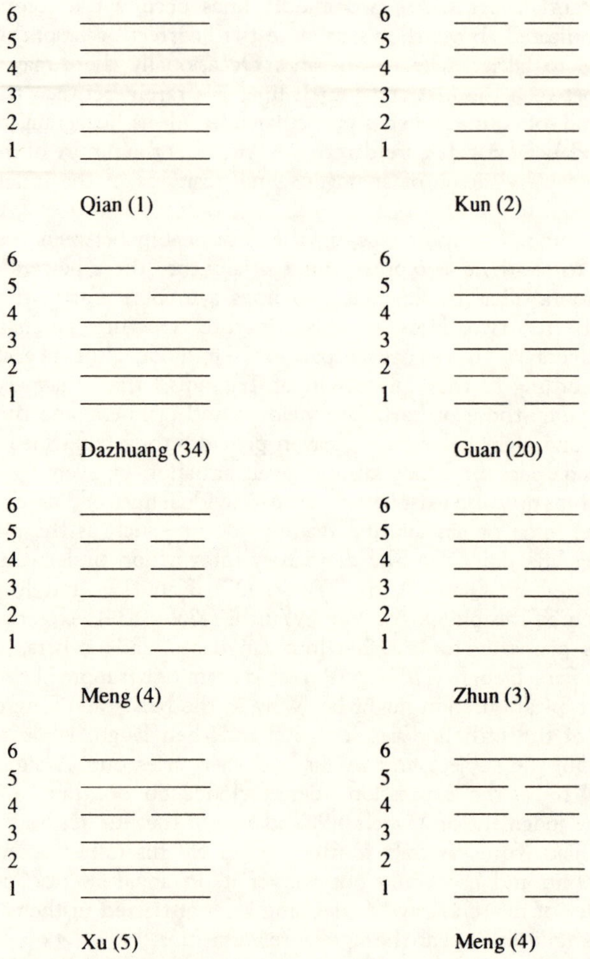

6 ——————   6 —— ——
5 ——————   5 —— ——
4 ——————   4 —— ——
3 ——————   3 —— ——
2 ——————   2 —— ——
1 ——————   1 —— ——

Qian (1)   Kun (2)

6 —— ——   6 ——————
5 —— ——   5 —— ——
4 ——————   4 —— ——
3 ——————   3 —— ——
2 ——————   2 ——————
1 ——————   1 —— ——

Dazhuang (34)   Guan (20)

6 ——————   6 —— ——
5 —— ——   5 ——————
4 —— ——   4 —— ——
3 —— ——   3 —— ——
2 ——————   2 ——————
1 —— ——   1 —— ——

Meng (4)   Zhun (3)

6 —— ——   6 ——————
5 ——————   5 —— ——
4 —— ——   4 —— ——
3 ——————   3 —— ——
2 ——————   2 ——————
1 ——————   1 —— ——

Xu (5)   Meng (4)

Figure 3.4 Hexagrams.

on structural principles.[56] One long-standing assumption was that a close affinity existed between two hexagrams of opposite form. There were two main types of contrast. One was line-for-line opposition (*pangtong*) throughout the entire hexagram, as with Qian (1) and Kun (2), or Dazhuang (34) and Guan (20). The other was based on "inversion" (*fandui*), as if one hexagram had been turned upside down to create another—for example Meng (4) to Zhun (3), or Xu (5) to Meng (4) (see Fig. 3.4). The prevailing order of the hexagrams for most of the imperial era reflected this principle of inversion. With the exception of the eight hexagrams that were paired with their polar opposites (since they were identical when inverted), all of the hexagrams in the *Yijing* were paired with their inverted form. The obvious assumption was that contemplation of

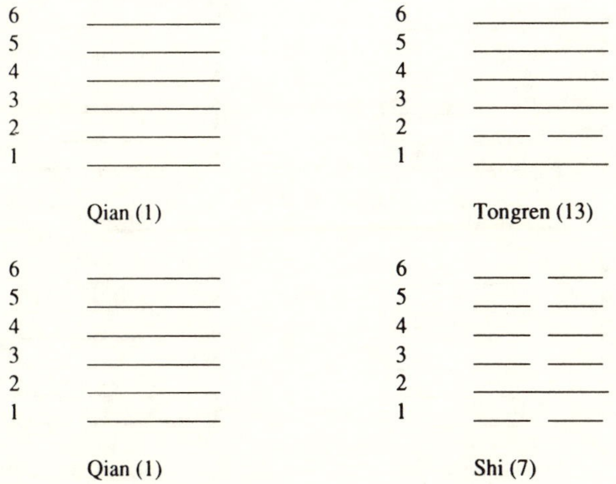

Figure 3.5 Hexagrams.

such contrasts, together with an appreciation of corresponding changes in trigram relationships, would bring a more complete understanding of the latent (*fu*) as well as the manifest (*fei*) possibilities in any particular situation.[57]

In addition to structural opposition based on entire hexagrams, we find hexagram relationships based on individual line transformations. For if whole hexagrams have latent potential, so, presumably, do their constituent lines. Thus, in considering line two of Qian (1) one considers its transformation into a *yin* line, producing the hexagram Tongren (13), in order to see how the new hexagram and the new lower trigram might affect the meaning of the original line. Similarly, the extension of line two of Qian sideways to its opposite, Kun (2), yields yet another hexagram, Shi (7), which may also have a possible connection with the original line (see Fig. 3.5).[58] And, of course, in the process of divination (see next section), certain lines are often "in movement" as a result of their assigned numerical value, which means that a new, integrally-related hexagram is formed out of the transformed line(s). This hexagram then becomes a "changed" or "derivative" hexagram (*biangua* or *zhigua*). Speculation about the way lines moved and related never ceased to fascinate devotees of the *Changes*.[59]

The relentless impulse of Chinese thinkers from the Han period onwards to integrate the hexagrams of the *Yijing* into ever more coherent patterns of meaning produced a number of schemes designed to show a "natural" evolutionary relationship between these dynamic symbols as well as a structural affinity. In late imperial times this impulse took several forms. Shao Yong, as is well known, developed in his "Former Heaven" sequence a mathematically logical but highly mechanical binary system of hexagram organization.[60] Less ambitiously, and with a different purpose in mind, Zhu Xi drew on Yu Fan in an effort to show how certain "hexagram changes" (*guabian*) explained the relationship between nineteen particular hexagrams in such a way as to make them compatible

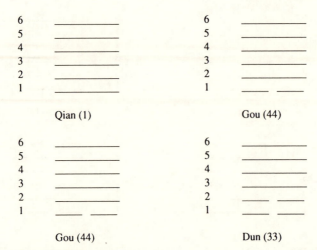

Figure 3.6 Hexagrams.

with certain obscure phrases pertaining to them in the "Commentary on the Judgment." Zhu also employed the so-called "eight palace" (*bagong*) system of Jing Fang to illustrate how the eight trigrams changed systematically into the sixty-four hexagrams.[61] Lai Zhide, for his part, devised a comprehensive theory of hexagram relationships (*guazong*) in which systematic line movement from bottom to top created new hexagrams—as when the first line of Qian (1) changes from *yang* to *yin* to produce Gou (44), and the second line of Gou changes to produce Dun (33) (see Fig. 3.6).[62]

These and other such systems underwent heavy fire from a number of Qing scholars—either for being too limited in scope, or for going too far.[63] Yet as had been the case with cosmological criticism generally in late imperial China (see chapter 2), Qing critiques of *Yijing* schemes such as those of Shao, Zhu, Lai and others stopped far short of fundamental reformulation. Iconoclastic individuals such as Hu Wei, Mao Qiling and Hui Dong found it easy enough to point out the limitations and mistakes of previous scholars, but they could not so easily shed other inherited assumptions about the *Yijing*. Mao, in particular, remained firmly in the grip of traditional ideas about hexagram and trigram relationships. Not only did he accept the fundamental principles of *pangtong* and *fandui* (which he described as changes of "correspondence" [*duiyi*] and of "reversal" [*fanyi*], respectively), but he also attempted to construct his own systematic theory of hexagram relationships, based on Han precedents, which he termed "changes of extrapolation" (*tuiyi*). Unfortunately, his effort revealed the same kind of arbitrariness, inconsistency and over-ambitiousness he had criticized in others.[64]

Like many Qing scholars, Mao devoted much attention to early historical examples of *Yijing* divination. One of his several books on the *Changes*, entitled *Chunqiu zhanshi shu* (Book on Milfoil Divination in the Spring and Autumn Annals), used well-known stories from the *Annals* to show the refinements of

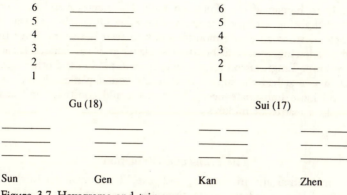

6	⚊⚊⚊	6	⚋ ⚋
5	⚋ ⚋	5	⚊⚊⚊
4	⚋ ⚋	4	⚊⚊⚊
3	⚊⚊⚊	3	⚋ ⚋
2	⚊⚊⚊	2	⚋ ⚋
1	⚋ ⚋	1	⚊⚊⚊
	Gu (18)		Sui (17)

Sun   Gen   Kan   Zhen

Figure 3.7 Hexagrams and trigrams.

Yijing symbolism.[65] One of the most famous incidents is Duke Mu of Qin's punitive expedition against Duke Hui of Jin in 645 B.C. Before the attack, Duke Mu asked his diviner, Tu Fu, to consult the *Changes* regarding the outcome. Tu drew the hexagram Gu (18) with no line changes. The judgment of this hexagram reads: "Work on what has been spoiled brings supreme success. It benefits one to cross the great water." Tu thus predicted victory, remarking that Duke Mu's troops would cross the river separating Qin from Jin, defeat the forces of Duke Hui, and arrest the duke. He explained that since the inner (lower) trigram of Gu was Sun (wind), and the outer (upper), Gen (mountain), the winds of Qin would blow down the fruits of Jin on the mountain and their timber would be seized.[66]

Mao Qiling's elaboration of this analysis is revealing. In the first place, he explains that the idea of "crossing the great water" in the judgment is derived from the lower four lines of Ku, which resemble the Kan trigram (the symbol of water) inasmuch as they consist of a pair of *yang* lines contained between two *yin* lines. Here, Mao interprets the four lines visually as if they were three. Secondly, he points out that the upper nuclear trigram (*hugua*) of Gu—that is, lines 3, 4 and 5—is Zhen, which is not only the symbol of a feudal lord, but also that of an upturned bowl (*yangyu*), which resembles the body of a chariot. Since the upper trigram (Gen) is Zhen turned upside down, this indicates the overthrow of Duke Hui. And because Gen symbolizes both the hands and the idea of stoppage (*zhi*), the meaning conveyed is the arrest of Duke Hui. This notion is reinforced by consideration of the hexagram Sui (17), the opposite of Gu, in which the line readings refer repeatedly to clinging (*xi*; lit. "binding") to someone, presumably Duke Hui[67] (see Fig. 3.7).

Much more analysis could be brought to bear on this or any other case. The important point is that for the purpose of divination (as well as for study and contemplation), all of the interpretive techniques mentioned above, and many others as well, were available for use by any literate Chinese, male or female.[68] Ideally, the more a person explored the hexagrams the more he or she discovered about the mysterious workings of the universe and their relationship to human affairs. Thus, an individual might spend days or even weeks contemplating a single hexagram. The early Qing scholar Qian Lucan, for example, devoted an entire month's study to each hexagram. Over time he acquired a following of several hundred students and was famous throughout the entire lower Yangzi region as an *Yijing* specialist.[69] On the other hand, not everyone in China had the luxury of leisurely contemplation. For those with simpler and more immediate needs, a diviner could construct and analyze a hexagram in a matter of minutes.

The *Yijing* and Divination

The fundamental aim in divining with the *Yi*, as explained in the "Great Commentary," was to understand the situation represented by a given hexagram, to identify the incipient moment (*ji*) of change within it, and to respond to the situation and its changing circumstances in an appropriate way. By internalizing the spiritual capacity of the milfoil as well as the mind of the sage, a person could not only know the future (that is, the pattern or principle [*li*] of unfolding events, which was already present in incipient form), but also develop the capacity to adopt a sage-like response. Timing was crucial, as were moral choices—at least in the eyes of the Confucian elite.[70] Most prominent Qing intellectuals followed Gu Yanwu in stressing the ethical dimension of *Yijing* consultation. Jiao Xun, for one, not only agreed with Gu that divination was the means by which the sage kings of old taught the people to "abandon profit and embrace righteousness," but he went so far as to apply mathematical principles to the *Changes* in order to determine comparatively the amount of good fortune or calamity that would ensue from various types of conduct.[71] Less distinguished exponents of the *Yijing* also stressed the theme of morality— some by their writings and divinatory pronouncements; others by their use of the document to mediate disputes or to urge other people to act properly.[72]

Since all Qing thinkers accepted the idea of the "Great Commentary" that the patterns and processes of cosmic change were knowable through the *Yijing*, the only question was exactly how much could (or should) be known. The "Great Norm" chapter of the *Shujing* indicates that milfoil divination should be reserved for resolving "doubts on great matters;"[73] yet by Qing times, and in fact well before, the *Changes* provided guidance in every realm of Chinese life, from life and death situations to the most mundane problems. The poet Yuan Mei (1716–1798), for instance, consulted the *Yi* to find out what to do about a toothache.[74] Individuals often divined on the first day of the first month of the lunar calendar, to see what the new year held in store. The scholar Jiang Kanghu (1883–1946), for example, writes of a friend of his father's who on New Year's day (January 30, 1911) correctly predicted that "there would be a great change in the middle of the autumn in the middle of China Proper"— the Wuchang Uprising of October 10 of that year which led to the overthrow of the Qing dynasty.[75]

The biographies of diviners in local gazetteers of the Qing period testify to the employment of an enormously wide variety of *Yijing*-related mantic techniques, from the conventional use of milfoil stalks and various substitutes (including bamboo sticks and coin-tossing) to all kinds of astrological and numerological systems—many of which, such as *liuren, taiyi* and *qimen dunjia* (see chapter 5), are related only tangentially to the *Changes*.[76] Of the more than three hundred Qing dynasty divination specialists I have studied whose biographies indicate a particular interest in the *Yijing*, the majority seem to have employed standard methods of consultation. On the other hand, many were either exponents of the *Hetu* and *Luoshu* or devotees of the "unorthodox" Yi-related mantic arts of Jiao Yanshou, Jing Fang, Guo Pu, and Shao Yong. And even among those who used relatively standard techniques, some emphasized the individual lines of hexagrams, while others focused primarily on trigrams. Some considered only a single hexagram in their divinations, while others devoted attention to hexagram relationships. At least one idiosyncratic diviner, by the name of Cheng Shirong, claimed to be able to evaluate three-year segments of time based on paired hexagram lines—two lines for each year.[77]

We can assume, I think, that the more weighty the issue, the more sophisticated the divination—not only in terms of considering the interpretive possibilities of any given hexagram, but also in matters of ritual. Orthodox divination with the *Changes* required an elaborate ceremony, as we can see from one of the appendices to Zhu Xi's *Zhouyi benyi* entitled "Milfoil Etiquette." In it, Zhu provides a complete account of the formal divination process and a description of the paraphernalia involved, which included a table (to be located ideally in a secluded room), a divining board, an incense burner and incense, a container of fifty milfoil stalks, and writing materials.[78]

According to Zhu's account, after engaging in preliminary ceremonies of ablution and purification, the diviner enters the room from the east, approaches the divining board (situated on a table extending west to east), and burns incense to "show reverence" (*zhijing*). Taking the bundle of milfoil stalks from a container located to the north of the divining board, the person consulting the *Changes* then holds the stalks with both hands and passes them through the smoke rising from the incense burner, located to the south of the container, below the board. The diviner then addresses the stalks: "Availing of you, great milfoil with constancy [i.e., reliability], I, official so-and-so, because of thus-and-such affair, wonder if I may express my doubts and concerns to the spiritual powers [*yushen yuling*]. Whether the news is auspicious or inauspicious, involves a gain or a loss, remorse or humiliation, sorrow or anxiety, you alone with your divine intelligence can provide clear information [about the situation]."

Following this petitionary statement, the diviner takes one milfoil stalk from the bundle and returns it to the container, symbolizing the unity of the "Supreme Ultimate" as indicated in the "Great Commentary."[79] Next the bundle of forty-nine stalks is divided into two, symbolizing the cosmic powers of *yin* and *yang*, and placed on either side of the divining board. The person now picks up the group of milfoils on the left side of the board with the left hand and takes a single stalk from the right side with the right hand, placing it between the small finger and the fourth finger of the left hand. This symbolizes the tripartite aspect of the *Yijing*, the connection between Heaven, Earth and

Man. Then the diviner counts off the milfoil stalks by fours—symbolizing the four seasons—until there are four or fewer stalks remaining. These remaining stalks are placed between the fourth finger and the middle finger of the left hand.

After returning the milfoils counted off by fours to the left side of the divining board, the diviner does the same thing with the bundle of milfoils on the right side. If the remainder from the left side is one stalk, then the remainder from the right must be three, and so forth. The total number of milfoils from the two remainders, together with the single milfoil initially taken up, equals either five or nine. The "five," having one four, is regarded as odd; the "nine," having two fours, is regarded as even. Following the return of the milfoils to the right-hand side, the diviner takes the stalks from between the fingers of the left hand and places them to the west (left) of the left-hand bundle.

Two more manipulations follow with a diminished number of stalks (either forty-four or forty). This set of three manipulations yields a *yin* or a *yang* line, based on the numerical value assigned to each composite remainder. For example, if, after three manipulations, the combination of milfoil stalks placed in three small groups to the west of the left-hand bundle is thirteen $(5+4+4)$ then the line is designated "old yang" (*laoyang*) with a numerical value of 9 and marked with a small circle to indicate that it is in movement (changing to its opposite). If the total is twenty-five (i.e. $9+8+8$), then the line is designated "old yin" (*laoyin*) with a numerical value of 6 and marked by an "x" (*jiao*) to show that it is moving. Totals of seventeen or twenty-one are "young yin" (*shaoyin*, value of 8) and "young yang" (*shaoyang*, value of 7), respectively, and neither is in motion. After obtaining this initial (bottom) line, the diviner continues the same three-phase process five more times, building an entire hexagram in a total of eighteen steps. After drawing, marking and identifying the hexagram(s) in question, the diviner burns more incense before leaving the room to contemplate the possible meanings.[80]

According to some commentators, if a hexagram drawn in this way has no changing lines, the diviner is obliged to take into account only the judgment, the commentary on the judgment, and the "great symbolism." In this view, changing lines alone merit reference to line readings and to the derivative hexagram. But, as I have tried to stress, the interpretive possibilities of *Yijing* consultation were limited only by the creative imagination of the person involved, and many individuals found inspiration in line readings, whether or not the line was in motion. Even sagely advice, if constraining, had its limits among Yi practitioners. Therefore, although Zhu Xi's *Yixue qimeng* (Beginner's Guide to Students of the Changes) suggests that if four lines of a hexagram are in motion then special attention must be given to the lower one of the two unchanging lines in the derivative hexagram, most diviners would still be inclined to study both of the hexagrams carefully, and to place primary emphasis on the moving lines.[81]

It is difficult to know how scrupulously scholars adhered to the practices suggested by Zhu Xi. Apparently, however, at least some individuals followed the rituals, if not all of the interpretive rules, quite closely. Consider, for example, a letter written by Zeng Jize (1839–1890) to his illustrious father, Zeng Guofan (1811–1872) in 1870. At the time, the elder Zeng found himself embroiled in delicate negotiations related to the so-called "Tientsin Massacre," an anti-foreign outbreak in North China precipitated by the rash actions of a French consul. In his letter, Jize indicated deep filial concern about his father's health under the unfavorable circumstances, and, not knowing how or when the affair would be settled, he divined in the late afternoon of a certain day, drawing the hexagram Shi (7), which changed to Xie (40). The augury, he suggested hopefully to his father, was at least slightly favorable (*weiyou jixiang*).[82]

What makes this letter so revealing is the appended "charge" to the milfoil stalks by Zeng Jize asking for information regarding the outcome of the "Tianjin affair" on behalf of his father. This document, which conforms precisely in language to the model suggested by Zhu Xi in his "Milfoil Etiquette" section of the *Zhouyi benyi*, includes an illustration of the Shi hexagram, together with the "x" mark indicating a changing *yin* line. To the left of the hexagram is the appropriate line reading, written in very small characters: "Six in the fourth place: The army retreats. No blame," as well as the commentary on the image: "'The army retreats. No blame,' for it does not deviate from the usual way."[83] Both the elder Zeng and his son knew that because line four was yielding and not central, retreat was natural; just as they understood that because its place was "correct" in the hexagram (i.e., a *yin* line in an even number), retreat was also appropriate. Significantly, Zeng Jize made no mention of the overall symbolism or significance of the Shi hexagram (the army needs perseverance and a strong leader), nor did he refer to the symbolism or significance of the derivative hexagram Xie, which normally refers to a time when tensions and complications begin to be eased.[84] These things were simply taken for granted.

Of course not all *Yijing* consultations involved recourse to the milfoil. A number of quicker and less elaborate methods of creating hexagrams existed, and although they lacked classical sanction, they had the virtue of ease and simplicity. One technique, sometimes called the "King Wen method" (*Wenwang ke*), involved throwing three copper coins simultaneously, and seeing whether they landed "heads" (*yang*) or "tails" (*yin*). Heads had a value of 3; tails, 2. Thus, three heads yielded a nine; three tails, a six, and so on. With this technique a hexagram could be constructed rapidly without sacrificing the interpretive possibilities of changing lines.[85] Some Qing scholars criticized this sort of "coin divination" (*qianbu*) for its base origins, its random nature, and its inconsistent application by professional soothsayers (see below), but it seems to have enjoyed widespread popularity nonetheless.[86]

Hexagrams could also be constructed in one's head. Shao Yong's popular "Plum Blossom" calculations (*meihua yishu*), for example, required neither stalks nor coins—only mental manipulations of one sort or another. One common method consisted of creating an upper primary trigram by assigning numerical value to a given situation or problem according to the numbers of the "Former Heaven" sequence (see chapter 2), and then choosing the lower primary trigram on the basis of numerical values associated with the year, month, day and hour in question. Related methods included basing both of the constituent trigrams on different aspects of a situation or problem, and composing both trigrams on the basis of time variables alone. In these and most other popular forms of divination, trigram correlations and "five agents" correlations played significant roles.[87]

Unfortunately, detailed accounts of divination with the *Changes* are difficult to come by. In gazetteer biographies and other Qing dynasty materials I have examined, references to the use of the *Yijing* are bountiful but relatively brief—in part, no doubt, because so much could simply be assumed by the writer. Diary entries and correspondence usually provide little more than a mention of the hexagram(s) drawn, and perhaps a general indication of the problem at hand. Few individuals indicate the method used to construct a hexagram, and fewer still provide concrete illustrations of the sort appended to Zeng Jize's letter to his father.

The best one can normally hope for is a diary like that of Yan Fu (1853–1921) for 1911. During this tumultuous year Yan kept two separate journals—one for describing events and the other for recording divinations. The latter work contains numerous references to Yi consultations undertaken on behalf of friends and relatives. It regularly includes information concerning not only the subject inquired about (generally wealth, official position, scholarship, business, travel, and family matters), but also the hexagram drawn, its changes, and its *yinyang/wuxing* correlations. Yan often mentions the advice he gave, and occasionally he discusses the actual outcome. Unfortunately, however, the specific techniques he employs are difficult to trace. And most Qing memoirs are far less revealing than Yan's. The lengthy diary of Weng Tonghe (1830–1904), for instance, refers to several divinations, but only in the most superficial way. A characteristic entry for March 3, 1862, notes only that he divined twice at night and got Xiao Chu (9), which changed to Sun (57), and then Dayou (14), which changed to Ding (50). Many Qing scholars, perhaps a majority, divined without mentioning it at all. Li Hongzhang, for example, is reported on reliable authority to have been very much attracted to *Yijing* divination; but one could hardly guess it from his extant writings.[88]

Despite limitations with source materials, there are enough details of Yi divination and consultation to illustrate at least some of the ways in which it was used by the various sectors of Chinese society. Let us begin at the top. Although every Qing ruler studied the *Yijing* and consulted it at least on occasion, the Kangxi emperor seems to have been particularly inclined to value its arcane wisdom. The official "Account of [Imperial] Activities" and "Veritable Records" of his reign, together with the writings of his close advisers, such as Li Guangdi, provide many concrete illustrations of his use of the Yi, both for specific advice and for general guidance. During the late 1680s and thereafter, Li's explanations of the *Changes* carried particular weight with Kangxi; but well before this time the emperor had already begun to study the classic and its major commentaries intensively, as part of his regular education. As a youth he received at least a rudimentary introduction to the Yi, and by 1680 he had begun a careful reading of the book together with his court lecturers, spending three days on each hexagram.[89]

The official account of the emperor's activities for December 12, 1680, reveals one of the ways in which the *Changes* figured in Kangxi's daily schedule of work and study. As usual, the emperor began his day with a dawn meeting to discuss matters of state with his Grand Secretaries and other high officials at the south gate of the Qianqing Palace. Later in the morning, the emperor received his court lecturers—Kulena, Ye Fang'ai, and Zhang Yushu in this case—at the Mouqin Hall to study and discuss the primary trigram images of Zhen (thunder) and Li (fire) in the hexagram Shihe (21). They also considered the first line reading which states: "Nine at the beginning means his feet are fastened in the stocks, so that his toes disappear. No blame." After the lecture, Kulena made a special point of emphasizing the different meaning of each line reading based on its position in any given hexagram, as well as the need to understand the meaning of the hexagram as a whole before examining the meaning of its constituent elements. He also presented the emperor with a text discussing the symbolic significance of the hexagrams Qian (1) and Kun (2). After examining this document, the emperor redirected his attention to the Shihe hexagram, which usually refers to criminal cases, observing that the fourth line represented the person meting out punishment, while the top and bottom lines in this case represented those receiving punishment.[90]

Although the "Account of Imperial Activities" does not point specifically to a connection between the *Yijing* lecture and the Kangxi emperor's earlier deliberations with his high officials, the two circumstances appear to be related, since the main issues discussed at the dawn audience both involved judicial matters. One concerned the appropriate penalty for a man named Ma Shan, accused of destroying imperial coins; the other had to do with the fate of Gao Heng, a high official in the Board of Punishments who seemed to be incompetent if not also corrupt. In effect, the formal lecture and informal discussion on the hexagram Shihe became an ex post facto "divination" which confirmed the judicial decisions made by the emperor. Although he ordered Ma executed after the autumn assizes, he merely requested a report on Gao from the former President of the Board of Punishments, Wei Xiangshu (1617–1687), who had recommended him in the first place. Presumably the advice offered in the fourth line of Shihe encouraged careful attention to both matters: "Nine in the fourth place means biting on dried gristly meat and receiving metal arrows. It benefits one to be mindful of difficulties and to be persevering."[91]

On another occasion, in 1683, the Kangxi emperor placed primary emphasis on trigram relationships rather than on individual line readings in seeking guidance from the *Yijing*. At this point, Taiwan had just been recaptured from rebel forces under the descendents of Zheng Chenggong (1624–1662). The emperor and his court lecturers discussed the image of the Lü (10) hexagram, in which the Li trigram, signifying fire, rests on top of the Gen trigram, representing a mountain. The "Commentary on the Image" reads: "Fire on the mountain; the image of the wanderer [*lü*]. Thus the superior man is clear-minded and cautious in imposing penalties, and protracts no lawsuits." To Kangxi, the calm of the mountain signified the need for care, while fire, which spreads rapidly, indicated that legal matters should be settled quickly and decisively.[92]

During 1684, in the course of studying the *Yijing* with his court lecturers, the Kangxi emperor noticed that they had placed in the category of "things there was no need to discuss" the sixth line of the Qian (1) hexagram, which reads: "Arrogant dragon will have cause to repent." The emperor pointed out, however, that the "Commentary on the Words" for the top line of Qian reads: "Arrogance means that one knows how to press forward but not how to draw back, that one knows existence but not annihilation, knows something about winning but nothing about losing." He went on to tell his court lecturers that "everything follows this principle as it is expressed in the *Yijing*, that arrogance will lead to sorrow. We should by rights take this as a warning; it is not something we should shy away from."[93]

The Kangxi emperor's interpretation of the hexagram Feng (55) provides yet another illustration of the way in which the Son of Heaven probed more deeply into the *Yijing* than his formalized lectures required. The basic judgment of Feng appears highly favorable: "Abundance indicates success. The king attains abundance. Be not sad. Be like the sun at midday." Yet in contemplating the hexagram, the Kangxi emperor emphasized that the circumstances defined by Feng in fact ebb and flow. He therefore cited the "Commentary on the Judgment," which states: "When the sun stands at midday, it begins to set; when the moon is full, it begins to wane. The fullness and emptiness of Heaven and Earth wane and wax in the course of time. How much truer is this of men, or ghosts and spirits." He also paid particular attention to the line reading of nine in the third place: "The underbrush is of such abundance that the small stars can be seen at noon." This statement, he remarked, warns of petty people who push themselves forward and prevent more able men from undertaking significant work. Kangxi's response was to give special consideration to personnel matters under the circumstances.[94]

In 1688, during a severe spring drought, and in the midst of factional struggle at court, the Kangxi emperor ordered his diviners to consult the *Yijing*. They drew the hexagram Guai (43), which refers to a "breakthrough," as in nature when a cloudburst occurs, or in human affairs when inferior people begin to disappear. The line readings of greatest concern were nine in the third place and nine in the fifth place. The former reads in part: "The superior man is firmly resolved. He walks alone and is caught in the rain. He is bespattered, and people murmur against him. No blame." The latter reads: "In dealing with weeds, firm resolution is necessary." From these indications, the emperor determined that a purge of the bureaucracy was necessary, and he therefore removed from office all the senior members of Grand Secretary Mingru's clique.[95] Perhaps the *Yijing* gave him the courage, if not the authority, to take this bold step.

The willful Kangxi emperor did not always accept the counsel of his court diviners, however, and even Li Guangdi's advice and explanations at times failed to move him. He is known to have commented, for example, that the senior statesman's interpretations occasionally left him in the dark; and at least once he completely reversed the meaning attached to one of Li's prognostications. When asked to use the *Yijing* to predict the outcome of a battle, Li indicated that on the basis of his investigations there would be a defeat—implying that Qing forces would lose the fight. The Kangxi emperor agreed with him, but stated that the defeat would be for the enemy, not for his own troops. Apparently he was correct.[96]

A more dramatic instance involving reversal of an "official" interpretation of the *Yijing* occurred in 1901, upon the return of the Qing court to Beijing from Xi'an after the humiliating Boxer episode and subsequent imperial retreat. While in Lintong, Shaanxi, the Empress Dowager, Cixi, heard about a famous itinerant diviner, named Zhang Yanyi, whom she ordered to set up an altar and divine regarding the best course of action for the future. Consulting the *Changes*, Zhang drew the Jiaren (37) hexagram, with an emphasis on nine in the third place: "When woman and child dally and laugh, it leads in the end to humiliation." He courageously interpreted this to mean that a woman ruler should not be in power. But a high official named Chen, who witnessed the divination, understandably did not want to be the bearer of bad news to the Empress Dowager. He therefore arranged for another more auspicious line reading (probably six in the fourth place: "She is the treasure of the house; great fortune."), which was duly forwarded to Her Majesty. Much to his surprise and relief, Zhang received a reward of 1,000 taels.[97]

Like the Son of Heaven, many Qing officials also resorted to *Yijing* divination, undertaken either by themselves or by others, both professionals and amateurs.[98] Often, the incentive was military exigency. During the 1760s, for instance, China had become embroiled in a border war with Burma, a "rebellious" tributary state. In mid-1768, the Manchu commander Agui (1717-1797) received orders to serve as governor-general in Yunnan and to assist in the campaign against the Burmese. Later in the year, Zhang Fengming, an Yi specialist who had joined Agui's service, divined for him, drawing the hexagram Li (30). Li, like its constituent trigrams of the same name, symbolizes fire and therefore the south—presumably the southern border area shared with Burma. But since the sixth line of the chosen hexagram, which refers to "marching forth to chastize [the enemy]" was not in movement, Zhang's interpretation was that Agui's campaign would not succeed. It did not, despite a few early Qing victories, and although a truce was soon arranged, it broke down in 1770, and Agui suffered punishment for this turn of events.[99]

Luo Shijing, a *jinshi* degree holder with considerable skill in divination, was recommended to the Manchu commander Fukang'an (d. 1796) during the latter's tenure as governor-general of Shaanxi and Gansu (1784-1788). Facing a difficult military decision in the war against Muslim rebels, Fukang'an had Luo divine with the *Yijing*. Luo drew the hexagram Jin (35), which, because it refers to the "Marquis of Kang"—the same *kang* that appears in Fukang'an's name— and because the hexagram as a whole denotes progress and success, was viewed as a highly favorable omen. It proved to be, and when the revolt was finally suppressed, Fukang'an received the rank of marquis from the throne, despite his well-deserved reputation for corruption.[100]

Sun Yiyan was a Daoguang *jinshi*, who became prefect of Anqing in 1858. At that time the city was threatened by the Taiping rebels, and Sun received timely inspiration and guidance from his study of the Yijing, particularly the hexagram Mingyi (36). This hexagram refers to a situation in which threatening circumstances require caution and inner strength, despite great difficulties and the criticism of others. Eventually the darkness yields to light, and goodness triumphs. As indicated by Sun's divination, the Taipings were repulsed from Anqing and before too long the movement collapsed. This sequence of events confirmed his belief that the Yijing "makes foreknowledge possible."[101]

Of course the Changes could also serve non-military purposes. During the late eighteenth century, for example, Ma Jinzhi, a specialist in the Yi from the town of Sijing, near Shanghai, was asked by his fellow townsmen to divine about the prospects for building a new bridge in a place where local conditions and problems with funding made construction difficult. He divined, and got the Guimei (54) hexagram, with nine in the second place. Although Guimei is usually associated with husband-wife relationships, Ma applied it to the local project. "Nine in the second place means: a one-eyed man who is able to see. The perseverance of a solitary man furthers." Ma drew additional inspiration from the first line: "Nine at the beginning means . . . a lame man who is able to tread. Undertakings bring good fortune." With this encouragement, which seems to have encouraged timely financial aid, local leaders found their way clear to build the bridge.[102]

Accounts of the personal "resolution of doubts" indicate that the Yijing, like other forms of divination, could promote action or counsel patience, inspire dedication or encourage passive resignation. In the late Ming period, for example, Lü Gong (1603–1664) divined regarding his future at a potential turning point in his scholarly career. He drew the hexagram Pi (12) changing to Tai (11). Pi signifies decline—a time in which "the great departs and the small approaches"— a period of retreat and seclusion. Tai, on the other hand, indicates a point at which "the small departs and the great approaches." Lü therefore bided his time, engaging in study, travel, and contemplation. After the Ming dynasty fell and the Qing was established, Lü divined again. This time, he got Qian (1), with an emphasis on nine in the second place: "Flying dragon in the heavens. It furthers to see the great man." Prodded into action by this highly auspicious omen, Lü participated in the grand examination of 1647 and took highest honors. He subsequently embarked on a distinguished career as a Qing official, and became a Grand Secretary in 1654. That same year, however, he fell victim to a factional struggle which forced him into ignominious retirement. Even so, the emperor granted him the title of Senior Guardian of the Heir Apparent as a reward for his services.[103]

The case of Le Zhixian illustrates a radically different theme. At age twenty, the young scholar divined with the Yijing, and drew the hexagram Dun (33), with an emphasis on nine in the sixth place: "Nine at the top means cheerful retreat. Everything serves to further." With this encouragement, Le ceased thinking about conventional advancement in society and withdrew to the contemplative life of a hermit. He continued to study the Yijing, as well as life-preserving Daoist techniques, and when he died at age eighty he had the complexion of a young man.[104] Liu Longguang met a very different end, but he seems to have accepted his fate with equal resignation. In 1672, after travelling great distances in search of his lost family, Liu divined with the *Changes* on New Year's Day to see what was in store for him. He drew the hexagram Daguo (28) changing to Jian (39). Jian indicates obstructions at every turn; and the last line of Daguo states: "One must go through the water. It goes over one's head. Misfortune. No blame." Upon receipt of these inauspicious omens, Liu simply sighed and said, "I cannot avoid this [fate]." Later in the year he drowned as he had predicted. Since the situation described by "six at the top" implies courageous perseverance, even in the face of death, we can assume that Liu died knowing that at least he had done his filial duty.[105]

Many individuals consulted the *Yijing* to find out whether they would be successful in the civil service examinations—an understandable obsession with Qing intellectuals.[106] Career questions were often posed in deadly earnest, but they could also be entertained in a more or less playful spirit, as a kind of diversion. Zou Shijin, a low degree-holder in the early or middle Qing period, excelled at predicting examination results with the Yi. On one occasion, while prognosticating for a group of examination hopefuls concerning the results of a test in the *gengwu* year (either 1690 or 1750), Zou drew the hexagram Lü (10) for a man named Chen, who, he predicted, would succeed at the exams but be last among the candidates. His prediction was based solely on the judgment: "Treading upon the tail of the tiger. It does not bite the man. Success." As Zou had indicated, Chen passed, and his name was found at the "tail" end of the list of successful candidates.[107]

Most Confucian sources tell us rather little of value about divination with the *Changes* by professionals and other commoners. In elite eyes, the *Yijing* was far too hallowed a document to be employed by "petty" individuals who were concerned only with personal blessings and profit.[108] In addition, many intellectuals (although presumably not Yan Fu) felt that only milfoil divination was truly orthodox, and that other techniques, such as coin-tossing, compromised the integrity of the classic—especially if they involved "crude" stem-branch and *wuxing* calculations of the sort used in personal horoscopes and related numerological systems (see chapter 5).[109] For this reason most Qing scholars also scorned the inclusion of various mantic techniques based on the *Changes* in popular almanacs.[110] Yet despite such prejudices, it is clear from a number of accounts by Western observers in the late Qing period that *Yijing*-inspired methods were ubiquitous in China at all levels of society.[111] And although many professional soothsayers undoubtedly composed and interpreted hexagrams with more speed than attention to ceremony, at least a few made a conscious effort to approximate orthodox rituals in their divining practices.

Justus Doolittle, a long-time resident of Fuzhou, in Fujian province, describes at some length coin-tossing practices that are still used today by professionals in Hong Kong and Taiwan. The fortune-tellers, he says,

first light incense and candles, placing them before the picture of an old man whom they worship as the deity who presides over this form of divination [probably Wenchang, the God of Literature]. They then take . . . [three copper cash of Tang dynasty vintage] and put them in a tortoise-shell, which they shake once or twice before the picture, invoking the aid and presence of the god. They then empty the cash out, and, taking them in one hand, they strike the shell gently three times with them, still repeating their formulas. The cash are again put into the shell, and shaken as before three times, when they are turned out upon a plate, carefully observing the manner in which they appear after having fallen out upon the plate. After noting how many have the reverse [uninscribed side] upward, the same cash are put into the shell, and a similar operation is repeated once and again. At the conclusion of the third shaking and the third observation of the relative positions of cash, they procede to compare the diagrams [trigrams] with the five elements, according to the abstruse and intricate rules of this species of divination.[112]

A similar account—written by another well-informed missionary, John Nevius—suggests a ritual even closer to Zhu Xi's orthodox model. He writes:

When a person wishing a response presents himself [to the fortune-teller], a small box, containing three copper cash, is handed to him, which he takes very reverently in both hands, and with which he describes a circle around incense-sticks burning before paintings of the patrons of the art of divination. After having made his prostrations before these paintings, he proceeds in the same reverent manner to the door, and then invokes the aid of heaven, in a form somewhat like the following: "Today, I ____ , residing near the temple ____ , on account of sickness in my family (or some other cause, as the case may be), present myself to obtain a true response respecting this matter. Let me know the event, whether it be favorable, or the contrary." This ceremony being performed, the applicant places the box with cash in the hands of the diviner, who also, after asking a few questions, waves it with even greater solemnity over the table of incense. He then repeats a form of prayer, generally addressed to the patrons of the mystic art. The form prescribed . . . is the following: "Though Heaven has no voice, when addressed, there is a response; the gods are living, and when invoked, are near. A man is now present who is harassed with anxieties, and is unable to solve his doubts and perplexities. We can only look to the gods to instruct us as to what is or is not to take place."[113]

Nevius goes on to describe yet another coin-tossing procedure in which, after the first three lines are drawn to yield the lower trigram, another "prayer" is offered before the upper trigram is produced. He notes: "Three distinct considerations combine to fix . . . [the interpretation of the hexagram in question], and give an endless variety to the meanings of each diagram. These are, the particular objects sought in the divination . . . [and] the meaning, or power, of the two characters designating the current month, and the meaning of the two characters designating the day." For guidance in forming his interpretation, Nevius reports, the fortune-teller consults a book that appears to be Wang Weide's well-known diviner's manual entitled *Bushi zhengzong* (Orthodox Divination), first published in 1709[114] (see Fig. 3.8). According to Nevius, after this consulting process is completed, the fortune-teller writes down the hexagram along with its explanation and hands it to the inquirer, who sometimes has it interpreted a second time in another place. Payment, he says, differs according to "the circumstances of the applicant and the importance of the matter in hand."[115]

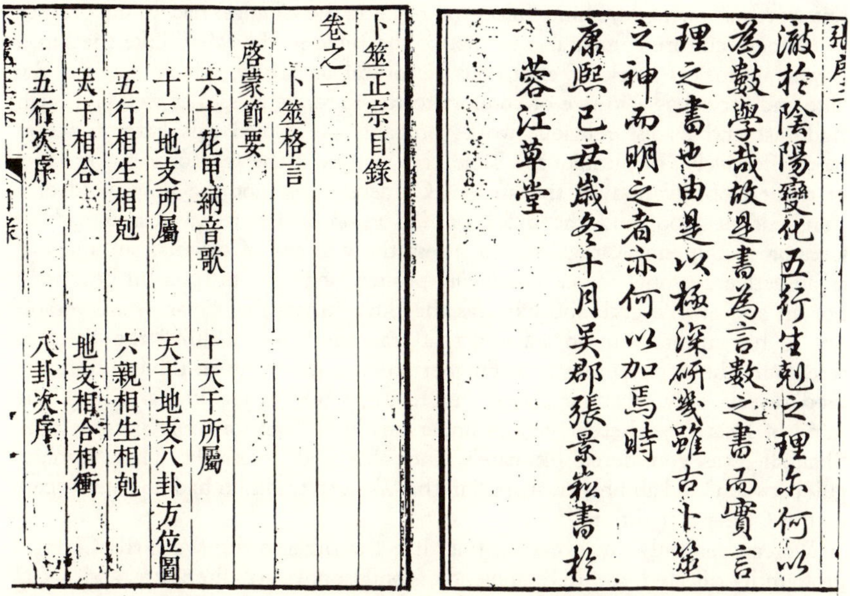

卜筮正宗目錄

卷之一

卜筮格言

啟蒙節要

六十花甲納音歌　　十天干所屬

十二地支所屬　　天干地支八卦方位圖

五行相生相剋　　六親相生相剋

天干相合　　地支相合相冲

五行次序

八卦次序

澂於陰陽變化五行生剋之理矣何以
為數學哉故是書為言數之書而實言
理之書也由是以極深研幾雖古卜筮
之神而明之者亦何以加焉時
康熙己丑歲冬十月吳郡張景崧書於
蓉江草堂

Figure 3.8 The last part of the handwritten preface (right) and first section of the printed table of contents (left) of Wang Weide's *Bushi zhengzong*. The preface indicates that although the book deals with calculations based on the changes of *yin* and *yang* and the cycles of *wuxing*, it is fundamentally a book of principle (*li*), by means of which spiritual intelligence can be fathomed. The table of contents suggests the importance not only of *yinyang*/five agents transformations but also of stem and branch correlations, including the *nayin* system. *Source:* Wang Weide, *Bushi zhengzong* (1709).

Significantly, Nevius asserts that "no small part of the gains of those who engage in this occupation is obtained by making business for priests and physicians, for doing which they receive a consideration from them." J. H. Gray makes a similar point with respect to the Buddhist and Daoist clergy at Canton (Guangzhou), whom, he says, "encourage all feelings of dependence on the unseen world, as it is sure to bring a reverence [and presumably financial support] to their monasteries."[116] We might dismiss such statements as nothing more than the usual ethnocentric railings of Westerners in nineteenth-century China; but Chinese sources make the same basic observation. A preface to the *Bushi zhengzong*, for example, harshly condemns the prevalence of self-interested agreements made between soothsayers, physicians, priests and nuns for mutual economic gain from human misery.[117]

Cultural Significance

Despite its inescapable association with such "unsavory" characters and alliances, the *Yijing* maintained its reputation as the embodiment of all that was worth knowing in China. In several respects the *Changes* had an importance in Chinese culture comparable to that of the Bible in the West. Like the Bible, it was a timeless work of enormous scriptural authority, which inspired the elite and served as a source of comfort to the illiterate masses as well (although Buddhist and Daoist religious works probably performed this latter function more effectively). But unlike the Bible, the *Yijing* was the self-conscious product of natural observation by the ancient Chinese sages, not the holy word of a transcendent God; and the order or *dao* upon which it was based had no Creator or Supreme Ordainer, much less the concept of original sin and evil as an active personal force. The *Yijing* posited neither a purposeful beginning nor an apocalyptic end; and whereas the Bible insists that "man is answerable not to his culture, but to a being that transcends all culture," the Yi takes essentially the opposite position. Furthermore, in the Western Biblical tradition God reveals only what he chooses to reveal, while in traditional China, the mind of Heaven—whether viewed impersonally as Tian, or more personally as Shangdi—was considered ultimately knowable and accessible. The "absolute gulf between God and his creatures" in the Western tradition had no counterpart in the Chinese tradition.[118]

We can certainly say, however, that, like the Bible in the West, the *Changes* profoundly affected the development of philosophy, art, literature and social life in imperial China—although not always with the same dramatic impact. A book that lacks such colorful elements as a jealous and angry God, an evil presence like Satan, a saviour like Jesus, or the sinfulness of Sodom and Gomorrah, operates at a certain disadvantage, after all. From this standpoint, divinely-inspired Buddhist and Daoist scriptures, with their richly textured mythology and explicit supernatural elements, provided textual color and drama that the secular classic lacked. A complete inventory of the *Yijing*'s influences would certainly require another book, but a few general indications of its cultural significance may not be out of place here.[119]

From a philosophical standpoint, the *Changes* exerted more influence in China than any other Confucian classic. In the first place, the Yi established the conceptual underpinnings for much of traditional Chinese cosmology, as well as the point of departure for most philosophical discussions of space and time. Not only did it inspire various early derivative schemes, such as Yang Xiong's highly-refined system of eighty-one tetragrams in the *Taixuan jing* (see chapter 1), but it also served as inspiration for alternative cosmologies—notably the world view of the iconoclastic Qing scholar Yan Yuan (1635–1704). Yan, an ardent enemy of Song Learning, developed a view of cosmic creativity and change that replaced the conventional "five agents" with the "four powers" (*side*), one of which corresponded with each of the four characters comprising the judgment of Qian (1)—usually translated "great and originating" (*yuan*), "penetrating" (*heng*), "advantageous" (*li*) and "correct and firm" (*zhen*).[120]

The *Changes* also provided a virtually indispensible philosophical vocabulary for a wide range of Chinese thinkers. It served as the locus classicus for such fundamental concepts as *yin* and *yang* and *Taiji*, as well as for such crucial ontological distinctions as between "what exists before physical form" (*xing er shang*)—for example "images," principles, and ultimately the *dao*—and "what exists after physical form" (*xing er xia*); that is "implements" (*qi*) or more generally, "things" (*wu*). And because so many provocative concepts in the *Yijing* were not well defined in the text itself, they could be used in many different ways. As a result of both the prestige and the ambiguity of the *Changes*, Confucians, Daoists, and Buddhists alike employed its terminology, and argued incessantly over its cosmological, epistemological, ontological and moral implications.[121]

The *Yijing* became, in fact, an important intellectual and cultural common denominator of the "Three Teachings"—even though its original messages were sometimes modified beyond recognition. For example, the Buddhist scholar Zhixu Ouyi (Wan Yi, 1598–1654) glossed the hexagram Qian (1)—conventionally identified with the assertive idea of a Confucian gentleman who "strengthens himself unceasingly"—as representing "the Buddha-nature and the essence of enlightenment." Similarly, the seventeenth century Daoist Liu Yiming maintained that Qian referred to creative energy that was "tranquil and unstirring, yet sensitive and effective."[122] Of course a number of Confucian scholars claimed that Buddhism and Religious Daoism were themselves derived from the *Yijing*, and at least a few Chinese went so far as to claim affinities between the Bible and the *Changes*.[123] But such efforts by Qing intellectuals to neutralize the effect of "strange doctrines" (*yiduan*) ultimately had the effect of bringing the "Three Teachings" closer together. Zhang Xuecheng, for example, might hold steadfastly to the view that Buddhism came "originally from the teaching of the *Changes*;" but his exposure to, and admiration for, Buddhist texts, impelled him to argue that the abstruse symbolism of the sutras could in fact be understood metaphorically, like the *Yi*, which referred to such things as "dragons with dark and yellow blood."[124]

Whatever its role in harmonizing divergent philosophies in China, the *Yijing* unquestionably contributed in significant ways to the shaping of Chinese discourse. In the earliest strata of the basic text we can already find a sensitivity to rhymes and homophony conducive to puns and double entendres, as well as a tendency to pair words and concepts with opposite or complementary meanings in such a way as to encourage associational or correlative thinking— a long-standing and integral feature of traditional Chinese thought.[125] Although a number of other classical texts exhibit similar tendencies, these linguistic forms are particularly well developed in the Ten Wings—which together display a highly refined if rather diversified system of symbolic logic. In this system, as I have tried to indicate, abstract ideas are embodied in concrete instances of things and their relations. The key notion of complementary opposition, for example, is vividly illustrated in the "Commentary on the Judgment" of the hexagram Kui (38), which states in part: "Heaven and Earth are opposites, but their action is concerted. Man and woman are opposites, but they strive for union. All beings stand in opposition to one another, and what they do takes on order thereby."[126]

The *Yijing's* numerological and metaphorical symbolism, together with its *yinyang*-oriented "logic of correlative duality" (to borrow a phrase from Chang

Tung-sun), contributed substantially to the Chinese preference for allegory, analogy, and the use of numerical and other forms of relational symbolism in making an argument (see also chapter 5). The "Great Commentary" describes the Yi's discursive style as one of using "words that are indirect but hit the mark" (yan qu er zhong). Although the names connected to the hexagrams and lines may appear trivial, the commentary states, "they embrace many categories and are far reaching and refined. Things are openly set forth, but they also contain a deeper secret."[127] Guided by this sort of an intellectual orientation, most Chinese scholars lacked a Western-style concern with separate qualities or "laws" of identity, and saw no need for anything approximating an Aristotelian syllogism as a form of logic. Nor did they deem it necessarily desireable to unpack and systematically elaborate the implicit symbolic connections that might exist within a given text. Put another way, the aphoristic and highly metaphorical nature of the Yijing encouraged an intuitive as well as an intellectual approach to understanding. Although Qing scholars distinguished between learning (xue) and thinking (si), and between erudition (bo) and grasping the essence (yue), traditional Chinese thought did not on the whole involve a conscious exaltation of "reason" over intuition.[128]

In the realm of art, the Yijing's brevity and paucity of parables and anecdotes diminished its importance as a direct source of representational inspiration. It is true, of course, that trigrams served as an extremely common decorative motif on craft productions of all types, including charms, and that certain specific animal symbols from the classic, such as flying dragons, were depicted vividly in Chinese paintings, as well as crafts. One can also find examples of paintings that represent the idea of scholars contemplating the Changes, such as Liu Songnian's Song dynasty work entitled "Reading the Yijing in the Pine Shade."[129] But the Yi did not—and could not, of course—provoke an artistic avalanche of the sort that Biblical stories did in the West. On the other hand, it did encourage an artistic preoccupation with nature, and provided an analytic vocabulary that proved as serviceable in art and literature as it did in philosophy.

As early as the fifth century A.D., Chinese art critics had already begun to assert that "Painting should correspond with the Yijing." This did not, of course, mean that brushwork should simply imitate trigrams and hexagrams; rather, it meant that the form and symbolism of paintings should reflect the patterns and ever-changing processes of nature that the Changes revealed in its own unique way. Thus, for example, the Jieziyuan huazhuan (Mustard Seed Garden Painting Manual) describes the symbolism of plum tree painting almost exclusively in terms of Yijing categories: "The blossoms are of the yang principle, that of Heaven. The wood of its trunk and branches is of the yin principle. Its basic number is five, and its various parts and aspects are based on odd and even numbers [like those of the Yijing]. [The base of the flower] symbolizes Taiji [the Supreme Ultimate] . . . the branches symbolize the six lines [of the hexagrams] . . . and the tips of the branches have eight knots or forks, symbolizing the Eight Trigrams."[130]

Yijing symbolism also informed literary and musical criticism. The hexagram Bi (22), for example, stood for beauty, grace and simplicity of form, while Yu

(16) indicated energy, enthusiasm and emotion. Guai (43) symbolized resolute, critical judgment, and Li (30), logical clarity. Qian (1) generally denoted creativity and spirituality, while Kun (2) suggested passive intelligence.[131] Thus we find the poet Yuan Mei justifying his preoccupation with landscape gardens by reference to "the grace of hills and gardens;" and Zhang Xuecheng, in a much-admired critique of Han dynasty historical scholarship, describing the writing of Sima Qian as "round and spiritual," and that of his successor, Ban Gu, as "square and sagacious." In both cases, the critical vocabulary employed by these scholars is drawn verbatim from the *Changes*.[132]

Significantly, the *Yijing* provided the single most compelling classical model of linguistic parallelism—a style of composition that was invariably prized in traditional Chinese literature. Liu Xie, the enormously influential literary critic of fifth and sixth century China, tells us in his *Wenxin diaolong* (The Literary Mind and the Carving of Dragons) that the "Commentary on the Words" and the "Great Commentary" of the *Changes* "embody the profound thought of the Sage. In narrating the four virtues of the hexagram Qian [1], the sentences are matched in couplets, and in describing the kinds of responses evoked by the dragon and the tiger, the words are all paired and paralleled." He goes on to say, "When describing the hexagrams of Qian and Kun [2] as easy and simple respectively, the passage winds and turns, with lines smoothly woven into one another; and in depicting the going and coming of the sun and the moon, the alternate lines form couplets. Occasionally there may be some variation in the structure of the sentence, or some change in word order, but parallelism is always the aim."[133]

The *Yijing* also affected the narrative tradition in China, although in very different ways than the Bible influenced Western literature. In the first place, the *Changes* deliberately avoids recourse to elaborated myth in presenting patterns of temporal flux, while the Bible, decidedly diachronic, revels in it. And whereas the latter work presents us with the image of a self-conscious alienation from civilization, an ever-present awareness of discontinuity, and the idea of "sacred discontent"—that is, joy over "breaking free from redundant patterns," in the words of Herbert Schneidau—we find in the *Yijing* precisely such recurrent, cyclical patterns. These patterns, in turn, were the foundation of Chinese aesthetics, whether expressed in art, music, landscape gardens or literature. Andrew Plaks has shown, for example, that the *Yijing*'s principles of bipolarity, ceaseless alternation, presence within absence, and infinite overlapping, are not only the key to the structure of China's greatest novel, *Honglou meng* (Dream of the Red Chamber), but also "basic to a major portion of the Chinese literary tradition."[134]

The *Changes* provided not only structural elements but also particular concepts that informed Chinese narrative works, both consciously and unconsciously. Wen Tong, a Manchu Bannerman and divination specialist in Qing times, developed the unusual but at least defensible theory that several of the main characters in the Ming novel *Shuihu zhuan* (Water Margin), as well as a few more minor figures, were directly related to images derived from the *Changes*. Thus, for example, he argued that events in the text foreshadowed

Song Jiang's identification with the hexagram Song (6), Li Kui's association with Sheng (46) and Liu Tang's affinity with Ding (50).[135] In the same spirit, Wang Mingxiong, a contemporary scholar/diviner in Taiwan, adduces evidence from *Honglou meng* to suggest that the author, Cao Xueqin (d. 1763) used images from the *Changes* as well as other divinatory systems, in constructing his narrative of events in "Prospect Garden."[136] Plaks suggests that the name itself (Daguan yuan; lit. Garden of Great View) may have been inspired by the "Commentary on the Judgment" for Guan (20), which refers to "a great view (*daguan*) from above."[137]

Chinese scholars wrote literally thousands of essays on the *Yijing* from the Han period to the Qing, many of which, along with various inscriptions, memorials, eulogies, and works of rhyme-prose (*fu*) focusing on the classic, found a place in the massive Qing encyclopedia *Tushu jicheng* under the heading "Literature" in the section on the Yi.[138] In addition, the editors brought together in the work thirty-four poems on the *Changes*—the earliest by Fu Xian in the third century. Most of the verses included in the encyclopedia are relatively undistinguished and about a third of them list no author at all. There are, however, a few well-known names in the collection, including such renowned *Yijing* specialists as Shao Yong, Ouyang Xiu, Zhu Xi, and Lai Zhide.[139]

The famous Tang poet Meng Jiao is also represented in the collection. His poem, entitled "Sent in Parting to the Hermit Yin, upon his Return to Seclusion after Talking About the *Changes*," reveals the joy of Yi explication by a close friend. It reads:

Your talk about Heaven and Earth
Was as if the spiritual turtle itself were speaking.
Mystery upon mystery unknown to men
One by one became confirmed for me.
The autumn moon illuminated the white night;
And the cold wind harmonized with the clear stream.
On the byway—then suddenly at a distance;
Spirit responds—then stillness, without display of words.
On first awareness all constraints are abandoned;
In the embrace of night I incline toward the troubles of the morning.
The traveler's boat does not stop on the waves,
And the departing horse neighs as the hitching-shaft is removed.
Yin, the diligent scholar of the thicket
Knows he has a close friend who understands.[140]

Most of the other poems included in the *Tushu jicheng* are significant more for their subject matter than for their style or sentiment. Needless to say, we do not find in this collection anything like Milton's epic *Paradise Lost*; nor, despite the theme of prophecy, mystic poetry akin to that of, say, William Blake. Specific references to the *Changes* abound, however. Many poems focus on the idea of *yinyang* interaction, and a number employ trigram and hexagram names and images. Some include lines from the *Yijing*, usually judgments; and one poem, by Shao Yong, reads like a miniature essay on hexagram relationships. Two works refer to Zhou Dunyi's "Diagram of the Supreme Ultimate" and another to the *Hetu* and *Luoshu*. Approximately one-fifth of the Yi-related poems in the *Tushu jicheng* mention the supposed inventor of the trigrams, Fu Xi (alternatively Bao Xi), and about the same number refer to Confucius. Several poems allude to the famous story about the Sage breaking the bindings of his copy of the *Changes* three times, and several more refer to Shao Yong, either by elliptical reference to plum blossoms or to the concept of "Former Heaven." Wang Bi merits specific attention in a poem by Xie Xuan (1389–1464) of the Ming.[141]

In the realm of Chinese social and political life, the *Yijing* exerted enormous influence. Quite apart from its use as a divination text and as a repository of moral knowledge, it provided a cosmologically-grounded justification for the political and social hierarchies of imperial China from Han times through the Qing. For just as the eight trigrams symbolized unequal family relationships, various hexagrams legitimated other relations of subordination in terms of *yinyang* inequality. The hexagram Guimei (54), for example, casts the role of women solely in terms of their subordination to men in marriage, concubinage, or slavery.[142] Jiaren (37) indicates that the woman of a household should submit totally to her husband's authority, attending only to her domestic chores and neither following her whims nor dallying and laughing.[143]

By definition all hexagrams had potential application to human affairs. Among those most relevant to Chinese social and political life, in addition to those mentioned above, were Qian (1), signifying male control; Kun (2), female compliance; Song (6) litigation; Shi (7), military affairs; Bi (8), union and accord; Li (10), circumspect behavior; Qian (15), modesty; Yu (16) comfort or satisfaction; Gu (18), decay; Shihe (21), criminal law; Fu (24), return; Wuwang (25), absence of falsehood; Daguo (28), excess; Heng (32), perseverance; Tun (33), retreat; Jin (35), advance in rank; Mingyi (36), failure to be appreciated; Kui (38), separation or alienation; Kuai (43), breakthrough; Gou (44) social intercourse; Cui (45), people gathered around a good ruler; Sheng (46) the career of a good official; Kun (47), difficulty; Ding (50), nourishment of talents; Jian (53), slow and steady advance; Feng (55), prosperity; Lü (56), travel and strangers; Huan (59), dispersion; Jie (60), restraint; Zhongfu (61), kingly sway; Jiji (63), accomplishment; and Weiji (64), something not yet completed.[144]

The influential neo-Confucian compilation known as the *Jinsi lu* (Reflections on Things at Hand) employs about fifty different hexagrams, including most of the above-mentioned, to illustrate various social and political themes. In the chapter on governing, for example, Zhou Dunyi is cited:

It is difficult to govern a family whereas it is easy to govern the world, for the family is near while the world is distant. If members of the family are separated, the cause surely lies with women. This is why the hexagram Kui [to part; 38] follows the hexagram Jiaren [family; 37], for "When two women live together, their wills move in different directions." This is why [the sage emperor] Yao, having put the empire in order, gave his two daughters in marriage to Shun in order to test him and see whether the throne should be given to him. Thus it is that, in order to see how he governs his empire, we observe the government of his family.[145]

Although invariably considered to be "first among the classics," the *Changes* had no special claim to moral authority over the others. Like the rest of the canon, the source of its ethical values was held to be human rather than divine, and it remained at the service of the imperial Chinese state, never independent of it. As a result, the *Yijing* could not occupy a position analogous to the Bible's with respect to the Church in the Western tradition. Secret societies might draw on its magical symbolism, and many did, but the *Yi* did not provide a radical alternative to prevailing conceptions of political power.[146] Nor, of course, did the *Changes* encourage a Calvinist concept of "the elect," which some have argued had significant, if not vitally important, social and economic implications in the West.[147] It did, however, play a role in the history of Chinese science, a theme that deserves a bit more attention.

One may say, I think, that for some two thousand years, the *Changes* occupied a position in the minds of most Chinese scholars analogous to the view of present-day Christian fundamentalists such as Harold Lindsell, who have argued that the Bible is inerrant by modern standards in all matters that it mentions, including "chemistry, astronomy, philosophy . . . [and] medicine."[148] The official eighteenth-century assessment of the *Yijing* by the editors of the *Siku quanshu* offers a similar assessment: "The way of the *Changes* is broad and great. It encompasses everything, including astronomy, geography, music, military methods, the study of rhymes, numerical calculations, and even alchemy."[149]

The scientific implications of this outlook in China were significant. For if, as the "Great Commentary" claimed, the trigrams and hexagrams of the *Yijing* truly expressed the principles and patterns of all phenomena in Heaven and on Earth through images and numbers, then everything was equally susceptible to interpretation and classification in terms of the classic—not only social and political life, art, literature and music, but also, as the *Siku quanshu* asserts, science, technology, and mathematics. And if the great sages of the past who invented these images did so on the basis of their direct observation of nature, further investigation often seemed unnecessary.[150] It is true that Western-style mathematics appealed to some Qing scholars—but not for the most part as a way of explaining natural phenomena in the Newtonian fashion. Rather, as we see vividly in the case of Jiao Xun, numbers served primarily to help in understanding "the Way of Fu Xi, King Wen, the Duke of Zhou, and Confucius." From a traditional Chinese perspective, the abstract significations of the trigrams and hexagrams were sufficiently abstract, and in addition they had the virtue of classical sanction. In the words of Ho Peng-Yoke: "If . . . [the Chinese] were fully satisfied with an explanation they could find from the system of the Book of Changes they would not go further to look for mathematical formulations and experimental verifications in their scientific studies."[151]

There was very little that the *Yijing* did not seem to explain, as a glance at any volume of Joseph Needham's monumental *Science and Civilisation in China* reveals. Not surprisingly, most "explanations" consisted primarily of established correlations or relationships. Thus, for example, the early Ming scholar Wang Kui could state confidently: "The upper eyelid of human beings moves, and the lower one keeps still. This is because the symbolism of the hexagram Guan (20) embodies the idea of vision. The trigram Sun (Wind) is moving above, and the trigram Kun (Earth) is immobile below." Similarly, the hexagram Jiji (63) came to be employed to describe human sexual activity. In this usage, the constituent trigrams Li (Fire) and Kan (Water) reflected, respectively, the responses of men (quick to heat; quick to cool) and women (slow to heat; slow to cool).[152] Qing scholars were similarly inclined to draw upon the authority of the Changes in making pronouncements about science, medicine, and mathematics.[153]

But hexagrams did more than simply represent correlative functions. As indicated briefly in chapter 2, they also "controlled" time, phenomena, and situations in a concrete way, rather like "force fields." Some were considered donators, others receptors; some involved movement, others immobility; some encouraged aggregation, others disaggregation; some entailed progression, others retrogression. Trigrams possessed similar attributes, whether paired as opposites in the "Former Heaven" sequence, or arranged developmentally in the "Later Heaven" sequence. The important point is that in exerting cosmic control, trigrams and hexagrams acted much the same way bureaucrats did in the Chinese administrative order, and spirits did in the supernatural world. Joseph Needham has observed in this regard that "The Book of Changes might almost be said to have constituted an organization for 'routing ideas through the right channels to the right departments.' "[154]

China's bureaucratic mentality served well enough in the conduct of government for literally thousands of years, but it did not conduce to the rise of modern science. Rather, the Yijing, with its great scriptural authority, became, in Needham's phrase, a universal filing system—a device for "pigeon-holing novelty and then doing nothing about it." It "tempted those who were interested in Nature to rest in explanations that were no real explanation at all."[155] In addition, the organismic outlook of the Changes militated against the rise of a concept corresponding to the European idea of Laws of Nature, or even the mundane notion of a Heavenly Clockmaker—although Chinese philosophical terms such as dao and li do suggest the idea of natural process and ordering principles. Westerners may not wish to recall that in 1474 their forebears sentenced a rooster to be burned alive for the "heinous and unnatural crime" of laying an egg, or that there was a similar legal prosecution as late as 1730; but such events indicate an attitude toward nature that encouraged Western scientists to search for natural laws—an impulse more or less absent in the history of traditional China.[156]

Of course, the scientific road was by no means smooth in the post-medieval West. Even during the Renaissance, we can find arbitrary correlative and numerological systems that rivalled those of the Chinese in complexity if not in breadth of appeal; and who could deny that the Inquisitions of the fifteenth and sixteenth centuries used Biblical authority to impede scientific progress? But the Renaissance itself grew out of dramatic political, social and economic changes that had no counterpart in China; and the Inquisitions were neither pervasive enough nor sustained enough to stem the tide of Western science.

Galileo, we might say, had the last laugh on his tormentors. Furthermore, the history of the Reformation in the sixteenth and seventeenth centuries abundantly illustrates that Biblical debate in the West had implications that went well beyond mere scholasticism.[157]

The situation was decisively different in imperial China—as Professors Elman, Henderson, Ho, Nakayama, Needham, Porter, Sivin, Zurndorfer, and a host of other Western and Asian authorities have indicated. Although a full discussion of the development of Chinese science would take us well beyond the realm of the Yijing, we should at least keep in mind the close relationship between governmental and intellectual authority that reverence for the classic in traditional times implied. Imperial power—manifest not only in the close supervision of the Buddhist and Daoist religious establishment but also in the monopolization of state sacrifice by the emperor and his officials—prevented any significant conflict between Church and State. Perhaps more important, the Chinese civil service examination system guaranteed the intellectual hegemony of the Yijing and other Confucian classics. This system, as is well known, rewarded scholars who had mastered the classics with extraordinary bureaucratic and social mobility. The state-sponsored exams tested moral knowledge above all, and encouraged an increasingly rigid intellectual and educational orthodoxy. From 1313 to 1905, this orthodoxy was based solidly on the idealistic and highly metaphysical interpretations of the classics by Zhu Xi, whose veneration for the Yijing was matched only by his disdain for natural science. In all, the close fit between Confucian orthodoxy and the omnipowerful Chinese state, allowed little room for what Lancelot Whyte has called "European schizophrenia:" the "great chasm of the West between the sacred and the secular, between Pope and Emperor, between the angels and the atoms."[158]

To be sure, as we have seen, the seventeenth and eighteenth centuries witnessed a burst of critical and creative kaozheng scholarship in China by individuals who applied rigorous scientific methods to the analysis of ancient texts, and who assailed certain elements of the inherited cosmology, including Daoist accretions to the Yijing. But these scholars remained steadfast Confucians, who continued to believe that the Changes and other classics were the repositories of the most profound and ultimately valuable knowledge. Individuals such as Fang Yizhi (d. 1671), who admired certain aspects of Western scientific learning and extended the Confucian concept of "investigating things" (gewu) to include not only human affairs but also physical objects, natural phenomena and technology, were few and far between in Qing China.[159]

The modern Chinese educator Hu Shi once offered the following assessment of the accomplishments of kaozheng scholars in the light of Western experience:

> When Gu Yenwu worked on his philological studies and reconstructed the ancient pronunciations [in the 1640s], Harvey had already published his great work on the circulation of blood, and Galileo his two great works on astronomy and the new sciences. Eleven years before Yan Ruoju began his critical study of the Book of History, Torricelli had completed his great experiment on the pressure of air, and shortly thereafter Boyle announced the results of his experiments in chemistry.

The year before Gu Yenwu completed his epoch-making Five Books on phonological studies [1667], Newton had worked out his calculus and analysis of light.

Professor Hu concluded:

> The striking similarity in the scientific spirit and method of these great leaders of the age of new learning in their respective countries makes the fundamental difference between their fields of work all the more conspicuous. Galileo, Boyle, Harvey, and Newton worked with the objects of nature; with stars, balls, inclining planes, telescopes, microscopes, prisms, chemicals, numbers and astronomical tables. And their Chinese contemporaries worked with books, words, and documentary evidence. The latter created three hundred years of scientific book learning; the former created a new science and a new world.[160]

Although this comparison is somewhat overdrawn, it captures, I think, the essence of two very different intellectual traditions. It is true that a number of scholars—both Western and Chinese—have noticed that certain elements of classical Chinese thought bear a striking resemblance to modern subatomic physics and relativity theory, and that the binary logic of the Yijing itself shows affinities with contemporary coding theory and computer technology.[161] But the fact is that science in premodern China never passed through a Newtonian phase of classical mechanics, with its emphasis on both direct observation and the mathematization of hypothesis. And although the binary structure of the Yijing entranced and inspired Leibniz when he learned of it through a Jesuit missionary to China in the late seventeenth century, the Chinese themselves did not develop the idea of using hexagrams as computational numbers. In short, the number symbolism of the Yijing remained numerological and never truly mathematical.[162]

Even after the traumatic impact of Western imperialism on China during the latter half of the nineteenth century—a development that brought a host of new ideas to the Middle Kingdom—many Chinese claimed, as they had done since the time of the Jesuits during the seventeenth century, that foreign science and mathematics were all based on the principles of the Yijing.[163] A few progressive scholars referred to the concept of change in the Yi to argue for fundamental reform, and the abortive "self-strengthening movement" of the period from 1860 to 1895 in fact derived its name from the "Commentary on the Image" for Qian (1).[164] But when radical change finally came after the Sino-Japanese War—first with the abolition of the civil service examinations in 1905, and then with the revolution of 1911—the Yijing as a classic of now-discredited Confucianism lost a great deal of its authority.

Nonetheless, a great many intellectuals continued to study it, as they do to this day. Moreover, in popular thought, the link between the Changes and other forms of divination remained as powerful as it had always been. This was nowhere more obvious than in the cosmology and symbolic vocabulary of geomancy.[165]

FOUR

The Ways of Wind and Water

Geomancy, or "siting"—the Chinese art of selecting auspicious locations for tombs, houses, and other structures—took many forms and went by a variety of names in the Qing period.[1] The best-known modern term in Chinese is *fengshui* (lit. "wind and water"), but practitioners in late imperial times generally favored descriptive names with a longer and more distinguished pedigree, such as *kanyu* (lit. "cover and support").[2] Regardless of the designation employed, all Chinese siting techniques were based on the principle of harmonizing dwellings for both the living and the dead with the immediate physical environment as well as the larger cosmic scheme. Such attunement, most Chinese believed, brought good fortune to everyone concerned. Thus geomancy came to be viewed not only as divination in the sense of "supernatural knowing," but also as a kind of magic—that is, the manipulation of cosmic forces to influence future events.[3]

Geomancy shared with traditional Chinese medicine a concern with maintaining a harmonious *yinyang* equilibrium in the midst of constant change. A given location, like the human body, represented a microcosm of the universe, which naturally required a balance of cosmic energy or *qi* for proper functioning. Any disruption in a geomantic system brought the functional equivalent of illness in human affairs; that is, misfortune. As specialists in siting, geomancers, often known as *fengshui* masters (*fengshui xiansheng*), were, in effect, "doctors of the earth." They often employed medical metaphors to explain their ideas, and in fact, a great many specialized in traditional Chinese medicine.[4] Before any significant building took place, geomancers determined the proper time and place for the construction, in order to assure maximum benefit to the parties concerned. If necessary, they prescribed "treatment" for an area, such as the erection of a pagoda, or the razing of a poorly-located structure. Quite often their clients sought second opinions. But whereas the influence of medical doctors was confined primarily to individuals, the pronouncements of geomancers could affect entire families, clans, villages, towns and even cities. As a result, *fengshui* specialists often found themselves in the midst of social controversies.

According to Chinese geomantic theory, the *qi* of an area, like that of the human body, might be either "alive" (*sheng*) or "dead" (*si*). These terms, which can also be found in Chinese medical texts, refer to qualitatively different functions, not different stuff: "[*Shengqi* refers to] the quality of energy during the *yang* hours of the rising sun (midnight to noon). It has a quickening and invigorating influence on active enterprises. . . . [*Siqi* refers to] the quality of the energy during the *yin* hours of the sinking sun (noon to midnight), which has a dampening influence on the activity and liveliness."[5] Since the object of *fengshui* calculations was to concentrate as much vital *qi* into one location as possible, this meant taking into account, and taking advantage of, virtually every relevant temporal and spatial variable known to traditional Chinese cosmology. In geomancy, as in most other forms of divination, time and space were inseparable.

Of the many forms of Chinese divination in the Qing period, geomancy came under particularly heavy fire from foreigners in the nineteenth century. They described it as "a ridiculous caricature of science," a "farrago of absurdities," an "abyss of insane vagaries," and "a perverse application of physical and meteorological knowledge."[6] In part, their animus grew out of a belief that *fengshui* was to blame for the difficulties Westerners experienced in promoting Christianity, trade, communications, and "progress" generally in China.[7] And, indeed, we know that certain Qing officials did use the argument that Western-style churches, railways, mines, and telegraphs would disrupt the *fengshui* of localities and create hostility on the part of Chinese residents.[8] But it is misleading to assert, as some scholars have done, that Western accounts of geomancy in Qing dynasty China overemphasized its importance and pervasiveness out of frustration with it.[9] Although the tone of Westerners is usually harsh and unsympathetic, their observations merely corroborate what Chinese sources—including imperial edicts, memorials, law codes, gazetteers, clan rules, and scholarly essays—abundantly document: that *fengshui* maintained a powerful hold on Chinese society at all levels, throughout the Qing period.[10]

Geomantic Theories

Although geomancy had to do with all sorts of structures related to the living and the dead, its primary focus was on the deceased. Specialists in "tomb divination" (*xiangmu* or *zhanmu*) were therefore ubiquitous in Qing times. Classical sanction for a concern with the proper place and time for burials may be found in such hallowed sources such as the *Chunqiu*, *Liji* and *Zhouli*. The *Xiaojing* (Classic of Filial Piety), often cited by proponents of *fengshui*, states: "[The filial son] determines the burial place [of his parents] by divination and puts them to rest" (*bu qi zhaizhao er ancuo zhi*).[11] But, as Qing critics of geomancy repeatedly pointed out, for a thousand years or more gravesites in China were chosen primarily to bring benefits to survivors rather than comfort to the departed. In the straightforward words of the *Huangdi zhaijing* (Yellow Emperor's Siting Classic), "If a site is proper (*an*; lit., peaceful), a family will have generations of good fortune; if not, then the family will decline."[12] Yet despite relentless condemnation by scholars and discouragement by the state (see last section), geomancy flourished throughout the empire, particularly in the southeastern provinces of Jiangsu, Zhejiang, Jiangxi, Fujian, and Guangdong.[13]

By late imperial times there were two main schools of *fengshui*, each tracing its lineage to the renowned third and fourth century scholar-diviner Guo Pu (see chapter 1).[14] In their review of the *Zangshu* (Burial Book), traditionally ascribed to Guo, the editors of the *Siku quanshu* cite the Ming scholar Wang Wei's discussion of the two basic approaches to geomancy. He is quoted as saying,

> One is called the Ancestral Temple method. It began in Fujian province [but] its origins are remote. In the Song dynasty it was popularized by Wang Ji. Its theory is based on heavenly bodies, trigrams, and the principle of non-opposition, by which a *yang* hill faces in *yang* direction and a *yin* hill faces in a *yin* direction. It places sole reliance on the eight trigrams and the five planets in determining the cycles of production and conquest [of the five agents]. The doctrines of this school are still transmitted in Zhejiang, but those who use them are very rare. The other approach is called the Jiangxi method. It commenced with Yang Yunsong and Zeng Wendi of Ganzhou, and was then refined by Lai Dayou and Xie Ziyi. Its theory emphasizes the position [*wei*] and orientation [*xiang*] of land forms [*xing*] and configurations [*shi*], determined by where they arise and where they stop. The sole concern [of the proponents of this school] is with the mutual pairing of dragons and lairs [*xue*], alluvial formations [*sha*] and water, and they stubbornly refuse to discuss anything else. These days, everyone south of the Yangtze follows [this school].[15]

The Qing scholar-practitioner Ding Ruipu made a similar distinction in his *Fengshui quhuo* (Dispelling Confusion about Geomancy). "The art of *fengshui*," he wrote, "is encompassed by the forms and configurations school [*xingshi*] and the directions and positions school [*fangwei*]. Today we refer to the former as the mountain peaks–vital embodiment school [*luanti*; also *luantou*], and the latter as the pattern-energy school [*liqi*]."[16] Another scholar-practitioner, Zhu Chou, in a book entitled *Zaoming qieyao* (An Aid to Creating [Good] Fate), refers disparagingly to a further differentiation among at least some *fengshui* specialists—between those who emphasized the cosmic patterns and principles that determined forms and configurations and those who emphasized their actual manifestations in material force.[17]

Some Qing scholars aggressively defended their geomantic turf. Shen Hao, for example, denounced the Pattern-Energy School for deluding people with its empty talk of heavenly bodies, trigrams, hexagrams and the esoteric *Hetu* and *Luoshu* charts of the *Yijing*. In his view, devotees of the Fujian School were lazy, impatient, and misguided. "Those struck by the poison," he tells us, "are like smoke dissipated and fire extinguished, and never have a chance to reason out the source of their misfortunes. . . . I grieve that the gentry will not interest themselves in [geomantic] lore, but put their trust in rustic masters and so imperil their parents and prepare disaster for their posterity."[18] But from the standpoint of the Pattern-Energy School, only an appreciation of cosmology could bring true understanding of how best to harmonize a site with the rhythms of nature. Using the language of the *Yijing*, cosmologically inclined geomancers stressed that the completion of earthly forms reflected the completion of heavenly images. Or, in a more popular formulation: "The stars of the Heavens above and the configurations of the Earth below mutually correspond [*xiangying*]."[19]

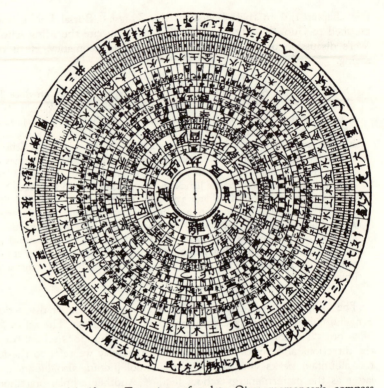

Figure 4.1 *Above:* Top view of a late Qing geomancer's compass (*luopan*). *Source:* J.J.M. De Groot, *The Religious System of China* (Leiden, 1892–1910), 3: 958. Reprinted by permission. *Opposite:* Late Qing representation of a geomantic search. The *luopan* is on a stand near the center of the scene. *Source:* Joseph Needham et al., *Science and Civilisation in China* (Cambridge, England, Cambridge University Press, 1969), 2: 362. Reprinted by permission.

Of course lines drawn sharply in theory tended to blur in practice, even among sub-sects, and exponents of geomancy in the Qing period drew freely upon the vocabulary and techniques of both major schools in a characteristic display of Chinese eclecticism.[20] By the nineteenth century, and no doubt well before, the schools had become "so fused together that no good expert in either . . . neglects to practise the methods of the other."[21] Like modern stockbrokers and economic forecasters in the contemporary West—who, in the face of a myriad of complex variables, make predictions based on commonly held economic theories as well as intuition and "instinct"—geomancers shared certain fundamental theoretical principles but differed in both emphasis and personal approach.

The Fujian School relied heavily on a device conventionally known as a "compass" (*luopan* or *luojing*) for determining the proper site and time for

matters relating to construction and burial, including the positioning of the coffin.[22] This device, which will be described in greater detail below, had a magnetized needle, the red tip of which pointed south, and a series of concentric rings or layers (*ceng*) that contained the major Chinese symbols used to deal with space, time and cosmic change: *yin* and *yang*, the four seasons and cardinal directions, the five "agents," the eight trigrams, the nine moving "stars" (*jiuxing*; also designated "star-spirits"), various "palaces" (*gong*), the ten stems and twelve branches, the twenty-four directions, the twenty-eight lunar lodges, the sixty-four hexagrams, and so forth (see chapter 2).[23] Particularly important to *fengshui* calculations were the numerical and other correlative schemes associated with the *Hetu* and *Luoshu*—linked, as we have seen, with the two major trigram configurations of the *Yijing* as well as the two primary sequences of the *wuxing* (see chapter 3).[24]

As mapping devices for the cosmos, compasses had enormous practical utility. Even exponents of the Jiangxi School used them, since virtually all geomancers sought sites that harmonized with the stars.[25] A Qing dynasty edition (1810) of a Ming work by Wu Wanggang known as the Luojing jie (Explanation of the Geomatic Compass) provides a detailed description of the ideal prototype. It consists of thirty-eight rings. The innermost circle, divided in half by the magnetic needle, is called the Heavenly Pool (tianchi). It represents the Supreme Ultimate, generator of yin and yang. The first ring contains the eight trigrams in the Former Heaven sequence. Then comes the Three Houses (sanjia) of the wuxing. This ring assigns one of the five "elements" to each of the twenty-four directions, which are in turn designated by the twelve branches, four of the eight trigrams, and eight of the ten stems. Next we find the Nine Stars (jiuxing), which are correlated not only with the trigrams and "elements," but also with certain branches and the twelve "stages of life" (see chapter 5) that determined the relative strength of the wuxing.[26] Another ring, called the Stars of Heaven (tianxing), depicts stars, constellations and star symbols, including some trigrams and some stems. The Earth Plate (dipan), representing the twenty-four directions, governs the inner region of the compass according to the Correct Needle (zhengzhen). Beyond it lie the rings associated with Inner and Outer Heaven (see Fig. 4.1).

The first of the Inner Heaven rings correlates the twenty-four directions with the twenty-four fifteen-day periods of the solar year, thus introducing a calendrical component into the calculations. It is followed by the Seventy-two Dragons (qishier long), based on the relationship between various stems and branches, trigrams, and the conventional seventy-two five-day divisions of the year. This ring is used specifically for evaluating mountain formations. The next, called the Nine Mansions, applies the numerology of the Luoshu to the seventy-two time divisions just mentioned, indicating yinyang positions and an appropriate number (from one to nine) for each of twelve sets. Another ring, also based on the seventy-two time divisions, correlates the symbolic animals of the twenty-eight lodges with various branches, allocating two or three lodges to each. From this point on the compass outward, the configurations of cosmic variables and the relationships between the rings become ever more complex. A number of rings apply stems, branches and other variables to numerical sets of sixty and 120. Many also involve elaborate hexagram groupings and line changes based on well-known calendrical schemes of Han and Song provenance.[27] The outermost ring, however, represents a return to simplicity. It divides the twenty-four directions of the compass into twelve pairs, each corresponding to a part of China Proper according to a highly arbitrary fenye plan (see chapter 2).[28]

The key to interpreting a geomantic compass was, of course, in identifying the relationship between the site in question and the overlapping variables contained in the rings. To take a simple example, if water flows from a point marked by a certain trigram (used here as a directional indicator) in a ring depicting the Former Heaven sequence, towards a point marked by the same trigram in another ring depicting the Later Heaven sequence, this situation is called "dispersion" (*xiao*); and if it flows from a point marked by a trigram in the Later Heaven sequence towards a point marked by the same trigram in the Former Heaven sequence, it is called "demise" (*wang*). In either case, since one sequence overcomes another, the site is considered unlucky.[29] By the same sort of correlational logic, if the compass shows a certain spot to be associated with the planet Mars (and hence fire), and if the "agent" wood is to the left of this point while "water" is to the right of it, then the location will be inauspicious because water destroys fire and fire destroys wood. On the other hand, if the compass indicates that earth is to the left of fire and wood is to the right, then the conjunction is favorable because wood produces fire and fire produces earth.[30]

But this might be just the beginning. In the first place, most compass readings involved the linking of several cosmic variables as well as the use of multiple sets of symbols, including stars, animals, and objects (see below).[31] Secondly, a geomancer could take any number of readings, depending on circumstances.[32] The assumption was that every ring of the compass made some contribution to the analysis of any given location, and that all variables were therefore related.[33] But how could they be reconciled? Changing trigram and hexagram relationships appeared in different configurations on different rings, and the trigrams themselves had geomantic connotations that went beyond the already complex conventional symbolism of the *Yijing*. The *Luojing jie*, for instance, ascribes a distinctive "killer nature" to each of the eight trigrams on the Earth Plate—that is, an animal quality that they assume whenever they are involved in "an element clash" with other symbols in bearings on the site.[34] Complicating matters was the use of separate but overlapping divination systems for siting, such as the *dunjia* ("hidden stem") method (see chapters 3 and 5), which applied in particular to the Nine Mansions ring. As if this were not enough, many, if not most, geomancers also found it essential to take into account the "eight characters" of a client's birth (see chapter 5) in their *fengshui* calculations.[35]

Relics from the Qing era and other bits of evidence from the period suggest a remarkable fit between the stipulations laid down in the *Luojing jie*—which does not, curiously, include a single illustration of a compass—and the devices actually used by geomancers. Most seem to have been about five inches in diameter, with between fifteen and twenty-five rings, although some larger versions had as many as forty *ceng* and some smaller ones as few as five.[36] They were generally made of lacquered wood and had a square base (symbolizing Earth, as the counterpart to Heaven) comprised of the same material. Some indicated auspicious and inauspicious directions for each degree of the compass by means of 360 separate marks—black crosses for bad fortune and red circles for good.[37] Although the particular features of these devices, such as the order of the rings, might differ substantially, virtually all of them contained the major cosmic variables outlined above.

It is fair, I think, to assume that the more complex the compass, the more impressive it was. Western observers in nineteenth century China describe the *luopan* as inspiring "reverential awe"—not only among commoners, as might be expected, but also among members of the educated elite. J.J.M. De Groot writes, for instance: "To the uninitiated, who know all the terms and cycles by name, but comprehend next to nothing of the numerous bewildering conjunctions that can be computed therefrom for any spot in particular, the compass becomes, in the hands of the professors, a powerful magical box containing an inexhaustible source of predictions which, promising money and bliss to every one, are sold at high price, forming thus a steady source of income to the professors [i.e. *fengshui xiansheng*]."[38]

It is difficult to know exactly how geomancers of the Fujian school made their calculations, much less how they reconciled the various errors, omissions and inconsistencies contained in *fengshui* manuals such as the *Luojing jie*.[39] Theoretical tracts on *fengshui* tell us very little about actual practice, and accounts of practice seldom reveal much about theory.[40] Furthermore, neither Chinese nor Western sources tend to indicate the extent to which a geomancer, in any particular situation, might draw upon sources of information and/or inspiration not directly connected to the compass, such as landforms and heavenly constellations (see below). Geomancers themselves were probably only partially aware of the myriad of influences playing upon their minds at any time, in any given situation. Moreover, we know that at least some geomantic practitioners, notably the blind soothsayer Li Sanyang, responded intuitively to the earthly and celestial environment, without recourse to either the compass or to visible shapes.[41] All that can be said with confidence is that *fengshui* specialists must have felt free to consider any of the enormous number of cosmological, topographical or other symbolic variables that might be of use to them and their clients.[42]

Timing remained crucial to all facets of *fengshui*, since, as in the case of both medicine and alchemy, the cosmos and all of its various microcosmic manifestations, including the earth, its subdivisions, and human beings themselves, were in interacting states of perpetual flux.[43] No situation remained static. In view of the importance of timing, specialists in "day selection" might be consulted to assist in, or check on, geomantic calculations (see chapter 5). Likewise, popular almanacs figured prominently in the interpretations of virtually all *fengshui* specialists.[44] De Groot writes:

> The chief use of the geomantic compass is to find the line in which, according to the almanac, a grave ought to be made, or a house or temple built. Indeed . . . in this most useful of all books it is every year decided between which two points of the compass the lucky line for that year lies and which point is absolutely inauspicious. This circumstance not only entails a postponement of many burials, seeing it is not always possible to find a grave, answering to all the geomantic requirements, in the lucky line of the year; but it regularly compels the owners of houses and temples to postpone repairs or the rebuilding of the same until a year in which the line wherein their properties are situate[d] is declared to be lucky. Many buildings for this reason alone are allowed to fall in ruin for years, and it is no rare thing to see whole streets simultaneously demolished and rebuilt in years auspicious to the direction in which they are placed.[45]

The Jiangxi method of geomancy, by virtue of its emphasis on physical forms and configurations, was far more comprehensible, or at least more generally familiar, to non-specialists in Qing China. It was also a more prevalent technique empirewide, judging from contemporary accounts.[46] In fact we find geomancers from Fujian travelling to Jiangxi to study their art.[47] In place of the abstruse cosmology and elaborate calculations of the Fujian school, which presumably provided more latitude for creative interpretations on relatively flat land, the school of forms might initially require only a visual, intuitive appreciation of a given site. Some authorities describe the experience of finding the right location in terms reminiscent of Chan-Buddhist enlightenment: "At a true site . . . the hills are fair, the waters fine, the sun handsome, the breeze mild; and the sky has a new light: another world. Amid confusion, peace; amid peace, a festive air. Upon coming into its presence, one's eyes are opened; if one sits or lies, one's heart is joyful. . . . Play with it, and it is as if you can catch it; put it off, and it cannot be got rid of. Try to understand! It is hard to describe."[48]

But while intuitive appreciation came easily, analysis was generally far more difficult. As might be expected, the metaphorical vocabulary of the Jiangxi school was vast, since every landform, waterway, and physical relationship looked like something. The imagery in *fengshui* manuals ranges widely, from animals (dragons, tigers, tortoises, birds, fish, etc.), to parts of the body (head, tongue, teeth, arms, elbows, etc.), to heavenly and earthly objects of every description (stars, constellations, buildings, boats, carts, nets, carpets, wash basins, spears, arrows, nests, leaves, etc.) to the written script itself.[49] Characteristically, these metaphors tended to acquire a symbolic significance in Chinese geomancy that made them, in effect, instruments of power—much as trigrams, hexagrams, stems and branches came to be viewed as the actual embodiment of cosmic forces. Thus we find geomantic evaluations such as the following: "If on the right and left [of a grave] the rocks assume the shapes of drums and flags, it presages military power. . . . If the hills opposite are in the shape of moth wings, it indicates that beautiful daughters-in-law and good daughters will appear" (see Fig. 4.2).[50]

Aside from such colorful metaphors, the focus of geomantic symbolism in the forms and configurations school focused on the notion of vital "life breath" (*shengqi*) and the processes of change, opposition, and interaction that affected it at a given site. Stephen Feuchtwang, who has analyzed a number of Qing tracts on the subject, writes: "[Geomantic] symbols themselves rarely stand for a static state, nearly always for a process or a state of being that is in flux and always in some kind of relation to another symbol. There is always some form of dialectic, basically between the Heaven and Earth aspects of a situation, but more specifically, even within a single series of symbols, one symbol implies another and interacts with it."[51] The most common verbs in the formal discourse of *fengshui* thus express action and especially relationship. For instance, the influence of qi on a site comes (*lai* or *chu*) and goes (*ru* or *qu*); qi is collected up (*shou*) or dispersed (*xiao*); yin and yang go with the flow (*shun*) or are at odds (*ni*); forces clash (*chong*) or harmonize (*he*); symbols transfer change to one another (*i*) or are matched or paired with one another (*pei* or *shuang*). Other terms that describe interdependency include *jiao* (interlocked with), *na* (contained in), *shu* (classified as) and *xiang* (in mutual relationship). Aside from

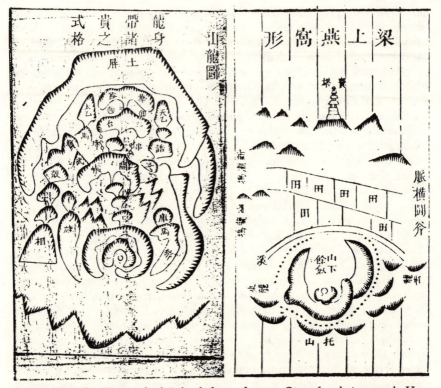

Figure 4.2 *Left:* "Dragon-body" land form, from a Qing *fengshui* manual. Here various topographical configurations are designated primarily by concrete symbolic terms such as sun, moon, pearl, horse, drum, and storehouse. *Source:* Ouyang Chun, *Fengshui yishu* (1814), 2: 11b. *Right:* This page from another *fengshui* manual shows the geomantic shape of a "swallow's nest on a beam." At the lower left is the entrance for the *qi* of the dragon's vein, and on the lower right, the exit. Fields occupy the middle ground (beyond a stream) between the gravesite and a "precious pagoda" on the higher elevation. *Source:* Ouyang Chun, *Fengshui ershu xingqi leize* (1831), 2: 11b.

the words for auspicious (*ji*) and inauspicious (*xiong*) situations, the most common adjectives in the lexicon of geomancy are beautiful (*mei*), elegant (*xiu*), pure and simple (*shun*), confused (*boza*), chaotic (*cuo*) and muddy (*ni* or *zhuo*).[52]

In essence, the study of forms centered on finding concentrations of vital *qi* embodied in physical configurations described as "dragons" or "dragon lairs" (*longxue*). In the straightforward words of an early nineteenth century *fengshui* manual: "The humane man and filial son obtain a lair with live *qi* for the burial of their parents."[53] Shen Hao tells us:

The beginning and end of geomancy is nothing more than the layout of mountain ridges, and all the authorities are alike in referring to them as dragons. Why is this? Because none but the magic dragon can lie low or fly, and be big or small; and the earth's forms may rise to mountain heights or fall away to deep springs; they open wide to cover counties and to extend through subprefectures; they contract and are like a thread or a string. Is this not like a dragon? The magic dragon writhes and changes, unknowable in its subtle origins; and mountain ridges that have life breath will start to run east, then suddenly turn west, or begin to run south then suddenly head north. You cannot pin them down—off they go in all directions. Surely nothing but the writings of the magic dragon is an adequate figure of the mountain ridges' permutations. That which does not resemble the permutations of the magic dragon does not realize the subtle geomantic essence. Therefore it is said: if it has permutations, call it a dragon; if it has none, call it barren mountain.[54]

Mountains receive more attention in *fengshui* manuals than any other landform; and so powerful was the dragon imagery in Qing China that the section on "dragon rules" (*longfa*) in such manuals would generally be consulted even in areas where the topography was essentially flat. To the trained eye, any undulation or outcropping had potential significance, but the designation "dragon" carried a special status in the lexicon of *fengshui*.[55] Despite the infinite variety of mountains and hills that actually existed in nature, twelve forms came to be viewed as paradigmatic. Yang Yunsong's Tang dynasty compilation entitled *Shier zhang fa* (The Twelve Staff Patterns) set the standard for later geomantic works.

The twelve staff patterns are: (1) "Going with the flow," in which the site or lair receives the influence of vital *qi* by "riding along" with the incoming "dragon vein" (*longmai*) of the dominating mountain or hill (*benshan*); (2) "going against the flow," in which the site receives influence by meeting the mountain vein head-on; (3) "coiled up" (*shu*), in which the site receives influence from surrounding and proximal but not directly connected mountains; (4) "connected" (*zhui*), in which the site is located amidst veins that are connected like threads in a piece of cloth; (5) "opened" (*kai*), in which the dragon vein is divided in such a way as to form two sites; (6) "threaded" (*chuan*), in which the vein enters a site from the side; (7) "discarded" (*li*), in which the site is influenced by the "cast-off" vein of the dominating mountain; (8) "sunken" (*mo*), in which a hollow (*wo*) is formed in the site; (9) "paired" (*dui*), in which the influences of the four directions are harmoniously matched in a site; (10) "severed" (*jie*), in which lack of protection by surrounding land formations makes part of the site vulnerable to being "snipped off;" (11) "invaded" (*fan*), in which a site is located too low in relation to surrounding mountains; and (12) "put in order" (*dun*), in which the site is built up artificially to receive vital *qi*.[56] In actuality, of course, landforms were frequently a composite of the characteristics of two or more of these configurations (see Fig. 4.3).

In most geomantic illustrations, the dragon's lair, located ideally in a place protected on three sides, is represented by a small circle. According to conventional wisdom, a perfect site should be cradled by the "arms" of a horseshoe-shaped formation. In *fengshui* parlance, flanking features are called generically

142

杖　順

杖　逆

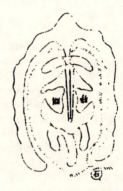

杖　縮

Figure 4.3 Three of the "Twelve Staff Patterns." Reading from top to bottom, they are "going with the flow," "going against the flow," and "coiled up." *Source:* Jiang Tingxi, ed., *Qinding gujin tushu jicheng* (Taibei, 1977 reprint), 47: 6881.

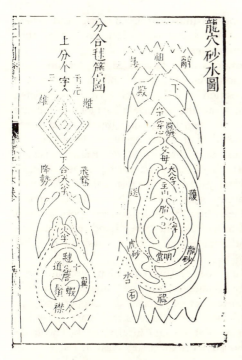

Figure 4.4 The "dragon lair" formation on the right uses the symbolism of water, land, animals (the dragon and tiger), family (parents and ancestors), buildings, and the shape of characters to describe the scene. The "rounded eave-tile" formation on the left uses some of the same imagery (notably configurations in the form of the character "eight") but draws more heavily upon animal symbolism. Source: Wang Qi, Sancai tuhui (1609), page indistinct.

sha, (lit. "lumps of stone" or "pebbles"). As indicated in the *Shier zhang fa*, a well-located site should be neither too high nor too low in relation to the surrounding landscape, but located at a transitional point, "where high and low meet." *Yang* influences, or "heavenly *qi*," symbolized by the seven constellations known as the Azure Dragon, should be on the left (east) side of a south-facing lair, while *yin* influences, or "earthly *qi*," symbolized by the seven constellations known as the White Tiger, should be on the right (west). In all cases the primary object is to keep life breath concentrated and to avoid harmful breath (*shaqi*) produced by unfortunate astrological influences and conflicting conjunctions (see Fig. 4.4).[57]

As a rule, whenever a geomancer encounters ground that shows no ridge-like indications of the dragon's veins, he looks for a secluded corner, where *yin* and *yang* influences (*diqi* and *tianqi*, respectively) are most closely intertwined and the life breath of the area is therefore most highly concentrated. Above all, a site must have protection from "noxious winds" (*fengsha*) emanating from the north—even if it does not actually face due south. A good site should enjoy only mild breezes and gently moving water, whether in rivers, streams, brooks, and gullies, or in oceans, lakes, and ponds. Too much wind or too fast a watercourse at a site causes harm and disperses good influences, while too little wind and sluggish water or marshy ground creates stagnation. Rolling hills that resemble a crouching tiger afford security, especially if the site is located near the head or paws. In flat terrain, single trees or groves may substitute for the protective function of hills and mountains. And where landforms seem to approximate animals, objects or written characters, they must be appropriate to the larger environment.[58]

The geomancer seeks both oppositions and affinities in the terrain itself. On relatively flat ground the site should be prominent, and in hilly areas it must be located in an intermediate position on a slope with a view unrestricted by walls, houses or boulders. Ideally, a site should have a harmonious balance of "male" ground (bold elevations) and "female" ground (uneven and softly undulating), as well as a congenial blend of the five "agents." This blend can be discerned cosmologically by means of a compass or determined visually. According to exponents of the Jiangxi school, softly undulating terrestrial forms suggest water; sharply pointed forms, fire; gently rounded forms, metal; elongated, trunk-like forms, wood; and squared forms, earth.[59] Naturally enough, a conjunction of hills or boulders representing fire and wood can pose a threat if located too close to graves and houses. On the other hand, combinations or fire-shaped and water-shaped landforms might offset one another (see Fig. 4.5).

Some geomancers identified certain types of land formations not only with the five "agents," but also with celestial bodies, such as the "nine stars" (jiuxing) of Daoist lore. These included the seven actual stars of the Dipper and two imaginary stars. Such xing were not, however, the same as the "stars" identified with the "nine palaces" referred to both above and in chapter 2. The latter referred to directions, and corresponded with the Later Heaven sequence of the eight trigrams (with the addition of one star for the center). These stars, represented by numbers and colors in the charts of popular almanacs, indicated auspicious and inauspicious directions for burials at certain times.[60]

The requirements for human residences were as detailed as those for graves. The Yangzhai jing (Classic of Houses for the Living) provides numerous stipulations for proper locations. It tells us, for example, that dwellings should not be at the mouth of a thoroughfare, nor in a temple complex. They must not come too near a shrine, nor be located where plants and trees do not grow to protect them. Neither should they be erected in former battlegrounds, at the gate or opening of a large wall, or opposite a prison gate.[61] Watercourses must not run straight into either a grave or a human dwelling, but should flow down from the left or right and drain off laterally. Similarly, roads should not run directly into homes. In fact, all direct lines were considered pathways for evil spirits and thus designated "secret arrows" (anjian)—to be avoided whenever possible. According to popular belief, a house must not be surrounded by appreciably higher houses, or be located at a point where the corners of other houses converge on it. Above all, nothing ought to oppress, obstruct, or sever a dragon "vein." Other geomantic considerations, reflected not only in fengshui manuals but also in popular almanacs, had to do with structures related to homes, such as pig sties, and even the placement of furniture.[62]

Few locations were ideal, but a truly bad site could usually be improved, either by the use of charms (see next section), or by physical changes in the environment. One such modification might be to break off the sharp point of

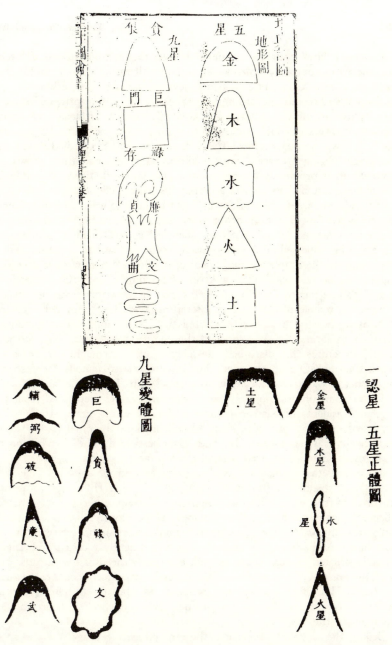

Figure 4.5 *Top:* These two illustrations depict various discrete land forms. To the right are those associated with (top to bottom) metal, wood, water, fire, and earth; to the left, those associated with five of the "nine stars." Compare with the forms illustrated in the drawing below. *Source:* Wang Qi, *Sancai tuhui* (1609), page indistinct. *Bottom:* Another depiction of land forms associated with the "five agents" and "nine stars." Note the differences. *Source:* Jiang Tingxi, ed., *Qinding gujin tushu jicheng* (Taibei, 1977 reprint), 47: 6767.

a dangerous "fire" rock to transform it into the harmless form of "wood." Building an appropriately-scaled water tank or redirecting a brook could achieve the same effect. "Geomantic pagodas" (fengshui ta), whether fashioned out of piled-up stones or built according to orthodox architectural principles, had the capacity to ward off evil influences if situated correctly. Artificial ridges behind a grave or dwelling could also serve this purpose. If no natural watercourse ran by a grave, house or temple, the deficiency might be remedied by installing a tank or digging a channel which collects rainwater and then allows it to drain off in a propitious direction, at a proper speed. Even dry tanks and gullets were assumed to possess a certain geomantic efficacy.[63]

In residential areas, walls or fences might be built to ward off evil influences, and protective images of lions or tigers strategically placed for the same purpose. These were termed "stabilizing" or "quelling" things (zhenwu). Modifications could also be made in buildings, from changes in the basic structure or external furnishings to the simple rearrangement of furniture.[64] Sometimes entire buildings had to be relocated. The gazetteer of Luoding county (Guangdong) tells of a magistrate named Dai Shilun, well-versed in geomancy, who in the 1830s ordered the temple of the God of Literature (Wenchang) moved to the town of Nanping because it adversely affected the literary fortunes of Luoding by virtue of its location with respect to the county examination hall.[65] And, of course, structures that disturbed the fengshui of a site might simply be torn down. One late Qing geomancer, Sun Buyun, was so famous for destroying things that he was known locally as Sun Pafang (Sun "Rake the House Down").[66]

Entire communities, no less than homes and graves, benefitted from good fengshui. Residents of Xiamen (Amoy) in Fujian, for example, attributed the city's prosperity to a pair of protective knolls flanking the inner harbor, known respectively as Dragon-head Hill and Tiger-head Hill. The thriving port of Guangzhou (Canton) enjoyed a similarly favorable location by virtue of two chains of hills that formed a horseshoe shape around the so-called Tiger Gate. Beijing was shielded from the north by the Golden Hills, not to mention nurtured by the gently flowing Jade River. Certain other cities, towns and villages throughout the empire also boasted well-positioned hills, rock formations and even individual boulders (known as a fengshui stones), that offered protection from harm. And where a community lacked sufficiently good natural fengshui, properly situated pagodas could be built to remedy the situation. On the other hand, ill-considered manipulation of the natural environment could cause serious problems. Thus, for example, the residents of Hankou in Hubei province attributed the frequency of fires in the city to unchecked quarrying in a mountain to the west.[67]

Beijing, the capital of China since the early fifteenth century, warrants special attention as an example of traditional fengshui considerations applied to an entire urban complex. Organized on a strict north-south axis, the metropolis in the Qing period consisted of an Inner (Manchu) City to the north and an Outer (Chinese) City to the south—both walled, like all major urban centers in China. Within the Inner City was the Imperial City, which, in turn, surrounded the Forbidden City, the Manchu palace area. Since Beijing was built almost de novo, one might think that the imperial architects would have designed it to conform closely to the classical model laid out in the *Zhouli*, which called for a perfectly square city with twelve symetrically placed gates, nine major north-south streets, nine east-west arteries, and so forth. In fact, however, the requirements of *fengshui* necessitated significant modifications in all parts of the city, placing two separate symbolic systems in perpetual tension.[68]

As indicated above, an ideally located site should contain topographical forms representing each of the five "elements." But according to some *fengshui* theorists, geographical locations could provide the cosmological equivalent of distinctive shapes by virtue of correlations between the trigrams (as directional indicators in the Later Heaven sequence) and the *wuxing* (in the mutual conquest sequence). They also suggest certain natural and man-made features of the environment that are appropriate to each direction. Thus, for instance, Kan, associated with the north, water, and the color black, implies an undulating shape, and is linked with rivers, brooks and lakes. Li, associated with the south, fire, and red, implies a pointed shape, and is linked to gardens, towers, *pailou*, schools, warehouses, and sheds. Dui and Qian, associated with the west and northwest respectively, as well as metal, and white, imply a round shape, and are linked with stone bridges, dams, and mountains. Zhen and Sun, associated with the east and southeast, respectively, wood, and green, imply a long shape, and are linked with rivers, brooks and lakes. Kun and Gen, associated with the southwest and northeast, respectively, and also earth and yellow, imply a square shape, and are linked with streets, walls, hills, and the banks of pools.[69]

In some respects, Beijing occupies an ideal geomantic position. It lies on a plain, with protective mountain ranges to the north, west and east. Its location, however, corresponds with the trigram Kan (Water), for which only the directions associated with Kan and Kun are considered auspicious. Qian, Li, and Zhen are all inauspicious. In Qing times, Beijing had no central northern gate for fear of allowing access to evil influences, and although the walled Forbidden City had a large central gate opening out to the north, it was protected from destructive winds by a huge artificial mound complex known as Prospect Hill (Jingshan), built with dirt from the moat surrounding the palace. The earth of Prospect Hill not only sheltered the Forbidden City but also related favorably to its wooden palaces, since earth produces wood. For added geomantic insurance, the Ming and Qing emperors added balanced convex and concave elements to the northern and southern walls of Beijing, and built a number of pagodas, both in the outlying hills and closer to the Forbidden City.[70]

Most other distinctive features of the city can also be understood in terms of *fengshui* considerations. Each of the gates on the southern wall, for example, occupied the dangerous Li position in relation to the Kan location of Beijing. For this reason, various modifications had to be introduced. Thus we find a wooden tower erected above the already massive Front Gate (Qian men) linking the Inner and Outer Cities, in order to facilitate the mutual production of "agents" rather than a stark opposition; that is, water to wood to fire, rather than the simple contrast of fire to water. Reflecting the same cosmological elements, but a somewhat different geomantic logic, an artificial stream known as the Golden Waters (Jinshui) in the southern part of the Forbidden City had the effect of neutralizing the "fire" of the southern Meridian Gate before it could reach the "water" of the Inner Court. In terms of *yinyang* influences, the *yang* of the northwest gate (Xizhi men) balanced the *yin* of Qian men, just as the *yang* of the east gate (Chaoyang men) stood harmoniously juxtaposed to Qian men.[71]

A more thorough discussion of the *fengshui* of Beijing, or that of any other Chinese city, would require another book, and present interpretive difficulties even greater than those attending the analysis of graves and homes. For in addition to considering the vast number of ordinary cosmological and topographical variables, one would also have to take into account the relationship of a myriad of man-made structures to one another, as well as their relationship to the larger celestial and terrestrial environment. Such an effort would bring to light all sorts of inconsistencies and apparent contradictions.[72] Yet complexity never disabled geomantic analysis; it only invited different explanations. Whether a geomancer was concerned with an entire city or a simple grave, he evaluated the site in much the same way that a traditional Chinese doctor diagnosed a patient, relying on fixed cosmological principles as well as direct observation, and trusting to both logic and instinct. In the words of Ye Tai's *Dili dacheng* (Great Synthesis of Geomancy): "Life breath cannot be conveyed in words, but only recognized by the eye. If you can recognize life breath, then you need not recognize the stars [shapes], nor analyze the stems and branches, nor investigate the site conditions, nor distinguish the eminences and the waters. Yet when you pick a site for someone, it will always be right—how is this? It is because all the multifarious methods were devised for no other purpose than to seek out life breath; when life breath is found, there is no longer the least need to discuss the methods."[73] In geomancy, as with medicine, the bottom line remained efficacy.

Geomancy in Practice

Practitioners of geomancy in Qing times ranged from high officials such as Zhao Zhixin (1662-1744), Li Wentian (1834-1895) and Zhang Zhidong (1837-1909) to commoners whose names are forever lost to history. According to the *Qingbai leichao* even some Qing emperors were considered conversant in the art.[74] The clients of *fengshui* specialists likewise spanned the entire Chinese social spectrum, from emperors to peasants, loyalists to rebels. Some geomancers were professionals; others, amateurs with varying degrees of expertise.[75] Some enjoyed excellent reputations and numerous clients, while others were no more than crass and opportunistic charlatans.[76] A few claimed unique supernatural skills, such as the ability to see deep into the earth; and, despite regulations in some monastaries prohibiting the practice of geomancy and certain other forms of divination, there were also a number of Buddhist and Religious Daoist *fengshui* practitioners, including the eminent Chan abbot Xuyun (1840-1959).[77]

Nineteenth and early twentieth century accounts of geomancers depict them as affecting a scholarly manner, wearing long gowns, travelling in sedan chairs, and carrying books—one or more *fengshui* manuals, an almanac and perhaps a copy of the *Yijing*. According to one knowledgeable Westerner: "About all their movements there is an air of classic decorum; and it is no wonder, therefore, that the masses regard the geomancers as fountains of wisdom, marvels of learning, capable of fathoming all the mysteries of heaven and earth."[78] This scholarly style may well have been only an affectation in some cases, but many of those who practiced geomancy in late imperial China actually came from literati backgrounds. Among the nearly five hundred Qing dynasty *fengshui* specialists I have studied there are dozens of degree-holders, not to mention a number of exam failures.[79]

No doubt because of the scholarly air that geomancers tried to cultivate, and the fact that scholarship was identified as a male domain in traditional China, biographies of women *fengshui* specialists in local gazetteers and other such sources are virtually impossible to find. We know, however, that in their daily lives Chinese women often took an active interest in geomancy, and that at least some of them "read books on the subject."[80] We should also remember that alternative sources of divinatory authority—from popular written texts such as almanacs, to professional fortune-tellers, spirit-writers and other mediums (see chapters 2 and 5)—could always be used for geomantic information. Geomancers naturally disdained these "outside" competitors, but in fact their own mantic skills were seldom confined exclusively to *fengshui*.

As diviners, geomancers operated at a point where the mental (and physical) worlds of the scholarly elite and commoners overlapped and interacted.[81] They were, in fact, self-conscious agents in this complex interactive process. Many served both social groups, but few felt entirely comfortable with either. As technical specialists, their geomantic talents were at once prized and looked down upon by the Confucian literati; while their scholarly pretensions stood in the way of closer relations with their less exalted clients. Generally speaking, geomancers seem to have enjoyed the highest social status in south China, where *fengshui* practices were most pervasive and deeply entrenched; but even in the north they were almost always accorded deference, at least by their clients.[82]

In some respects *fengshui* specialists stood apart from the ordinary religious system as "observers of nature" who, like Zhu Chou, appealed to an orthodox neo-Confucian metaphysics. On the other hand, they often operated like priests, employing methods familiar to all devotees of Chinese popular religion. Not only did they actively manipulate the physical environment in various ways for the purpose of improving the fortunes of their clients, but many also performed graveside rituals, and some wrote charms or chanted spells for anxious constituents. Tales of their power were perpetuated in traditional Chinese folklore, both by word of mouth and by means of vernacular literature.[83]

Fengshui manuals devote considerable attention to the charms and spells used for amplifying the normal "strength" (*shi*) of a location and in "stabilizing" (*zhen*) a structure. Activated by geomancers themselves or by Daoist priests, these talismans were reportedly capable of warding off "sickness, injury and calamity"[84] (see Fig. 4.6). Many had quite specific applications. The geomantic

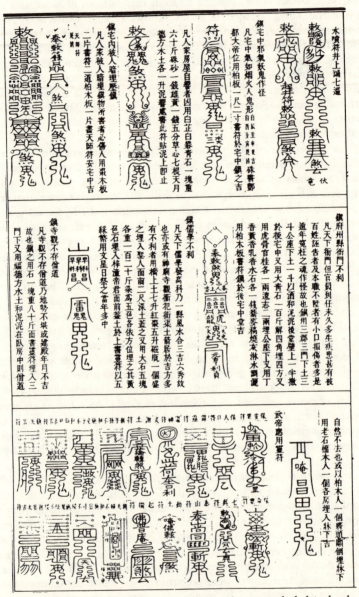

Figure 4.6 A few of the many geomantic charms included in book four of the *Yangzhai*. The charms on this page are concerned primarily with the protection of places such as yamens, educational buildings, and temples. *Source*: Jiang Tingxi, ed., *Qinding gujin tushu jicheng* (Taibei, 1977 reprint), 47: 7042.

guidebook entitled *Yangzhai*, for instance, provides written charms appropriate for houses sited too near monasteries or temples, houses whose inhabitants' children do not perform well in school, and so forth.[85] Such works often provided guidelines regarding the size of charms, the kinds of materials on which they should be written, and the type of writing ink to be used. Some invoked the names of popular deities, such as Guandi, the God of War, while others relied on ferocious natural images, such as that of the tiger, for protection. Octagonal representations of the eight trigrams, with either the *yinyang* symbol (*Taiji tu*) or a mirror in the middle to ward off evil spirits, graced many homes and buildings throughout China, complementing devices such as "shadow walls" (*yingbi*), which were placed in front of doorways and designed to prevent access by evil spirits on the theory that *gui* could only travel in straight lines. The use of certain painted colors on buildings, depicting one or another of the five "agents," might compensate for deficiencies in location or orientation; and graves commonly had felicitous inscriptions and/or the *yinyang* motif carved on the headstone, since such symbols in effect "created" the reality they represented.[86]

As already indicated, the most important application of geomancy in Qing China was to identify the proper burial place for one's deceased parents and other ancestors. This instantly placed *fengshui* at the vortex of Chinese mortuary ritual, with all of its perplexing variety across space and time.[87] Yet despite significant differences in specific burial practices from region to region, there were several important common denominators. At all levels of Chinese society, in most parts of the empire, professional geomancers gave advice to bereaved families on matters such as the placement of the body on the deathbed (and the coffin in the hall), the siting and depth of the grave, and the orientation of the coffin at the gravesite. They determined the most auspicious times for the encoffining, procession, and burial rituals, and provided information on which individuals outside the immediate family might be too vulnerable or astrologically unsuitable to be allowed near the corpse. And, as indicated above, they also often wrote charms to "stabilize malevolent forces," and to purify the home.[88]

In southeastern China, the reburial of ancestral remains was widely practiced, requiring the multiple employment of geomancers. Sometimes the deceased were placed in temporary graves until a proper gravesite could be located or until arrival of the most propitious time for permanent interment. On other occasions, a decline in family fortunes provided the incentive for reburial. If for any reason an ancestral grave lost its "good *fengshui*," a new site and time for burial had to be chosen by a geomancer. The bones of the deceased were then exhumed and placed in an urn—although only the urns belonging to families for whom geomantic reburial had become important and financially possible were actually placed in new graves: "Urns awaiting second burial are stored in the open air, near the fields or on a hillside; and in reality most of them are never moved from this position. They may begin by being tended as the potential contents of a final grave, but after the lapse of a generation they are more likely to turn into anonymous pots, weathered until they crack and spill their irrelevant bones on the ground."[89]

Fengshui was not normally a hereditary occupation.[90] Fathers and grandfathers occasionally provided geomantic guidance to their progeny, but most *fengshui* specialists, quite naturally, directed the attention of their children toward success in the civil service examination system rather than perpetuation of a geomantic family tradition. Jia Yanling, for example, orphaned at nine and forced into the self-study of geomancy and medicine in order to support his mother, provided a much-admired model for filial piety by educating two sons who, in fulfillment of their grandmother's ardent wishes, passed the exams.[91] A number of aspiring *fengshui* practitioners served an apprenticeship, and some made long pilgrimages of study to renowned centers of geomantic activity, such as Ganzhou, in Jianxi, or Shanghai, in Jiangsu.[92] But even respected teachers of the geomantic arts did not always encourage emulation. Zhang Yanhua, for one, bluntly told his followers to study the Four Books and Five Classics of Confucianism rather than his own writings.[93] In the absence of a well-developed tradition of either hereditary transmission or systematic apprenticeship, book-learning became a common means by which geomantic knowledge could be acquired in Qing dynasty China. Judging from nineteenth century accounts, *fengshui* manuals were available everywhere in great profusion—a reflection of the dramatic expansion of both printing and literacy in late imperial times.[94]

Most extant works on geomancy cover the same basic ground, although individual formats differ substantially. Some manuals are highly abstruse and technical while others are relatively easy to understand. Many works commence with a general discussion of *fengshui* principles, often couched in explicitly Confucian terms, and perhaps an introduction to the topographical features of China as a whole—notably its great river systems and mountain ranges. Sometimes they also subdivide China into provincial units or into various *fenye* schemes, since the *fengshui* of any given locality is, of course, subordinate to the large macrocosm. Works that include an historical overview generally trace the origins of geomancy to the *Yijing*, citing passages that emphasize the relationship between heavenly patterns and earthly forms. They also refer reverentially to such great early practitioners of the art as Guan Lu and Guo Pu. The main body of each text discusses the concrete celestial and terrestrial variables involved in geomancy and how to interpret them. Most works contain a large number of illustrations, including not only depictions of celestial configurations and their relation to landforms, but also various charts and diagrams (many based on the eight trigrams, the *najia* and *nayin* schemes, etc.) The most noteworthy feature of this vast literature is its sophistication, eclecticism, and correlative emphasis.[95]

Perhaps the single most influential book on *fengshui* produced in the Qing period was Jiang Pingjie's *Dili bianzheng* (Distinguishing Orthodoxy in Geomancy). Jiang, also known as Jiang Dahong, received his initial instruction in geomancy from his grandfather during the late Ming, and proceeded to study the art assiduously for the next thirty years, investigating written materials as well as natural topography. He invented a widely-used compass, and many people considered his book to be the only reliable source on the subject in the early Qing period.[96] Even his admirers considered the language of his opus obscure, however, and so they attempted to clarify his ideas. The most successful effort of this sort was made by Jiang Guozi, whose *Dili zhengzong* (Correct Standard of Geomancy) is cited repeatedly as authority in the *Tushu jicheng* section on practitioners of the geomantic arts.[97] Other popular works of the Qing period included Hao Jibao's *Kanyu zhinan* (A Guide to Geomancy), Jiang Yitang's *Dili beiyao* (Essentials of Geomancy), and Cheng Sile's *Dili sanzi jing* (Three-Character Classic for Geomancy).[98]

The biographies of geomancers in Qing gazetteers attest to what many *fengshui* manuals aver: that field investigation is indispensable for the proper evaluation of a site. "Climb the heights, look into the depths, bear hunger and thirst and every discomfort," one authority advised an aspiring disciple.[99] Although some sources describe the search for a good site as a rather dignified affair, with travel by sedan chair and somber evaluations of the terrain, other accounts suggest that a geomancer might trundle off on foot for four or five *li* (over a mile) and display unbridled enthusiasm over the discovery of the right location.[100] Many *fengshui* specialists traveled extensively in the course of their profession, not only at the behest of clients, but also in the pursuit of geomantic knowledge.[101] At the same time, the localism of Chinese culture resisted the full assimilation of such sojourners, and they almost invariably invited suspicion wherever they went.

Why would a literate Chinese go to the trouble of studying geomancy? According to local gazetteers, which naturally reflect the biases of their Confucian compilers, filial piety offered one compelling reason. Concern for the well-being of one's parents, both in life and after death, found expression in a popular adage: "No man's son should be ignorant of mountains [i.e. *fengshui*] or medicine."[102] Thus we read of Xia Bingnan, who took up geomancy after having been fooled by unscrupulous *fengshui* specialists in the course of trying to find a gravesite for his ancestors.[103] Li Xingyu, orphaned as a child, was unable to bury his parents in a good location. When he grew older, however, he went to Jiangxi to study geomancy, and returned to give them a proper burial.[104] The upright and filial scholar Feng Wenyao read up on geomancy for the same reason.[105] Lou Yu spent several years of his life looking for the proper spot to bury his mother, and so on.[106]

The idea of geomancy as a morally-inspired enterprise finds expression in the titles of works such as Zhou Meiliang's *Dili renxiao bidu* (Book on Geomancy That Must Be Read by the Humane and Filial).[107] It was also articulated forcefully by a number of individuals, such as Zhu Ying, who argued that the purpose of selecting of a proper burial site was only to put the mind of the deceased to rest, not to seek good fortune. To do otherwise, he maintained, would be unfilial.[108] Liu Shijun, an exam failure, held a similar view—for which the compilers of the Nanling (Anhui) gazetteer felt obliged to applaud him.[109] Meng Hao, for his part, is credited with having a Confucian concern for "the investigation of things" [*gewu*] in his geomantic endeavors, not simply with "the position of spirits and stars" or the techniques that diviners use to "frighten people."[110]

In the minds of many practitioners, efficacious geomancy required moral rectitude, for in the end, "heavenly principle" (*tianli*) would always triumph over "earthly principle" (*dili*).[111] Viewed cynically, this emphasis on morality might appear to be nothing more than a convenient way for geomancers to explain away wrong predictions.[112] On the other hand, it seems evident that a substantial number of *fengshui* specialists genuinely believed in the ultimate power of moral action.[113] Although separated by time, space, and social class, individuals such as Huang Zhuocheng, Nie Ting, Li Qingxi, and Zhao Dongzhou all refused to talk about wealth or poverty, stressing instead the need for their clients to accumulate virtue (*jishan* or *jide*).[114] Guan Wenkui emphasized "moral grounding" in choosing auspicious land, and Liu Xianjia told his clients that a good heart/mind was better than a good site.[115] Ma Bailang tried to assure that his clients were virtuous, and Lin Shihe likewise expressed his steadfast determination to help only those who were upright and honest.[116]

Altruism apparently motivated many *fengshui* specialists, for a large number are reported in gazetteers to have enjoyed simply "helping people."[117] Wang Huaguo assisted those who could not afford to bury their relatives, while Wu Zhenchuan provided the poor with both medical aid and free burials.[118] Wang Xingzhen and Yang Shutai likewise served the poor in their local communities, asking nothing in return.[119] Local sources of the Qing era record a large number of geomancers who refused to accept any money for their services, and a few who would take it only if their client's family became prosperous.[120] Significantly, at least a few public-spirited geomancers, notably Wang Xingzhen and Yang Shutai—like the *Yijing* specialists noted in the previous chapter—played important roles in their local communities as mediators.[121]

Some *fengshui* experts took as their task the improvement of entire cities. Thus, Fang Zhengming brought geomantic benefits to Guichi, Anhui, by determining the proper time and location for the construction of a temple to Wenchang, the God of Literature.[122] When Qin Luhai's home county of Qingyun (Hebei) failed to produce an examination success for more than forty years in the mid-nineteenth century, he sought the causes in the physical structure of the county seat. After a careful investigation of the situation, he made his recommendations to the local gentry for the renovation of several buildings. They followed his instructions to the letter, and the county soon began to produce successful civil and military candidates.[123] Li Youlong, from Yongxing county in Hunan, showed a similar commitment to his local community, but he enjoyed far less satisfaction. When the leaders of Yongxing decided to build a pagoda in the southern sector of the city, he advised them not to, on the grounds that the structure would harm its "scholarly air" (*wenfeng*). They went ahead with the building, however, and examination hopefuls from the town suffered for several decades until the pagoda was finally destroyed.[124]

Of course not all *fengshui* specialists were altruistic. Some individuals took up geomancy under financial duress, in order to support their families.[125] Others, such as Gao Jiyang, sought to alter their own personal or family fortunes. Because Gao's ancestors tended to have only one son per generation, he studied geomancy in the hope of finding a graveyard for his father that would produce more male heirs for the family. Apparently he found the right spot, for subsequently he had five sons, and his eldest son in turn fathered five sons.[126]

Wang Chenglie helped find the right place and time to build a house for a relative who, at the age of sixty, had no male heirs. After construction of the house, he produced two sons.[127] Family interests also impelled individuals like Xie Xianting to select a site for his own burial that would benefit future generations. When, thirty years after his death, one of his sons (Xie Lanjie) helped suppress the Taiping Rebellion, Xianting received a posthumous reward from the throne.[128]

At times altruism and self-interest intermingled. Consider the case of Li Yiqing, a low degree-holder described in the Xincheng (Jiangxi) gazetteer of the Tongzhi period as "invariably successful in divining auspicious burial grounds for clients." Employed by one Chen Yuan of Zhongxi, Li found a suitable resting place for his client's father, but pointed out to his employer that although the location would bring prosperity to Chen's family, it would not be beneficial to either himself or Chen personally. He therefore wanted assurances that his own heirs would be taken care of in the event that something happened to him. As it turned out, Chen died at the age of thirty and Li became blind. But Li's daughter married Chen's younger brother according to agreement, and the two families prospered together, enjoying a harmonious relationship.[129]

Some *fengshui* masters clearly hoped to make a windfall by sharing in the prosperity of their clients—either those who were wealthy or those who would become so.[130] Significantly, however, the geomancers who merit biographies in local gazetteers are seldom explicitly described as professional diviners (*maibu*).[131] One reason may be that they often had other occupations as teachers, doctors, and so forth, making *fengshui* a sideline rather than a full-time profession. We may also assume that for those of a scholarly background or self-image receipt of a salary or fee would be considered too demeaning. Sometimes, however, a rich family or lineage would keep a geomancer on retainer, providing him with his entire livelihood. This made particular sense for lineages, since they had to consider the proper location of the ancestral temple as well as individual and collective gravesites.[132] At least a few individuals struck bargains with their clients for shared profits, on the assumption that a well-chosen site, particularly a grave, would bring financial prosperity.[133]

Quite often geomancers received a comparatively small salary, but were entertained lavishly during the period of their employment, which might last several days or more. For this reason we find that gazetteers often refer to *fengshui* specialists being "invited" (*qing*) by their clients, rather than simply employed.[134] One late Qing source indicates that for even a simple and straightforward divination the geomancer must be "treated well, with good food and good things to drink." First, we learn, the head of the family invites the *fengshui* specialist into his house. He then asks him to sit down in the guest room. "The stove is lit; the teapot rinsed; and the finest tea, costing 960 cash, is used for the infusion. The guest is asked . . . to take the place of honor and tea is served to him." In all this, he is shown the greatest respect (*gonggong jingjing*). At dinner, four special dishes and a jar of wine are ceremoniously placed before him. After choosing the gravesite, the geomancer returns to his host's home. At this point, "someone is sent to the silk storehouse to buy for him the material for an outer coat and inner robe, a pair of boots, and a cap. He is also given about ten strings of cash [i.e., about ten ounces of silver]. Finally, he is brought home in a two-horse cart."[135]

Geomancers naturally sought the prestige of high places, whether or not the quest brought them wealth (which it often did). After all, metropolitan officials and the Qing court were no less anxious than local elites and commoners to find auspicious locations for tombs and other structures. The historical record abounds with anecdotes concerning the private employment of *fengshui* specialists by the throne. As early as the Shunzhi reign, Wan Guoning placed first in a set of special metropolitan examinations on the geomantic topic "dragon lairs, sand and water" (*longxue shashui lun*); and the scholar Kang Zhengji was only one of several private individuals called upon by the Shunzhi court to find graveyards for the royal family. In recognition of Kang's services, the throne gave him a temporary position in the Board of Astronomy and subsequently appointed him to be a prefect.[136]

Later on in the Qing period, another well-regarded geomancer by the name of Ping Zhang was ordered by royal decree to chose an auspicious burial spot for the family of the Duke of Yansheng, direct descendent of Confucius.[137] Similarly, Li Genchang of Shanxi, who initially learned *fengshui* from a "strange man" (*yiren*) who crossed his path, captured the attention of some high officials because of his mantic skills, and went to Beijing, where he soon became famous. Imperial princes and other nobles invited him to their palaces as a consultant, and he was amply rewarded by them.[138] Zhou Yingji, for his part, divined a site for Prince Xian, and was later rewarded with a calligraphic inscription from the prince as well as official rank.[139] And Guan Zhining gained important positions within both the provincial government of Shaanxi and the metropolitan bureaucracy for his assistance in finding auspicious land for the throne during the first year of the Yongzheng emperor's reign.[140]

Not all geomancers employed by the throne sought prestige. Some already enjoyed it, such as Gao Qizhuo, a *jinshi* and high metropolitan official who was summoned by the Yongzheng emperor to improve the *fengshui* of the Qing tombs.[141] Nor was the employment of individuals like Gao always for the purpose of enhancing *fengshui*. In 1899, for example, Yingnian, a high-ranking Manchu official known for his geomantic ability, was reportedly walking together with the Empress Dowager, Cixi, and her entourage near the grave of the first Prince Chun, Yihuan (1840–1891), father of the Guangxu emperor. The Empress Dowager, ever mindful of politics, asked Yingnian whether the site was auspicious or not, whereupon Yingnian replied that its *qi* was still quite powerful, and that in the next generation it would produce another emperor. At that time, Pujun, son of Cixi's political ally, Zaiyi, was presumed to be the successor to the Guangxu emperor. Fearing that her plans might be spoiled by the positive *fengshui* of the garden, the Empress Dowager wanted to know how to counteract its influence. Yingnian's advice was to chop down an old Ginko tree near the grave; but when Cixi's attendants tried to cut the tree down it proved to be "as hard as iron." Finally, after much effort, they toppled the tree, exposing a huge nest of snakes—which in Chinese folklore are associated with dragons, the symbol of imperial rule. Yingnian's prophecy proved true when, after Pujun had been deprived of his status as heir apparent in the wake of the Boxer Rebellion, Puyi, grandson of Yihuan, became emperor in 1908.[142]

Although the Empress Dowager boldly sought to disturb the *fengshui* of Prince Chun's garden, she would not have had the temerity to disrupt Yihuan's grave itself. Qing law provided harsh punishments for all such activities, and enforced them with a vengeance.[143] On the other hand, the throne had no compunction against destroying the graves of rebel leaders in order to damage their *fengshui* fortunes. In fact, this was one of its first reactions to organized popular movements such as the Taiping Rebellion. For the same reasons, but with a somewhat different method, the Qing government reportedly tried to ruin the geomantic fortunes of a place called Dragon Pool in Taiwan, where, rumor had it, a new (non-Manchu) emperor would be born.[144]

More positively, Qing law specifically provided for the services of geomancers in the construction of public buildings, since the location, direction and even design of windows and doors could affect the fortunes of the entire community.[145] Officials at all levels of government sought specialists in siting who could not only supervise the details of construction and/or repair of walls, gates, yamens, schools and temples, but also determine the most propitious time for beginning work. Liu Xiandi's employment by Chen Hongmou (1696–1771) is only one of many examples of such geomantic service.[146] The accomplishments of these individuals were duly recorded in local gazetteers—sometimes with a sense of awe. During the Qianlong era, for example, Zhao Tingdong, an official in retirement, mourning the death of his mother, was invited by the magistrate of Pengxian, Sichuan, to give advice concerning the repair of his yamen as well as changes in the gates of the city. Prior to the modifications suggested by Zhao, a number of candidates from Pengxian had failed the civil service examinations, but thereafter the city boasted several noteworthy successes. "Is this not," the compilers of the Pengxian gazetteer asked, "reason to believe in the theories of *fengshui?*" Zhao later published two books on geomancy, one entitled *Yangzhai sanyao* (The Three Essentials of Site Selection for Housing for the Living) and *Dili wujue* (The Five Secrets of Geomancy).[147]

A number of geomancers served the Qing government in a military capacity, although the exact nature of their service is not always clear. Presumably they were employed not only for their expertise in divination, which many Chinese soldiers practiced, but also for their knowledge of landforms and weather. Some, such as the military *jinshi* Ma Wenzhi, seem to have had a more or less academic interest in *fengshui*,[148] but others, such as Li Zonghui, Zhao Caidong, Xiong Deqian, and Gui Jipan, served actively as military advisers, entering the *mufu* of both field commanders and civil officials engaged in temporary operations against rebel forces.[149] During the Taiping Rebellion, a young man by the name of Shen Zhureng, who later attained great fame as an *Yijing* specialist and geomantic expert, joined the Sino-foreign Ever-Victorious Army and became a close personal adviser of its Western commanders, Frederick Townsend Ward and Charles G. Gordon.[150]

By virtue of their knowledge of terrain and waterways, *fengshui* experts often assisted officials in the management of public works. Thus, when the

Wen river near Qianshan, Anhui, flooded, Wang Baile helped local officials to bring it under control.[151] Sometimes low-ranking bureaucrats undertook geomantic work themselves. When, for example, the Qianlong emperor wanted to build a canal to avoid the hazards of travel on the Yangzi River from Zhenjiang to Jiangning, Zhang Panggui, a military intendant from the Shanghai area, observed the situation and offered valuable advice for construction.[152] During the Guangxu reign, the dikes of the Yellow River broke in several places, flooding dozens of counties. Governor Li Bingheng, hearing of magistrate Xu Guifen's reputation as a geomancer, summoned him to help contain the situation. After "looking up at the heavenly patterns and down on the terrestrial lines" (a rather presumptuous cliché drawn from the *Yijing* by the compilers of the Xu clan genealogy),[153] Xu made geomantic calculations and determined a day for dike repairs on which the "stars of the earth" (*tuxing*) were powerful and those of the water (*shuixing*) were weak. Needless to say, considering the source, the repairs were completely successful, and Xu received an official promotion for his efforts.[154]

Naturally enough, Qing officials, like other elites, sought to take personal advantage of *fengshui* specialists.[155] They even invited to their homes men such as the eccentric Fu Sheng of Jiangsu, who, because he went without shoes year-round, was known as the "Barefoot Immortal on Earth" (*chijiao dixian*).[156] Geomancers such as Wang Jihong were in constant demand because of their reputation for picking ancestral land that yielded examination successes.[157] Among the many famous officials for whom geomancers selected auspicious gravesites were Chen Hongmou, Wei Yuan (1794–1856), Tao Zhu (1779–1839) and Ding Richang (1823–1882).[158] Not all specialists in *fengshui* bent to political or social pressure, however. The proud scholar Xie Hong, for one, self-righteously declined to find a graveyard for an official's deceased mother.[159]

Although the selection of sites involved elaborate cosmological calculations based on both compass readings and the symbolism of landforms, geomancy was also a matter of aesthetics. All Chinese appreciated the rhythmic quality of lines sweeping east and west and converging on a single focal point. *Fengshui* involved a beauty of movement, not just of static proportions.[160] In the words of Ye Tai, "The hills, with their dragons in transit and their coalescing sites, make certain definite patterns. Nowadays everyone who speaks of the geomantic forms of hills says 'a thousand changes, ten thousand permutations.'" Ye likened these differences to differences in human faces. He went on to say, however, that although geomantic sites were unlike in detail they were similar in their general structures, just as the faces of all people had foreheads high and mouths low, eyebrows above eyes, a nose in the middle, and ears at the sides. "If in the absence of definite patterns one were to hunt the hills and seek the dragon, how could even an earthly immortal [*dixian*; a term used to describe particularly gifted diviners] be clear in his understanding and without doubts?"[161]

Even nineteenth-century Western critics of *fengshui* occasionally acknowledged the aesthetic appeal of certain sites. One of the most hostile among them, Storrs Turner, observed: "In some mountain valley the traveller remarks a handsome, well kept tomb of a horse-shoe shape, resting against the side of a rounded hill, backed by loftier heights and flanked by declivities gently falling on either hand into the plain, over which a broad and silvery stream meanders. The beauty and peacefulness of the retired scene impresses his mind and he muses half-aloud, 'There must be poetry in the Chinese soul after all.' "[162]

The aesthetics of *fengshui* were closely related to the *yinyang* complementarity of traditional Chinese landscape paintings and landscape gardens.[163] According to the *Dili dacheng*: "On a rock hill you must take an earthy site; on an earth hill you must take a rocky site. Where it is confined, take an open place; where it is open, take a confined place. On a prominence, take the flat; where it is flat, take the prominent. Where strong comes, take weak; where weak comes, take strong. Where there are many hills, emphasize water; where there is much water, emphasize hills." And again, "If the dragon curls left, the water has to curl right; if the dragon curls right, the water has to curl left."[164] Compare these remarks to those of the famous Qing garden connoisseur Shen Fu (1763-?): "In laying out garden pavillions and towers, suites of rooms and covered walkways, piling up rocks into mountains, or planting flowers to form a desired shape, the aim is to see the small in the large, to see the large in the small, to see the real in the illusory, and to see the illusory in the real. Sometimes you conceal, sometimes you reveal, sometimes you work on the surface, sometimes in depth."[165]

Geomancy as a Social Phenomenon

The aesthetics of *fengshui*, together with its assumed efficacy, gave geomancy extraordinary appeal and staying power in traditional Chinese society. For hundreds of years it remained a prominent feature of the ancestral cult, and provided a potentially valuable tool by which individuals with the means could not only understand cosmic forces but also manipulate them. Yet *fengshui* was by no means an unmixed blessing. Geomancers, like fortune-tellers generally, were often stigmatized as unscrupulous people; and indeed, the word "deceit" (*huo*) is commonly found in elite descriptions of their mantic activities. Although many practitioners performed noteworthy social and political roles, the application of their diagnostic and prognostic skills did not always seem to be in the best interest of their clients. A popular Qing proverb went: "If a family employs a geomancer, it might as well move" (*jia you yinyang zhai fangzi nuoqilai*)— suggesting that a *fengshui* specialist would tinker with a dwelling until it is completely transformed, presumably out of selfish concern for his own financial benefit.[166] But then again, what filial son or devoted parent could afford to take the chance of selecting an inauspicious location for a grave or dwelling?

Uncertainty, together with the power of popular folklore, produced a profound ambivalence toward *fengshui* in Qing China on the part of the elite. Emperors denounced the practice at the same time that they employed it.[167] Although some Chinese genealogies and "clan rules" expressed disbelief in geomancy, others affirmed it, and many adopted an openly equivocal stance.[168] Thus we read in the genealogy of the Zhang lineage of Yunyang (1887): "Although we should not completely believe in geomancy, yet if a location is damaged, those involved seldom escape the harmful effect."[169]

The individual testimony of many Qing scholars reveals a similar uncertainty about *fengshui*. The illustrious Zeng Guofan, for example, dutifully championed his grandfather's "three disbeliefs" (in geomancy, doctors, and priests) in his home-letters; yet after the death and auspicious interment of his grandmother in 1847 he remarked: "Since . . . [her proper burial] all the household matters have prospered. My grandfather's illness is already cured, my ailment is healed, and I have gone up to the second rank; from this can be seen the good in our *fengshui*. Under no circumstances must the burial place be changed." Furthermore, when the Zeng fortunes later declined temporarily, Guofan and his brothers readily relocated the graves of his mother and father in order to "secure better fortune for the family."[170] Similarly, Dong Xun (1807–1892) once stated that he would not allow books on *fengshui* and other divinatory arts in his library because fortune-telling merely encouraged blind fatalism; yet on another occasion he fervently asked a neighbor not to build a high chimney near his house lest it harm the *fengshui*.[171] Such examples can easily be multiplied.[172]

In part, this equivocation reflects a more general uncertainty about spiritual concerns and afterlife in China. As I have argued in this book and elsewhere, the line between neo-Confucian "rationalism" and popular "superstition" has never been easy to draw, and Qing elites in their day-to-day affairs made all kinds of compromises in the realm of religion.[173] Some such compromises were inspired by essentially pragmatic considerations. Hong Liangji (1746–1809), for instance, argued cogently (though not always consistently) against popular notions of fate, immortality, and karmic retribution, yet he maintained that religious beliefs should be encouraged among uneducated commoners as devices for social control. In Hong's view, if peasants did not submit to the idea of a heavenly ordained and morally-grounded fate, they would behave recklessly and bring chaos to the countryside; and if they did not believe in either the Daoist idea of the accumulation of merits and demerits or the Buddhist notion of karma, they would not know the difference between right and wrong.[174]

Hong's scholarly friend, Yuan Mei, is even better known for his skeptical attitudes toward fate and fortune-telling, ghosts and spirits, Daoist immortality and Buddhist concepts of the afterlife. Yet it appears that he believed in at least a limited notion of karmic retribution, and allowed his family members and servants to undertake religious sacrifices within his home.[175] A story Yuan tells about these domestic devotions is most revealing:

My concubine Miss Fang worshipped a small sandal-wood image of Guanyin, four inches high. I am by nature very tolerant. I did not join her in her performances; but I did not forbid them. An old servant called Mrs. Zhang worshipped this same image with great devotion and would never begin her house-work in the morning till she had gone and burnt incense in front of it and bowed her head. I happened one day to get up earlier than usual. I called out to Mrs. Zhang to bring my hot water immediately for washing my face . . . [but] she had not finished her prostrations and took not notice. I was so angry that I took the image, flung it on the floor, and kicked it. Miss Fang, my concubine, heard of this, and said weeping, "Last night I dreamt that Guanyin came and said goodbye to me. 'Tomorrow,' she [Guanyin] said, 'there is going to be a wicked assault upon me, and I shall not be able to stay here.' Now you have kicked her, which is certainly the fulfilment of my dream." She then took the image to be looked after at the Cundi Shrine. I thought to myself, "Buddhism is an abstract philosophy. It does not deal in prophecy or clever tricks of that kind. Some evil spirit must certainly have 'possessed' the image." After that I never allowed my household to worship Buddhas.[176]

Yuan's capacity to reject Buddhist worship and yet accept the notion of spirit possession indicates a characteristic oscillation on the part of the Qing elite between belief and disbelief in supernatural forces (see also chapter 6). This tension was especially great in the case of *fengshui* precisely because the stakes were so high. Ancestors were not to be trifled with. Thus we find that Confucian households often employed monks, priests, geomancers and other religious agents as a kind of filial insurance, since no one could possibly know for certain what happened to a person after death. The desire to do everything possible for one's departed ancestor fostered, in the words of Holmes Welch, "the development of an extraordinarily rich assortment of posthumous rites in China."[177]

We should not assume, however, that elite critiques of geomancy were for this reason less powerful than criticisms of other forms of divination. In fact, indictments of *fengshui* often took a quite virulent form, particularly when motivated by personal antagonisms.[178] The well-known author Wu Jingzi (1701–1754), for example, apparently believed in *fengshui* until his examination career went bad, and then he turned against it with a vengeance. Wu clan lore ascribed the enormous literary success of his family during the early Qing period to an auspicious gravesite chosen by a geomancer named Jian Yaopo; but Jingzi never attained the advanced degrees and official rank expected of him. Meanwhile, for reasons beyond his control, he had to live with the discomfitting knowledge that a permanent gravesite for his mother had still not been chosen by his family seventeen years after her death. As a result of these experiences Wu rejected geomancy and other such beliefs. In chapters 44 and 45 of his famous novel *Rulin waishi* (The Scholars), he harshly satirizes *fengshui* specialists, debunking their ideas and showing them to be either frauds or fools.[179]

More successful scholars assailed geomancy through more conventional means. The influential compendium entitled *Huangchao jingshi wenbian* (Qing Dynasty Writings on Statecraft), for example, contains several essays by high-ranking officials condemning *fengshui* specialists for encouraging practices such as late burial and reburial, both of which were considered to be unorthodox and unfilial.[180] In the straightforward words of Xu Qianxue (1631–1694), "There is no greater crime a son can commit than to fail to bury a parent [promptly]."[181] Clan rules often repeated this refrain, as did local gazetteers and the throne itself.[182] In popular Buddhism there was even a special purgatorial "court" in the underworld for the punishment of those who, in the name of *fengshui*, delayed burials and committed other such unpardonable sins.[183]

The Qing legal code, which devoted enormous attention to matters pertaining to proper burial, included specific provisions designed to prevent "ignorant people, deluded by geomancy" (yumin huo yu fengshui) from delaying interment, or disturbing the remains of their own descendents (or those of others), in order to secure personal advantage. But reports from cities such as Suzhou in Jiangsu, of thousands of coffins lining rivers and covering fields, all awaiting a propitious time for burial, suggest that many people simply ignored the law.[184] As a matter of principle and of record, the official commentary to the Qing Code forthrightly denounced fengshui for being "basically absurd and false, unworthy of belief."[185] Significantly, however, this denunciation—like other critiques of geomancy by Qing scholars—did not assail the fundamental cosmological assumptions of fengshui, nor did it question the idea of determining a proper gravesite by means of divination. Rather, it derided the idea that "future blessings" could be transmitted to descendents by the bones of their ancestors, and condemned as "the worst of unfilial acts" the narrowly self-interested practice of leaving the coffin of a parent unburied. In the same spirit, an Enxian (Hubei) gazetteer of 1864 explicitly distinguished between orthodox "site divination" (budi) for proper burial and the deception (huo) of fengshui specialists. As with the Yijing, scholarly criticisms were not directed toward the use of divination per se, but simply to its misuse.[186]

One of the most vehement critics of geomancy in Qing times was a comparatively obscure individual by the name of Chen Que, a classmate and friend of the renowned early Qing intellectual, Huang Zongxi. Chen was willing to grant that some forms of Chinese divination, including astrology and physiognomy, might be beneficial, at least some of the time. But geomancy, he asserted, was the most harmful and illogical of all popular beliefs—a poisonous influence among the people.[187] Like earlier enemies of fengshui, as well as his contemporaries, including Huang, Chen condemned the practice on both ideological and practical grounds.[188] Citing the Zhouli, he pointed out that families were meant to live, die, and be buried together, and that burial separate from one's clan had once been a form of criminal punishment. How, then, could decent people encourage separate burials out of self-interest? And if geomancy was indeed practiced for reasons of filial piety, why did not the great culture heros of the early Zhou dynasty, such as King Wu and the Duke of Zhou, practice it? Finally, if geomancers had special knowledge of luck-producing sites, why were they and their families not all rich and powerful rather than poor and weak?[189] In a letter to a local geomantic society, Chen frankly advised its members that if they wanted to improve their fortunes, they ought to begin by burying their family members together, rather than seeking separate sites. By doing this, he said, they might accumulate enough virtue to help enrich their descendents.[190]

Chen openly attacked Zhu Xi for once suggesting that geomancers should find an auspicious burial site for the Song emperor Xiaozong (r. 1163–1189); and he praised Sima Guang for having recommended the destruction of all "burial books" (zangshu).[191] Furthermore, he ridiculed the popular notion that "dragon veins" could be "broken" by a house or grave built perpendicular rather than horizontal to them. The earth, he argued, was far too wide and deep to be affected by such minor disturbances. Addressing himself to the popular story that the Qin general Meng Tian (d. 209), famous for having overseen the construction of the Great Wall, had lost his life because the wall severed innumerable dragon veins, Chen wrote, following the Han historian Sima Qian, that Meng died and the Qin dynasty itself fell not because the dragon veins were broken, but "because the strength of the people was exhausted."[192]

Chen also condemned the practice of geomancy for taking scarce fertile land out of cultivation, and putting it to use only by the rich.[193] A kindred intellectual spirit, Cheng Tingzuo (1691–1767), friend of Wu Jingzi and a follower of the iconoclastic philosopher Yan Yuan, argued that since only the rich could afford the best-known geomancers, if they were successful in choosing auspicious this would indicate that Heaven favored the wealthy, clearly a preposterous idea. Like Chen, Cheng took the orthodox view that Heaven, not earth, determined fate, and that moral exertion alone brought Heaven's favor.[194] "The superior man," as Qing scholars such as Quan Zuwang were fond of repeating, "does not speak of calamities and blessings."[195] In the same spirit, a late nineteenth-century circuit intendant at Xiamen, Fujian, in a long and illuminating document reaffirming the state's general prohibitions concerning delayed burial, reminded people in the area that "wealth and status in human life are fundamentally fixed by Heaven" (*rensheng fugui ben yu Tian ding*), and that the greatness and glory of future generations could not possibly be secured by the mere selection of auspicious gravesites.[196]

One of Chen Que's most powerful arguments was that *fengshui* disturbed society. "The world is not enlightened," he wrote; "people fight for land, making enemies of local communities; [they] fight for material profit, making enemies [even] in clans. Men are imprisoned; others are implicated. There are even families which are broken and destroyed. . . . Nothing causes more heartbreak [than geomancy]."[197] This theme can also be found in Qing popular literature, such as the late nineteenth-century novel *Jiuming qiyuan* (The Strange Case of the Nine Deaths), by Wu Woyao (1867–1910), one of the most accomplished popular writers of his time. In Wu's work, a clan feud precipitated by a geomantic quarrel over the location of a stone house leads to a chain of homicides. Eventually justice is done by a judge who, significantly, assumes the guise of a fortune-teller.[198]

The historical record attests to both the validity of Chen Que's critique and the verisimilitude of Wu Woyao's fictional narrative. Throughout the Qing period, *fengshui* beliefs produced numerous social conflicts. One primary source of tension was, of course, economic. Because of the high demand for good burial land, and the fact that certain auspicious locations were intuitively obvious, even to the untrained observer, opportunities for fraud and exploitation abounded. Landowners and unscrupulous geomancers could, for example, conspire to inflate the value of real estate by identifying cosmological factors that made a site more attractive than it might otherwise appear. But even without such deception, landowners knew that an individual who had already identified an auspicious burial plot might well pay more for the land than it would ordinarily be worth.[199]

A late Qing vernacular account of *fengshui* negotiations in a north China village highlights this point. It describes the efforts of a middleman (*shuohe di*) to purchase land from one Wang Laosan after a local geomancer had selected an appropriate plot. In the process, the middleman asks Mr. Wang his price for the land, but does not indicate that his client wants it for a gravesite. Wang gives his price, sixty strings of copper cash per *mu* (c. one-sixth of an acre), but then makes secret inquiries and discovers the use to which his land is to be put. When the middleman returns to seal the transaction, Wang unexpectedly raises the selling price, whereupon the middleman becomes enraged and the two men almost come to blows. Peace is restored by yet another middleman, but the incident underscores the possibility for misunderstandings and deceit created by the search for good *fengshui*.[200]

Even more disruptive to society was competition for the advantages supposed to flow from an auspicious site—especially if it affected the Chinese family system. Brothers, it seems, often struggled among themselves to secure a gravesite for a deceased parent that would bring them and their descendents maximum benefit, at the expense, if necessary, of other sibs. According to one late Qing authority on the problem: "Different positions [for the grave] are canvassed as to their bearings upon different scions of the house, and the geomancer is at a loss as to what to do. Sometimes each brother will engage a different [*fengshui*] professor, and years will elapse before the matter is settled, the coffin remaining in a temporary receptacle."[201] A famous story by Pu Songling (1640–1750) centers precisely on this theme. It describes how two brothers surnamed Song, each leading "his own little army of geomancers," battled for three years over where to bury their father, a former high official. Eventually both men died without resolving the issue, whereupon their wives, after jointly enlisting another set of *fengshui* specialists, found an auspicious spot in a matter of days. Pu's commentary to this story notes that geomancy "may or may not be based upon sound principles;" but for brothers to fight for personal advantage while a coffin is relegated to the roadside is hardly in accordance with either the dictates of filial piety or those of fraternal love. Pu also considers it worthy of remark that two women should have quietly settled this matter.[202]

Fraternal conflict was built into the *fengshui* system, since after the death of a parent, each surviving brother stood in a different cosmological relationship to the grave in question. Each had a different horoscope (see chapter 5), and each occupied a different symbolic position on the geomancer's compass. Thus, one or another brother might insist on having the burial of a parent postponed for a longer or shorter period of time, because the year of the Chinese sexegenary cycle clashed with his particular horoscope. Furthermore, the location of each brother's tomb usually depended on the location and orientation of the father's tomb:

> The position on the left side of the tomb [looking outward from it] is the place of honor, and belongs to the first son; the nearest place on the right belongs to the second son, and thus the relative positions of the different members of the

family with reference to the tomb are fixed. . . . [But] the position of one individual being in the direction of a hill or water-course, may be propitious; while that of another, being in the direction of a hill or another tomb, may be unpropitious. Under the circumstances, one brother is as earnest to secure a certain place as the other is opposed to it, and quarrels and litigation ensue respecting the place of burial of a parent that may last for life.[203]

Complicating matters was the fact that in elite families, where concubinage was prevalent, sons of the same father but different mothers often sought paths to fortune through their respective maternal graves. As Maurice Freedman has noted, men descended agnatically from one ancestor could "differentiate them-selves in respect of the women married to him, and so escape from the inconvenience of sharing geomantic fortune with those whose success it is their very last wish to promote." Viewed from this perspective, women ancestors were necessary "not only to discriminate among agnates but also for swelling the number of chances [for geomantic success] open to a man when he is unwilling to look to higher generations [beyond parents and grandparents for assistance]."[204]

Regardless of how individual sons might try to manipulate fate, the distribution of benefits from favorable *fengshui* was still likely to be unequal. These inequalities could easily be explained, however, by a moral argument: "[If] one brother is poor and another is rich, [this] is simply a consequence of the latter's neglecting to give the former his fair share in the profits the grave produces [for] him." Selfishness, in other words, assured that good *fengshui* would eventually be driven away by bad behavior. All this was fully in accordance with the theory mentioned previously, that "heavenly principle" can always overcome "earthly principle." From this standpoint, good behavior brought good fortune. In the words of the scholar-diviner Song Yishi, "An unlucky man [i.e., an immoral individual] can get lucky land and [yet his] good fortune can become misfortune; a lucky man may encounter unlucky land and yet turn misfortune into good fortune."[205]

In order to prevent sons from competing for favorable *fengshui*, with the concommitant problems of delayed burial and family tensions, some well-to-do fathers chose a gravesite for themselves and their wives prior to death. This did not always ease the strain, however. In the first place, several geomancers might still be consulted, introducing the same sorts of professional and family rivalries that prevailed under other circumstances. And in any case a parent still might not be buried promptly if the timing of his or her death was considered inappropriate for immediate interment from the standpoint of the location of the grave in a given year.[206]

Fengshui disputes between neighbors in traditional China occurred frequently, owing to the fragility of the geomantic balance in any given area. In the words of J.J.M. De Groot, writing about Fujian province: "A slight alteration made in the course of a brook for agricultural or other purposes; the modification of the brow of a hill or the outlines of a rock by the erection of a house or a shed; in short, any little trifle may seriously disturb the Fung-shui of villages or valleys, which is usually evinced by a decadence of their prosperity, bad crops, calamities, etc." He goes on to say:

> Quarrels and litigation arising from Fung-shui questions are of daily occurance in towns. The repairing of a house, the building of a wall or dwelling, especially if it overtops its surroundings, the planting of a pole or cutting down of a tree, in short, any change in the ordinary position of objects may disturb the Fung-shui of the houses and temples in the vicinity and of the whole quarter, and cause the people to be visited by disasters, misery and death. Should anyone suddenly fall ill or die, his kindred are immediately ready to impute the cause to somebody who has ventured to make a change in the established order of things. . . . Instances are by no means rare of their having stormed his house, demolished his furniture, assailed his person; sometimes they place the corpse in his bed, with the object of extorting money and avenging themselves by introducing the influences of death into the house.[207]

Normally, the parties involved in any *fengshui* dispute first tried to negotiate an amicable settlement.[208] If discussion or mediation failed, however, the case might then find its way to the local magistrate's yamen. Here, litigation was both costly and time-consuming. It involved, among other things, an elaborate on-site "official geomantic inspection" (*kan fengshui*), undertaken by the magistrate personally and paid for by the plaintiff. It also often entailed bureaucratic peculation by yamen underlings. In the words of a popular ditty: "The yamen stands open as wide as the character 'eight;' but without money, there is no way to enter" (*yamen bazi kai wuqian wushi lai*).[209] R. F. Johnston, a British district officer at Weihaiwei in Shandong near the end of the Qing period, reports in unusual and illuminating detail a typical case. It involved a local villager named Zhang Yingmu, who wished to transfer the bodies of his descendents from their old burial ground to a new spot selected by an intinerant geomancer surnamed Xiao. According to Xiao, who claimed to follow the Pingyang (Zhejiang) tradition of geomancy, Zhang's *fengshui* was irrevocably bad in the old location and would be much better in the new one.

Xiao's deposition in the case shows how geomancers conveyed their ideas to lay audiences:

> As to the present site, all along the front of the graveyard there is a gully as deep as the height of two men. This is unlucky. The deep gully presses against the tombs like a wall, obstructing the passage of benign influences. This has a disastrous effect on the women of the family, who will have excessive difficulty in childbirth. Secondly, a small stream of water trickles from the graveyard and after flowing a distance of half a *li* [c. one-third of a mile] it vanishes in the sand. The result of this on the family is that children are born as weaklings and die in infancy. Thirdly, another stream of water flows away to the northeast. This carries off all the wealth-making capabilities of the family and the good qualities of sons and grandsons. Regarding the proposed new site: first, there are hills on the southwest, their direction being from east to west. Their formation so controls the courses of four streams that they all unite at the eastern corner of this site. Just as these streams of water come together and cannot again separate, so will riches and honors flow from various quarters and finally unite in the hands of

the family that has its graveyard in this fortunate locality. Secondly, the ceaseless flow of water has formed a long sandbank, four feet high, on the southern and southeastern sides of the site. Just as the water brings down innumerable grains of sand and piles them up near the point where the waters meet, so will the family that buries its dead here be blessed with countless male descendents.[210]

Zhang's neighbors objected to the move, however—in part because they would be forced to look at the new graves upon leaving their houses, which would certainly bring bad luck to them. Furthermore, they argued that the new gravesite, which Zhang had already acquired in a land trade, was inauspiciously located for the village as a whole—at least if utilized as a burial ground. In an effort to placate his neighbors, Zhang offered to plant a row of trees in order to obstruct the malevolent view, but his neighbors refused to accept this arrangement, presumably on the advice of their own geomancer. Zhang then offered to build a stone wall as a permanent *fengshui* screen, with the auspicious characters "happiness" and "long life" painted on the side. This time, however, Xiao himself objected, on the grounds that such a ponderous structure would certainly obstruct the free circulation of *qi* at the new gravesite.

With matters at an impasse, Zhang's neighbors added a new wrinkle to their argument: that Xiao the geomancer was "a stranger to our village and . . . quite evidently a rascal." "We fail to see," they remarked in a supplementary petition, "why the customs of . . . [Jiangnan] should be made applicable to our province [of Shandong]." This charge of foreignness and unreliability, predicated on the fact that Xiao's original home had been in the lower Yangzi River region, was quite common in the Qing period. From a traditional Chinese perspective, sojourners were inherently untrustworthy, and most likely disruptive as well. The argument had particular force since the regional stereotype of Jiangnan people was that they were unscrupulous.

Xiao, assuming his best scholarly airs, responded that these rude northern villagers were mere "children," who knew nothing about *fengshui;* and he reiterated his point that, based on long personal experience, if the coffins of Zhang's ancestors remained where they were, his family would inescapably "have bad luck, no honours and short lives." His arguments fell on deaf ears, however. Since the dispute originated in the British concession area at Weihaiwei, under Johnston's administrative jurisdiction, no geomantic site inspection took place. Nor, as far as we know, was there any bribery or influence-peddling involved. In the end, Johnston sided with Zhang's neighbors, and ordered Xiao to withdraw from Weihaiwei in three days or to be arrested "as a rogue and vagabond."[211]

Another case, this one from a Chinese source, provides less detail on geomancy but a bit more on the legal process. According to the records of Fan Fanshan, a Weinan county magistrate in Shaanxi province during the late Qing period, an old man by the name of Gao Mingde filed suit against Zhang Hongru, a gentry member, for disturbing the *fengshui* of a gravesite that had recently been selected for him (Gao) by a geomancer. According to Gao, Zhang, who owned a house near Gao's gravesite, had dug a pit as a prelude to building a wall on one side of the house—presumably to shield his home from the grave. But from Gao's perspective, the pit, and the wall Zhang planned to build, would assuredly "wound" (*shang*) the gravesite.

Gao's hope had been to take advantage of what he presumed to be the animosity of the magistrate toward Zhang because of a family disturbance that had arisen the previous year. But Fan pointed out in his remarks on a petition by one of the Zhang clan (Zhang Huaide), that he was an impartial official, who decided right and wrong solely on the merits of the case. In his view, it was unreasonable of Gao to prevent the Zhang family from building a wall, particularly since there was not yet a body in the grave. If Gao dared to obstruct the building of the wall, Fan threatened to have him brought to his yamen and punished. The Gao clan appealed this decision, but the magistrate, using maps supplied by the Zhang clan, pointed out, in the technical language of geomancy no less, that the grave was situated on a southeast-northwest axis (*sunshan qianxiang*), with the mound oriented to the southeast. Zhang's house was to the west, several dozen steps away. Magistrate Fan could not see how a wall put up by Zhang would harm Gao's *fengshui*, and he suggested that if Gao continued to be concerned about the matter he ought to seek another divination. In Fan's opinion, the fact that the site was the cause of so much quarreling and litigation gave proof enough that it was "unlucky land;" and in his comments to a petition by Gao Zhaoxiang, he baldly observed: "I have never believed in *fengshui*. Those of you who do believe in it need not come to litigate."

Gao Mingde persisted, however, claiming that because the grave was basically oriented west-to-east and because Zhang's house lay to the west of the site, the digging of a pit and the building of a wall would harm the "dragon vein." To this Fan replied disdainfully (but somewhat illogically, given the premises of geomancy) that Gao should have considered this problem when the grave was first sited. After all, the weight of the house itself would presumably have had an oppressive effect on the vein. Furthermore, he asked Gao sarcastically whether he would not be concerned that the "breath of the earth" would blow horizontally across his body, creating discomfort. From Fan's point of view, Gao's case had no merit whatsoever. After all, the house was old, the grave was new, and the digging done by Zhang Hongru was on his own property. "I still reject this petition," he said firmly.[212]

By far the worst kind of geomantic dispute involved the deliberate wounding of another person's *fengshui*—either to harm that person or to enhance one's own family fortunes. Such selfish and utterly irresponsible activity, like delayed burial and geomantically motivated reburial, was not only outlawed by statute but also punished in one of the purgatorial "Ten Courts" of the Buddhist underworld.[213] Yet it seems to have been quite common. "Not unfrequently," writes John Nevius, "a family seeks satisfaction or revenge from another family with which it is at enmity by breaking or injuring its *fung-shwuy*. This consists in defacing a noted tomb, or cutting trees connected with it. Prosecutions before the officers on the charge of breaking *feng-shwuy* are entertained by them as offenses of the gravest character, and are treated with great severity."[214]

Sometimes simple jealousy motivated the wounding of *fengshui*. A concrete example may be found in Sichuan province:

Between Suifu and Li Chuang, on the south bank of the Yangzi River, is a large stone that is the *fengshui* stone of the Luo family, who for generations have lived on the north side of the river opposite the stone, and who in the past prospered and accumulated great wealth through the help of this wonderful stone. It is said that when wood was split in the home of the Luo family the stone would move. The Zang family lived on the other side of the river and owned the land on which the *fengshui* stone was situated. The Zangs were jealous of the prosperity of the Luo's, so they chiseled and "broke" the stone whose power and influence helped the Luo family. Thereupon the Luo family accused the Zang family at court, and a long period of litigation ensued, consuming much of the wealth of both families.[215]

A version of the theme of altering *fengshui* for personal gain informs the plot of Wu Woyao's novel *Jiuming qiyuan*. In it, Ling Guixing, the villain, wants to tear down Liang Tianlai's stone house in order to improve his own luck in the examination system. Liang, however, refuses to sell the house. In desperation and anger, Ling and a few of his family members excavate the grave of Liang's deceased father in order to harm his good fortune. They also put a curse on Liang, destroy his garden, and finally take his furniture, crops and money.[216] Naturally such activities could escalate and erupt into outright warfare between clans or villages. De Groot reports, for instance, that in the area of Xiamen there were "instances on record of the whole male population of a village having worked hard for several days to destroy the felicity of a hated neighbor by digging away a knoll, levelling down an eminence, or amputating a limb from a Dragon or Tiger."[217] Similarly, John Macgowan writes of Guangzhou: "When a place has been discovered that is found to enrich the family that owns it, desperate attempts are often made by stronger clans to wrest it from them. Some of the fiercest feuds that have turned a certain district into a battle-field, where hundreds on each side have come out to wage war upon each other, have been stirred up by the desire to possess some piece of land that the geomancers have said will bring wealth and honours to those that possess it."[218]

As already indicated, at least a few Qing officials used *fengshui* as a weapon in their fight to limit Western evangelical and economic influence in nineteenth century China. In fact, a clause in the unequal treaties, insisted upon by the Chinese authorities, alluded to the widespread belief in geomancy in stipulating that foreigners could purchase land in designated areas only if the local inhabitants offered no objection—presumably on the grounds that their *fengshui* might be disturbed by foreign excavations or construction.[219] Despite this stipulation, however, Sino-foreign tensions involving geomancy periodically and inevitably arose. W.A.P. Martin cites the case of a hill above the city of Fuzhou, on which some British missionaries built a church, a schoolhouse, and a few other dwellings, only to see them demolished by angry Chinese concerned over the negative effect this construction would have on the *fengshui* of the city. Martin also cites a case in Hangzhou, where the sudden death of a county magistrate was ascribed to the position of a mission building on a hillside overlooking his yamen. In this instance, however, the offer of another location (and Western fears that the foreign establishment would be destroyed) averted a showdown between the missionaries and the local populace.[220]

Not all geomantic conflicts came to be resolved by force or negotiation. In the early 1850s, for instance, the inhabitants of Shanghai ascribed the death of the magistrate to the detrimental influence of a church tower looming to the north of the magistrate's yamen. Before they could take action, however, the Small Sword Society captured the city (1853) and held it until 1855. During this time the yamen was destroyed. After the Small Sword rebels had been expelled (with foreign assistance, ironically), the local inhabitants, on the advice of several geomancers, reoriented the rebuilt structure to deflect evil influences, thus saving the situation.[221] At the treaty-port of Ningpo, the residents were "much alarmed" by the building of a Roman Catholic cathedral in the city. This steeple portended misfortune for the whole city, but it was particularly threatening to the bell-tower, from which it had "usurped the pre-eminence of height." The worst fears of the Chinese community came to be realized when a fire destroyed the tower. Soon thereafter, however, the authorities employed an eminent artist to paint a tiger-like animal on a wall confronting the church, and "in a short time the cathedral crumbled and fell." The Chinese bell-tower was then, as if in defiance, built two or three stories higher than before, and again "peace and tranquility reigned in the city."[222]

Geomantic conflicts of this sort, like those involving attempts to build foreign-sponsored railways, telegraphs, and mines in China, created genuine resentment on the part of nineteenth-century Western "modernizers," who vigorously denounced *fengshui* as a "superstition" inimical to progress.[223] Yet well before geomancy became a weapon in the hands of anti-foreign Chinese officials, it had already worked its will on the Chinese landscape. Mining and building projects that had no connection with foreigners were also constrained by *fengshui* considerations. Canals could not be opened and bridges could not be built if they disrupted the *fengshui* of a given neighborhood.[224] And if alterations in the landscape were made without the geomantic consensus of the local community, feuds and lawsuits inevitably ensued. These could often be settled by payment of a certain amount of money by the party presumed to have the advantage in the matter to the less fortunate neighbor.[225]

So far I have emphasized the socially divisive aspects of Chinese *fengshui*. But there is another side to the phenomenon, one that goes well beyond the salutory official and community services of geomancers discussed in the previous section. *Fengshui* also played an integrative role in late imperial China. In the first place, it provided all Chinese with a heightened awareness of their place in the cosmic, social and ecological order, as well as a concrete sense of their community obligations. It affirmed and reinforced status distinctions, and relieved, or at least diminished, anxieties associated with the traumas of death, sickness, crop failure and so forth. It provided, in other words, a way not only of perceiving reality, but of dealing with it.[226] Furthermore, for all the complexity of its theory and the diversity of its practice, geomancy served remarkably well as a shared metaphorical and aesthetic lingua franca for Chinese at every level of society. De Groot remarks, for instance, that even the least educated Chinese "show an astounding amount of knowledge of Fung-shui."[227] Virtually everyone in China recognized its basic symbolic repertoire and knew intuitively a good geomantic location on first glance—just as nearly everyone could repeat tales that illustrated the marvelous skills of geomancers. These stories circulated freely in Chinese popular lore, enhancing the reputation of practitioners everywhere.[228] It is true that *fengshui* specialists could be made to look foolish in vernacular writings, but then so could scholars.[229] In any case, the stigma attached to frauds, whether diviners or intellectuals, was not nearly powerful enough to undermine their pervasive social role in late imperial times.

FIVE

Reading Fate

In Qing times, everyone believed that in certain respects destiny was fixed at birth. Classical texts, the Sacred Edict, clan rules, Buddhist and Religious Daoist writings, and a raft of popular proverbs and rhymes left no doubt on this score: "You can't control fate;" "Riches and honor depend on Heaven;" "[Fate] is fixed in former lives;" "Listen to fate; everything comes from Heaven;" "Bandits and fires are invited by fate;" "A doctor can heal illness but cannot affect fate;" "For good health it is better to call a lucky doctor than a renowned one;" "If one has sons, the reason is fate; if there are no sons, it is Heaven's determination."[1] Some proverbs were devastatingly deterministic: "One's life is completely fated, even the slightest thing cannot be obtained by exertion."[2]

Fate could account for personal failure, such as lack of success in the examination system—a perennial Chinese fear. Hence expressions such as "His essays despise fate," or "The *xiucai* [lowest] degree is earned by oneself, but the *juren* [middle] degree is produced by Heaven."[3] The great Qing scholar Zeng Guofan once wrote that while human effort might determine the quality of examination essays, "whether the officer selects them or you secure the degree early or late are matters governed by the will of Heaven."[4] Yet few Chinese scholars were rigidly deterministic, including Zeng; and even proverbs that emphasized the importance of fate, *fengshui*, and the accumulation of "hidden merits" (*yingong*) to literary success might nonetheless acknowledge the importance of dedicated "book-learning."[5] The *Yijing* established the premise that by knowing one's place in the larger pattern of cosmic change and responding appropriately to situations, a person could actually "establish fate;" and geomancy, as a specific technique, endowed individuals and groups with the capacity to avail of, or manipulate, heavenly and terrestrial influences in order to bring benefits to themselves as well as past and future generations.

Yet the question remained: How much of one's entire life was fated? How specific, in other words, was a person's individual allotment (*yuanfen*) from Heaven? There were two primary ways of gaining this sort of information, of "reading fate" (*kanming*). One was "extrapolation" (*tui*), which involved the construction of "horoscopes" (to borrow a Western term); the other was direct observation (*xiang*), which applied not only to geomancy, but also to the analysis of the body (physiognomy)—not to mention mundane objects, the stars, the weather, and even written characters.[6] A popular proverb from the Qing period implicitly recognized that people were like geomantic sites, reflecting not only distinctive physical features but also celestial influences: "Man has a human destiny [just as] places have an earthly destiny" (*ren you renyun di you diyun*).[7] The early Qing scholar Chen Wen suggested the cosmological link in the organization of his book on divination, entitled *Sancai fami* (Secrets of the Three Powers). The section on Heaven dealt primarily with astrology and the selection of lucky days, while the one on Earth focused on geomancy. The one on Man embraced fate extrapolation and numerology.[8]

Techniques of Fate Calculation

As Chen's book implies, the realms of fate extrapolation, geomancy, numerology and astrology were inextricably linked.[9] Although the expansive vocabulary of Chinese divination made extraordinarily fine distinctions between different techniques and approaches, their shared ground remained vast, and few Qing fortune-tellers specialized narrowly in any case. The biographies of diviners in local gazetteers and other sources indicate that most individuals were familiar with at least two major techniques, and many claimed a considerably greater range of mantic skills. Some were high-ranking metropolitan officials, such as the scholar-inventor Qian Daxin (1728–1804), who had an interest in astrology, milfoil divination, and various numerical systems. Other diviners enjoyed less-exalted reputations, but had equally broad interests. Ding Huan, for one, gained great fame in Jiangxi as an exponent of astrology, physiognomy, geomancy and *Yijing* divination. Liu Mouji of Anhui, had a similarly impressive set of credentials. Yao Dian, from Jiangxi, excelled at fate calculation, physiognomy, and numerology. Wang Chun of Jiangsu knew milfoil methods, fate extrapolation, numerology, and astrology. Xing Congyang of Liaoning, employed the *Yijing*, meteorological divination, numerology and physiognomy. And Ma Bailiang, from Yunnan, was conversant with numerology, geomancy, and physiognomy. These examples could be multiplied indefinitely, irrespective of reign period or place.[10]

Qing divinatory cosmology did not differentiate between spatial, temporal, astrological, numerical and "spiritual" variables except as a matter of analytical convenience—even in such comparatively narrow and "natural" realms as weather prediction.[11] Similarly, mantic approaches that applied to particular situations, and those designed to provide individuals with a sense of what they might encounter throughout their lives, all centered on the idea of a cosmic continuum linking past, present and future. Any attempt to separate them is therefore artificial and misleading. Although the emphasis in this section is clearly on horoscopic divination, my larger purpose is to show how the terminology, techniques, categories of analysis and cultural concerns embedded in several prominent Chinese mantic systems intersected and overlapped to form a vast, plush and colorful tapestry.[12] Naturally enough, the symbolism of the *Yijing* provided one important common denominator for these systems.

Historically, Chinese horoscopes assumed a variety of forms. The *Tushu jicheng's* section on "Astrology" includes samples of about forty "star-based" horoscopes from the fourteenth century, all appended to a work entitled

Xingzong (Astral Bodies; attributed to the eighth century scholar-diviner Zhang Guo). Each is in the form of a dodecagonal "spider-web," above which rests a group of squares and rectangles with information regarding the sex and status of the subject of the horoscope, the cyclical characters of his or her birth (see below), general indications of happiness (*xi*) and misfortune (*ji*), as well as several dozen specific "stars" identified with either one of the five "agents," the sun or the moon, or one of four malevolent influences linked to the planets Mars, Saturn, Venus and Mercury (see Fig. 5.1).

Inside each "spider web," at the center under the character for "fate" (*ming*), is the name of one of the lunar lodges, as well as the number of degrees (*du*) by which the horoscope is aligned. It indicates, in other words, what Western astrologers would describe as that particular horoscope's "ascendant." The parallel with Western star charts should not be taken too far, however, for Chinese astrological systems are much more loosely based on observable planets and stars than those of the West. The first layer of the horoscopic web displays the twelve earthly branches, with *zi* at the base, indicating north. The next layer contains various "real" (*shi*) and "empty" (*xu*) celestial influences (star-spirits; see chapter 2), followed by a thin layer referring to twelve aspects of human experience: longevity, wealth (parents), siblings, land, sons, servants, marriage (women), illness, movement, official position, happiness, and bodily appearance or constitution.[13] A grid follows, indicating the position of heavenly bodies at the time of the person's birth. Next comes a layer with the twenty-eight lunar lodges, in groups of two and three. Then we find a layer of "harmonized" sexagenary signs and finally an outer layer that includes, among other things, the twelve phases of change in the *wuxing*.[14]

Most Qing dynasty horoscopes contained the same set of variables, but their formats were far more diverse. The majority had a rectangular shape, although some were circular. The client's sex might be indicated in several ways. One was to leave it unspecified, in which case people invariably assumed a male. A female, on the other hand, would be designated by the character *nü* (woman). Another common approach employed the heirarchical vocabulary of the *Yijing*, in which the character Qian (for the first hexagram) denoted a male, and Kun (the second hexagram), a female. Similarly, the character *zuo* ("left," the honored position) signified a male, and *you* ("right," the secondary position), a female.

Nineteenth century Western accounts of fate extrapolation suggest a powerful continuity with Ming dynasty astrology. One reads in part:

> The events of men's lives are supposed to be under the influences of twenty-eight stars [of the lunar lodges], each of which is an object of worship. In telling fortunes by this method, a representation on paper of a man's horoscope is prepared for each individual applicant. It has, first, a circular map or table, on the periphery of which are arranged the twenty-eight stars in longer or shorter segments, to which they are severally assigned. The . . . [cyclical characters] determine under the influences of what particular star an individual's life begins. Starting from this point, the life is supposed to revolve in this fixed circle, passing, in regular succession, under different and varying stellar influences. The length of time during which one's life is under the influence of any particular star, is

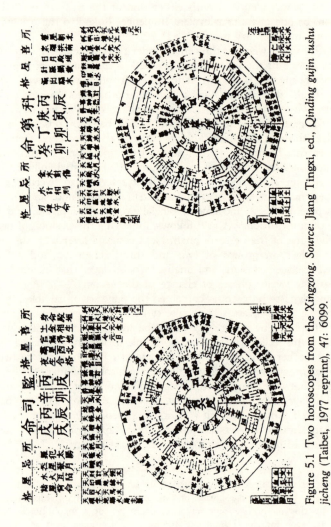

Figure 5.1 Two horoscopes from the *Xingzong*. *Source:* Jiang Tingxi, ed., *Qinding gujin tushu jicheng* (Taibei, 1977 reprint), 47: 6099.

ascertained by a computation based upon the Chinese festivals. . . . It commands the confidence of the people more, perhaps, than any other [form of divination], either because it is more mysterious, or because of the natural disposition of mankind to connect their destinies with the influences of the heavenly bodies.[15]

The primary textual authority for fate extrapolators in Qing times was the *Sanming tonghui* (Compendium of the Three Fates), commonly attributed to the Ming astrologer Wan Mingying. Reprinted in both the *Siku quanshu* and the *Tushu jicheng*, it remains to this day a standard work of fortune-tellers in Hong Kong and Taiwan. Like the *Xieji bianfang shu* and most geomantic handbooks as well, the *Sanming tonghui* begins with an explanation of general principles, laying out in detail the cosmological variables pertinent to fate extrapolation: *yin* and *yang* the five "agents," stems and branches, solar periods, and the usual inventory of celestial influences, including palaces, stars and star-spirits. Somewhat surprisingly, it does not devote much explicit attention to the trigrams and hexagrams of the *Yijing*—although it does discuss certain correlative schemes such as the *nayin* and *fenye* systems at some length.[16] The *Sanming tonghui* also describes the relationship of various divination techniques to different kinds of people (men, women, children, parents, wives and concubines, siblings, etc.), and provides a history of the development of fate extrapolation from its origins in the Han period to its culmination in the techniques of Li Xuzhong of the Tang and Xu Ziping of the Song (see chapter 1).

Both the Xuzhong and Ziping extrapolation systems place primary emphasis on permutations of the *wuxing*. Particularly critical are the "seasonal" and "life-cycle" phases alluded to briefly in chapters 2 and 4. The five seasonal phases consist of: (A) assisting (*xiang*), (B) flourishing (*wang*), (B) retiring (*xiu*), (D) imprisoning (*qiu*) and (F) dying (*si*). The twelve life-cycle phases are those of: (1) the womb (*tai*), (2) nourishment (*yang*), (3) birth (*sheng*) or long-life (*changsheng*), (4) bathing (*muyu*) or spoiling (*bai*), (5) coming of age (*guan* or *guandai*), (6) becoming an official (*guan, lingguan,* or *lu*), (7) flourishing (*wang*), (8) declining (*shuai*), (9) becoming ill (*bing*), (10) dying (*si*), (11) burial (*zang* or *mu*), and (12) receiving breath (*shouqi*) or extinction (*jue*).[17] In all circumstances, the strength of the *wuxing*, as determined by the stem-branch combinations of any given horoscope, waxes and wanes.

Significant differences existed, however, between the Xuzhong and Ziping methods. The former determined fate on the basis of the year, month, and day of a person's birth—each indicated by stem-branch combinations. Of these three variables, the year was most significant, and was therefore called the Heavenly Beginning (*Tianyuan*).[18] The latter method, although derived from the Xuzhong system and closely related in both fundamental assumptions and analytical vocabulary, calculated fate on the basis of the year, month, day and hour of a person's birth—making a total of "four pillars" (*sizhu*) or "eight characters" (*bazi*). For Xu Ziping, the day of birth was the Heavenly Beginning. Judging from the biographies of diviners in local gazetteers, the Ziping method was by far the most popular system of fate extrapolation in Qing times.[19] For this reason, among others, the following discussion will focus primarily on the Ziping system.[20]

In Ziping divination, as in most other schemes of fate extrapolation, one's allotment is divided into years (known generally as "minor destiny," *xiaoyun*) and decades ("major destiny," *dayun*). Exponents of the Ziping method often compare the "four pillars" metaphorically to a plant, in which the year is the root, the month is the sprout, the day is the flower, and the hour is the fruit. Thus, the first two decades of one's life are subsumed under the year, the next two under the month, and so on. For men, the annual period of fate begins in the first year with the stem-branch combination *bingyin*, and proceeds in the conventional sexegenary order; for women, it begins in the first year with *renshen* and proceeds in the reverse order. The formula used to calculate when the decennial periodization process commences suggests in a small way the complexity of fate extrapolation techniques. The formula is based on the relationship of the birth day to the calendrical system of twenty-four solar divisions. For a man with a *yang* stem in his birth year, or a woman with a *yin* stem, the number of days from the birth to the next solar division is divided by three. The quotient is the number of years from which age he or she will begin the first decennial period of fate. For a man with a *yin* stem in his birth year, or a woman with a *yang* stem, the number of days from birth to the preceding solar division is divided by three to yield the starting point.[21]

The four main terms used to describe an individual's "circumstances" (*geju*) in Ziping divination are "official position" (*guan*), "wealth" (*cai*), "seal" (*yin*) and "food" (*shi*). The *Sanming tonghui* discusses these terms at length, but only a brief summary can be attempted here. Each stem of the birth day or Heavenly Beginning belongs to one of the *wuxing*, and the "agent" that overcomes it in the "mutual conquest" sequence (see chapter 2) is the dominant "official" over that individual. Thus, for example, if a person is born on a day marked by the *yang* stem *jia*, which belongs to wood, then metal—associated with the stems *geng* and *xin*—becomes that person's "official," since metal conquers wood. But because *geng* is a *yang* stem and *xin* is a *yin* stem, they occupy different relationships with respect to *jia*.[22]

Since *jia* and *xin* are complementary to one another, *yang* to *yin*, they are considered correct or "upright" (*zheng*). But *jia* and *geng* are both *yang*, and therefore they incorrectly "lean to one side" (*pian*). *Xin* is an "upright official" (*zhengguan*) in terms of *jia*, but *geng* is "an official leaning to one side." Because a leaning official, also known as a "seventh killer" (*qisha*), may harm one's chances for prestige and power, it becomes important to find in an individual's eight characters a stem (in this case, *bing* or *ding*, indicating fire) to conquer or control that wayward official. Ideally the controlling stem should be found in the stem-branch combination of the month, since the stem-branch of the year, determining fate before the age of fifteen, is too early for official life, and the hour, which determines fate after fifty, comes too late. Also beneficial to someone born in a *jia* year would be the branch *mao*—identified with wood but *yin* to the *yang* of *jia*—in one of his or her other "pillars," preferably the month.[23]

With respect to wealth, the relationship of one stem to another is different than that governing official position, although both circumstances reflect the *wuxing* conquest mode. In this case, what is "conquered" constitutes wealth. Taking again the example of an individual born on a *jia* day, the "correct" stem would be *ji*, since the (*yang*) wood of *jia* overcomes the (*yin*) earth of *ji*. Although *wu* also signifies earth, it is *yang*, and it therefore becomes the "one-sided" wealth of *jia*. Similarly, *ji* becomes the one-sided wealth of *yi* (*yin* and wood). "Correct" wealth suggests that it can be anticipated, while one-sided wealth is unexpected. Wealth can be "plundered," however, by two stems that belong to the same "agent," such as *jia* and *yi*, if they appear together in the same year, month, day or hour—even though one is always *yin* and the other always *yang*.

In contrast to official position and wealth, the "seal" and "food" both operate in the "mutual production" mode (see chapter 2). The seal, however, produces, while food itself is produced. Thus, for an individual born on a *jia* day, *gui* becomes the "correct" seal (*yin* and water)—also known as the "seal ribbon" (*yinshou*)—while *ren* (*yang* and water) becomes the one-sided seal. By the same token, *ding* (*yin* and fire) becomes the correct food for *jia*, while *bing* becomes the one-sided food (see Fig. 5.2).

The force that determines the balance of *yin* and *yang*, and thus the processes of mutual production or mutual conquest, in Ziping divination is called the "operational spirit" (*yongshen*). In the simplest terms, if the official position, wealth, seal and food are harmonized by favorable stem-branch combinations, one's fate is good. If, however, they conflict, producing certain cosmic configurations marked by "death" (*sha*), "injury" (*shang*), "plunder" (*jie*) or "a cutting edge" (*ren*), the situation becomes bad. Naturally enough, all kinds of possibilities exist. *Xin*, the upright official of the Heavenly Beginning, *jia*, may be "injured" by *ding*; but *gui* can control *ding* and thus save *xin*. *Geng* may be the "killer" of *jia*, but *bing* can both control the killer and produce one-sided wealth.[24]

Of course it is quite possible for an individual's eight characters to contain no official position, wealth, seal, or food. Let us take an actual late Qing horoscope as illustration. The diviner, Yuan Shushan, is known to have been a practitioner of the Ziping method as well as a doctor. His client in this case, Zhao Houan, was born on October 24, 1853, between the hours of 11 P.M. and 1 A.M. In Chinese terms, this means that his birth year was *guichou*; the month, *renxu*, and both the day and hour, *jiazi*. From the standpoint of his stems and branches, Zhao had no official position (*xin* or *geng*), wealth (*ji* or *wu*), seal (*gui* or *ren*), or food (*ding* or *bing*). Yet clearly he had both a past and future. How was it calculated?[25]

As is readily apparent, Zhao's day and hour stems "contain" (i.e. signify) *yang* and wood, while their branches contain *yang* and water. His monthly stem also indicates *yang* and water, while his yearly stem connotes *yin* and water. The branches for his year and month supply a certain amount of earth, but not enough to counterbalance the "flood" of water that threatens the wood. In his written explanation of Zhao's horoscope, Yuan points out that metal, contained in the earth of *chou* and *xu*, cannot secure the "operational spirit" that will harmonize the "elements;" hence Zhao's wood cannot be "fashioned into beams" [*zaozuo dongliang*]—a common Qing metaphor referring to the

Heavenly Yuan	Official		Wealth		Seal		Food		Robber of Wealth
	Cor-rect	One-sided	Cor-rect	One-sided	Cor-rect	One-sided	God of Food	Injurer of Official	
jia	xin you	geng shen	ji chou wei	wu chen xu	gui zi	ren hai	bing si	ding wu	yi mao
yi	geng shen	xin you	wu chen xu	ji chou wei	ren hai	gui zi	ding wu	bing si	jia yin
bing	gui zi	ren hai	xin you	geng shen	yi mao	jia yin	wu chen xu	ji chou wei	ding wu
ding	ren hai	gui zi	geng shen	xin you	jia yin	yi mao	ji chou wei	wu chen xu	bing si
wu	yi mao	jia yin	gui zi	jen hai	ding wu	bing si	geng shen	xin you	ji chou wei
ji	jia yin	yi mao	ren hai	gui zi	bing si	ding wu	xin you	geng shen	wu chen xu
geng	ding wu	bing si	yi mao	jia yin	ji chou wei	wu chen xu	ren hai	gui zi	xin you
xin	bing si	ding wu	jia yin	yi mao	wu chen xu	ji chou wei	gui zi	ren hai	geng shen
ren	ji chou wei	wu chen xu	ding wu	bing si	xin you	geng shen	jia yin	yi mao	gui zi
gui	wu chen xu	ji chou wei	bing si	ding wu	geng shen	hai you	yi mao	jia yin	ren hai

Figure 5.2 A summary of the Ziping system. *Source:* Adapted from Chao Wei-pang, "The Chinese Science of Fate-Calculation," *Folklore Studies* (1946), 5: 313.

outstanding ability of a civil or military official. This accounts for hardships in Zhao's past. However, the stem-branch combination that marks the beginning of the second decade under the month (*renxu*), at thirty-five years of age (thirty-six *sui*), contains *yang* and fire, which has the potential of invigorating the wood of *jia*. Timing, Yuan affirms, is critical to success, and he offers hope that gratifications will come to Zhao later in life.

The horoscope of former governor-general of Liang Jiang, Wei Guangtao, a relative of Wei Yuan, provides a counter-case, also based on the theme of "wood." Born on November 27, 1837, between the hours of 1 and 3 P.M., Wei's "eight characters" were *dingyu* (year), *xinhai* (month), *jiaxu* (day) and *xinwei* (hour). Like Zhao, his Heavenly Beginning was dominated by wood; but unlike Zhao his year-stem supplied fire and his month-stem, metal. Yuan Shushan, citing Mencius on the timely entry of the woodsman into the forest, points out in his analysis that the fire of Wei's year-stem not only has the capacity to invigorate his wood but it can also temper metal for use in "fashioning [wood] into beams." "Your 'four pillars,'" he writes, "indicate clearly . . . that your life [has been and] will be one of riches and honor." Weaving together information about Wei's past and future, Yuan remarks that although his client's "early fate" (*zaoyun*) left him without a distinguished examination career (in fact, Wei possessed only the title of *jiansheng*, or Student of the Imperial Academy), his "middle fate" (*zhongyun*) brought high office and substantial rewards from the throne. Later in life, says Yuan, Wei will encounter some difficulties, but if he retires by the age of seventy-eight *sui* he can look forward to a peaceful life, with a wife, several concubines, and numerous sons and grandsons.[26]

As the above examples suggest, the language of fate extrapolation, like that of geomancy, tended to be highly metaphorical; and characteristically, the metaphors assumed a kind of social and cosmological "reality"—rather like the images of the trigrams and hexagrams in the *Yijing*. The horoscope of an unnamed but semi-educated courtesan, born in 1895, offers another illustration. It focuses on the imagery of flowers, identified with the *yin* wood (*yi*) that appears in three of her "four pillars." In this horoscope we find phrases such as: "Up to the age of about twenty *sui* [character missing] your life has been unsettled, like falling flowers." Later, however, the woman will enter the home of a respectable man and give birth to a son, Yuan confidently asserts.[27] For Zhang Xingwu, a former Qing magistrate born in 1845, the defining metaphor is that of a lamp, since his birth day is marked by the *yin* fire of *ding*. According to Yuan, the flame of this lamp, fueled by the wood supplied by his year and hour stems (*yi* and *jia*, respectively), has the capacity to "burn all night," ensuring continuous blessings and longevity. His later career will, however, involve certain setbacks.[28]

Chinese horoscopes, like the *Sanming tonghui* itself, reflect distinctive cultural preoccupations. We find, therefore, that in addition to predictions concerning such universal human concerns as financial prosperity, marriage, children, and health, a number of Qing horoscopes and works on fate calculation refer specifically to the civil service examination system and to official careers (see also last section). Not surprisingly, lack of success is most often explained horoscopically in terms of the absence or conflict of certain specific "elements." Former magistrate Dou Diangao, for instance, born in 1842, had too much fire and earth in his fate and not enough water. Since "without the nourishment of water there must be drought," Dou did not enjoy distinction in the exams and experienced various disappointments in his bureaucratic career—despite his noteworthy integrity and obvious literary ability. Although he finally did become a Qing official, fate conspired against him, negating in large measure the two personal qualities that should have brought sustained gratification to him in China's inveterately literary and bureaucratic culture. Only late in life, during the years 1905–1906, was Dou both happy and successful.[29]

Another feature of Chinese horoscopes is their persistent moral advice and encouragement. Thus Yuan Shushan admonishes Zhang Xingwu at a turning point in the latter's life (sixty-two *sui*) to be diligent in his work and not self-indulgent. An unnamed Buddhist monk, born in 1884, hears from Yuan that at the age of forty-one *sui* he must be careful and cast away both greed and anger. Yuan also encourages an unnamed woman, born in 1877 and widowed in her mid-twenties, to remain chaste and morally strong. She must, he commands, maintain her will, which he approvingly describes as "hard as metal and stone." Sometimes Yuan's advice is medical, and purely pragmatic. For instance, he advises an older woman, born in 1839, to be particularly careful to guard against diseases of the lungs, liver and blood.[30]

My general impression is that most fate calculators sincerely tried to understand their clients, and to give them the best possible advice under the circumstances. On the whole, they did not mince words. Although very few horoscopes were one-sidedly negative, few were overwhelmingly positive; and when necessary fortune-tellers did not hesitate to point out flaws in the character or personality of their clients. We may take as illustration the horoscope of an unnamed male, born on June 14, 1881, who was 23 *sui* at the time it was drawn. Calculated according to the methods of both Shao Yong and Xu Ziping, this man's fate is linked to the hexagram Gou (44), which appears comparatively favorable for the time of his birth. However, the man lacks any sort of water in his "eight characters" (a clear sign of obtuseness in the traditional view), and although he is vigorous and strong, and possessed of great ambition, his mind is described as "coarse" (*cu*).[31]

For amusement and perhaps inspiration, some Qing scholars used the Ziping method to measure the lives of historical figures against the prognostications implied by their eight characters. One such individual was Liu Yusong, who lived during the Daoguang period and recorded his studies of fate extrapolation in a work entitled *Tongyi tang wenji* (Literary Collection from the Hall of Penetrating Meaning).[32] But most Qing diviners required a living client in order to take fully into account the myriad of factors relating not only to time, space, direction, and environment, but also to human relationships. In Chinese cosmology, as in social life, one's individual fate always intermingled with that of others, requiring, at least theoretically, consideration of their horoscopes as well. This was particularly true of women, since their lives were so often dominated by men. Yuan Shushan provides several examples of women whose fate was inextricably bound up in the "stars" of their husbands and/or sons.[33]

Yet as with all major forms of divination, the complexities of fate calculation could be, and often were, radically simplified. Local almanacs in the Qing period contained several devices designed to demystify the process. One of these depicted the "Emperor of the Four Seasons" (*Siji huangdi*), whose head, body, arms and legs bore cyclical characters indicating one of the twelve two-hour segments of the twenty-four hour day. These characters were explained by fifty-six accompanying verses of five characters each. When a child was born, the parents consulted the appropriate figure for the season to discover what the future held for anyone born in any particular two-hour time period. On the whole, a birth time located on the head, hand, shoulder, belly and groin was fortunate, while one on the leg or foot was less auspicious. This was particularly true of birth on the leg, which presaged a hard life of toil and deprivation as a youth—although mercifully relieved by blessings late in life. As with most other forms of fate calculation, these poems offered advice. Thus, we read that neither a male nor a female "born on the emperor's foot" should remarry if their spouse happened to die.[34]

One of the simplest and most widespread notions related to fate calculation was that of astrological "signs" comparable with, and perhaps related to, the zodiac of the Western tradition. In traditional China, each person's birth came to be identified with one of twelve animals correlated with the twelve earthly branches: the rat (branch zi), ox (chou), tiger (yin), rabbit (mao), dragon (chen), snake (si), horse (wu), sheep (wei), monkey (shen), rooster (you), dog (xu) and pig (hai). According to popular belief, each of these animals had its own personality or character. The rat, for instance, generally symbolized wit and sociability; the ox was known for its stability and tenacity; the tiger epitomized courage and independence; the rabbit stood for virtue and reserve; the dragon signified vitality and good fortune. The snake was seen as wise and persistent; the horse, as elegant and strong; the sheep, graceful and adaptable; the monkey, clever and capricious; the rooster, methodical and straightforward; the dog, loyal and reliable; the pig, honest and innocent.[35]

Of course these stereotypes varied somewhat from region to region, and a few proved more powerful and evocative than the others. The dragon, mentioned often in the Yijing, remained a particularly potent symbol in Chinese divination—as it had been for centuries in virtually all realms of traditional Chinese mythology. Many if not most people in Qing times believed that birth in a dragon year was extremely auspicious, especially for boys—a belief that still exists today in Hong Kong and on Taiwan. On the other hand, birth in a horse year was considered unlucky for girls, since the horse implied movement rather than domestic stability.[36] Although not all Chinese imputed specific character traits to individuals born in certain years, few were immune to this tendency. One reason was that reference to an animal was the most common way to indicate the year of one's birth.[37] Another was the influence of Chinese vernacular literature, which not only described personalities in broad brush strokes that bordered on stereotype, but also reinforced certain animal images, such as the capricious monkey "hero" Sun Wukong in the enormously popular novel Xiyou ji (Journey to the West).[38]

Naturally each animal had a yin or yang designation, although these iden-tifications did not necessarily correlate with those of the twelve earthly branches. Nor were wuxing identifications the same for both animals and branches. According to one scheme based on odd (yang) and even (yin) numbers, the rat, related to water and possessing five claws, was yang; the ox, related to earth and possessing two divisions of the hoof, was yin; the tiger, related to wood and possessing five claws, was yang; the rabbit, related to wood and possessing two claws, was *yin*; the dragon, related to earth, and possessing five claws, was *yang*; the snake, related to fire and possessing a forked (double) tongue, was *yin*; the horse, related to water and possessing an undivided hoof, was *yang*; the sheep, related to earth and possessing two divisions of the hoof, was *yin*; the monkey, related to metal and possessing five fingers, was *yang*; the rooster, related to metal and possessing four claws, was *yin*; the dog, related to earth and possessing five claws, was *yang*; and the pig, related to water and possessing two claws, was *yin*. According to another system of categorization, the pig, rat, and ox were identified with water (north and winter); the tiger, rabbit, and dragon with wood (east and spring); the snake, horse, and sheep, with fire (south and summer); and the monkey, rooster, and dog, with metal (west and autumn).[39]

The belief in a relationship between one's birth and one's fortunes had several important implications in traditional Chinese society. In the first place, the requirements of a cosmological "fit" in everyday life were such that a person regularly needed to know whether his or her horoscope conformed with the requirements stipulated in state calendars and popular almanacs. Although such works provided specific indications of "appropriate" and "inappropriate" days for various mundane and ritual activities, not all days were equally auspicious for everyone. In planning important events, then, one would have to make certain that the *bazi* of the person in question harmonized with the *wuxing*, constellations, stars and "star spirits" that dominated a particular day, time, location and direction.[40] Even Qing officials were not immune to these considerations. Thus we find that in trying to decide when to open the bureaucratic offices at Guangzhou after they had been closed for the New Year's holiday, Shizeng, a high-ranking member of the Imperial Household during the 1860s, had to find a day compatible with his own "eight characters."[41]

Many aspects of Chinese domestic ritual also depended heavily on the day and time of one's birth. As indicated briefly in the previous chapter, *fengshui* considerations were closely linked with the personal horoscope of a client, or, in the case of mortuary ritual, the deceased. J.J.M. De Groot remarks, for example, that "no burial place can answer to the geomantic requirements if the cyclical characters expressing the year of the birth of the occupant stand in the compass on the lower end of the line which the almanac has decreed as auspicious for the current year and in which, of course, the coffin is to be placed." He goes on to indicate that the month, day, and hour of the deceased may also prove to be unlucky—although certain conjunctions of influences might be found to "neutralize such dangers." If no such offsetting factors could be discovered, a family was "constrained to adjourn the burial until the almanac assigns another direction as peculiarly auspicious."[42]

A significant part of traditional Chinese marriage ritual revolved around a comparison of the horoscopes of bride and groom, and the selection of "lucky days" for various related activities, including the all-important transfer of the bride (*qinying*). Calendars, almanacs, and ritual handbooks of the Qing period give considerable attention to these matters, for Chinese marriages, as affairs of truly cosmic consequence, required cosmic validation. But in Chinese folklore, certain pairs of animals came to be considered incompatible. At least some Qing subjects believed, therefore, that individuals born in years marked by antagonistic animals should not marry. According to one scheme, the horse and the ox were bad for each other, as were the sheep and the rat, the rooster and the dog, the tiger and the snake, the rabbit and the dragon, the pig and the monkey. Another system pitted the rat against the horse, the ox against the sheep, the tiger against the monkey, the rabbit against the rooster, the dragon against the dog, and the snake against the pig.[43] Usually, however, the process of comparing horoscopes involved Ziping-style calculations, which considered the day of birth as most significant.

After preliminary investigations by a matchmaker, the "eight characters" of a prospective bride were sent to the home of the prospective groom, where they would be placed in front of the ancestral altar for three days. If no inauspicious omens appeared during this period, the girl's horoscope would then be sent to a professional diviner by the boy's parents. If this divination proved favorable, the go-between took the boy's horoscope to the girl's family, where it underwent similar scrutiny. If this divination also proved successful, the marriage ritual could proceed to the next stage, the exchange of presents and contractual agreements that attested to the marriage (*nazheng*).[44]

The choice of an auspicious day and time for the transfer of the bride might be made in various ways. One was, of course, to consult a state calendar or popular almanac. John Nevius tells us: "Nothing strikes the attention of an observer so much on [officially designated] lucky days as the large number of bridal chairs, with their accompanying retinue and music, which on these days may be seen passing in every direction through the streets, and through the country."[45] But, as I have indicated, such general stipulations might not be sufficient in all cases. For this reason, specialists in "day selection" (*xuanze*) were extremely popular in traditional China.[46]

Many such specialists employed numerological techniques such as *liuren*, *qimen dunjia*, and *taiyi* (see chapter 3), which were closely linked to the concerns, methods and symbolism of fate extrapolation. In a sense, the charts of these practitioners applied to discrete slices of human experience the way horoscopes did to entire lives. They involved a similar set of cosmological variables, and the calculations they entailed were often similar to, or even congruent with, those of Fujian-style geomancy.[47] But while numerologists might use complex devices like the *luopan* to make predictions, their methods did not always require elaborate calculations. Qing almanacs describe a *liuren* technique by which even illiterates could determine the proper timing of a given enterprise by counting on their finger joints (see next section); and Western observers describe a simple *liuren/qimen dunjia* process by which diviners rolled a red ball around a wooden tub until it landed in one of twelve holes marked by the earthly branches. They then combined the selected branch with one of the ten stems, and consulted a guidebook for the appropriate reading. In the case of day selection for marriage, bridegrooms were represented by the ten stems and brides by the twelve branches.[48]

Popular proverbs, songs and verses provided an alternative source of information for individuals interested in determining auspicious days for various marriage-related rituals. One ditty, designed to reveal the appropriate month for the transfer of a bride, went: "In the first and seventh months, invite the rooster and the rabbit; in the second and the eighth, unite the tiger and the monkey; in the third and the ninth, join the snake and the pig; and in the fourth and the tenth, combine the dragon and the dog. The cow and the sheep belong to the fifth and eleventh, and the rat and the horse to the sixth and the twelfth."[49]

After choosing a month, the concerned parents might then consult an almanac which had a circular chart consisting of the *Taiji tu* surrounded by eight characters, reading clockwise in the following order: *fu* (man or husband), *gu* (husband's mother), *tang* (main hall), *weng* (husband's father), *di* (younger brother), *zao* (stove), *fu* (woman or wife) and *chu* (kitchen). *Fu* denoted the first day of the month, *gu* the second, and so on. Depending on whether a month had thirty or twenty-nine days, the person consulting the chart proceeded to mark off days, clockwise or counterclockwise. If the day chosen for the marriage corresponded to *di, tang, chu* or *zao* it was felicitous. On the other hand, if it corresponded with *weng* or *gu*, one of two situations prevailed. If either the father or the mother of the bridegroom was still living, this day became inauspicious, unsuitable for the transfer ceremony. But if one or both of the groom's parents had already died, then the marriage might take place on that day.[50]

Not surprisingly, many Qing scholars were hostile to such systems of fate calculation. Individuals such as Gu Yanwu, Lu Shiyi, Feng Jing, and Quan Zuwang, for example, took pleasure in pointing out statistical and logical flaws in extrapolation techniques.[51] We also know that popular Chinese novels such as *Rulin waishi* (The Scholars) are filled with glaring examples of faulty divinations by fate calculators and even outright admissions of fraud.[52] And a statistical study by Wolfram Eberhard of over 3,700 married couples from the Rong clan of Guangdong province in the period from 1600 to 1899 suggests that the members of this illustrious clan, at least, "did not let themselves be influenced by the auspicious and inauspicious combinations of signs in their selection of marriage partners."[53]

But scholarly criticisms seem to have had little impact on most traditional Chinese households; and the negative image of fortune-tellers projected in novels such as *Rulin waishi* should not obscure the fact that in these "realistic" works diviners are continually consulted by rich and poor alike to match horoscopes and choose auspicious days for all important events. It is true that Zeng Guofan, a mainstay of the late Qing social and intellectual establishment, generally scoffed at "eight-character" lore; yet when his eldest son finally had a child at the age of thirty-three, Zeng wrote that in the child's *bazi*, "fire and water are lacking among the [five] elements and I do not know whether he can live long or not." When the child died later in the year, Zeng sadly acknowledged the accuracy of his prediction, commenting that such things were "entirely in Heaven's control." The only thing to be done, he said, was to "receive fate calmly and obey it quietly."[54]

Furthermore, Eberhard's conclusions are unconvincing. In the first place, he does not seem to be aware that there were at least two major systems of measuring marital compatibility and incompatibility in Qing times. Secondly, he takes only the year of birth into account, assuming, at least implicitly, that the Xuzhong method of fate extrapolation, with its emphasis on the year, was more pervasive than the Ziping method, with its stress on the day of birth. This assumption is not, I believe, warranted for the Qing period. By ignoring *yinyang/wuxing* configurations and variables relating to time and place, Professor Eberhard oversimplifies the very complex process by which families contemplating marriage negotiated the future of their children.[55] It is true, of course, that a diviner always had the power to manipulate a horoscopic reading (or any other revelation) to suit the various interests involved (including his own). In fact, it was not unknown for families to deceive fortune-tellers regarding the "eight characters" of a son or daughter.[56] But malpractices of this sort do not mean that *bazi* divinations were not taken seriously; and even in those cases where the matching of horoscopes was highly ritualized, the rituals remained important.[57]

Testimony from local gazetteers in the Qing period indicates that practices such as fate-extrapolation, day selection, and the exchange of the eight characters remained extremely prevalent throughout the Chinese empire, from Chuxiong district in remote Yunnan province to Liaoyang, in Manchuria (Liaoning).[58] And even in areas of China where traditional rituals such as "capping" had fallen into disuse, the exchange of horoscopic information continued unabated.[59] Foreign observers, like the authors of local gazetteers, often commented on the importance of choosing auspicious times for various activities, and the need for exchanging horoscopic information in Qing dynasty China. John Nevius, for example, refers to "the universal practice" of comparing horoscopes in the course of negotiating marriage contracts. In the same vein, Justus Doolittle writes: "Whether certain parties may or not be engaged in marriage is always submitted to some fortune-teller." Numerous other Western writers corroborate this testimony.[60] So pervasive was the Chinese preoccupation with the selection of auspicious days that we find instances when a lucky day was chosen for a divination![61]

The Shape of the Future

An enduring fascination with numerical correlations and cosmological calculations did not deter the Chinese from observing tangible objects closely for possible clues to the future. Indeed, as we have seen in the case of geomancy, certain shapes represented cosmic correspondences. For this reason, among others, the divinatory analysis of forms—both natural and man-made—attracted considerable attention in late imperial China.

Since many Chinese considered the human body to be a microcosm of nature, it is hardly surprising that physiognomy (*xiangren, kanxiang, fengjian,* etc.) offered unique insights into the fate of individuals. Although gazetteer biographies of diviners in the Qing period mention expertise in the *Yijing,* geomancy, astrology, numerology, and fate extrapolation far more often than other techniques of fate calculation, nineteenth century Western accounts testify to the popularity of physiognomy and related practices, particularly among the Chinese elite. John Gray writes, for instance, "it is surprising to find what a number of respectable and influential men throughout the empire resort to the professors of the art."[62] A great many Qing civil and military officials relied on physiognomers for advice (see next section), and among those who actually practiced the art were such notables as Zeng Guofan, Shen Baozhen (1820–1879), Li Wentian (1834–1895) and Zhao Shuqiao (d. 1900).[63]

The Shenxiang quanbian (Complete Guide to Spiritual Observation [and Analysis]) was to physiognomy what the Sanming tonghui was to fate extrapolation. Compiled in the Ming dynasty by Yuan Zhongzhe, a practicing physiognomer, it was reprinted in the Tushu jicheng (although not the Siku quanshu) and it remains to this day the single most important Chinese reference work for "body divination." Like the Sanming tonghui, Yuan's book is a composite work—comprehensive, but neither systematic nor particularly coherent. It, too, contains a cosmological overview, devoting, however, more explicit attention than the Sanming tonghui to the eight trigrams, and to matters of "spirit" (shen), "life force" (qi), and "form" (xing). In many respects it looks and reads like an enormous fengshui manual, a "geomancy of the person," so to speak.[64]

Like works from the Jiangxi "School of Forms," the Shenxiang quanbian reflects an obsession with classification. It identifies several dozen different body types, and all manner of individual parts—nearly forty kinds of eyes, thirty kinds of eyebrows, twenty-four kinds of noses, and so on. The "logic of interpretation" involves standard numerical categories, cosmological correlations, and a wide range of colorful metaphors that find expression not only in other realms of Chinese divination, but also in traditional Chinese medicine. The emphasis in all such realms is, of course, on balance and harmony.[65]

Generally speaking, the Chinese believed that large features were signs of good fortune. They thus spoke approvingly of the "six bigs" (liuda), referring to the head, eyes, nose, mouth, ears and stomach. But features that were ordinarily considered favorable might be offset by others that were less auspicious. Thus, for example, a big head that lacked protruding bones on each side of the forehead would invite poverty, as would eyes that were big but dull, a nose that was big but flat at the bridge, a mouth that was big but had drooping corners, ears that were large but ill-defined, and a stomach that was large but did not hang downward.[66] Popular proverbs suggest, moreover, that big was not always better: "He whose steps sound like a drumbeat will have a life of bitterness." "A large person is sure to be stupid; and if not stupid, then treacherous." And again: "To be big and not stupid is truly rare."[67]

The Shenxiang quanbian evaluates bodies in terms of both wuxing correlations (including the "Five Constant Virtues") and animal categories. Classified by "agents," individuals are either relatively "pure" or a combination of two primary qualities. In general, a pure "metal" person, standing straight and "square," represents right behavior and the quality of endurance. A "wood" person, who is tall and thin, with sturdy bones, symbolizes humaneness and prosperity. A "water" person, with a heavy, round appearance, reflects knowledge and wisdom. A "fire" person, who appears broad at the bottom and "sharp" at the top, represents propriety, courage, and adaptability. And an "earth" person, thick, straight, and heavy, symbolizes faithfulness and reliability.[68]

In accordance with the principle of mutual production, a "metal" person with some earth qualities will be successful and content, since earth produces metal; similarly, a "wood" person with some water will enjoy wealth and honor; a "water" person with some metal is destined for fame and fortune; a "fire" person with some wood will succeed early in life. An "earth" person with some fire will attain spiritual fulfillment. But from the standpoint of mutual conquest, a "metal" person, with some fire will have difficulties as a youth, since fire conquers metal; a "wood" person with some metal will suffer throughout life; a "water" person with some earth is destined for poverty and illness; a "fire" person with some water will lose portions of both wealth and family; and an "earth" person with some wood will either die prematurely or suffer loneliness.[69]

It would be tedious to ennumerate the fifty or so "animal" types that appear in the *Shenxiang quanbian*, but a brief discussion of those representing the twelve animals of the Chinese zodiac may shed further light on how cultural stereotypes, derived from many different sources, including divination, overlapped and interacted to create social profiles for individuals in traditional China. Each entry contains a general description of the facial and body characteristics of the animal/person, followed by a simple, four-line poem designed to serve as a mnemonic device. Not surprisingly, a dragon appearance indicates great things: power, resourcefulness, and high rank—perhaps as a minister of state. The look of a tiger suggests intelligence, ambition, and the position of a general. A monkey, intelligent and ingenious, but also inconsistent, can look forward to a lower-ranking military career. The ox, quiet and modest, will probably encounter wealth and happiness. Snake-like people can expect difficulties because they are cruel and unpredictable; horses, a better life, since they are worthy of respect. Pigs are foolish and self-absorbed; dogs, loyal; rats, comfortable (well-fed), and chickens, at least trustworthy. A sheep might aspire to a middling official position, but could also anticipate marital difficulties. A rabbit would probably attain a higher rank than the sheep, and enjoy a more satisfactory marriage.[70]

Chinese physiognomers in Qing times, as today, believed that the face revealed the most about a person. Generally speaking, a face that was full, straight, smooth and lustrous was best; a crooked, gloomy or pointed one, far less desireable. In the *Shenxiang quanbian*, facial features are categorized in several different ways. One of the simplest classification schemes divides the face into "six storehouses, three powers, and three stops." The three powers, symbolizing Heaven, Earth, and Man, are represented by the forehead, nose, and chin, respectively. The "stops," as illustrated in Figure 5.3, mark specific vertical sections of these three parts of the face. The "storehouses," referring symbolically to the five "agents," plus grain, can be seen in three pairs: on both sides of the forehead, on the upper cheeks, and on the lower cheeks. Qing physiognomers believed that the shape of each area, and its relative size, revealed something significant about the client. A round and smooth (and therefore heavenly)

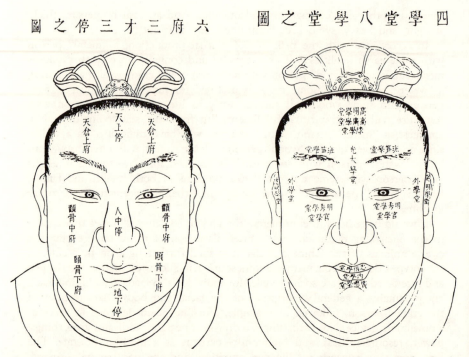

圖 之 停 三 才 三 府 六   圖 之 堂 學 八 堂 學 四

Figure 5.3 *Left:* "The Six Storehouses, Three Powers, and Three Stops." *Right:* Study halls. *Source:* Jiang Tingxi, ed., *Qinding gujin tushu jicheng* (Taibei, 1977 reprint), 47: 6657 and 6549.

forehead, for example, was viewed as a sign of honor, just as a broad and square "earthly" chin signified wealth. A long upper "stop" was preferable to a long middle stop, but both were more desireable than a long lower "stop."[71]

Another system of classification in the *Shenxiang quanbian* divides the face into two groups of "study halls" (*xuetang*), one of four and one of eight. As Figure 5.3 reveals, the four consist of: a "hall of emolument" on the forehead (the lowest of the three sets of horizontally printed characters); an "inner hall" depicted on the lower lip (but referring to the two upper front teeth); and a pair of "outer halls"—one for each temple. The eight halls correspond respectively to the top two areas of the forehead (the "high and bright" and "high and broad" halls, each marked by horizontally printed characters); the area above the bridge of the nose (the "glorious and great" hall); each ear (the "intelligence" halls), with the area under each eye (the "bright and refined" halls); with the top lip (the "loyalty and faithfulness" hall—again, indicating teeth); and with the area beneath the lower lip (the "broad virtue" hall). Handsome features naturally augured well for the realm in question.[72]

The "five planets, six luminaries, five mountains and four rivers" represent an approach to facial classification that not only overlapped with the "study halls," but also resonated powerfully with the topographical and astrological

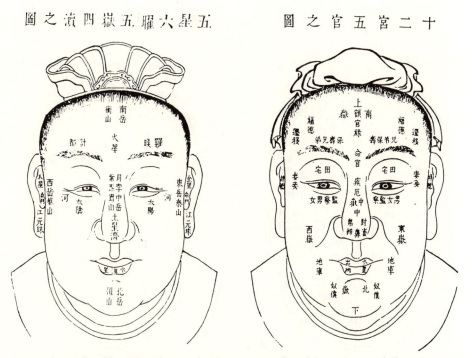

Figure 5.4 *Left:* "The Five Planets, Six Luminaries, Five Mountains, and Four Rivers." *Right:* "The Twelve Palaces and Five Officials." *Source:* Jiang Tingxi, ed., *Qinding gujin tushu jicheng* (Taibei, 1977 reprint), 47: 6547 and 6556.

symbolism of geomancy, including *fenye* (see chapters 2 and 4). The *Shenxiang quanbian* does not explore systematically the cosmological relationship between one's facial features, celestial bodies, and China's great mountain and river systems; but it does correlate the compass points associated with the "five sacred mountains" with regions of the face, and it links the Yangzi, Ji, Wei and Yellow Rivers with the ears, nose, eyes, and mouth, respectively.[73] At the same time it ascribes to each area of the face a certain relevance to particular preoccupations such as wealth, rank, honor, and longevity. Thus, for example, the "Earth Star," Jupiter, located on the end of the nose, pertains to one's lifespan, while the "Purple Luminary," Ziqi, on the upper part of the nose, has relevance to official position (see Fig. 5.4).[74]

The "twelve palaces and five officials" represent yet another overlapping system of metaphorical interpretation. The latter term, *wuguan*, refers to the five basic senses—sight, smell, sound, taste and touch—although not all Chinese sources agree on the part of the body responsible for "feeling." (Some authorities point to the tongue, others to the eyebrows, still others to the heart/mind.) The twelve palaces (*gong*) of the face do not correspond directly to the "palaces" of Chinese astrology, although they strongly suggest implicit parallels. Like the "five planets and six luminaries" they provide indications regarding the prospects

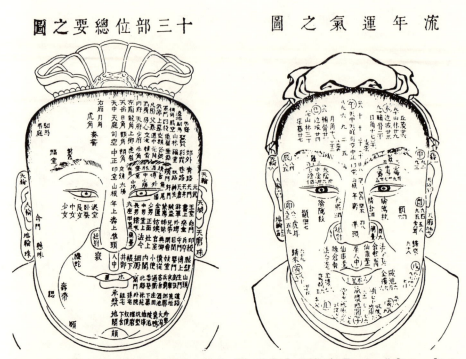

Figure 5.5 *Left*: "The Thirteen Parts of the Face." *Right*: "Yearly Fortune." *Source*: Jiang Tingxi, ed., *Qinding gujin tushu jicheng* (Taibei, 1977 reprint), 47: 6545 and 6556.

for health, wealth, property and status; but in addition they apply to more specific realms of domestic life, including the well-being of parents, siblings, wives and children (see Fig. 5.4).[75]

Two other classification schemes deserve brief mention. One divides the face into "thirteen parts," each of which, in turn, has about a dozen subdivisions. This system may be viewed as an elaboration of the themes and concerns discussed above, with each subdivision pertaining to an ever more narrowly defined realm of human activity. The other system, of "yearly fortune" (*liunian yunqi*), comes closest to providing a "facial horoscope" analogous to the charts of fate extrapolators. It groups various phases of life up to the age of ninety-nine under the twelve earthly branches, beginning in the general region of *shen*, near the top of the left ear, and ending at *xu*, on the left cheek. According to the *Shenxiang quanbian*, if all the parts of one's face are well formed, a person can expect good luck at each juncture of life; but wherever a deformity exists, trouble will strike (see Fig. 5.5).[76]

As the face is the most important single feature of the body, so the eyes are the most important single feature of the face. Symbolically they represent the sun and the moon, the father and the mother (left and right respectively), and the key to one's inner spirit. From the standpoint of *wuxing* correlations, the eyes (identified with wood) reveal the heart (correlated with fire), just as wood "produces" fire. Long, deep and bright eyes signify great honor; narrow, delicate and deep eyes, longevity; eyes "like dots of black varnish" reflect intelligence; short and small eyes, stupidity; more white than black, a hard life. Round and protruding eyes are considered a sign of early demise; prominent, protruding and watery eyes, the mark of debauchery and lawlessness. Red eyeballs suggest evil; triangular (pyramid-shaped) eyes, cruelty.[77]

Like bodies, most eyes are classified in the *Shenxiang quanbian* according to animal types—in this case, about thirty-five in all. Again taking certain members of the Chinese zodiac as representatives, we find that dragon eyes, large and clear, signify wealth, honor and talent. Tiger eyes, large, with golden irises, also suggest wealth and honor—although they indicate that those who possess them face the possibility of harm to their children later in life. Monkey eyes, spirited with black irises, signify wealth and honor, with some difficulties (and a persistent craving for fruit!). Snake eyes, round and red, portend treachery and an unhappy family life. Horse eyes, spiritless and triangular, signify a toilsome existence. Pig eyes, blurred and watery, promise hardship and trouble. Sheep eyes, blackish-yellow and cloudy, suggest poverty later in life.[78]

The *Shenxiang quanbian* devotes an enormous amount of space to other facial features, including the hair, forehead, nose, ears, mouth, teeth, lips, and tongue. All such features are minutely categorized by shape and sometimes by size, each type forecasting certain features of personality and/or fortune. The *Shenxiang quanbian* also analyzes at length distinctive features such as bumps on the back of the head (known as "pillow bones"), lines on the face, and moles. For the most part, moles were a sign of bad luck. In the words of an ancient proverb: "The head has no bad bones; the face has no good moles." As the accompanying illustrations indicate, moles on the face had specific designations. Figure 5.6 identifies generally auspicious and inauspicious moles; Figure 5.7 illustrates the particular significance of moles for men and women respectively.[79]

Like doctors, physiognomers paid close attention to complexion (*qise*). According to the *Shenxiang quanbian*, facial colors not only indicated different kinds of personalities; they also suggested certain kinds of fate. Skin that was tinged with red, yellow or purple (a category related to red in one extension of *wuxing* correlative thought, and yellow in another) came to be considered auspicious, while white, green, black or deep red skin was viewed as inauspicious.[80] In traditional Chinese medicine, a healthy face, like a "lucky" face to physiognomers, was slightly shiny and moist, but to doctors distinctive colors were usually signs of health problems. A green complexion, for example, indicated the stagnation of one's *qi*, and a yellow skin implied a weakened spleen and excessive dampness. A red complexion suggested excessive heat, while a white complexion indicated deficiencies of blood and *qi*. Black facial color was a sign of weakened kidneys.[81]

It would be surprising if physiognomers ignored the medical implications of a person's complexion and other external features as some Western commentators have asserted.[82] In the first place, works such as the *Shenxiang quanbian* specifically encouraged an awareness of the connection. Furthermore, a large

圖之凶吉痣面

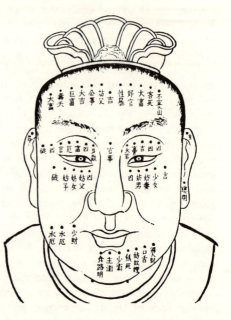

Figure 5.6 "Auspicious and Inauspicious Facial Moles." *Source:* Jiang Tingxi, ed., *Qinding gujin tushu jicheng* (Taibei, 1977 reprint), 47: 6641.

number of fortune-tellers, including physiognomers, were also practicing physicians. At least fifteen percent of the 1200 or so biographies I have examined for the Qing period refer to individuals who were doctor/diviners—or who at least knew both medicine and divination (*yibu*).[83] And even among those physiognomers who did not claim a specific medical expertise, most probably had at least a passing acquaintance with traditional Chinese medicine. A Qianlong period gazetteer from Shandong explicitly links medicine and divination as arts of prognostication that "understand *yin* and *yang*, investigate *li* and *qi*, know the way of transformation [*bianhua*] and have efficacy in everyday affairs."[84]

The four standard categories of Chinese medical examination—visual inspection, hearing and smelling, questioning the patient, and touching the body—correspond closely to the approach of most physiognomers. In their observation of external signs, both doctors and physiognomers focused on a client's facial expression, posture, speech, responsiveness, and clarity of eyes and thought. They also took note of unusual sounds and secretions.[85] If a person had an "unlucky" coloration by the standards of physiognomy, but was nonetheless bright and alert, with moist skin, the diviner's verdict, like the doctor's, might be that the individual in question was on the verge of good fortune. Conversely, a person with a "lucky" face who nonetheless exhibited signs of a serious illness might be judged unfortunate.[86]

Of course the *Shenxiang quanbian* has a more explicitly divinatory emphasis than most of the medical treatises reprinted in the *Tushu jicheng* or *Siku*

圖 之 痣 面 人 女 　　　　　 圖 之 痣 面 子 男

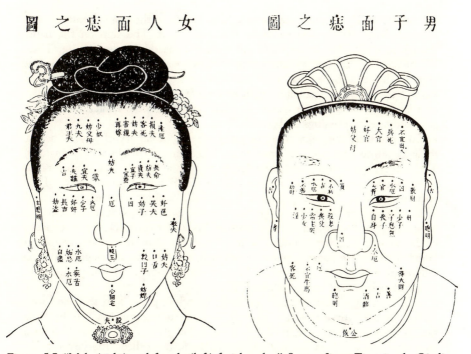

Figure 5.7 "Male (right) and female (left) facial moles." *Source:* Jiang Tingxi, ed., *Qinding gujin tushu jicheng* (Taibei, 1977 reprint) 47: 6641 and 6642.

quanshu. But a tract entitled *Taisu mofa* (Elementary Pulse-Reading Methods), reviewed at length in the *Siku quanshu zongmu*, demonstrates that this universally applied "medical" technique could also be used to determine good or bad fortune, high or low status, blessings or calamities.[87] And even such standard medical references as the *Huangdi neijing taisu* (Elementary Aspects of the Yellow Emperor's Inner Classic) link health not simply with physiology, state of mind, and temperament, but also with cosmic variables, including atmospheric conditions, the time of year or day, stellar influences, locality and evil spirits.[88] Virtually all of the best-known medical authors of the Ming and Qing periods, including Xu Dachun (1693–1771) and Sun Derun (fl. 1826), acknowledged the pathogenic influence of "demons," and many physicians, like most diviners, prescribed charms as remedies.[89]

Hand-reading (*zhangxiang* or *shouxiang*), which followed closely the principles of face-reading, proved more generally significant to physiognomers than to doctors.[90] Normally, men had their left (*yang*) hand read; women, their right (*yin*). Variables in hand-reading included shape, size, color, firmness, bumps, and lines. For men, at least, large was better than small; long was better than short; thick, better than thin. Ideally, the skin should be glossy and mottled red. "The inside of the hands," we discover, "should be like cinnabar, with the sheen of water and as warm as fire. The back of the hand should resemble the curved back of a prostrate tortoise. The center of the palm should be deep [depressed] so that an egg could be contained in it. The skin on the hands should be slack, the sinews thick but hidden beneath the flesh. [. . . These all] indicate a rich and noble person."[91] The relationship of the hands and arms to the rest of the body also held significance. Hands that did not extend beyond the waist, for example, indicated a life of poverty—as did possession of a large body with small hands. A small body and large hands, by contrast, gave promise of blessings and wealth.[92]

Like the face, the palm could be categorized in a variety of ways. One was to divide it into eight main sectors surrounding a central "Bright Hall" (*mingtang*). These areas were designated by trigram names, although their configuration (as shown in Fig. 5.8) below reflects neither the Former Heaven nor the Later Heaven sequence. Subsections went by colorful designations such as "the eye of Confucius," or by terms designating family relationships, such as "wife and concubine," or "elder and younger brother." Another approach was to conceive of the palm as a square bounded by four trigrams: Qian, Kun, Gen, and Zhen. Hand shapes were sometimes correlated with the *wuxing*, although the forms differed from those of geomancy.[93] Within either framework, bumps and lines could then be "read" and evaluated.

The most significant "bumps" (*roufeng*; lit. "flesh-peaks") on the hand were known as the "three wonders" (*sanqi*). They rested at the base of the three middle fingers, on the outer edges of the palm. According to the *Shenxiang quanbian*, the bump at the root of the index finger, called "the virtue peak" and correlated with the trigram Kun, represented wealth. It also governed the first twenty-five years of one's life. The middle bump, called the "emolument peak" and correlated with the trigram Sun, represented official position. It governed the second twenty-five years. The third bump, called the "blessings peak" and correlated with the trigram Li, represented longevity and governed the third twenty-five years of one's life.[94] Clearly a complete reading of a client's fate required reconciliation of indications expressed in one part of the body with those expressed in other parts.

Lines had a special importance in Chinese palm-reading, as they did in many other chiromantic traditions. In the words of the *Shenxiang quanbian*, they reflected human quality "like the patterns [of grain that reveal quality] in wood." The most prominent lines on the palm were called the "three powers." The top one, correlated with Heaven, the sovereign, and the fire element, determined status; the lowest, correlated with Earth, the minister, and the earth element, determined wealth. The middle one, correlated with Man and the sage but having no specified element, determined longevity. The depth (*shen*), length (*chang*) and refinement (*xi*) of these and other lines held great meaning to the Chinese, as did their relationship to points of reference, such as trigrams. Also of significance were lines that took the shape of physical objects or written characters. For example, the character for "well" (*jing*), or "seal" (*yin*) on the part of the palm designated by the trigram Sun indicated protection against loss of money. Similarly, the character for "ten" (*shi*) on the "virtue peak" portended assistance from someone who is wealthy.[95]

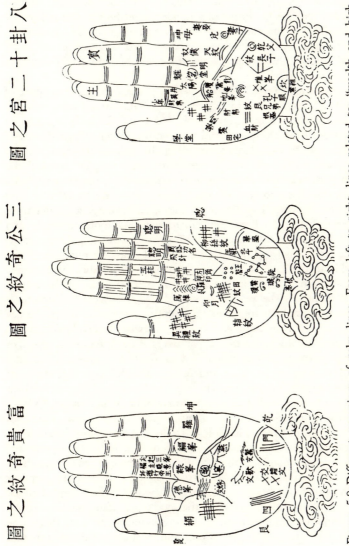

Figure 5.8 Different groupings of palm lines. From left to right, lines related to: "wealth and high position," lines signifying the "three dukes," and lines defined in terms of the "eight trigrams and twelve palaces." Naturally, the meaning of many lines derived not only from their position in the palm but also from the written characters they seemed to resemble. Source: Jiang Tingxi, ed., *Qinding gujin tushu jicheng* (Taibei, 1977 reprint), 47: 6619.

According to some physiognomic analysts, the four fingers and the thumb represented the five "agents," which have to be properly balanced. The thumb, as "the foundation of life," should be straight rather than crooked, and longer than the little finger—just as the dragon is superior to the tiger. The same metaphoric logic dictates that the middle finger, "ruler of the hand," should be longer than the palm. On the whole, slender, long fingers, conical at the tips, indicate intelligence and moral rectitude; short fingers with thick ends, the reverse. Large gaps between the fingers at the base denote misfortune. Long and slender nails suggest intelligence, while thick and hard nails give evidence of longevity.[96]

The fingers could also reveal fate by means of their joints, in a form of *liuren* calculation called *dashi* (lit., "hitting the time"). This activity was reportedly "much in vogue among the common people" in Qing China because of its simplicity and straightforwardness. It did not require either a high degree of literacy or a third party. Calculations regarding the month, day and hour of an event were made on the six main joints of the three middle fingers of the left hand. Each joint represented a general prognostication, usually elaborated upon in popular almanacs, in the following order: (1) "great security" (*daan*) on the index finger, below (2) "patience" (*liulian*); (3) "prompt joy" (*shuxi*) on the middle finger, below (4) "red mouth" (*chikou*, signifying quarrels and disappointment); and (5) "a little luck" (*xiaoji*) on the remaining finger, below (6) "loss and death" (*kongwang*). By adding in succession the numbers of the month, day and hour of a given occurence, a person could predict the outcome. If, for example, a woman fell ill at the second hour (1–3 A.M.), of the second day, of the first month of the year, and wanted to know what the prognosis might be, she would simply count joints representing the month (one), the day (two), and the hour (two), arriving at *xiaoji*, a somewhat favorable reading.[97]

The *Shenxiang quanbian* devotes comparatively little attention to parts of the body other than the head and hands. It does, however, give some attention to the neck, chest, belly, waist, back and feet. It also explores differences in the physiognomy of men, women and children, and discusses matters such as bone structure, the human voice and various kinds of body movements.[98] Other physiognomic works included in the *Tushu jicheng* amplify the picture in important ways. The *Xiang'er jing* (Classic of Evaluating Children), for instance, indicates the life and death significance of different sounds and movements made by newborns and infants.[99] Significantly, most physiognomic manuals of the late imperial era evaluate only those parts of the body that would normally be visible to the public, in contrast to pre-Song works, which tended to be far more explicit about other parts of the body, including sexual organs. Stereotypes of feminine beauty in the *Shenxiang quanbian* such as the "Nine Good Points of Women," also reflect Song and post-Song values—although several sections of the work clearly date from an earlier era.[100]

Standards of male and female attractiveness seem to have been remarkably uniform and persistent throughout the Qing period: Proverbially, the ideal for men was: "clear eyebrows, refined eyes; a square face and large ears; a straight nose and broad mouth; a face that looks as if it had been powdered; and lips that seem to have been rubbed with vermillion." For women: "eyebrows like the leaf of a willow; eyes like the pit of an apricot; a mouth like a cherry; a face shaped like a melon seed; a waist like the poplar and the willow."[101] According to the *Shenxiang quanbian*, the "Nine Good Points of Women" consisted of: (1) a round head and flat forehead, (2) delicate bones and smooth skin, (3) red lips and white teeth, (4) long eyes and refined eyebrows, (5) pointed fingers, with thick palms and delicate lines that look "like tangled threads of silk," (6) a voice "as clear as water," (7) a smile that does not reveal the teeth, (8) grace and dignity both in movement and at rest, and (9) a "delicate and moist" appearance.[102]

John Gray, writing in the 1870s, provides several guidelines for physiognomic prognostications that correspond closely to the stipulations of the *Shenxiang quanbian*. A high forehead, he tells us, with "eyebrows thin and of equal length, large and thick ears, the upper parts of which extend above the eyebrows, a large mouth in the male and a small one in the female, a large chin, a high and firm nose, high cheek bones . . . are regarded as most favorable indications." For men, "a silky beard, a dark moustache with a tendency to curl upward, a large neck, a powerful voice, and eyes long and angular, and with much expression," are also desireable. He goes on to say that a "thick hand with a soft red palm without wrinkles is a sign of much good fortune, and [when] . . . the fingers fit closely together, it is regarded as an indication of a happy and prosperous life."[103]

A person whose forehead is "singularly low," however, is "likely to suffer punishment from the magistrate, and is invariably advised to . . . become a monk and seek the retirement of a cloister." If his eyebrows are thick, he "is told that he can never attain to celebrity, but must remain in a subordinate position all the days of his life." To be without high cheek bones "is to be born without character, and to be shut out from the hope of attaining any position of trust or honor." The wife of a thin-necked man "will die shortly after marriage," and a woman with a large mouth "has a life of shame predicted for her." A man with an effeminate voice will be "the slave of vicious practices, who cannot attain to a good old age." One whose ears are neither large nor thick is told that "he will die at an age varying from fifty to sixty years, and that, should he continue to attain a good old age, he will die in a state of destitution."[104]

The social importance of impressive features in Qing China can scarcely be underestimated. In the first place, physiognomic stereotypes unquestionably influenced the way people responded to one another, as did regional stereotypes. These physical stereotypes were reinforced not only in popular proverbs, but also in folktales, novels, and the persistent banter of fortune-tellers (see next section).[105] Comprehensive almanacs depicted different types of faces, as did public displays that advertised, "with painted representations of the human countenance," the special skills of professional physiognomers. People walking the streets constantly encountered graphic depictions of faces representing the best and the worst of Chinese character types: the wise and the stupid, the fortunate and the unfortunate, the powerful and the weak, the affluent and the poor, the upright and the degenerate.[106]

Facial stereotypes could even affect a man's bureaucratic career. If, for example, a middle degree holder repeatedly failed the next highest examination (for the *jinshi* degree), he could still enter official life at a comparatively high level if he possessed what was considered to be "the right kind of face." There are numerous stories in the *Qingbai leichao* of physiognomers who passed judgment on the examination prospects of aspiring scholars (including their own classmates), as well as tales of official examiners who evaluated the facial features of candidates along with their essays. One such examiner, well known for his ability to judge talent and morality in this fashion, was the scholar-calligrapher and Grand Secretary Ji Huang, who received his *jinshi* degree in 1730.[107] Criticisms of physiognomic evaluations were never in short supply, but the practice continued unabated.[108]

Virtually anything about a person could be forecast by reference to various parts of the head, face, body, hands, and feet, from personality traits to lifespan; from marriage prospects to the number of children a couple might have. No concern was so trivial as to lack some sort of bodily manifestation.[109] One physiognomer, Fan Lai, author of a well-known book on divination prefaced by Huang Zongxi, even claimed to be able to predict the fate of temples by reading the faces of the gods contained therein.[110] Specific techniques employed by physiognomers varied enormously, however, since there were over seventy distinct analytical traditions recognized in the Qing period and innumerable points of reference on the body. All sighted physiognomers relied heavily on direct observation, but some also employed the techniques of blind fortune-tellers (see next section), who touched the faces and hands of clients, felt their bones (*chuai'gu*), and listened to their voices (*tingsheng*). Presumably a number also felt the pulse (*zhenmo*) in the manner of physicians. Rigid and long-standing notions of Confucian propriety limited male-female contact in traditional China, however. For this reason, male physiognomers generally used different techniques to "read" men and women, and blind exponents of the art seem to have relied almost entirely on sounds in dealing with members of the opposite sex.[111]

The *fangji* sections of local gazetteers provide numerous examples of the way different physiognomers approached their art. Some emphasized purely external features. Li Xuan, a colonel in the Green Standard army, required only one look at a person to decide his or her fate. Li Liuming, apparently a professional, told fortunes with remarkable accuracy based solely on a client's complexion. Liu Lu, a scholar, used both "appearance and speech" (*rongmao yanyu*) to determine whether a person would be rich or poor, lucky or unlucky, long-lived or not. Qu Fuhou, for his part, felt bones (*mogu*) and gauged proportions (*chidu*) to judge a person's fate. Yang Pang had a more complex method. He "examined the complexion to determine financial prospects, bone structure to determine lifespan, sounds to determine status, and movements to determine birth and death." In Yang's view, physiognomy was not simply a matter of evaluating the "five officials and six storehouses," but also of "spiritual communication." According to the gazetteer of Dantu county (Jiangsu province), he was "invariably successful [in his prognostications]" (*wan wu yi shi*).[112]

Many other physiognomers also emphasized the "spiritual" side of their enterprise. Teng Yunlong, a professional fortune-teller who once served as an adviser to the leader of the Taiping movement, Hong Xiuquan (1813–1864), claimed that in physiognomy, "analyzing shapes is not as good as evaluating the mind/heart." In Teng's view, a "bad face" would not necessarily bring harm to a superior man, while a "good face" could not redeem a petty man.[113] Liao Chunshan, an examination failure, compiled a book in the early 1860s entitled *Xingshen xiangfa* (Methods of Evaluating Shape and Spirit) which argued that physiognomy required attention to the inner spirit as well as the outer form of a person.[114] Armed with such information, physiognomers could make very specific predictions. For instance, Jin Daoren, reportedly "invariably successful" as a prognosticator in the fashion of Yang Pang, laid out in detail the timetable of a client's examination career, from his initial failure, to physical changes in his hair and body that were to be regarded as omens, to his eventual success.[115]

Related to physiognomy in its emphasis on the interpretation of forms, not to mention spirituality, was the art of "fathoming" or "dissecting" written characters (*cezi; chaizi*). The ideographic nature of the Chinese script made it eminently well suited to this sort of "word analysis" (*xiangzi*), which could be used either by itself or together with other methods of fate calculation.[116] Written characters can be classified according to four basic types: (1) representations of objects (*xiangxing*); (2) indicative words, whose forms suggest meaning (*zhishi*); (3) grouped elements that indicate meaning through the relationship of two or more represented objects (*huiyi*); and (4) semantic and phonetic combinations (*xingsheng*). Of these four types, Qing word analysts prized *huiyi* above all.[117]

The vast majority of Chinese characters (about ninety percent) are semantic and phonetic combinations, sometimes called phonograms. Each has a semantic indicator, or "radical," and a phonetic component that provides clues as to how the character is probably pronounced. The radical, one of 214 possibilities, suggests the general class or category of phenomena to which the character belongs. These categories include animals (humans and other mammals, reptiles, birds, fish and mythical beasts), parts of animals, minerals, natural phenomena and physical formations, structures, utensils, descriptives (colors, shapes, smells, and so on), and actions. Because phonetic components can usually stand alone as individual characters, each with its own set of meanings, most phonograms can be broken down into at least two semantically significant units; and many can be "dissected" into three, four or more constituent parts. By the same token, simple characters can be amplified—either by the addition of individual strokes, new radicals, or new phonetic components—to form new words. The great number of similar sounds in any given dialect, and the visual similarities between many different characters, make the Chinese written language an especially congenial medium for both puns and visual plays on words.

From earliest times, Chinese characters possessed a magical, mystical aura, derived in part from their sacred use in Shang dynasty oracles and as inscriptions on bronze sacrificial vessels. Written prayers were generally considered more efficacious than spoken prayers, just as written charms were more powerful than mere incantations. Calligraphy, whether in the form of elegant scrolls, auspicious inscriptions, or protective charms, adorned every home in traditional

China, and word games were always a favorite social diversion of the literati. During the Qing period, an official could be degraded for miswriting a single character in a memorial to the throne, and so venerated was the ancient script that anything with writing on it was not simply to be thrown away, but rather to be ritually burned on special altars known as "pagodas for cherishing the written word" (*xizi ta*).[118]

Written characters had, then, a special "spirit"—a life and power of their own.[119] They were, in a very real sense, the things they represented, and like trigrams and hexagrams, they could not only reveal the future but actually cause things to happen. The great Qing scholar Ji Yun (1724–1805) described the "omens" of word analysis as developing from the same sort of "spiritual communication" as the selection of milfoil stalks or the cracking of turtle shells.[120] In Qing popular culture, charms often took the form of written "orders" from superior deities to lesser ones, and many Chinese believed that a piece of paper with the character "to kill" on it, or one that bore the word for a disease, a destructive animal, or an evil spirit, could actually harm other people. Written words could even remedy deficiencies in one's natural endowment of the *wuxing*. No more vivid illustration can be found than the common practice of giving children names that compensated for the perceived shortage of one or more "agents" at birth.[121] If, for example, the horoscopic "eight characters" of a child indicated a shortage of wood, a given name might be chosen for him or her that had one or more wood components (*mu*). The most extreme case I have seen is the diviner Lin Sen, whose surname consists of two wood elements, and his given name of three.[122]

The *Tushu jicheng* contains a section devoted to word analysis based on pre-Qing works such as the *Chaizi shu* (Fate Through the Dissection of Characters), and the *Xinding zhi mingxin fa* (New Edition of Methods for Pointing to a Clear Heart/Mind). These materials describe, often in verse or song, techniques for evaluating characters based not only on their structure, but also on a surprisingly wide range of cosmological correlations, including yin and yang, the *wuxing*, stems and branches, trigrams and hexagrams, the *nayin* system, and so forth. They even devote attention to styles of calligraphy and their relationship to what Westerners term "graphology"—that is, the link between handwriting and personality. But while Chinese calligraphy could never be detached entirely from the character and style of the writer, handwriting analysis in the Western sense never became an independent divination technique in China.[123]

Works such as Zhou Lianggong's *Zichu* (Handling Characters), written in the mid-seventeenth century, and later compendia, notably the *Cezi mizhi* (Secret Guide to Fathoming Characters), describe at length various types of word analysis.[124] Six of the most common were: (1) adding strokes (*tianbi*), (2) reducing strokes (*jianbi*), (3) extracting components (*zhequ*), (4) connecting opposites (*duiguan*), (5) devising puns (known technically as *xiesheng*, lit. "harmonizing the sounds"), and (6) relating characters having common constituent parts. The first technique enabled the analyst to transform a simple character into a more complex one, such as *mu* ("eye") into *gui* ("honorable"). Subtraction reversed the process, as when *nan* ("difficult") became *xie* ("shoe"). Extraction allowed the diviner to break a complex character down into its constituent parts, and to examine one or more of them, as with the character *yan* ("swallow;" also the area of Beijing), comprised of semantic components meaning "grass," "mouth," "north" and "fire." By "connecting opposites," a word analyst could interpret a character such as *xian* ("in front") as having "life on the top and death on the bottom" (*sheng tou si zu*). Rebus-like puns linked concepts by either the sound or the general shape of a character—and sometimes both, as in the case of "bat" (*fu*) and "blessings" (*fu*). Characters with common constituent parts expanded the scope of analysis to include, among other things, a comparison of radicals—such as that of earth in the word "place" (*di*) and that of water in the word for "pool" (*chi*)—both of which have the component *ye* (which carries the general meaning of "also").[125]

Refinements of these basic techniques allowed virtually limitless scope for creative interpretations. In the hands of skilled practitioners, characters with normally negative meanings, such as "death" (*si*), could yield positive readings when dissected, just as positive terms, such as "flourishing" (*feng*), could be read in a decidedly negative way. Fortune-tellers could also give different clients different breakdowns of the same character, thus producing different interpretations.[126] The logic of word analysis, like that of physiognomy and most other forms of Chinese divination, was inveterately associational, allowing, perhaps even compelling, diviners to link all relevant concepts, cosmological as well as personal, to the client. Thus, for example, the "sun," "fire" and "wood" radicals normally carried male significations, while the "moon" and "water" radicals indicated female qualities. But interpreters still had enormous latitude in investing these symbols with personalized meaning.[127]

Word analysts often used analogies drawn from the literal meaning(s) of a character as well as the meaning(s) of its constituent parts. We may take one illustration from the career of Fan Shixing, a professional fortune-teller from Suzhou who lived during the Qianlong era. When a soldier-client selected one of three possible versions of the character for "chess piece" (*qi*), Fan first discussed the implications of the man's choice (a version that contained the wood radical rather than the stone radical). He then went on to interpret the man's past life and future prospects based primarily on the style of play characterizing the two main kinds of Chinese chess—*xiangqi* ("elephant chess"), in which pieces are subtracted from the board as the game progresses, and *weiqi* ("surrounding chess"), in which pieces are added over time. Fan's basic conclusion was that the man had suffered the loss of a close family member in the past (the *xiangqi* metaphor), and that in the future he would have to proceed gradually and cautiously, a step at a time (the *weiqi* metaphor).[128]

Whether directed toward the reading of an entire life or a discrete event, effective word analysis could not be done by just anyone. It required a quick wit, mastery of the written language (including knowledge of the many associations and levels of meaning attached to any given character), and shrewd psychological insight. A good calligraphic hand was also an advantage. Some diviners reduced the mental pressure on themselves by limiting the number of characters a client could choose. One common device was to carry around a paper lantern on which slips of paper were pasted, each with a character written upon it. For a few cash, the customer tore off a slip and had the character analyzed. Other word analysts carried a box full of characters, which were randomly chosen by clients and similarly evaluated.[129] For such practitioners, handbooks such as the *Chaizi yi* (Ideas of Character Dissection), edited by a "Mr. Liang" in 1801, provided invaluable guidance. This work explains in careful detail how to evaluate each of sixty-four characters, ranging from such simple words as *wei* ("not yet"), *you* ("to have") and *jian* ("to see") to more complex characters such as *long* ("dragon"), *bi* ("azure") and *guan* ("a large fish;" "widower").[130] Literate customers, who wrote their own word choice down, probably demanded more analytical expertise from diviners; but by their conscious decisions, and perhaps by their calligraphy as well, they undoubtedly revealed far more about their state of mind and character than less literate clients. They also generally paid more for a divination session.[131]

A number of word analysts also specialized in the interpretation of actual objects selected by their clients—inkstones, scarves, pipes, and so forth. This technique, sometimes called "borrowing" (*jiajie*), was loosely identified with Shao Yong's "plum blossom" method of divination (see chapter 3). Clients would write down the name of an object, draw it, point to it, or place it before the diviner to be evaluated. Like the choice of a character, the selection of an object for analysis might be psychologically revealing.[132] On the other hand, randomly encountered objects also begged for interpretation. Thus we find that after a scholarly client, Chen Hansheng, encountered a frog on the way to Xing Congyang's divining establishment, known as the Parlor of Premonitions (Xianjue guaguan), he wanted to know the meaning of this particular event. Xing, for his part, likened the frog (*wa*) to the striped toad (*chan*) thought to reside in the moon, and used the phrase "plucking cassia in the toad's palace" (*changong zhegui*) to predict that Chen would be successful in the examinations at the *juren* level.[133] Other interpretations rested primarily on the form or composition of objects.[134]

The heightened attunement of the Chinese to shapes—whether exemplified in the landscape, the body, in writing, or everyday objects—influenced other Chinese divination techniques, from the analysis of "chops" or seals (*yinxiang*) to meteorological divination, known generally as *zhanhou*, discussed briefly in chapter 2.[135] *Zhanhou* techniques, like those of seal interpretation, were not, of course, as obviously "psychological" in orientation as word and object analysis, which involved a degree of conscious or unconscious choice; and they relied to a far greater extent on explicit stem-branch correlations and astrological configurations in the process of making predictions. Furthermore, the category *zhanhou* included a number of non-visual divination methods, such as the analysis of wind sounds (*fengjiao*; lit. "wind corners") as part of its repertoire. Nonetheless, techniques such as "observing the rain" (*xiangyu*), "watching the vapors" (*wangqi* or *houqi*) and "divining on the basis of clouds" (*zhanyun*) required the same kind of careful attention to visual detail required of geomancy, physiognomy, word analysis, and the evaluation of objects. According to works such as Huang Zifa's *Xiangyu shu* (Book on Observing Rain), Tao Luzi's *Yunqi zhanhou* (Divination by Cloud Vapors), and Zhou Lüjing's *Tianwen zhanyan* (Predictions Based on Heavenly Patterns), *zhanhou* exponents took into account not only spiritual, temporal, spatial and directional factors, but also the shapes and colors of phenomena, and even the relationship of meteorological conditions to grass, wood, insects, animals, fish, and minerals.[136]

Style and Substance

Who were the astrologers, numerologists, fate extrapolators, physiognomers, word analysts and meteorological diviners of Qing China, and how did they go about their business day to day? As with geomancers and *Yijing* devotees, the information is at best incomplete. The masses remain nameless and all but voiceless in the historical record. Gazetteer biographies display a distinct bias in favor of diviners who for one reason or another favorably impressed the local elite with their erudition, their morality and/or their public service. Few clerics appear in the individual record, and even fewer women. Most fortune-tellers accorded biographies in gazetteers appear literate, and a great number are members of the local elite. Although the majority of scholars are lower gentry, holders of higher degrees are surprisingly well represented, as a few examples will illustrate. Shi Kui, a Kangxi *jinshi*, proved himself to be an expert practitioner of Ziping divination. Lin Lan, also a Kangxi period scholar, used a wide variety of numerological and meteorological techniques to tell fortunes "as if [he were] a spirit." Qian Tang, a clansman of Qian Daxin and a Qianlong *jinshi*, mastered both milfoil divination and fate extrapolation. Wang Guangxie (1711–1779), a *jinshi* degree holder from the Qianlong era with a military background, was also good at fate calculation. And Ding Shoucun, a Daoguang *jinshi*, excelled at astrology, weather prediction, and numerology.[137]

Apparently a large number of Chinese fortune-tellers were blind—although very few such diviners appear in either gazetteer biographies or in collections of anecdotes such as the *Qingbai leichao*.[138] According to nineteenth century Western accounts, some blind diviners occupied street stalls, but the majority wandered from place to place, often travelling vast distances. They generally marked their presence in a neighborhood by means of a musical instrument or a wooden clapper. "Blind soothsayers are to be met in all parts of the empire," remarked John Gray, a close observer of Chinese customs. "When young they are placed under the care of others of the calling, and commit to memory from their lips several volumes regarding the mysteries of their trade. . . . They are chiefly called into dwelling-houses where the inmates are in perplexity through domestic affliction."[139] According to John Nevius, "blind fortune-tellers may be continually seen in the streets of Ningpo, led by an attendant, and giving notice of their approach by playing lively airs on a kind of guitar of three strings." He writes that they are "great gossips," and that they "become familiarly acquainted by mutual consultations with the neighborhoods in which they carry on their business, and . . . [deliver] their responses [to questions] in ambiguous language. They make their disclosures in a chanting tone, with musical accompaniment on their instruments." Similar accounts exist for other parts of China.[140]

The vast majority of both sighted and unsighted fortune-tellers in urban areas were men. According to some accounts, itinerant blind fortune-tellers catered primarily to women clients—perhaps in part because so many females in traditional China were confined to their homes most of the time. ("Their services," Nevius reports, "may be secured for eighteen or twenty cash—less than two cents.")[141] In the countryside, a number of female fortune-tellers, known generally as *guagu* ("divining women"), served an exclusively female clientele. *Guagu* were one of three classes of "female devotees" (*sangu*)—the other two being Buddhist and Daoist nuns—as distinct from the six classes of so-called "old women" (*liupo*), which included spirit mediums and professional "praying women." Some such women were doubtless literate, but most tended to be "the wives of itinerant tinkers . . . found in villages and hamlets."[142]

Most divinations were public affairs. Although well-to-do clients of fate extrapolators, astrologers and numerologists almost invariably received written horoscopes at some point in the divining process—often the day after an initial consultation with the diviner—those with more modest means (or less education) had their fortunes calculated and told on the spot. In either case, the explanations took place at the diviner's stall, located in front of a temple, in a marketplace, or on the street (Fig. 5.9). Palm and face readings, word analysis and the evaluation of objects likewise generally proceeded in the full gaze of others. Reginald Johnston tells us that "The telling of fortunes takes place, as a rule, in the open air, and within view and hearing of a large body of interested spectators and auditors."[143]

I have not discovered any detailed discussions by either Chinese or Westerners of the banter between fate-calculators, physiognomers or word analysts and their clients in Qing times. It is clear, however, that a great deal of conversation took place, and that a number of diviners were clever talkers and shrewd psychologists.[144] Justus Doolittle remarks that fate calculators and physiognomers, like geomancers and other popular diviners, were all "very fluent in speech, and . . . ever ready to say something on the multifarious points which are submitted to them for examination and decision." Similarly, John Nevius avers that blind fortune-tellers were "particularly skilled in eliciting facts by indirect questions," and that sighted practitioners of Ziping divination were "astute observers of character." He adds that "the circumstances and appearance of the applicant, together with the information derived by subtle questions, have much to do in each case in determining the nature of the response."[145] An anecdote in the *Qingbai leichao* concerning fate extrapolation by means of "River Chart numerology" confirms the accuracy of these observations.[146]

More recent ethnographic evidence, including my own field research in Hong Kong and Taiwan, suggests patterns of diviner-client interaction that probably prevailed throughout the Qing period. In these interactions, fortune-tellers were at pains to tell their clients something meaningful about the past in order to establish credibility concerning the future. The point of their divination was to develop a consistent, logically closed biographical account of the client from

Figure 5.9 A late Qing fortune-teller and his female client (center) form one of a group of "street industries." *Source:* John Thomson, *Through China with a Camera* (Westminster, A Constable & Co., 1898), p. 116. Photo courtesy of the General Research Division of the New York Public Library, Astor, Lenox and Tilden Foundations.

birth to death. In the process, the diviner, working from *bazi* calculations and personal observations, moved from specific statements establishing the social identity, background and character of the client, to those that bore on future situations, activities and strategies.

Futures were thus negotiated.[147] In these exchanges, however, the client almost always occupied a subordinate position, for, like doctors, diviners possessed esoteric and valuable knowledge, which they dispensed carefully and calculatingly. Doolittle refers to their "patronizing manner," and Johnston writes that the physiognomers at Jiuhua Mountain in Anhui demonstrated "a degree of skill which is only surpassed by their remarkable self-confidence." On the other hand, despite their superior airs diviners no doubt consciously tried to close the interpersonal distance between themselves and their clients, in order to gain their trust as well as their respect.[148]

In conversation with a client, a diviner not only made assertions but also sought information. This process served the interests of both parties, for the more a diviner discovered about a client by whatever means, the more accurate his or her "predictions" or advice might be; and the more appropriate the counsel of the diviner, the more likely a client would return for further consultation. According to the *Qingbai leichao*, some fortune-tellers were not above gathering information about their clients from local "spies" who then relayed this intelligence to the diviners, thereby enhancing their credibility.[149] But even in the absence of such informants, fortune-tellers always received from their clients unconscious messages as well as conscious responses. As Nevius correctly inferred, clothing, manner, body language, possessions, and speech patterns all provided clues about the personality and social status of a client. Furthermore, conscious responses not only revealed factual information, but also indicated the client's acceptance or rejection—or ambiguity concerning—statements made by the fortune-teller. A quizzical expression on the client's face, for example, might provoke the search for additional clues, a more thorough explanation of the problem, an elaboration of an earlier statement, or a basic recalculation of the personal and cosmological variables involved. Often, in fact, a negotiated reconsideration of the many relevant factors was essential to a successful transaction.[150]

Another central feature of verbal horoscope interpretation, physiognomy, and word analysis was the use of moral maxims, which the fortune-teller might address to his entire audience as well as to his client. More intimate remarks were, however, naturally confined to a closer circle of friends or family, who themselves might become active participants in the interpretive process. As I have stressed, ethical concerns were central to virtually all forms of Chinese divination. Thus Qing fortune-tellers were anxious not only to identify the moral character of their clients, but also to give them morally-grounded advice. To the skills of the clinical psychologist they added the judgmental impulses of both Confucians and clerics. At the same time, they seem to have been intent on encouraging patrons to realize their full human potential, and on indicating that the future holds some hope for improvement.[151]

Liu Heng illustrates one form of mantic moralism. A lower degree holder in the late Qing period, he twice took the metropolitan exams in the Daoguang era, but each time he failed. Subsequently he made a name for himself as a physiognomer. A distinctive feature of his divinatory approach was an emphasis on Buddhist notions of karmic retribution. In fact, he wrote a book, informed by both Confucian and Buddhist values, entitled *Quancheng jiyao* (A Digest of Exhortations and Warnings) to promote his ideas.[152] Buddhist doctrine blended well with physiognomy because of the common belief that one of the primary ways karma expresses itself is in the body. Hence the claim made by some monks that they could "read" three lives (*sanshi;* lit., generations)—those of the past, the present, and the future.[153] The majority of clerics identified as diviners in the *fangji* sections of Qing gazetteers were Buddhist monks specializing in physiognomy, and Buddhist monasteries often served as a base for physiognomers.[154] But, as with most other Chinese concepts of fate, the idea of negative karma expressed in a "bad face" did not preclude the possibility of modification by good behavior. By the same token, a "good face" did not necessarily mean success in life. Destiny to Buddhists, as to Confucians, was variable.

Religious Daoist diviners seem to have been attracted more to astrology and numerology than to physiognomy, despite their well-known preoccupation with the human body and its "alchemical" transformation. They appear less often than Buddhists in gazetteer biographies, and seem less intent overall on championing moral values explicitly. Several Daoist clerics did, however, perform useful community services. A colorful example—and one of the very few individuals of his religious persuasion I have found described as "excelling in physiognomy"—is the nameless "Mad Daoist Priest" (Dian Daoshi) of Xingshan, Hubei, who lived in the local Guandi Temple, always sat up, even when he slept, never took a bath, and told fortunes for a fee. According to the Xingshan gazetteer, he "never missed" (wushuang) in his divinations, and although he gave a certain amount of money to the poor and hungry, he spent the rest of the day's income on liquor for himself.[155]

Of course neither clerics in general nor physiognomers in particular had a monopoly on moral high ground. Fate extrapolators, astrologers, numerologists and word analysts were as anxious as any other diviners to establish their ethical credentials. Yu Chuntan, an accomplished professional astrologer, emphasized that selfish desire could adversely affect one's destiny. Xiong Deqian, a scholar-diviner who specialized in numerology and military studies as well as astrology, went so far as to assert that although numbers basically determined the fate dispensed by Heaven, man could in effect overcome numbers by following (moral) principle. The astrologer Luo Hao, for his part, pointed out that since the time of Li Xuzhong, people interested in fate had been preoccupied with wealth, status and longevity; but to Luo, these things were distinctly inferior to virtue. He considered it far better to live a virtuous life fated to poverty, and even to face the prospect of a premature death, than to enjoy wealth and longevity in a morally misspent existence.[156]

Not all fortune-tellers were somber moralists, nor was divination invariably a serious affair. Mistaken pronouncements provided one source of potential amusement. During the Shunzhi period, for example, an official by the name of Wu Ziying, at home to mourn the death of a parent, went to a divination parlor to have his fate read according to the Ziping system of fate extrapolation. The diviner, fooled by his appearance in simple mourning attire, told Wu, a high degree holder, that he would never be successful in the civil service examinations![157] Skeptics loved such stories, and undoubtedly enjoyed testing the skills of diviners in various ways as a kind of game. Even Qing monarchs toyed with fortune-tellers on occasion. According to the Qingbai leichao, the Qianlong emperor once asked an astrologer by the name of Liu to extrapolate his fate according to the Ziping method on an incognito stroll around the city of Jiangning during one of his legendary southern tours.[158]

Joseph Needham has remarked on the strong possibility of a "genetic connection" between Chinese games, gambling techniques, and methods of divination—a point amply supported by anecdotes in local gazetteers and the Qingbai leichao. In some instances, it is clear that a frivolous atmosphere attended the dissection of written characters—a mood rather like what one would expect in polite social circles with the ancient but in Qing times still practiced guessing game known as *shefou* ("shooting the cover"). Scholars undoubtedly enjoyed socializing with professional word analysts precisely because they shared the same basic interest in word-play; and it is no accident that the section on "dissecting characters" in the *Tushu jicheng* follows the sections on *shefou* and another game-like divining practice, loosely related to the imagery of the *Yijing*, known as "hanging shadows" (*guaying*).[159]

It would be quite wrong, however, to take playful indulgence in divination and stories of faulty prognostications as evidence that fortune-telling was not taken seriously in Qing dynasty China. For every account of a missed divination there were dozens that told of unerringly accurate predictions. The biographies of diviners in local gazetteers and other Qing sources indicate that a great many fate extrapolators, astrologers, numerologists, and physiognomers were highly regarded for their mantic skills.[160] De Groot writes that even word analysis, often a source of scholarly amusement, was "cultivated as a most serious art, and omens, obtained from it, are considered not a whit less valuable than those derived from any other branch of necromancy."[161] In all realms of Chinese divination, the questions asked most frequently by clients related to success in the examinations, bureaucratic careers, family, wealth, honor, good health and longevity.[162]

Tales of predictions regarding the civil service examinations found an especially receptive audience in China's literary culture—particularly from the eighteenth century onward, a time when rapid population growth exacerbated already fierce competition within the exam system. These tales not only added a supernatural twist to the age-old Horatio Alger–like myth of social mobility, but also enhanced the reputations of individual diviners. Of the huge number of exam-related stories, a few examples should suffice to indicate their mythic appeal. One concerns a fate extrapolator named Yu Mingsheng, who predicted correctly that his two grandsons would both become holders of the highest literary degree—even though his home county in Fujian had produced no examination successes in a century. Another story involves the scholar-official Ji Yun, who, before he became famous as chief editor of the *Siku quanshu* project, was told by an unnamed word analyst in 1754 that the particular character Ji had written to be evaluated (*mo*; ink) indicated that although he would not be associated with "the head of the dragon" (that is, achieve the highest ranking in the metropolitan examinations of that year), he would nonetheless be allowed to enter the prestigious Hanlin Academy. Similarly, Gu Fengwei, a self-taught fate extrapolator, told Liu Lun (1711–1773), then only a licentiate, that he would enter the Hanlin Academy without an advanced degree. As it happened Liu took the special *boxue hongci* examination in 1736, passed first among 180 candidates, and became a Hanlin compiler.[163]

Predictions by diviners concerning more mundane matters, also became a part of local and sometimes even national lore, enhancing the aura of fortune-tellers and contributing to their collective mystique. Lu Jun, a gifted fate extrapolator, numerologist and astrologer, acquired an outstanding reputation in Jiangsu for his predictions regarding domestic affairs, from the birth of twins to the return of a long-lost husband. After Jin Ma predicted the death of a

Green Standard colonel by numerology, people flocked to his door. Xia Sheng, who took up the study of astrology and numerology during the mid-nineteenth century in the hope of using these skills against the "British barbarians," foretold the Taiping invasion of Zhejiang by means of "star divination;" and Zhang Shao predicted floods with uncanny accuracy by a similar method. Huai Zhenxi, conversant in *rendun* calculations and the related art of meteorological prediction, had a special knack for anticipating bad weather without the usual obvious clues.[164]

Stories of accurate divinations naturally attracted the attention of Qing officials and the throne. The historical record is therefore full of accounts of astrologers, fate extrapolators, physiognomers and word analysts, who, like geomancers, served the royal household or Qing bureaucrats. Some served only in a temporary capacity—as when royalty and officials on tour asked fate extrapolators to cast their horoscopes or physiognomers to read their faces. Thus we find Prince Zheng (Duanhua, d. 1861), on a visit to the south, requesting a meeting with Huang Yizhi to analyze his features, and Qian Wenmin, a lower official, seeking out the Buddhist cleric known as "The Old Monk with Penetrating Intelligence" for the same purpose.[165] Liu Lü, a specialist in physiognomy and *fengjiao*, periodically served the Kangxi emperor as a diviner and personal adviser, but he repeatedly refused to accept an official appointment.[166] Xiong Deqing, a professional astrologer, reportedly accumulated a small fortune for his occasional services to nobles and high ministers and used the money for famine relief.[167] Members of noble families also vied to win the favor of Zhang Xinheng, an itinerant professional, whose predictions based on *liuren* and *dunjia* methods occasioned considerable praise.[168]

Other diviners took more permanent employment, often as private secretaries. As governor-general of Sichuan in the early 1730s, Huang Tinggui (1691–1759) greatly valued the predictions of Yang Fengting, a scholar-diviner whose vast expertise included astrology, numerology and medicine. During the 1860s, Zeng Guofan, then governor-general of Liang Jiang, recruited Xue Fucheng (1838–1894), a scholar conversant in both astrology and numerology, to serve in his *mufu*. Later Xue entered the service of Li Hongzhang, and eventually he became the Chinese Minister to England, France, Italy and Belgium. Another prominent scholar-diviner, Li Fengbao (d. 1887), also pursued a diplomatic career, serving as Minister to France. At a less exalted level, Xu Honggao, a specialist in word analysis and astrology, worked for his uncle, a prefect, performing dutifully as a fortune-teller while the latter was in office. Later on he took divination as a business in order to support himself.[169]

The specific tasks performed by diviners for their employers varied enormously. Sometimes they simply gave reassurance. In 1709, for example, the Hunan Provincial Treasurer, Dong Zhaozu, found himself in political hot water. He therefore invited Yang Zixiu, a specialist in fate extrapolation, to divine for him. Yang's prediction was that Dong would weather the storm within a month, which proved correct—much to the latter's relief. In 1857, after the dismissal in disgrace of Yu Yue (1821–1907) as Commissioner of Education in Henan, Xu Guangdi predicted by means of fate extrapolation that Yu would still wield literary authority. Yu did not believe him, but a decade later he received an appointment as head of the prestigious Refined Study for the Explication of the Classics (Gujing jingshe) in Hangzhou, where he taught for about thirty years. In the realm of military affairs, Gong Bu, a numerologist and former official himself, provided peace of mind to Qing authorities in Yunnan when he informed them that on the basis of his divinations timely assistance against local bandits would be forthcoming. Gong also correctly predicted the capture of four rebel leaders.[170]

Some fortune-tellers assumed technical responsibilities in local government. One vitally important realm was the prediction of weather and harvests, where astrologers and *zhanhou* specialists in particular had important contributions to make. Many diviners undertook these tasks, including Qu Donghai, a professional fortune-teller from Anhui, who performed admirably in both capacities for local officials during the Jiaqing years.[171] His fellow provincial, Zhang Lun, a specialist in *yinyang* arts and *fengjiao*, once predicted that misfortune would befall the person ritually responsible for constructing a "Pavillion to Honor the Virtue of Water" (Shuide ting) in Guichi—a structure which the county magistrate, Zhao Yan, earnestly hoped would help to prevent local flooding. Zhang altruistically assumed the position, only to die the same day. His fellow townsmen asked Zhao to establish a shrine to honor his memory.[172] Wang Chun, a scholarly specialist in fate extrapolation, *taiyi* and other numerical arts, provided Director-General of River Conservancy Li Shixu (1773–1824) with useful predictions concerning floods and advice about water control.[173]

A significant number of fortune-tellers found official employment in law enforcement and local control. Some, such as Chen Shou, greatly esteemed by the governor of Guangdong province for his skill as a fate extrapolator, served as negotiators—presumably because of their psychological insights and facility with words.[174] Others worked within the judicial system, using the same talents.[175] Numerologists often assisted Qing officials with police work, since their techniques were deemed valuable in recovering lost items. In Yunnan province, for instance, Li Weixin, a low degree holder, used *liuren* methods to track down a murderer for his uncle, a local official. Using the same approach in Anhui, the scholar Zhou Jiaxiang divined on behalf of a local prefect in order to find six escaped prisoners. In his prediction he not only told the prefect where and when the men would be found, but also informed him that a total of seven bandits would be recaptured. According to the Anhui provincial gazetteer, his prediction proved correct; the extra man turned out to be an escapee from another province.[176]

Other such stories abound: In Hubei, Yuan Chengyu, a specialist in medicine and numerology, helped the local authorities to find an escaped prisoner. So did He Futang, a Sichuanese diviner with no specified expertise, and the astrologer/numerologist Luo Xizhu in Jiangxi. An interesting variation on the theme of locating escaped prisoners can be found in the case of Shen Hengzhang, a professional fortune-teller in Jiangsu during the late eighteenth and early nineteenth century. Shen helped local officials in Songjiang to find an escaped prisoner by offering a detailed analysis of the written character for parrot (*ying*), based on both the nature of the bird ("an animal that can talk") and the individual components of the word itself.[177]

An extremely important sphere of service for diviners was the evaluation of personnel—and, one suspects, the examination and interrogation of individuals accused of committing crimes. The physiognomer Shi Hulian seems to have been employed by a local civil official in Fujian with at least one of these two purposes expressly in mind.[178] Liu Lü also appears to have done work of this sort for the Kangxi emperor. Military commanders regularly enlisted the assistance of specialists in "reading" people as part of the process of selecting their subordinates.[179] The case of Enming (1846-1907) illustrates, at least symbolically, the perils of ignoring the advice of physiognomers. In Beijing after an audience with the emperor upon his appointment as governor of Anhui, he met a fortune-teller outside the Zhongyang Gate and had his face read. According to the diviner, although Enming had an auspicious complexion, he should nonetheless guard against unanticipated calamities, and take special care in choosing his subordinates, military personnel in particular. As it turned out, Enming did not take sufficient care; for one of his officers, the revolutionary Xu Xilin (1873-1907), assassinated him.[180]

Zeng Guofan, himself an amateur physiognomer of considerable reputation, had a standard formula for measuring men: "To gauge depravity or rectitude, look at the eyes and nose; for honesty or dishonesty, look at the lips; for [the possibility of] merit and fame, look at the level of energy [qigai]; for wealth and nobility, look at the spirit; for ideas and intentions [zhuyi], look at the fingernails; for volatility [fengpo], look at the tendons of the feet." The physiognomer Gao Renjian reportedly "discovered" Peng Yulin (1816-1890), who later became one of the many famous military commanders recruited by Zeng during the anti-Taiping campaigns of the 1850s and 1860s.[181] Not surprisingly, a number of Zeng's other subordinates, including the diplomat Xue Fucheng and such renowned military figures as Li Hongzhang (1823-1901), Zuo Zongtang (1812-1885), and Liu Mingchuan (1836-1896), also took divination seriously. Liu in particular had a deep interest in physiognomy.[182]

Many if not most Qing commanders viewed divination—particularly numerological techniques such as qimen dunjia and meteorological ones such as wangqi and fengjiao—as potentially valuable in field operations.[183] Both types of divination were, after all, historically linked to strategy and tactics, although by no means confined exclusively to them.[184] Throughout the Qing period, fortune-tellers played important roles in military affairs. Diviners such as Jin Guang, who served commander Shang Kexi (d. 1676) for a full fifty years, facilitated the Manchu conquest—although he was later executed for refusing to go along with the rebellion of Shang's son, Zhixin (d. 1680). Chen Zhibing, an astrologer and milfoil expert, was one of several soothsayers who contributed to the consolidation of Manchu rule by helping to suppress local disturbances. Dong Yi, a Kangxi period numerologist, followed government forces under Lieutenant General Wu Ge and others in their 1720 campaign against the Eleuths in Tibet, earning the respect of his superiors for both his rectitude and his intelligence. He divined for them often, and was reportedly invariably successful. Later he attracted the notice of Li Wei (1687–1738), governor-general of Min-Zhe, who also valued his advice and expertise, and who appointed him to an official position.[185]

During the early reign of the Yongzheng emperor, General Nian Gengyao (d. 1726), charged with suppressing the Kokonor uprising in the 1720s, heard about the talents of a diviner named Shi, who specialized in *fengjiao*. Shi joined Nian's staff, and in the fighting at Qinghai he made "many unusually accurate predictions." He left Nian's service, however, well before the latter got into trouble for his infamous "ninety-two crimes." Perhaps out of disgust, Shi subsequently gave up divination completely. When Yang Yuchun (1762–1837), one of the most illustrious generals of the late eighteenth and early nineteenth centuries, returned from one of his border campaigns in Chinese Turkestan, he invited Chen Yiyun, a Daoguang scholar conversant in both numerology and fate extrapolation, to serve in his staff office. Jealous people obstructed him, however, and Chen eventually returned home, like Shi, never to engage in divination again. Even so, several decades after his death at the age of ninety-seven *sui*, his neighbors still revered him for his problem-solving abilities.[186]

Domestic rebellion provided many opportunities for fortune-tellers to utilize their mantic skills. When Wu Sangui (1612–1678) was contemplating revolt against the Qing, he requested funds from the Jiangsu provincial treasury; but on the advice of a word analyst named Zhu, who divined Wu's treacherous intentions, the local authorities rejected his request. After Wu actually rebelled in 1673 and invaded the city of Changsha in Hunan, Liu Erhuan, a lower degree-holder who excelled in the arts of *taiyi*, *qimen*, and *liuren*, predicted that the threatening situation would pass, "like floating clouds." Later, Prince An (Yolo, 1625–1689), the Manchu warrior sent to oppose Wu's forces, recruited Liu for his field staff in appreciation of Liu's divinatory talents and insights. Xiong Yingxiong, a low degree holder who specialized in Xuzhong divination, also assisted the Qing authorities against Wu. Sangui, for his part, employed his own fortune-tellers—sometimes against their will.[187]

The Miao minority uprising in southwestern China during the late eighteenth century provided a number of fortune-tellers with the opportunity to display their prognostic gifts. Perhaps the most noteworthy example is Dai Shangwen, a low degree holder, who learned secret *liuren* techniques from a Buddhist monk in Jiangnan, and who served his local community by recovering items that had been lost or stolen. When the Manchu general Fukang'an took over the campaign against the Miao, he sought people with "unusual talents" (*qicai*). Dai was one such person. As a military adviser he predicted when the rebels would attack, made weather forecasts, and helped the army find springs for water. He also predicted Fukang'an's untimely demise.[188] At about the same time, the White Lotus Rebellion of 1796–1804 broke out in north China. Hu Yuanjing, author of several works on astrology, numerology, and military strategy, predicted the rise and fall of the rebels. Meanwhile, Xie Tian'ao, who learned Sunzi's *Bingfa* (Military Methods) and *qimen* techniques together as a youth, assisted his neighbor, Zhu Cheng, in organizing and training mercenary "braves" to combat the rebels in Hubei in 1798.[189]

In the nineteenth century numerologists were no less involved in the suppression of rebellion. During the Lin Qing uprising of 1813, for example, the Jiaqing emperor sought experts in the mantic arts, hoping desperately to contend with the rebels—who themselves availed of divination to determine the most auspicious time for an attack on the Forbidden City. The Grand Council recommended Kang Wenduo, a scholar-official renowned at the capital for his expertise in *liuren* divination. Kang's predictions proved successful, and the emperor duly rewarded him with a present of fine silk.[190] Later in the century, Ba Jianlong, a skilled practitioner of astrology, *qimen* and military tactics, helped local officials in his home county of Taihe, Anhwei, to devise "invariably successful" plans for local defense in the early stages of the Nian Rebellion (1853-1868).[191]

During the Qing-Taiping War, an especially large number of diviners served as military advisers—among them, Xie Tian'ao's son, Xie Xinzhi, also a *qimen* specialist; the scholar Kong Jilian, who excelled in *liuren* techniques; Xu Xigong, an expert in the *Yijing*, *fengjiao*, and numerology; and Xiong Deqian, an exam failure of wide-ranging mantic expertise, who "threw down his writing brush and followed the [Qing] army" when rebellion broke out in the 1850s.[192] Zhou Fu (1837-1912), a professional numerologist, assisted Li Hongzhang in selecting "lucky days" for battle, and eventually parlayed his association with the powerful Li into his own governor-generalship.[193] Zhao Caidong, a specialist in *taiyi*, *qimen dunjia* and *liuren* as well as geomancy, rendered valuable military assistance to general Feng Zicai (1818-1903) during the war; and Li Suzhen—one of only three women from the Qing period to be included in Yuan Shushan's monumental collection of diviner-biographies—joined her brother, Li Mengqun, to fight the Taipings in south China in the early stages of the war. The daughter of an illustrious family, Li Suzhen knew horseriding, archery, military tactics and astrology, and as a strategist and adviser, she rendered valuable service against the rebels. She died a heroic death in an attack on Hanyang, Hubei, in 1855.[194] The Taipings, meanwhile, also tried mightily to recruit fortune-tellers, despite their alleged antipathy toward divination.[195]

Of course numerology and astrology, like other forms of prophecy, could serve personal and community as well as bureaucratic interests. Again, one or two examples should suffice. Li Taichu, a specialist in *liuren* and *qimen dunjia*, was able to "know the future," and to make predictions that were "extraordinarily accurate." One day, he suddenly closed the door to his home and warned his family to stay inside. Later, a woman in the area hanged herself after a quarrel, and because Li had shielded his family members from any possible suspicion, they were protected from collective responsibility and punishment.[196] The astrologer Liu Zhong, who divined for his neighbors without pay in times of crisis, was only one of many fate calculators who helped their local communities by providing solace and personal services in difficult circumstances.[197] Whether motivated by altruism or self-interest, such individuals played a genuinely "psychotherapeutic" role in Chinese society by offering hope to distressed individuals and groups.[198]

But while premonitions could provide protection or comfort, they could also be a source of difficulty. In the first place, prophecies were not always positive, and sometimes they angered people. Ling Kun, a Daoguang *juren*, predicted by means of physiognomy that one of his scholarly associates, He Guiqing (1816–1862), would become a high official. As foreseen, He eventually received an appointment as governor of Jiangsu province. Later, however, when the two men again met, He once more asked Ling to predict his future. This time, Ling reported that Governor He would be decapitated. The governor was furious, but the prediction proved true, and He was soon thereafter executed for dereliction of duty against the Taipings.[199] At another level, the scholar Li Fangchun predicted on the basis of a woman's appearance that she would be hit by lightning on a certain day. When she heard of this, she hated him; but on the specified day she was indeed struck. Li felt very remorseful, and from that time onward he no longer engaged in physiognomy.[200] Facing such pressure, it is small wonder that some fortune-tellers did their best work after drinking wine, and that some refused to divine without it.[201]

The assumed power of astrologers, fate extrapolators, numerologists, and physiognomers made them vulnerable to charges of witchcraft. Like other types of diviners, such as the geomancer called "Immortal Eyes" Zhang by his contemporaries, many had peculiar habits, an unusual appearance, or the stigma of having learned their skills from "strange men" (*yiren*). Song Xiance bore a double stigma in China: He was not only a dwarf, but also a fortune-teller for Li Zicheng, the "dashing prince," who toppled the Ming dynasty before succumbing to the Manchus.[202] But even soothsayers who lacked such distinctive features or such backgrounds invited suspicion. The professional fortune-teller Huang Mingzhuang, for example, had to pay the funeral expenses of a client who died soon after a divining session, because friends of the man (an actor) accused Huang of having caused his death through a form of "nightmare magic" (*yaoyan*), and they threatened to report him to the local authorities.[203]

The personal prophecies of diviners could also become self-fulfilling. Sometimes this could happen in tragicomic ways, as when the physiognomer Gu Heming told a client that his face revealed murderous tendencies, wherepon the man became enraged and beat Gu to death.[204] Lu Qimeng, an astrologer and geomancer, predicted to friends that he would die on a certain day after falling from a high place; and when the appointed day arrived, he tumbled from the stairs in his own home and was killed.[205] Other situations, however, had implications that were more threatening to the Qing authorities. When the physiognomer Li Benshan innocently predicted that three prisoners sentenced to public execution would not die because their faces showed "the breath of life," he was naturally blamed when they escaped.[206]

From the Chinese government's standpoint, political predictions were particularly unsettling.[207] For nearly two thousand years, since at least the Han dynasty, prophetic books of one kind or another circulated more or less clandestinely. Most of them relied heavily on word play of the sort associated with the dissection of characters, and by late imperial times there were a number that seemed to pass judgment on the Qing. One, the "Eternal Song of the Universe" (*Qiankun wannian ge*), appeared to contain oblique references to the rebellion of Li Zicheng that toppled the Ming dynasty and allowed the

Manchus to invade and rule China for over two hundred years.[208] Another, based on Zhuge Liang's "Before the Horse" method of divination (*maqian ke*), predicted the founding of the Qing by foreign invaders from an analysis of lines that included the characters for "water, month, and ruler" (*shui yue zhu*), which together formed the word Qing, and the characters "ancient and month" (*gu yue*), which together formed the word "barbarian" (*hu;* i.e., the Manchus).[209]

Shao Yong's "Plum Blossom Poems" (*Meihua shi*) also proved to be a popular source of prophetic wisdom in the Qing. Of the ten poems in this collection, one in particular seemed to apply to the.reigning dynasty. It read:

> The barbarians rode by horseback into Chang'an,
> Opening the Central Plain up to the borders of the sea.
> The vast waters receded and then rose up again,
> And the pure light could readily be seen in the midst of the Han.

According to the interpretation offered in the *Qingbai leichao*, this poem refers to (1) the Manchu invasion into China, specifically when the Shunzhi emperor entered the strategic pass of the Great Wall known as Shanhai guan; (2) the relaxation of trade restrictions with foreign countries after a period of maritime isolation; (3) the tumultuous Taiping Rebellion under Hong Xiuquan ("Hong" can mean "vast"); and (4) the fall of the Qing dynasty after a revolutionary uprising at Wuchang (Wuhan) led by Li Yuanhong in 1911.[210]

Perhaps the most famous book of political prophecy in Qing times was the *Tuibei tu* (Chart of Extrapolation from the Back), attributed to Li Chunfeng (602–670) and Yuan Tiangang (d. 627) of the Tang dynasty. Although officially prohibited, it circulated widely. Arthur Smith, writing at the end of the Qing period, observed that

> The influence which the T'ui Pei T'u has exerted, and still continues to exert upon the Chinese mind, is a remarkable phenomenon. It is popularly regarded in much the same light in which Christian nations view the Apocalypse of St. John the Apostle, . . . [and] there is good reason to believe that this chart is known and accepted as an authority all over the empire. . . . It is cherished in imperial households, and handed down from generation to generation, and is not to be lightly perused. Those who are fortunate enough to inspect its concealed wisdom may escape the calamity of flood, fire, and violence.[211]

Qing dynasty versions of the *Tuibei tu* often contained a preface purporting to have been written by the famous necromancer Liu Ji (also known as Liu Bowen) of the early Ming dynasty. The work is organized into sixty parts, each indicated by a hexagram. Much of its interpretive logic revolves around the use of stems and branches (particularly branches, marked by the twelve cyclical animals), and principles of word analysis that have already been discussed. A comparison of two late Qing editions of the *Tuibei tu* from different provinces— both handwritten rather than printed—reveals a number of inconsistencies in the number and order of verses and illustrations, the number of characters per line, the particular characters used, and the illustrations used. The format, however, is basically the same.[212]

The sections of the *Tuibei tu* pertaining to the Qing dynasty begin with the "image" numbered thirty-three, the cyclical characters *bingshen* (the first appearance of which occurs in the Qing in 1656) and the hexagram Daguo (28). It contains a phrase in the prophecy (*chen*) with the characters for the first Qing emperor's reign title (Shunzhi), and therefore came to be seen by subsequent generations of Chinese as portending the Manchu takeover of China after 1644. The thirty-fourth image, marked by the cyclical characters *dingyu* (which occurs in 1837) and the hexagram Sun (57), contains characters and phrases in the prophecy that seem to refer to a number of distinctive features of the Taiping Rebellion (which had its origins in the late 1830s)—from the name of the movement and its primary leader, to the long hair that distinguished its adherents from loyal Qing subjects. The thirty-fifth image, with the cyclical characters *wuxu* (which occurs in 1898) and the hexagram Sui (17) has a prophecy that appears to refer to the inroads of Western aggression on China in the period from the Tongzhi Restoration (1862–1874) to the Scramble for Concessions and Boxer Fiasco (1898–1900). The thirty-sixth image, marked by the cyclical characters *yihai* (1899) and the hexagram Xiaochu (9), contains a prophecy that suggests the problems of succession that plagued the Qing dynasty in its final years; and the thirty-seventh image, marked by *gengzi* (1900) and the hexagram Yi (42), can be construed to refer to the process leading to the fall of the Qing dynasty in 1911 and the establishment of the Republic of China in the following year.[213]

During the 1880s other prophetic documents were unearthed which, in cryptic passages decipherable only through word analysis, conveyed messages about the future. The most famous "discovery" of this sort was the so-called "Baked Pastry Song" (*Shaobing ge*), attributed to Liu Ji. Although undoubtedly written in the late Qing and amplified after its fall, this document purports to record an intimate conversation between Liu and the first Ming emperor, chronicling in obscure language the history of the Ming and Qing dynasties. As usual, the names of people and special terms are derived in large measure from word analysis. Thus, for example, the text uses the four characters "rain, water, grass and head" (*yu shui cao tou*) to refer to the Manchus, since the character *Man* can be dissected into three components: water (on the left) and rain (on the right), with grass on top (at the head) of the rain. Similar devices were used to refer to particular individuals. For instance, the characters "stream, water, page (or head) and exalted" (*chuan shui ye tai*) refer to the Shunzhi emperor's reign name, because the word *Shun* is a combination of stream and page, while the components of *zhi* are water and exalted (see Fig. 5.25). Even more complex constellations (and occasional distortions) of basic characters yielded the reign names of other Qing monarchs up to the Tongzhi emperor. Thereafter, other devices—including the use of *wuxing* and stem-branch correlations—identified late Qing notables such as Liu Kunyi (1830–1902) and Zhang Zhidong (1837–1909).[214]

According to Arthur Smith, the appearance of prophetic documents was "a phenomenon of constant occurrence at any crisis in the affairs of the government, in times of rebellion, and even when there is no visible exciting cause." He goes on to say that these "so-called 'inscriptions,' and other compositions of the sort . . . are put in circulation by the leaders of the various Secret Societies or Sects, with which the Chinese Empire is honeycombed."[215] Of all such groups, the popular religious organization known as the White Lotus Society offered the most sustained challenge to the Qing dynasty. Blending millenarian Buddhism with elements of orthodox cosmology, the White Lotus sectarians forged a powerful prophetic appeal. Summoning up terrifying images of destruction and doom, they predicted the turning of a new kalpa and the arrival of the so-called Buddha of the Future. The most likely time for this "coming" was a *jiazi* year—the onset of a new sexegenary cycle—but the calamities that presaged it could always be predicted by using the standard stem-branch calculations of conventional fortune-tellers. Impelled by political considerations, White Lotus sect-masters manipulated these cyclical characters and "used them to prove conjunction between current events and the prophecies set forth in sect scriptures."[216]

But while such sectarian organizations had an unorthodox, indeed heretical, political agenda, they invariably looked to the orthodox cosmology for symbolic sustenance. This entailed not only the appropriation of conventional time markers such as stems and branches, but also concepts such as *yinyang* and *wuxing*, the eight trigrams, the nine mansions, the twenty-eight lunar lodges, and so forth. Rebel groups published almanacs, wrote protective charms, and engaged in word play similar to that employed in prophetic books. All such groups employed diviners, and many promised to teach their adherents ways to "encourage good fortune, . . . avoid bad fortune, and be saved from poverty."[217] In short, the urge to divine, as well as the techniques employed, transcended the divide between orthodoxy and heterodoxy.

SIX

Spirit Mediums and Spirit Messages

All forms of Qing divination were spiritual, but some were more spiritual than others. Consultation of the *Yijing*, as well as the observations and calculations of geomancers, astrologers, fate extrapolators, numerologists, and physiognomers, implied some sort of spiritual communication, some kind of special cosmic access to hidden knowledge. Dreams and omens also had a spiritual dimension, since both provided a means by which supernatural intelligence might manifest itself.[1] But the actual embodiment of spirits, as in the case of spirit-possession, presented special problems of interpretation and management to members of the orthodox Chinese elite.

In discussing supernatural questions, Qing Confucians repeatedly cited the famous maxim from the *Lunyu*, "Respect the spirits, but keep them at a distance" (*jing guishen er yuan zhi*). In the orthodox view, this meant that one should "devote one's effort to what is proper in the way of man and not be deluded by spiritual beings which are unknowable."[2] Yet gods, ghosts and monsters did exist, even if only as creations of the mind; and they became powerful precisely because people believed in them.[3] From an elite standpoint the problem was to keep the noble spiritual powers of the mind from being deflected by illusory ideas. "Ignorant or stupid people" (*yumin*), it seemed, were far too prone to worship false gods, engage in wanton sacrifices (*yinsi*), make disorderly pilgrimages, and succumb to the "misleading" words of shamans, fortune-tellers and other forms of Chinese lowlife.[4]

Here again we see evidence of a double standard on the part of the Qing elite. On the one hand, scholars considered it proper, indeed essential, for the Son of Heaven and his designated representatives to worship a host of deities, including spirits of nature and deceased humans, as part of an elaborate system of state-sponsored sacrifice. They also believed that it was perfectly acceptable for educated people, who "extended their sincerity and reverence to the utmost," to engage in divination and even to patronize soothsayers and shamans.[5] On the other hand, the Qing government and its agents did everything in their power to limit contact between the common people and non-elite ritual specialists. For this reason the throne not only prohibited "false" prophecy and sorcery (see chapter 2), but also outlawed shamans who, under various names, claimed the ability to "summon heterodox spirits, write charms, pronounce spells on water, and petition the sages by means of spirit-writing [*fuluan*]."[6]

The influential scholar-official Wu Rongguang (1773–1843), in an effort to draw the sharpest possible distinction between the orthodox state rituals connected with sacrifices to the City God (Chenghuang) and the seemingly raucous popular celebrations surrounding the City God's "birthday," spoke for his entire social class in condemning commoners who "flatter spirits to seek blessings" (*meishen qiufu*).[7] Yet this is precisely what most Qing elites themselves did in one way or another. Quite apart from conducting officially-mandated sacrifices, scholars and officials earnestly prayed to deities such as the God of Literature (Wenchang) for assistance in their careers, and Xu Dishan informs us that in provinces such as Jiangsu and Zhejiang, where the "scholarly fashion" prevailed, the common attitude in Qing times was simply that "if one did not believe in the spirits of the planchette [*jixian*], he could not be successful in the examinations."[8]

Shamans and Spirit-writing

Shamans, both male (*shigong, shentong, jitong, duangong*, etc.) and female (*shipo, wupo, nüwu, xipo, duanpo*, etc.), played a significant role in Qing society at all levels, despite rising elite antagonism toward them in late imperial times. Prior to the Ming dynasty, shamans enjoyed a relatively high social position in China as healers, fortune-tellers, exorcists and magicians; but the neo-Confucian revival of the Song undermined their status, helping to relegate them primarily to peripheral areas in the provinces rather than to "core" centers of commerce or culture.[9] Ming and Qing law, the Kangxi emperor's Sacred Edict, intermittent proclamations by local officials, and various clan rules all contributed to this process of marginalization. Some clan rules, for example, forbade members to consult shamans, and others ordered that males who became shamans be removed from the clan registers. Local gazetteers generally cast shamans in a far less flattering light than more conventional diviners, and they were seldom, if ever, accorded individual biographies.[10]

Nonetheless, spirit mediums of various sorts continued to treat patients, tell fortunes, and perform various kinds of magic. They exorcized demons, communicated with the dead, undertook local community rituals (including disease and drought prevention ceremonies), and sometimes officiated in religious pilgrimages as well.[11] Some assumed shamanistic roles without formal discipline; others, notably *shigong*, underwent training and purification rituals overseen by a Daoist "master" (*jiaozhu*) as part of an involved process of apprenticeship, often hereditary.[12] Almanacs designated propitious times to "transmit [the calling] to disciples" (*chuantu*). Younger shamans, known as *shentong* (lit., "spirit fellows"), were generally individuals of low social class who discovered their gifts as seers and exorcists spontaneously.[13]

J.J.M. De Groot provides a first-hand description of how spirit possession might take place on the occasion of a local religious festival:

[A] young man suddenly begins to hop, dance and waddle with wild or drawsy [sic] looks, and nervous gestures of arms and hands. . . . All onlookers at once realize the fact that one of the gods whose images stand in the temple, or some other spirit has "seized the youth" [*latong*] . . . [who] now begins to moan; some incoherent talk follows, mingled with cries; but all this is [obscure] oracular language which reveals unknown things. . . . Some moments pass by, and the patient relapses into his normal condition because the spirit leaves his body.[14]

As this account suggests, shamans literally spoke for a deity—usually a low ranking local spirit unconnected with the official pantheon of state worship. Their pronouncements thus had substantial oracular authority, if considered authentic.[15] The god in question generally inhabited a small local shrine, or resided at the domestic altar of a shaman. At these venues, friends and neighbors, and even gentry and officials, gathered for mantic advice, "paying fees of gratitude, to be theoretically converted by the owner of the altar into sacrifices . . . and for the support of the altar and the house."[16] Ideally, shamans did not accept money for their services, but clients usually supplied them with gifts of cash or kind, in amounts dictated by local custom; and if the mediums claimed an association with a local temple or shrine, their clients might also provide an offering to the god or gods therein.[17] A club or association might also arrange for one or more of its members to become a *shentong* for its patron deity.[18]

On the whole, shamanistic activities were far more common in south China than in the north, with the exception of Manchuria.[19] Throughout most of the empire, minority peoples as well as the Han Chinese indulged in shamanism.[20] At the capital, within the Qing Imperial Household, shamanistic activities, which had long been part of the Manchu tribal heritage, fell under the administrative jurisdiction of the Office of Ceremonial.[21] Shamanism also naturally flourished in the extreme northeast, beyond the Great Wall, in the Qing homeland, where among the Manchus, mediumistic "exorcism" (*tiaoshen*; "jumping of [or with] spirits") was practiced not only whenever an illness occurred, but on other occasions as well—at least in relatively affluent households.[22]

Qing period gazetteers leave no doubt that shamanistic healing was extremely popular in many parts of China Proper. In Yongxin county, Jiangxi, for instance, the prevalent custom was "to believe in shamans and not in traditional Chinese medicine."[23] The gazetteer of Dengfeng county, Henan, tells us that "in time of illness, many people seek the spiritual [aid of] shamans."[24] Like traditional Chinese doctors and diviners, shamans performed a useful psychotherapeutic function in providing a sense of hope to their clients (see next section)—not to mention physical reinvigoration and psychic release to themselves. In relatively primitive areas of China, marked by poverty, low literacy, and isolation from the orthodox elite, shamans were perhaps more integral to their local communities than literate physicians and fortune-tellers. When they danced and sang, family and neighbors joined in, partaking of supernatural power. In this way, they could vicariously do battle with demons or wander into the netherworld with the shaman—all in an effort to reestablish social and supernatural harmony.[25]

A gazetteer from western Hunan describes the healing rituals of one type of male shaman known as a *duangong*:

When the shaman appears it is always nighttime. He puts up a small table and arranges pictures of gods, and wooden images of the *fantan*, the five demons and others. The sick person's family brings one pint of rice, and places tablets and incense candles on top of it. The shaman wears a Guanyin hat or a Seven Buddha hat, and a red Buddhist robe, holding in his left hand a ring knife, popularly called the master's knife, which clatters noisily; and in his right hand a Daoist tablet [*lingpai*] rounded at the top and square at the base, inscribed with charms and taboo words. He blows a horn, sings and dances, rises and falls, bows and kneels, in order to please his god. He spins like lightning, whirls like the wind, and scatters and burns paper money. During this time come the motions of beseeching the master, withdrawing the sickness, summoning the soul [*zhaohun*] and "destroying the temple [*pomiao*]." Earlier, reeds have been cut to make a human figure, dressed in the sick person's clothes. It is offered wine and food, carried in a reed boat through the door and burnt. This is called "substituting the reeds." Also the shaman bears the mask of the dragon spirit. It is said that if it is not carried properly he will catch the disease after the substitution. Sometimes, too, he prays to the birth star and dipper and requests thirteen men to present a guarantee before the God of the Eastern Mountain. This is called "insuring happiness [*dabaofu*]."[26]

Other accounts of exorcisms emphasize the use of caustics, hempen "spiritual whips" (*lingbian*), cosmic symbols such as the *Taiji tu* and eight trigrams, and various devices used by shamans to mortify their own flesh, including a terrifying spiked object known as a "thorn ball" (*ciqi*). This spirit-inspired self-mortification in the service of an individual patient paralleled the techniques employed by shamans in large-scale Daoist rituals of exorcism designed to protect entire communities from pestilence. In both cases, bleeding released *yang* forces that counteracted the evil influence of *yin*.[27] At the same time, these *yang* forces also extended the life of the shaman, at least in theory. According to popular belief, most *shentong* had a "light" (*qing*) fate—that is, their "eight characters" endowed them with a weak constitution and therefore a short life. But when a *yang* spirit possessed them, their otherwise insubstantial fate could be enhanced.[28]

Not all shamanistic healers effected cures through exorcisms. Oracular pronouncements could also serve more conventional medical needs; and apparently *shentong*, acting as soothsayers, received more health-related questions than any other kind. Prior to a formal consultation, one or more of the patient's relatives prepared the altar of the god by lighting candles, offering food, and burning incense. The assistant(s) of the *shentong* then "invited" the deity to descend, perhaps with an eloquent incantation in the classical language.[29] Eventually the god "entered into communication with the medium" (*guantong*), who began to jump and twitch. De Groot reports: "His limbs shake vehemently; his arms knock on the table; his head and shoulders jerk nervously from side to side, and his staring eyes, half closed, seem to gaze straight into a hidden world." Questions are asked to him, and he answers in a shrill, incoherent voice. An assistant translates his responses, which, in the case of illness, often consist of medical prescriptions. Meanwhile, the medium goes into a swoon, revives, rubs his eyes, and returns to normal with no recollection of what he has said or done.[30]

Sometimes in the course of his medical revelations, a god might express the desire to see a sick patient in person. This required that his image be carried to the individual's house on a small litter, where it was then placed ceremoniously on the domestic altar. The same basic preparations took place, but now the shaman could deal with the responsible demon directly. A significant feature of this ritual is that the litter (*lian*) of the god was usually left in the home of the patient for a few days to act as a stabilizing device in the fashion of a geomantic charm (see chapter 4). To a far greater degree than most non-shamanistic diviners would care to admit, *shentong* played their own fortune-telling game, particularly in thinly settled or newly settled areas where mantic competition was not great enough to encourage specialization. Shamans evaluated buildings, landforms and waterways in the fashion of geomancers; showed a concern with propitious times, directions and locations in the manner of numerologists and day selection specialists; took celestial influences into account as if they were astrologers; and even engaged in various kinds of word analysis.[31] At the same time, however, their approach was much more self-consciously supernatural than that of most Qing fortune-tellers, and their connection with Daoism far more obvious.

A particularly noteworthy feature of exorcisms was the "bureaucratic" appeal made by a medium in the event that a healing ritual failed to achieve its object. Typically, the unsuccessful *shentong* would pay a visit to the local City God temple in hopes of bringing higher spiritual authority to bear on the case. If such a visit revealed that the City God himself was responsible for ordering the "punishment" of his sick patient, the *shentong* might then call upon a *shigong* who, by virtue of his superior rank, could perform an elaborate series of rituals designed to save the afflicted individual by returning his or her "vital spirit" (*jingshen*). If this, too, failed, the shaman might be forced to acknowledge that the demon in question could not, in fact, be exorcized unless the patient personally atoned for past misdeeds. The moral burden of effecting a successful cure then fell on the patient rather than on the spirit medium.[32]

The most authoritative oracular pronouncements by spirit-mediums were those written down on a table or planchette (*jipan*) with the blunt end of a two-pronged stick made of protective peachwood or willow. The planchette was covered with sand, ashes from incense, or some other substance that allowed the writing to be revealed. The stick (*ji* or *jibi*), normally about two feet long, was cut from the southeastern side of a tree (exposed to the *yang* influence of the rising and culminating sun) on a day and at a time that were deemed auspicious.[33] Spirit-writing also required an altar, located either in a religious temple (usually Daoist but sometimes Buddhist), an association hall (*huiguan*, etc.), or a domestic residence. Although the Qing government officially discouraged spirit-writing, it could not curtail the practice, even in urban areas. According to Xu Dishan, spirit-writing altars (*jitan*) could be found in virtually every prefectural and county capital during the Ming-Qing era; and the *Qingbai leichao* tells us that in one (unnamed) urban center, two or three thousand petitioners from Hunan, Hubei, Henan and Sichuan converged on a single *huiguan* altar.[34]

Some spirit-writing associations were "a shabby lot," appealing only to "the very lowest class" of Chinese society. But others were decidedly of "a better sort." De Groot describes "large temples to which people of the best classes and even high officials, resort to oracles in numbers so great every day, that it is necessary to register their names and their subjects for consultation, in order that everybody may duly have his turn." Ironically, spirit-writing enjoyed the ardent support of the very class responsible for enforcing the state's provisions against it. The interest taken by scholars in the *fuji* system was apparently so great that,

> desireous of oracles thoroughly reliable, many will enable the god to prepare properly for an answer . . . [by first writing] a letter to him, in which they lay down their questions with such precision of detail as they think is warranted. This document at the same time informs the god that they intend to set out a sacrifice on his altar on such-and-such a day, and that they humbly invite him then to come and partake of it and at the same time give his answer.[35]

The rituals of spirit-writing varied from place to place and time to time, but tended to follow certain basic patterns. Prior to the actual descent of the spirit, the diviner and his assistants usually provided offerings of food or flowers, candles and incense, wrote charms, and engaged in other ceremonies of purification. In anticipation of the spirit-writing session, which might last for several hours, the medium held (*fu*) one prong of the stick in his right hand, while his assistant grabbed the other in his left—hence the term *fuji*, "to support the divining instrument."[36] The spirit was then "invited" to descend directly into the stick: "Suddenly the tip comes down upon the writing table; like a hammer it jumps up and down, two, three, even more times, its violence being tempered by the automatic resistance of the other holder." The spirit identifies itself in writing, or is asked politely to do so. A question from the petitioner follows. "With remarkable insight and quickness the reader dictates the scrawl to the scribe, who puts everything on paper."[37]

Some spirit-writers were literate and others were not. Naturally in the latter case the message had to be interpreted, and occasionally negotiated, before a final version could be committed to paper. The end product took many different forms. Whether lengthy or brief, the *fuji* revelation characteristically contained ethical advice. Thus a student might be told that moral development was more important than literary proficiency; and an official might learn that maladministration resulted in a shortened life.[38] Some oracular responses were delivered poetically, in two or more lines, often of equal length, while others consisted of a longer prose statement. Still others took the form of a dialogue between the spirit and his interlocutor. (Most *fuji* spirits in Qing times were male, although occasionally a female spirit would descend.)[39] The spirit's advice, as conveyed in writing, might be relatively straightforward or almost hopelessly obscure. Part of the appeal of spirit-writing, at least for the literati, seems clearly to have been its literary emphasis and elaborate word play.

Sometimes the "conversation" between a *fuji* spirit and his interlocutor took the form of an effort to "match couplets"—a traditional literary technique long used by Chinese scholars to demonstrate their erudition and mastery of poetic style. A scholarly patron might even impose specific stylistic requirements on the poetry of a spirit. In many instances, interpretation of a *fuji* revelation required skills closely akin to, if not identical with, conventional word-analysis (see chapter 5).[40] Zeng Guofan's elation over the capture of Jiujiang from the Taipings in 1858 was tempered considerably by the somber advice of a *fuji* spirit that he should replace the *wu* (military) element in the character *fu* (rhymed prose—one poetic form of spirit-writing) with *wen* (civil) to see what the process would yield. This "supplanting of the military by the civil" seemed natural enough after the pacification of the rebels in this area, but it produced the unpropitious character, *bai* (defeat). Zeng questioned how such a great victory could be viewed in such a way until he learned that the Jiujiang battle had set the stage for a disastrous debacle at Sanhe later in the year—a defeat, as the oracle predicted, not only for the Qing government, which lost several of its best commanders, including Li Xupin (d. 1858), but also the Zeng family, which suffered the loss of Zeng's younger brother, Guohua (1822–1858).[41]

In contrast to the wild gyrations characteristic of most forms of spirit possession, *fuji* divination, particularly when undertaken in the homes or in the presence of the Qing elite, was often a decorous affair. Under these circumstances each question was "made in a soft and solemn tone," or "carefully written on paper, and burned with an additional quantity of sheets of paper money to enrich the god." A scholar familiar with the writing stick might himself assume the role of a *shentong* without exhibiting any symptoms of possession or ecstacy; and even regular *fuji* specialists became somewhat more subdued in the presence of true literati. Lacking wild enthusiasm on the part of the medium, a delicate writing instrument might be substituted for the sturdy but cumbersome twin-pronged stick.[42]

Although *fuji* divination was highly ritualized, it offered periodic surprises. Spirits did not, for example, always answer the questions put to them. They might instead digress on subjects unrelated to those at hand, or chastize individuals for asking about the wrong things, or for seeking unworthy objectives. Sometimes, a writing stick would force the medium and his assistant into another part of the room or temple, or even out into the street. On occasion the wrong spirit entered the stick. If this spirit had evil intentions, the result might be an oracle that was either unpropitious or unintelligible. On the other hand, occasionally a deceased family member, or even a high-ranking deity in the official pantheon, such as Guandi, the God of War, might occupy the writing-stick, lending great prestige and authority to the oracular pronouncement.[43]

In part, Qing scholars esteemed *fuji* divination for its explicitly moral emphasis. By the early seventeenth century, books of ethical teachings composed by means of spirit-writing had begun to appear in China. These works, part of a continuous tradition extending throughout the Qing period and into the present, consisted of alternating passages of prose and verse written in a simple classical style.

Many employed the technical vocabulary of *fuji* consultation, providing names, times and places for significant revelations. The God of War, the God of Literature, and the Daoist immortal Lü Dongbin (also considered a patron saint of literary studies in the Qing period) appeared most frequently as revealing deities; and although the values expressed in *fuji* texts were unmistakably Confucian, the sanction was predominantly religious. Buddhist concepts of karma and the Ten Courts of Judgment assumed particular importance, and divinations sometimes took place in Buddhist as well as Daoist temples. The presence of these elements of Chinese popular culture did not, however, dissuade Qing officials and gentry from either supporting publication of these works or writing colophons.[44]

Of course the primary reason *fuji* divination attracted the attention of Qing scholars was its utility in answering questions of ultimate importance to them. These included matters of life and death, sickness and health, problems of civil and military administration, and career issues.[45] The *Qingbai leichao, Tushu jicheng*, Xu Dishan's collection of anecdotes on spirit-writing and other sources provide a wealth of examples concerning these types of divination. Like professional fortune-tellers, *fuji* spirit mediums predicted disasters such as droughts, floods, epidemics and rebellions. They also advised individuals on how to conduct their lives for maximum personal advantage, assisted officials in their administrative affairs (including legal decisions), and helped them to defeat pirates and bandits.[46] Ye Mingchen (1807–1859), governor-general of Liang-Guang in the turbulent 1850s, had a particularly great faith in *fuji* oracles, and resorted to them often. Occasionally he even included the pronouncements of *fuji* deities in his own official proclamations.[47]

A great many *fuji* stories from the Qing period, both factual and fictional, revolve around the examination system. Pu Songling tells of a scholarly *fuji* specialist named Wang Ruiting, who, speaking for the spirit that possessed him, evaluated the essay of one Li Bian. He pronounced the essay to be of the highest quality, but predicted that the man's literary ability and fate were out of harmony, and that therefore he would not do as well as expected in the examinations. Because of malpractices in the system, Wang's prediction proved true. But he advised Li, again through the spirit, that he should be patient and continue to strive for improvement, and that the next time he took the examinations he might well gain distinction—which he did.[48] Anecdotes from the *Qingbai leichao* attest to the verisimilitude of Pu's tales, offering many variations on the theme of morality and rectitude. They also demonstrate that *fuji* divination involved some of the most illustrious scholar-officials in the land, including early Qing worthies like Peng Dingqiu (1645–1719) as well as later notables such as Ye Mingchen and Zeng Guofan.[49]

Zhu Mouxiang's dramatic spirit-writing story of Yue Baohe, a student preparing for his triennial exams, underscores the importance of morality to the scholarly enterprise. According to Zhu's account, Yue established a *fuji* altar to inquire about his prospects for the upcoming examinations. Without warning, the spirit of Guandi suddenly appeared, and in response to Yue's query wrote:

When celestial officials select scholars they discuss literary essays last, and first look at moral conduct. All those who are filial and friendly pass, those who are sincere and genuine pass, those who share their merit with others pass, those whose mind and mouth are one pass, those who are not perverse and do not ask from others pass, those who look on others as themselves pass, those who err by speaking ill unintentionally pass, those who abstain from lust and immorality pass. I have examined your life and find not one good thing. I have therefore ordered [my standard bearer] Zhou Cang to destroy your family and extinguish its traces.

A year later an epidemic wiped out Yue's entire family.[50]

Morality aside, scholars wanted help with their careers, and spirit-writing offered hope from several quarters. In the first place, it held out the possibility of magical instruction. The *Qingbai leichao* instances Li Yuhong, a scholar in Tongzhou (Shandong), before whom a "writing spirit" (*bishen*) revealed itself. The spirit promised that if Li would pay proper respect, it would help Li win a name for himself in the examination system. With the spirit's assistance, Li was able to write elegant essays in an attractive hand. He thus passed the examinations, became an official, and continued to use the spirit as an aid in administration.[51] Furthermore, Qing scholars were not above trying to find out which questions would appear on the examinations. Stories of *fuji* divinations that revealed this type of information circulated widely in China, contributing immensely to the popularity of spirit-writing throughout the empire. The fact that spirits as exalted as Guandi sometimes participated in the revelations made these tales all the more plausible, or at least more attractive.[52]

In divination concerning examination topics, word play loomed large—though the game itself was deadly serious. Yuan Mei, in his *Zi buyu* (Things of Which the Master Did Not Speak), provides an illuminating example. He recounts the case of an unnamed *juren* degree-holder who, prior to the metropolitan examinations of 1688, asked a *fuji* spirit for insight into the question. The spirit answered "[I] don't know" (*buzhi*). Incredulous, the scholar wanted to know why. The spirit replied: "[I] don't know, [I] don't know, and again, [I] don't know" (*buzhi buzhi you buzhi*). The scholars who had gathered at the *fuji* altar for the occasion were amused by this response, but they remained unenlightened. Only later did they discover that the three-part examination theme was taken from the last chapter of the *Analects* (20: 3): "Without knowing [*buzhi*] fate it is impossible to be a gentleman; without knowing [*buzhi*] ritual it is impossible to establish [character]; and without knowing [*buzhi*] words, it is impossible to know men."[53]

As with other forms of spirit possession, *fuji* divination could always find a medical application—not only for families but also, at least occasionally, for whole communities. In cases involving individual illness, if the patient needed to be seen in person, the medium and his assistant would take their divining stick to the person's home, where they passed it over the patient several times. They then returned to the original planchette, where medical advice, often in the form of a charm or a prescription, was forthcoming.[54] Spirit-writing designed for an entire community was an even more complicated matter. One example, illustrating an elaborate link between *fuji* divination, fate, medicine and morality, can be found in 1894, during a widespread outbreak of bubonic plague in south China.

In Hong Kong, one of many cities ravaged by disease, the God of War reportedly descended into a writing stick several times. During one of these visits, he wrote a long announcement in forty-two lines of six characters each, reporting that it was Heaven's inescapable will that one or two out of every ten people in the city would die of the plague. But, as the administrative agent of Heaven, he, Guandi, could bring relief to those willing to rectify their minds and atone for their sins. In yet another revelation, he stated that his protection could not be gained by sacrifice, worship or any means other than virtue and sanctity. No dwelling, he maintained, will be entered by any plague-demons if "filial devotion and friendship prevail." He urged people to read and recite one of his *fuji* morality tracts, adding that "in the case of women who cannot read," protection could be gained by "one incense-stick kindled in the morning and one in the evening." Finally, for good measure, Guandi provided charms and a medical prescription consisting of seventeen ingredients for use by the population at large. Local benevolent societies disseminated these messages, embellishing them in various ways.[55]

In Qing times women normally did not engage in spirit-writing. They did, however, perform most other shamanistic services, primarily for members of their own sex. Although a number had bound feet, their preliminary ritual and "dancing" approximated that of male shamans, as did their medical remedies, exorcisms and oral prognostications.[56] The most popular female deity for spirit possession in Qing times was Zigu (lit., the Purple Aunt), also known as Sangu (the Third Aunt), and, less flatteringly, as the "Goddess of the Privy" (Ceshen). Her use as the primary focus for a pre-literate divination cult can be traced to the Tang dynasty, and by Song times she had come to be considered a talented writer and artist.[57] During the Qing, however, she seems to have reverted to her Tang role as a pre-literate oracle. Local gazetteers indicate that Zigu was worshipped by women primarily on the fifteenth day of the first month, usually at night, and asked about prospects for the coming year.[58] This was not, however, the only time she could be called upon to shed light on the future.[59]

A number of women shamans specialized in communicating directly with the dead, perhaps because so many unplaced spirits in traditional China were female—*gui* who had an axe to grind against the oppressive patriarchal society that caused them so much misery in life.[60] These women mediums, known as "feeble aunts" (*wangyi*), "spirit ladies" (*xianpo*), "rice-inquiry ladies" (*wenmipo*) and so forth, were often blind, which people generally considered conducive to clairvoyance (see chapter 5). Such shamans usually met with groups of women on an auspicious day, and for a small fee agreed to help them find out about loved ones or discover the source of their *gui*-related family problems.[61] By means of a trance-like state the shaman entered the nether world (*yinfang*; lit., "the dark realm"), made direct contact with deceased relatives or friends, and spoke both to them and for them. As with male shamans, the answers given to the questions of clients were sometimes difficult to understand. They did not always address the queries raised, and they often gratuitously offered advice, even rebukes, to clients.[62]

Another technique used by women shamans to communicate with the deceased friends and relatives of other women involved a small wooden image, made of willow wood. This image, endowed with spirituality by various occult rituals, was placed on the stomach or chest of the shaman to whom it belonged. There it served as a secondary medium, to be inhabited temporarily by someone from the nether world. According to Justus Doolittle, "questions are addressed to the [primary] medium; the replies appear to come from her stomach. . . . The medium makes use of no incense or candles in the performance of this method. Widows who desire information in regard to their deceased husbands, or childless married women who wish to learn in regard to the future, not infrequently call upon this class of spiritualists or mediums."[63] Apparently one means of investing the carved image with supernatural power was to write upon it the "eight characters" of "some clever living person whose spirit is desired, and then worshiping the image, and leaving it out-doors until this person dies, . . . which it is said will surely take place in a very short time." Needless to say, this approach occasionally gave rise to the charge of murder.[64]

In part because of such practices and accusations, Qing elites tended to be particularly critical of women shamans and their "foolish" women followers.[65] But all spirit mediums proved threatening to the scholarly class by virtue of their willingness to flout social norms openly. They were everything people in traditional China were not supposed to be: extravagant, vulgar, unlettered and unrestrained. With the exception of elite-oriented spirit-writers, they lacked any semblance of decorum or any sensitivity to the social distinctions that defined Confucianism as the "teachings of status" (*mingjiao*). Furthermore, those who indulged in self-mortification (a practice confined largely to Fujian and Taiwan) were deplorably unfilial, since the body was a treasured gift of one's ancestors.[66]

Elites also feared the spiritual power of shamans, which smacked of "black magic." The capacity to heal implied the capacity to harm, and many stories circulated of the use of shamanistic skills for both purposes.[67] A vigorous but typically ineffective late Qing proclamation by the acting governor-general of Min-Zhe, outlawing religious processions (*yingshen saihui*) in Fujian and Zhejiang, took pains to point out that such activities not only encouraged young men and women to act improperly, but also provided the occasion for spirit mediums to "delude the masses" (*huochong*) and even to use magical incantations that "kill people."[68]

Above all, the elite felt threatened by the social power of shamans. As with other traditional Chinese service groups, including doctors, the more literate they were, the more power they wielded. But while possessed, even illiterate peasant mediums enjoyed a status and influence disproportionate to their normal standing in society. They spoke, after all, for the gods, and not always in a comforting voice. Sometimes they championed the specific interests of the spirit that possessed them, as in the case of a low-ranking deity who longed for a higher post in the supernatural world, and who, through a medium, advised the local population to petition the emperor for a promotion.[69] But shamans could also wield power for other purposes. They could, for instance, criticize elites or ask officials for the redress of grievances in the name of the gods.[70] And even when shamanistic oracles worked to the advantage of the elite— such as when a local spirit-writer advised thousands of angry and recalcitrant peasants that they should honor the wishes of the local magistrate, who had cancelled a procession honoring the Qingpu City God on his "birthday"—the scholarly class could hardly fail to recognize the political potential of such utterances.[71]

It was the capacity of shamans to influence large numbers of people that most terrified Qing officials. In contrast to more conventional doctors and diviners, spirit mediums often worked with groups of individuals. They thus became a possible rallying point, or at least source of support, for politically threatening sectarian movements (see chapter 5). This was particularly true of diviners whose gift for summoning spirits attracted a large band of loyal supporters.[72] A memorial to the throne by Ying Shan, financial commissioner of Sichuan, suggests the dangers. In 1792 Ying reported that he had recently seized a writing stick which had been used in the composition of "rebellious poems and prefaces," including verses that "recklessly claimed" that a local rebel named Liu Wanchong was a descendent of the Han house. This man, together with a number of others, formed a group that pledged brotherhood—"an extremely illegal business," in Ying's words. Similarly, in 1815, the governor-general of Zhili reported that an itinerant physician by the name of Jiang Yinglong, who used *fuji* divination to seek prescriptions for doubtful or difficult illnesses, summoned a spirit that implicated him and others in a plot to restore the Ming dynasty.[73] Healing practices had long been identified with sectarian movements, and since *fuji* often united medicine, revelation, and groups of people, it posed a particularly potent threat.[74] *Fuji* groups could serve as convenient covers for anti-social associations.

Yet despite hostility on the part of the Qing elite that far outweighed its antipathy toward doctors and professional diviners, changes in the patterns and prevalence of shamanism came slowly in China.[75] Why? In large part the answer lies in their multifaceted social role, particularly in "peripheral" areas. In the first place, Chinese mediums were entertaining, and literally entrancing. Their esoteric speech, wild gesturing, and colorful costumes gave them genuine dramatic appeal, placing them firmly and quite comfortably in a larger framework of culturally satisfying activities that included plays, festivals, and pilgrimages.[76] For this reason, among others, members of the Qing elite sometimes classified shamans with performers and prostitutes as entertainers.[77] Furthermore, the use by shamans of aesthetically appealing symbols—notably the *Taiji tu* and eight trigrams—on ritual clothing, spirit altars, litters for carrying gods, and flags—both reflected and reinforced, if only subliminally, a powerful sense of shared culture at all levels of Chinese society.

As seers, healers and advisers, spirit mediums fulfilled a variety of individual needs—both social and psychological—in traditional Chinese society, overlapping and complementing the responsibilities of physicians and professional fortune-tellers in a variety of ways.[78] And, as ritualists for families, temples, shrines, associations and entire communities, they contributed to group solidarity, not least by acting as arbitrators and cultural intermediaries. Finally, looking at matters from yet another perspective, the practice of shamanism allowed traditionally powerless people a way to approach figures of distant, autocratic authority by providing an idiom—possession by a superior but "related" being—that made sense from the standpoint of their own perception of social reality.[79]

Personal Omens and Oracles

One did not, of course, require shamans to receive spiritually-inspired messages. Signs portending the future were visible everywhere. All sectors of Qing society had an acute awareness of the importance of omens, from the Son of Heaven to the lowliest peasant. In government, the emperor and his officials depended heavily on the proper interpretation of a wide variety of celestial and earthly phenomena in order to maintain effective administration and forestall criticism or outright rebellion (see chapter 2). Chinese scholars naturally shared this concern, whether in or out of office.[80] Commoners, too, displayed a high sensitivity to portents, for those who lived in the countryside always paid close attention to changes in their physical environment, and those who resided in urban areas were often called upon by Qing officials to participate in public rituals designed to restore cosmic harmony in the face of anomalies such as eclipses.[81]

Elites and commoners also felt the need to seek personal guidance from omens, whether in the form of plants, animals, sounds, and sensations, or their own dreams (see next section). The *Qingbai leichao* devotes considerable attention to various portents (*zhao*) involving a wide range of individuals, and an even wider array of unusual phenomena.[82] Other sources reflect a concern with more mundane signs and situations.[83] Qing almanacs, for example, generally include a section on personal omens that people might encounter at any time in their daily lives. The most common categories were: twitching of the eyes (*yantiao*), ringing in the ears (*erming*), a burning or itching sensation in the face or ears (*mianre* or *erre*), quivering flesh (*rouchan*), palpitations (*xinjing*; lit., a startled heart/mind), sneezing (*tipen*), clothes left behind (*yiliu*), the sounds made by a hot pot on the stove (*fuming*), a fire growing out of control (*huoyi*), a dog barking (*quanfei*), and a magpie chirping (*qiaosao*) (see Fig. 6.2).[84]

With all such phenomena, considerations of time, direction, or location were critical to correct interpretation. Thus, almanacs invariably divided omen categories into twelve two-hour periods marked by "earthly branches." A ringing in the left ear at the *zi* hour (11 P.M.–1 A.M.), for instance, indicated that a loved one was thinking of you, while a ringing in the right ear during the same time period indicated that you would lose money. Ringing in the left ear at the *chou* hour (1 A.M.–3 A.M.) signified a quarrel, and in the right ear, a lawsuit. By the same token, the chirping of a magpie at the *zi* hour indicated that a relative would arrive from afar, bringing "great good fortune;" at the *chou* hour, it signified great happiness, celebration, and good fortune; and at the *yin* hour (3 A.M.–5 A.M.), a small amount of good luck in the midst of litigation.[85] Most of the omens contained in popular almanacs were favorable, and the majority dealt with down-to-earth themes of the sort outlined above: visits from friends, relatives and others (including Buddhist and Daoist clerics), feasting, and the accumulation of wealth. Unfavorable events included injuries, disputes, lawsuits, and the loss of money. As with most other features of traditional Chinese almanacs, the specific content of these omen texts remained remarkably consistent over time and space, not only during the Qing period, but down to the present.

Nicholas Dennys, in his *Folk-Lore of China* (1876), provides an illuminating comparison of Chinese and Western beliefs respecting omens and portents, showing a number of parallels between the two cultures. He equates, for example, the misfortune of spilling salt in the West with the upsetting of an oil jar in China, and shows that Chinese and European attitudes toward certain physical sensations (such as sneezing or a "burning" in the ears), events (encountering a funeral or hearing the "unseasonable" crowing of roosters), natural phenomena (such as comets), animals (including dogs, magpies and crows), and activities (such as the breaking of mirrors) were remarkably similar.

When it comes to the question of how seriously such beliefs were taken, however, Dennys seems ambivalent. On the one hand, he remarks that "omens exert, as might be expected, a telling influence on Chinese everyday life;" and he claims that the cry of a crow is "considered so unlucky [in China] that when any one about to undertake an affair hears it, he generally postpones action." On the other hand, Denny takes pains to point out that the "superstitious beliefs" of China do not differ "to any material extent from those current amongst humanity elsewhere." He resolves this apparent conflict by writing: "The one grand distinction between Chinese and European folk-lore lies . . . in the different powers they exert over the respective communities. In the one case it is either a matter only of amused indifference or of interested research to all but the lowest classes of the population. In the other it represents an all-pervading system of regulations believed in or complied with by high and low alike."[86] Perhaps Dennys underestimates the pervasiveness of what he calls "superstitious beliefs" in the nineteenth century West; but the fundamental point he makes is, I think, valid and significant.

What other forms of personal access to "spiritual" knowledge existed in traditional Chinese society? One of the most pervasive—available to literates and illiterates alike—was the use of paired divining blocks known variously as *jiao, bei, jiaobei, beijiao,* or *jiaogua.* These blocks, each carved out of wood or bamboo root into the shape of a crescent moon, with one side rounded and the other side flat, allowed individuals to determine a god's will—at least with respect to questions that could be answered "yes" or "no."[87] The usual procedure was to hold the blocks, which might be anywhere from three to eight inches in length, about head high, and either throw them or allow them to fall on the floor, after posing a silent question in the form of a prayer. Three configurations were possible: both blocks might land with the flat side down (*yin*); both with the flat side up (*yang*); or one with the flat side up and the other with the flat side down ("victorious" [*sheng*] or "holy," another term for the same combination, also pronounced *sheng*). If both flat sides landed down, the answer was "no;" if one remained up and the other down, the answer was "yes;" and if both landed with the flat side facing upward, the answer was equivocal. Often this configuration was interpreted as amusement (*xiaobei*; lit., "laughing blocks") on the part of the god in question.[88]

Divining blocks were used to communicate with all kinds of spirits, from ancestors and household deities to the innumerable gods ensconced in Buddhist and Daoist temples. Mediums and professional fortune-tellers occasionally employed them, and some Buddhist monasteries even used them to select abbots.[89] In ordinary divination, the blocks were most often dropped in multiple rounds of three; and although the questions posed required only a "yes" or "no" answer, many temples and individual fortune-tellers possessed books that provided additional advice, often highly metaphorical, based on the possible results of a three-round series of tosses.[90] One such work, organized into sections corresponding to the twenty-eight lunar lodges, offers the following oracle for a *yin/sheng/sheng* series: "The end will be as the beginning, neither cold nor hot. Travellers must stop at once and wayfarers must seek a village to rest in." Three *yang* tosses yields: "The bright moon is in the clouds and the fish are rushing madly up the rapids. If you want to catch fish or see the moon, there will be difficulties in either case." Three *sheng* tosses reveal that "The Constellation Can has always been a lucky one. Have no doubts [or fears], everything you seek you shall find, and everyone shall hear of your good fortune."[91]

In some temples, a local priest might cast the blocks for patrons, who would then promise a gift to the god or the temple if the cleric would keep dropping them until a favorable result ensued. The logic behind this approach was that the god in question could change a person's fate if he or she demonstrated sufficient devotion.[92] In the home, questions directed to the ancestors focused primarily on aspects of life-cycle ritual, such as whether they (the deceased) agreed with a proposed marriage. Other commonly asked questions, both at home and in temples, shrines, and non-domestic altars, had to do with the usual range of personal problems, from health and finances to career concerns.[93] But the primary application of divining blocks outside the home was to determine whether another method of divination, the selection of bamboo lots or "spiritual sticks" (*lingqian*), would yield a satisfactory result.

The pervasiveness of *qian* divination in Qing times, which extended to all areas of the empire, including Tibet, gave rise to the cliché, "If anything happens, seek [advice from] *qian* slips" (*you shiqing qiuqian*).[94] *Qian* divination, like the use of *jiao* blocks, tended to be undertaken primarily by unlettered women—for whom trips to the religious temples where they could invariably be found constituted one of the few forms of non-domestic recreation available to them.[95] But members of the elite also employed them. The great Qing scholar Yan Yuan, for example, resorted to bamboo lots in an effort to locate his father, from whom he had been separated since the age of three, during the Manchu conquest.[96] Other prominent scholars who are known to have practiced *qian* divination at one time or another include Wang Shizhen (1634–1711), Han Tan (1637–1704), Bi Yuan (1730–1797) and Enming (1846–1907).[97]

One practical reason for the popularity of *qian* divination, aside from its usually negligible cost, was its close connection with traditional Chinese medicine. Many temples, Buddhist as well as Daoist, offered petitioners "spiritual sticks" that identified prescriptions and other specific medical remedies (see below).[98] Another reason for its popularity was its presumed relationship to the hallowed *Yijing*. Although most fortune-telling systems ultimately tried to trace their lineage to this exalted classic, works such as Lu Han's *Qian Yi* (The [Spiritual] Stick Changes) made the connection a direct one. The editors of the *Siku quanshu*, in reviewing Lu's book, likened bamboo lots to the use of coins (rather than milfoil stalks) as derivative techniques in a long tradition of *Yijing* evolution undertaken by mantic "technicians" (*fangji*).[99] Rong Zhaozu, for his part, shows how Qing dynasty *qian* handbooks with sixty-four passages show structural affinities with the *Yijing* and its derivatives—notably the *Yilin* and the *Lingqi jing* (see chapter 1)—and he describes the *Yi* as a "distant ancestor" of *qian* divination books.[100]

Lot sticks came in sets that varied in number from twenty to more than a hundred. Sets of fifty, sixty-four, and one hundred seem to have been most popular in Qing times, as they are today.[101] The sticks, each about twelve to eighteen inches in length and numbered consecutively, were contained together in a bamboo tube. When a person (let us presume a woman) was ready to divine, she would burn incense, supplicate the god of her choice in a reverential spirit, and shake the container until a single bamboo stick emerged further than the others (see Fig. 6.1). A system of coin divination, involving ten copper cash, might also be used to find the appropriate *qian*.[102] After the spiritual stick had been selected, the petitioner determined with divining blocks whether it was an appropriate one. If not, the procedure would be repeated until the god gave its assent. At this point, the person consulted a written oracle corresponding to the number of the stick.[103]

As Wolfram Eberhard has observed, these short inscriptions, based on history and myth, often refer to events and themes derived from popular dramas. He provides several examples, three of which may serve to illustrate the point. One reads: "Xiangru Returns to Zhao with the Entire Ring." This reference, drawn from a play entitled "The Complete Ring," alludes to the trials and tribulations of one Lin Xiangru, entrusted by the ruler of Zhao in the Warring States period to negotiate with the state of Qin for fifteen cities in exchange for a famous jade ring. It warns of manifold dangers for a man and his wife. A second allusion, "Sun Bin Meets Pang Quan," comes from a play known as "Pang Quan Flees at Night on the Maling Road," in which Pang, a classmate of Sun, cuts off the latter's legs out of envy so that he (Sun) will not be able to serve as a general. Although Sun eventually defeats Pang in battle, the oracle draws its lesson not from the winner but from the loser, offering the warning that plans which initially seem successful may later turn out badly. The third case, "Xu Jia harms Fan Ju," takes its theme from a play entitled "The Vituperation of Fan Ju." In it, both men are sent as hostages to a neighboring

Figure 6.1 *Qian* divination at the Wang Daxian Temple.

state in the Zhou period. Xu believes that Fan is collaborating with the enemy and he denounces Fan, who is stripped of his honors and nearly beaten to death. Fan later retaliates and causes Xu equal misery. The clear message concerns the wages of slander and revenge.[104]

Commoners who knew such plays by heart (and many apparently did) could appreciate the allusions; but few could actually read them. Most people who consulted *qian* slips were illiterate, or at best, semi-literate. Each temple therefore needed someone to identify and explain the allusion; if not a monk, priest,

第一籤　甲甲　大吉　巍巍獨步向雲間　玉殿千官第一班　聖意　功名遂　福祿全　訟得理　病即痊
十八学士登瀛洲　富貴榮華天付汝　福如東海壽如山　桑麻熟　婚姻圓　孕生子　行人還
解曰　此籤謀望事緒。無不遂意。但各有所主。官員占此。有超越之喜。士人有功名之慶。占前程者。福壽綿長。占事業者。根基穩固。若謀望求財。多主有名無實。為語多空虛也。
釋義　雲間。青雲之上也。巍巍獨步。許其足踏青雲也。玉殿千官。乃是天曹仙吏。第一班。仙吏之最貴者也。榮華富貴。自天作主。天已付之。自然福壽無涯。如海。言福之廣遠。如山。言壽之堅永。上上大吉。須要人地相當則應。
〔東坡解〕　雲間獨步　拔萃超羣　名登甲第　談笑功勛　終身光顯　皆天所相　祿厚壽高　意稱謀望
〔碧仙註〕　月裏攀丹桂　成名步玉墀　求謀皆稱意　萬事足無疑

第二籤　甲乙　上吉　盈虛消息總天時　自此君當百事宜　聖意　訟宜和　病宜禱　功名有　遲莫躁
韓蘄王西湖騎驢　若問前程歸縮地　須憑方寸好修為　求財平　問婚好　若妄為　身莫保
解曰　此籤前運不佳。前事蹭蹬。自此以後。漸見順利。若問究竟歸結。全在存心種德。方得成實。倘值境遇逆意。須忘前因。暗損心術。必至有始無終。自貽後悔。勉之慎之。
釋義　盈虛消息。天運之常。人生窮通得喪。亦似比無有定在。言占者未曾遇時也。自此相宜。困極而亨。所謀遂意也。前程歸縮。是收成結果之地。方寸修為。戒占者勿損心田。勿害天理。及早積德修因。遂終有慶矣。君子修之吉。小人悖之凶。唯所自擇何如耳。
〔東坡解〕　萬事乘除　隨時而處　否極泰來　事無齟齬　收成結果　方寸修為　切莫妄動　萬福來宜
〔碧仙註〕　禍福從天降　存心萬事宜　若還無妄作　禍散福相隨

第三籤　甲丙　中吉　衣食自然生處有　勸君不用苦勞心　聖意　問名利　自有時　訟和吉　產尚遲
張公藝九世同居　但能孝悌存忠信　福祿來成禍不侵　病可治　婚未宜　宜謹守　免憂疑
解曰　此籤只宜守舊。不可貪求。但存中直。卻得兩平。須以孝弟忠信為本。自有福祿來成之應。若思強取強求。反招意外之禍。占者循理守分則吉。
釋義　衣食自然。言衣食各有定分。生處有。言係人生命理所載。不可強也。不用勞心。勸人安分。孝弟忠信。勸人務本。孝弟所以盡倫。忠信所以處事。如此為人。自蒙上天鑑佑。福祿來成。言福集而祿臻。俯仰稱意。禍不侵。凡事有吉無凶也。全在修為。不可背本。慎之。
〔東坡解〕　富貴前定　何須強求　徒勞心力　反致傷憂　事親待人　動合循理　天必佑之　有泰無否
〔碧仙註〕　隨緣安分　直道而行　心中無愧　自然和平

Figure 6.2 Excerpt from a popular *qian* booklet. This page provides complete interpretations for the first three "spiritual sticks" of the "God of War," Guan Yu. *Source: Guan Shengdi lingqian* (n.d.), p. 2.

caretaker or other low-ranking functionary, then a professional fortune-teller—one or more of whom could always be found in the immediate vicinity. The Buddhist clergy's official position was that *qian* divination had no real utility, "since it did not change the future of the worshipper, which was determined by the karma of his deeds." Nonetheless, Buddhist temples tolerated the use of "spiritual sticks" as a "popular custom," and even some of the most prestigious monasteries allowed their vergers (*xiangdeng*) to accept small "tips" in exchange for their assistance in interpreting the *qian* slips.[105]

Interpreters of this sort either elaborated on an oracle from memory or consulted a *qian* booklet (see Fig. 6.2). These works, many of which could be purchased at very low cost and were sometimes distributed without charge, contained, in addition to a full set of verses, a more extensive explanation for each. Although regional tastes and gender preferences make generalizations about these handbooks difficult,[106] it appears that of the several dozen different kinds of *qian* booklets available in various Qing dynasty temples and bookstores, the most popular was the one associated with the name of Guandi, the God of War.[107] Other widely used *qian* handbooks included those connected with deities such as Guanyin (The Goddess of Mercy), Tianhou (The Empress of Heaven) and Lüzu (Ancestor Lü; Lü Dongbin).[108]

The best way to capture the flavor of these works is to provide a detailed discussion of one representative entry and its subtexts. The following example comes from the *Wusheng Guandi lingqian* (Spiritual Sticks of the Military Sage Emperor Guan [Yu]) reprinted in a late Qing almanac entitled *Guanshang kuailan* (A Quick Reference for Officials and Merchants, 1903). Although this version lacks the color of more recent editions (see below), it is remarkably similar in both substance and style, and contains instructions for using coins as well as *qian*. Let us take the first of its one hundred entries, this one marked by the doubled stem combination *jiajia*.

The introductory phrase is: "The Eighteen Scholars Ascend to Yingzhou." This refers to a group of famous individuals in the Tang dynasty who lived during the reign of Emperor Taizong (r. 976–996). The term Yingzhou has the double meaning of a prestigious College with which the eighteen men were associated, and one of the legendary Daoist Islands of the Immortals. The four seven-character verses that follow read:

Walking alone majestically toward the clouds;
First class among a thousand officials in the Jade Palace.
Heaven bestows upon you wealth, nobility and glory;
Blessings like the Eastern Sea and longevity like a mountain.

The "sagely meaning" (*shengyi*) comes next, expounded in eight groups of three characters each. "You will attain merit and fame. Your blessings and wealth will be complete. [If you are involved in] litigation you will obtain a proper settlement [of your case]. If sick, you will become well. [If you are a farmer] your crops [lit., mulberries and hemp] will ripen fully. Your marriage [will be] satisfactory [lit. round]. Pregnancy will yield a son. Travellers will return home."

The next section provides an "explanation" (*jie*) of the four preliminary verses. Reportedly written by the great Song dynasty scholar Su Dongpo, it reiterates the opening themes in eight rather more elegant four-character phrases, ending with the judgment: "All you wish for you will have, and everything you plan will be as you had hoped" (*yicheng mouwang*). The last section, a "commentary" attributed to Bi Xian (lit. "The Azure Immortal"), does the same in four five-character phrases, alluding to literary success, fame, the fulfillment of desires, and "indubitable satisfaction in everything" (*wanshi zu wuyi*).

At the top of the *jiajia* column in the Guandi handbook is the phrase "great good luck" (*daji*), one of six possible designations for each of the one hundred "spiritual sticks." The others are: extremely good (*shanshang*), very good luck (*shangji*), medium good luck (*zhongji*), middling (*zhongping*), medium bad luck (*zhongxia*) and extremely bad (*xiaxia*). From a traditional standpoint, only the last two categories represent bad fortune.[109] A content analysis of the Guandi handbook of 1903 reveals a total of three *daji*, eight *shanshang*, eighteen *shangji*, twenty-seven *zhongji*, twenty-four *zhongping*, one *zhongxia*, and nineteen *xiaxia*. In other words, only twenty percent of the *qian* fortunes are bad, nearly twenty-five percent represent "average" luck, and over fifty percent are notably auspicious.

How does this handbook compare with other *qian* handbooks in this respect? In a pioneering and still valuable study of the history of Chinese divination, first published in 1928, Rong Zhaozu analyzes several *qian* booklets he gathered in Guangzhou at some unspecified time. Although Rong points out that works identified with different supernatural authorities may vary significantly in content (see below), those identified with the same authority are virtually the same in content over long stretches of time. Thus, I was not surprised to discover that his statistical analysis of the seven categories of fortune found in the Guandi handbook he had acquired corresponded precisely with the breakdown in my own 1903 version. For this reason among others, I assume that the other *qian* booklets he gathered also reflect long-standing Qing dynasty categories and contents.[110]

The Guanyin handbook Rong cites contains one hundred fortunes, thirty of which are designated superior (*shang*), fifty-five middling (*zhong*), and fifteen inferior (*xia*). Another lesser-known handbook of one hundred entries, the *Caibaixing jun qian* (Sticks of the Honorable Wealth Star), contains one extremely good (*shanshang*) slip, thirty-four designated very good luck (*shangji*), one medium superior (*zhongshang*), thirty medium good luck (*zhongji*), three ordinary luck (*pingji*), one average (*pingping*), four lower average (*xiaping*), and twenty-one lower luck (*xiaji*). Of the 101 fortunes in the *Dongyue qian* (Eastern Mountain [i.e., the God of Mount Tai] Sticks), twenty slips are considered extremely good (*shangshang*), twelve indicate very good luck (*shangji*), seven are upper middling (*shangzhong*), fifteen are great good luck (*daji*—apparently this is not the top category, as it is in the Guandi handbook), four are middling (*zhongzhong*), nineteen middle average (*zhongping*), one middle good luck, two middle lower (*zhongxia*) and twenty-one lower lower. Of the 103 fortunes in the *Tianhou qian* (Empress of Heaven Sticks), three special sticks, identified with levels of distinction in the examination system, are considered extremely good (*shangshang*), thirty-four, superior (*shang*), thirty-two, middling (*zhong*), and thirty-four, inferior (*xia*).[111]

Among handbooks with less than one hundred sticks, similar patterns of distribution prevail, with some exceptions. Of the two works with sixty-four, one contains thirty-five slips designated as superior, twenty-two as middling and seven as lower; while the other identifies thirty-two as superior, fifteen as middling, and seventeen as inferior. Among the three handbooks providing information on fifty slips, one has twenty-two superior designations, twelve middling, and fifteen inferior, with one "unclear." Another is broken down into twelve extremely good (*shangshang*) fortunes, ten involving great good luck (*daji*; again, apparently not the top category), one designated "peaceful" (*ping'an*; presumably corresponding to "middle average"), one middle average (*zhongping*), seven lower (*xia*) and ten extremely bad (*xiaxia*). The third contains a similar breakdown: twelve extremely good, ten great good luck, one "peaceful," twelve middle average, seven middle lower (*zhongxia*), and eleven extremely bad. The *Huatuo qian* (Sticks of Huatuo [the God of Medicine]), with only thirty-six sticks, designates fifteen of them as superior, twelve as middling and nine as inferior, while the *Tudi qian* (Sticks of the Earth God), with even fewer fortunes (twenty-eight), has eight superior, ten middling, and ten inferior.[112]

On the whole, the striking feature of these handbooks is of course the positive character of their messages. Statistically speaking, under most circumstances a person consulting one or another *qian* oracle in Qing times had a much better than average chance of drawing at least a satisfactory fortune. A content analysis of four unnamed but obviously popular *qian* handbooks from Taiwan in the 1970s reveals a similar pattern of positive readings. The author of this study, Jin Xu, a professional physician (M.D.), divides the oracles for each of these works into four categories: very lucky, lucky, average luck, and bad luck. According to this breakdown, about fifty percent of the oracles indicate good luck, twenty-five percent suggest average luck, and twenty-five percent indicate bad luck. As Jin points out, not all cultures display such patterns of positive reading in divination systems of this sort.[113]

Virtually anyone in traditional China could learn to recognize the characters for "great good luck" and "lower misfortune," but, as I have suggested, illiterate patrons who desired further information on the chosen oracle needed someone to explain the basic text and commentaries.[114] Such explanations, provided in colloquial prose for modern *qian* handbooks, were probably supplied verbally much of the time in the Qing period.[115] A recent version of the Guandi handbook discussed above, entitled *Guan Shengdi lingqian* (The Spiritual Sticks of Guan [Yu] the Sage Emperor), which I picked up in Hong Kong in 1986, contains vernacular explanations that I strongly suspect were prevalent in Qing times—particularly since the main text of the handbook (primary verses, "sagely meaning," and commentaries by Su Dongpuo and Bi Xian) is identical with the 1903 edition.[116]

According to the colloquial "explanation" of *jiajia*: "This stick indicates that plans are fulfilled and affairs are accomplished, but everything has a purpose. If an official gets this divination, it will mean the pleasure of a promotion. If a scholar gets it, he will celebrate merit and fame. For someone looking ahead, the future holds extended blessings and long life. For one concerned with business, the foundation is solid. If a person seeks wealth, it is mainly in the name and not the reality, for words are often empty." A further "explication of the meaning" (*shiyi*) elaborates on the metaphors contained in the primary verses, investing some of them with explicitly religious significance. Thus, for example, the "thousand officials of the Jade Palace" are identified with "heavenly officials and immortal deputies" (*tiancao xianli*) of the nether world.

The most characteristic feature of *qian* divination, aside from its optimistic tone, is its decidedly moral emphasis. The preface to a Guandi handbook, dated 1793, ends with the following simple admonition: "Preserve a good mind; carry out good deeds; read good books; and speak good words."[117] The title page of a Guanyin handbook from about the same period displays the following couplet, reminding the reader that ultimately behavior is the foundation of fate: "Divining omens of auspiciousness and inauspiciousness before one's eyes; indicating the source of fortune and misfortune in the world of human affairs."[118]

Ethical advice sometimes, but not invariably, occurs in the basic verses of *qian* handbooks. Slip number three of the 1903 Guandi text, identified as one of "medium good luck," reads:

Clothing and food exist naturally in life;
The gentleman should be encouraged not to worry [about such things].
Instead practice filial piety, fraternal devotion, loyalty and faithfulness;
And blessings and wealth will come without the threat of calamity.

The "sagely meaning" of this oracle provides basic information and advice without explicitly moral overtones: fame and profit will arrive at the proper time; harmonious settlement of litigation will be fortunate; production will be delayed; sickness will be cured; the time is not right for marriage; conserve what you have; and avoid worry and doubts. The commentaries by Su Dongpuo and Bi Xian, however, as well as the vernacular explanation, lay heavy stress on ethical behavior: "paying attention to fundamentals" (*wuben*), "serving parents" (*shiqin*), and so forth.[119]

As with many other types of Chinese divination, *qian* oracles had several levels of meaning, not all of which were explicated in handbooks. A line from Su Dongpuo's "explanation" of stick number three provides one illustration. Translated roughly and superficially, it reads: "There is good [*tai*] rather than bad [*pi*]"—a line reminiscent of the hoary cliché "when things are at their worst they then get better" (*pi ji ze tai*). But below the surface of this simple phrase are all kinds of interpretive possibilities based on *Yijing* principles, for the hexagram Tai (11) offers a fascinating contrast with Pi (12)—not only in basic meaning and hexagram structure, but also in imagery and line readings.[120] Moreover, as Rong Zhaozu has shown, the structure and content of a number of *qian* books reflect the influence of *yinyang/wuxing* theory as well as mantic elements derived from the Yi tradition.[121]

Of course temple caretakers, priests, and professional fortune-tellers did more than simply explain the text and commentaries of *qian* handbooks. They also offered concrete advice on matters of critical concern: personal well-being, business, marriage, travel, household affairs, litigation, farming, animal husbandry, the loss of personal property, moving, sickness and so forth.[122] The distribution of specific topics varied somewhat from work to work according to the target audience. Some handbooks, for instance, had a specifically medical emphasis— notably those connected with healers such as the legendary Han physician, Hua Tuo. Oracles of this sort supplied pharmacological prescriptions as well as other forms of medical advice.[123] Other works, particularly those identified with the Guanyin cult, were directed primarily toward women, and tended to focus on domestic concerns even more than most *qian* books. Some handbooks, such as the *Shuilu zongguan lingqian* (Spiritual Sticks of the General Manager of Land and Water), gave special attention to travelers,[124] while others reflected regional concerns. Thus, for example, the *Tianhou qian* devotes inordinate attention to the preoccupations of a constituency located predominantly in coastal as opposed to inland areas.[125]

Information on how interpreters actually explained texts and gave advice in late imperial China is extremely difficult to come by, but recent field work in Taiwan and Hong Kong suggests a process that probably took place in Qing times as well. One feature of this process, characteristic of Chinese fortune-telling generally, is an inquiry into the background of a client—including, in the case of professional *qian* analysts, an examination of the person's "eight characters."[126] Clerics and temple caretakers in the Qing period, although not normally conversant with specific techniques of fate extrapolation, tended to be older people, experienced in giving advice to people in need. Many had at least a passing acquaintance with the Chinese classics and histories, and all were familiar with the *qian* poems and the historical or mythological events they described. Their clients, usually women,[127] presented their problems to the interpreter, usually a man, who would then ask for additional information if the situation seemed to require it.[128]

A description of the advice given by an old interpreter to a younger client in Taiwan two decades ago sounds very much like what one might have expected to hear under similar circumstances in the Qing dynasty:

> A woman of forty asked the interpreter whether it was good for her to leave home and take up residence in a temple with the intention of becoming a nun. When questioned by the interpreter, she told him that she had only an adopted son, who did not care for her very much. She was so disappointed that she decided to donate all her money to the temple and stay there the rest of her life. The interpreter advised her not to go to the temple because she would be taken care of only so long as she had money to donate. "But," the woman said, "I have lots of money." The interpreter said: "There is an old Chinese saying that even a mountain will break down if you keep digging at it. How long do you think your money will last if you continue to donate it?" When the woman failed to reply, he again advised her to stay home with her son. He said: "A son is a son. He is still young and does not appreciate the invaluable relationship between mother and son. Give him a little time. When he grows older he will learn to treat his mother better."[129]

Let us take another example from a recorded conversation. The *qian* interpreter begins by asking his client: "What is the problem?"

> Client: Marriage. The man has a concubine.
> Interpreter: Don't marry him. The *qian* says not to marry.
> Client: I'm already married to him. Should I separate?
> Interpreter: Do you have children?
> Client: Yes.
> Interpreter: Does he give you money?
> Client: Yes, he gives me at least half the money.
> Interpeter: Then don't separate from him. It is not good to separate.[130]

As with astrologers, fate extrapolators, physiognomers and others, *qian* interpreters negotiated the future with their clients. In Arthur Kleinman's words, "the chief concern is not the beauty and consistency of the explanatory models, but their utility in providing meaningful psychosocial interpretations of difficult situations."[131]

There were a number of related mantic systems by which people in Qing times could obtain written oracles and have them interpreted by specialists. One of the most popular involved trained birds and the use of sixty-four small pieces of paper—each containing a prophetic verse, usually of four seven-character lines, and perhaps an illustration. These sheets would be arranged so as not to reveal any visual message, and a bird released from its cage to select a slip or two. The fortune-teller then interpreted the message(s) in light of the client's particular needs. According to Justus Doolittle, writing of mid-nineteenth century Fuzhou, "Females and the lower classes of the populace largely patronize this kind of fortune-teller."[132]

Henrietta Shuck provides a colorful account of the practice as she witnessed it in the 1850s:

A pretty cage, containing eight Java sparrows, having three different apartments, with a little door to each apartment, was set upon a table, before sixty or seventy cards, placed upon their edges. The applicant was a person who labored under disease, and he came to enquire with regard to his recovery. From a cylinder containing a dozen or two, he drew a slip of bamboo, and the diviner then spead open one of the doors of the cage. One of the birds immediately hopped out, and with its red bill, dexterously drew out one of the cards, and receiving only one grain of paddy for its trouble, re-entered the cage of its own accord. On opening the card, the soothsayer produced two slips of paper; one of which informed the enquirer of his certain recovery, and the other contained a picture of a doctor feeling the pulse of his patient, and also pointing out his identical disease.

The divination cost six cash, "a little more than a half cent."[133]

Another system employed cards with *qian*-like inscriptions. Clients first chose a card from a pack of one hundred, each of which had an oracle indicating very good, good, middling, bad, or very bad fortune. After a card had been selected, the client returned it to the deck, making note of the inscription on it. The fortune-teller then shuffled the cards and released a bird to select a card by itself. If the bird's choice matched that of the client, the prediction would be verified.[134] In Sichuan, a fortune-teller by the name of Jin Dayu established such a reputation for his "trained bird method" of divination that he earned a place in the Nanquan county gazetteer. His technique, similar to the one described above, used pieces of paper marked with the sixty cyclical characters, together with twenty-eight slips of bamboo representing the twenty-eight lunar lodges.[135] According to John Gray, in the city of Guangzhou (Canton) "female fortune-tellers who predict the future of females only," used the same basic system, but had turtles choose the cards instead of birds. Other professional soothsayers allowed snakes to indicate a choice with their heads.[136]

These mantic displays often had the quality of sideshows, drawing crowds and evoking appreciative astonishment.[137] For this reason we may wonder how seriously the oracles themselves were taken. Perhaps they were simply a diversion, a form of recreation like gambling, with which they were sometimes associated. We can be reasonably certain, however, that *qian* divination played a more important social role in Qing China. After all, *qian* interpreters proffered medical advice, counselled clients on how to overcome misfortune through the use of charms and religious rituals, and offered "common sense" advice based on their own personal experience and a knowledge of the client's background.[138] The Confucian values embedded and expressed in *qian* oracles tended to reinforce traditional patterns of behavior, including submission to authority,[139] but from a psychological point of view, *qian* divination helped to eliminate anxiety and strengthen self-esteem. In the words of Jin Xu, "part of the therapeutic effect of *qian* lies in its ability to mobilize hope, inspire a feeling of well-being, and thus spur actions that lead to the fulfillment of the hope. The widespread acceptance of *qian* and faith in its reputed high rate of accurate prediction is probably due to its self-fulfilling nature."[140]

Of course not all "spiritual" media conveyed moral messages, and not all relied on the authority of either experts or written texts. A number of Chinese divining techniques, such as listening to the language of passers-by or balancing chopsticks upright in a bowl of water (an approach reportedly used exclusively by women in seeking answers to domestic questions), had no explicitly ethical dimension and required no professional intervention at all.[141] The same was often true for a practice known as *yuanguang* (lit. "round reflections," or "aura"), by which individuals saw things reflected in water (bowls, ponds, etc.) or in objects such as mirrors and even pieces of paper. It took a variety of forms, and was employed for many different purposes, from finding lost articles and determining the source of problems to healing the sick.[142]

The *Qingbai leichao* describes *yuanguang* as a kind of hypnotic art (*cuimian shu*), which could be either "genuine" or "false." Viewed from the standpoint of psychology—as suggestion or auto-suggestion—it is easy to see how reflected shapes might appear to be "things," particularly when viewed by impressionable young boys, as was often apparently the case.[143] But the practice could also have an explicitly supernatural dimension; and, when undertaken by professional specialists, it involved elaborate preliminary rituals, including incantations, the burning of incense, and the writing of charms.[144] Several anecdotes in the *Qingbai leichao* deal with *yuanguang* and related practices, but it is difficult to know how widespread they were.[145] *Yuanguang* specialists warranted no biographies in gazetteers and are rarely even mentioned in them. It is evident, however, that at least in some parts of China, women gathered in special divination houses, where they stared intently at a stone placed on a tripod until a figure appeared on its surface to reveal future events.[146]

Dream Divination

There were special locations for acquiring other kinds of personal revelations as well. Often, supplicants would "pray for dreams" (*qimeng*) in religious temples, spending the night in hopes of receiving clues to the future. Justus Doolittle writes of Fujian: "Many people, in case they find great difficulty in deciding what course to take in regard to an important subject under consideration, visit some popular temple and, having burned incense and candles, beg the divinity worshipped to favor them with a dream shedding light on the subject of their perplexity, which they briefly state. They frequently sleep before the idol, burning incense and candles." Doolittle goes on to say that after having a dream, supplicants used divining blocks to determine whether the dream was indeed sent by the god in question, and if "an affirmative answer is received, they proceed to study the character of the dream, and endeavor to decide from its teachings what they should do in regard to the subject under consideration, and whether they will be successful." Reportedly, individuals who did not use divining blocks to ascertain the source of their dreams were likely to be led astray by "wild dreams" that did not proceed from the god in question.[147]

Qing accounts of dream divination centers abound. Zhou Lianggong (1612–1672) describes locations in Fujian such as the Cave of the Immortals' Gate (Xianmen dong)—a picturesque site surrounded by Buddhist monasteries, Daoist temples, waterfalls and trees—where the dreams procured were "as marvelously efficacious as those at Carp Lake."[148] Of the literally dozens of stories of dream divination contained in the *Qingbai leichao*, no less than ten focus on temple dreams obtained by means of prayers. Most of the individuals involved in seeking them are reputable scholars—among them, such notables as Li Guangdi, Jiang Yi (1631–1687), Zhang Ying (1638–1708), and Xu Ben (1683–1747).[149]

City God temples in urban centers often attracted dream seekers. In Hangzhou, for example, people gathered in large numbers at the West Lake to pray for dreams on the eve of the winter solstice, enduring extreme cold in the hope of procuring auspicious dreams at a time when "the night is long and dreams are plentiful." The Qing scholar Huang Junzai tells of a certain Qin Zhongyuan who had a series of inauspicious dreams and went to the City God temple, where he offered a large amount of sacrificial money and a prayerful essay, the gist of which was: "Amidst the sundry glitters of this world, human fortunes are predetermined. The momentariness of a dream surely does not matter one way or another. This sum of money is hereby offered in payment for auspicious dreams." According to Huang, when this prayer was over, ghostly voices were heard squealing, as if disputing [over the money]. "From then on his dreams became more agreeable."[150]

Anecdotes in the *Qingbai leichao* and other sources testify to the importance attached to dream divination by all sectors of Chinese society. "Dreams have their fulfillments" (*meng you zheng ye*), went a well-known Qing dynasty proverb. And because dream prophecies often seemed to come true, whether unsolicited or not, they, like other omens, easily acquired explicitly political implications. Thus, when an individual named Zhi Tianbao made predictions concerning the length of the Qianlong emperor's reign based on dream revelations (purportedly emanating from the Shunzhi emperor himself), the pronouncements were treated like a curse, and both Zhi and his disciple, Zhang Jiuxiao, were executed.[151]

The tradition of dreams as harbingers of future events had a long and distinguished pedigree in China.[152] The Confucian classics contain a number of references to dream divination. The *Shijing*, for example, reads:

Your herdsman dreams of multitudes [locusts] and fish, of turtle
and serpent and falcon banners.
The chief diviner elucidates their meaning:
The multitudes and fish mean plentiful years.
The turtle and serpent and falcon banners signify an increasing
population.[153]

And again:

Divine my dreams for me; what dreams are auspicious?
They have been of bears;
They have been of serpents.
The chief diviner elucidates their meaning:
The bears are auspicious intimations of sons;
The serpents are auspicious intimations of daughters.[154]

The section on literature in the *Hanshu* (History of the Former Han Dynasty)
refers to these specific lines in acknowledging the importance of dream divination
in Chinese culture: "There are many [miscellaneous] mantic arts, but the greatest
of them concerns dreams. Thus, during Zhou times, officials were appointed
to take charge of them. The *Shijing* records dreams of black and brown bears,
of locusts and fish, and of flags and banners, showing how the prognostications
of the great men [dream interpreters] were conducive to the verification of
good and bad omens."[155]

Other Confucian classics are rich in dream accounts. The *Zuozhuan*, for
instance, contains about thirty such episodes. The *Zhouli* discusses at length
the dynasty's official system of dream divination; and the *Liji* recounts, among
other portentious dreams, the premonition by Confucius of his own demise.
Virtually all of the early Daoist philosophers—from Laozi and Zhuangzi to Liezi
and Huainanzi—contributed significantly to the literature on dreams in China.
The Han scholar-skeptics Wang Chong and Wang Fu had much to say about
dream divination (in which, incidentally, both believed), and the authors of
Religious Daoist and Buddhist texts often filled them with dream stories. By
late imperial times a great number of Chinese works on dream interpretation
existed—at least a few of them written by women.[156]

Of the several different ways to classify dreams in China, two of the best
known come from the *Zhouli* and Wang Fu's *Qianfu lun* (see chapter 1). The
Zhouli distinguishes six types of dreams: (1) regular or positive dreams (*zhengmeng*);
(2) horrible dreams (*emeng*; i.e., nightmares); (3) yearning dreams (*simeng*); (4)
wakeful dreams (*wumeng*); happy dreams (*ximeng*); and (6) fearful dreams (*qumeng*).
Wang Fu identifies ten categories of dreams: (1) straightforward or literal (*zhi*);
(2) symbolic (*xiang*); (3) earnest (*jing*); (4) pensive or longing (*xiang*); (5) personal
(*ren*); (6) climatic (*gan*; lit., "stimulation"); (7) seasonal (*shi*); (8) paradoxical or
oppositional (*fan*); (9) pathological (*bing*); and (10) affective (*xing*).[157] As these
typologies suggest, dreams reflected different emotions, were inspired by different
stimuli, and could be interpreted in different ways.

One common view, expressed as a proverb in Qing times, was that "Dreams come from what one thinks about [during the day]."[158] Naturally enough, preoccupation with the examinations, official careers, producing sons, and so forth led people to dream about these subjects. The *Qingbai leichao* contains numerous accounts illustrating this sort of connection, such as the case of the renowned scholar Lu Longji (1630–1693), widely respected for his uprightness, whose dream of the loyal but maligned Ming official Yang Jisheng (1516–1555) related directly to his dismissal as county magistrate of Jiading in 1677.[159] The time that a dream occurred was also considered significant. According to some traditional Chinese dreamworks, if a night vision takes place before midnight, the event indicated will be in the distant future; and if it takes place after midnight, the event will be in the near future.[160]

Most Chinese, following Wang Fu as well as traditional medical authorities, believed that one's physical condition, the weather, and seasonal factors all influenced the nature and specific content of dreams.[161] A famous dream work of late imperial times begins with a quotation from the *Huangdi neijing suwen*:

> When *yin* influences flourish, one dreams of wading through great [bodies of] water in fear. When *yang* influences flourish, one dreams of great fires burning. And when both *yin* and *yang* flourish, there are dreams of mutual destruction. When the upper [pulse] flourishes, one dreams of flying; when the lower [pulse] flourishes, one dreams of falling. Overfed, one dreams of giving; famished, one dreams of taking. When the breath [*qi*] of the liver thrives, one dreams of being angry. When the breath of the lungs thrives, one dreams of crying. An abundance of short worms [in the bowels] brings about dreams of gathering a throng. An abundance of long worms causes dreams of beating and hurting one another.[162]

The *Lingshu jing* (Classic on the Vital Pivot) confirms these points and adds others: "When the breath of the heart thrives, one dreams of being prone to laughter or of fear and timidity. When the breath of the spleen thrives, one dreams of song and music, or of one's body growing heavy and unwieldy. When the breath of the kidneys thrives, one dreams that the waist and backbone are loose and disjointed."[163]

A Chinese proverb states: "Dreams come when the connection between body and soul [*xingshen*; lit. shape and spirit] is broken."[164] In Qing times, virtually all Chinese believed that the human soul consisted of two parts: a *yang* component, identified with wood and known as *hun*; and a *yin* component, identified with metal and known as *po*.[165] Dreams arose from the activity of one or both of these souls. Most people assumed that the *po* component activated dreams from the lungs or liver, and that the *hun* part of the soul could temporarily leave the body during periods of sleep or unconsciousness.[166] According to Chen Shiyuan's *Mengzhan yizhi* (An Easy Guide to Dream Divination), dreams reflected the wandering spirit's ability to apprehend what has not yet come to pass as well as the stable spirit's capacity to remember things. In his words: "The *hun* soul can know the future; the *po* soul is able to treasure experience. In the daytime a person's *hun* is connected with the eye, and at night the *po* lodges in the liver. Because of the *hun*'s connection with the eye, sight is possible; and because the *po* resides in the liver, dreams are possible."[167]

The *Mengzhan yizhi*, written in the late Ming and informed by Buddhist as well as Confucian and Daoist ideas, remained a highly influential work on dream interpretation throughout the Qing period.[168] The work is divided into eight chapters and thirty subsections. The first ten subsections introduce various aspects of dream lore in a series of disjointed and heavily annotated essays. Some of these tracts, such as the one on "Causation" (*Zhenzai*; lit. "the true ruler"—an allusion to Zhuangzi's famous remark on the difficulty of proving the existence of a God-like creator), are highly metaphysical. Others, including an essay entitled "Day and Night," are equally metaphorical. Taken together, these essays refer to virtually all of the best-known dream episodes recorded in either the official dynastic histories or the various Confucian, Daoist and Buddhist "classics." The subsections that follow organize dreams according to conventional and often overlapping Chinese cultural categories: (1) Heaven; (2) the Sun and the Moon; (3) Thunder and Rain; (4) Mountains and Streams; (5) Appearances; (6) Food and Clothing; (7) Utensils; (8) Wealth and Property; (9) Brush and Ink; (10) Written Scrolls; (11) Scholarly Ranking; (12) Spirits and Strange Things; (13) Longevity; (14) Phoenixes and Birds; (15) [Four-Legged] Animals; (16) Dragons and Snakes; (17) Turtles and Fish; (18) Grass and Woods; (19) Giving and Receiving; and (20) Vague Indications.[169]

A close reading of the various subsections of the *Mengzhan yizhi* reveals three main types of traditional Chinese dream interpretation: meanings derived from classical and historical accounts; straightforward messages, often of explicitly "spiritual" inspiration; and word analysis. By Qing times, of the hundreds of dream accounts in circulation, about thirty historical episodes—dating from the Shang dynasty down to the Ming, and covering a wide range of personalities, from the inveterate dreamer King Wu Ding to the romantic Tang poet Li Bai—came to epitomize the tradition of Chinese dream interpretation. These stories were summarized in works such as the *Yuxia ji guangji* (Expanded Collection of the Jade Box Record; c. 1700). In this influential compendium we find, in a section entitled "Analyzing Dreams by Categories," headings such as "Omen of Dreaming about the Sun Entering the Breast." Under it appears a summary of the vision that accompanied the pregnancy of Han Wudi's mother. Likewise, under the heading "Omen of Dreaming about Gaining and Losing Grain" there is a brief description of Cai Mao's famous dream, recorded in the *Hou Hanshu* (History of the Later Han), in which he grabbed hold of a stalk of grain, only to drop it. The interpretation of this event, based on a form of word analysis, was that Cai would gain high rank (*zhi*), since the character *zhi* is comprised of the characters for grain (*he*) and loss (*shi*).[170]

As already indicated, many Chinese believed that dreams conveyed messages from the spirit world. The *Qingbai leichao* and other sources contain many accounts of dreams in which ancestral spirits or powerful gods render advice or assistance to the dreamer, even when no direct appeal is made to them. Thus, for example, the governor of Gansu, Tong Guoxiang, while visiting the county seat of Fuqiang on a tour of inspection, received word from an unidentified spirit that he must leave the place. He did so, just before a flood devastated the city and surrounding countryside. Later, in Jianchang, Tong discovered that the spirit offering assistance was none other than the great Guandi.[171] Spirits could offer dream advice to groups of people as well as individuals. A modern compilation entitled *Renwu fengsu zhidu congtan* (Collected Anecdotes on Personalities, Customs, and Institutions) tells of an episode during the early Qing in which a deceased elder appeared in a dream to the entire congregation of a Buddhist monastery at the same time.[172]

Helpful spirits did not have to be those of deceased individuals. A story in the *Qingbai leichao* indicates, for instance, that the spirit of a person who was asleep could communicate with others who were awake. It tells of a man named Tong Ershu, whose friends were engaged elsewhere in *fuji* divination at the same time that he was sleeping at home. All of a sudden, to their surprise, Tong's spirit began writing poetry with the divination stick. Startled, they went to his house to discover that he had just awakened from a dream in which he and they were composing verse together. The verses he dreamt about, according to this account, were exactly the same as those written down in the *fuji* session.[173]

Naturally, orthodox neo-Confucians attempted to rationalize the process of dream divination. According to Zhu Xi, as cited in the *Mengzhan yizhi*, "Man's spirit [jingshen] flows freely with Heaven and Earth, yin and yang; thus our dreams during the night are classified according to their auspiciousness or inauspiciousness, just as our acts during the day are classified according to whether they are good and bad."[174] Among Qing scholars, Wei Xiangshu (1617–1687) equated the "evil spirits" that misled dreamers with the evil thoughts of one's mind, and the "good spirits" with good thoughts. Bad dreams, in Wei's view, were simply projections of an unsettled mind. "If our mind is at ease, so will be our speech and action. If our speech and action are at ease, so will be our dream soul [hun]." He went on to say: "To be able to hold one's own while dreaming is a sign of consummate scholarship. Such an ability ensures orderliness in the management of important affairs. My own experience has attested to this."[175]

Wei's clear implication was that a strong mind could manipulate the content of one's dreams. To some, it was then a relatively short step to using the mind as a means of fulfilling those dreams. Thus we find in the Qing period individuals such as Lu Yixian, who claimed that they could teach people to employ dreams as a way of satisfying their own desires. Their methods of dream fulfillment, although similar in some ways to the techniques employed in "praying for dreams," also involved a kind of hypnotic suggestion akin to that of *yuanguang*.[176]

Word analysis played a significant role in all facets of dream divination, including analogies drawn from classic accounts and direct messages from spirits. The subsection entitled "Written Scrolls" in the *Mengzhan yizhi* is devoted almost entirely to this sort of interpretive approach. One of the most famous examples concerns the legendary Yellow Emperor, who dreamt one night that he saw a great wind blowing away the "dust and dirt" under Heaven. He then dreamt that he saw a man with a very heavy cross-bow herding great numbers of sheep. Upon awakening, he interpreted these dreams to mean that he should seek two particular people to serve in his administration. One would be a civil official named Feng ("wind") Hou (the "earth" radical taken away from the character for "dirt")—since the wind was like a royal command and the person who executed the command was like a person sweeping away dirt from a place and making it clean. The other would be a military official named Li ("strength," required of a man with a heavy bow) Mu ("shepherd;" used also in the sense of an official who "cares for the people;" *mumin*). Later, moved by this event and apparently satisfied with the performance of Feng Hou and Li Mu, the Yellow Emperor reportedly wrote the book entitled *Huangdi changliu zhanmeng* (see chapter 1).[177]

One can find many examples of dream divination in the Qing period based on word analysis. Two should suffice as illustration. According to the *Qingbai leichao*, the famous scholar Li Guangdi, before he became well-known, sought dream advice from a spirit in the Nine-Dragon Rapids Temple in his home province of Fujian. In this dream, he received a poem which read in part: "There is no hope for wealth and honor; merit and fame will both be incomplete." Although quite unhappy with this message, he persevered in his academic career, and eventually achieved the *jinshi* degree in 1670. It was then that he recognized on the basis of an elaborate dissection of the above-mentioned lines, that the proper time for success was the year marked by the cyclical characters *wuxu* (1670).[178] Likewise, Zhang Ying, who also became a high-ranking official and close associate of the Kangxi emperor, went to the Guandi temple outside the city gates of Beijing in order to seek dream-inspired information about having sons, since at that time he had none. In this dream, Guandi gave Zhang a bamboo pole (*gan*) that had no leaves or branches. Zhang was quite disappointed, since the lack of any offshoots seemed to indicate no progeny. But a dream interpreter explained that the meaning of this episode was in fact quite propitious. The bamboo (*zhu*) represented two sons, he said, for when the character *zhu* was "split" according to the methods of word analysis, it yielded two *ge*, numeratives of sons (*ge nanzi*) in this particular instance.[179]

Of course the interpretation of Chinese dreams was seldom straightforward. In the first place, as the *Mengzhan yizhi* and other such sources point out, different types of people have different kinds of dreams. In the traditional Chinese view, status differences affect dreams, as do other personal factors, including individual destiny. Thus, according to Chen Shiyuan, when unlucky people have propitious dreams, they do not necessarily turn out well; and by the same token, lucky people who have unlucky dreams may not encounter any misfortune.[180] Furthermore, as with the interpretation of dreams in any culture, context counts heavily, not only in terms of manifest meaning but also symbolic content. An anecdote concerning Zhou Xuan, a renowned dream specialist of the Three Kingdoms period, highlights the way different situations could affect the same basic symbolism. In this well-known story, a man dreams of straw dogs three times, and each time Zhou attaches a radically different meaning to the dream. When questioned about the three divergent prognostications, each of which came to pass, Zhou explained: "Straw dogs are sacrificial offerings to the gods. Hence, your first dream meant that you would get food and drink. When the sacrifice is over, the straw dogs are crushed under a wheel, thus your second dream prefigured your fall from a carriage, which ended in broken legs. When the straw dogs have been crushed, they are bound to be carted away as kindling. And so your last dream warned you of fire."[181]

Complicating the process of Chinese dream interpretation was a long-standing tendency, already identified by Wang Fu in the Han period, to invest certain dreams with the opposite of what one might assume to be their "obvious" meaning. For example, a dream of crying indicated a joyful event; to murder a person or to be killed was usually considered auspicious; and filth often denoted good fortune. "To dream of living brings death," went a Qing period cliché.[182] This mentality of opposition and transformation (*fan*) found expression in another proverb: "If you have an inauspicious dream, write it on the south wall [and it will turn into an auspicious one]."[183] Although I have examined a large body of Chinese dream literature, including the writings of Wang Fu on "paradoxical" dreams, I have not been able to find a consistent principle for applying this type of oppositional interpretation.[184]

For the many Chinese interested in dream interpretation but lacking either the time, inclination, or educational background to wade through Chen Shiyuan's densely illustrated and ponderously documented tome, a convenient alternative existed in Qing times. This work, known as the *Zhougong jiemeng* (The Duke of Zhou's Explanation of Dreams), consisted of a certain number of fixed interpretations of presumably common dreams, each reduced to a pithy seven-character phrase. The central idea was that all one needs to interpret a dream is its main motif; one event, image or set of images constitutes the decisive omen.[185] It is clear that the interpretive principles contained in the *Mengzhan yizhi*, as well as a substantial number of specific historical allusions, are reflected in the *Zhougong jiemeng*; but they remain implicit. The same is true of the interpretive possibilities introduced by newly evolved forms of literature in late imperial China, including not only plays and short stories, but also Ming and Qing novels—notably *Honglou meng*.

The origins of the *Zhougong jiemeng* are uncertain, but the work plainly draws on a wide variety of sources that include not only ancient classics, histories and early dream books but also more recent vernacular writings.[186] According to the preface of Zhang Fengyi's *Mengzhan leikao* (An Examination by Category of Dream Divination), written in 1585, the Duke of Zhou's name came to be appropriated by dream book writers sometime during the Song-Yuan period. This remark suggests that by Ming times at the latest the *Zhougong jiemeng* had already become an influential dream work.[187] During the Qing period, several editions of the *Zhougong jiemeng* circulated—some in popular almanacs. The most extensive version, boasting a general introduction and several additional explanatory sections, consists of nearly one thousand seven-character dream interpretations. It is called, appropriately enough, the *Zhougong jiemeng quanshu* (Comprehensive [Edition of] the Duke of Zhou's Explanation of Dreams). The earliest copy I have seen, which conforms remarkably with contemporary editions of the work, is contained in a fragment of the British Museum's *Yuxia ji guangji* (c. 1700).[188]

Like the Mengzhan yizhi, the Zhougong jiemeng quanshu divides dreams into a number of overlapping categories. These include (1) heavenly phenomena (the sun, moon, stars, planets, etc.; 64 entries); (2) terrestrial phenomena (mountains, rocks, plants and trees; 56 entries); (3) the body (including face, eyes, teeth and hair; 30 entries); (4) clothing (caps, robes, shoes, etc.; 50 entries); (5) items such as knives, swords, banners, bells and drums (40 entries); (6) administration (rulers, civil and military officials, orders, etc.; 28 entries); (7) buildings (palaces, houses, granaries, etc.; 52 entries); (8) domestic structures (gates, doors, stoves, wells, and privies; 52 entries); (9) precious items (gold, silver, pearls, jade and silk; 28 entries); (10) toiletries, including mirrors, bracelets, hairpins and combs (24 entries); (11) household items (bedding, carpeting, and utensils; 58 entries); (12) transportation vehicles such as boats and carts (32 entries); (13) roads, bridges and marketplaces (16 entries); (14) married life (husbands, wives, pregnancy, etc.; 24 entries); (15) food and drink (meat, wine, fruit, etc.; 40 entries); (16) matters related to burial (cemeteries, graves, coffins, etc.; 14 entries); (17) writing materials and weaponry (40 entries); (18) happy and sad occasions (particularly involving music or singing; 30 entries); (19) religion (Buddhism, Daoism, monks, priests, nuns, ghosts and spirits; 20 entries); (20) killing, fighting, wounding and cursing (36 entries); (21) criminality (arrests and punishments; 28 entries); (22) fields, orchards, gardens and agriculture (32 entries); (23) water, fire, lamps, bandits and rebels (36 entries); (24) filth and cleansing (16 entries); (25) dragons, snakes and wild animals (68 entries); (26) farm and domestic animals (32 entries); and (27) tortoises, fish, shrimp, and insects (38 entries).[189] A few entries from the section on heavenly phenomena in the Zhougong jiemeng quanshu will illustrate the style of the work:

When [one dreams that] the gate of Heaven opens, an illustrious person will make recommendations and introductions [on the dreamer's behalf]. When heavenly light shines, illness will be eradicated. When the skies are clear and rain has dissipated, all worries will disappear. When the sky brightens, a woman will bear an illustrious son. When the gate of Heaven turns red, there will be a great beginning. When one's face turns upward toward Heaven there will be great wealth and honor. When one rides a dragon up to Heaven, great honor will follow. Ascending to Heaven in search of a wife signifies illustrious sons and daughters.

Not all entries are positive, however. Indeed, about a third of the total number of entries in the massive dreamwork have decidedly negative connotations. For instance, in the section just cited we find: "If Heaven splits open, there will be the sorrow of a divided nation. . . . If the sun or moon descends from the sky, a parent will die. . . . If the sun or moon is obscured by a mountain, servants will cheat their master. . . . If a star descends from heaven, there will be illness and lawsuits."[190]

Shorter versions of the Zhougong jiemeng, such as those included in popular almanacs, were generally known as "Books of Good and Bad Fortune [Based on the Duke of Zhou's] Explanation of Dreams." These works might have only a half dozen or so categories and only about a hundred seven-character interpretations. The *Daquan qizheng tongshu* (Comprehensive Almanac Based on the Seven Regulators) of 1858 provides a typical example. It has a total of 118 stanzas divided into sections on heavenly patterns (19 entries), earthly configurations (9 entries), spirits (9 entries), the body (19 entries), sorrow and joy (9 entries), hitting and cursing (9 entries), and miscellaneous (44 entries, most of which deal with officialdom, domestic life and structures, plants and animals).[191]

On the whole, both the specific interpretations and the ratio of auspicious to inauspicious dreams in these "Books of Good and Bad Fortune" correspond closely with the *Zhougong jiemeng*. Only a few minor differences exist. In the longer version, for example, the opening of Heaven's gate refers generally to recommendations and introductions, while the shorter version specifies the acquisition of wealth. Other almanac dreamworks, such as the "Explanation of Dreams," contained in various editions of the *Wanbao quanshu* (Complete Book of Myriad Treasures), indicate more substantial variations. According to the *Zhougong jiemeng*, for instance, to dream of seeing a deer indicates emoluments, while the *Wanbao quanshu* identifies the deer with food and drink. In the former work, burning incense and making devotions suggest good fortune generally, while the latter specifies great honor and emoluments. In the former, to dream of beating one's wife portends a loss of profit, while in the latter, such a dream indicates the loss of one's strength.[192] Occasionally interpretations will differ significantly. Thus we find that whereas the *Zhougong jiemeng* tells us that a pregnant wife in a dream signifies adultery, the *Wanbao quanshu* maintains that it portends good fortune for the "sagely man."[193]

Some of the dream interpretations offered in the *Zhougong jiemeng* would seem to be at least plausible in almost any culture.[194] One might assume, for example, that the positive imagery of a rising sun or new vegetation, like the negative connotations of storms and damaged property, would resonate in most societies, past and present. Many cultures could also probably accept as plausible the notion that a dream in which a gate opens on its own symbolizes a wife's infidelity. But the vast majority of images and interpretations contained in the *Zhougong jiemeng* are quite specific to Chinese tradition. Without knowing about the sage emperor Shun's dream life, who could guess that long eyebrows would have a decidedly positive oneirocritical connotation? The image of a flying swallow entering a person's breast might well not conjure up the idea of a noble birth in the absence of information about the jade bird dream of Zhang Yue's mother in the Tang dynasty. And without appreciating the pervasive Chinese principle of paradoxical interpretation, one could hardly imagine that good fortune would arise from a dream about being covered with urine and feces, or that a dream of a man and wife beating each other would indicate marital harmony.

Although the *Zhougong jiemeng* does not usually specify the gender of the dreamer, it seems to have been written primarily from a male point of view. Much of the symbolism is dominated by traditionally masculine images. The dragon appears about four times more often in the text than its female counterpart, the so-called phoenix (*fenghuang*). In the *Zhougong jiemeng*, as in the rest of traditional Chinese literature, dragons have very positive connotations, whether waking or sleeping, flying or at rest. Riding a dragon into the sky, up a mountain, into a marketplace, or into the water (unless it is a well) indicates good fortune in various forms. Dreaming of a dragon portends the birth of an honorable son. Likewise, the tiger, king of Chinese land beasts and the symbol of Chinese scholar-officials, is also almost invariably a good omen: "If [one dreams] of tiger roaring loudly, one will get official rank." "A person riding a tiger will not suffer any harm." "If a tiger enters a house, one's official rank will be high."

Snake dreams in the *Zhougong jiemeng* reflect a characteristic ambivalence toward serpents on the part of the Chinese. On the one hand, snakes were rather like dragons in appearance, and they sometimes served as objects of worship. On the other hand, they could be extremely dangerous. Generally speaking, snake images in the *Zhougong jiemeng* are positive. When snakes and dragons appear together in a dream, the prophecy is favorable, unless they kill someone. To be bitten by a snake in a dream generally indicates great wealth, unless the bite is fatal. Some snake symbolism is clearly sexual. A snake following someone indicates a wife with adulterous intentions. If a snake enters a woman's bosom or winds around her body, it signifies that an honorable son will be born.[195]

The analogical logic of the *Zhougong jiemeng* is, for the most part, quite straightforward. Books are equated with high social position, since status is what successful scholars in traditional China could reasonably expect from their literary pursuits. Virtually every reference to books, paper and writing in the *Zhougong jiemeng* is positive. The main hall (*tang*) in Chinese dream lore often refers to one's parents, an association derived from domestic imagery as well as common family terminology. The message, however, could be either encouraging or discouraging, depending on the specific situation. Going up into a high hall, for example, indicates good fortune, but a dream in which the floor of the hall collapses signifies that one's mother is in distress. Similarly, although the color red is highly auspicious under most circumstances—even when it appears in the form of blood—it is not invariably positive. Blood on the bed, for example, indicates that a wife or concubine has committed adultery. Although a dream about a green snake is auspicious, one involving a red or black one signifies a quarrel. And even so seemingly positive an image as consulting the hallowed *Yijing* may not auger well. The one reference to Yi divination in the *Zhougong jiemeng* associates it unambiguously with illness.

Many Chinese dream interpretations are drawn from the symbolism of puns, which explain certain features of oppositional analysis. One reason for the large number of very positive interpretations to be found in the *Zhougong jiemeng*'s section on matters related to burial is undoubtedly the similarity in sound between coffins (*guan*) and official position (*guan*). Likewise, the turtle (*gui*) often serves as a rebus for honorable (*gui*). In Chinese folklore, including dream interpretation, deer (*lu*) symbolize official emoluments (*lu*)—although they are also associated with the well-known Daoist quest for longevity by virtue of their supposed capacity to find the life-enhancing plant known as *lingzhi*. Fish (*yu*) usually signify good fortune in the sense of abundance (*yu*; lit. "excess")—though they may also connote success in the examinations (the image of a carp swimming ambitiously against the current), the idea of fertility (since fish lay many eggs), or simply water (either as a natural habitat for fish or in the form of rain, since the characters for both fish and rain share the *yu* sound).[196]

The most common desires expressed in the *Zhougong jiemeng* are for good luck, wealth, health, high position, honorable children (particularly sons) and longevity. The greatest fears are of death, illness, violence, poverty, lawsuits, and the usurpation of authority. Significantly, a number of entries focus on the themes such as family quarrels and the prospect of wives committing adultery. This suggests that these problems were more intractable in Chinese society than members of the Qing elite would normally be willing to admit. In a sense, the *Zhougong jiemeng* reveals the same sort of lack of fit between Chinese social theory and social reality evinced in many Qing legal cases.[197]

It is particularly difficult to know, of course, how seriously Chinese of the Qing period, particularly members of the elite, took the interpretations of one or another version of the *Zhougong jiemeng*. I cannot recall any references to this particular work in the writings of the Chinese scholars I have investigated for this study. However, J. H. Gray, writing of Guangzhou in the 1870s, suggests that the book had wide appeal, at least in south China. "Being earnest believers in dreams," he writes, "the Chinese pay great attention to their interpretation"—adding that the pronouncements of the Duke of Zhou are "now regarded as the greatest authority upon such matters."[198] Furthermore, we know that in more recent times, up to the present, versions of the *Zhougong jiemeng* have always been abundantly available in Hong Kong and Taiwan, and that they have obviously influenced the dream interpretations of modern Chinese men and women.[199]

In any case, as with so many other types of Chinese divination, the predictions of Chinese dreams were seldom inescapable.[200] As indicated above, an inauspicious dream, written down at the proper time on a wall facing the proper direction, could be transformed into an auspicious one. In addition, professional dream interpreters and dream books, including the *Zhougong jiemeng*, provided charms or incantations to offset the bad influence of certain dreams. These charms, generally written on yellow paper and attached directly to the clothing of the person involved, varied according to the day of the month on which the impropitious dream occurred.[201]

Professional dream interpreters activated these charms by means of rituals similar to Daoist exorcisms. According to J. H. Gray,

> The dreamer is . . . made to look towards the east, with a sword in his right hand and his mouth full of spring water. In this position he ejects the water from his mouth, and beats the air with the sword, repeating in an imperative tone certain words of which the following is a translation: "As quickly, and with as much strength as rises the sun in the East, do thou, charm or mystic scroll, avert all the evil influences which are likely to result from my bad dream. As quickly as lightning passes through the air, O charm, cause impending evils to disappear."[202]

If necessary, professional diviners could also give personal advice on how to contend with dreams, taking into account the time and other circumstances of the event, including cosmological variables related to *yinyang/wuxing* correlations. Naturally their interpretations did not always agree, and were sometimes diametrically opposed.[203] This should not surprise us, however—particularly in light of the seemingly inconsistent application of oppositional analysis in Chinese dream lore.

SEVEN

Conclusion

In 1934, the celebrated Chinese writer Lu Xun produced a short essay entitled "Fate" (*Yunming*). With a characteristic blend of insight, wit, and sarcasm, he observed that the Chinese

> believe in fate, but a fate that can be averted. To say "there is no way out" is sometimes a method of trying another way out—a means of averting fate. When a person really believes that this is "fate" and there is "no way out," that is in fact the time when all means have failed or one is about to perish. For the Chinese, fate is not something determining events but an easy explanation to give after events have happened. . . . Geomancy, magic charms, prayers . . . however grave the fate, the expenditure of some money or a few kowtows would make it quite different from that predestined. Among our wise ancestors were some who knew that the uncertainty of "certain fate" could not suffice to give people a sense of certainty; they therefore said that the outcome of all the methods tried was the genuine "fate," and that the use of various methods to avert fate was predestined too. . . .
>
> To my mind, it is a good thing that the Chinese who believe in fate also believe that fate can be averted. Only so far, we have used superstition to counteract some other superstition, so that the final result is the same. If in the future we use rational ideas and behavior—science in place of superstition—the Chinese will discard their fatalistic outlook. If such a day comes, indeed, the thrones of Buddhist monks, Daoist priests, witch-doctors, astrologers, geomancers and the rest will be ceded to scientists, and we shall be able to dispense with all this nonsense the whole year round.[1]

In this passage, Lu Xun not only identifies a significant feature of China's "feudal" past, but he also expresses an aspiration common to many Chinese intellectuals of his generation—to modernize the Middle Kingdom by self-consciously emulating the West. "Superstition," it seemed, was China's mortal disease; Western "science," the only cure. But Lu Xun and like minds faced a formidable enemy, for the inertia of tradition was strong in every realm of Chinese life, not least divination. It is worth recalling that all major fortune-telling techniques existing in the Qing period could be traced back at least a thousand years, if not twice or three times as long. Furthermore, these techniques were not simply long-standing; they were also deeply woven into the fabric of Chinese society—its institutions, its values, and even its aesthetics.

The Legacy of the Past

Virtually everyone in Qing dynasty China believed in divination. The problem was not whether to believe in it, but who to believe. In the words of a popular proverb: "Do not say that King Wen's hexagrams are ineffective [buling]; fear only that the fortune-teller's reading is untrue [buzhen]."[2] From an elite perspective, divination was much too important a matter to be left to fortune-tellers. This helps account for the many high-ranking Chinese scholar-officials of the Qing period who had an active and well-documented interest in divination.[3] Further research would undoubtedly reveal large numbers of other notables who engaged in the practice—probably as part of the regular literati networks that defined so much of social and political life in late imperial China. It cannot be accidental, for example, that so many distinguished scholar-generals in the Qing-Taiping war used fortune-tellers and/or fortune-telling techniques. Perhaps Zeng Guofan's fame and success as both a scholar and a military commander, together with his widely-known reputation as a devotee of physiognomy, spirit-writing and the Yijing, encouraged his colleagues and their associates to make more substantial use of these mantic methods.[4] It is also possible, of course, that the chronic instability of the times contributed to the popularity of divination as a way of making sense out of things and seeking new solutions to China's manifold problems. Mao Qiling's frequent and sustained use of the Yijing as a fortune-telling device during the tumultuous Ming-Qing transition, followed by his abrupt abandonment of Yi divination after his own personal crisis had passed, serves as a reminder of this phenomenon.[5]

It is unfortunate and somewhat ironic that so little contemporary Chinese documentation exists on exactly how commoners viewed divination in the Qing period. Yuan Shushan's indispensable Zhongguo lidai buren zhuan, which includes well over a thousand biographical entries for Qing diviners, most drawn from local gazetteers, is heavily biased in favor of individuals who were either scholars (many, if not most, are degree holders), or moral exemplars, or both.[6] My own work with gazetteers reveals the same source bias. Comparatively few commoners appear as diviners in the fangji sections of local gazetteers, and even fewer clerics. At present, I can identify only about twenty Buddhist monks, including three Tibetan lamas, and a few Daoist priests, whose divinatory talents merit mention in these sources.[7] Furthermore, there are only about a dozen additional diviners included in Yuan's compendium who seem to have had strong Buddhist or Daoist inclinations.[8] Yet we know that divination played an important role in Chinese religious life at all levels, and that the Qing religious establishment itself supported certain practices such as physiognomy, spirit-writing, and qian consultation.

Minorities, including Manchus, do not figure significantly in gazetteer biographies, although there are a number of scattered references to ethnically distinctive mantic techniques, as well as standard procedures, in the fengsu (customs) sections of these works.[9] Chinese Muslims (Hui), heirs to a long and distinguished Islamic tradition of astronomy and astrology, did not generally designate auspicious and inauspicious days, and this naturally limited their divinatory activity.[10] Aside from a few Tibetan lamas, I have come across no biographies of non-Manchu minority diviners, although virtually all minority peoples throughout the Qing empire practiced divination. I have found only a few biographies of Manchu practitioners of the fortune-telling art—three of whom were Banner military officers.[11] Yet there must have been countless other Manchus who, while maintaining their native interest in shamanism, became sinicized and succumbed to Chinese fashions in divination as they did with so many other aspects of Han culture. Certainly all of the Qing emperors, not to mention many empresses, consorts and imperial princes, were vitally interested in divination, and resorted to it often.

Also conspicuously absent from the pages of gazetteers are women diviners. I have found only three biographies of such individuals—all daughters or wives of prominent scholars, and all well educated. Two, in fact, wrote books on divination.[12] The paucity of women diviners in *fangji* biographies and other Qing sources does not mean, of course, that they were a negligible influence in traditional Chinese society. Quite the contrary, we know that they often played significant mantic roles, particularly in South China. We should also remember that among some minority peoples—for instance, the Lolo in Sichuan— women assumed roles that were reserved almost exclusively for men among the Han population (such as physiognomy). But most Chinese women in the Qing period lacked access to the kind of formal education that brought enhanced prestige and influence to male fortune-tellers; and because most women diviners in China were illiterate, they tended to engage in fortune-telling practices that were scorned, at least theoretically, by the orthodox elite.

Shamanism, one of the most important spheres of female divinatory activity in the Qing period, drew particularly heavy fire from the literati, even as scholars themselves freely patronized mediums who were experts in spirit-writing. Significantly, *fuji* does not normally occupy a place in the discussions of diviners and other "technicians" in works such as the *Tushu jicheng*, the dynastic histories, or local gazetteers—presumably because as a shamanistic technique it was considered too unorthodox, too far removed from conventional types of prognostication. Likewise, Yuan's book ignores spirit-writing entirely as a category of divination.[13] Encyclopedias, histories and gazetteers do, of course, contain some information on male and female "spirit mediums," but they are not treated as diviners per se and are not in any case afforded individual biographies. It is revealing that the "Arts and Occupations" section of the *Tushu jicheng* devotes a mere fifteen pages to shamans, as against 2,172 pages on divination.[14]

Although most of the 1200 or so individuals I have studied divined for other people in addition to themselves, only about 100 appear unambiguously to be professional diviners (*maibu*).[15] This undoubtedly under-represents the proportion of professional fortune-tellers to amateurs in Qing society as a whole (if we put aside divinations by scholars that were designed only for themselves or their families). These professionals usually earned between a few hundred cash and, say, one or two taels per day. Wang Weixiong, who compared himself with the great Han diviner Yan Junping, reportedly closed shop every day after earning only 100 cash; Rong Bangda quit as soon as he made 300 cash; and Fan Shixing closed his door after bringing in 600 cash.[16] The man known only as "The Spring and Autumn Pen" accepted 200 cash for every written character he analyzed, but he never dissected more than ten words a day; and the Buddhist eccentric Wan Shouqi would periodically go to the city of Huaiyin, occupy a fortune-telling stall that had been temporarily vacated, and make 2,000 cash for the diviner before the man returned.[17] Pay was best when the stakes were high, as Cixi's 1,000 tael reward to Zhang Yanyi abundantly attests.[18]

Competition between professional diviners naturally occurred, as each tried to gain a larger (or more affluent) share of a given market. Fengshui specialists seem to have been particularly intent on defending their geomantic territory, not only against incursions by non-specialists—notably spirit mediums, who might well ascribe problems of the living to improper siting—but also against exponents of rival schools of interpretation. Although criticisms by geomancers of their competitors were usually couched in terms of either high-mindedness or expertise, there can be little doubt that financial considerations were also at issue. This competitive situation continues to exist in the environments of both Hong Kong and Taiwan, where mediums periodically pass judgment on geomantic sites, much to the disgust and dismay of fengshui xiansheng. At yet another level, divinatory competition can still be found between rival spirit-writing sects who vie for members, motivated by social as well as economic concerns.

What can we say about the relative popularity of different divining practices in Qing China as a whole? Undoubtedly the most widely practiced techniques were the use of divining blocks and "spiritual sticks." They had the advantage, after all, of being both inexpensive and easy to use, and they appealed to all social classes. They were not illegal to use, and they did not in any way threaten the political or social status quo. Elites naturally preferred one or another form of Yijing divination, but not all techniques were equally "orthodox."

Beyond these broad generalizations, the question of popularity is difficult to answer. One reason is, of course, China's extraordinary diversity (see below). Another is the fact that fortune-tellers who merit biographies in local gazetteers often practiced two or more techniques, but we do not always know which one (or ones) predominated. Yet another problem is the ambiguity of many divinatory terms, and a significant overlap in various mantic techniques. Normally, for instance, Qing scholars distinguished between the study of Yili (the principles of the Yijing) and Yishu (techniques of Yijing divination, especially numerology); yet the distinction is often unclear in individual biographies.[19] The Tushu jicheng's section on "Arts and Occupations" also blurs distinctions. It is organized according to five basic types of divination: (1) "Oracle Bones and Milfoil Stalks" (bushi; in late imperial times this term generally meant orthodox Yijing consultation, although a few diviners continued to use Shang style pyromantic techniques); (2) "Astrology;" (3) "Physiognomy;" (4) "Geomancy" (kanyu; I have lumped this category together with "the selection of [auspicious] days," *xuanze*); and (5) "Computational Arts" (*shushu*, in which I have also included the stem-and-branch calculation techniques of *taiyi*, *qimen dunjia* and *liuren*).[20]

In terms of these five basic categories, and based on the number of times each is mentioned in the 1200 or so biographies I have examined, it appears that in Qing China as a whole, geomancy (including the selection of auspicious days) was the most popular form of divination (c. 400 mentions), followed by various *Yijing*-related divining systems (c. 250), and then by other computational techniques (c. 250), including "fate-extrapolation." Next in popularity were various kinds of astrology (c. 200), followed by physiognomy (c. 50).[21] Judging from the relative number of biographical entries in gazetteers and/or dynastic histories for the Song, Yuan and Ming periods, as well as biographies for the same time frame under the five major categories of the *Tushu jicheng*, these general patterns of popularity remained relatively constant for most of the late imperial era in China.[22] Unfortunately, it is impossible to say whether they reveal anything more than the prejudices of elite editors. The entries may well reflect prestige rather than true popularity.

Regional representation of different mantic techniques is even more problematical. In the first place, many fortune-tellers were itinerant; it is often difficult to know how widely they travelled, and for what specific purposes. Secondly, as Donald Sutton has noted in his pioneering spatial analysis of Chinese shamans, the comparative poverty of the peripheral counties in each Chinese macroregion made it difficult for them to produce extensive gazetteers, forcing editors in these areas to deal more perfunctorily with social customs. Sutton also indicates—and my own research confirms—that local gazetteers tend to take non-shamanistic divination largely for granted, giving comparatively little attention to it in their sections on "customs." Standard forms of divination are unworthy of detailed discussion not because of their insignificance, but precisely because of their ubiquitousness.[23]

Moreover, even if gazetteers did devote greater attention to mantic methods, we would not necessarily discover how the practices in one area of China compared with those of another. Biographies concentrate on diviners rather than their clients, and hence they do not usually indicate which techniques were most popular in a given locale—much less other areas of China. Although the gazetteers of some counties clearly contain more biographies of one type of diviner than another,[24] we cannot be certain that these sources reflect actual patterns of popularity. More likely, as with encyclopedias, they indicate the interests of the compilers, which might be informed by their own personal preferences, or by the fact that a famous diviner, identified with a particular skill, came from that county and was therefore seen as the local "model."

If anthropological fieldwork in modern Taiwan and Hong Kong is any indication (and I think it is), there was probably enormous local variation in Chinese religious practices, including shamanism and certain forms of non-shamanistic divination, during the Qing period. Variables included patterns of historical settlement, ease of travel, ethnic composition, individual and community wealth, kinship organization, the ritual structure of "territorial cults," and so forth. Even areas in relatively close proximity to one another might have decidedly different ritual structures. David DeGlopper notes, for example, that in the county of Changhua (west-central Taiwan) there are two towns, Erlin and Lugang, only eighteen kilometers apart. In the late 1960s, Erlin had a population of about 12,000, with six temples (one for every 1,900 people) and a flourishing spirit-writing (bailuan) cult. Lugang, with approximately 28,000 people, had thirty-nine temples (one for every 690 people); its residents undertook many more processions and small-scale public rituals than did the people of Erlin, but they claimed never to have heard of bailuan.[25]

It seems logical to assume that during the Qing period non-literate diviners, like shamans, were located primarily in "peripheral" areas, where they presumably undertook a variety of mantic responsibilities, while more literate practitioners gravitated toward "core" areas and tended to specialize. Unfortunately, I do not have the data to make the case. It is safe to say, however—based both on Qing sources and on modern anthropological fieldwork—that fortune-telling, like "a belief in ghosts and spirits" generally, was more common in south China than in the north.[26] We can also say that certain shamanistic practices and mantic techniques were more prevalent in some sub-regions of the south than others. Self-mortification of mediums, for example, seems to have been limited largely if not exclusively to Fujian and Taiwan. Geomancy, although practiced empire-wide, was most solidly entrenched in the provinces of Jiangxi, Fujian, and Guangdong.[27]

An inventory of Yuan Shushan's biographical entries for the Qing period yields a very different and obviously distorted picture. For instance, although Guangdong was by all accounts a hotbed of fortune-telling activity in late imperial times, Yuan includes only 32 Qing biographies for the province— compared to 246 for Jiangsu, 118 for Hubei, 105 for Zhejiang, 103 for Anhui, 90 for Jiangxi, 68 for Hebei, 51 for Shandong, 49 for Sichuan, 48 for Fujian, 41 for Yunnan, and 40 for Henan. (All other provinces have less than 30 biographical entries.) Similarly, out of a total of about 400 references to geomantic expertise in Yuan's book, 46 are from Jiangxi, 18 from Fujian and only 10 from Guangdong. By contrast, Jiangsu has 82 references, Zhejiang, 47, and Anhui, 35. The northern province of Hebei has more references (23) to geomancers than Fujian, and Shandong has more (13) than Guangdong![28]

In all five major categories of divination, Jiangsu, Zhejiang and Anhui lead the other provinces—except that, as noted, geomancers in Jiangxi outnumber those of Anhui by eleven.[29] There are two primary reasons for this skewed distribution. One is the scholarly emphasis of the biographies in Yuan, which reflect the predominance of the lower Yangzi region in Qing intellectual life (including scientific activity).[30] The other is the fact that Yuan's own cultural center of gravity (and primary source of information) was his home province of Jiangsu, bordered on the north by Shandong, the west by Anhui and the south by Zhejiang.

Reliance on gazetteers naturally affects assessments of change over time. Although works produced after 1905 often give considerable attention to changes in local customs such as marriage ritual, they seldom show an interest in documenting trends in local divination—not only for the reasons already mentioned, but also because so much seems to have remained the same (see next section).[31] Complicating matters is the fact that a large number of the biographies of diviners in gazetteers can be located no more precisely in time than one or another long reign period, and many are identified only by dynasty. Gazetteers from the late Qing and early Republican eras, which naturally tend to emphasize recent developments and personalities, are comparatively numerous, further distorting the sample. Twice as many gazetteers were produced in China from 1880–1899 than from 1680 to 1689, and at least three times as many in the former period as in any other twenty-year span of the Qing.[32] All that can be said with confidence is that divination tended to be particularly prevalent in insecure times and places.[33] Several biographies of diviners make this point more or less explicitly, as does the scholar Liang Qichao (1873–1929), who correlates a rise in the popularity of both Buddhism and divination in the late Qing period directly with China's widespread internal and external problems.[34]

But the remarkable feature of Qing divination at any time was its pervasiveness at all levels of society, in cities as well as the countryside, and in every corner of the empire. Why did divination last so long and penetrate so deeply into Chinese society? One important reason is that it both embodied and reflected many of the most fundamental features of traditional Chinese civilization. Although divination always had a certain heterodox potential, it was not fundamentally a counter-cultural phenomenon. On the contrary, it remained an integral part of the most important state and domestic rituals, from official sacrifices to life-cycle ceremonies. In fact, Qing fortune-telling may perhaps best be understood as a highly personalized ritual of empowerment, which, like other Chinese rituals, synthesized ethics, aesthetics, and world view.

Enjoying abundant classical sanction and a long history, Chinese mantic practices, in their richness and variety, followed the main contours of Chinese thought. Most forms of Qing divination were eclectic, "spiritual," associational, tradition-bound, and highly moralistic. These qualities fit comfortably in a syncretic society whose dominant class esteemed ancient Confucian values, relied heavily on correlational logic, believed in a spiritual link between Heaven, Earth, and Man (which made divination possible, after all), and saw "knowing" as an activity in which "the rational operations of the intellect were not sharply disconnected from what we [Westerners] would call intuition, imagination, illumination, ecstacy, aesthetic perception, ethical commitment, or sensuous experience."[35] The Yijing epitomized both the philosophical and the mantic tradition of the Middle Kingdom, and served as an extremely important source of legitimation for the latter.[36]

Divination also had a visceral appeal, quite apart from the obvious aesthetics of geomancy. Even mundane practices, such as the use of jiaobei and qian, generally took place in comforting and familiar environments, either at home or in religious temples. Professional fortune-tellers, for their part, employed a colorful and universally resonant symbolism in conveying their often poetic messages. This symbolism was deeply embedded in the consciousness of Chinese at all levels of society. Allusions to historical, classical, and mythological figures in divinatory statements—derived not only from the Confucian canon and the official dynastic histories, but also from vernacular literature and oral folk traditions—evoked powerful responses in clients, as did appropriate references to certain symbolic colors, numbers, plants and animals.[37]

Fortune-tellers invariably surrounded themselves with culturally familiar paraphernalia. Even the most rudimentary fortune-telling table on the street would be adorned with writing materials, books, and calligraphic inscriptions— the marks of scholarly refinement and moral cultivation. More elaborate settings in homes or divination parlors might boast religious icons or spirit tablets, as well as incense and candles, in the fashion of temples and shrines. Visual representations of cosmic power such as the *Taiji tu* and the eight trigrams, which often adorned divination handbooks, almanacs, and fortune-telling stalls, were also ubiquitous as decorative elements (and charms) in elite and commoner households alike.[38]

The rituals of divination were similarly satisfying and culturally familiar to all clients. Ceremonies such as the burning of incense, which invested divinatory procedures with an explicitly spiritual if not a magical aura, had a truly universal appeal. The use of writing by diviners not only enhanced their social prestige, but it also gave them cosmic leverage, since so many Chinese believed that written words had magical power.[39] Meanwhile, the theatrical performance of fortune-tellers contributed to their public charm. In several respects patronizing a diviner was like watching a play, or even participating in one.[40] Dramatic forms of divination such as spirit-writing and other types of spirit possession held audiences spellbound; but even the more subdued rituals of physiognomy, fate extrapolation and word analysis attracted passers-by on the streets, in marketplaces, and at temples throughout China.[41] Although private fortune-telling parlors existed, and a number of people consulted diviners in the privacy of their homes, Chinese divination was fundamentally a public affair. This was yet another reason why most Qing subjects simply took it for granted.

The close link between divination and traditional Chinese medicine in the Qing period probably contributed to the tenacity of both. Much of *qian* divination revolved around illness and remedies for it (including prescriptions), and physiognomy overlapped considerably with the professional practice of physicians. Despite the great diversity of medical and mantic theory in late imperial times, doctors and diviners shared many of the same cosmological assumptions about systematic correspondence as well as demonology. In fact, in the early twentieth century some medical associations sponsored the publication of fortune-telling manuals.[42] Although the Confucian classics and a number of popular proverbs emphasized that health and longevity were predestined, few individuals in Qing China accepted their fate passively.[43] All segments of Chinese society sought to know and alter their future, medical or otherwise, and they attempted to do so with the assistance of shamans and other fortune-tellers, as well as more conventional healers—sometimes in combination.[44] From an elite perspective, the more room for autonomous moral choice, the more esteemed the method of divination; but all forms of fortune-telling were considered valuable if the fate divined could somehow be modified.

As Lu Xun correctly observed, people in traditional China believed that they could manipulate their destiny by moral or magical means. In truth, the two sources of power were closely related. For the scholarly elite, the same "spiritual" capacity that made foreknowledge possible, gave those who had developed their sincerity to the utmost the ability to transform their own lives in concert with Heaven and Earth. Theirs was a kind of cosmological mind-magic, sanctioned by no less authority than the Zhongyong and Yijing. For commoners, charms and the advice of soothsayers might do the trick.[45] One could even circumvent the stipulations of calendars and almanacs if armed with the proper cosmological information or assistance.

Chinese attitudes toward fate, then, seldom crippled initiative.[46] On the other hand, as Lu Xun plainly understood, the idea of inescapable destiny served as a convenient explanation for adversity and disappointment. Thus, we find that even Zeng Guofan, a staunch Confucian known for his rectitude and determination, once remarked during a difficult phase of the Taiping Rebellion that fate determined seventy percent of a situation, leaving only thirty percent to man's exertions.[47] And Guo Songtao, a hard-working and dedicated scholar who had the misfortune to assume a career in late Qing foreign affairs, went so far as to ask that his obituary end with the following remark: "I don't believe in books; I believe in luck" (buxin shu xin qiyun).[48]

Another point to keep in mind is that in Qing China, divination did not stand as starkly opposed to either "science" or religion as it did in, say, contemporary Europe, especially after the seventeenth century. To be sure, Chinese scholars in the late imperial era were well aware of the expanding parameters of knowledge about the natural world, and of an increasing ability to predict accurately; but scientifically-minded individuals of the Qing period had neither a religious belief in "order" of the sort that inspired their European contemporaries (see next section), nor did they hold the conviction that in time all phenomena would yield their ultimate secrets. The typical belief was that "natural processes wove a pattern of constant relations too subtle and too multivariant to be understood completely by what we would call empirical investigation or mathematical analysis. Scientific explanation merely expressed, for finite and practical human purposes, partial and indirect views of that fabric."[49] The influential Song dynasty scientist Shen Gua (1031–1095) vividly articulated this notion in the following way:

> Those in the world who speak of the regularities underlying phenomena, it seems, manage to apprehend their crude traces. But these regularities have their very subtle aspect, which those who rely on mathematical astronomy cannot know of. Still, even these are nothing more than traces. As for the spiritual processes described in the Book of Changes . . . [which] penetrate every situation in the realm, mere traces have nothing to do with them. This spiritual state by which foreknowledge is attained can hardly be sought through traces, of which in any case only the cruder sort are attainable.[50]

Divination thus passed often for science in Qing times.[51] Although the period witnessed a revival of interest in mathematics, mathematical astronomy, and geography, stimulated in part by the Jesuit educational effort, astrology remained integral to the Chinese scientific tradition.[52] The Jesuits themselves apparently practiced divination in the Imperial Bureau of Astronomy.[53] New technologies for exploring the heavens brought valuable scientific knowledge to China, but they did not pose a significant challenge to traditional mantic methods—at least in part because the great number of invisible operators in Chinese astrology, such as "empty" stars or star-spirits, made astronomical falsification difficult.[54] Furthermore, and more importantly, divination categorized and explained experience in culturally significant ways. The elaborate schemes used by fortune-tellers to analyze heavenly phenomena, earthly forms, personality types, and so forth were undoubtedly more generally well known and persuasive than other systems of scientific explanation available in Qing dynasty China. To the extent that science can be viewed as an "ordering device" for managing data,[55] divination served Chinese scientific purposes nicely. Certainly this was true, for better or worse, of the hallowed Yijing.

The "spiritual" preoccupations of diviners did not necessarily preclude empirical investigation. It is true that experts in wind, rain, and cloud divination—like other types of Chinese fortune-tellers (and most of the rest of the Qing population)—believed in the influence of supernatural forces. But they were also close and insightful students of meteorology. Exponents of qimen dunjia and other numerological systems, although concerned primarily with cosmological calculations to determine auspicious times and locations, often studied military science as part of their training. Geomancers used mystical "compasses" to identify lucky sites and times for building and making repairs, but they also knew a great deal about land forms and hydraulic systems—information of value in public works as well as military affairs. In all, geomancy probably exerted a more profound influence on the physical environment, and the way the Chinese responded to it, than most other "natural sciences" of the time.[56]

An especially significant reason for the prevalence and persistence of divination in Qing China was the multi-faceted social role it played. In the first place, it contributed to social order by regulating the rituals and rhythms of daily life. Few devices were more powerful as mechanisms for structuring society than the stipulations regarding lucky and unlucky days in Chinese calendars and almanacs. In fact, private tongshu were sometimes proscribed precisely because they did not follow the official calendrical model closely enough, thus inviting confusion of the social order. Secondly, Chinese fortune-tellers served as the functional equivalent of modern-day psychologists. As therapists and personal counsellors, they helped individuals in China to cope with their anxieties, whether inspired by bureaucratic problems, the examination system, or more mundane concerns. Divination clarified the source and nature of difficulties, alleviated doubt, and invested lives with longed-for meaning. It also empowered people with a special kind of cosmic knowledge and perhaps endowed them with greater self-confidence.

Furthermore, the optimistic thrust of techniques such as qian divination and dream book interpretation provided hope in time of uncertainty and fear, as did geomancy, with its alluring promise of cosmic control. Exponents of fate extrapolation and physiognomy gave individuals a glimpse of their long-term future, as well as concrete advice on how to contend with seemingly inescapable problems. Methods such as word analysis did the same for more immediate issues, while personal consultation of the *Yijing* offered ways of "resolving doubts" that emphasized introspection and personal initiative. Spirit-writing associations not only provided a sense of group identity outside the family, but also offered hope for individuals excluded from conventional routes to social and economic advancement. By various means, not all equally effective, divination in Qing China restored "value and significance to lives in crisis."[57]

But fortune-tellers were more than personal therapists. In a society such as China's, where so many aspects of life and thought hinged on compromise and conciliation, and where intermediaries were essential to all forms of social intercourse, diviners proved to be cultural middlemen par excellence, mediating not only between the client and the cosmos, and between Confucian, Buddhist and Daoist versions of "reality," but also between contending elements within their own local communities, from quarreling couples to feuding clans. Some relied primarily on their psychological skills and verbal ability to settle disputes. Others made use of their comparatively intimate knowledge of the personal histories and local connections of many community members. Still others, notably shamans, called upon supernatural authority to develop and maintain group consensus, thus bringing "order out of confusion."[58]

Diviners also helped bridge the gap between commoners and the elite in Qing dynasty China. Robert Weller is correct, of course, in pointing out that people involved in different social relations may well interpret rituals—including those of divination—in different ways, and that their divergent interpretations may, in turn, lead them to different political and social strategies. On the basis of research in modern Taiwan he argues, for example, that whereas popular geomancy "ties into the personified bureaucracy of gods, ghosts and ancestors," and thus tends to support prevailing community and kinship values, elite geomancy "channels reinterpretation through its institutions, and has greater possibilities to justify politically improper behavior (like fraternal competition) because it relies on impersonal forces."[59] But this contrast may be a bit too stark; for popular geomantic practices did not always conduce to social harmony, and elite *fengshui* practices did not always reflect a potentially divisive reliance on "impersonal forces."

Despite its obvious merits as a strategy for contending with the complexity of traditional Chinese society, Weller's stress on the diversity of social inter-pretation over the uniformity of cultural codes may lead us to underestimate the power of such codes—at least with respect to divination. On the whole, I am struck by the degree to which Qing dynasty mantic methods not only reflected shared assumptions but also supported the prevailing social order, regardless of who undertook them or for whom they were undertaken. Most Chinese divination techniques offered no possibility for social subversion, and although geomancy undeniably created family and community tensions, it is hard to imagine that the Chinese scholarly elite would have given so much support to a practice fundamentally detrimental to its own interests. Even *fuji* divination was probably used more often to maintain local power structures than to overthrow them.

By summoning up visions of orthodox heros and urging clients to embrace conventional values, fortune-tellers of all social classes reinforced the hegemonic literati culture. For this reason, among others, certain of them received commendation by local officials for their skill as prognosticators. Peng Tianlun, for one, got an honorific plaque that read "He is able to know the future" (keyi qianzhi)—a phrase instantly recalling the rare and admirable quality of foreknowledge touted by Mencius (who claimed, incidentally, to possess it).[60] But the process of cultural transmission was not one of downward movement only. Popular values also found their way to the upper levels of Chinese society in the course of divination. Although the exact nature of this two-way interaction cannot be documented with precision, we know that at least some fortune-tellers had both elites and commoners as clients and that a number of non-elite diviners enjoyed close relations with the literati by virtue of their unusual and much-coveted skills.[61] Furthermore, it is clear that certain divinatory media, spirit-writing in particular, conveyed messages that were suffused with elements from the Chinese folk tradition as well as Confucian "high culture." As with the Ma Yuan and Qu Yuan cults of the late imperial era, elites and commoners drew on "overlapping repertoires of images and associations," cycling and recycling "symbols, motifs and attitudes between the oral and regional and the literary and cosmopolitan sectors of Chinese culture."[62]

The special talents of diviners, from weather prediction and siting to the evaluation of personnel, made them valuable not only to Qing officials but also to the leaders of their own communities. Fortune-tellers helped to maintain the mechanisms of local defense and control, undertook famine relief, managed schools, and supervised public works projects. Some used their special talents to help neighbors find lost or stolen property, while others provided free advice and medical assistance to their local areas in times of crisis. These altruistic activities helped diviners to overcome the common stereotype of being devious and selfish, and brought them more fully into the mainstream of Chinese community life.[63]

Finally, in attempting to account for the remarkable staying power of divination in China, we should bear in mind institutional factors. For one, the Qing religious establishment did not actively attempt to suppress divination in the fashion of the Christian Church in the West. Rather, Buddhist and Daoist temples and monasteries supported a wide range of divinatory activity, undertaken by religious functionaries and professional fortune-tellers as well as lay persons. In fact, the apocrypha of both religious traditions in China included special texts on divination, such as the Zhancha shano yebao jing (Classic of Divining the Requital of Good and Evil Actions). Furthermore, Chinese monks and priests did not have the institutional power to challenge long-standing mantic traditions, even if they had the will, for the Buddhist and Daoist establishment in China remained ever subordinate to the imperial Confucian state.

The Qing government, for its part, reinforced the inherited cosmology and sanctified orthodox mantic practices at all levels. Edicts and other official announcements constantly referred to auspicious and inauspicious dates, times, events and omens; the state calendar institutionalized divination empirewide by designating certain days as "appropriate" and "inappropriate" for various activities; and bureaucrats availed of divination in all kinds of civil and military situations. Without fully realizing it, the Qing government was as much in the grip of the future as it was of the past. For the emperor to dispense with divination would be to abandon his cosmological claim to kingship—an abdication of his role as mediator between Heaven and Earth.

Divination in the "Modern" Era

The ubiquitousness and persistence of divination throughout the Qing period suggests that despite the importance of seventeenth and eighteenth century *kaozheng* scholarship in some realms of Chinese life, it did not succeed in effecting the kind of radical transformation of consciousness that occurred in Europe at about the same time.[64] Keith Thomas, in *Religion and the Decline of Magic*, describes the circumstances which made traditional modes of magical thought such as divination appear "increasingly out-dated" in the West. The first of these was "the series of intellectual changes which constituted the scientific and philosophical revolution of the seventeenth century." The second was the development of new ideas and technologies, such as insurance and new fire-fighting methods, which lessened the incidence of human misfortune and enhanced the capacity of people to control their own environment. A third had to do with the rise of new social and economic explanations of misfortune; and a fourth was the development of statistical probability.[65] Finally, the newly established Protestant Church powerfully reasserted the distinction between magic and theology that had been blurred by medieval Christianity.

Of all these factors, Thomas identifies the intellectual transformation as the most critical one. "The change which occurred in the seventeenth century," he writes, "was . . . not so much technological as mental. In many different spheres of human life the period saw the emergence of a new faith in the potentialities of human initiative." At the same time, a religious belief in order provided "a necessary prior assumption upon which the subsequent work of the natural scientists was to be founded."[66] Thomas goes on to say that in England, "magic lost its appeal before the appropriate technical solutions had been devised to take its place. It was the abandonment of magic which made possible the upsurge of technology, not the other way around." Similarly, he argues that supernatural theories of medicine went out of fashion before effective techniques came in. Meanwhile, superior methods of prediction could not of themselves overcome the uncertainty produced in an increasingly complex society. Thomas concludes: "The technological primacy of Western civilisation owes a sizeable debt to the fact that in Europe recourse to magic was to prove less ineradicable than in other parts of the world."[67]

This analysis probably underestimates the degree to which new ideas, attitudes, technologies, and techniques interacted to undermine a belief in magic and divination in the West. But the argument is nonetheless useful in highlighting certain features of the Chinese counter-example. For if we agree that "scientific" *kaozheng* scholarship in the seventeenth and eighteenth century brought a new epistemology to China, and with it, "a fundamental pattern of intellectual change" roughly analogous to that of Western Europe at the time,[68] why did this new outlook have so little effect on divination and other magical practices during the Qing period? On the other hand, if, as some scholars have intimated, the "rejection of traditional cosmology" in the early Qing inhibited the de-velopment of modern science in China by denying that a uniform world order of any kind was accessible to human intelligence (or even immanent in the cosmos),[69] why was Western science so enthusiastically embraced by Chinese intellectuals so soon after the fall of the dynasty in 1912? These questions suggest, in turn, a related but more fundamental one: Could China have generated "fresh forms of social and political organization from within itself" in the absence of an unprecedented political, economic, and intellectual challenge from the West?[70]

We will never know the answer, of course, since historical events have a nasty habit of intervening to prevent something else from happening. But in the light of my own research on Chinese divination, I would answer a qualified no. At least the process would not have occurred nearly as rapidly as it did in the late nineteenth and early twentieth centuries. To put the matter somewhat differently, although *kaozheng* scholarship succeeded in breaking the neo-Confucian epistemological lock, it took the combined influence of Western imperialism and Chinese nationalism to open the door to a radical restructuring of Chinese thought and society. And even then, the civil service examination system continued to reward orthodox patterns of thought and behavior until the throne abolished it in 1905 as part of a Western-inspired Chinese reform movement.[71]

Of course, as Thomas Metzger argues in *Escape from Predicament*, the complex political, social and intellectual movements of late Qing times cannot be reduced to a simple contrast between "imported transformative orientations and indig-enous, stagnative ones." The emergence of revolutionary thought in China did not, after all, depend on "the importation of any Promethian or Faustian will." The process was, however, profoundly affected by a belief that "modern [Western] technology, new techniques of political participation . . . and new forms of knowledge" could solve seemingly intractable problems in the "outer" realm of Chinese economics and politics (as opposed to the "inner" realm of mental and moral development). For at least some Chinese intellectuals who viewed the question of "the people's livelihood" as philosophically of the utmost importance, the possibilities presented by Western material progress had an almost religious appeal. And as transformative action in the "outer" realm appeared ever more feasible to Chinese intellectuals, they relaxed their search for transformative power within the mind. As a result, "The 'inner' predicament of moral purification and metaphysical linkage became less acute and central."[72]

Meanwhile, as Chang Hao has demonstrated, nationalistic Chinese intellectuals launched an attack on the concept of "cosmological kingship"—the notion of the emperor as Heaven's earthly agent charged with maintaining cosmic harmony.[73] This vigorous assault, which was far more revolutionary in its political implications than the early Qing critique of correlative cosmology, occurred by stages, as Chinese intellectuals learned more about the outside world through translations and direct contact with Westerners. Their awareness was "deepened and exacerbated by the repeated defeats China suffered at the hands of the outside world"—most particularly Japan's humiliating victory over China in the Sino-Japanese War of 1894–1895.[74] The Treaty of Shimonoseki produced a powerful surge of Chinese nationalism, and with it, a heightened clamor for Western-style political, military, economic, and educational reforms.

These reforms had revolutionary consequences. The establishment of new-style schools with both Chinese and Western curriculum, for example, contributed significantly to the abolition of the civil service examination system as the state tried desperately to encourage enrollments. And as ever greater numbers of able Chinese students entered such schools, their minds became transformed. Jiang Menglin (1886–1984), the son of a Shanghai businessman, inventor and landowner, describes the liberating process:

> The first thing I learned in . . . [my Sino-Western school] was that the earth is round like a ball. To me it was decidedly flat. I was dumbfounded on being further told that lightning is created by electricity and is not the reflection from the mirror of a goddess; that thunder is a by-product of the same electricity and not the beating of a drum by the god of thunder. In elementary physics I learned how rain is formed. It made me give up the idea that a gigantic dragon showers it from his mouth like a fountain high above in the clouds. To understand the meaning of combustion was to banish the idea of fire gods from my mind. One after another, the gods worshipped by my people melted away in my mind like snowmen in the sun. It was the beginning of what little science I know and the end of animism in me.[75]

Yet it is clear that even among the most progressive intellectuals of the era, some still held traditional cosmological notions. The brilliant visionary Kang Youwei (1858–1927), for instance, advocated constitutional government and the adoption of Western science and technology as part of a far-reaching late Qing reform program; and his communalistic utopian ideas, developed in the 1880s but not widely disseminated until after his death, were even more radical. Yet he also believed in omens, physiognomy and geomancy. In 1877, Kang delayed the burial of his grandfather in deference to the advice of a geomancer; and in 1898 he confided to Liang Qichao that the physical features of two of his most prominent supporters in the reform movement were too "light" for the weighty positions they would soon assume. As late as 1923, on a visit to Shandong, he suggested that the entire city of Jinan be relocated because it violated geomantic principles.[76] Similarly, the great translator of Western works and champion of Western ideas, Yan Fu, reserved a special volume of his diary for recording traditional Chinese-style divinations for friends and family.

The political, military and educational reforms of the early twentieth century, although designed to keep the Manchus in power, ultimately achieved the opposite effect. Republican government replaced imperial rule in 1912, and the fall of the Qing dynasty brought an end to state-sponsored cosmology. The newly-established Republic of China, intent on distancing itself from the old regime, and anxious to promote a progressive image both at home and abroad, made no effort to legitimate itself with the Mandate of Heaven idea. Nor did it attempt, in promulgating a "new" Gregorian calendar, to preserve any traditional cosmological elements, such as the designation of various activities as auspicious or inauspicious for a given day. Rather, it actively attempted to discourage "superstitious" practices of all kinds.[77] But the fragile democratic institutions of the infant regime proved too weak to hold China together, much less to outlaw traditional practices, and the Republic soon degenerated into over a decade of destructive warlordism. In the midst of internal strife and external aggression, Chinese intellectuals such as Chen Duxiu (1879–1942) blamed China's pressing problems squarely on the conservatism and traditionalism of the past.

During the iconoclastic New Culture Movement (c. 1915–1925), which erupted dramatically in the midst of warlord chaos, Chen and his disciples championed the twin saviours of "Mr. Science and Mr. Democracy." Many intellectuals abandoned their idealistic belief in a "spiritual" link between Heaven, Earth and Man, although a number also reacted negatively to the aggressive "materialism" of the West, particularly in the aftermath of World War I. Critics of the old order railed against Confucian values and ridiculed old-fashioned "superstitions," including Buddhism, Daoism, divination and most aspects of traditional Chinese medicine. Chen wrote in 1918 that only by first casting away practices such as geomancy, fortune-telling, spirit-writing and the use of charms, spells and alchemy, could people begin to put their minds right (zheng renxin).[78] He was not attacking a straw man, for old-style mantic techniques and cosmological assumptions remained in force, judging from the remarks of a well-informed foreign observer in the midst of the New Culture Movement: "At the present day," he wrote, "soothsayers, diviners and fortune-tellers abound throughout the land, and the people place implicit faith in their vain forecasts."[79]

Throughout the Republican era, divination of all kinds remained popular in China. Western and Chinese accounts testify not only to its persistence, but also to its continuity with Qing dynasty practices. As in the past, elite powerholders relentlessly attempted to manipulate the masses by reference to their foreknowledge, while lowly professional diviners and prophets out of power attempted to employ divination to serve their own, sometimes antithetical, ends. Fuji techniques proved to be particularly well suited to these divergent efforts and self-interested motives.[80] Of course, significant social and political changes took place in the period from 1912 to 1949, particularly in the cities, where new ideas spread comparatively rapidly. Literacy increased, the position of women improved somewhat, and new roads and railways reduced the isolation of certain remote areas of China. At the same time, and significantly, the gap between urban and rural culture widened.[81] But in both the cities and the countryside the desire to "know fate" persisted. A brief history of traditional-style almanacs reveals patterns of development that apply, more or less, to divination as a whole in the post-imperial period.

Immediately after the Republican Revolution of 1911, various provincial authorities, following the lead of the central government, published their own local calendars, designed—like the Beijing prototype—to replace almanacs and to "destroy superstition" (*po mixin*).[82] But neither the feeble government in Beijing, nor local provincial officials, could eradicate centuries-old traditions by fiat. Like the Taiping effort to introduce a calendar devoid of lucky and unlucky days during the 1850s and 1860s, the new Republic's attempt to introduce a secular calendar met with pronounced resistance.[83] Traditional-style almanacs continued to appear in huge numbers.

An examination of several dozen of these works from the early Republic to the present reveals a remarkable continuity in form, style and content with Qing period almanacs.[84] To be sure, most of them include new information of practical use, from domestic and foreign postal rates to maps and even pronunciation guides for English words (transliterated into Chinese characters). But they also perpetuate the old-style cosmology and reflect other long-standing cultural concerns. Every Republican-era almanac I have seen, from 1912 to the present in Taiwan, contains information on lucky and unlucky stars, divining methods, and auspicious and inauspicious days—as well as the usual array of charms, charts, tables, morality tales and woodblock illustrations. They also indicate agricultural prospects in time-honored fashion, through the familiar symbolism of the "spring ox" and herdsman.[85]

Although after 1912 there was no central government authority to sanction these works, they remained closely tied to politics. During the warlord era, for example, a number of almanacs carried pictures of local military leaders; and after reunification of the country in 1927 and an abortive effort by the Nationalist (Guomindang) government in Nanjing to outlaw *tongshu*, at least four different editions of the almanac for 1930 boasted Sun Yatsen's portrait and "will" on the front page.[86] It is not clear, however, whether the publishers of these almanacs sought legitimation through association with the recently deceased (1925) Dr. Sun, or whether the Nationalists sought to promote Sun's image by means of an undeniably popular medium—despite its "superstitious" orientation. It is also possible, of course, that the producers of almanacs simply wished to demonstrate their loyalty to the new regime in an obvious, unmistakable way. To my knowledge, the only large-scale and sustained effort to revive a state-sponsored traditional Chinese cosmology occurred when the Japanese established the puppet state of "Manchukuo" in 1931, and installed Puyi as their puppet emperor. At that time, they published a state calendar based almost exactly on the old Qing dynasty model, in hopes of once again putting the inherited cosmology to work in the service of the state. Although the calendar was confined only to Manchuria, and did not outlast the Japanese conquest, it suggests that in the mind of the Japanese, at least, the association between the imperial institution and the traditional cosmology was still strong enough to exploit.[87]

For several years after the establishment of the People's Republic of China in 1949, private publishers continued to print traditional-style almanacs on the Mainland, as they did also in the Republic of China on Taiwan. One Mainland edition, published in 1953, bears the title of the new regime and contains the usual cosmological and astrological information as well as political slogans such as "Oppose America and Assist Korea" (kang Mei yuan Chao).[88] At about the same time, however, the state had begun to issue "new almanacs" (xin tongshu) as part of a deliberate and widespread campaign to discredit old-fashioned "superstitions."[89] These almanacs, which the People's Republic continues to produce, are devoid of all so-called "feudal" elements, and are instead full of rudimentary practical knowledge regarding agriculture, hygiene, science, and technology.[90] In recent years, however, I have noticed the appearance in several cities of thin, crudely printed traditional-style almanacs, which give lip service to the "Four Modernizations," but which also include rudimentary astrological information and basic indications of auspicious and inauspicious activities for each day of the year.

I have one such work, published privately in Changsha, Hunan, and entitled *Gongyuan yijiu baba nian wuchen lishu* (Almanac for 1988 A.D.). It consists of only sixteen crudely-printed pages, and, unlike either pre-1949 almanacs or those published today in Hong Kong and Taiwan, it supplies very little practical, historical, or cultural information beyond the traditional features I have mentioned above. It does, however, include a list of important dates, including the National Youth Festival (commemorating the May Fourth Incident of 1919), the founding of the Chinese Communist Party (1921), and the anniversary dates for the deaths of several Marxist luminaries, from Mao Zedong, Zhu De, Zhou Enlai and Liu Shaoqi to Lenin and Stalin (but not Marx). This feature, like a brief reference in the foreword to the "Four Modernizations," appears to be a sop to the authorities.[91]

An article in the *Guangming Daily*, dated April 20, 1981, highlights the difficulties facing the People's Republic in its general effort to eradicate traditional patterns of thought and behavior. The article begins:

> When we talk about feudal superstition, we usually mean telling fortunes by the eight trigrams, feeling a person's bones and looking at his appearance to forecast his future, practicing geomancy, . . . exorcising spirits to cure illness, spirit-writing, offering sacrifices to the gods, beseeching gods to bestow children on people, offering prayers to gods to ward off calamities and to ask for rain, and so on. These are the dregs handed down from the old society in our country.

The author, Ya Hanzhang, goes on to say that while the state made great progress after 1949 in eradicating these evils, the Cultural Revolution of 1966–1976 allowed them to "float to the surface" again. Even worse, "Since the smashing of the 'Gang of Four' [in 1976], various kinds of feudal superstitious activities have been spreading unchecked."[92] According to Ya, one reason for this rampant spread is the government's new emphasis on "freedom of belief," and the failure of party cadres under the new, more liberal, policy, to distinguish between religion and superstition. "Religion," he writes, "is a way of viewing the world, while feudal superstition is a means by which some people practice fraud."[93] As in the past, the ruling elite sees the problem in terms of popular practice rather than abstract theory.

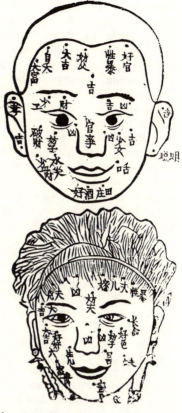

相 理 说 明

人有五官，眉毛叫保寿官，眼睛是检察官，鼻子叫审辨官，
口为出纳官，耳为采听官。

秘传十字面相图解

天下之貌众多，可用十字尽之。善观理者以一本而贯通
万卷。善观相者以五行而包万壮。人有形非五行（金木水火
土）之精气，人之有貌离不五行了之休质。虽经千百亿人，
不能出乎十字之外。现且说明，上尖下阔谓由字面。上阔下
尖谓甲字面，园而肥者谓园字面，方而厚者谓同子相。上下
俱尖者谓申字面上下大中间小谓风字相。上下俱方而长目
瘦者谓目字面，方而尖方而露者谓用字相和王字相，众貌虽
多，不能离开五行。十字虽少，实能包乎万状。

甲字相　　　由字面相解说

凡人天庭窄狭，地阁丰满，此乃有地
无天谓之由字面，男人得此相，初主二十
年孤苦。祖业少根基薄，直到中年进福进
财。所谋皆遂心愿，四官，五官好小贵（
做小官的意思）五官都不好，主富足只是
不贵，女人得此相。乃中寿之相。珠皆别
埠，五产它山，若五都官好，女孙得名才
有成，有缘有太之份，一生福禄。

1

Figure 7.1 The first and last pages of a privately printed contemporary Chinese physiognomy book (Beijing). *Source: Mayi xiang jieshuo* (n.d., c. 1989).

At present, despite continual propaganda in the Chinese press and periodic campaigns of suppression, evidence abounds of old-style mantic practices in the People's Republic, including use of the *Yijing* as a divinatory text.[94] The number of people who either engage in divination or resort to it is difficult to judge, but the manifestations are everywhere. Fortune-tellers ply their trade in urban areas as well as in rural villages. Divination books—some produced in Hong Kong and most put together amateurishly in the fashion of privately printed almanacs—circulate freely, sold openly by enterprising street vendors even in Beijing. Although very rudimentary, these fortune-telling manuals cover a wide variety of traditional techniques. Some give advice on how to choose marriage partners, or how to produce a child of the desired sex, and one even claims to show, by means of "physiognomy," how to determine whether a woman is lewd or licentious (*yindang*) (see Fig. 7.1).[95] Geomancy has experienced a marked revival, particularly in South China. According to one press report, oil drilling on Hainan Island was actually disrupted by concerned local residents, who believed that the oil rig and drilling had disturbed the *fengshui* in the area.[96] Shades of nineteenth century China's "response to the West!"

Meanwhile, on Taiwan, in Hong Kong, and in many overseas Chinese communities around the world, divination of all sorts thrives, unencumbered by government interference as long as it does not pose a direct political threat. The evidence is overwhelming, and does not require elaboration. One index of its popularity is the enormous amount of space devoted to mantic works in Chinese bookstores. Some merchants have, in addition to almanacs, literally hundreds of different fortune-telling books on their shelves—many of them reprints of Qing and earlier works. These books, which appeal to huge numbers of amateurs as well as practicing professionals, cover every conceivable form of traditional Chinese divination, from physiognomy and *fengshui* to fate extrapolation and word analysis. The Secretary of the Chinese Fortune-teller's Association in Taibei reports that there are presently some 3,000 registered diviners among its membership, but this represents only a fraction of the fortune-tellers who operate in both urban and rural areas throughout the country (Figs. 7.2 and 7.3). One well-known amateur fortune-teller in Taibei, Mr. Wang Mingxiong (Wang Ming-hsiung), estimates that at about eighty percent of the population in Taiwan has consulted a diviner at least once, and from thirty to forty percent of the population, several times.[97] Even "modern" Chinese intellectuals, who claim to be above such popular "superstitions," will often confess, when pressed, to an interest, and perhaps even an active belief, in divination.

One such person told me recently: "*Fengshui* is part of the makeup of nature, and therefore practiced by intellectuals. Like nature, it may be misused . . . but that does not diminish the truth of its existence. . . . Practices [such as *fengshui*] have universal spatial and temporal appeal and are closer [than crude superstitions] to man's universal apprehensions about the future." Like Kang Youwei, such individuals are quite capable of embracing dual cosmologies— one the product of Western science, the other a remnant of long-standing Chinese beliefs in a universe of cosmic resonance.[98]

Virtually every major anthropological field study undertaken in either Taiwan or Hong Kong over the last thirty years devotes considerable attention to divination as a distinctive feature of urban and especially rural life. The mantic techniques that these works describe are uncannily similar to those of the Qing period, despite the encroachments of Western culture in both Chinese environments.[99] At the Huang Daxian temple in Kowloon, many of the more than 200 registered diviners have radios, tape-players and other electric appliances in their fortune-telling stalls, and some even carry beepers to play the stock market. Yet their techniques and banter conform to long-standing conventions. In both Hong Kong and Taiwan, the form of astrology known as *Ziwei doushu* is presently the rage, not only among members of the working class, but also among white-collar workers, including stock market speculators. Although sometimes popularized almost beyond recognition, its roots remain firmly fixed in Qing dynasty soil.

Sydney Greenblatt conjectures that the continued popularity of traditional-style divination in such places "owes much to the syncretistic character of the

Figure 7.2 Contemporary fortune-teller in Hong Kong.

fortune-teller's stock of knowledge in-trade." Compared to more "doctrinaire" systems of knowledge, he asserts, the culture of Chinese fortune-telling is flexible and adaptable. "Though the social types and typified values and motives belong to an era that is passing, they still survive when fleshed out with new contents. Marriage is not what it once was, but the typification of marital behavior in the fortune-telling literature is sufficiently flexible to accomodate changing mores."[100] Almanacs in Taiwan and Hong Kong give partial support to Greenblatt's thesis. For instance, they now refer more frequently than in

Figure 7.3 Contemporary spirit-writing in Hong Kong.

the past to traditionally stigmatized phenomena such as lawsuits (*cisong*), presumably because litigation has become somewhat more acceptable to the Chinese in modern times and environments.

Yet the striking feature of contemporary Chinese almanacs—in addition to their widespread use—is the persistence of their traditional form and content, including virtually all standard categories of concern regarding lucky and unlucky activities for the various days of each lunar year. The old-style cosmology remains intact, despite the pervasive influence of modern Western science.

Moreover, divination continues to perform time-honored social and psychological roles for the Chinese. It is still linked closely with medicine, and for the most part it still draws upon traditional metaphors, symbols and homilies. One may argue that part of the reason for the continued appeal of old-style divination is not only its adaptability in the face of modernization, but also its value as an alternative to the acceptance of a personal identity defined largely in terms of modernizing change. As David Jordan and Daniel Overmyer have perceptively noted in their study of spirit-writing (bailuan) in present-day Taiwan, bailuan "provides satisfactory self-esteem by redefining traditionalism as superior to modernity." It thus serves as a convenient way of integrating the individual with the "merit-gaining aspects of selected features of the Chinese great tradition."[101]

Some Comparative Reflections

What does Chinese divination look like in broad cross-cultural perspective? Although the topic is vast and understudied, I would like to make a few general observations. The first is that modern Western works on divination tend to focus either on "dead" civilizations (such as ancient Mesopotamia, Greece and Rome), so-called "primitive" cultures (associated with village systems in Africa and South America), or "occult" counter-cultures (such as those connected with astrology and witchcraft in the modern West).[102] Qing China does not easily fall into any of these categories, and even present-day divination in Hong Kong, Taiwan, and overseas Chinese communities cannot justly be described as counter-cultural. Yet precisely for this reason traditional China offers a valuable comparative example for students of philosophy, history, psychology, anthropology, and religious studies.[103]

All kinds of questions leap to mind: What would a systematic comparison of the attitudes toward divination on the part of such highly influential thinkers as Socrates and Zhu Xi (both of whom believed in the limited use of oracles) yield? How does the ambivalence of the Western Judaic and Christian traditions toward divination compare historically with that of the Confucian elite in China? To what extent can we compare the social purposes of divination in urban Taiwan and Japan, or in the village cultures of Hong Kong's New Territories and Africa? What affinities does Chinese dream divination share with the phenomenon of induced dreams in the ancient civilizations of Egypt and the Middle East? How closely in both theory and practice does the astrological matching of horoscopes for prospective marriage partners in India correspond to the Chinese system? In what particular ways does Ifa divination in Nigeria, with its spiritual framework, moral concerns, poetic verses, and binary divinatory ritual, resemble use of the Yijing and related Chinese mantic techniques?

In their massive work La Divination, André Caquot and Marcel Leibovici identify about 160 forms of fortune-telling.[104] Evan Zuesse, writing in the Encyclopedia of Religion (1988), reduces these to three main types: intuition, possession, and decoding. The first entails a spontaneous "seeing" or "knowing" of the future, from hunches and premonitions to the insights of spiritual masters. The second involves messages communicated by spiritual beings through intermediaries—either human (in the form of dreams, body sensations, trances, spirit possession, etc.) or non-human (stars, planets, fire, water, objects, animals and lots). The third implies a logical analysis of "impersonal patterns of reality," including divination based on celestial movements, earthly patterns, body forms and mathematical correspondences.[105] All three types of divination existed (and still exist) in China, although most would fall under the third category.

According to Zuesse, spontaneous "seeing" has no particular social character, although it may have any number of distinctive cultural manifestations. Mediumistic divination, he maintains, is more characteristic of agricultural societies than hunting and fishing societies, since the latter tend to emphasize individual self-reliance more than group solidarity. Decoding, based on "a unified field of impersonal and universal processes that can be studied, harmonized with, and above all internalized by non-ecstatic sages," is most often found in "complex civilizations that have been defeated by equally powerful cultures and therefore must integrate their own indigenous views with other perspectives."[106]

Although the pervasive use of spirit-mediums in traditional China seems to support the idea of a relationship between agrarianism and shamanism, it does not help to explain the popularity of spirit-possession in more nomadic cultures of the world, including East Asia. Nor does it serve as an effective illustration of Zuesse's conquest theme. Alien ideas such as Indian astrology came to China in peace rather than as a result of war, and in any case they never fundamentally altered, or even significantly amplified, the Chinese system. Defeat and political domination by the Mongols and Manchus brought nothing new to Chinese cosmology; and by the time Western imperialism brought new perspectives to the Middle Kingdom, "decoding" in the form of indigenous practices such as astrology, geomancy, and numerology had been in place for literally thousands of years. Although a few Chinese fortune-tellers, both in Qing times and later, adopted Western foreign-telling techniques or tried to synthesize Chinese and foreign methods, they never gained widespread influence.

Why do people of different cultures believe in divination? One common (Western) answer is their ignorance of modern (Western) science. Yet not all societies that lack a modern Western viewpoint esteem the mantic arts. In fact, two of the cultures of the world *least* interested in divination appear to be the traditional Australian Aborigines and the American Plains Indians.[107] On the other hand, in the twentieth century West, where science seems to be something of a god, divination and magical practices are surprisingly prevalent. A study of the "English character" in 1955 concluded that about a quarter of the population held a view of the universe that could "most properly be called magical;"[108] and a recent (1988) Gallup poll, based on a representative national cross-section of 506 American teenagers from 13–17 years old, revealed that fifty-eight percent believed in astrology—up from fifty-five percent in 1984 and forty percent in 1978.[109] Roger Culver and Philip Ianna, authors of *Astrology: True or False* (first published in 1979) lament: "We are in the midst of an astrological renaissance such as the world has not seen in over four centuries."[110]

One reason for a persistent interest in divination—not only in the West but throughout the world—is that regardless of how powerful science may be as an explanatory tool, it is not very emotionally satisfying, especially as a replacement for the mantic arts.[111] By design it is impersonal and abstract, and it does not seek to express itself in culturally distinctive ways. Its aesthetic appeal rests in the elegance of its equations rather than the color of its symbols or the richness of its metaphors. Furthermore, science has not answered, and will probably never answer, certain fundamental human questions: Does God or some other form of supernatural intelligence exist? Is there a purpose or meaning to our lives? How should we behave as human beings? What is the life well-lived? Such questions are the province of philosophers and theologians, not scientists.

Divination, as a "pseudo-science,"[112] attempts to bridge the gap between "hard" science, which purports to describe impersonally the way the universe works, and religion, which attempts to invest human lives with cosmically-derived but individualized meaning. Like science, divination is concerned with natural phenomena and predictable, orderly processes; but like religion, it relies heavily on faith and presupposes some sort of personal connection with the constantly unfolding but mysterious patterns of cosmic change. Divination satisfies a basic human need to know about the future, and to make sense of it all.[113] Westerners who pray to God for guidance and assistance, and Chinese who consult fortune-tellers and use charms, are, it would appear, motivated by the same basic impulses. To put the matter another way, the sharp lines drawn in the early modern (seventeenth century) West between religion and more "primitive" sacramental magic, between prayers and spells, and between sovereign deity and manipulable divine being(s), begin to blur on closer inspection and in cross-cultural perspective.[114]

Western scholars (and others as well) often characterize divination as a "primitive" form of knowing, in the sense that it appears naive, crude, rudimentary and "lacking in sophistication or subtlety." Such characterizations can be traced to the late nineteenth and early twentieth century formulations of individuals such as Lucien Lévy-Bruhl, who divided human mental processes into "primitive" or "precausal"—which he defined as mystical, prelogical, and above all participatory—and "modern," which he described as causal and bound by the principles of modern logic, including the laws of contradiction and the rules of inference and proof. Participation, as an aspect of "primitive" thought, signified to Lévy-Bruhl an association between persons and things that invested them with mutual identity and consubstantiality. Thus, what modern Westerners would presumably consider logically distinct aspects of reality, such as a man and an animal, or the living and the dead, so-called primitives might fuse into a single "mystic unity."[115] Unfortunately, as Don LePan points out, "primitive" thinking bore the stigma of inferiority, since Western scholars have long tended to assume that a close relationship exists between rationality and moral goodness.[116]

Clearly this idea of moral inferiority is as untenable as the term "primitive" is unfortunate. In fact, Chinese philosophy provides an apt illustration of the limits of such pejorative labels. Much if not most of Chinese formal thought can be described as precausal—yet it is undeniably highly sophisticated and extraordinarily moralistic. Even the "rationalist" philosopher Wang Fuzhi, a harsh critic of neo-Confucian systematizers such as Shao Yong and ardent admirer of the scientific empiricism of his contemporary, Fang Yizhi, believed that participation, not detachment, was the key to meaningful knowledge. This participation included value judgment, moral commitment, and "a sense of ease." To Wang, as to all Chinese thinkers, participation was a critical function of the morally-grounded, organic and expressive universe of which he and they were a part.[117]

Stanley Tambiah's *Magic, Science, Religion, and the Scope of Rationality* (1990) juxtaposes this sort of "religious" participation to "causality," drawing upon the epistemological paradigm of Lévy-Bruhl but providing a more satisfying (or at least less judgmental) formulation. Causal thinking, he writes, is "quintessentially represented by the categories, rules and methodology of positive science and discursive mathematico-logical reason." Participatory thinking, by contrast, exists when "persons, groups, animals, places, and natural phenomena are in a relation of contiguity . . . [translated into] existential immediacy and contact, and shared affinities."[118] Tambiah goes on to argue that people in all cultures have not only the capacity but also the inclination to think in a participatory or "mystical" fashion in some contexts and more "rationally" in others. There are, in other words, multiple "orientations to reality," defined by specific situations as well as factors such as gender and social class.[119]

Modern Western culture has no more of a monopoly on "reason" than so-called primitive cultures do on mystical intuition.[120] The anthropologist Bronislaw Malinowski offers an especially apt illustration of this point in the second volume of *Coral Gardens and Their Magic* (1935). Although Malinowski, as a cultural product of twentieth century Europe, distinguishes between the language of "technology and science" and the language of "magic and persuasion," he takes pains to point out that "word magic" can be found not only in "primitive" peoples such as the Trobriand Islanders, whom he studied, but also among modern Westerners. Advertising slogans, political campaigns, and legal formulas, for example, all provide illustrations for Malinowski of the magical power of words.[121]

Malinowski further observes that word magic can describe conditions that are "objectively" false, but subjectively true—that is, language is capable of reflecting a kind of "pragmatic" truth (as per William James) that is "reasonable" in terms of addressing certain psychological needs of the individual, and sociologically true in the sense that it "affects intentions, motivations and expectations."[122] Much of the appeal of divination as an explanatory device can be understood as a product of this sort of word power—especially in societies such as traditional China's, where the written language exerted inordinate social influence by virtue of its seemingly intrinsic magical qualities.[123] Efficacy, in turn, depends on the successful application of "cultural belief systems which order reality through ritualized activities."[124] These activities may range from individual acts as simple as randomly touching a phrase in the Bible (or the Chinese equivalent, a character in a text—not necessarily a religious one), to elaborate ceremonies involving entire communities, designed to identify and expose the source of discord.

A number of writers have commented on the role of divination in structuring and harmonizing society. Eugene Mendonsa asserts, for example, that among the Sisala people of Northern Ghana, the "symbolic management and control of social reality through the divinatory process periodically provides social power and a means of reaffirming and altering the social order."[125] Victor Turner writes that among the Ndembu tribe of Northwest Zambia, divination is "a form of social analysis, in the course of which hidden conflicts are revealed so that they may be dealt with by traditional and institutionalized procedures."[126] And George Park, comparing several different traditional societies, asserts that divination "has as its regular consequence the elimination of an important source of disorder in social relationships."[127]

Park's perspective is particularly interesting, since it is explicitly cross-cultural and at least touches on China. He acknowledges that from an individual standpoint, divination may indeed eliminate "doubt and indecision" and provide a certain psychological release for people who become convinced that their subsequent actions will be "in tune with the wishes of supernatural forces."[128] But he argues that a more important feature of divination is the way fortune-tellers intervene in and affect social processes "with rather definite and socially useful results." Thus, for example, the Chinese diviner who takes into account delicate status concerns in matching the "eight characters" of a prospective bride and groom contributes to the Chinese social order by legitimating its hierarchies.[129] A Yoruba diviner who chooses a housing site for a client "remove[s] the agency and responsibility for a decision from the actor himself, casting it upon the heavens where it lies beyond cavil and beyond reproach." Under these circumstances, divination sanctions the social order by "depersonalizing the various types of action which may normally be required in the process of sorting and resorting local living arrangements."[130]

Curiously, Park does not mention Chinese geomancy in his analysis. Perhaps he is aware that it might weaken his case, since *fengshui* conflicts often proved to be so disruptive in traditional Chinese society. Yet as I have argued, geomancers did contribute to community solidarity, not only by resolving status questions, but also by holding out hope that the educational and financial prospects of a given area could be improved by the creative manipulation of the environment. Furthermore, *fengshui* played a discernible role in "controlling and channeling public opinion and belief"—a critical social function Park ascribes to divination. Listen to the revealing remarks of a Chinese Christian convert in 1885: "When any villager builds a house, he must select a lucky day, and employ the priests to drive away the evil spirits. If we, who believe in Jesus, refuse to do this, and then any of the villagers are taken sick and die, the responsibility of the death is laid at our doors, and we are required to make a recompense for the man's life."[131] We should not assume, however, that geomancy diminished class tensions in the course of building consensus. More often than not, Chinese geomancers, like spirit writers, probably served the interests of the scholarly elite. Nonetheless, as in the case of Yoruba diviners, their calculations at least had the occasional effect of "depersonalizing" difficult decisions concerning land allocation, status and power.

Of course divination could always be put to counter-cultural purposes, as in the case of Chinese secret societies. But even when employed by political dissidents it was only a practical tool, not itself an expression of alienation from the existing order. In the modern West, by contrast, divination—like other so-called occult practices—"serves usually as a muted protest against everyday social identity or generally accepted scientific values and cosmology." According to Zuesse, in an increasingly fluid, anonymous, and heterogeneous society, practices such as divination restore a sense of control to personal life "through the aesthetic and probabilistic terms in which predictions are couched." Thus, he says, astrology appeals particularly to women because it "desubstantializes oppressive personal relationships, offering instead an exotic alternative identity in which faults are erased or elevated into association with a 'star family' embracing strangers."[132] Putting aside the condescending tone, his basic point seems valid: Oppression and marginalization invite esoteric, or at least irregular, means of escape.[133]

Divination does not necessarily provide an alternative identity, however. As I have already indicated, experience in traditional China suggests that most forms of divination affirmed and reinforced existing power structures rather than undermining them—especially since recourse to fortune-tellers and fortune-telling methods was by no means confined to the margins of Chinese society. Disadvantaged groups in China, including women, may well have been particularly inclined to seek personal advice and assistance through mantic methods in order to enhance their sense of personal control, but they could also be victimized by these methods. Consider the case of a mother in the late Qing period who was told by a diviner that her son would die unless her daughter was removed from the family. The daughter later recollected that her parents "were very sorry to have me go, but as a boy is of so much greater value than a girl, they would not risk my brother's life by keeping me."[134] In any case, the assumption of an alternative identity in China demanded a more dramatic step than simply consulting a fortune-teller. It generally required becoming one—in the case of women, most commonly as a spirit medium. And even then, the oppressive, male-dominated environment of Qing China provided few opportunities for women mediums to assume the sort of high-profile roles as prophets and mediums enjoyed by, say, the spirit-rapping Fox sisters in mid-nineteenth century America.[135]

These comparative remarks are nothing more than a brief reminder that ultimately China belongs in a universal world of discourse. Cross-cultural comparisons should be attempted, if only to show why analogies fail. In the words of Joseph Levenson, "We have to see darkly, through cultures, to see one culture clear. Only from this nettle, intellectual danger, may we pluck this flower, safe assurance."[136] I do not claim to have presented a definitive interpretation of Chinese divination, much less a comprehensive comparative analysis of divination as an historical phenomenon. My project is little more than a preliminary survey of some vast and endlessly fascinating territory. I hope, however, that this book will at least inspire further investigation and analysis, not only of the rich Chinese mantic tradition but also of its relationship to other such traditions.

Notes

Unless otherwise noted, translations from Chinese sources are my own. In some cases I have modified the translations of others for consistency and clarity after consulting the Chinese originals. Also, in the interest of brevity, I have generally cited only the author, and not the title, of articles included in collections—for example: Liu Ts'un-yan in de Bary, ed. (1970). For abbreviations used in notes, see lists of abbreviations in the Bibliography of Asian-Language Works and the Bibliography of Western-Language Works.

Introduction

1. On Yuan's background and interests, see the several prefaces, both by the author and others, in Yuan (1948).

2. For a characteristic expression of the ambivalence of Qing intellectuals toward divination, see Quan Zuwang's essay "On Fate," in JSWB, 69: 15b-16a. Cf. CC, 3: 338.

3. Williams (1883), 2: 260; Shuck (1853), p. 71; Milne (1820), p. 30; Parker (1888), p. 66; Arthur Smith (1894), p. 164. For other representative statements, consult Dennys (1876), pp. 56-57; Douglas (1882), p. 289; Nevius (1869), pp. 170 and 188; Johnston (1910), p. 175; Gray (1878), 2: 2; CC, 3: 335; etc.

4. See David Johnson in Johnson, et al., eds. (1985), p. 292. See also the articles by James Watson and Evelyn Rawski in Watson and Rawski, eds. (1988).

5. See, for example, Wei (1981), esp. pp. 134-137.

6. I have discussed these factors at some length in R. J. Smith (1983) and in an article entitled "Ritual in Ch'ing Culture," in Liu, ed. (1990). See also Barbara Ward in Jain, ed. (1977).

7. R. J. Smith (1983), esp. pp. 31-79 passim. Cf. the caveats and excellent general discussion in Zurndorfer (1988a).

8. See R. J. Smith in Liu, ed. (1990); cf. Barbara Ward in Jain, ed. (1977).

9. For variations in Chinese customs over space and time, consult Hu Puan (1968) and Shang Binghe (1966). On regional development and regional stereotypes, see Rozman (1982), pp. 121 and R. J. Smith (1983), pp. 18-21. Sutton (1981) provides an excellent example of a "spatial approach" to Chinese social history. The quotation on the people of Yue is from JSWXB, 61: 8b; the Kangxi emperor's views are cited in Spence (1975), pp. 49-50. See also the sources cited in my concluding chapter, note 25.

10. See Guldin (1984), esp. pp. 140-143; also Barbara Ward in Jain, ed. (1977), p. 187.

11. Arthur Wolf in Wolf, ed. (1974), p. 9; also Weller (1987), passim, on this point. Cf. Maurice Freedman in Wolf, ed. (1974), p. 40. See also note 12 below.

12. Marjorie Topley in Topley, ed. (1967), pp. 13 ff., esp. p. 14; Maurice Freedman in Skinner, ed. (1979), p. 316; Skinner (1971); Arthur Wolf in Wolf, ed. (1974), p. 132. See also Sangren (1984 and 1988), Joachim (1988), Weller (1987), and McRae et al., eds. (1989), esp. pp. 85 and 112-113.

13. David Johnson in Johnson, *et al.*, eds. (1985), pp. 45 ff.

14. Margery Wolf is cited in the excellent analysis of Chinese women by Joachim (1988), pp. 28 ff., esp. pp. 38–41. See also the illuminating articles by Stevan Harrall and Alison Black in Caroline Bynum, *et al.*, eds. (1986).

Chapter 1

1. Wilhelm (1967), pp. 328–329, slightly modified; cf. Yuan (1948), *juanshou*, p. 1.

2. Yuan (1948), p. 1; cf. Wilhelm (1967), p. 314. See also Yuan (1926), 1: 1a.

3. See ZWDCD, 24: 7–30 passim; esp. 7–8 and 15 (155). Cf. Peterson (1982), pp. 103 ff.; Harper (1985); Schafer (1977), p. 290, note 21.

4. See the discussions in Yuan (1926), 5: 9a ff. and Metzger (1977), pp. 127 ff.; also notes 88, 102–107 below and chapters 3, 4 and 5. Fate was supposedly something Confucius "seldom talked about" (*hanyan*), but he clearly said a good deal about it. See Yuan (1926), 8: 6a and 33a.

5. On the notion of resolving doubts (also *jue xianyi; duanyi*), see Yuan (1926), 5: 4a; Wilhelm (1967), pp. 316–317; CC, 5: 334–338; ESLS, *Shihji, liezhuan,* 68: 1b; Chai and Chai, (1967), 1: 94. The TSJC, *yishu,* 47: 5849 ff. provides many examples of the use of the phrase *jueyi* from sources as diverse as the *Baihutong* (Comprehensive Discussions from the White Tiger Hall) and the *Yanshi jiaxun* (Yan Family Instructions).

6. Rong (1969) provides a convenient, though somewhat dated, overview. For a wealth of material on diviners and divining practices from the Zhou to the Ming, consult in particular TSJC, *yishu,* 47: 5681–7854 and Yuan (1948), passim. The TSJC contains excerpts from a great many books on divination, as well as comments on divining practices recorded in a wide variety of classical, literary, historical and other sources. It also includes 348 biographical entries for diviners, organized under five major (and overlapping) categories: Oracle Bones and Milfoil Stalks (*Bushi;* 112 individuals), Astrology (*Xingming;* 24), Physiognomy (*Xiangshu;* 46), Geomancy (*Kanyu;* 115) and Computational Arts (*Shushu;* 51). Of these individuals, the majority are from the Six Dynasties (45), Tang (55), Song (82), and Ming (108). Computational Arts seems to be a catch-all category, containing biographies that reflect not only calendrical and astrological skills, but also the practice of geomancy and divination by means of the *Yijing,* dreams, and even sounds and smells. Cf. the breakdowns in the *Siku quanshu,* chapter 5, note 9 and in Yuan (1926), 4: 3b–9a and 7: 12b–17a.

Yuan Shushan's compendium, organized by provinces and provincial subdivisions, identifies 778 diviners by both name and specialization (twenty or so different techniques), and provides information on a total of well over three thousand practitioners. Of the smaller sample, over 400 are pre-Qing—most of them, following the general pattern of the TSJC, from the Six Dynasties (68), Tang (58), Song (100) and Ming (164) dynasties. It may be added that these two sources overlap somewhat and neither is by any means exhaustive. Although Yuan's bibliography includes several hundred local gazetteers, a spot check of the sections on *fangji* (technicians) in forty or so gazetteers from various parts of China reveals a number of significant omissions. See Smith (1990), p. 2 and note 8. Similarly, the TSJC does not include biographical entries for all diviners mentioned in the *fangji* sections of the dynastic histories. Furthermore, by personal inclination as well as by the nature of their primary sources, both Yuan and the editors of the TSJC ignore certain "unorthodox" types of divination, such as "spirit writing" (*fuji*), and tend to emphasize individuals who exemplify conventional Confucian virtues. For an illuminating discussion of Yuan's sources and approach, see his prefaces and introductory remarks.

7. Keightley (1978), pp. 1–2; slightly modified.

8. *Ibid.*, p. 155. For an example of elite criticism of divination as "superstition," see Rong (1969). J. P. Vernant, "Parole et signes muets," in J. P. Vernant, *et al.*, eds. (1974) discusses the close relationship between divinatory and "normal" thinking.

9. Ho (1975), p. 323; Keightley (1978a), p. 222; Chang (1976), pp. 93 ff.

10. Chang Kwang-chih in Roy and Tsien, eds. (1978). The ten "heavenly stems" (*tiangan*) and twelve "earthly branches" (*dizhi*) were combined to yield a cycle of sixty. Later, the "earthly branches" became linked with twelve symbolic animals and twelve zodiacal signs, which marked the birth year of every individual in China. As with Western astrology, these signs were supposed to symbolize the personality characteristics of an individual born in that year. Fu (1972). See also chapters 2 and 5.

11. See SCC, 3: 242 ff.

12. Vandermeersch (1983); also Chang Cheng-lang (1980-1981).

13. See Keightley (1983 and 1978a); cf. Unschuld (1985), p. 25 and McRae, *et al.*, pp. 63-64. On the social role of shamans in early Chinese history, consult TSJC *yishu*, 48: 8453-8468; also Loewe (1982), pp. 104-113. See also chapter 6.

14. Nivison (1982).

15. See Mendosa (1982), esp. pp. 1-30; also the discussions in Bouché-Leclerq (1963); J.P. Vernant, *et al.*, eds. (1974); Ngo (1976); Loewe and Blacker (1981); Park (1963); etc.

16. Ong (1985), pp. 17-18.

17. *Ibid.*, p. 9. Then, as now, dreams tended to be more unsettling to Chinese than to Westerners.

18. Keightley (1978), pp. 117-123, 177-182.

19. David Keightley in Keightley, ed. (1983), p. 556.

20. ESLS, *Shiji, liezhuan*, 68: 1a-25a, passim; cf. Shaughnessy (1983), pp. 69 ff.

21. On Zhou feudalism and the Shang background, see Cho-yun Hsu and Katherine M. Linduff, eds. (1988), esp. pp. 24-32, 46-48, 147 ff. For the use of pyromancy by the early Zhou rulers, see Shaughnessy (1983), pp. 59 ff.

22. *Ibid.*, pp. 94-96; cf. CC, 3: 291-292.

23. See the initial preface by Yuan (1948), p. 1; also DeWoskin (1983), p. 3; SCC, 3: 190

24. CC, 5: 750 and 752. See also Timoteus Pokora in Le Blanc and Blader, eds. (1987), p. 231.

25. On the Mandate of Heaven, see ZWDCD, 8: 304 (600, 602); cf. CC, 2: 354-359. On the link between astronomy, astrology, divination and calendrical science, consult SCC, 3: 190-423, passim; 6.2: 58-244 passim; 5.1: 25, 151-226; 4.2: 489 ff; also the "Great Plan" of the *Shujing* (CC, 3: 320-344) and the "Calendrical" and "Heavenly Office" sections of the *Shiji* (*juan* 26 and 27). Sima Qian, author of the *Shiji*, describes the concerns of astronomy and the calendar as "close to divination and the world of spirits."

26. Yuan (1948) provides biographies of these individuals. See also Teboul (1982), pp. 155-156; Forke (1925), p. 7; TSJC, *yishu*, pp. 5862-5863, 5902-5903; CC, 5: 169; 466-467, 478-479; 523, etc. On recent excavations related to divination, consult Yü, ed. (1981), pp. 23-27, 95; also Li (1983 and 1985). Although the Zhou court persisted in using bone and shell for divination, oracular inscriptions were increasingly written separately on bamboo and silk. See SCC, 5.1: 25.

27. CC, 3: 367. See also SCC, 3: 351, 355-356, 360, 367, 369, 374, 421, 436-438, 479.

28. SSC 4: 305-306.

29. *Ibid.*, 4: 266.

30. For a discussion of some possibilities, consult Vandermeersch (1983); also Shaughnessy (1983a); Chang Cheng-lang (1980-1981); Liu (1986). Rong Zhaozu (1969) provides

an interesting, although somewhat dated, narrative of the evolution of Chinese divining practices and texts, together with charts showing these "genealogical" developments in convenient summary form. See also Yuan (1926), 1: 4a ff.

31. The description of the Yi is from Michael Nylan and Nathan Sivin in Le Blanc and Blader, eds., p. 43. For a detailed account of one standard procedure, consult Zhu (1979), shiyi appendix, pp. 1a–5a; cf. Shaughnessy (1983), pp. 60 ff., esp. pp. 82–90; Kidder Smith, et al. (1990), pp. 11 ff.

32. R. J. Smith (1989); see also the sources cited in note 31 above.

33. CC, 5: 124–125. Cf. Wilhelm (1967), pp. 10–20. For other examples from the Zuozhuan, see Kidder Smith (1989); Shaughnessy (1983), pp. 72 ff.

34. R. J. Smith (1989); cf. Shaughnessy (1983), pp. 70–71, who compares divination topics in different sources from the Shang period to the Han dynasty.

35. See R. J. Smith (1989); also Kunst (1985), passim, esp. pp. 30–51. The appendix to Li Jingchi (1978), pp. 378–397, provides an illuminating discussion of "normal" (chang) and "unusual" (guai) symbols of divination in the Yijing.

36. Even the relatively straightforward symbolism of color is problematic. Consider, for example, the different interpretations of, say, yellow (huang) as applied to animals ("yellow ox," Wilhelm (1967), p. 131; cf. ZYJJ, p. 212), elements ("yellow metal," Wilhelm (1967), p. 89; cf. ZYJJ, p. 152), garments ("yellow skirt," Wilhelm (1967), p. 15; cf. ZYJJ, p. 40), implements ("yellow ears [of vessels]," Wilhelm (1967), p. 196; cf. ZYJJ, p. 198), phenomena ("yellow light," Wilhelm (1967), p. 120; cf. ZYJJ, p. 300), etc. See also chapter 3, notes 24 and 27.

37. On "omen songs," see Riegel (1983) and Chang (1980–1981), p. 91. For changes, see the discussions in Shaughnessy (1983) and Kunst (1985), esp. pp. 82–95.

38. On Ni Yuanlu, see Ray Huang in de Bary, ed. (1970), esp. pp. 433–436. For discussions of the Yijing commentarial tradition, consult SKQSZM, 1: 1a ff.; also Schulz (1982), chapter 1 and Shchutskii (1980), chapters 2 and 9.

39. See, for example, Han (1955), p. 106; cf. Wilhelm (1967), pp. 7–8, 379. For a discussion of dragon symbolism and its connection with early astronomy, see Shaughnessy (1983), pp. 268 ff.

40. See, for example, CC, 5: 165–167; 194–195; 818–819; Chang (1980–1981), pp. 89 ff.; Shaughnessy (1983), chapter 2, esp. pp. 72–73.

41. CC, 5: 102–103; 123–125; 127–129; 600; 604; 615; 619.

42. Ibid., 5: 573, 580–581.

43. See R. J. Smith (1983), pp. 85–99, esp. 92–93; see also Cheng (1987); Liu (1974); Swanson (1974), 31–62; Kunst (1985), 19–30 and passim.

44. On the moral framework of the Yijing, see Luo (1981), pp. 529 ff., esp. 542, 623, etc.; also ESLS, Shihji, liezhuan, 67: 3a–b and note 88 below. For concrete examples, consult CC, 5: 437, 439–440; 637, 640, 573, 581, etc.

45. CC, 1: 272–273; slightly modified. Cf. Waley (1938), pp. 177 and 249. For another version of this quotation, from the Liji, see Chai and Chai (1967), 2: 363.

46. For a summary discussion of the dramatic changes in the late Zhou period, consult CHC, 1: 21–30. On calendrical concerns, see Rao (1981 and 1983); also Rao and Zeng (1982).

47. Yuan (1948) provides biographies of these individuals. See also TSJC, yishu, 47: 5865, 6689–6690; Forke (1925), p. 7; SCC, 3: 197; Timoteus Pokora in Le Blanc and Blader, eds. (1987), p. 231.

48. Unschuld (1985), pp. 35–40; cf. Harper (1985), esp. pp. 462 ff..

49. Schwartz (1985), pp. 356–366.

50. R. J. Smith (1983), pp. 85–98; 102–104. For details on yinyang/wuxing correlations, consult Forke (1925), pp. 163–200 and 227–300.

51. For some indications of the emphasis on divination in the *Liji*, see Chai and Chai (1967), 1: 92, 94, 103, 109, 119, 235, 259, 297–298, 380–381, 367, 385–386, 428–429, 472; 2: 4, 51, 53–54, 71, 74, 84, 135–136, 156, 223, 233, 289, 295, 349, 363.

52. CHC, 1: 69–72.

53. Fung (1952–1953), 1: 379–395. On the "Ten Wings" in particular, consult Swanson (1974), esp. his "Sinological Introduction," pp. 4–12; also Peterson (1982).

54. Wilhelm (1967), pp. 293, 295, etc.

55. Chan (1963), pp. 280–282, slightly modified. Correspondence theory also found expression in The "Treatise on Astrology" of the *Shiji*, which drew an explicit analogy between the stars and asterisms of the celestial realm and the bureaucratic offices of the Han government. See Nakayama (1966), p. 447–448; also Kalinowski (1982). For other examples of correlative thinking, consult Ho (1966) and Henderson (1984), chapter 1.

56. Chan (1963), p. 279; slightly modified. On the relationship between correlative cosmology and music see Fung (1952–1953), 2: 118–122 and 127–128.

57. Henderson (1984), p. 37.

58. Wong and Wu (1936), p. 19; also Unschuld (1985), pp. 83–100.

59. Unschuld (1985), pp. 67–68, 72–73, 100; DeWoskin (1983), pp. 14–20; CHC, 1: 671–673; Loewe (1982), pp. 104–113.

60. Unschuld (1985), p. 79; Nakamura (1966), p. 146.

61. The primary reason was, of course, that they shared the same basic cosmological assumptions. See Li (1986); Smith (1986), p. 169–170.

62. Unschuld (1985), pp. 79, 85–86, 91. See also Nathan Sivin in Fraser, *et al.*, eds. (1986).

63. SCC, 2: 304 ff., esp. 312–325. Cf. Wilhelm (1967), pp. 262–355, passim.

64. Ho (1972), pp. 31 ff.

65. Wilhelm (1967), p. 295; slightly modified.

66. See SKQSZM 1: 1a ff. for Qing views of Meng Xi and his legacy. Cf. Shaughnessy (1983), pp. 3–4.

67. For a full discussion of Han scholarship on the *Yijing*, consult Xu (1975a).

68. ESLS, *Hanshu, liezhuan*, 58: 6a–10a.

69. Qu (1984), pp. 77 ff. elaborates on these and other early interpretive schemes. It should be noted that there were two well-known individuals named Jing Fang in the Former Han, both of whom were interested in the *Yijing* and linked with the name of Jiao Yanshou. Their identical names have given rise to much confusion. See ESLS, *Hanshu, liezhuan*, 45: 6a–11b and Yuan (1948), 28: 20–21; cf. ESLS, *Hanshu, liezhuan*, 58: 8b–10a (esp. 8b). Consult also CHC, 1: 692; Fung (1952–1953), 2: 111–118; Toda (1963), pp. 17–18; Schulz (1982), pp. 13–16, 21–25; Henderson (1984), pp. 14–15; DeWoskin (1983), pp. 12–13, 27, 55, 62–63, etc.

70. For a discussion of the different versions and interpretations of the *Yijing*, see Xu (1975a); also Liebenthal (1947), esp. pp. 135 ff.

71. *Ibid.* (both sources); see also Chen (1968); Liu (1986); Schulz (1982), pp. 16–18; Fung (1952–1953), 2: 86 ff. Both Zheng and Yu embraced correlative schemes. The former correlated the twelve lines of the hexagrams Qian and Kun with the twelve months of the year, while the latter refined the ancient *najia* sexegenary system by correlating various hexagrams with the ten heavenly stems and twelve earthly branches.

72. Itano (1976 and 1978).

73. Fung (1952–1953), 2: 88 ff., esp. pp. 97–101.

74. On Yang Xiong, consult *ibid.*, 2: 136–150; Yuan (1926), 5: 14b; and Yuan (1948), 19: 5–6; also Michael Nylan and Nathan Sivin in Le Blanc and Blader, eds. (1987).

75. See Henderson (1984), p. 262, note 62; also Walters (1983), pp. 9–12.

76. See Michael Nylan and Nathan Sivin in Le Blanc and Blader, eds. (1987); cf. Henderson (1984), pp. 16–19. For a long and illuminating Qing evaluation, consult SKQSZM, 108: 2a–5a.

77. Sima Guang, a Song scholar (see next section), cited by Michael Nylan and Nathan Sivin in Le Blanc and Blader, eds. (1987), p. 50. Slightly modified.

78. See Yü, ed. (1981), pp. 23 ff.; also Harper (1985); Liu (1986); Rao and Zeng (1982); Li (1985), p. 419.

79. On the social and political role of *fangshi*, see DeWoskin (1983); also Ngo (1976) and CHC, 1: 665–667, 751–752, etc.

80. These biographical sections can also be found in early encyclopedias such as the *Taiping yulan* (Imperial Digest of the Taiping Reign [976 A.D.]) as well as later compendia such as the TSJC. See note 6 above; also Li (1960), *juan* 720–737.

81. CHC, 1: 483 and 683 ff., esp. 686–688; cf. Rao (1981 and 1983) and Rao and Zeng (1982). Chapter 26 of the *Shiji* traces the evolution of calendrical science in China from earliest times to the inauguration of the Taichu (Great Beginning) Calendar of Han Wudi in 104 B.C., emphasizing the need to study celestial movements in order to maintain cosmic harmony. Of the legendary sage-king Yao, for example, it says that having appointed Xi He to head his calendrical office, he clarified the seasons, corrected the divisions (*du*) of earth and sky, harmonized *yin* and *yang*, regulated the wind and rain, and revitalized the "breath" (*qi*) of the cosmos. As a result, "the people did not suffer from pestilence." ESLS, *Shiji, lishu*, 4: 1a–4a, esp. 2a.

82. DeWoskin (1983), p. 10–13; see also Timoteus Pokura in Le Blanc and Blader, eds. (1987). Throughout the imperial era, the throne employed unofficial fortune-tellers as well as its regular stable of official diviners. See Smith (1986), p. 175.

83. DeWoskin (1983), pp. 23–29 provides an inventory of these and other techniques, as well as a brief description of some of the most prominent practices. See also Ngo (1976); ESLS, *Hanshu, yiwen zhi*, 30: 27a–34a; CHC, 1: 673–682; Loewe (1982), pp. 73–103; Bodde (1981), pp. 351–372; Chü (1972), pp. 124–126, 307, 329, 407, 457.

84. See Yuan (1948), passim.

85. DeWoskin (1983), pp. 3–6, 32–38; slightly modified. Cf. Timoteus Pokura in Le Blanc and Blader, eds. (1987), pp. 226 ff. and Yuan (1926), 5: 1a–3b. By late imperial times, the remarks on *fangshi* in the dynastic histories had become somewhat more restrained. The *Mingshi* (History of the Ming Dynasty), for example, acknowledges the need for, and the accomplishments of, several diviners and other technical specialists, both past and present. On the other hand, it displays a certain amount of skepticism regarding their exploits, and asserts that in the end the most important thing is to study the classics and learn from the ancient sages. ESLS, *Mingshi, liezhuan*, 187: 1a–b.

86. Cited in Watson (1961), 2: 468–475; cf. Timoteus Pokura in Le Blanc and Blader, eds. (1987). See also Yuan (1926), 5: 2a, 3a, 11b; 6: 11b–13a; SKQSZM, 109: 23a–b.

87. See ESLS, *Hanshu, liezhuan*, 42: 1b–3a; also Yuan (1948), 19: 2–5, 22: 25, 22: 32–33, 22: 34, 37: 31, etc.

88. See, for example, CHC, 1: 680–682; also Chan (1989), pp. 216–218. Wang Fuzhi's *Zhouyi neizhuan fali* (Introduction to the Inner Commentary on the Book of Changes), reprinted in volume 141 of YJJC, provides an excellent example of how Chinese scholars tended to link fatalistic divination to the problem of moral decline. For, the argument went, if all questions of life and death, rise and fall, were assumed to be immutably fixed, what need was there for right behavior? Sovereigns could simply be inhumane to their subjects, subjects could be disloyal to their rulers, children could be inattentive to their parents, and parents could be neglectful of the moral education of their children. See esp. pp. 2a–b.

89. See XBZZJC, 7: 5–7, 10–12, and 232–240; also Peng (1985), pp. 291–296 on Wang Fu (c. 90–165 A.D.). Cf. CHC, 1: 681–682 and Yuan (1926), 5: 9a–9b, 15a, 16a–b; 6: 2b–3a.

90. For an overview of the Six Dynasties period, consult CHC, 1: 808–878; also DeWoskin (1983), passim.

91. On these sources, consult Bodde (1981), pp. 331–350; DeWoskin (1983), pp. ix, 2, 21; Mather (1976). Mather's translation of *Shishuo xinyu*—like DeWoskin's translation of *fangshi* biographies—provides many illuminating examples of divination in the Six Dynasties period. See for example, pp. 92–93, 115, 277–280, 359–360, 347, etc.

92. See CHC, 1: 837–867, passim.

93. Bergeron (1986). See also Liebenthal (1947); Fung (1952–1953), 2: 168–189; Schulz (1982), pp. 18–21; CHC, 1: 830 ff. On the complex evolution of Daoism, see Sivin (1978) and Strickmann (1980).

94. See Wilhelm (1967), p. 315–316. Wilhelm translates *ji* as "seeds." See also Peterson (1982), p. 107.

95. Shchutskii (1980), pp. 63–64, 92–93, 209.

96. Schafer (1977), pp. 5, 10, 60, 79, 81; Nakayama (1966), pp. 445 ff.

97. Henderson (1984), pp. 68–71. On conceptions of the universe, see Forke (1925), pp. 12 ff.; SCC, 3: 210 ff.; also John Major in Rosemont, ed. (1983).

98. See the introduction to Welch and Sidel (1979); also Saso (1978), pp. 21 ff., esp. pp. 31–32; Strickmann (1980); Kristoper Schipper in Fraser, *et al.*, eds. (1986).

99. Forke (1925), pp. 137–142.

100. R. J. Smith (1986), pp. 137–138; see also Strickmann (1980 and 1983).

101. See the sources cited in notes 93 and 98 above.

102. CC, 2: 449–450. See also Hsü (1975).

103. Cited in Fung (1952–1953), 2: 162–163; slightly modified.

104. See Mencius in CC, 2: 185, 189, 239, 253, 289, etc. Cf. CHC, 1: 701–703, 775–776, 780–783; Chan (1963), pp. 78, 79, 82, 101–102, 266–267, 303–304.

105. CC, 2: 449; slightly modified.

106. This was, of course, the central premise of the *Yijing*. The idea of moral assertion is well reflected in the story of Emperor Taiwu of the Shang, whose minister Yi Zhi is supposed to have told him: "Strange [omens] cannot triumph over virtue" (*yao busheng de*). ESLS, *Shiji, fengshan shu*, 6: 1b.

107. For a convenient summary, consult Wei (1974), pp. 181–184. Yuan (1926), 1: 3b, discusses Mozi's belief in spirits but his denial of fatalism.

108. See, for example, Yuan (1948), 38: 10–12; Chao (1946), p. 283; Unschuld (1985), p. 148; etc.

109. Strickmann (1983); Yuan (1948), 38: 10–12.

110. Strickmann (1983). See also Whalen Lai in Buswell, ed. (1990) on the *Zhancha shano yebao jing* (Classic of Divining the Requital of Good and Bad Actions).

111. See Yuan (1926), 5: 2a; 6: 3b–4a, 13a–b, 20b–21a; TSJC *yishu* 47: 5865–5877; 6523, 6690, 7047, 7063; SCC, 2: 360; 4.1: 296 ff.

112. TSJC *yishu* 47: 7047; cf. SKQSZM, 109: 1a ff. Carole Morgan has an illuminating but as yet unpublished manuscript on the early development of geomancy in China entitled "Tang Geomancy: The Wuxing School and Its Legacy."

113. This self-interested use of geomancy was heavily criticized. See, for example, TSJC *yishu* 47: 7055 ff.

114. *Ibid.*, 47: 5865–5872, 6523, 7830; Yuan (1926), 6: 3b–4a; 13a–b, 20b–21a, 24; DeWoskin (1983), pp. 91 ff. On the relationship between divination and games, see SSC, 4.1: 326–330; also Schafer (1977), p. 291 note 37.

115. See note 69 above.

116. SCC, 2: 358; Chao (1946), p. 283.

117. DeWoskin (1983), p. 103; slightly modified. As DeWoskin indicates (p. 182, note 38), all of the signs and symbols in interpretations of this sort change meaning with changing contexts, and none has particular significance in isolation.

118. *Ibid.*, pp. 93, 128–130; TSJC *yishu* 47: 5862, 5902, 6689–6690. DeWoskin's book provides biographies of thirty-four *fangshi* from the *Hou Hanshu*; three from the *Sanguo zhi*; and one from the *Jinshu*. Since many of these individuals were diviners, his material sheds valuable light on our general concerns. See also the similar study by Ngo (1976). There are, however, a great many diviners from the Han, Three Kingdoms and Six Dynasties periods whose biographies are not included in the works of either DeWoskin or Ngo. See note 6 above. Furthermore, there are numerous examples of individuals who were well known for their prognosticating skills, but not considered professionals or *fangshi*. The famous strategist Zhuge Liang immediately comes to mind. See Yuan (1926), 6: 4b, 8a.

119. De Woskin (1983), p. 100. For the invidious comparison of Guan, Jing and Guo, see TSJC, *yishu* 47: 5850–5851.

120. Xiao (1925), preface, esp. 1b. Biographical material on Xiao is included in the subsection on geomancy in the TSJC *yishu* 47: 7048, 7063–7064; see also Chao (1948), pp. 283–284. Marc Kalinowski is presently translating and annotating the *Wuxing dayi*.

121. On Sui-Tang ritual, religion, and divination, consult Wechsler (1985), esp. pp. 14–20, 32–34, 37–77, 212–223; also CHC, 3, passim.

122. Weschler (1985), pp. ix–x.

123. Schafer (1977), p. 12.

124. *Ibid.*, p. 54. For pre-Tang precedents, see Ho (1966), p. 22.

125. Weschler (1985), pp. 69–73; Bokenkamp (1983).

126. Nakayama (1966), p. 450; see also Soymié (1981). The famous *Tuibei tu* (Chart of Extrapolation from the Back) is the most famous prophetic book from the Tang. See chapter 5, note 211.

127. SCC, 5.1: 151.

128. Schafer (1977), pp. 37 ff., esp. 42–51, 55–57, 78–84, and 120–162; also Birnbaum (1980). Oddly enough, the TSJC subsection on astrology contains no biographies of Tang exponents of the art, and only one pre-Tang exponent, Wei Ning—although the Tang scholar Lü Cai's critique appears in this subsection. See note 130 below.

129. Cited in Schafer (1977), p. 58; slightly modified. See also *ibid.*, pp. 48–49, 52, 59, 69, etc.; Fu (1972), pp. 33–34; Riegel (1983).

130. TSJC *yishu* 47: 6524–6525 and 7057, 7061. See also Doré (1914–1933), 4: 383, 387; ZDLZ, 416: 13a; JSWP, 63: 9a; etc. Lü, it should be noted, believed in divination, but criticized its misapplication.

131. Chao (1948), esp. 285; Nakayama (1966), pp. 448–449. Li's *Mingshu* and Han's epitaph are discussed in SKQSZM, 109: 22b–25a.

132. Yuan (1948), 38: 13–23. For secular women diviners of the Tang period, consult *ibid.*, 38: 1–4. The various TSJC subsections on divination include many biographies of male diviners in the Tang.

133. See TSJC *yishu*: 47: 7048; Yuan (1948), 38: 20–21 and 31 and Yuan (1919), Wu Yinsun's preface, 1a; SMTH, 7: 2b–4b. See also Schafer (1977), pp. 14–15, 48, 58, 78–79; SCC, 4.1: 301.

134. On Song and post-Song changes in Chinese society, consult Johnson, *et al.*, eds. (1985), esp. pp. 3–72; Unschuld (1985), pp. 166–188.

135. The literature on these individuals is voluminous. For a convenient overview, consult Fung (1952–1953), 2: 434–592. On the *Yijing* in particular, see Kidder Smith,

et al. (1990); also Chan, ed. (1986), esp. pp. 34–36, 61–62, 81–82, 204–205, 292–307, 506–507, 526–528 and Chan (1990), pp. 111–115, 212–219, 406, etc.

136. See Kidder Smith, *et al.* (1990); also R. J. Smith (1986), pp. 158–159; Henderson (1984), pp. 120–131.

137. Chan, ed. (1967), pp. 107–108.

138. Kidder Smith, *et al.* (1990); Chan, ed. (1967), p. xxxiv; Chan (1986), p. 552.

139. Wyatt (1985), esp. pp. 656–662; Wang (1976), pp. 409–414. See also chapters 2 and 5.

140. See Yuan (1926), 5: 4a; also notes 88, 93, and 102–107 above.

141. SCC, 4.1: 305; modified; see also *ibid.*, pp. 293 ff.

142. *Ibid.*, 4.1: 304; modified.

143. On Xu Ziping, consult Chao (1948), esp. pp. 286 ff.; Yuan (1926) 5: 11b; SMTH, 7: 2b–4b; SKQSZM, 109: 26b–29a. On the origins and authorship of the *Sanming tonghui*, see SKQSZM, 109: 34b–35b; cf. Yuan (1948), 22: 13–14.

144. See Hansen (1990), esp. pp. 61–75.

145. See QBLC, *fangji*, p. 90; also Yuan (1948), 21: 4. For origins of the practice, consult notes 42 and 83 above.

146. See Strickmann (1983); also Rong (1969), pp. 2–3 and Morgan (forthcoming). The *Lingqi jing* is reviewed in SKQSZM, 109: 12a–13a.

147. Jordan and Overmyer (1986), pp. 36–88; Xu (1940).

148. Overmyer (1972), esp. p. 65; ZWDCD, 8: 322.

149. See Yuan (1926), 7: 11a–b; Yuan (1948), 38: 30–31; also Langlois (1981), pp. 218 ff.

150. SCC, 3: 381; Zhu (1934).

151. On Chinese influence in Tibet as well as indigenous Tibetan divining techniques, consult Strickmann (1983); Yuan (1948), 20: 36; cf. Loewe and Blacker (1981), pp. 6 ff.

152. Langlois and Sun (1981).

153. See Liu (1971).

154. Liu Ts'un-yan in de Bary, ed. (1975), p. 291; also Liu (1971), pp. 70 and 82.

155. Ho (1969), pp. 140, 148, 151; Peterson (1986).

156. Ho (1969), pp. 150 ff; Dunne (1962). For background, consult Yuan (1926), 7: 10a–12b.

157. Ho (1969), pp. 142–143, 152. For denunciations of the practice of selecting "lucky days" by one who, ironically, had to engage in divination as an employee of the Qing government see Nan Huairen (Ferdinand Verbiest; 1669 and 1669a).

158. R. J. Smith (1986), p. 161; also SCC, 2: 357.

159. Cited in R. J. Smith (1986), p. 161.

160. For Lai Zhide's critique of Han and Song *Yijing* scholarship, consult Lai (1971), original preface, pp. 1a–2a. Schulz (1982) offers a detailed analysis of Lai's thought. On Wang and Lü, see Henderson (1984), pp. 186, 189–191, 214, 242–243. See also *ibid.*, pp. 219–220 for criticisms of Song versions of the *Hetu* and *Luoshu*.

Chapter 2

1. See R. J. Smith (1983), p. 2. See also Guy (1987), pp. 16 ff.; Ropp (1981), pp. 11 ff., and the sources cited in note 2 below.

2. Wakeman and Grant (1975), p. 2; Naquin and Rawski (1987), pp. 21 ff.; 99 ff.; see also Wakeman (1986) and Spence and Wills, eds. (1979), passim.

3. See Elman (1984) on *kaozheng* scholarship; also Guy (1987), esp. pp. 16–49 and 134–156; Struve (1988), etc.

4. See Henderson (1984).

5. Elman (1984), pp. 232 ff.

6. Henderson (1984), p. 150; see also Struve (1988), esp. pp. 490-493.

7. Henderson (1984), p. 173. Cf. my conclusion, note 78.

8. Henderson (1984), pp. 196-197.

9. CC, Mengzi, 2: 363, 370.

10. Sivin (1969), pp. 7, 52-54.

11. R. J. Smith (1988), p. 127.

12. The clearest and most concise statements regarding the complex relationship between cosmic variables may be found in the memorials (zouyi) that follow the preface to the XJBFS. Reliable Western-language sources that discuss such matters include Morgan (1980), Forke (1925); Parker (1888 and 1888a); and Graham (1989), esp. chapter 4. See also Walters (1987).

13. See, for example, XJBFS, zouyi, p. 10a; also the reviews of the Xingli kaoyuan and Xieji bianfang shu in JSWB, 69: 18a-19a.

14. Unschuld (1985), pp. 57-58; see also ibid., pp. 194 ff., esp. 215-228; Black (1989), pp. 54-55, 108-109, 143-144, and 152-157; Birdwhistell (1989), pp. 7 ff., and esp. 228-232; Graham (1989), esp. chapter 4; and Nakayama, p. 446, 449.

15. XJBFS, preface, 1a.

16. Wilhelm (1967), p. 297; modified.

17. Chan (1967), p. 22; see also ibid., pp. 26, 31, 33, 36, 74, etc. Cf. Black (1989), pp. 71-73.

18. See Luo (1982), esp. pp. 21-32; Luo (1981), pp. 529-610, passim; also Black (1989), pp. 63-64 and 69; Forke (1925), pp. 200 ff. For applications in medicine, consult Liu (1988), pp. 32 ff. and Unschuld (1985), pp. 283-285.

19. Zhu (1979), preface, pp. 1a-2b; JSWXB, 61: 2a-b. For details, see the sources cited in note 18 above.

20. XLKY, 1: 1a; cf. Wilhelm (1967), p. 264.

21. Zhu (1979), diagrams, 3a ff.; cf. Wilhelm (1967), p. 318; Fung (1952-1953), pp. 459-460.

22. There were other graphic conceptions of the Supreme Ultimate, but they did not capture the popular imagination in the same way.

23. Wilhelm (1967), p. 301; cf. Peterson, pp. 104-110. The commentaries to the passage in ZYJJ, pp. 380-381 discuss the meaning of "spirit" at considerable length. See also note 24 below.

24. See, for example, Wilhelm, pp. 294, 296, 310, 313 316; ZYJJ, pp. 375, 376, 396, 398-399, 403, 405. Cf. Kidder Smith, et al. (1990), esp. pp. 199-203; Black (1989), pp. 72-74, 79-81, 227-229 and 236-241.

25. ZYBY, preface, p. 2a; also Chan (1967), p. 8. Cf. Yuan (1948), 23: 9-11. For additional remarks on shen, see note 24 above and chapters 3 and 6.

26. See also Chan (1967), pp. 366-367 and Graham (1958), pp. 108 ff.; cf. JSWXB, 61: 2a-3a; JSWB 69: 18b. Some classical entries do not lend themselves well to a rationalist explanation. See, for example, CC, Shujing, 3: 63-64; cf. ibid., 3: 337 ff.

27. Chan (1986a), pp. 142-168.

28. Ibid., p. 143, slightly modified.

29. Ibid.; cf. JSWXB, 61: 2a.

30. JSWXB, 61: 2a-3a; cf. Xu Dachun (1693-1771) cited in Unschuld (1985), pp. 337-340.

31. Chai and Chai (1967), p. 381, modified.

32. R. J. Smith (1983), pp. 101-102. See also Nathan Sivin in Ropp, ed. (1990), pp. 169-170; Ng (1986) and Liu (1988), pp. 48 ff.

33. Chan (1967), p. 31. For details, see the articles by Stanislaus Lokuang, Teng Aimin and Chiu Hansheng in Chan, ed. (1986).

34. Luo (1982), pp. 21 ff.; see also Forke (1925), p. 187, 213, 266–267 and Yuan (1919), passim.

35. Wilhelm (1967), pp. 265–267; cf. Zhu Xi's comments on *bian* (sudden change) and *hua* (gradual transformation) in Zhu (1979), 3: 13a. See also SCC, 2: 253 ff., esp. p. 259; Henderson (1984), pp. 8–9; Loewe (1982), pp. 39–42; Schulz (1982), pp. 168 ff., esp. pp. 175–176; JSWB, 69: 18b.

36. See the convenient summary in SKQSZM, 109: 47b; also JSWB, 69: 18a–b and Yuan (1919), 6: 23b–24b. Cf. note 39 below.

37. Yuan (1919), 2: 3a ff. and Luo (1982), pp. 34 ff, esp. 44–47; Cf. Unschuld (1985), pp. 58–61, 86–88, 171–172 and Graham (1989), pp. 340–356. On the twelve phases of change, see Morgan (1980), pp. 237 ff.; also Ho (1985), pp. 28–29 and Chao (1946), pp. 299–303; also chapters 4 and 5.

38. XLKY, 1: 4a–b; cf. Black (1989), p. 120; Schulz (1982), pp. 174 and 199.

39. Cited in Shegehisa Kuriyama in Kawakita, ed. (1987), pp. 55 ff.; see also Luo (1982), pp. 53–61; cf. Morgan (1980b), p. 213; Wilhelm (1967), pp. 265–72; Schipper (1978), passim.

40. See the illuminating discussion in Walshe (1906), pp. 189–195. Cf. Doré (1914– 1933), 1: 141–142. Day (1969), p. 80 remarks that Chinese peasants worship the stems and branches as gods. Hodus (1929), pp. 22–23, describes the popular notion that a written character is not merely the sign of an idea, but a "double" of the object it signified, and thus possessed of real power. To put the matter another way, stems and branches, like trigrams and hexagrams, had an "objective" existence beyond their graphic depiction, even though they could not otherwise be apprehended. See also chapter 3, note 23 and chapter 5, note 119.; cf. the discussion in Tambiah (1990), pp. 73–83.

41. For details, see Luo (1982), pp. 45 ff.; also Ho (1985), p. 28 and Morgan (1980), pp. 232 ff.; cf. XLKY, 1: 24b–25a.

42. See the diagrams in XLKY, 1: 24b–26a.

43. R. J. Smith (1983), p. 104. On the *nayin* system of correlations, consult Yuan (1919), 1: 6a ff.; cf. Chao (1946), pp. 292–294 and Morgan (1980), pp. 241–242. See also XLKY, 1: 27a–28a. The Chinese commonly considered cycles of sixty years to be part of larger recurrent cycles of 120 years, known collectively as the three phases (*sanyuan*). These phases were: a beginning period of growth (*shangyuan*), a middle period of flourishing (*zhongyuan*), and an ending period of decline (*xiayuan*). For an illustration of their relationship to cosmic variables, consult XLKY, 2: 1a–5a.

44. Luo (1982), pp. 44–47 and 59–61; also XLKY, 1: 6b–9a and 23b–24a; cf. XJBFS, *zouyi*, pp. 26 ff.; Chao (1946), pp. 288–294; Ho (1985), pp. 27–29.

45. Wilhelm (1967), p. 320; cf. ZYJJ, p. 411.

46. XJBFS, *zouyi*, p. 11a; cf. Zhu (1979), 3: 13a. See also the excellent discussion in SCC, 5.5: 52 ff.

47. Wilhelm (1967), pp. 308–310; see note 35 above on Zhu Xi's commentary to this passage regarding *bian* and *hua*.

48. XLKY, 1: 5a–6b.

49. Ho (1985), pp. 7, 18, 27, 115, 173; cf. Chang Liwen in Chan, ed. (1986), pp. 301– 306.

50. For examples in the Qing, consult Yuan (1948), 2: 4; 2: 7; 2: 10–11; 2: 23; 5: 16–17; 5: 19–20; 5: 26–27; 6: 17; 7: 17–18; 7: 27; 8: 12–13; 8: 37; 18: 7; 18: 24; 19: 33– 34; 20: 26–27; etc. Yuan's book contains a great many more relevant entries. See also Jiao Xun, cited in Elman (1984), pp. 181–182.

51. See chapter 1 and chapter 3; also the convenient summary in Schulz (1982), pp. 168 ff.

52. Schulz (1982), pp. 147, 179.

53. See, for example, XLKY, 1: 28a–32b.

54. Wilhelm (1967), p. 300 and 314; cf. ZYJJ, pp. 380 and 401.

55. XLKY, 1: 1a–9a. Schafer (1977), chapter 6 provides a useful overview. See also Morgan (1980b), pp. 211–213.

56. Morgan (1980), pp. 178 ff.; Ho Peng Yoke (1961), pp. 121 ff. One of the earliest Chinese horoscopic treatises employing the sun, moon, and five planets as variables is the ninth century work known as the *Qiyao rang zai jue* (Formulas for Avoiding Calamities According to the Seven Luminaries). See Nakayama (1966), p. 450.

57. XLKY, 1: 40b–45a. Cf. Morgan (1980), pp. 178–183; Morgan (1980b), pp. 212–213; and Schafer (1977), chapter 7 on "embodied stars."

58. XLKY, 5: 8a ff.; see also Eitel (1984), pp. 12–14. Giles (1912), pp. 26–27, provides a convenient list of the "determining asterisms" of the twenty-eight Chinese "lodges," together with their corresponding elements and animals, as well as astronomical equivalents in terms of Western constellations. In Qing popular thought, as expressed in almanacs, each lodge was associated with fortune or misfortune under various circumstances. See Gray (1878), 2: 14–15 and DuBose (1886), pp. 415 ff.

59. E-tu Zen Sun (1961), p. 197. See also chapter 5, note 136. On the importance of *zhanhou* to the Qing emperors, consult, for example, SCSX, Kangxi, 10: 3a–b; DQHD, 77: 2a; Cf. Henderson (1986), p. 138. For methods of interpretation, see the works cited in CSJCXB, 25: 1–23, esp. 11–16; also SKQSZM, 110: 21a–35b; SCC, 3: 432–433, 462–464, 467–471. Biographies of specialists in techniques such as *wangqi* ("watching the vapors"), *zhanyun* ("cloud divination") and *fengjiao* ("wind angles") may be found in Yuan (1948); 1: 19–20; 2: 1–2; 2: 3; 2: 4; 3: 10; 3: 11; 3: 19; 5: 10; 5: 10–12; 7: 17–18; 20: 29–30; 36: 11; 36: 15–16; etc. At least twenty-six of Yuan's biographies of Qing diviners mention *fengjiao*, and about 200 of these biographies indicate an interest or expertise in astrology—often termed *tianwen xue* (lit., "the study of heavenly patterns"). *Tianwen xue* also included scientific astronomy. For a few representative entries on various forms of astrology, see *ibid.*, 1: 7–9, 1: 16; 1: 20; 2: 1–2; 2: 3; 2: 9; 2: 13; 2: 14; 2: 27–28; 3: 3–4; 3: 11; 5: 17–18; 7: 18–19; etc.

60. See SKQSZM, 109: 47b.

61. XJBFS *juan* 3–8; cf. XLKY, *juan* 2–4; DQHD, 77: 1a ff. and 80: 1a ff. See also Ho (1966), pp. 66 ff.

62. Parker (1888a), p. 550; cf. JSWB, 69: 18b and Morgan (1980), pp. 178 ff. On popular "star worship," consult Du Bose (1886), pp. 417 ff.; also Doré (1914–1933), 4: 347 and De Groot (1892–1910), 6: 929 ff., esp. 1107–1124.

63. See, for example, CC, 4: 291; Chai and Chai (1967), 1: 94; 1: 259; 2: 51; 2: 156; 2: 349; etc.; also TSJC, *yishu*, 47: 7071 ff. See also note 146 below.

64. Morgan (1980), p. 177.

65. *Ibid.*; also Fei (1984), esp. pp. 48–51. In terms of celestial movement, the "yellow road" (*huangdao*) is considered auspicious; the "black road" (*heidao*), retrograde; see also XLKY, 5: 3a–4.

66. Morgan (1980), chapters 9–10, esp. pp. 208 ff.; cf. XLKY, 2: 5a ff. and XJBFS *juan* 3, passim.

67. See Ching-lang Hou in Welch and Sidel (1979), p. 193.

68. *Da Qing tongli*, 13: 1a–7b; see also DQHD, 80: 3a.

69. Ching-lang Hou in Welch and Sidel (1979) p. 194 ff. Cf. Chard (1982), pp. 25–29.

70. Wei (1967), 15: 4a; cf. JSWB, 69: 15a.

71. See, for example, SCSX, Kangxi, *jingtian*, 10: 7a; ZDLZ, 415: 9b-10a; etc. Abundant evidence can be found in the "Basic Annals" (*benji*) and "Portents" (*zaiyi*) chapters of the *Qingshi*. The "Basic Annals" of the Shunzhi emperor provide one useful illustration of the different types of portents recorded for posterity, from those surrounding Fulin's birth, to earthquakes, eclipses and other anomalies during his reign. Consult QS, 1: 32 ff. See also note 77 below.

72. Metzger (1973), p. 51. A commonly held assumption was that maladministration, particularly in law, caused natural calamities.

73. Spence (1975), p. 52; cf. *ibid.* pp. 150 and 174. Similarly, Prince Gong (Yixin), brother of the Xianfeng emperor, wrote in the 1860s that good fortune "could not be divined from Heaven" (*bubi bu zhi yu Tian*), but could only be manifested in the condition of the people. Yixin (1867), 2: 33b.

74. See SCSX, Kangxi, *jingtian*, 10: 1a ff.; cf. Tongzhi, *jingtian*, 11: 1a ff.

75. *Ibid.*, Kangxi, *jingtian*, 10: 8a-b; see also 2b, 3a, 7a, etc.

76. Spence (1975), p. 52.

77. See, for example, *Huangpo xianzhi* (Hubei; 1871), *tianwen zhi*, 1: 9a-b; *Xiangshan xianzhi* (Guangdong; 1750), *xiangyi*, 8: 49a; *Xuxiu Shunning fuzhi gao* (Yunnan; 1904), *tianwen zhi*, 2: 4a; *Yicheng xianzhi* (Hubei; 1866), *fangyu zhi*, 1: 1a-b; also notes 56, 57, 64, 65, and 66 above. Cf. SCSX, Kangxi, *jingtian*, 10: 3b. Johnston (1910), pp. 59-68 provides an illuminating list of celestial signs and other significant events from the Han era to the Qing, taken from a local gazetteer for the area around Weihaiwei.

78. Cited in Ho (1966), pp. 66-67; slightly modified; see also Nakayama (1966), pp. 445 ff. Cf. Eitel (1984), pp. 12-14 and my chapter 4, note 26.

79. ZDLZ, 415: 6a. Cf. Wylie (1897), p. 110; Ho (1966), p. 66 ff.; SCC, 3: 265 ff.

80. Henderson (1984), pp. 162, 210-211, 237-239.

81. Nakamura, p. 449.

82. ESLS, *Mingshi, tianwen*, 25: 2a ff.; cf. JSWB, 69: 19b-22b. See also notes 77 above and 83, 84 and 88 below. Geomantic manuals naturally gave attention to this relationship. See chapter 5.

83. Yu Minzhong, *et al.* (1981), pp. 1-12. See also Meyer (1976), pp. 134 ff.; cf. Schafer, pp. 75 ff., esp. p. 77. An essay in JSWB, 69: 19b-22b discusses various other *fenye* systems. See also Henderson (1984), pp. 68-71 and 216.

84. Yu Minzhong, *et al.* (1981), p. 1; cf. Ouyang Shun (1814), author's preface, esp. 1a, and other prefaces, *passim*. See also Eitel (1984), pp. 9 ff. and Morgan (1980), p. 166, citing Zhang Heng.

85. Cf. JSWB, 69: 21b.

86. Yu Minzhong, *et al.* (1981), pp. 2-12; see also Meyer (1976), pp. 139-40.

87. Meyer (1976), pp. 45-51.

88. For an example of skepticism, consult *Xuxiu Shunning fuzhi gao* (1904; 1968), *tianwen zhi*, 1: 1a-b. Cf. note 77 above.

89. Wang (1986); Wang (1976), pp. 409-414. On Yan's divinatory interests, see my concluding chapter, note 76.

90. See esp. Henderson (1984), pp. 159-163, 181-199, and 218-224, *passim*; also Birdwhistell (1989), p. 217-219; Black (1989), ff.; JSWB, 69: 18a ff.

91. See Henderson (1984), pp. 184-191 and 214-215.

92. *Ibid.*, pp. 184-191; Henderson (1986). See also chapter 3.

93. *Ibid.*, p. 182.

94. *Ibid.*, p. 249. See also *ibid.*, pp. 178, 193, 197-200; Black (1989), pp. 109 ff., esp. p. 127. Cf. Kidder Smith, *et al.* (1990), p. 193, note 94.

95. Henderson (1984), pp. 193-201; see also Graham, (1989), esp. pp. 319 ff. on the power of correlative cosmology.

96. See, for example, Yuan (1948), 8: 12-13; 8: 37; 18: 17; 18: 24; 19: 33-34; 20: 26-27; 20: 29-30; 28: 2; 28: 20; etc.

97. *Ibid.*, 28: 15-16; cf. Birdwhistell (1989), p. 228.

98. Henderson (1984), esp. p. 197.

99. There were, in fact, several versions or configurations of the *Hetu* and *Luoshu.* See TSJC, *jingji*, 55: 564 ff. On the popularity of the *Hetu*, consult Saso (1978); also chapter 3, note 31. Pi is cited in Henderson (1984), p. 224.

100. On Qing ontology, see Ng (1986). Henderson (1984), p. 159, discusses Hu Wei's understanding of the terms *xiang* and *shu*, but he exaggerates, I think, the cosmological implications of Hu's "redefinitions." See also Henderson (1986), pp. 134-135. Cf. Wilhelm (1967), pp. 300, 304, 310-314; Black (1989), pp. 112 ff. Yuan (1948) is full of biographies of Qing scholars who continued to hold conventional views regarding the "images" and "numbers" of the *Yijing*; see also chapter 3.

101. We do find, however, Wang Xishan (1628-1682) attempting to overhaul Tycho Brahe's world system in a conservative effort to provide a new cosmological foundation for traditional Chinese astronomy. See Sivin (1969), p. 68; also QS, *shixian*, 46: 723.

102. The *Tushu jicheng*, for example, devotes over one hundred *juan* to the subject (see chapter 1, note 6). For specific acknowledgements of the obvious, consult SKQSZM, 108: 1a-b; also JSWB, 69: 16a-17a, 23a-25a. Significantly, the major critics of unorthodox divination represented in the TSJC are the ones most often mentioned by Qing scholars in their private essays—namely, Xunzi, Wang Chong, and Lü Cai.

103. See my article on Qing ritual in Liu. ed. (1990); also JSWXB, 61: 2b-3a; cf. Chan (1986a), pp. 156-167; Strickmann (1980), p. 226.

104. CC, 1: 340-341. Cf. Lu Yao's essay on "technicians" in JSWB, 69: 13b-14a. For representative remarks on *xiaodao* from the introductory sections on *fangji* in local gazetteers, see for example, *Wuhe xianzhi* (Anhui; 1894), *fangji*, 15: 10a; *Fuyang xianzhi* (Zhejiang; 1906), *fangji*, 28: 30b-31a; *Longling xianzhi* (Yunnan, 1917), *fangji*, 11: 26a-b; *Qixian xianzhi* (Henan, 1788), *fangji*, 18: 13a; *Nanle xianzhi* (Hebei, 1903), *fangji*, 5: 50a-b; etc.

105. See Ouyang Shun (1814), preface, 7a; also Unschuld (1985), p. 203. Cf. Wong and Wu (1936), p. 179 and Hail (1927), pp. 338 and 340.

106. Quoted in Wang Fuzhi's *Zhouyi neizhuan fali*, p. 3b in YJJC, 141. See also chapter 3, note 108. Cf. Strickmann (1980), p. 226.

107. JSWB, 69: 14b-15a (Feng Jing), 15b-16a (Quan), 23a-b, 24a-25a (Gu); 23b-24a (Lu Shiyi). See also *ibid.*, 69: 13b-14b; *ibid.*, 63: 1a-b, 8b-9b, 10b-11a; Wu (1832), 19: 3a-7b; and the critiques cited in Ropp (1981), pp. 161-165, 171-179, 183-187, 189, 232. Cf. Henderson (1986), p. 141.

108. JSWB, 69: 15b-16a; cf. Wang's *Zhouyi neizhuan fali*, pp. 2a-b, reprinted in YJJC, vol. 141; Wu (1832), 9: 10a.

109. JSWB, 69: 16a; cf. Gu's statement that when there are "human actions below, there are changes in heavenly images above." *Ibid.*, 69: 23a. That is, Heaven responds to human activities rather than causing them.

110. *Ibid.*, 69: 23b.

111. Spence (1975), pp. 58-59.

112. Boulais (1924), 360-395, 467-474; JSWP, 68: 8a-12b. See also Jordan and Overmyer (1986), pp. 45-46.

113. JSWB, 69: 23b.

114. Chen Chun provides an illuminating discussion of the importance of "sincerity" in Chinese divination. See Chan (1986a), pp. 153 ff. esp. p. 162; Kidder Smith, *et al.* (1990), p. 199, note 112; and the examples cited in Yuan (1948), 3: 20, 20: 29-30 and 23: 9-10; also the preface to Wang Weide's *Bushi zhengzong*, quoted in Nevius (1869),

p. 181. On the self-confirming character of popular beliefs generally, consult Thomas (1971), pp. 642–643. Like diviners in various other cultures, Chinese fortune-tellers often complicated their maneuvers in order to increase the possibilities of associations while at the same time mystifying their clients. See Henderson (1984), pp. 52–53; also *ibid.*, p. 150. Cf. Rossi, ed. (1980), pp. 524–526.

115. See note 107 above; also Yao Nai's preface to *Xuanze zhengzong* in JSWB, 69: 15a. Even a cursory glance at Yuan (1948) indicates that far more scholars wrote books (or prefaces to books) on divination than wrote essays criticizing the practice. For additional evidence concerning the ambivalence of scholars toward fortune-telling, consult Ropp (1981), pp. 159–161; also CC 3: 338 (Legge's note).

116. Wang (1709), *geyan*. See also note 114 above.

117. See, for example, Anonymous (1868).

118. Wakeman (1986), 2: 857; QS, *benji*, 4: 34. See also R. J. Smith (1986), p. 172; R. J. Smith (1988), p. 174; Sivin (1969), pp. 7–9, 52–54.

119. See ZDLZ, 415: 1a ff.; JSWP, 68: 8a–12b; E-tu Zen Sun, p. 199. See also Morgan (1983), pp. 364–365; Williams (1899), 1: 79.

120. ZDLZ, 415: 4a–8b. The language of the warning is the same as on Ming calendars; see, for example, those of 1511, 1524, and 1543 in the Library of Congress.

121. DQHD, 36: 4b–5a; ZDLZ, 417: 1a–b. See also Morgan (1980), pp. 17–19; Hoang (1904), pp. 4–5.

122. ZDLZ, 417: 1a–b.

123. *Ibid.* See also Guo (1984), pp. 9–13; Morgan (1983), pp. 370–375; Hoang (1904), pp. 5–6; Gray (1878), 2: 14–17. The Harvard-Yenching Library has a calendar dated Daoguang 14 (1834) annotated by a Japanese scholar in the 13th year of Meiji rule (1880).

124. DQHD, 77: 1a. See also Porter (1980).

125. For a summary, see QS *shixian*, 46: 723–731; ZDLZ, *juan* 415 and 416, provide extensive documentation.

126. ZDLZ, 415: 1a–2b; also Huang (1990) and Konings (1990). Cf. Cummins (1962), 2: 190; Hummel, pp. 488–489, 570–571 and esp. 889–892; Yuan (1948), 38: 45–51.

127. XJBFS, preface, p. 1b–2a; cf. ZDLZ, 415: 5a ff., esp. 8a; XSCL, 1: 126 ff. For an example of the kind of mistake that could be made, see Huang (1904) on the intercalary month of 1813.

128. See note 132 below. For a discussion of different calendrical formats, consult ZDLZ, 417: 1a–b; also Morgan (1983), pp. 366–369; Smith (1988), pp. 124–125. A few calendars, such as the 1859 version at the Harvard-Yenching Library, insert the characters *zhupi* ("imperially endorsed") before *Shixian shu*. The only unquestionably authentic "official" calendars are in the Pelliot collection of the Bibliotheque Nationale.

129. R. J. Smith (1988), pp. 124–125; cf. DQHD, 77: 1a–b, 80: 1a–3b; Guo (1984), pp. 9–13.

130. QBLC, *shiling*, 1: 6. Differences in the color and quality of calendar covers also distinguished status within the Qing socio-political hierarchy. ZDZL 417: 1a–2a. For a discussion of the distinctive features of calendars for the emperor's use, see QBLC, *shiling*, 1: 6–8. See also note 132 below.

131. See ZDLZ, 415: 4a–8b, especially the case of Huang San. Morgan (1983), pp. 370–378 provides an excellent summary of the problems involved.

132. See Morgan (1983), pp. 366 ff., esp. 381–382. The analogy with the Sacred Edict is suggested in R. J. Smith (1988), p. 125, citing Victor Mair in Johnson, *et al.*, eds. (1985). The British Museum's three different versions of a calendar for 1841—all styled *Shixian shu*—provide an excellent illustration of how non-official and/or pirated calendars could be tailored to satisfy different audiences. The two smaller versions, which differ slightly from each other, and more fundamentally from the larger version, are clearly

pirated, while the larger edition seems simply to be non-official or quasi-official. The smaller versions are local in orientation, poorly printed on cheap paper, have red covers, and contain illustrations of the "spring ox" (*chunniu*), usually seen only in almanacs. See notes 164 and 166 below.

133. See Morgan (1983), p. 380; also ZDLZ, 415: 4a–b and 8b. I have seen the same inscription on an obviously unofficial calendar (*Shixian shu*), dated 1886, at the University of California, Berkeley. The cost of Qing calendars apparently varied considerably, depending on quality and availability. Although most versions were quite inexpensive, the diary of the late Qing scholar-official Li Ciming (1830–1894) indicates that he paid from 500 cash (one-half tael) in 1863 to as much as 1,300 cash in 1882 for "a new calendar for the coming year" (*mingnian xinli*). See Zhang (1970), pp. 106, 170, 183, 187, etc. Cf. Morgan (1983), p. 371; Williams (1883) 2: 79–80.

134. Consult ZDZL, 417: 3a–b and 8b ff. For an excellent example of a broad-ranging calendar devoted primarily to regional and temporal concerns, see the 1877 *Shixian shu* contained in the East Asiatic collection of the University of Washington, Seattle. Cf. the three calendars of 1841 discussed in note 132 above.

135. For details, consult Morgan (1980), pp. 198 ff.; also ZDLZ, 417: 2b, 5a–6a.

136. ZDLZ, 417: 2b.

137. *Ibid.*, 415: 4a and 417: 2a, 7b–8a; cf. DQHD, 80: 3a.

138. See esp. Morgan (1983) pp. 366–370 and Morgan (1980), chapters 9 and 10, esp. pp. 208 ff.; cf. Walters (1987), pp. 199 ff. and pp. 264 ff.

139. Consult Morgan, 367–368; also Hoang, 7–9 on animal correlations. The illuminating account by Parker (1888) is clearly based on an irregular version of the calendar (which he calls an almanac).

140. ZDLZ, 415: 4a–b; 416: 13b; 417: 2b; etc. Cf. Chang (1940).

141. For concrete examples, see Doré (1914–1933), 4: 399; also Parker (1888), pp. 67 ff.

142. R. J. Smith (1988), p. 131.

143. The calendar cited in note 134 above provides a relatively rare example of a work in which no spirits appear above or below the daily columns.

144. See Chang (1940), pp. 51 ff; cf. Huon de Kermadec (1983), pp. 104 ff.; Walters (1987), chapter 4.

145. ZDLZ, 417: 2a–b. The pattern for expressing a specific time was: " 'x' hour is appropriate for doing 'y' " ("y" *yiyong* "x" *shih*).

146. See note 63 above; also chapter 5. Walshe (1906), pp. 186–209 provides a useful overview of how choices were made in practice.

147. See, for example, Yuan (1948), 8: 19–20 and 23: 5.

148. XJBFS, *juan* 4; cf. Doré, 4: 385–386; Dennys (1876), 28–31. For Han precedents, see Rao (1981 and 1983); also Rao and Zeng (1982).

149. See DQHD, 80: 2b ff.; cf. Ho (1969).

150. R. J. Smith (1988), p. 130.

151. *Ibid.*, p. 131. For an excellent example of activities encouraged or discouraged for the first month of 1853, consult Milne (1858), pp. 139–140.

152. These statistics come from an 1886 calendar at the East Asiatic library of the University of California, Berkeley. R. J. Smith (1988), Appendix A contains an inventory of Chinese calendars held in the Bibliotheque Nationale, the British Library, the Library of Congress, and the Harvard-Yenching Library.

153. Yuan (1948), 8: 6. On this sort of fate manipulation, see Morgan (1980), pp. 232–233.

154. Yuan (1948), 24: 4.

155. Ren (1737), 3: 17b–18a; Wang (1711), *diji*, 1: 2a–4b; also Morgan (1980), pp. 232–233.

156. Cited in Parker, (1888a), p. 551.

157. See R. J. Smith (1988), esp. Appendix A, which contains a partial listing of Qing almanacs I have consulted. On problems related to the distribution of both almanacs and forged versions of the state calendar in south China, see ZDLZ, 415: 4a–b; also Hoang (1904), pp. 2, 4 and 6.

158. Cited in Yuan (1948), 33: 22. Wylie (1897), part 2, p. 87, says that Hong's almanac had a reputation equal to that of Francis Noore's "Vox Stellarum" in England, and could be found for sale "in many of the principal cities of southern and middle China."

159. R. J. Smith (1986), pp. 173–174.

160. *Ibid.*

161. Editions of this almanac I have seen for the years 1797, 1820, and 1865 contain the same preface, but it is sometimes handwritten and at other times printed.

162. R. J. Smith (1986), pp. 173–174.

163. Almanacs, like calendars, varied in price. See Lister (1872–1873), p. 239; cf. note 132 above. Simple prints of the "spring ox" (see note 169 below) could be bought for only a single "cash" (one one-thousandth of a tael) or two. One might add that just as the Qing government sold officially-sanctioned (*qinding*) editions of the *Wannian shu*, so private entrepreneurs marketed their own versions of "perpetual calendars." One of the most popular of these was Wang Weide's *Yongning tongshu* (Almanac of Perpetual Peace), first published in 1711. Wang (1711); see also Yuan (1948), 3: 20. I am grateful to Dr. James Hayes for photocopying his own edition for my use.

164. Morgan (1983), p. 371, note 23, correctly points out that one major difference between Chinese calendars and almanacs is the absence in the former of the "spring ox" (*chunniu*; see note 169 below). Yet both she and I have found at least a few works entitled *Shixian shu* that contain representations of the ox (see notes 132 and 139 above).

165. See R. J. Smith (1986 and 1988).

166. Among the exceptions I have found are those almanacs prefaced by Fei Chun, which have yellow covers. See note 161 above. On the other hand, some unofficial *Shixian shu* have red covers. See note 132 above. For a fine example of Buddhist and Daoist symbolism on the cover of an almanac, see the *Riyong jifu tongshu* (Almanac of Collecting Blessings, for Daily Use; 1757) in the British Library.

167. Ebrey (1981), pp. 187–188; cf. Parker (1888), p. 73.

168. For details and illustrations, see Morgan (1980), pp. 3 ff., 118 ff., and 188 ff.; also my chapter 4, notes 44, 45, and 60. Cf. Walters (1987), pp. 270 ff.

169. Morgan (1980), pp. 23–24 and 92 ff.

170. See DQHD 77: 11 and XJBFS *juan* 12–13. Cf. Morgan (1980), p. 27.

171. See, for example, Doré (1914–1933), 5: 665; Bogan (1928), p. 12; Johnston (1910), pp. 181–182; Morgan (1980), p. 94.

172. For details, see Morgan (1980), pp. 23–24, 59–113, esp. 96 ff. and 247; cf. Parker (1888a), p. 552.

173. See *Yicheng xianzhi* (Hubei, 1866), *yudi zhi*, 1: 4a. See Doolittle (1865), 2: 18–23; Williams (1923), p. 208; Burkhardt (1955), 1: 11–12; etc.; also note 171 above.

174. Cf. Morgan (1980), pp. 26–27.

175. Cf. Doré (1914–1933), 1: 26–27. The *Daquan tongshu* of 1819 (London School of Oriental and African Studies) and the Liwen tang edition of the *Zouji tongshu* for 1876 (East Asiatic Library of the University of Chicago) provide excellent examples of the common features of nineteenth century Chinese almanacs. See also Lister (1872–1873) and Morgan (1980), esp. pp. 26–28. For discussions of twentieth-century almanacs,

see *ibid.*, pp. 28-28; also Chang (1940), chapter 4; Burkhardt (1955), 2: 1-13; Marjorie Topley in Topley (1967); Palmer (1986), passim; etc.

176. See, for example, *Daquan tongshu* (1819), *Zhongzi fangfa*, 1a ff. Morgan (1980) emphasizes and illustrates the close relationship between almanacs and geomancy. See also Wang (1711), passim.

177. These and other features may be found in the *Guanshang kuailan* (A Quick Reference for Merchants and Officials; 1908) of the Library of Congress. An even greater range and amount of new information is contained in the *Yisi nian Yingxue zhai fenlei guanshang bianlan qibai zhong* (1905 Guide for Officials and Merchants, Classified According to Seven Hundred Categories, from the Study of Dazzling Snow) in the British Library. On the "Methods for Producing Children," see the *Daquan tongshu* of 1819 (note 175 above).

178. See R. J. Smith (1988), p. 128.

179. R. J. Smith (1986), p. 174.

180. XJBFS, preface, p. 1a.

181. See my discussion in Liu, ed. (1990).

182. ZDLZ, 416: 13a-b; cf. *ibid.* 415: 5a-b. Significantly, the compiler of a comprehensive sourcebook for almanacs made a similar distinction. See the preface to Wei (1721), which denounces magicians and tricksters who depart from "the orthodox way of [day] selection" (*ze zhi zhengdao*).

183. Nan Huairen (1669 and 1669a).

184. See Konings (1990), p. 4; Cummins (1962), 2: 190. For succinct and illuminating evaluations of the Chinese attitude toward the scientific accomplishments of the Jesuits, consult Guy (1987), pp. 137-138 and Graham (1989), pp. 318-319; also Black (1989), pp. 167 ff.

185. For Taiping efforts to recruit fortune-tellers to their cause, see Yuan (1948), 19: 36-37; 24: 20.

186. *Taiping tianguo genghao [sic] sannian xinli* (New Calendar for 1853 for the Heavenly Kingdom of Great Peace), preface. This book is part of the British Library collection.

187. Hawkes (1973), p. 61.

188. *Chinese Repository*, 7.8 (December, 1838), p. 399 and Walshe (1906), p. 198. For additional evidence on the popularity of almanacs, consult Milne (1858), pp. 135-138; Douglas (1882), pp. 277-278; Gray (1878), 2: 15-16 and 26-27; Lister (1872-1873), Parker (1888), p. 66. See also Morgan (1980), p. 29, and the essays by Evelyn Rawski and James Hayes in Johnson, *et al.*, eds. (1985), esp. pp. 23-24 and 82-83; Ebrey (1981), p. 187.

189. Lister (1872-1873), p. 239. Despite his hostile tone, Lister provides a basically solid account.

190. Xie Xingyao (1934 and 1936).

191. On Western almanacs, see Capp (1979), esp. p. 25; Stowell (1977), esp. p. 81. Dennys (1876), pp. 27-32 compares the pervasive "superstitions of the Chinese concerning lucky and unlucky days" in the nineteenth century with similar beliefs in the West during the sixteenth century.

192. Doré, (1914-1933), 5: 501-502.

193. Alfred Lister (1872-1873), p. 239.

194. See, for example, Robert Hart's unpublished journals, December 31, 1867 (Queens University Library, Belfast, Ireland); *North-China Herald*, January 25, 1865; Cummins (1962), 2: 190; Dennys (1878), p. 7; also R. J. Smith (1986), pp. 161 and 178 (note 76); R. J. Smith (1988), pp. 132-133; Parker (1888), p. 61.

195. Martin (1897), p. 310; cf. Gray (1878), 2: 13-15 and 26-27.

196. Parker (1888), p. 65.

197. Williams (1883), 2: 80. See also Douglas (1882), pp. 277-278 and Milne (1820), p. 30.

198. Preface to the 1853 Taiping calendar; see note 186 above.

199. See R. J. Smith (1983), chapter 4, esp. pp. 125-126; cf. Williams (1923), p. 209; *Chinese Repository*, 7.8 (December, 1838), p. 400.

200. Ren (1748), preface, p. 1a, and 3: 17a-18a; cf. Dennys (1878), p. 7.

201. R. J. Smith (1986), pp. 179-180.

202. On late Qing proposals for calendar reform, see QS 46: 731.

203. R. J. Smith (1988), p. 133.

Chapter 3

1. Wilhelm (1967), p. 314; modified.

2. See, for example, the 1755 foreword to Xu Wenjing's *Zhouyi shiyi* (Recovered Remnants of the Zhou Changes) in YJJC, vol. 132. The claim regarding Confucius was first made by Sima Qian in the *Shiji*.

3. Wilhelm (1967), p. 293; modified. Cf. Fan Lei, *Suichu tang Yilun* (Discussions of the Changes from the Suichu Hall), preface, 1a, in YJJC, vol. 122: "The teaching of the Changes is to extrapolate [tui] from the Way of Heaven in order to illumine human affairs." For a discussion of the place of the *Yijing* in Chinese philosophy, see Luo (1981), pp. 529-662; also Cheng Chung-ying in Allison, ed. (1989) and Kidder Smith, *et al.* (1990), esp. pp. 3-8.

4. See CC, *Zhongyong*, 1: 416, slightly modified. Cf. Yuan (1948), 23: 9-11.

5. Cited in Toda (1963), p. 104. Similar views can be found in many of the works reproduced in YJJC. See, for example, the foreword to Xu Wenjing's book cited in note 2 above. For additional evidence of Qing attitudes toward the *Yijing*, including the views of commoners, consult Williams (1883), 1: 632; Doolittle (1865), 2: 309; etc.

6. See SKQSZM, juan 1-10. Ibid., 1: 2b-3a provides a summary of scholarly trends over time. For other conceptions, see, for example, the prefaces to Chen Shirong's *Duyi zashuo* (Miscellaneous Theories on Reading the Changes) in YJJC, vol. 137; Hui Dong's *Zhouyi shu* (Commentary on the Zhou Changes), ibid., vol. 85; and Ding Yan's *Zhouyi jiegu* (An Explanation of Ancient Writings on the Zhou Changes), ibid., vol. 135. Cao Yuanbi's *Zhouyi xue* (Studies on the Zhou Changes), vol. 124 of YJJC, discusses about a dozen major Yi scholars, from Zheng Xuan and Xun Shuang of the Han dynasty to Zhang Huiyan and Yao Zhongyu of the Qing. For Western language summaries, see Schulz (1982), pp. 3-47 and Shchutskii (1979), pp. 56-125 and 196-211.

7. Toda (1963), passim, esp. p. 99; cf. Shchutskii (1979), pp. xxxvi-xliii.

8. Zheng Xianfu, *Du Yi lu*, (Record of Reading the Changes), preface, 1: 1a in YJJC, vol. 135. For additional examples of the polarization of opinion, see, for example, Kidder Smith et al. (1990), pp. 167-176, 182-189, 191-205, 212, and 234-235; the prefaces to Li Daoping's *Zhouyi jijie zuanshu* (Supplementary Commentary to the Collected Explanations of the Zhou Changes), in vol. 93 of YJJC, and Mao Qiling's *Zhongshi Yi* ([My Elder Brother] Mr. Zhong's Changes), in vol. 77; also Toda (1963), passim.

9. Cited by Chang Liwen in Chan (1986), p. 308, slightly modified. Many individuals, including the Kangxi emperor, saw no real conflict between the two conceptions of the *Changes*: "Though it is hard to fathom Heaven's signs," the emperor once wrote, "if you approach them openly you can attain a kind of foreknowledge. . . . I have never tired of the *Yijing*, and have used it in fortune-telling and as a source of moral principles." Spence (1975), p. 59, slightly modified. On Zhu Xi's influence, see, for example, Toda (1963), p. 99; also Hu Wei, *Yitu mingbian* (Clear Distinctions Regarding the Illustrations of the Changes), preface, 1a, in YJJC, vol. 141.

10. Cited by Chang Liwen in Chan (1986), p. 308, slightly modified. Cf. Wilhelm (1967), pp. 289–290, 293–294, 313, 314, 317, 319–320, 321, 327, 338, 342, 344. Popular wisdom in Qing times expressed the mantic purpose of the *Yijing* in a pithy aphorism: "If you read the *Changes* you will know how to calculate [the future] with hexagrams" (*Nianguo Yijing hui suangua*).

11. Chan (1989), pp. 111–115; cf. SKQSZM, 108: 1a–b. In discussing the methods of Shao Yong, Zhu quoted a verse from the *Shijing* to the effect that accordance with right behavior is good fortune and following evil is bad fortune. Good and bad fortune, he said, do not concern tomorrow's weather. See Birdwhistell (1989), pp. 212–213. Significantly, Shao himself distinguished between "genuine foreknowledge" and the vulgar predictions of popular diviners." See *ibid.*, p. 30; also note 8 above.

12. CC, *Zhongyong*, 1: 417, modified.

13. See R. J. Smith (1983), pp. 93–98, 120–121.

14. Quoted in *ibid.*, p. 120. Cf. Eno (1990), pp. 92–93 and 248–249, notes 48 and 50; also his chapter 5, passim.

15. See the biographies of Wan Shouqi, Zeng Guangyan and others in Yuan (1948), 38: 39–43; also Shchutskii (1979), pp. 205–206, 223, 225, 229; and note 122 below.

16. See SKQSZM, 1: 2b; 108: 1a-b; 146: 8b, etc.; also Guy (1987), p. 115. For a tirade against individuals such as Jing Fang and Jiao Yanshou, who allegedly corrupted the *Yijing* by using it for "petty calculations and *wuxing* divinations," consult Ding Yan, *Zhouyi jiegu* (An Explanation of Ancient Writings on the Zhou Changes), 1: 1a, in YJJC, vol. 135.

17. See chapter 1, note 6 for a discussion of the contents of the "Arts and Occupations" section on divination in the TSJC.

18. For a discussion of the basic features of Yi-related exegetical scholarship, see the sources mentioned in note 6 above. Zhuang Zhongyu's *Zhouyi tongyi* (Comprehensive Meaning of the Zhou Changes), written in the late nineteenth century, provides a convenient inventory of the kinds of textual problems addressed by Qing scholars. See YJJC, vol. 123.

19. The following generalizations are based on a perusal of the 100 or so Qing works on the *Changes* reprinted in YJJC. Literally dozens of these works employ a topical format based on individual words and phrases from the *Yi*. For several examples, see notes 29–30 below.

20. Many of the systematic tracts are discussed in Toda (1963), passim. Quan Zuwang's *Zhouyi dawen* (Answers to Questions on the Zhou Changes) and Feng Dengfu's *Yijing dawen* (Answers to Questions about the Classic of Changes) in vol. 141 of YJJC provide excellent examples of the question/answer format.

21. See, for example, Li Daoping's *Zhouyi jijie zuanshu* (Appended Commentary to the Collected Explanations of the Zhou Changes), in vol. 93 of YJJC; Lin Qingping's *Zhouyi jijie bujian* (Supplementary Gloss on the Collected Explanations of the Zhou Changes) in *ibid.*, vol. 93; and Cao Yuanbi's *Zhouyi jijie bushi* (Supplementary Explication of the Collected Explanations of the Zhou Changes), *ibid.*, vol. 122.

22. See Toda (1963), passim. The most common schemes discussed were the calendrical correlative systems known as *guaqi*, *najia*, and *xiaochen*, usually ascribed to Meng Xi, Jing Fang and Zheng Xuan, respectively.

23. On the concept of "word magic" as it applies to the *Yi*, see Kunst (1985), pp. 58–60. Cf. chapter 2, note 40.

24. For a few representative works, see Wang Fuzhi, *Zhouyi daxiang jie* (Explanation of the "Big Images" of the Zhou Changes), in YJJC, vol. 122; Li Suiqiu, *Zhouyi yaowu dangming* (Appropriate Names for the Things Referred to in the Lines of the Zhou Changes), *ibid.*, vol. 73; and Zhai Junlian, *Zhouyi zhangju zhengyi* (An Examination of

Discrepancies in Phrases from the Zhou Changes) in *ibid.*, vol. 164. See also chapter 1, note 35 and note 27 below.

25. Legge (1882), pp. 154–157, modified; cf. Wilhelm (1967), pp. 171–173, also Kunst (1985), pp. 326–327.

26. On problems of translation, consult Kunst (1985), esp. pp. vi–ix and 21 ff.; also Shchuskii (1979), pp. xi–xii.

27. The appendix to Li (1978), pp. 378–397, provides a good general discussion of the problems involved in interpreting the *Yijing's* divinatory symbolism. Consult also Li Suiqiu, *Zhouyi yaowu dangming* (Appropriate Names for the Things Referred to in the Lines of the Zhou Changes), YJJC, vol. 73. On the "emaciated pig" in particular, see Li (1978) p. 389; also Kunst (1985), p. 59.

28. See Kunst (1985), pp. 58–60; also p. 224, note 49.

29. I have seen well over a dozen essays on this problem in the YJJC collection. The editors of the SKQSZM indicate that there are three main schools of interpretation: those of (1) Meng Xi; (2) Xun Shuang, Yu Fan and Wang Bi; and (3) Shao Yong and Zhu Xi. The translation given in the text follows Shao and Zhu. See Zhai Junlian, *Zhouyi zhangju zhengyi* (An Examination of Discrepancies in Phrases from the Zhou Changes) in YJJC, vol. 164; also Wu Yi, *Yidu kaoyi* (An Examination of Discrepancies in Readings on the Changes), 1: 1a–b.

30. See Zhuang Zhongyu, *Zhouyi tongyi* (Comprehensive Meaning of the Zhou Changes), *juan* 3 in YJJC, vol. 123.; also the introductions to Jiang Fan's *Zhouyi shubu* (A Supplement to [Hui Dong's] Discourse on the Zhou Changes), 1b, in YJJC, vol. 87 and Jiao Xun's *Zhouyi bushu* (Supplementary Commentary on the Zhou Changes), 1a, in *ibid.*, vol. 135. According to most Qing commentators, Jizi was Prince Ji, uncle of the Shang dynasty tyrant Zhou Xin. Although opposed to the evil king's policies, he could not retire from government without personal risk. He therefore "darkened his light," tattooing his body and pretending to be insane. For a general discussion of historical allusions in the Yi, consult Wilhelm (1977), pp. 52 ff. On Hui Dong's involvement in the Jizi controversy, see Toda (1963), p. 111.

31. TSJC, *jingji*, 55: 543–625. Yuan (1948) contains a great many references to advocates of the Hetu and Luoshu. See, for example, the biographies of Li Zhonghui, Zhou Ziqian, Yang Yiliang, Wang Jiucheng and others in *ibid.*, 1: 19, 1: 27–28, 5: 2, 6: 17, etc. For a more complete inventory, see Smith (1990). Toda (1963), pp. 102–104 and 116 discusses the Hetu/Luoshu controversy. See also Elman (1990), pp. 126–135, esp. pp. 129–130.

32. For an excellent discussion of the Ten Wings, consult Shchutskii (1979), pp. 60–62 and 158–176; also Wilhelm (1967), pp. 256–261; Legge (1882), pp. 26 ff.; Swanson (1974), passim.

33. See Toda (1963), pp. 104–105.

34. *Ibid.*, pp. 110–114, 116. Hui also wrote an influential but incomplete tract entitled *Zhouyi shu* (Discourse on the Zhou Changes), which was finished by Jiang Fan (1761–1831). See his *Zhouyi shubu* (A Supplement to [Hui Dong's] Discourse on the Zhou Changes) in YJJC, vol. 87.

35. Toda (1963) pp. 114–117. See also Jiao Xun's *Zhouyi bushu* (Supplementary Commentary on the Zhou Changes) in YJJC, vol. 135.

36. Toda (1963), pp. 99–100, 127. Dai Zhen draws on an extraordinarily wide range of scholars in addition to Zhu and Cheng in his *Zhouyi kao*. See YJJC, vol. 132.

37. These prominent scholars all have biographies in Hummel (1943–1944). For some lesser known advocates of Song scholarship on the Yi, see the biographies of Zhang Xinyan, Lao Shi, Chen Rongguang, Qian Chengzhi, and others in Yuan (1948), 8: 12–13, 9: 19–20, 12: 4, 12: 7, etc. R. J. Smith (1990) contains a more complete inventory.

38. Spence (1975), p. 59. Cf. Wilhelm (1967), p. 322.

39. All of the points mentioned in the following paragraphs are thoroughly discussed and illustrated in the works I have noted above and others in the YJJC. For a few convenient summaries of interpretive techniques, consult Jou (1984), chapters 1 and 2; Luo (1981), pp. 631–640; Wei (1970), chapter 10; Wei (1987), chapter 6; Swanson (1974), pp. 148–209; Wilhelm (1967), pp. 356–365; and Whincup, appendix "C."

40. See Wilhelm (1967), pp. 283, 288–289, and esp. 326–327. Divided lines are designated zhai (broken); solid lines, dan (single, or simple).

41. For details, see Shchutskii (1979), p. 8.

42. See Spence (1975), pp. 147, 171, slightly modified. Cf. Wilhelm (1967), pp. 129, 550.

43. For examples of the way Fu (24) might be interpreted, see Chan (1967), pp. 11–12, 26, 146–147, 157, 203, 269; also Kidder Smith, et al. (1990), pp. 237–254.

44. See Toda (1963), esp. pp. 100–101 and 114.

45. Zhu (1979), guage, 1a.

46. Zhu (1979), yitu, 12a-b.

47. See SCC, 2: 312–313.

48. For details and refinements, see Wilhelm (1967), pp. 262 ff.

49. Wilhelm (1967), p. 33; translation slightly modified. Cf. Legge (1882), p. 276.

50. See Wilhelm (1967), pp. 48–55 and 244–252.

51. For details, consult Wilhelm (1967), pp. 361–362.

52. Wilhelm (1967), p. 264; cf. p. 289.

53. See CC, Mengzi, 1: 559–560. Also note 70 below.

54. See Wang Yinzhi's Zhouyi shuwen (Narrations on the Zhou Changes) in YJJC, vol. 137 and Feng Dengfu's Yijing dawen (Answers to Questions about the Classic of Changes) in ibid., vol. 141. On the phrase wuyong, consult Kunst, pp. 389–390.

55. On Jiao, see Toda, pp. 119–127. Both of the questions mentioned in the text are discussed in Feng Dengfu, 1: 1a-b (see note 54 above).

56. Toda (1963) provides a detailed analysis of these schemes in the light of Qing scholarship. See also Mao Qiling, Tui Yi shimo (A Complete Account of Change Extrapolation), vol. 122 of YJJC.

57. Ibid., esp. pp. 106–109. The concepts fandui and pangtong were also known by other names. Lai Zhide, for example, described them as zong ("inverse") and cuo ("antipode"). See Schulz (1982), pp. 44–45, 133 ff. and 213 ff.; also note 64 below. The idea of latent and manifest (feifu; lit., "flying" and "hidden") meanings is usually attributed to Jing Fang.

58. See Wei (1970), pp. 167–170.

59. See Toda (1963), esp. pp. 106–107.

60. See Birdwhistell (1989), chapters 4 and 5, passim; esp. pp. 86 ff. For illuminating reviews of Shao's Huangji jingshi shu and related works, consult SKQSZM, 108: 9a ff. and 111: 24b ff.

61. Zhu (1979), tu, pp. 27–38; guage, pp. 9–12.

62. See Schulz (1982), pp. 133 ff., 196 ff., and 213 ff.

63. For details, consult Toda (1963), pp. 100, 103–105, 107, and 127.

64. Ibid., pp. 105–106. See also the case of Jiao Xun in ibid., pp. 119 ff.

65. This book, like all of the other works mentioned in the text of this chapter, is reprinted in the YJJC. For Mao's early interest in Yi divination, consult Wu (1990), pp. 176–177.

66. CC, 5: 164, 167.

67. See the summary in Wei (1970), pp. 100–102; cf. Zhu (1979), p. 9; Wilhelm (1967), pp. 73–74.

68. There were at least a few women who, by virtue of their elite status, acquired the education necessary to explore the refinements of *Yijing* scholarship. See, for example, the case of Zhang Tun, who not only divined with the *Changes*, but also studied its principles (*Yili*) and wrote a book entitled *Yidao rumen* (Introduction to the Way of the Changes). Yuan (1948), 38: 8.

69. Yuan (1948), 4: 2–3.

70. On timing, see Peterson (1982), passim, esp. 106–111 and Kidder Smith, *et al.* (1990), pp. 194–199. Cf. Wilhelm (1967), pp. 262, 265, 313 and 342; Black (1989), pp. 148–149; Wilhelm (1977), pp. 3 ff.; also note 53 above.

71. Toda (1963), pp. 30, 119–127; also Hummel (1943–1944), p. 145.

72. See, for example, individuals such as Wang Hengyu, Yuan Xuekong. Chen Changsi, Qian Jingxun, and Lei Guangyi. Yuan (1948), 1: 21–22, 5: 23; 8: 37, 13: 28, 13: 32. For other examples, consult R. J. Smith (1990).

73. CC, *Shujing*, 3: 337.

74. See Waley (1970), p. 98.

75. Kiang (1925), p. 263. See also the citations in Peterson (1979), pp. 18, 44, 82, 151, 164 and esp. 120–122.

76. See Rong (1969), pp. 2–3 and Zhang (n. d.), pp. 10–28 for these relationships; also SKQSZM, 109: 43b–45b; 111: 15b–24a and 41a–49a. For illustrations from Qing biographies, consult R. J. Smith (1990). Most Chinese believed that every major divination system had its foundations in the Yi. See, for example, SKQSZM, 108: 1a. Cf. the discussion of Shen Zhureng's popular nineteenth-century manual entitled *Zhouyi yijie* (An Easy Explanation of the Zhou Changes) in Yuan (1948), 7: 20–21 and the views of Sun Meng and Zhang Xinheng in *ibid.*, 13: 3 and 18: 18. Most Chinese mantic methods drew heavily upon the vocabulary of the Yi—including those that employed stem-branch and *wuxing* correlations. See, for example, TSJC, *yishu*, 48: 7136–7438 (on *taiyi, qimen* and *liuren*); also Zhuang Zhongyu, *Zhouyi tongyi* (Comprehensive Meaning of the Zhou Changes), 14: 1a ff. in YJJC, vol. 123; Luo (1981), pp. 535, 546–548; Yuan (1948), 34: 22–23, etc. For an indictment of *wuxing* divination with the Yi, consult Ding Yan, *Zhouyi jiegu* (An Explanation of Ancient Writings on the Zhou Changes), 1: 1a, in YJJC, vol. 135.

77. Examples of the approaches mentioned in the preceding paragraph, too numerous to cite individually, may be found in R. J. Smith (1990). See also note 76 above, note 87 below, and chapter 5.

78. The following account is drawn from Zhu (1979), *shiyi*, pp. 1a–5a. cf. Yan (1989).

79. See Wilhelm (1967), pp. 310–313, 721–724.

80. Cf. Wei (1970), pp. 99 ff.

81. *Ibid.*, pp. 99–100.

82. Zeng Jize to Zeng Guofan in *Xiangxiang Zengshi wenxian* (1965) vol. 10, pp. 6021–6022. I am grateful to Professor K. C. Liu for calling this letter to my attention and photocopying it for me.

83. Wilhelm (1967), p. 423.

84. *Ibid.*, p. 155.

85. For a detailed description, consult Doré (1914–1933), 4: 340–343. See also the biography of Cheng Liangyu in Yuan (1948), 12: 30 and QBLC, *fangji*, pp. 60–62, esp. p. 61.

86. Coin divination was reportedly first used by Jing Fang. See Huang Shi, *Jing Fang Yi zazhan tiaoli fa* (Rules for the Various Divination Methods with the Changes Employed by Jing Fang) in the YJJC. On the elite aversion to coin tossing and related mantic techniques, see the views of Li Ruicang in Yuan (1948), 37: 21–22; also Doolittle (1865), 2: 337–339; Doré (1914–1933), 4: 431–432. According to Doolittle, professional specialists

in coin-tossing charged about 100 cash (theoretically one-tenth of an ounce of silver) per consultation.

87. Consult Liu (1979) and Jou (1984), pp. 86 ff.; also the biographies of Duan Wenya and Sun Sumian in Yuan (1948), 20: 29–30 and 28: 2. Cf. Hu Cuishun's *Zhouyi bianlan* (Guide to the Zhou Changes) discussed in Yuan (1948), 5: 16–17.

88. Wang (1986), 5: 1506–1511. See also Weng (1970), 1: 129. Normally, one did not divine twice about the same matter on the same occasion. For examples of Yi divination other than those noted below, consult QBLC, *fangji*, pp. 73 ff., esp. p. 77. Doré (1970), p. 101, discusses Li Hongzhang's attraction to a form of Yi divination—no doubt encouraged by his association with the professional fortune-teller Zhou Fu. *Ibid.*, p. 103. See also chapter 5, notes 182 and 193.

89. Spence (1975), pp. 44–45. Hummel (1943–1944), pp. 473–475 discusses Li Guangdi's career. For examples of Li's *Yijing* divinations, consult Li (1829), 1: 40b–41b; 1: 45a–b; 1: 50a–b; etc. Also note 96 below.

90. *Kangxi qiju zhu*, pp. 628–629.

91. *Ibid.*; cf. Wilhelm (1967), pp. 86–89, slightly modified.

92. Spence (1975), p. 29; cf. Wilhelm (1967), p. 221.

93. Spence (1975), pp. 44–45, slightly modified; cf. Wilhelm (1967), pp. 9 and 383.

94. Spence (1975), pp. 45–46; cf. Wilhelm (1967), pp. 213–216 and 670, slightly modified.

95. Spence (1975), p. 57; cf. Wilhelm (1967), pp. 166–168; see also Hummel (1943–1944), p. 577.

96. Hummel (1943–1944), pp. 474–475. See also note 89 above.

97. Yuan (1948), 30: 21–22.

98. R. J. Smith (1990) indicates the various ways Qing officials employed the Yi; see also Doré (1917–1933), pp. 101–103 and note 88 above, as well as the examples cited below.

99. Yuan (1948), 17: 10–11. See Wilhelm (1967), p. 118–121; Hummel (1943–1944), p. 7.

100. Yuan (1948), 13: 31; Wilhelm (1967), pp. 136–139; Hummel, pp. 253–255.

101. Yuan (1948), 11: 22; Wilhelm (1967), pp. 139–142.

102. Yuan (1948), 2: 12–13; Wilhelm (1967), pp. 208–211.

103. Yuan (1948), 4: 10; Wilhelm (1967), pp. 48–49, 52–53; Hummel (1943–1944), pp. 550–551.

104. Yuan (1948), 18: 31; Wilhelm (1967), p. 132. The period in which he lived is not clear. See also the fatalism of Fan Tengfeng in Yuan (1948), 22: 24.

105. Yuan (1948), 3: 19; Wilhelm (1967), p. 114.

106. See Yang (1961), pp. 265–272.

107. Yuan (1948), 33: 9–10; Wilhelm (1967), p. 44. See also the example of Wang Xuan in Yuan (1948), 4: 22–23.

108. See chapter 2, notes 106–109; also Doré (1917–1933), 4: 341–342; Doolittle (1865), 2: 337; Nevius (1869), pp. 181–182. Ironically, Jiao Xun's father was himself a professional diviner. See Yuan (1948), 5: 25.

109. See, for example, the late Qing horoscope reproduced on the inside cover of Doré (1917–1933), vol. 4, which Walters (1987), pp. 322–325 reproduces and describes in part, but apparently does not fully understand. See also the discussion in Schulz (1982), pp. 16 ff. and 195–196; SKQSZM, 109: 22a–b; and notes 16, 77 and 86 above and 110 below.

110. See, for instance, the Yi-related schemes in the *Jiqing tang xingzong qizheng* (Astrological Guide from the Hall of Celebrating Good Fortune; 1820), London School

of Oriental and African Studies and the *Zengbu qimeng Tianji duan Yi daquan* (Supplement to the Primer of Heavenly Power Change Divination Compendium, 1825), British Library.

111. See, for example, Williams (1883), 1: 632; Arthur Smith (1894), p. 164; Doré (1970), pp. 98 ff. etc; also notes 76 and 77 above.

112. Doolittle (1865), 2: 336-337. Milne (1858), p. 108, asserts that "the whole art of divining is ascribed to the god of literature [Wenchang] as its inventor."

113. Nevius (1869), pp. 182-184.

114. See Yuan (1948), 3: 20.

115. Douglas (1882), p. 157 reports a similar practice for doctors, in which fee scales ranged from about six pence in the case of poor people, to about five shillings in the case of the rich. For other pay scales and practices, see my conclusion, note 18.

116. See Gray (1878), 2: 5.

117. Cited in Nevius (1869), pp. 181-182, 184.

118. On the Western biblical tradition, consult Schneidau (1976), esp. pp. 3-4, 10-11, cited in R. J. Smith (1987).

119. For a related discussion, see R. J. Smith (1989); also Kidder Smith et al. (1990), esp. pp. 231-235.

120. On Yan's idiosyncratic cosmology, consult Fung (1953), 2: 636 ff. Cf. SKQSZM, 97: 9b-11b, which criticizes Yan for going "too far" in his hostility to Song learning. Chan (1963), p. 263 testifies to the Yi's philosophical importance. See also note 3 above.

121. See, for example, Yü (1981), p. 116; Chan (1963), pp. 151, 392-393, 396; Boltz (1987), pp. 165, 222, etc.; notes 120 above and 122 below. Whalen Lai considers the late sixth century text entitled *Zhancha shano yebao jing* (Classic of Divining the Requital of Good and Bad Actions) to be "the Buddhist answer to the *Yijing*." Whalen Lai in Buswell, ed. (1990), p. 175.

122. On Wan Yi, see Cleary (1986 and 1987); cf. Shchutskii (1979), pp. 205-206 and 220-222.

123. See, for example, the views of Hang Xingzhai in Yuan (1948), 7: 27-29.

124. Cited in R. J. Smith (1983), p. 136.

125. *Ibid.*, pp. 85-86, 91-98; also Smith (1990b).

126. Wilhelm (1967), p. 575, slightly modified. On the numerous polarities of the *Yijing*, particularly within the "Great Commentary," consult Swanson (1974), pp. 31-43; also Kunst (1985), pp. 46-51; R. J. Smith (1983), pp. 93-96.

127. Wilhelm (1967), p. 345. *Ibid.*, p. 322 remarks on the limitations of words in expressing ideas. On the analogical logic of the Yi, consult Swanson (1974), pp. 43-62; see also Graham (1989), pp. 365-370; Kunst (1985), pp. 19 ff. Cf. Birdwhistell (1989), pp. 63-64.

128. R. J. Smith (1983), pp. 85-88, 91-93; Shchutskii (1979), pp. 166-172 and 224 ff. See also Black (1989), pp. 155-159 and the articles by Cheng Chung-ying and Chad Hansen in Allison, ed., (1989).

129. Liu's painting is reproduced opposite the title page in Kidder Smith, et al. (1990). For a discussion of *Yijing*-related symbols, consult R. J. Smith (1983), p. 160 and R. J. Smith (1990b).

130. Sze (1959), p. 325. See also pp. 39 ff.

131. See Wilhelm (1979), pp. 43 ff.

132. See Plaks (1976), p. 147; R. J. Smith (1983), p. 96. Cf. Wilhelm (1967), p. 316.

133. Cited in R. J. Smith (1983), p. 87, slightly modified.

134. Plaks (1976), pp. 23, 46-47; cf. Schneidau (1976), pp. 11 ff.; 265-266. See also note 118.

135. Yuan (1948), 21: 4-5.

136. Wang (1988), p. 39.

137. Plaks (1976), p. 178; cf. Wilhelm (1967), p. 286, slightly modified.

138. TSJC, jingji, 55: 971-993; about 100 works altogether.

139. Ibid., 55: 986-995; cf. Shchutskii (1979), pp. 229-235, who includes translations of one essay and several poems.

140. TSJC, jingji, 55: 993.

141. Ibid., pp. 993-995.

142. Wilhelm (1967), pp. 208-212, 663-668. Cf. Kunst (1985), pp. 49-50.

143. Wilhelm (1967), pp. 143-147, 569-573.

144. See Ho (1972), pp. 26-29; cf. SCC, 2: 315-321.

145. Chan (1967), p. 202, slightly modified; cf. Wilhelm (1967), pp. 143-150.

146. See, for example, Naquin (1976).

147. See the discussion in Tambiah (1990), esp. pp. 4-15; cf. R. J. Smith (1989). Chinese Buddhist and Daoist scriptures did, however, have a strong sense of the elect. On the issue of Max Weber's theory of capitalism as applied to China, see Gary Hamilton's critical essay in Buss, ed. (1985).

148. Lindsell is cited in R. J. Smith (1989).

149. SKQSZM, jingbu, 1: 3a. See also Yuan (1948), 7: 20-21; 13: 3.

150. On these early investigations, see Wilhelm (1967), pp. 316, 320, 324, 328, etc. Cf. note 151 below.

151. Ho (1972), p. 38. See also R. J. Smith (1990a); Porter (1990); Kidder Smith et al. (1990), p. 193, note 94. Cf. Henderson (1986).

152. SCC, 2: 329-335. See also ibid. 2: 322-325, 334-337; 3: 56-59, 119-120, 464, 625; 4.1: 14, 16; 4.2: 143, 530; 4.3: 125; 5.3: 51-53, 60-66, 69-74, 128, 217; Ho (1972), pp. 30-38; Tang Mingbang, et al., eds. (1986), "Editors' Introductory Note" and pp. 423-552, passim.

153. See Legge, cited in SCC, 2: 335-336; Spence (1975), pp. 11, 74. See also the link between the Yijing and medicine in Shanghai guoyi xueshe, ed., (1961) and Yuan (1948), 12: 9-10; 13: 3; 13: 33, etc. R. J. Smith (1990) provides a more complete inventory.

154. SCC, 2: 337.

155. Ibid., 2: 336.

156. Ibid., 2: 518 and 2: 574 ff.; cf. Black (1989), pp. 54-55 and 108-109. See also Tambiah (1990), esp. pp. 13-24. Derk Bodde in Borei and Le Blanc, eds. (1981), pp. 299-315, discusses Chinese concepts that might be considered "laws of nature," but he points out that the lack of an all powerful creator-deity in the early Chinese philosophical and religious tradition probably limited the concept in significant ways as compared to the West.

157. See Tambiah (1990), pp. 12-20.

158. Cited in R. J. Smith (1978a), p. 5.

159. See Willard Peterson's article on Fang in de Bary, ed. (1975); also Henderson (1986) and Porter (1982). Cf. Black (1989), pp. 164-180 on the limits to empirical investigation in China.

160. Cited in R. J. Smith (1989), pp. 575-576. Cf. Elman (1984), pp. 83-84.

161. See R. J. Smith (1989), pp. 575-576.

162. Ibid., esp. p. 576; also Black (1989), pp. 109-116, 122-134 and esp. 164. Cf. Henderson (1986).

163. See, for example, Spence (1975), p. 74; also note 153 above.

164. "The superior man strengthens himself unceasingly [Junzi yi ziqiang buxi]." Cf. Wilhelm (1967), p. 6.

165. See, for example, QBLC, fangji, p. 139 and the book by Xiao Gonghui entitled Zhouyi tu dili zhengzong (Standard Geomancy Based on the Diagrams of the Zhou Changes). Yuan (1948), 17: 9; also note 76 above and chapter 4, note 96.

Chapter 4

1. Among the many commonly used terms are: *qingwu shu, dili, dixue, budi, kanyu, yinyang jiayan; xing jiayan, fengshui, zhanzhai, xiangzhai,* etc. see Yuan (1948), passim.

2. Gazetteers generally refer to *kanyu, dili,* or *qingwu shu;* see *ibid.* Bennett (1978) argues correctly that "geomancy" is a poor translation for such terms, but it is too commonly used to abandon at this point.

3. See, for example, Freedman in Skinner, ed. (1979), pp. 324–325. As indicated above (note 1), a common term for geomancy in Qing times was *budi,* lit. "divining the earth."

4. See Yuan (1948), 1: 16; 1: 17; 1: 22–23; 1: 29; 2: 2; 2: 11; 2: 16; 3: 6; 3: 11; 4: 16–17; 5: 7; 5: 8; 5: 9; 5: 9–10; 5: 10; 5: 18–19; 5: 25–26; 6: 7–8; 8: 9–10; 8: 10–11; 8: 14; 10: 13–14; 11: 3; 12: 3; 12: 7; 12: 14; 12: 22–23; 12: 30–31; 13: 14; 13: 32 (two entries); 14: 31; 15: 27; 15: 31; 16: 25–26; 16: 34 (two entries); 17: 19–20; 17: 26; 17: 28–29; 18: 22; 18: 35; 18: 40; 20: 2; 20: 12; 20: 20; 21: 25; 21: 31; 21: 39; 22: 10; 23: 3; 23: 11; 25: 13; 25: 14; 25: 19–20; 25: 21–22; 26: 10; 29: 18; 29: 29; 30: 30; 32: 3–4; 32: 5; 32: 9; 32: 10; 33: 5; 33: 8; 33: 11–12; 33: 25; 35: 6–7; 35: 9; 36: 3; 36: 5; 36: 7; 36: 12; 36: 22; 36: 26–27; 36: 28–29; 37: 6–7; 37: 11; 37: 14–15; 37: 19; 37: 29. For the use of medical analogies in geomantic writings, see, for example, the preface to the *Huangdi zhaijing* (The Yellow Emperor's Siting Classic), TSJC, *yishu,* 47: 6724. See also Shigehisa Kuriyama in Kawakita, ed. (1987), pp. 55 ff.; Schipper (1978); and chapter 5, notes 83 and 84.

5. Porkert quoted in Bennett (1978), p. 7; slightly modified. On the importance of *shengqi* to the well-being of ancestors, consult Ouyang (1831), author's preface, 2b.

6. See March (1968), p. 253–254.

7. See, for example, Du Bose (1886), p. 431; Macgowan (1909), pp. 94–95; Johnston (1910), p. 119; Edkins (1879), pp. 327–328; etc.

8. See Maurice Freedman in Skinner, ed. (1979), pp. 315, 320–321; also Wright (1962), p. 274.

9. See, for example, Cohen and Schrecker, eds. (1976), p. 80.

10. For some representative Western views, see De Groot, (1892–1910), 3: 936; Nevius (1869), pp. 170–171; Macgowan (1909), p. 87–88; Williams (1883), 2: 246; Johnston (1910), p. 265; Martin (1897), pp. 41–42; Edkins (1879), chapter 21; Doré, (1914–1933), 4: 412, 415, etc. Cf. *Xiangshan xianzhi* (Guangdong, 1750), *fengsu,* 3: 29b–30a; *Dongwan xianzhi* (Guangdong, 1921), *fengsu,* 9: 1a; *Yongxin xianzhi* (Jiangxi, 1874), *fengsu,* 4: 23a–b; *Hexian xianzhi* (Anhui, 1770), *fengsu,* 15: 14a; *Neixiang xianzhi* (Henan, 1693), *fengsu,* p. 362 (Western pagination, 1976 reprint); *Naxi xianzhi* (Sichuan, 1813), *fengsu,* 6: 1a; *Chuxiong xianzhi* (Yunnan, 1910), *fengsu,* 2: 24b; *Chongming xianzhi* (Jiangsu, 1924), *fengsu,* 4: 4a–b; *Enxian xianzhi* (Hubei, 1864), *fengsu,* p. 4 (Western pagination,1975 reprint); *Hanyang fuzhi* (Hubei, 1747), *fengsu,* 47: 83b–84a, etc. See also Ocko (1983), pp. 40–41 and Ropp (1981), pp. 160, 174, and 293, note 85. Arthur Smith (1914), pp. 318–319, includes some proverbs on geomancy.

11. CSJCXB, *kanyu,* 25: 350, 360, etc. See also De Groot, (1892–1910), 3: 984.

12. TSJC, *yishu,* 47: 6724; see also Freedman (1966), pp. 126 ff.; cf. Ahern (1973).

13. See Freedman (1958), pp. 77 ff. and (1966), chapter 5. Johnston (1910) points out that faith in *fengshui* was "much less strong in Weihaiwei than in many other parts of the Empire." See also *Fuping xianzhi* (Shaanxi, 1890), *fengsu,* 3: 7b, which indicates a lack of concern with choosing lucky land (*zedi*). Part of the popularity of *fengshui* may be attributed to the prestige of individuals such as Cheng Yi and Zhu Xi, who reportedly believed in it. See Kidder Smith, *et al.* (1990), p. 205, note 138; also Doré, (1914–1933), 4: 411–412; De Groot (1892–1910), 3: 1049–1050. Cf. Chan (1989), pp. 119–120.

14. Carole Morgan points out that each major school had a variety of branches, such as the Sanyuan branch of the Jiangxi school. See Morgan (1980), pp. 160 ff. For examples of other approaches, consult the biographies of Meng Hao, Liu Daoren, Yin Jinyang, Zhou Li and Zhu Bangdian in Yuan (1948), 13: 14, 15: 10, 18: 8, 20: 3, and 20: 21, respectively; see also De Groot (1892–1910), 3: 1016–1017 and note 40 below.

15. SKQSZM, 109: 3a–3b; for three geomantic books attributed to Yang Yunsong, see ibid., 109: 4a–9a.

16. Cited in Bennett (1978), p. 2, slightly modified. See also the discussion of Zhu Bangdian in Yuan (1948), 20: 21.

17. See the excellent discussion by Zhu Chou in Yuan (1948), 34: 22–2; cf. the views of Yin Jinyang in ibid., 18: 8.

18. March (1968), p. 262; see also Li Guangcheng's remarks in Yuan (1948), 15: 34. Cf. Zhu Chou cited in note 17 above.

19. De Groot (1892–1910), 3: 954, slightly modified; cf. Jiang (1813), 1: 1a–b; Ouyang (1814), preface, p. 4a; QBLC, fangji, p. 134; Yuan (1948), 34: 22–23. See also Nevius (1869), pp. 173–174; Morgan (1980), p. 166; Feuchtwang (1974), pp. 87, 112–114; and Edkins (1879), pp. 336–337, 345–349.

20. See, for example, Yuan (1948), 34: 22–23. Liang (1982) provides a convenient dictionary of geomantic terms.

21. See Doré (1914–1933), 4: 406.

22. See, for example, Morgan (1980), pp. 171–172; also SKQSZM, 111: 10b and notes 23 and 36 below.

23. R. J. Smith (1983), pp. 147–148. For details, consult TSJC, yishu, 47: 6724 ff.; cf. SCC, 4.1: 293 ff.; Feuchtwang, pp. 18 ff. and 255–257 ff.; De Groot (1892–1910), 3: 958 ff.; Eitel (1984), pp. 27 ff.; etc.

24. Morgan (1980), pp. 205–206 and Morgan (1980b), pp. 211–212; see also chapter 2, notes 38, 45, 46 and 49, and note 212 below.

25. See, however, the views of Zhou Puan in Yuan (1948), 5: 3. Cf. the sources cited in note 19 above.

26. For a detailed discussion of the so-called "nine stars," see Edkins (1879), pp. 345–349, drawing on the Hanlong jing (Classic of the Shaking Dragon). Cf. the discussion in SKQSZM, 109: 4a–5a and ibid., 111: 5a-b. Consult also Morgan (1980), pp. 175–184 and Morgan (1980b), pp. 212–213. For a discussion of the twelve "stages of life," see chapter 2, note 37 and esp. chapter 5, note 17.

27. See the discussion in Feuchtwang (1974), pp. 76–80. Cf. SCC, 4.1: 294–295 and chapters 2 and 3 of this book.

28. Feuchtwang (1974), pp. 18 ff. and 255–257; cf. De Groot, (1892–1910), 3: 958 ff.; Eitel (1984), pp. 27 ff.

29. See Feuchtwang (1974), p. 75; cf. ibid., pp. 129–130; also Edkins (1879), p. 329.

30. Eitel (1984), p. 29.

31. See Ahern (1978), pp. 56–57; also Edkins (1879), pp. 330–331 and note 49 below.

32. See Feuchtwang (1974), pp. 30–31.

33. See, for example, Eitel (1984), p. 34; cf. Carole Morgan's illuminating discussion of a similar set of geomantic variables contained in the liunian dali of popular almanacs. Morgan (1980), pp. 188–225. See also notes 44 and 45 below.

34. Feuchtwang (1974), p. 79.

35. See Morgan (1980), pp. 169 and 232 ff., esp. p. 234; also the concrete illustration in De Groot, (1892–1910), 3: 976; cf. Feuchtwang (1974), pp. 70–71, 76–77; Johnston (1910), pp. 265–266.

36. See SCC, 4.1: 293–301; also Eitel (1984), pp. 27–35 and 45; De Groot, (1892–1910), 3: 959–975; Carus (1974), 58–63; Feuchtwang (1974), pp. 18 ff. and 255–257.

37. Yip (1989), 30-38 provides several excellent photographs of *luopan*; for other illustrations, see the sources cited in note 36 above.

38. De Groot, (1892-1910), 3: 975; cf. Eitel (1984), pp. 34-35. On the obscure pronouncements of some practitioners, consult Yuan (1948), passim.

39. See the discussion in Feuchtwang (1974), p. 107.

40. For some examples of the theoretical positions taken by Qing geomancers, consult Yuan (1948) 1: 19; 2: 5-7; 4: 14; 4: 16-17; 4: 18-20; 4: 26-27; 5: 8; 7: 26-27; 8: 7; 8: 12-13; 14: 11; 16: 26; 17: 7-8; 18: 8; 20: 3; 20: 4; 20: 21; 21: 24; 21: 25; 22: 26; 22: 33; 24: 6; 25: 19; 34: 8; 34: 22-23; etc. See also note 95.

41. *Luquan xianzhi* (Yunnan, 1925), *fangji*, 11: 51a. Li became blind late in life, after he had already practiced geomancy for a long time. Apparently he was of the Fujian school, for the gazetteer tells us that he indicated celestial movements with his hands.

42. See, for example, Feuchtwang (1974), p. 171.

43. See the *Yangzhai shishu* (Ten Books on Housing for the Living) in TSJC, *yishu*, 47: 7010 ff. On the link between geomancy and alchemy, consult Seaman (1986); on medicine and geomancy, see Shigehisa Kuriyama in Kawakita, ed. (1987).

44. Morgan (1980), pp. 117-123 and 188-225; cf. Doolittle (1865), p. 346. On day-selection, consult Walshe (1906), chapter 24, esp. pp. 197 ff. See also note 33 above.

45. De Groot, (1892-1910); 3: 974-975 and 1033-1034; see also Eitel (1984), pp. 28, 30; Doolittle (1865), p. 346.

46. De Groot, (1892-1910), 3: 1008-1009.

47. See the biographies of Zhang Ding and Li Xingyu in Yuan (1948), 33: 13 and 33: 23, respectively. Ganzhou, in Jianxi province, was something of a mecca for geomancers.

48. Cited in March (1968), p. 259.

49. See, for example, Ouyang (1814 and 1831); cf. Feuchtwang (1974), pp. 120 ff., esp. 126-127; Ahern (1978), pp. 56-57; Seaman (1986), p. 12; Edkins (1879), p. 349, etc.

50. Cited in Freedman (1966), p. 135.

51. Feuchtwang (1974), pp. 108-112.

52. *Ibid.* For a valuable discussion of *fengshui* terminology, and a critique of Feuchtwang, consult Morgan (1980b). Liang (1982) provides a more detailed lexicon.

53. Ouyang (1831), author's preface, p. 2b; Jiang (1813), preface, pp. 1a-b. See also Yuan (1948) 1: 19, 2: 5-7, 14: 11, 17: 7-8, 20: 3, 20: 4, 21: 24, 22: 26, 24: 6, 34: 22-23, etc.; cf. Henry (1885), pp. 140 ff.

54. Shen Hao, cited in March (1968), p. 256-257, slightly modified.

55. See, for example, TSJC, *yishu*, 47: 6923 ff.

56. See Miu Xiyong's *Zangjing yi* (Appendix to the Burial Classic), CSJCXB, 25: 253-256; cf. TSJC, *yishu*, 47: 6881-6884 and *ibid.* pp. 6885-6889; also Feuchtwang (1974), pp. 121-124.

57. The geomantic works reproduced in CSJCXB and TSJC provide many useful discussions (and numerous illustrations) of the variety of both *xue* and *sha*. See, for example, Wu Yuanyin's illustrated annotation of Guo Pu's *Zangjing* (Burial Classic) in CSJCXB, 25: 211-225 and the anonymously edited *Zangtu* (Burial Illustrations) in *ibid.*, 25: 246-248. Cf. Edkins (1879), chapter 21; Feuchtwang (1974), pp. 113 ff.; Eitel, pp. 41 ff.; De Groot, (1892-1910), 3: 948 ff.

58. This discussion is drawn from the sources cited in note 57 above; see also DuBose (1886), p. 432.

59. Morgan (1980), p. 167; SKQSZM, 109: 4a-5a and *ibid.*, 111: 5a-b. As with the shape of rocks, different waterway configurations indicated different "elements." For a further discussion of these and other considerations, consult Weller (1987), pp. 147-155 and 173-184; March (1968), pp. 258 ff.; Edkins (1879), pp. 345-349; De Groot, (1892-

1910), 3: 939 ff., esp. 954–956; SCC, 2: 359–360; Feuchtwang (1974), pp. 129–134; etc. See also note 69 below.

60. See Morgan (1980b), pp. 211–212; also Morgan (1980), pp. 175 ff.; Weller (1987), 173–184.

61. TSJC, yishu, 47: 7004.

62. Ibid. See also Ahern (1978), p. 56; Feuchtwang (1974), pp. 168–171; De Groot, (1892–1910), 3: 943–945; Nevius (1869), pp. 176–177; Edkins (1879), p. 338.

63. On the importance of watercourses, see in particular Jiang Pingjie's Mizhuan shuilong jing (Secretly Transmitted Water Dragon Classic) in CSJCXB, 25: 275 ff. Cf. TSJC, yishu, 47: 6953 ff.; Feuchtwang (1974), pp. 129 ff. Consult also De Groot, (1892–1910), 3: 941, 946, and 1043–1044; Macgowan (1909), pp. 90–91; Doré (1970), p. 118; Yuan (1948), 27: 15–16; and the sources cited in note 62 above.

64. See, for example, the discussion in the Qing work entitled Yangzhai cuoyao (Selected Essentials Regarding Houses for the Living) in CSJCXB, 25: 307. Consult also QBLC, fangji, 135, 140, 141, 142; also Nevius (1869), pp. 174–175 and 177; De Groot (1892–1910), 3: 1041–1042.

65. Cited in Yang (1961), p. 264; cf. QBLC, fangji, p. 140.

66. Yuan (1948), 37: 8–9; see also the interesting case of Yu Zhizhong in ibid., 35: 20.

67. Rowe (1989), p. 160. For illustrations of favorable fengshui, consult De Groot, (1892–1910), 3: 949–950; Macgowan (1909), pp. 88–90; Graham (1928), pp. 33–34.

68. Meyer (1978), esp. pp. 139–142.

69. Ibid., p. 145; cf. note 59 above.

70. Ibid., pp. 146–148, drawing on Peng Zuozhi (1961).

71. Ibid., pp. 144–145.

72. For some examples, see ibid., pp. 148 ff.

73. Cited in March (1968), p. 259. Cf. note 4 above. On Ye Tai, see Yuan (1948), 16: 26–27.

74. QBLC, fangji, p. 221 On Zhao, Li and Zhang, consult Yuan (1948), 35: 6–7; 35: 16; see also Hummel (1943–1944), pp. 71 and 495.

75. Professionals went by a variety of names, such as fengshui xiansheng; xiansheng, yinyang xiansheng; xingjia, and dishi. For an example of an amateur praised by professionals, see Pu Zhishang in Yuan (1948), 13: 24.

76. For some examples of famous geomancers, see Yuan (1948), 2: 22, 14: 11, 20: 2, 26: 6, 37: 16, etc.

77. Welch (1967), pp. 122 and 483–484; Nevius (1869), pp. 170–171. See also Yuan (1948), 38: 40; 38: 42; 38: 43. Among geomancers who were not clergymen, but who claimed supernatural power, Deng Junshan asserted that he could see five feet (chi) into the ground. Yuan (1948), 15: 36.

78. De Groot (1892–1910), 3: 1010; cf. Freedman in Skinner, ed. (1979), p. 323. For a detailed but not entirely flattering Chinese account of the activities of a late Qing geomancer, see Wieger (1913), pp. 547 ff.; cf. Henry (1885), pp. 166 ff.

79. Yuan Shushan (1948) identifies about 480 geomancers for the Qing period. Not all were literate of course. This is true also for modern Taiwan and Hong Kong. See, for example, Gallin (1966), p. 245.

80. See Giles (1916), p. 447; cf. Johnston (1910), pp. 198 and 203. I have noticed no women geomancers in Yuan (1948) or the numerous gazetteers I have consulted.

81. See De Groot (1892–1910), 3: 939. Most of the geomancers whose biographies appear in Yuan (1948)—see note 79 above—are credited with one or more divinatory specialties in addition to geomancy. Not surprisingly, these specialties tended to bear

directly on the concerns of *fengshui*, such as *Yijing*-related numerology (including *taiyi*, *liuren* and *qimen dunjia*), astrology, and day-selection. See also note 4 above.

82. See Naquin in Watson and Rawski, eds. (1988), p. 56; for the case in north China, consult, for example, Wieger (1913), pp. 547–549.

83. See De Groot (1892–1910), 3: 1080 ff.; also Yuan (1948), 23: 16 (on expelling *gui* from a house by removing buried coffins); cf. Freedman in Skinner, ed. (1979), pp. 323–324. Traditional folktales also emphasized the special power of *fengshui* specialists. See, for example, Eberhard (1965), pp. 77–79; cf. Seaman (1986). Feuchtwang (1974), p. 194–195 argues that recourse to priests was the norm, and that geomancers were "not religious functionaries." This conclusion seems overstated—although presumably the more exalted the self-image of the geomancer, the more reluctant he would be to use charms and spells.

84. For examples of such charms, see TSJC, *yishu*, 47: 7037–7043; cf. Feuchtwang (1974), p. 194; Doré (1970), pp. 88 ff. Doctors also commonly used charms, of course. See chapter 6.

85. *Ibid.* (all sources).

86. See, for example, Wu Ding's *Yangzhai cuoyao* (Selected Essentials Regarding Houses for the Living) in CSJCXB, 25: 312–313; also QBLC, *mixin*, pp. 33–34; De Groot (1892–1910), 3: 978–979, 1041–1042; Edkins (1879), pp. 337–338; Doré (1970), pp. 90 ff.

87. See Watson and Rawski, eds. (1988), esp. pp. 33, 55–59, 66, 104, 109–110, 204, 207, 213–218.

88. See Naquin in Watson and Rawski, eds. (1988), esp. p. 55; also Feuchtwang (1974), pp. 175 ff. and note 84 above.

89. Freedman (1966), pp. 119 ff., esp. p. 120.

90. For one of relatively few exceptions, see Yuan (1948), 6: 2 on Li Shilian.

91. Yuan (1948), 23: 3; see also *ibid.*, 13: 14.

92. See De Groot (1892–1910), 3: 1009. On pilgrimages see note 47 above.

93. *Ibid.*, 36: 23; also *ibid.*, 14: 32. On apprenticeship, see Feuchtwang (1974).

94. See, for example, De Groot (1892–1910), 3: 1009. On the expansion of printing and literacy, see the articles by Evelyn Rawski and James Hayes in Johnston, *et al.*, eds. (1985), esp. pp. 17–28 and 93–100.

95. Many manuals included songs and rhymes to facilitate memorization. The correlative emphasis of such works is highlighted in the preface to Ouyang (1814), 4b–5a, which indicates: "Heaven has five elements [i.e., "agents"] and Earth has five mountain ranges; Heaven has nine paths [*dao*] and Earth has nine continents." My brief summary of *fengshui* manuals in the text is based on works such as those of Jiang (1813), Ouyang (1814 and 1831); the reviews in SKQSZM, 109: 1a–11a and 111: 1a–14b; and the various books on geomancy reprinted in the TSJC and CSJCXB. See also De Groot (1892–1910), 3: 996 ff., esp. pp. 1009–1010.

96. On Jiang and his influence, consult Yuan (1948), 2: 22; also *ibid.*, 2: 7–8; 2: 30–31; 16: 32; 18: 6; Ouyang (1814), author's preface; see also note 63 above. A late Qing *luopan* in my possession bears an inscription on the base by one Fang Xiushui ("Elegant Waters" Fang) of Xin'an (Guangdong) in which Fang, in obvious admiration of Jiang, quotes him to the effect that the *Yijing* is the embodiment of all cosmic truths.

97. Yuan (1948), 16: 32 and 18: 6; see also TSJC, *yishu*, 47: 7047 ff.

98. On these three works, see Yuan (1948), 12: 2–3, 12: 20 and 17: 3. For other examples, consult *ibid.*, 1: 27–28; 2: 7–8; 2: 8; 2: 15; 2: 27; 3: 4; 4: 26–27; 4: 27; 5: 9; 8: 7; 8: 12–13; 8: 16–17; 8: 24; 9: 10–11; 9: 28; 11: 8–9; 12: 11; 12: 30–31; 13: 14; 13: 8; 13: 23; 13: 32–33; 15: 9; 15: 38–39; 16: 4; 16: 11; 16: 12; 16: 25–26; 16: 26; 16: 32; 16: 34; 17: 4; 17: 9; 17: 12; 18: 14; 18: 25; 19: 38; 21: 27; 26: 25; 29: 37–38; 34: 8; 35: 18 (two entries); 35: 24; 36: 16; 37: 3.

99. Cited in March (1968), p. 259. See also note 101 below.

100. See Wieger (1913), p. 549, which includes an excellent account of the geomancer's banter.

101. See the examples of Mao Shuyou, Chen Xuwen, Wei Duan, Guan Zhining, Hu Tongyu, Zhou Li, Kuang Chaofan, Zhao Zifeng and others in Yuan (1948), 10: 13–14; 12: 4; 14: 18; 15: 8–9; 16: 7; 18: 17–18; 20: 3; 20: 4; 24: 37; etc. Cf. March (1968), p. 259; QBLC, *fangji*, p. 138.

102. Cited in De Groot (1892–1910), 3: 938; cf. Ouyang (1814), preface, 7a; see also Unschuld (1985), p. 203.

103. Yuan (1948), 13: 23.

104. *Ibid.*, 33: 23.

105. *Ibid.*, 1: 18–19.

106. *Ibid.*, 2: 2; see also 6: 6–7; 17: 27; 22: 34–35; 27: 23; 29: 37–38; 33: 13; 33: 23; etc.

107. *Ibid.*, 9: 21–22; also 1: 29–30; 12: 17–18; see also the prefaces to Jiang (1813) and Ouyang (1831).

108. Yuan (1948), 12: 17–18.

109. *Ibid.*, 13: 14.

110. *Ibid.*, 13: 13–14.

111. See the discussion in De Groot (1892–1910), 3: 1013 ff.; cf. Yuan (1948), 5: 8; also note 205 below.

112. De Groot (1892–1910), 3: 1013–1014.

113. See, for example, the interesting account of retribution in Yuan (1948), 8: 21–22; also notes 111 above and 205 below.

114. *Ibid.*, 14: 32; 23: 5; 26: 25; 36: 19; see also 22: 34–35. Cf. Freedman (1966), p. 128 and De Groot (1892–1910), 3: 1014.

115. Yuan (1948), 37: 18 and 17: 19–20

116. *Ibid.*, 36: 10 and 35: 24; see also 21: 23; 23: 14–15; 34: 10, etc. and the case of Zheng Keshi in *Chongxiu Xiangshan xianzhi* (Guangdong, 1879), *fangji*, pp. 29b–30a.

117. See, for example, Lin Guizhi, Liu Yuanxi, Huang Qizhu, Wei Chengqing, Luo Jinjian, Xue Mei, and Chen Wenzao in Yuan (1948), 6: 7–8; 6: 8; 16: 5; 16: 34; 18: 14; 23: 14–15; 25: 21–22 and 36: 12.

118. *Ibid.*, 19: 25 and 20: 12.

119. *Ibid.*, 12: 14 and 36: 23.

120. *Ibid.*, 2: 14; 3: 8; 6: 7–8; 6: 8; 16: 32; 18: 22; 19: 24–25; 23: 14–15; 25: 13; 25: 21–22; 26: 10; 26: 25; 28: 3; 33: 13; 35: 25; 36: 23; 37: 21; etc.

121. *Ibid.*, 12: 14 and 36: 23; see also 15: 10.

122. *Ibid.*, (1948), 13: 17.

123. *Ibid.*, (1948), 21: 24; cf. QBLC, *fangji*, p. 140.

124. Yuan (1948), 18: 32.

125. See, for example, the case of Sun Meng in *ibid.*, 13: 3; also 33: 23.

126. *Ibid.*, 22: 18. See also the case of Zheng Keshi, cited in note 116 above.

127. *Ibid.*, 10: 13–14.

128. *Ibid.*, 18: 29.

129. *Ibid.*, 14: 15.

130. See De Groot (1892–1910), 3: 1018–1020 on salaries; cf. Johnston (1910), p. 119.

131. For a comparatively rare example, see Yuan (1948), 20: 30.

132. On types of employment and payment for geomancers, consult Feuchtwang (1974), p. 176; Freedman (1966), p. 138; Gray (1878), 2: 7; Doolittle (1865), 2: 339; etc. Doolittle, who discusses payment for several other kinds of divination as well, remarks that "Oftentimes, in the case of rich families, several scores of dollars are paid to the

geomancer for selecting a propitious site for a grave. The poorer families who employ such a helper in fixing the site for a grave sometimes only pay a few thousand cash, or even a few hundred cash for his services." One American dollar was worth about .625 taels or 4s 2d at prevailing exchange rates. Theoretically a tael (one ounce of silver) was worth 1,000 cash, but in fact it might be worth 1,300 cash or more.

133. See the example of Wang Chuzhen in Yuan (1948), 15: 7.

134. *Ibid.*, 10: 14, 12: 3, 15: 38, etc.; cf. Johnston (1910), pp. 118-119.

135. Weiger (1913), pp. 547-551, slightly modified; cf. Feuchtwang (1974), p. 176.

136. On Liu, see Yuan (1948), 14: 11; Kang is discussed in *Qianjiang xianzhi* (Hubei, 1880), *fangji*, 18: 32 a-b. In testimony to the royal family's patronage of *fengshui*, Prince Guo wrote an appreciative preface for a book on geomancy by Fan Yibin. See Yuan (1948), 37: 16.

137. Yuan (1948), 22: 11.

138. *Ibid.*, 26: 6; see also the similar case of Wang Shangheng in *ibid.*, 18: 34.

139. *Ibid.*, 14: 11

140. *Ibid.*, 16: 7. See also the examples of Dai Zetong, Zeng Mingxun and Xu Erchao in *ibid.*, 27: 15-16, 34: 26 and 36: 15; also Gao Silong in Feuchtwang (1974), p. 177.

141. Yuan (1948), 37: 2-3.

142. *Ibid.*, 21: 10-11; cf. Hummel (1943-1944), p. 385. See also note 144 below.

143. See De Groot (1892-1910), 3: 869 ff. In fact, even the cutting down of the tree was against the law, strictly speaking. *Ibid.*, p. 907.

144. *Ibid.*, 3: 1051-1052; Morgan (1980), 164. See also Feuchtwang (1974), p. 8 and Hummel (1943-1944), p. 741. For the example of Dragon Pool, consult Jordan and Overmyer (1986), pp. 93 ff.

145. Yang (1961), pp. 263-264; see also Yuan (1948), 33: 21 on the benefits of even minor changes.

146. Yuan (1948), 18: 16. See also the biographies of Jiang Gao and Li Jixiang in *ibid.*, 18: 16, 19: 33 and 19: 38, respectively; also *ibid.*, 13: 17, 15: 8-9, 15: 38, 16: 4-5, 19: 33, 33: 22, 35: 16, 37: 7-8, etc.

147. *Ibid.*, 19: 32-33.

148. *Ibid.*, 4: 16-17.

149. *Ibid.*, 1: 19, 1: 22, 4: 16-17, and 29: 29.

150. *Ibid.*, 7: 20. See also the several biographies of Shen appended to Shen (1969 and 1983). On the Ever-Victorious Army and its divinatory practices, consult Smith (1978b).

151. Yuan (1948), 12: 11.

152. *Ibid.*, 12: 6-7.

153. See Wilhelm (1967), p. 294. This phrase is often cited in *fengshui* manuals as classical justification for the practice of geomancy.

154. Yuan (1948), 5: 18-19.

155. See, for example, *ibid.*, 18: 34; 20: 20, 26: 5, 26: 6, 37: 7-8, etc.

156. *Ibid.*, 3: 8-9; see also 21: 3; 22: 11, etc.

157. *Ibid.*, 18: 13.

158. *Ibid.*, 18: 14 and 18: 16; also Ocko (1983), p. 230, note 53.

159. Yuan (1948), 5: 2.

160. On rhythm in Chinese aesthetics, see R. J. Smith (1983), pp. 157 ff., esp. pp. 172-174.

161. Cited in March (1968), p. 257; cf. Feuchtwang (1974), pp. 146-147. See also note 73 above.

162. Cited in March (1968), p. 255.

163. In fact, the geomantic metaphors of dragons and veins were also employed as evaluative terms in painting. See Feuchtwang (1974), pp. 143 and 146.

164. Cited in March (1968), p. 258; cf. Feuchtwang (1974), p. 110.

165. Cited in R. J. Smith (1983), p. 172.

166. Arthur Smith (1914), p. 318.

167. For some denunciations, see *Da Qing shichao shengxun* (1980), Gaozong, 261: 3a; 262: 5a, 263: 5a, etc.; also the paraphrase of the Yongzheng emperor's "Sacred Edict" cited in Anonymous (1868); De Groot (1892-1910), 3: 1051.

168. Liu Hui-chen Wang in Wright, ed. (1964), pp. 45-46; cf. Freedman (1966), p. 132; Yang (1961), pp. 264-265.

169. Yang (1961), p. 264.

170. Hail (1927), pp. 338, 340, 343-344, slightly modified.

171. R. J. Smith, et al., eds. (forthcoming), diary entry for August 20, 1864; cf. Martin (1897), pp. 355, 358.

172. See, for example, Ropp (1981), pp. 160 and 290, note 37; also Doré, (1914-1933), 4: 415-416.

173. See R. J. Smith in Liu, ed. (1990), esp. pp. 307-308; also R. J. Smith (1983), chapter 7, esp. pp. 152-154.

174. Cited in Ropp (1981), p. 187.

175. Ropp (1981), pp. 183-186.

176. Waley (1970), pp. 130-131, slightly modified; see also Ropp (1981), 185-186 and notes.

177. Holmes Welch, cited in R. J. Smith (1978a), p. 44. See also De Groot (1892-1910), 3: 1034-1035.

178. See Yuan (1948), 13: 13-14; 19: 25; 24: 15; 25: 19-20; also QBLC, *fangji*, p. 141.

179. Ropp (1981), pp. 174-179; for background, see *ibid.*, pp. 62 ff.

180. JSWB, 63: 1a ff., esp. 1a-2a, 8b-13a, 18a, etc.; see also Wu (1832), 19: 2a-7b. For details on these practices, consult Freedman (1966), pp. 119 ff.

181. JSWB, 63: 1a; cf. Yuan (1948), 1: 6-7; Ocko (1983), p. 40.

182. See Liu Hui-chen Wang in Wright (1964), pp. 27, 44-46; also Freedman (1966), p. 132. For critical comments in gazetteers, see, for example, *Xiangshan xianzhi* (Guangdong, 1750), *fengsu*, 3: 29b-30a; *Dongwan xianzhi* (Guangdong, 1921), *fengsu*, 9: 1a; *Hexian xianzhi* (Anhui, 1770), *fengsu*, 15: 14a; *Neixiang xianzhi* (Henan, 1693), *fengsu*, p. 362 (Western pagination, 1976 reprint); *Naxi xianzhi* (Sichuan, 1813), *fengsu*, 6: 1a; *Chongming xianzhi* (Jiangsu, 1924), *fengsu*, 4: 4a-b; *Yongxin xianzhi* (Jiangxi, 1874), *fengsu*, 4: 23a-b; etc.

183. See Thompson (1973), p. 190.

184. De Groot (1892-1910), 3: 869 ff., esp. pp. 878-882 and 887. See also note 185 below. For the description of unburied coffins, see Ocko (1983), p. 40.

185. *Ibid.*, 1: 133.

186. *Enxian xianzhi* (Hubei, 1864), *fengsu*, p. 4 (Western pagination, 1975 reprint). For various Qing critiques, see the essays by Huang Zongxi, Cai Shiyuan (1682-1733), Quan Zuwang, Qian Daxin and Mei Wending, in HCJSWB, 63: 9b-13a. Cf. De Groot (1892-1910), 3: 1016-1017; Wu (1832) 19: 2a-b. Consult also Ropp (1981), pp. 164-166, 184-186, 189-190; Doré, (1914-1933), 4: 407 ff.; and notes 166, 167, 178, 179, 180, 182, 184 and 185 above.

187. Ropp (1981), p. 162.

188. For earlier critiques, see Zhao Fang and others cited in TSJC, *yishu*, 47: 7054 ff.

189. See the sarcastic ditty cited by Morgan (1980), pp. 170-171. The answer sometimes given by geomancers was that they could not afford to buy the best land in the first place.

190. Ropp (1981), pp. 162–163; 290, note 47; cf. JSWB, 63: 10b–11a; see also Doré (1914–1933), 4: 407–416, esp. p. 412.

191. De Groot (1892–1910), 3: 1021–1026 provides the text and translation of Sima Guang's memorial.

192. Ropp (1981), p. 163–164, 290, note 47; Doré (1914–1933), 4: 407–416. For a relevant excerpt from the story of Meng Tian in the Shiji, see March (1968), pp. 260–261.

193. Ropp (1981), p. 163.

194. Ibid., p. 165.

195. HCJSWB, 63: 1a ff., esp. 11b.

196. De Groot (1892–1910), 1: 134–135, slightly modified.

197. Ropp (1981), p. 162.

198. For an overview, see Gilbert Fong in Dolezelova-Velingerova (1980), pp. 116–118. The novel is based on an actual eighteenth-century murder case.

199. See, for example, Wieger (1913), pp. 554 ff.; cf. Yongxin xianzhi (Jiangxi, 1874), fengsu, 4: 23a–b.

200. Wieger (1913), pp. 554–555. On go-betweens in business transactions, see Doolittle (1865), 2: 134–138.

201. Cited in Freedman (1966), p. 136. See also Maurice Freedman in Skinner, ed. (1979), p. 329 and Feuchtwang (1974), p. 212 ff.

202. Giles (1916), pp. 447–449.

203. Nevius (1869), p. 172; cf. DuBose (1886), pp. 434–435. Variations in the practice of fengshui naturally reflected, among other things, variations in local kinship organization. See Feuchtwang (1974), p. 215.

204. Freedman (1966), pp. 131–132.

205. De Groot (1892–1910), 3: 1029; cf. Freedman (1966), pp. 124–125. For the views of Song, consult Yuan (1948), 3: 1. Zhao Dongzhou held a similar stance. Ibid., 36: 19.

206. De Groot (1892–1910), 3: 1031–1034. Feuchtwang (1974), p. 215, argues that the mutual affection of brothers and their affection for their mother diminished sibling rivalry somewhat.

207. De Groot (1892–1910), 3: 1041–1042. See also Johnston (1910), pp. 118–119, 120, 198, 203, 251, 333–334; Doré, (1914–1933), 4: 414–415; and note 210 below.

208. For details, see De Groot (1892–1910), 3: 1035–1036, 1039–1040.

209. Cited in De Groot (1892–1910), 3: 1036–1037.

210. Johnston (1910), p. 269, slightly modified.

211. For the complete acccount, see Johnston (1910), pp. 267–270.

212. Fan (1933) 1: 134–137. My thanks to Jon Ocko for calling this case to my attention and photocopying the text for me.

213. See notes 183 and 184 above.

214. Nevius (1869), pp. 171–172. See also Freedman (1966), pp. 139–140; Hayes (1983), p. 151.

215. Graham (1928), p. 34. I have modified family and place names to be consistent with the pinyin romanization system used in this book.

216. See note 200 above.

217. De Groot (1892–1910), 3: 1034–1037, 1040–1041.

218. Macgowan (1909), pp. 91–92; cf. Yongxin xianzhi (Jiangxi, 1874), fengsu, 4: 23a–b.

219. Martin (1897), p. 41.

220. Ibid. For details of the latter case, see Dennys (1876), p. 66. See also Robert Hart's journal entry for May 7, 1865, in R. J. Smith, et al., eds. (forthcoming).

221. De Groot (1892–1910), 3: 1042–1043.

222. Nevius (1869), p. 175.

223. See the sources cited in notes 7 and 10 above; also *North-China Herald*, January 5 and May 7, 1865; January 5, 1867.

224. *Hanyang fuzhi* (Hubei, 1747), 47: 83–84, cited in Rowe (1989), p. 358, note 25; SCC, 4.3: 53; Henry (1885), p. 147. See also note 225 below; Hayes (1983), chapter 10, passim; and Robert Hart's unpublished journals, entry for June 5, 1868 in the Queens University Library, Belfast.

225. See note 224 above; also Nevius (1869), p. 175; Macgowan (1909), pp. 94–95 and DuBose (1886), p. 431. For indications of the pervasiveness and power of geomancy in Hankou, consult Rowe (1989), pp. 20, 32, 160, etc.

226. See Feuchtwang (1974), pp. 242 ff. for similar observations; also Nathan Sivin in Ropp, ed. (1990), pp. 189–190.

227. De Groot (1892–1910), 3: 939.

228. See, for example, Yuan (1948), 13: 33; Eberhard (1965), pp. 77–79; cf. Seaman (1986).

229. See Ropp (1981) on the novel *Julin waishi* (The Scholars), passim.

Chapter 5

1. See Plopper (1926), pp. 291–315; also Giles (1912), pp. 229, 987; Arthur Smith (1914), pp. 299, 310. These examples, most of which have several variants, have been modified somewhat to conform more closely to the Chinese originals.

2. Plopper (1926), p. 311. See also Allan (1926), pp. 176–190, passim.

3. Plopper (1926), p. 302; cf. Yang (1961), pp. 257 ff.

4. Hail (1927), p. 348.

5. Plopper (1926), p. 302. On Zeng's attitudes toward fate, see Hail (1927), p. 348; also R. J. Smith (1986), p. 171.

6. See Zhang (n.d.), pp. 10 ff., esp. pp. 12–13. Among the many general terms for fate extrapolation were *tuiming*, *tuibu*, and *tui luming*; for physiognomy, *kanxiang*, *xiangren*, and *fengjian*. The two types of divination are linked explicitly in the SKQSZM. See note 10 below.

7. Arthur Smith (1914), p. 310.

8. See Yuan (1948), 12: 30–31.

9. The blurring of categories in both the TSJC and SKQSZM suggests this inter-relationship. See esp. SKQSZM 108: 1a–b. The SKQSZM, *juan* 108–111, reviews a total of forty-five works on numerology (*shuxue*); twenty-eight on meteorological divination (*zhanhou*); twenty-six on geomancy (*xiangzhai*, *xiangmu*); twenty-nine on general divination (*zhanbu*); thirty-two on fate calculation (*mingshu*) and physiognomy (*xiangshu*); thirty-one works on *yinyang/wuxing*; and six miscellaneous works on medical divination (*zhenmo*; lit. "pulse-reading), word analysis and dream analysis. Cf. chapter 1, note 6, and the breakdown and analysis in Zhang (n.d.), pp. 10–23. See also Yuan (1948), 34: 8 and note 12 below.

10. Yuan (1948), 3: 6–7 (Qian), 14: 11–12 (Ding), 13: 17 (Liu), 15: 9 (Yao), 5: 12–14 (Wang), 37: 9–10 (Xing), and 36: 10 (Ma); see also *ibid.*, 3: 6; 3: 19; 5: 16; 5: 32; 7: 17–18; 17: 11; 22: 33; 24: 40; etc. Yuan's work, which is vast but not completely comprehensive, contains the biographies of nearly two hundred individuals with a stated interest in astrology, and well over two hundred references (many overlapping with the above-mentioned) to an interest in various kinds of numerology.

11. See the twenty-eight reviews of works on *zhanhou* in SKQSZM, 108: 27b–31a and 110: 20b–35b; also the works on weather divination in CSJCXB, 25: 1–23, esp. Tao

Luzi's Yunqi zhanhou (Divination by Cloud Ethers), ibid., 25: 11–16 (Qing dynasty edition by Wang Zongyi).

12. Unfortunately, as with my discussions of both the Yijing and geomancy, I can provide only a brief glimpse of the terrain. The English-language study of Hetu/Luoshu astrology by Chu and Sherrell (1976) provides one indication of the complexities involved.

13. See the discussion in Walters (1987), pp. 292 ff.; cf. SCC, 2: 352, which equates these segments with the twelve "houses" or cusps (loci, topoi) of Hellenistic astrology. The horoscopes can be found it TSJC, yishu, 47: 6096 ff.

14. See chapter 2, note 37; also note 17 below.

15. Nevius (1869), pp. 186 and 191; see also Doré (1914–1933), 4: 346–348; Gray (1878), 2: 13 ff.; Du Bose (1886), pp. 414 ff. Cf. Chu and Sherrill (1976), pp. 7–57 and Sherrill and Chu (1977), pp. 71–177 and the long note appended to the biography of Zhang Wenhu in Yuan (1948), 2: 28–29.

16. Some schools of fate extrapolation did include trigram and hexagram interpretation, however—notably the so-called Plum Blossom Method (Meihua yishu) of Shao Yong. See Liu (1979), Chu and Sherrill (1976), and Sherrill and Chu (1977). Consult also SKQSZM, 111: 31a-b; the note appended to the biography of Zhang Wenhu in Yuan (1948), 2: 28–29; and Doré (1914–1933), vol. 4, figure 152.

17. XSCL, 4: 76 ff; cf. Morgan (1980), pp. 236 ff. See also SKQSZM, 109: 32b-35b; Chao (1946), p. 298 and Doré, 4: 346 ff.

18. For a useful summary of Li's ideas, see Chao (1946), pp. 299–308; also the long review of his Mingshu (Book of Fate) in the SKQSZM, 109: 22b-24a.

19. Explicit references to the Ziping method in Yuan (1948) outnumber those to the Xuzhong method by about 3: 1. For some biographies of practitioners of the Xuzhong method, consult Yuan (1948), 1: 25; 3: 31–32; 20: 8; etc.; for exponents of the Ziping method, see ibid. 1: 20–21; 2: 9–10; 3: 6–7; 4: 12–13; 9: 14; 22: 25; 22: 33; 27: 15; etc. At least some diviners dutifully studied both approaches. Ibid., 24: 28–30. Shen Ziyuan, a professional fortune-teller and extremely able exponent of the Ziping method, wrote a book on divination with the ironic title Zi hanyan (Things of Which the Master [Confucius] Seldom Spoke). Yuan (1948), 7: 6. For provocative remarks on the Confucian quotation from which this book title is taken, consult Yuan (1926), 8: 6a.

20. This discussion, which gives only a slight hint of the enormous complexity of fate extrapolation, is drawn primarily from Chao (1946); the Sanming tonghui; books attributed directly to Xu (see SKQSZM, 109: 26b ff.), and works inspired by him—notably Yuan (1919). I have also found Zhang (n. d.), pp. 168–217, and the summary article by Chen Yiqing in XSCL, 4: 70–131, extremely helpful.

21. For details, see Chao (1946), p. 297; cf. Yuan (1919), 5: 8a-b, 16a.

22. TSJC, yishu, 47: 6284 ff. For a convenient and well illustrated overview, see XSCL, 4: 69 ff.; also Morgan (1980), pp. 213–214, 240–241.

23. For additional detail, see Chao (1946), p. 310; cf. XSCL, 4: 70 ff.

24. See Yuan (1919), 4: 27a ff.; also Zhang (n.d.), pp. 195–198 and XSCL, 1: 63–100, 3: 150–172, and 4: 72.

25. This horoscope is one of over thirty collected by Yuan Shushan in 1915 from previous divinations. They cover the entire Chinese social spectrum, from former Qing civil and military officials to Buddhist monks. Significantly, Yuan includes several horoscopes for women. See Yuan (1919), 7: 1a-3a, esp. 2a; also 5: 20a ff., esp. 22b-23b.

26. Ibid., 7: 5a-6a. Cf. the discussion concerning wood and fire in Yuan (1948), 18: 9–10.

27. See Yuan (1919) 7: 11b–12b.

28. Ibid., 7: 19b–20b.

29. *Ibid.*, 7: 23a–23b; 7: 43b. Cf. the horoscope of ⌐ ang Xingwu in *ibid.*, 7: 19b–20b. Consult also QBLC, *fangji*, p. 110.

30. See Yuan (1919), 7: 20a (Zhang); 7: 27a–b (monk); 7: 24a–b (widow); 7: 22a–23a (older woman). On Yuan's medical background, consult Yuan (1926), 8: 1a ff.

31. Reproduced in Doré (1914–1933), vol. 4, figure 152; cf. QBLC, *fangji*, 106 and esp. 110. See also the last section of this chapter. For illustrations of the link between astrology and hexagram analysis, consult Chu and Sherrill (1976), pp. 7–57 and Sherrill and Chu (1977), pp. 71–177.

32. Yuan (1948), 6: 4–5; see also *ibid.*, 9: 20–21. In the same spirit, but with even greater ambition, a recent book by Xu Lewu entitled *Gujin mingren mingjian* (A Mirror into the Fate of Famous People, Past and Present) interprets the horoscopes of twenty-three emperors (and three empresses) from the late imperial period, as well as those of over a hundred notables from the time of Confucius up to the end of the Qing dynasty. Xu (1975).

33. Yuan (1919) 7: 22a–23a. See also the example of an unnamed widow, born in 1877, in *ibid.*, 7: 24a–b. Cf. SMTH, 7: 28b–29b (TSJC, *yishu*, 47: 6356) on the fate of women. For an excellent English-language discussion of the five kinds of variables mentioned, see Sydney Greenblatt in Richard Wilson, *et al.*, eds. (1979), p. 77; cf. Chu and Sherrill (1976) and De Kermadec (1983), passim.

34. *Guangxian tang daquan tongshu* (1819); cf. Dennys (1876), pp. 8–10.

35. See, for example, De Kermadec (1983), pp. 97–102; cf. Walters (1987), pp. 62 ff.

36. See Wang (1988), pp. 105–122. Chinese friends and informants have told me about many other related beliefs—for example, that people born in the year of the tiger are not supposed to witness marriages or births—but I cannot gauge how widely held such views are (or were).

37. Everyone in China, contends Justus Doolittle, "is said to be born under a certain animal, or to 'belong' to a certain animal. The Chinese usually express this idea by saying 'his animal is the rat,' or 'his animal is the monkey,' as the case may be." Doolittle (1865), 2: 342.

38. See R. J. Smith (1983), chapter 9, esp. pp. 204–207, on these points; also the flawed but interesting article by Mortier (1936).

39. See Walshe (1906), pp. 192 ff. Cf. Huon de Kermadec (1983), p. 97; Chang (1940), p. 24. The twelve cyclical animals were also among the beasts associated with the twenty-eight dominant constellations of the lunar lodges—each of which had its own identification with either the sun, the moon or one of the five "elements." Most had no connection to the correlative systems just mentioned. In addition, many Chinese believed that in any given sexegenary cycle each animal would be associated in turn with all of the five "elements" (one for every twelve years).

40. See Wang (1711), *fanli*, 1a; also Walshe (1906), pp. 198 ff., esp. pp. 202–204; Gray (1878), 2: 13; Nevius (1869), pp. 190–191; De Groot (1892–1910), 5: 919–920, 6: 1121–1124, and 1269. Cf. Morgan (1980), pp. 232 ff. Many Chinese believed that the *bazi* of a child determined the time at which he or she would encounter one or another of the dangerous "passes" in life stipulated in almanacs (see chapter 2). Chang (1940), p. 66. At least some diviners believed, moreover, that one's *bazi* could even overcome almanac stipulations regarding proper location and time. See Yuan (1948), 8: 5–6.

41. See Robert Hart's journal entry for January 25, 1865, in Smith, *et al.*, eds. (forthcoming). Cf. Yuan (1948), 4: 10–11 and the illuminating discussion by James Hayes in Johnson, *et al.*, eds. (1985), pp. 99–100.

42. De Groot (1892–1910), 3: 976; cf. Morgan (1980), pp. 232 ff. See also Wolf, ed. (1974), p. 214 and the views expressed by Huai Zhenxi in Yuan (1948), 8: 5–6. Not all

diviners placed such reliance on the "eight characters," however. Consult Li Tong in Yuan (1948), 1: 23.

43. See Doré (1914–1933), 1: 35 and 4: 326–327; also Walshe (1906), pp. 194–195. Burkhardt (1955), 3: 122 presents yet another scheme. Cf. Walters (1987), pp. 69–70 and Chang (1940), pp. 79–80.

44. For particulars, consult Zhang (1723), 1: 27a-b; Liang (1895), 1: 27a-b; Lü (1975), pp. 91 ff., esp. pp. 106–112, etc.; also Weiger (1913) pp. 453 ff.; Doré (1914–1933), 1: 29 ff., esp. 30–31; Doolittle (1865), 2: 344 ff.; Nevius (1869), pp. 188 ff. Cf. R. J. Smith in Liu, ed. (1990), esp. pp. 302–303.

45. Nevius (1869), p. 191.

46. See TSJC, *yishu*, 48: 7811. Apparently these individuals were often the ones who evaluated the "eight characters" of prospective brides and grooms. See Walshe (1906), pp. 186 ff.; also Doolittle (1865), 2: 344 ff. and James Hayes in Johnson, *et al.*, eds. (1985), pp. 98–99. According to the *Qingbai leichao*, some such diviners even gave advice on the best times for married couples to have intercourse in order to produce male children. QBLC, *fangji*, p. 81.

47. For a useful summary and brief analysis, consult Zhang (n.d.), pp. 10 ff., esp. pp. 12–13, and pp. 218 ff., esp. pp. 282–285; cf. TSJC, *yishu*, 48: 7136 ff., esp. 7231–7239 and 7810–78. See also the review of the *Liuren daquan* (Great Compendium of *Liuren*) in SKQSZM, 109: 18a–20b and the biographical entries for Mao Zhidao and You Ping in Yuan (1948), 1: 18 and 33: 13–14, respectively. According to Zhang Yaowen, from the standpoint of relative sophistication, *liuren* can be compared to the astrological calculations known popularly as *Ziwei doushu*; *qimen dunjia* to the Ziping method of fate extrapolation; and *taiyi* to the system of divination exposited in Shui Zhonglong's *Xingping huihai* (Comprehensive Astrology). Zhang (n.d.), pp. 10 ff., esp. 12–13 and 16–17.

48. See Doré (1914–1933), 4: 345. For other applications of the process, consult *ibid.*, 345–346. Cf. the categories of *qimen dunjia* divination discussed in TSJC, *yishu*, 47: 7347 ff. *Liuren* calculations, I might add, even found expression in vernacular literature, such as the late Qing novel *Jinghua yuan* (Flowers in the Mirror). See Kalinowski (1983), p. 383.

49. Arthur Smith (1914), p. 311. Doré (1914–1933), 1: 32, has a separate auspicious month for every animal, except the rooster and rabbit, both of whom should be married in the seventh month.

50. Doré (1914–1933), 4: 368.

51. See chapter 2, note 107; also Yuan Jianzhai cited in Doré (1914–1933), pp. 325, 364–365. On the question of ideological commitment, see the remarks of Johnston (1910), p. 412.

52. Ropp (1981), p. 172.

53. See his "Auspicious Marriages" in Eberhard (1970).

54. Hail (1927), p. 350; cf. Wenxiang (1971), 3: 43b, 3: 55a, etc. De Groot (1892–1910), 6: 1121–1124 discusses the popular belief that harm can be done to individuals by meddling with their "eight characters." See also Nevius (1869), pp. 166–167.

55. See esp. Yuan (1926), 5: 20b ff.; XSCL, 4: 15–32 and 132–197; also James Hayes in Johnson, *et al.*, eds. (1985), pp. 98–99; Walters (1987), pp. 69–70; Doré (1914–1933), 1: 30 ff.; Chang (1940), pp. 78 ff.; R. J. Smith (1986), p. 178; etc.

56. See, for example, QBLC, *fangji*, pp. 107–108.

57. See R. J. Smith in Liu, ed. (1990).

58. See, for example, *Chuxiong xianzhi* (Yunnan, 1909), *dili*, 2: 23b; *Liaoyang xianzhi* (Liaoning, 1918), *fengwu men*, *fengsu*, p. 30a.

59. Compare *Changsha xianzhi* (Hunan, 1810), *fengsu*, 14: 9a and *Guidong xianzhi* (Hunan, 1867), *fengsu*, 9: 5a.

60. Nevius (1869), pp. 166–167 and 188; Doolittle (1865), 2: 340–345; De Groot (1892–1910), 5: 919–920. See also Graham (1961), p. 135; Gray (1878), 2: 13–14; Douglas (1882), pp. 277–278; Dennys (1876), pp. 53–54; Arthur Smith (1914), pp. 310 and 320; James Hayes in Johnson, et al., eds. (1985), pp. 98–99; etc.

61. See De Groot (1892–1910), 6: 1333; cf. Nevius (1869), pp. 190–192; Arthur Smith (1914), p. 320.

62. Gray (1878), 2: 3. See also Dennys (1876), p. 63 and Lessa (1966), p. 10. I have found only about fifty explicit references to physiognomy as a specialty in gazetteer biographies, as against nearly five hundred for geomancy, and more than three hundred for the Yijing. See also notes 10 and 19 above.

63. See Yuan (1948), 18: 10–11 (Zeng), 30: 21–22 (Zhao) and 33: 8–9 (Shen); also Hummel (1943–1944), p. 495 (Li); . For some other illustrious individuals who practiced physiognomy, consult Yuan (1948), 3: 19 and 14: 27–28.

64. Zhang (n.d.), pp. 12–13 and 16–17 identifies both geomancy and physiognomy as forms of "observation" (xiang). For references to spirit, life force, and form, see TSJC, yishu, 47: 6537–6538, 6542, 6559–6560, 6579–6581, 6625–6626, etc.; cf. Doré (1914–1933), 4: 338–339. Although the Shenxiang quanbian is not reviewed in the SKQSZM, other similar works are. See SKQSZM, 109: 38a–39a; 111: 28b–29a.

65. For a useful summary and analysis of the Shenxiang quanbian, consult Kohn (1986); cf. Ho et al., eds. (1986). On the "logic of interpretation," see Lessa (1968), pp. 14–33. Not surprisingly, the Shenxiang quanbian often draws upon the vocabulary of landforms to explain the "terrain" of the body. See, for example, TSJC, yishu, 47: 6642.

66. See Lessa (1966), p. 28; also the proverbs in Arthur Smith (1914), pp. 306–307.

67. Arthur Smith (1914), p. 308, modified slightly.

68. Drawn from Lessa (1966), pp. 38–39; cf. TSJC, yishu, 47: 6542. The Shenxiang quanbian discusses wuxing correlations in several other sections. See, for example, ibid., 47: 6559–6560; cf. CSJCXB, 25: 145 ff., esp. 150.

69. Drawn from Lessa (1966), pp. 38–39; cf. TSJC, yishu, 47: 6542.

70. TSJC, yishu, 47: 6633–6636; cf. Lessa (1966), pp. 36–38 and Burkhardt (1955), 1: 93–94. Although the facial and other characteristics of all fifty animals are described in the text of the Shenxiang quanbian, it contains no illustrations of them.

71. For details, see Lessa (1966), p. 43.

72. Ibid., p. 44.

73. Ibid,, pp. 147–148 remarks on the absence in China of an astrologically grounded physiognomy comparable to that of the West, but Chinese physiognomy was more astrologically oriented than he supposes—particularly the so-called Mayi school. See TSJC, yishu, 47: 6623 and Kohn (1986), pp. 235–236. Cf. Doré (1914–1933), 4: 332–333.

74. TSJC, yishu, 47: 6556. See Lessa (1966), p. 46.

75. Lessa (1966), p. 46.

76. For details, consult ibid., p. 52. Kohn (1986), p. 253 provides another explanation of the relationship between the parts of the face or head and the "limits" of life.

77. TSJC, yishu, 47: 6566; cf. Lessa (1966), p. 59.

78. See TSJC, yishu, 47: 6566–6568; cf. Lessa (1966), pp. 55 ff. Dog, rat, chicken and rabbit eyes are not listed as separate categories in the Shenxiang quanbian.

79. For a convenient analysis of moles and other features of the head and face, see Lessa (1966), pp. 61–88.

80. Ibid., pp. 38–39; Arlington (1928), 7: 229. For various refinements, including seasonal and other variables, see TSJC, yishu, 47: 6642 ff., esp. 6657–6665.

81. Liu (1988), pp. 195–196.

82. Arlington (1928), 7: 229 makes this claim. See, however, CSJCXB, 25: 141; also TSJC, yishu, 47: 6645–6665, esp. 6662.

83. Yuan (1948), 1: 14; 1: 16; 1: 17; 1: 22–23; 1: 24; 1: 29; 2: 2; 2: 5; 2: 16; 2: 24; 3: 4; 3: 11; 3: 20; 4: 16–17; 5: 6–7; 5: 8; 5: 9; 5: 10; 5: 18–19; 5: 19–20; 5: 25–26; 5: 30–31; 6: 1; 6: 6; 6: 7–8; 7: 4; 7: 6; 8: 10–11; 8: 14; 8: 22–24; 10: 13–14; 11: 3; 11: 23; 12: 3–4; 12: 5; 12: 7; 12: 9; 12: 14; 12: 14–15; 12: 22–23; 12: 28; 12: 30–31; 13: 22; 13: 23; 13: 27–28; 13: 32; 13: 33; 15: 27; 15: 30; 15: 31; 16: 15; 16: 25–26; 16: 27; 16: 34; 17: 2; 17: 19; 17: 21; 17: 26; 17: 28–29; 18: 11–12; 18: 13; 18: 24; 18: 35; 18: 40; 19: 28–29; 20: 2; 21: 23; 21: 25; 21: 31; 21: 34; 21: 39; 22: 10; 22: 18; 22: 23; 22: 34; 23: 3; 23: 11; 24: 37; 25: 13; 25: 14; 25: 19–20; 25: 21–22; 26: 3; 26: 4; 26: 5; 26: 8; 26: 10; 28: 3; 28: 15; 29: 18; 29: 29; 29: 35; 30; 31: 3; 31: 7–8; 31: 16; 31: 26; 32: 3–4; 32: 5; 32: 9; 32: 13; 33: 5; 33: 8; 33: 11–12; 33: 14; 33: 24; 33: 24; 34: 24; 35: 6; 35: 6–7; 35: 8; 35: 9; 35: 11; 35: 23; 36: 3; 36: 5; 36: 7; 36: 9; 36: 11; 36: 12; 36: 22; 36: 26–27; 36: 28–29; 36: 29; 37: 6–7; 37: 7; 37: 11; 37: 14; 37: 14–15; 37: 15; 37: 19; 37: 23; 37: 29. Although women doctors constituted a special occupational class in Qing China, I have found no biographies of women physiognomers among the Han Chinese. On the other hand, among certain minority people, such as the Lolo in Sichuan, women physiognomers were apparently quite prevalent. See Graham (1961), p. 135.

84. *Pingyuan xianzhi* (Shandong, 1748), *fangji, juan* 8, p. 400 (Western pagination).

85. Liu (1988), pp. 194 ff. Some physiognomic handbooks, like medical texts, even advocated the examination of urine and feces. See, for example, CSJCXB, 25: 113–115.

86. See Ho, *et al.*, eds. (1986), pp. 128–129; cf. TSJC, *yishu*, 47: 6351 ff.

87. SKQSZM, 111: 51b–52b; cf. Liu (1988), pp. 213–223. For medical works in the TSJC and SKQS, consult Wong and Wu (1936), pp. 169 ff. See also Yuan (1948), 17: 2.

88. See Wong and Wu (1936), p. 38 and Unschuld (1985), pp. 68–73, 179–180, 195, 215, 218 ff., esp. pp. 263–276; also Shigehisa Kuriyama in Kawakita, ed. (1987), pp. 54–60; cf. Lessa 1968, pp. 14–33.

89. See Unschuld (1985), pp. 216–226 and 337–340; cf. De Groot (1892–1910), 6: 1024 ff., esp. 1051–1057, 1071–1089, and 1121–1124. Wong and Wu (1936), pp. 186–187 discuss the "non-medical" features of Qing prescriptions.

90. Note, however, the function of the hand in Religious Daoist healing rituals. Saso (1978a), pp. 218 ff., esp. 220–221.

91. Arlington (1928), 7: 175; cf. Doré (1914–1933), 4: 332–333.

92. TSJC, *yishu*, 47: 6619; cf. the proverb cited by Arthur Smith (1914), p. 308: "Small hands and large feet indicate a life of misfortune."

93. TSJC, *yishu*, 47: 6623; see also Lessa (1966), p. 90 and Arlington (1928), 7: 229–230; cf. chapter 4, note 59.

94. TSJC, *yishu*, 47: 6625; cf. Lessa (1966), pp. 90–92; Arlington (1928), 7: 232–233.

95. TSJC, *yishu*, 47: 6619–6625; CSJCXB, 25: 132–136. Cf. Lessa (1966), 95–111; also Arlington (1928), 7: 230–235. For a similar analysis of facial lines, see TSJC, *yishu*, 47: 6638–6639.

96. Arlington (1928), 8: 70–74.

97. Doré (1914–1933), 4: 374–379.

98. For details, see TSJC, *yishu*, 47: 6625–6632; Lessa (1966), pp. 111–115; Doré (1914–1933), 4: 333–334.

99. TSJC, *yishu*, 47: 6537.

100. See, for example, the sections entitled "Analyzing Women," "Song about Analyzing Women," and "Nine Bad Points in Women" in TSJC, *yishu*, 47: 6626–6632, 6642, etc. For a useful discussion of the dating of these and other texts, see Kohn (1986), esp. pp. 235, 248–249, 250, and 254–255.

101. See Arthur Smith (1914), p. 307, slightly modified; consult also Gray (1878), 2: 2–3. Cf. Sidney Greenblatt in Wilson, *et al.*, eds. (1979), pp. 80–81.

102. TSJC, *yishu*, 47: 6631.

103. Gray (1878), 2: 2–3; cf. Douglas (1882), pp. 281–284.

104. *Ibid.* (both sources). Cf. Nevius (1869), p. 190 and Doolittle (1865), pp. 332–333; Arlington (1928), passim.

105. On characterization in novels, see Robert Ruhlman in Wright (1964); note also the prominent role of physiognomers in several popular novels, including *Jin Ping Mei* (conventionally translated Golden Lotus).

106. Gray (1878), 2: 2; Doré (1914–1933), 4: 330, figure 155; Dennys (1876), p. 63.

107. QBLC, *fangji*, pp. 125–126; Hummel (1943–1944), p. 120. See also QBLC, *fangji*, pp. 118 ff., esp. pp. 121, 123, 124 and 125; R. J. Smith (1986), p. 166.

108. For some criticisms, consult QBLC, *fangji*, p. 129; also Doré (1914–1933), 4: 329 ff. For earlier critiques by Xunzi and others, see *ibid.*, pp. 334–338; cf. TSJC, *yishu*, 47: 6686–6687.

109. For details, see Lessa (1968), esp. pp. 189–194; also Arlington (1928), passim.

110. Yuan (1948), 7: 27. For additional evidence, consult Nevius (1869), p. 190.

111. See QBLC, *fangji*, pp. 118 ff., esp. p. 121.

112. See Yuan (1948), 32: 2–3 (Li Xuan); 18: 35 (Li Liuming); 28: 5–7 (Liu); 37: 10 (Qu); 1: 14–15 (Yang).

113. Yuan (1948), 17: 8–9. Here Teng follows Xunzi. See note 108 above. This moral emphasis can also be found in scholarly prefaces to various editions of the *Shenxiang quanbian*, such as the one of 1797 (Qian Tang).

114. Yuan (1948), 33: 5–6.

115. *Ibid.*, 14: 7–8.

116. See note 130 below; also the biography of Wang Quan in Yuan (1948), 10: 9 and the discussion by Wolfgang Bauer in Allan and Cohen, eds. (1979), pp. 84 ff. Dennys (1876), p. 62 discusses the Chinese practice of randomly selecting for analysis a character (rather than an entire phrase or sentence) from a book. He notes that characters with the "female" (*nü*) semantic indicator are generally considered unlucky because of the disproportionally large number of words with this indicator that have negative connotations.

117. See, for example, the preface to Zhou Lianggong's *Zichu* (Handling Characters) in CSJCXB, 25: 176.

118. The foregoing discussion of language is drawn primarily from R. J. Smith (1983), chapter 5. See also Barbara Ward in Jain, ed. (1977), esp. p. 190.

119. See Rawski (1979), pp. 141–143 on Chinese "word magic;" also chapter 2 note 40, chapter 3, note 23, and the articles by Lindy Li Mark and Wolfgang Bauer in Allan and Cohen, eds. (1979), esp. pp. 62–65 and 71–72. Cf. Doolittle (1865), 2: 167–170; De Groot (1890), pp. 246–247 and (1892–1910), 6: 1024 ff.

120. See Yuan (1948), 21: 3–4; cf. *ibid.*, 20: 29–30.

121. De Groot (1892–1910), 5: 918–920; 6: 1043 and 6: 1135–1136; cf. Walshe (1906), pp. 202–204; Yuan (1948) 27: 13–14.

122. Yuan (1948), 33: 5. For examples of a similar type of logic, see QBLC, *fangji*, p. 106 and esp. 110. On the bestowing of auspicious "fate names" (*mingming*), consult De Groot (1892–1910), 6: 1134.

123. TSJC, *yishu*, 48: 7832 ff., esp. 7835–7849; *Chaizi yi* (1801), preface; Yuan (1948), 27: 13–15. Cf. Wolfgang Bauer in Allan and Cohen, eds. (1979), p. 76.

124. See Zhou's book in CSJCXB, 25: 176–202 and his biography in Yuan (1948), 27: 13.

125. Yuan (1948), 35: 18; QBLC, *fangji*, pp. 90–91; etc. For a more extensive discussion of the possibilities, see Wolfgang Bauer in Allan and Cohen, eds. (1979), pp. 75 ff.

126. Yuan (1948), 7: 5 and De Groot (1890), p. 240.

127. Consult Yuan (1948), 27: 13–15; De Groot (1890), pp. 239–240; Williams (1883), 2: 261. For additional illustrations, see Yuan (1948), 3: 30–31, 4: 17; 5: 5–6, 7: 5, 7: 5–6; etc.; also the examples in Zhou Lianggong's *Zichu*, CSJCXB, 25: 177–201; *Chaizi yi* (1801), preface and passim; QBLC, *fangji*, pp. 91 ff.

128. Yuan (1948), 8: 26–27.

129. The verb for choosing a character was usually *nian*, lit. "to pick up with the fingers." The common forms for describing the process were: "Someone used the character 'x' to ask about 'y'," or "So-and-so wrote character 'x' and asked about it." See the many illustrations in Zhou Lianggong's *Zichu*, reprinted in CSJCXB, 25: 176 ff. Consult also De Groot (1890), p. 239; Gray (1878), 2: 4–5; Doolittle (1865), 2: 335–336.

130. See *Chaizi yi* (1801), passim.

131. Yuan (1948), 20: 29–30. Usually a client selected only a single word, but not always. See, for example, Yuan (1948), 4: 17. QBLC, *fangji*, p. 91 mentions a word analyst named Zhu, who charged one tael per character.

132. See Yuan (1948), 20: 29–30. Parents in traditional China often indulged in a rudimentary version of this practice by placing certain career-related objects in front of newly born children to see which one might first be touched or grasped.

133. Yuan (1948), 37: 9–10.

134. See, for example, Yuan (1948), 32: 3.

135. On the analysis of seals and names, see Zhang (n.d.), pp. 356 ff.; cf. QBLC, *fangji*, p. 118.

136. See chapter 2, note 59; also CSJCXB, 25: 5 ff. For a discussion of *fengjiao* and other forms of wind analysis, consult Ngo (1976), pp. 186–190; cf. Needham, 3: 432–433 and 4.1: 135–141.

137. Yuan (1948), 2: 9–10 (Shi); 7: 17–18 (Lin); 3: 7 (Qin); 4: 10–11 (Wang); and 24: 40 (Ding).

138. For two such disadvantaged individuals, see Yuan (1948), 21: 38–39 and 23: 7. Note also the case of Du Hui, a deaf fortune-teller, in *ibid.*, 28: 17. Presumably blind or deaf diviners had special credibility, since they could not make full use of conventional senses.

139. Gray (1878), 2: 3–4. The biographies in Yuan (1948) include a number of popular books from which aspiring fate extrapolators might learn. See for example, Gu Fengwei's use of the *Suanming jue* (Secrets of Fortune-telling), *ibid.*, 9: 20–21.

140. Nevius (1869), p. 187. See also Doolittle (1865), 2: 332.

141. Doolittle (1865), 2: 339 indicates that fate extrapolators charged from twenty to forty cash for simple divinations, about half the fee for *Yijing* divination by means of coins.

142. For details on professional women diviners and personal divination by women, consult chapter 6; also Wieger (1913), p. 242; Gray (1878), 2: 6–7; Graham (1961), p. 135; Doré (1914–1933), 4: 369 and 374.

143. Johnston (1913), p. 234. Cf. Gray (1878), 2: 1, 3–4.

144. For some evidence from Chinese sources, see QBLC, *fangji*, p. 48 and esp. p. 112; also Yuan (1948), 3: 30–31; 4: 17; 5: 5–6; 8: 28–29; 18: 39–40; 20: 29–30; 25: 18; 28: 5–7; 32: 3; and 35: 8. See also TSJC, *yishu*, 47: 6439 ff.

145. Doolittle (1865), 2: 339; Nevius (1869), pp. 186–187. See also Johnston (1913), p. 234; Doolittle (1865), 2: 333.

146. QBLC, *fangji*, p. 112.

147. See especially Sydney Greenblatt in Richard Wilson, *et al.*, eds. (1979) and Osgood (1975), 2: 861–863. Their observations and conclusions conform closely with my own field experience.

148. Doolittle (1865), 2: 339; Johnston (1913), p. 234; cf. Greenblatt in Richard Wilson, et al., eds. (1979), pp. 77–78, 83 ff.

149. See QBLC, fangji, pp. 100 and 133.

150. See the excellent discussion by Sydney Greenblatt in Richard Wilson, et al., eds. (1979), esp. pp. 86–87; also Osgood (1975), 2: 863.

151. See, for example, the case of Gao Dingyu in Yuan (1948), 2: 24; cf. Sydney Greenblatt in Richard Wilson, et al., eds. (1979), pp. 73, 89 ff.

152. See Changle xian xuzhi (Shandong, 1944), fangji, 35: 4a.

153. QBLC, fangji, p. 120; see also the case of Li Yinbo in ibid., p. 121.

154. See, for example, Yuan (1948), 38: 41–43. For other evidence of the affinity between Buddhism and physiognomy, consult QBLC, fangji, p. 124 and esp. p. 127; also Graham (1961), p. 136; Johnston (1913), p. 234 and Welch (1967), p. 121 and p. 483 note 31. Buddhist monks, including Tibetan lamas, also consulted physiognomers. See QBLC, fangji, p. 133.

155. Yuan (1948), 38: 41.

156. Yuan (1948), 17: 17–18 (Yu); 20: 4–5 (Xiong) and 6: 20 (Luo). Not all Buddhist diviners were physiognomers, of course. See, for example, the case of Chen Qing in Yuan (1948), 32: 13; also QBLC, fangji, p. 81.

157. QBLC, fangji, p. 104. See also ibid., pp. 105, 107, and esp. the case of Chen Wenqin, pp. 119–120.

158. QBLC, fangji, pp. 108–109. See, however, note 161 below.

159. On Needham's observation, consult SCC, 4.1: 326–330; cf. Yuan (1948), 6: 14; 17: 4; 32: 3; QBLC, fangji, p. 67. On shefou, see also TSJC, yishu, 48: 7830–7832. For examples of socializing between word analysts and scholars, consult Yuan (1948), 13: 33 and 14: 31–32.

160. For a small sample, see Yuan (1948), 1: 21–22; 3: 5–6; 3: 28; 5: 10; 12: 8–9; 14: 11–12; 14: 27–28; 15: 16; 25: 9; 19: 33–34; 21: 10; 32: 8–9; 36: 11; also QBLC, fangji, pp. 11, 17, 91–98, 103–106, 116, 119, 121–125, 127.

161. De Groot (1890), p. 241. Significantly, in the case cited above (note 158), the Qianlong emperor appointed astrologer Liu as a prefect in appreciation of his honesty and insight.

162. For a more detailed analysis, see Lessa (1966), pp. 189–195; cf. the categories in TSJC, yishu, 48: 7611 ff., ibid., 48: 7835 ff., and the inventory of topics reflected in QBLC, fangji, pp. 91–132.

163. Yuan (1948), 34: 24–25 (Yu); 21: 3–4 (Ji); 9: 20–21 (Gu). For a few other stories regarding the examination system, consult ibid., 2: 21–22, 2: 27; 3: 23; 3: 28–29; 5: 28–29; 7: 5; 12: 8–9; 14: 24–25; 15: 16; 17: 27; 18: 19–20; etc.

164. Yuan (1948), 12: 10 (Jin); 3: 19–20 (Lu) 9: 27 (Xia); 2: 3 (Zhang); 8: 5–6 (Huai).

165. See ibid., (1948), 12: 18 and 38: 41–42; also 38: 43 and QBLC, fangji, p. 124.

166. Yuan (1948), 27: 10. Cf. Liao Ming, the Buddhist monk who reportedly became a special diviner to the Qing royal family. Graham (1961), p. 136.

167. Yuan (1948), 16: 12.

168. Ibid., 18: 19.

169. Ibid., 19: 28–29 (Yang); 4: 25 (Xue); 3: 11 (Li Fengbao); 2: 25 (Xu). See also ibid., 14: 17 (Mao Jie), 17: 5 (Jin Peng), and 19: 26 (Wang Wenjing).

170. Yuan (1948), 18: 36 (Yang); 27: 15 (Xu); 36: 12 (Gong). Note also the prediction of Hu Yuanjing, ibid., 17: 21. Fortune-tellers played a more active role under Li Zicheng, who employed them as spies. See Wakeman (1985), 1: 258.

171. Yuan (1948), 12: 17; for other accounts of this sort of expertise, consult ibid, 1: 20 (on Xu Changling); 2: 1–2 (Wu Guhuai); 12: 17 (Yu Lifang); 16: 33 (Chen Luzhang);

20: 4–5 (Xiong Deqian); 21: 34 (Gao Feng); 22: 25–26 (Gao Deliang); and 23: 18 (Li Shuang).

172. *Ibid.*, 13: 17.

173. *Ibid.*, 5: 12–14. See also *ibid.*, 5: 12–14; 5: 18–19; 12: 11; 12: 6–17; etc.

174. *Ibid.*, 35: 8.

175. See, for example, *ibid.*, 12: 17; 36: 6; etc.

176. *Ibid.*, 36: 12.

177. *Ibid.*, 18: 40 (Yuan); 19: 33 (He); 16: 8 (Luo). On Shen, see *ibid.*, 2: 14–15. We are not told why the character *ying* came to be chosen. See also QBLC, *fangji* p. 76.

178. Yuan (1948), 33: 22–23; see also 14: 27–28; QBLC, *fangji* pp. 79, 84–85.

179. See, for example, QBLC, *fangji* p. 131.

180. *Ibid.*, pp. 132–133.

181. See Yuan (1948), 18: 10–11 (Zeng); 18: 21 (Gao); also *ibid.* 14: 25.

182. Yuan (1948), 4: 25–26; 13: 18–19. See also QBLC, *fangji*, p. 130–131.

183. See, for example, Yuan (1948), 1: 22; 4: 10–11; 4: 12–13; 7: 17–18; 12: 2–3; 14: 8; 15: 9; 16: 12; 17: 11; 17: 19; 18: 36–37; 31: 13; 37: 28; 37: 9–10.

184. See Tao Luzi's *Yunqi zhanhou* (Divination by Cloud Vapors) in CSJCXB, 25: 11–16; also SKQSZM, 110: 29a ff. and 111: 40a ff. Cf. Zhang (n.d.), pp. 282–308 and Xu (1986) passim. Technically, *qimen dunjia*, *liuren* and *taiyi* were three separate methods of fate calculation, but all utilized the same basic set of cosmic variables, and all sought to "avoid misfortune and hasten toward good luck" (*bixiong quji*) through the selection of proper times, locations and directions for various activities. See Xu (1986), p. 1; TSJC, *yishu*, 48: 7810–7812, esp. 7811.

185. Yuan (1948), 11: 1 (Jin); 32: 14 (Chen); 36: 6 (Dong). See also the military contributions of Wang You in *ibid.*, 13: 13.

186. *Ibid.*, 31: 13 (Shi); 32: 8–9 (Chen).

187. QBLC, *fangji*, p. 91 (Zhu); Yuan (1948), 18: 4–5 (Liu) and 20: 8 (Xiong). For Wu's use of diviners, see *ibid.*, 18: 15; 33: 11; also QBLC, *fangji*, pp. 67–68 and 91.

188. Yuan (1948), 18: 36–37. See also chapter 3, note 100 and the cases of Sun Zhi and Chen Yuanchang in *ibid.*, 21: 13 and 23: 6, respectively.

189. Yuan (1948), 17: 23 (Dai); 17: 19 (Xie).

190. Yuan (1948), 25: 9. See also QBLC, *fangji*, pp. 84–85 and De Groot (1903), p. 430.

191. Yuan (1948), 13: 26.

192. *Ibid.*, 17: 19 (Xie); 1: 30 (Kong); 17: 11 (Xu). See also *ibid.*, 26: 5.

193. Doré (1970), pp. 101, 103; Yuan (1948), 13: 18–19.

194. Yuan (1948), 1: 22 (Zhao); 38: 9 (Li).

195. See, for example, *ibid.*, 19: 36–38 and 24: 20; also QBLC, *fangji*, pp. 87 and 113. For "official" Taiping attitudes toward lucky and unlucky days, consult R. J. Smith (1988), p. 133.

196. Yuan (1948), 21: 26.

197. *Ibid.*, 13: 22.

198. See Lebra, ed., (1976), pp. 174–176; Kleinman, *et al.*, eds., (1978), pp. 314–319; Tseng and Wu, eds., (1985), pp. 72–73; Kleinman and Lin, eds., (1981), pp. 101–106. For other examples of this role as performed by diviners in the Qing period, consult Yuan (1948), 2: 12–13; 4: 10; 18: 36; 19: 25; 27: 15; 36: 12; etc.

199. Yuan (1948), 8: 22–24. Ironically, not long thereafter the rebels captured Ling, wanting to make use of his mantic skills. He refused, however, and was himself executed.

200. *Ibid.*, 17: 26. For some other negative prophecies, consult *ibid.*, 7: 5–6, 12: 10; 12: 14; 13: 9–10; 13: 17; 13: 26; 13: 33; 15: 10; 20: 12; 20: 23–24; 21: 24; 33: 22–23; 36: 23; 37: 9–10; 38: 41–42. See also QBLC, *fangji*, pp. 97, 101, 120, 123, 124, 126, etc.

201. Yuan (1948), 3: 2; 21: 19–20.

202. Wakeman (1985), 1: 289. For examples of other "strange" diviners, see Yuan (1948), 1: 14–15; 2: 13; 2: 23; 3: 2; 3: 8–9; 5: 25; 7: 27–29; 9: 13–14; 13: 13; 17: 11; 18: 10; 18: 12; 18: 24; 18: 36–37; 18: 38; 19: 26; 19: 36; 21: 22; 22: 1–2; 24: 37; 25: 14; 26: 6; 28: 5–7; 32: 9; 36: 19; 37: 10.

203. *Ibid.*, 13: 13. This seems obviously to have been a case of blackmail perpetrated by unscrupulous associates of the deceased client. After losing his money, Huang quit his profession and burned his books in anger and disgust.

204. QBLC, *fangji*, pp. 126–127.

205. Yuan (1948), 17: 28.

206. *Ibid.*, 18: 19–20.

207. Yang (1961), pp. 232 ff., esp. 236–237. For examples of predictions regarding the founding of the Qing and similar prophecies, see QBLC, *mixin*, pp. 46 ff.; Yuan (1948), 3: 21; 18: 15; QBLC, *fangji*, pp. 3–4, 62; Wakeman (1985), 1: 258; Wu (1990), p. 175; Jordan and Overmyer (1986), pp. 44–45, 93–94, etc.

208. QBLC, *fangji*, p. 3.

209. *Ibid.* For information on this method, see *ibid.*, p. 61.

210. *Ibid.*, p. 5.

211. Arthur Smith (1914), p. 327; cf. Yang (1961), pp. 235–236. The Tibetans had their own analogue to the *Tuibei tu*. See QBLC, *fangji*, pp. 2–3.

212. Arthur Smith (1914), pp. 329–338. The London School of Oriental and African Studies has a handwritten and illustrated, but undated and otherwise unidentified, version of this work.

213. QBLC, *fangji*, pp. 4–5.

214. *Ibid.*, pp. 7–8. For background, consult Goodrich, ed. (1976), p. 62; Yang (1961), p. 236. Arthur Smith (1914), pp. 333–336 discusses late Qing "discoveries" of prophetic works.

215. Arthur Smith (1914), pp. 334–335.

216. See Naquin (1976), pp. 9 ff., esp. pp. 16–17; also the essay by Susan Naquin in Johnson, *et al.*, eds. (1985) and Yang (1961), pp. 232 ff.

217. See, for example, *ibid.*, esp. pp. 15, 18, 26, 31, etc.; also R. J. Smith in Liu, ed. (1990), pp. 303 ff.

Chapter 6

1. See the interesting and illuminating discussion in Chard (1982), pp. 9–14. For background, consult chapters 2, 3 and 5.

2. Chan (1986a), p. 167, slightly modified; cf. *Lunyu*, 6: 20.

3. Chan (1986a), p. 164; cf. Zhou Yuanding in JSWXB, 61: 2a–3a and Xu Dachun in Unschuld (1985), pp. 337–340. The perspective that gods, ghosts and monsters were simply "creations of the mind" seems to have been a distinctly minority view, even among members of the Qing elite.

4. See JSWXB, 61: 2b ff. and JSWB, 68: 1a ff.; cf. the illuminating official proclamation by the acting governor-general of Min-Zhe, cited in Doolittle (1872), pp. 516–518.

5. See R. J. Smith in Liu, ed. (1990), esp. pp. 297 and 308.

6. See De Groot (1892–1910), 6: 1242; also De Groot (1903), pp. 115 and 265–266; Doolittle (1872), pp. 516–518.

7. Wu (1832), 9: 10a; cf. De Groot (1892–1910), 6: 988–990. On state worship, see R. J. Smith in Liu, ed. (1990).

8. Xu (1941), p. 32; see also Woodside in Liu, ed. (1990).

9. This distinction is discussed in Sutton (1981), p. 40. There were, of course, suppressions prior to the Song period.

10. See the excellent treatment of shamans in Sutton (1981, 1981a, 1990, 1990a) and Sutton in Barnes and Stearns, eds. (1989). Cf. De Groot (1903), pp. 115 and 265–266; Doolittle (1872), 2: 516–518. Yuan (1948) ignores shamanistic diviners entirely.

11. Sutton (1981, 1981a, 1990 and 1990a); also Sutton in Barnes and Stearns, eds. (1989); Tseng Wen-shing in Kleinman, *et al.*, eds., pp. 178–180 and Yih-Yuan Li in Lebra, ed. (1972), passim.

12. De Groot (1892–1910), 6: 1245–1253 describes the process and the effort by the Qing authorities to monitor it; cf. Macgowan (1909), pp. 100–104. De Groot blurs distinctions between writing mediums, speaking mediums, exorcists, and mediums for the dead, but authorities such as Elliot (1955) and Jordan (1972) note that Chinese populations in modern Singapore and Taiwan differentiate between them. See also the distinctions noted in Chen (1962), 2: 258–259. One major difference between Daoists and shamanistic mediums is that the former use written texts (scriptures) and the latter do not.

13. They were also known as *jitong*, "divining fellows;" *tongji*, "fellow diviners;" etc. Often, but not invariably, such individuals were young—hence the common translations "divining youths" or "youthful diviners."

14. De Groot (1892–1910), 6: 1270–1271.

15. *Ibid.*, 6: 1721; cf. Gary Seaman in Kleinman and Lin (1981), pp. 70–72; Jordan (1972), pp. 67 ff., esp. pp. 73–74 and 85; Gallin (1966), pp. 242–244.

16. De Groot (1892–1910), 6: 1257; 1271–1272; 1278–1279.

17. In sessions involving self-mortification, a client might pay 500 cash for a single knife wound.

18. De Groot (1892–1910), 6: 1272; also QBLC, *fangji*, p. 42.

19. Sutton (1981), p. 43; QBLC, *fangji*, p. 29.

20. QBLC, *fangji*, p. 34; Graham (1961), pp. 104–105; cf. Sutton (1981), pp. 45–46; see also Eberhard (1968), pp. 303 ff.

21. See De Harlez (1887), pp. 26–29, also pp. 71 ff.

22. See, for example, *Ning'an (Songjiang) xianzhi* (Jilin, 1924), *fengsu, gusu,* 4: 6b; also QBLC, *fangji*, p. 29; cf. De Groot (1892–1910), 6: 1332.

23. *Yongxin xianzhi* (Jiangxi, 1874), *dili, fengsu,* 4: 24b; also 4: 25a.

24. *Dengfeng xianzhi* (Henan, n. d.), *fengtu ji,* 9: 6a. See also *Taoyuan xianzhi* (Hunan, 1892), *fengsu,* 1: 1a; *Suichang xianzhi* (Zhejiang, 1896), *fengsu,* p. 1191 (Western pagination), etc. Cf. the generalizations in Sutton (1981 and 1990).

25. Sutton (1981), p. 42–43.

26. *Ibid.*, pp. 41–42, modified.

27. See, for example, De Groot (1892–1910), 6: 981–990; 1256–1257; 1276–1284; 1292–1293; etc. For other Western accounts, consult Gray (1878), 2: 17–20; Macgowan (1909), pp. 104–105; etc.

28. De Groot (1892–1910), 6: 1121–1122, 1269–1270.

29. *Ibid.*, 6: 1278 provides an example.

30. *Ibid.*, 6: 1272–1274.

31. *Ibid.*, 6: 1257–1263; 1275–1285; 1306; etc.; see also Graham (1961), pp. 104–105; Gray (1878), 2: 17–21. In a recent personal communication, David Jordan observed that "in a long settled and densely settled area, one might expect to find a wide range of religious specialists with a fairly stabilized division of labor among them. In a more thinly settled area, it would make sense that only a smaller number of specialists could be sustained."

32. De Groot (1892–1910), 6: 1275–1285 and 1288–1289.

33. See Dennys (1876), pp. 57–58; cf. De Groot (1892–1910), 6: 1321–1322.

34. Xu (1941), p. 32; QBLC, *fangji*, p. 28.

35. De Groot (1892–1910), 6: 1297 and 1301; cf. Doolittle (1865), 2: 112–114; Graham (1961), p. 103; Gray (1878), 2: 21–22.

36. For other terms and distinctions, consult QBLC, *fangji*, p. 14.

37. See De Groot (1892–1910), 6: 1295 ff.; cf. Douglas (1882), pp. 285–288; Dennys, pp. 58–59; Doolittle (1865), 2: 110–114; Gray (1878), 2: 21–22; Douglas (1882), pp. 285–288; etc. As a rule, spirit-writers were not possessed in the same powerful way as other mediums.

38. See Xu (1941), pp. 42 and 44.

39. *Ibid.*, p. 31; QBLC, *fangji*, p. 20–21.

40. For illustrations of these points, see Xu (1941), pp. 33 and passim, esp. pp. 59–60; also QBLC, *fangji*, p. 15.

41. See Xu (1941), pp. 47–48. For other examples of this sort of word analysis, consult QBLC, *fangji*, esp. pp. 15–19, 21–22, 26, etc.; also Xu (1941), esp. pp. 32 ff.

42. De Groot (1892–1910), 6: 1307–1308; Xu (1941), p. 21; Gray (1878). 2: 21–22.

43. De Groot (1892–1910), 6: 1300; Doolittle (1865), 2: 112.

44. For details on *fuji* books consult Jordan and Overmyer (1986), pp. 45–63; cf. De Groot (1892–1910), 6: 1313–1314.

45. See the breakdown in Xu (1941), pp. 32 ff.

46. See, for example, Xu (1941), p. 44; QBLC, *fangji*, pp. 17 and 19; also Jordan and Overmyer (1986), pp. 41–44.

47. See Hummel (1943–1944), p. 905; also Gray (1878), 1: 145.

48. Giles (1912), pp. 433–435.

49. See, for example, QBLC, *fangji*, p. 15; also Jordan and Overmyer (1986), pp. 43–44.

50. Jordan and Overmyer (1986), p. 42, citing Xu (1941), p. 63; slightly modified.

51. QBLC, *fangji*, p. 19; cf. Xu (1941), p. 95 cited in Jordan and Overmyer (1986), p. 44.

52. See, for example, QBLC, *fangji*, p. 22.

53. Xu (1941), p. 33. Like a number of Xu's anecdotes, this story is included in QBLC, *fangji*, See *ibid.*, p. 16. For other stories of this kind, consult *ibid.*, pp. 16–18, 22; Xu (1941), pp. 33–36.

54. For details, consult De Groot (1892–1910), 6: 1299–1300 and 1316–1318. See also QBLC, *fangji*, pp. 22–26 and Xu (1941), pp. 66–73, passim.

55. De Groot (1892–1910), 6: 1302–1306; Unschuld (1985), pp. 226–228. Cf. Macgowan (1909), pp. 105 ff.

56. See De Groot (1892–1910), 6: 1323 ff., esp. 1330–1341; also QBLC, *fangji*, pp. 29 and 32; Eberhard (1968), pp. 304 ff.; Doolittle (1865), 2: 110–116; Jack Potter in Wolf, ed. (1974); Doolittle (1865), 2: 114–116; etc.

57. Jordan and Overmyer (1986), pp. 38–39, 42 and Xu (1941), 10–11, 16–18. For additional background, consult De Groot (1892–1910), 6: 1323–1329.

58. See, for example, *Taoyuan xianzhi* (Hunan, 1892), *fengsu*, 1: 2b; also *Linyi xianzhi* (Shandong, 1917), *fengsu*, 3: 1b–2a; *Yicheng xianzhi* (Hubei, 1866), *yudi zhi*, 1: 4a; cf. *Sihui xianzhi* (Guangdong, 1841), *fengsu*, 1: 66b.

59. See Doré (1970), pp. 105–106; De Groot (1892–1910), 6: 1335–1336.

60. See the analysis by Jack Potter in Wolf, ed. (1974), esp. pp. 228–231.

61. Doolittle (1865), 2: 115, mentions a cost of only two and a half cents per person, about fifteen cash. Rice, like blood, had apotropaic properties.

62. De Groot (1892–1910), 6: 1332–1336; Gray (1878), 2: 22–23; Dennys (1876), pp. 59–61; Doolittle (1865), 2: 116–117; Nevius (1869), pp. 166–167. See also Potter in Wolf, ed. (1974) and Jordan and Overmyer (1986), p. 85.

63. Doolittle (1865), 2: 114–115; see also QBLC, *fangji*, pp. 42–43. Cf. *ibid.*, pp. 41–42.

64. Nevius (1869), p. 167.

65. See Sutton (1981a), p. 17; Sutton (1981), p. 43; and Sutton in Barnes and Stearns, eds. (1989), pp. 108–109. Cf. QBLC, *fangji*, p. 39; JSWB, 68: 1a ff., esp. 8b–10a; and Doolittle (1872), 2: 516–518.

66. See in particular Jordan (1972), pp. 82–86; Sutton (1990), pp. 99–100; and Sutton in Barnes and Stearns, eds. (1989), pp. 108–109 and 111. On *mingjiao*, consult R. J. Smith in Liu, ed. (1990).

67. See, for example, QBLC, *fangji*, pp. 29–54, passim; also Graham (1961), pp. 104–105; Nevius (1869), p. 167; Dennys (1876), pp. 61–62; Doolittle (1865), 2: 114–115; De Groot (1892–1910), 6: 1338–1340.

68. Doolittle (1872), 2: 516–518.

69. See De Groot (1892–1910), 6: 1308; cf. Sutton in Barnes and Stearns, eds. (1989), pp. 112–113 and 116–118.

70. See, for example, QBLC, *fangji*, p. 16.

71. Yang (1961), p. 261; cf. William Hinton cited in R. J. Smith (1986), p. 178.

72. See, for example, the case noted in Xu (1941), p. 95.

73. Jordan and Overmyer (1986), pp. 44–45.

74. *Ibid.*, pp. 32, 36, etc.; see also Weller (1987), pp. 156–158; De Groot (1892–1910), 6: 1319 ff.; Naquin (1976), p. 292, note 44.

75. See Sutton (1981), pp. 47–48 and esp. Sutton in Barnes and Stearns, eds. (1989), passim.

76. See Bernard Gallin in Kleinman, *et al.*, eds. (1975), p. 277; also Barbara Ward in Jain, ed. (1977), esp. p. 196 and Tanaka Issei in Johnson, *et al.*, eds. (1985).

77. See, for example, the case of Shen Zinan, cited in Sutton (1981a), pp. 16–17.

78. See Unschuld (1985), pp. 223 ff.; Tseng Wen-shing in Kleinman, *et. al.*, eds. (1975); Yih-Yuan Li in Lebra, ed. (1972); etc. Sutton in Barnes and Stearns, eds. (1989), pp. 114 ff. makes a strong case for the social value of "ritual reversal" on the part of shamans.

79. See Gary Seaman in Kleinman and Lin (1981), pp. 61 ff., esp. pp. 71–72; also Jordan (1972), p. 85. Cf. Jordan and Overmyer (1986), pp. 274–276.

80. See, for example, the views of Zeng Guofan cited in Hail (1927), p. 345.

81. See, for example, the vivid account of one such ritual in Gray (1878), 2: 15; also Douglas (1882), pp. 274–275. For a similar rural response, consult Wieger (1913), p. 439.

82. See QBLC, *mixin*, pp. 46 ff.

83. For some late Qing accounts of everyday omens, consult, for example, Dennys (1876), pp. 33 ff. and Doolittle (1865), 2: 321 ff.; see also Doré (1914–1933), 4: 370–373 and Doré (1970), pp. 96–98.

84. Of the several dozen Qing almanacs that I have consulted—most dating from the 1820s to the early 1900s—the vast majority contain such categories and virtually identical interpretations. See, for example, the *Liwen tang zouji tongshu* (Almanac for Selecting Good Fortune from the Hall of Beneficial Literature; 1876).

85. See note 84 above; cf. Doré (1914–1933), 4: 370–373 and Dennys (1876), pp. 33–34.

86. Dennys (1876), p. 2; cf. *ibid.*, pp. 33 ff.

87. According to Doolittle (1865), 2: 107, the blocks were generally made of wood if for private homes and bamboo root if for temples. Cf. QBLC, *mixin*, p. 9. For additional background, consult Rong (1969), p. 53; Doré (1914–1933), 4: 353–355; and Yuan (1948), 2: 7.

88. De Groot (1892-1910), 6: 1285-1286; Doolittle (1872), 2: 504-505. Cf. Jordan (1972), pp. 61-63—especially his discussion of an awareness of statistical probability, at least on the part of modern Chinese. It is not clear to me whether there was such an awareness in Qing times, although there probably was.

89. On the pervasive use of divining blocks in these and other contexts, consult Doolittle (1865), 2: 108; De Groot (1892-1910), 6: 1282, 1285-1287, 1321; Gutzlaff (1856), pp. 85, 88, 91; Welch (1967), p. 155; Yuan (1948), 2: 7; etc. Cf. Jack Potter in Wolf, ed., pp. 217-218. In Chinese villages divining blocks are still used to select members of temple committees and for other similar purposes.

90. Doré (1914-1933), 4: 354; Doolittle (1872), 2: 504-505; cf. Kulp (1925) p. 297. Some almanacs also provided this information.

91. Doolittle (1872), 2: 505-506, modified. *Ibid.*, pp. 505-507, provides a complete list of readings. Cf. *Guanyin qian* (c. 1800), pp. 28a ff.

92. Graham (1961), p. 136; cf. Roe (1910), pp. 323-324 and Kulp (1925), p. 297.

93. Doolittle (1865), 2: 106-109; De Groot (1892-1910), 6: 1321. See also the discussion of *qian* slips below.

94. For a useful discussion of the spread and significance of *qian* techniques, consult Morgan (1987), esp. p. 166. See also Pas (1984), pp. 11 ff.

95. See, for example, Nevius (1869), pp. 103-105; also Gutzlaff (1856), pp. 85, 88, 91.

96. For details, see Rong (1969), pp. 43-44.

97. See QBLC, *mixin*, pp. 10-13.

98. See, for example, Nevius (1869), pp. 104-105; also QBLC, *mixin*, p. 9; Rong (1969), pp. 44 and 52; Morgan (1987), pp. 183-184.

99. SKQSZM, 111: 26a-b.

100. Rong (1969), pp. 48 ff.; cf. Morgan (1987), pp. 166 ff.; Banck (1976), pp. ii-vii. Oracle slips are generally considered to be *fuji* products.

101. Rong (1969), p. 44, provides a convenient breakdown of various sets. See also Banck (1976 and 1985); also Pas (1984).

102. See Rong (1969), p. 51 for details; cf. Doré (1914-1933), 4: 350.

103. For accounts of the process, consult Doolittle (1865), 2: 108-110; Doré (1914-1933), 4: 349-352; Dennys (1876), pp. 62-63; Graham (1961), pp. 136-138; etc. Cf. Rong (1969), pp. 46-50; Morgan (1987); Jordan (1972), pp. 63-64; Wolfram Eberhard in Eberhard, ed. (1970), pp. 191 ff.; Welch (1967), p. 212; Jin Hsu in Lebra (1972); Pas (1984) and Banck (1976 and 1985).

104. Eberhard, ed. (1970), pp. 195-196; cf. Rong (1969), p. 47.

105. Welch (1967), pp. 121, 155 and 483 note 31; also C. Gutzlaff (1856), p. 85. Generally speaking, tips were more substantial if the news was good.

106. See the discussion in Rong (1969), pp. 44 ff., esp. 49-51.

107. See, for example, QBLC, *mixin*, pp. 10-13; also Eberhard, ed. (1970), pp. 191-193 and Rong (1969), pp. 43 ff.

108. Eberhard, ed. (1970), p. 193; Rong (1969), pp. 44 ff.

109. In modern handbooks these designations are sometimes printed in black, while the rest might be printed in auspicious red.

110. See Rong (1969), pp. 44-45. Cf. Banck (1985), pp. 270 ff.

111. Rong (1969), pp. 44-45.

112. *Ibid.*, p. 46.

113. Jin Hsu in Lebra, ed. (1972), pp. 213-214; cf. Pas (1984), pp. 15 ff.; also Whalen Lai in Buswell, ed. (1990), p. 178 and note 105 above. A cynic might say that it was in the economic self-interest of the temple (or interpreter) to give good news.

114. Wen-Shin Tseng in Kleinman, *et al.*, eds. (1978), p. 315 cites a recent Taiwan survey indicating that half of the more than 700 *qian* diviners patronizing three urban

temples in a one week period were illiterate, and that the rest had "at best" a grade-school education.

115. I am certain, however, that some such written explanations also existed in the Qing. See Rong (1969), pp. 48-50.

116. It also corresponds verbatim with the excerpts cited by Rong (1969), p. 48. See discussion below.

117. *Guan shengdijun wanying lingqian* (1793), 2: 5a.

118. *Guanyin qian* (c. 1800).

119. Cf. Rong (1969), p. 48.

120. See Wilhelm (1967), pp. 48-55 and 440-450.

121. Rong (1969), pp. 44 ff., esp. 51.

122. On these common categories, also found in some Qing almanacs, see the introductory sections of the *Guanyin qian* (c. 1800).

123. Wong and Wu (1936), pp. 188-189 provide several excellent examples; see also Rong (1969), pp. 44 and 52 and Morgan (1987), pp. 183-184.

124. Cf. Doolittle (1872), 2: 504-507.

125. See the illuminating discussion of different emphases in Rong (1969), pp. 48-52; cf. Morgan (1987), pp. 175-183; Jin Hsu in Lebra, ed. (1972), esp. pp. 213 ff.

126. For contemporary studies, consult Jin Hsu in Lebra, ed. (1972); also Wen-Shing Tseng in Kleinman, et al., eds. (1978), pp. 314-316.

127. In contemporary Taiwan about eighty percent of the people who visit religious temples for the purpose of *qian* divination are women. Constraints on the mobility of women today are, of course, far less severe than they were in the Qing period. Nonetheless, I would guess that the ratio of women to men petitioners was roughly the same in both periods.

128. Perhaps the religious environment of the temple made male-female interactions of this type more comfortable than they would normally be in Qing society, but it was precisely this sort of contact that made elites so critical of temple-centered popular culture.

129. See Jin Hsu in Lebra, ed. (1972), p. 212.

130. See Arthur Kleinman in Kleinman, et al., eds. (1979), p. 349, modified.

131. *Ibid.* Kleinman provides several illustrations of the negotiating process.

132. See Doolittle (1865), 2: 333-334.

133. Shuck (1853), pp. 72-73. Cf. Yuan (1948), 19: 38; Dennys (1876), p. 63; Nevius (1869), p. 189. Doolittle (1865), 2: 339 indicates that bird divinations usually cost between four and six cash.

134. Gray (1878), 2: 6.

135. Yuan (1948), 19: 38. Cf. Doolittle (1872), 2: 504-507.

136. Gray (1878), 2: 6; Nevius (1869), p. 189.

137. For an example, see Gray (1878), 2: 6.

138. See Jin Hsu in Lebra, ed. (1972); also Wen-Shing Tseng in Kleinman, et al., eds. (1978), pp. 314-317; Arthur Kleinman in Kleinman, et al., eds. (1979), pp. 347 ff. and Yang (1961), pp. 262-263.

139. See Jin Hsu's illuminating comparison of Chinese and Western psychotherapy in Lebra, ed. (1972), pp. 219-220.

140. *Ibid.*, p. 217; slightly modified. See also Wen-Shing Tseng in Kleinman, et al., eds. (1978), pp. 314-317; Arthur Kleinman in Kleinman, et al., eds. (1975), pp. 351-352; and Yang (1961), pp. 262-263.

141. For examples of these and other such forms of divination, consult Doolittle (1865), 2: 330; Doré (1914-1933), 4: 369; QBLC, *fangji*, pp. 62, 67; QBLC, *mixin*, pp. 5, 9-10, 40, etc.

142. QBLC, *fangji*, p. 55; cf. Doré (1970), p. 105. Giles (1912), p. 806 defines *yuanguang* as "a medium, especially one who pretends to discover a thief or other evil-doer by a process of magical incantations, etc." The term also refers generally to the gift of "second sight." *Ibid.*, p. 1697.

143. See, for example, QBLC, *fangji*, pp. 56–58.

144. *Ibid.*, p. 55.

145. See, for example, *ibid.*, pp. 55–59 and 72–73.

146. Gray (1978), 2: 6–7. Apparently this was usually done without the assistance of professional mediums.

147. Doolittle (1865), 2: 130.

148. Cited in Ong (1985), p. 41.

149. QBLC, *mixin*, pp. 75, 79, 86, 87, 89, 95, 96, 106, 119, 120.

150. Both anecdotes are related in Ong (1985), pp. 42–44. I have modified the translations slightly. For discussions of similar Chinese dream centers in more recent times, consult Drege (1981) and Thompson (1988).

151. QBLC, *fangji*, p. 80.

152. See SKQSZM, 111: 54b–55a.

153. CC, 4: 309, modified.

154. *Ibid.*, 4: 306, modified.

155. Cited in Ong (1985), p. 145, slightly modified.

156. See, for example, the *Mengshu* (Book of Dreams) by Wang Zhaoyuan (1763–1851). Hummel (1943–1944), p. 278. On the background of Chinese dream works up to Qing times, consult Michel Strickmann in Brown, ed. (1988); also Ong (1985), passim, esp. pp. 2–5, 11–20, 35–36, 40–41, and 74–108; Chard (1982), pp. 33 ff.; SKQSZM, 111: 53b–55a.

157. Ong (1985), pp. 130–143; Chard (1982), pp. 34 ff. and pp. 50–51. See also the *Mengzhan yizhi* in CSJCXB, 25: 324–325.

158. Giles (1912), p. 967; cf. Ong (1985), p. 59.

159. QBLC, *mixin*, p. 84.

160. See, for example, the *Yuxia ji guangji*, 6: 20a; cf. Eberhard (1971), p. 81.

161. See Michel Strickmann in Brown, ed. (1988), pp. 29–31; also Ong (1985), pp. 53–54 and Chard (1982), pp. 44–50.

162. See *Yuxia ji guangji*, 6: 20a; cf. Veith (1949), p. 163. A portion of this passage is included in Zhou Fujing's *Zhanyan lu* (Record of Fulfilled Divinations), CSJCXB, 25: 7.

163. Ong (1985), p. 51. Ong provides additional examples of the relationship between physiology and dreams from the *Lingshu jing*, together with a detailed analysis of the *wuxing* correlations involved, pp. 52–53; cf. the *Mengzhan yizhi* in CSJCXB, 25: 325.

164. Giles (1912), p. 967.

165. For these and the traditional numerical correlations that accompany them—both attributed to Zhu Xi—consult the *Mengzhan yizhi* in CSJCXB, 25: 322.

166. Unschuld (1985), p. 36 and Liu (1988), p. 77; cf. Ong (1985), pp. 21–29 and De Groot (1892–1910), 4: 108–120, passim.

167. CSJCXB, 25: 322.

168. See, for example, Ohlinger (1905), p. 385; see also SKQSZM, 111: 54a–b.

169. CSJCXB, 25: 322 ff.

170. *Yuxia ji guangji* (c. 1700), 6: 31b ff.; cf. *Xiangmeng Yuxia ji* (1950), pp. 75 ff.

171. See QBLC, *mixin*, p. 80.

172. Cited in Ong (1985), pp. 38–39.

173. QBLC, *fangji*, p. 21; cf. De Groot (1892–1910), 4: 103–106.

174. CSJCXB, 25: 322–323; cf. Ye Cai's commentary to the *Jinsi lu,* cited in Chan (1967), pp. 148–149.

175. See Ong (1985), pp. 61–62.

176. QBLC, *fangji,* p. 48. Cf. note 143 above. In both cases the techniques are likened to hypnotism (*cumian shu*).

177. See Ong (1985), pp. 8–9; cf. Ohlinger (1906), 16–17 and CSJCXB, 25: 323.

178. QBLC, *mixin,* p. 87.

179. *Ibid.,* p. 79. Eventually Zhang had four distinguished sons. See Hummel (1943–1944), pp. 64–65.

180. CSJCXB, 25: 325.

181. Cited in Ong (1985), pp. 128–129, slightly modified. See also the discussion in *ibid.,* pp. 34–35 and 158–159.

182. Giles (1912), p. 967.

183. *Ibid.;* cf. Arthur Smith (1914), p. 318.

184. See note 196 below; also Eberhard (1971), pp. 80–81.

185. This tendency was always powerful in Chinese dream interpretation, regardless of the sophistication of the dreamer. See, for example, Li Guangdi's dream of three crows "invading" (*fan*) the sun, in which he interprets the sun as the sovereign, the crows as rebellious elements, and the event as the rebellion of Wu Sangui. Li (1829) 1: 18b–19a.

186. See Drege (1981), p. 272 ff.; cf. Eberhard (1971), p. 80; see also *ibid.,* p. 95, note 48.

187. Ong (1985), pp. 4–5. On the *Mengzhan leikao,* consult SKQSZM, 111: 54a.

188. Although this particular edition is in very poor shape, it seems to conform closely to the *Xiangmeng Yuxia ji* (1950), which I have used for all subsequent quotations from the *Zhougong jiemeng,* unless otherwise noted.

189. See also the discussions in Thompson (1988), pp. 74–75 and Drege (1981), p. 272.

190. *Xiangmeng Yuxia ji* (1950), p. 81. For some of these illustrations, as well as several other examples drawn from the same or similar versions of the text, see Ong (1985), pp. 151–152 and Gray (1878), 2: 10–12.

191. *Daquan qizheng tongshu* (1858).

192. In this latter case, the difference can be accounted for by the homophone *li* for both profit and strength.

193. See Drege (1981), pp. 273 ff., esp. p. 273.

194. For useful discussions of dream interpretation from a cross-cultural perspective, see Ong (1985), chapter 7 and Brown, ed. (1988), passim.

195. The above examples have all been taken from the *Xiangmeng Yuxia ji* (see note 188 above). See also the discussion in Eberhard (1971), pp. 51–52.

196. For details on traditional Chinese symbolism, consult Eberhard (1986); see also the discussion in Eberhard (1971), pp. 76 ff. and Ong (1985), pp. 151 ff.

197. See, for example, Jonathon Ocko in Liu, ed. (1990); also Bodde and Morris (1968), pp. 160–165.

198. Gray (1878), 2: 10; cf. Ong (1985), p. 157.

199. See, for example, Eberhard (1971), esp. p. 82.

200. *Ibid.,* pp. 83–84.

201. See *Xiangmeng Yuxia ji* (1950), p. 91; cf. Gray (1878), 2: 12–13.

202. Gray (1878), 2: 12–13.

203. See Drege (1981), p. 276–277.

Chapter 7

1. Yang and Yang, eds. (1980), 4: 135–137, slightly modified.

2. Allan (1926), p. 179; cf. *Qixian zhi* (Henan, 1788), *rewu*, 18: 18b–19a, which expresses a similar view.

3. Most of the high-ranking scholar-officials I have discussed in the text are at least mentioned in Arthur Hummel's *Eminent Chinese of the Ch'ing Period* and many have substantial biographies. Most are also discussed at length in the *Qingshi*, and a number have biographies in Ruan Yuan's *Chouren zhuan* (Biographies of Mathematical Calculators). Yet in only a few cases—notably those of Cheng Enze, Ye Mingchen, and Li Wentian—do we get even a hint of their interest in divination beyond conventional (although sometimes highly iconoclastic) *Yijing* scholarship.

4. See Yuan (1948), 1: 16; 1: 22; 4: 25–26; 9: 21; 13: 18–20; 18: 7; 18: 10; 33: 8–9; also QBLC, *fangji*, p. 86. It is significant, I think, that a number of the individuals considered by Jonathan Porter (1982) to be "leading scientists" of the Qing period also had an interest in divination. See, in addition, note 30 below.

5. Wu (1990), pp. 176–180. For a useful discussion of the argument that "occultism" is a manifestation of historical crisis, consult Robert Galbreath in Kerr and Crow, eds. (1983), pp. 23–26. See also note 33 below.

6. Yuan (1948). This work, although invaluable, is far from comprehensive. For example, since Yuan used the Jiaqing edition of the gazetteer for Changle county (Shandong) rather than the 1934 edition, he neglected several important Qing period diviners, including Liu Heng, Liu Dun, Gao Liankui, Gao Siyu, and Gao Peilian.

7. Yuan (1948), 20: 8–9; 20: 33; 38: 39–43. See also QBLC, *fangji*, pp. 68, 83, etc.

8. Yuan (1948), 7: 19; 13: 22; 15: 32; etc. also QBLC, *fangji*, pp. 55–56; *Changle xianzhi* (Shandong; 1934), *fangji*, 35: 4a, etc.

9. See, for example, *Maguan xianzhi* (Yunnan; 1932), *fengsu*, 2: 20a–b on the "heretical arts" (*xieshu*) indulged in by the Yao people. For Mongol, Miao and other minority forms of divination, see QBLC, *fangji*, pp. 34–35, 61–62. On Tibetan divination, consult Yuan (1948), 20: 36; cf. Loewe and Blacker, eds., (1981), pp. 3–37; QBLC, *fangji*, pp. 2–3, 34. Strickmann (1983) ably documents the spread of Chinese divination practices throughout the Chinese empire and beyond, including both Korea and Japan.

10. See, for instance, *Liaoyang xianzhi* (Liaoning; 1928), *lisu*, 25: 3b.

11. On Manchu diviners, consult Yuan (1948), 18: 36–37; 37: 1–2; 37: 7–8; 37: 18; 37: 23.

12. Women diviners are also poorly represented in the *Qingbai leichao* section on *fangji*. See, however, QBLC, *fangji*, pp. 39 and 43; also chapter 5, note 83.

13. For this reason, presumably, Yuan fails to mention Zeng Guofan's interest in "spirit-writing" in Zeng's biography (18: 10–11); and he omits Ye Mingchen, who was passionately devoted to spirit-writing, altogether.

14. See TSJC, *yishu*, 48: 8453–8468.

15. I have found only about twenty entries in Yuan Shushan indicating that divination was transmitted from father to son (or grandfather to grandson), and only about a half dozen suggesting a family tradition of three generations or more. See Yuan (1948), 6: 2; 12: 17; 12: 30; 19: 30–31; 20: 4; 20: 28; 33: 24.

16. Yuan (1948), 3: 5–6; 21: 13; 8: 26–27. See also *ibid.*, 37: 25; 18: 10; 20: 26–27; etc.

17. *Ibid.*, 14: 31–32; 38: 39–40.

18. On types of payment, see chapter 3, notes 86, 97, and 115; chapter 4, notes 131, 132 and 145; chapter 5, notes 129, 131 and 141; and chapter 6, notes 15, 16, 61 and 133.

19. See SKQSZM, 146: 8b and 108: 1a. Cf. Yuan (1948), 27: 25. *Yijing* divination is probably undervalued in any arbitrary breakdown of specialties because so many systems were related to it—including techniques that are often described generically as "computational arts" (*shushu*). Also, we can find numerous examples of individuals who used the *Yi* for divination, even though *bushi* techniques are not listed in their biographies as a specialty. See, for instance, Yuan (1948), 30: 21-22.

20. For various other ways of grouping divination techniques, consult SKQSZM, 108: 1a-b; CSJCXB, vols. 24-25; Yuan (1926), 7: 12a-16b and 4: 3a ff.; QS, *wenyi zhi*, 148: 1803 ff; QBLC, *fangji*. The TSJC *yishu* subsection lists the numerological techniques of *taiyi*, *qimen* and *liuren* separately, and, unlike the five major categories, includes no biographies for practitioners. Cf. Yuan (1926), 5: 5b-6a. The same is true for the selection of auspicious days. See chapter 1, note 6.

21. These biographies come largely from Yuan (1948) and the several dozen gazetteers I have consulted. Other popular forms of divination were various forms of wind and weather prediction (c. 40 mentions) and word analysis (c. 20 mentions). A great many other techniques are mentioned less frequently, including one reference to reading the cracks of dried cakes (*shaobing*) in the fashion of oracle bones. Yuan (1948), 20: 26. It should be remembered that most diviners included in Yuan's collection of biographies are listed as having two or more "specialties." See also note 24 below.

22. Based on a breakdown by specialties of 778 diviners in Yuan (1948), the divining technique most often mentioned was geomancy (nearly 300), followed by *Yijing* divination (*bushi*; c. 225), astrology (c. 150), computational arts (c. 100) and physiognomy (c. 100). Most of these 778 biographies come from Song, Yuan, Ming and Qing sources. The breakdown of biographies in the five main categories of the TSJC from the Song to the Ming yields 74 for geomancy, 59 for *Yijing* divination, 26 for computational arts, 25 for physiognomy, and 23 for astrology. Cf. chapter 1, note 6.

23. Sutton (1981), pp. 39 and 45. When gazetteers do mention divination in discussing local customs, it is usually connected with either geomancy or "day selection."

24. See, for example, the highly disproportionate number of Qing *liuren* specialists in Yanghu county, Jiangsu. Yuan (1948), *Zhongguo lidai buren biao*, p. 7. See also note 27 above.

25. Donald DeGlopper in Wolf, ed. (1974), p. 45. See also Michael Saso in Cardarola, ed. (1982). Sangren (1987) insightfully discusses territorial cults and problems of integration.

26. See, for example, JSWXB, 61: 8b; *Yongxin xianzhi* (Jiangxi, 1874), *fengsu*, 4: 23a-25b; *Chongming* xianzhi (Jiangsu, 1930), *fengsu*, 4: 4b; *Suzhou fuzhi* (Jiangsu, 1883), *fengsu*, 3: 1b, 11a-b,18a and 37a; Doolittle (1872), 2: 516; etc. Cf. Sutton (1981), p. 43. On the core/periphery distinction, see Johnson, *et al.*, eds. (1985), p. 70; also chapter 6, note 9.

27. See, for example, Naquin and Rawski (1987), chapter 5, esp. p. 172. I would certainly add Jiangsu to the list, at least for the nineteenth century. On self-mortifying shamans, consult Sutton (1990), p. 117.

28. The breakdowns for the top seven provinces in each category are as follows: *Kanyu/xuanze*: Jiangsu (82); Zhejiang (47); Jiangxi (46); Anhui (35); Hebei (23); Sichuan (21); Fujian (18)

Yijing/bushi: Jiangsu (58); Anhui (28); Zhejiang (23); Hunan (20); Hebei (19); Hubei (17); Jiangxi (16)

Shushu: Jiangsu (43); Zhejiang (30); Anhui (26); Yunnan (14); Jiangxi (13); Hunan (11); Fujian (10)

Xingming: Jiangsu (37); Anhui (25); Zhejiang (18); Jiangxi (17); Hunan (12); Hebei (11); Sichuan (10)

Xiangshu: Jiangsu (10); Jiangxi (6); Hunan (5); Anhui (2); Hubei (2); Hebei (2); Fujian (2)

This breakdown contrasts with Sutton's findings (1981) for shamanism, and has to do, of course, with the "peripheral" role of non-literate *wu* as compared to the "core" role of literate diviners (note 26 above). If more data on non-literate diviners were available, I suspect the distribution would be similar to that outlined by Sutton.

29. See Yuan's first preface, pp. 1–2; also note 27 above. It is interesting to note that of the 230 references to the five major categories of divination for Zhejiang province, only about fifteen percent (37) are to astrology. Yet John Nevius (1869), p. 187, writing primarily (I presume) about Ningpo, tells us that astrology "commands the confidence of the people more, perhaps than any other [form of divination]."

30. See note 27 above. Significantly, the provinces of Jiangsu, Anhui, and Zhejiang are also the places of origin for most of China's "leading scientists" in the Qing period. See Porter (1982), pp. 540–541 and note 4 above.

31. Cf. *Yongnian xianzhi* (Hebei, 1877), *fengsu,* 17: 2a, on changes in beliefs with respect to shaman spirits. As indicated in note 22 above, continuity of mantic practice was the norm in late imperial China. This seems to have been the case both for China as a whole and for individual provinces. If, for the sake of convenience, we take the example of Zhejiang, and use the breakdown by specialties of 778 diviners in Yuan (1948) from Song times through the Qing, it is apparent that the percentage of references to astrology compared to other forms of divination is about the same as for the Qing (i.e. fifteen percent or so—twenty-two out of 140). This is, however, only the roughest approximation.

32. Brook (1988), p. 51.

33. Cf. Robert Galbreath in Kerr and Crow, eds. (1983). As I have mentioned in an earlier chapter, heightened competition in the civil service examination system from the eighteenth century onward produced an acute sense of insecurity on the part of aspiring scholars, leading many to explore divination as a means of gaining an advantage.

34. For Liang's opinions, consult Hsü (1959), pp. 116–117. See also Yuan (1948), 13: 22–23; 17: 11; 20: 4–5; 36: 2; 36: 23; etc.

35. See Nathan Sivin in Ropp, ed. (1990), pp. 169–170; also notes 118–123 below. Cf. Bloom (1980) and Bloom in Kao and Hoosain, eds. (1986); Chang (1939); Cheng (1987); Hansen (1983) and esp. Hansen (1987). On the aesthetics of Chinese religion, consult Paper (1985).

36. Cf. Deuteronomy 18: 9, which describes divination, augury, sorcery, and other such activities as "abominations" to God.

37. See the illuminating discussion in Jordan and Overmyer (1986), pp. 276–280; also Feuchtwang (1974), pp. 141 ff. and 236 ff., esp. pp. 243–244.

38. R. J. Smith (1990a).

39. On Chinese word magic, see chapter 2, note 40, chapter 3, note 23, chapter 5, note 119, and notes 121–123 and 132 below; also R. J. Smith (1990b).

40. *Ibid.* See also note 41 below.

41. Park (1963), pp. 200 ff. insightfully discusses the dramatic impact of divination from a comparative perspective.

42. On the diversity of medical theory and practice, see Unschuld (1985), esp. p. 197. For an example of a book published by a medical study association in the 1920s or 1930s, consult Shanghai guoyi xueshe (1961).

43. See Plopper (1926), pp. 291–315, passim, esp. p. 294.

44. For an interesting modern polemic on the issue of medicine and fate, see Unschuld (1985), pp. 340–352.

45. Jiang Menglin describes his father, a late Qing entrepreneur, as occupying a kind of middle ground between Confucian moralism and common spiritualism, closer to the former than the latter. Jiang writes: "He believed in *fengshui*, the spirits of wind and water, and in fortune-telling and therefore—with a sort of fatalism—that a man's life was predetermined by supernatural forces. However he also believed that by virtuous conduct and clean thinking one could make these forces respond by bestowing blessings upon oneself as well as one's family; thus the predetermined course of life would gradually shift its ground to a better course." Chiang (1947), p. 29. Cf. Kulp (1925), p. 171, cited in Gallin (1966), p. 238.

46. QBLC, *fangji*, p. 105 provides a good example of the emphasis on self-exertion (in this case, dedicated study) as a means of establishing fate. For other variables and strategies, consult Yuan (1948), 17: 8–9; 17: 19–20; 18: 10; 20: 4–5; etc.

47. Cited in R. J. Smith (1986), p. 171, note 56; see also Yuan (1926), 5: 14a. Cf. Hail (1927), p. 348, where Zeng asserts that "The accomplishment of a great task rests half on human planning and half on Heaven's will." Metzger (1977), pp. 127–134, ably outlines the tensions inherent in neo-Confucian conceptions of fate.

48. Yuan (1948), 18: 11.

49. See Nathan Sivin's article in Ropp, ed. (1990), pp. 169–170; cf. Thomas (1971), p. 657. Consult also Henderson (1986), pp. 143–148.

50. Cited by Nathan Sivin in Ropp, ed. (1990), p. 170, slightly modified.

51. I have in mind here Thomas Kuhn's notion of science as a pragmatic search for the solutions to "puzzles" within a generally accepted, socially constructed paradigm of understanding. See also Everett Mendelsohn in Kleinman, *et al.*, eds. (1974), pp. 659–666. SSC, vol. 2, passim, documents the contributions of divination to the history of science and technology in China.

52. See Elman (1984), pp. 62–66, 79–85 and 137; Nathan Sivin in Ropp, ed. (1990), esp. pp. 180–181.

53. See Konings (1990); also Porter (1980). Cf. Feng (n.d.), 1: 1a.

54. See R. J. Smith (1990a); cf. Thomas (1971), p. 645. For the argument that *fengshui* is "scientific," see Liu (1966).

55. Henry Vetch, cited in Leahey and Leahey (1983), p. 240.

56. See R. J. Smith (1990a); also Feuchtwang (1974) and Nathan Sivin in Ropp, ed. (1990), pp. 189–190.

57. Evan Zuesse in Eliade, ed. (1987), p. 380. On the psychology of divination, consult Vernant (1948); cf. Park (1963), pp. 195–196. Gallin (1966), p. 238, argues that a belief in fate "is especially valuable in preventing a weakening of the general belief structure. See also Jordan and Overmyer (1986), pp. 274 ff.

58. See Jordan (1972), p. 85–86. On the role of intermediaries and mediation in traditional China, see H.G. Creel in Charles LeBlanc and Susan Blader, eds. (1987); also R. J. Smith (1983), pp. 55, 221–222; Doolittle (1865), 2: 134–138.

59. Weller (1987), chapter 6, esp. pp. 147–155. See also the remarks of Sutton (1989), p. 113.

60. Yuan (1948), 28: 2. Cf. CC, 2: 363 and 370.

61. See, for example, the case of Zhou Chunxi in Yuan (1948), 26: 5; also Tang Suizu's friendship with professional diviners. *Ibid.*, 5: 22. The monk Yishan had many good friends among officials and gentry in Guangzhou, as did Zhiyuan at Zhangzhou. *Ibid.*, 38: 43. For other instances of close relations between diviners and members of the scholarly elite, see *ibid.*, 1: 24; 3: 8–9; 5: 13; 7: 17–18; 7: 22–23; 10: 9; 12: 13; 18: 13–14; 14: 12–13; 15: 8–9; 18: 19–20; 18: 24–25; 20: 18; 20: 27; 21: 19–20; 23: 16–17; 26: 6; 28: 15; 34: 22; etc. Often, it appears, officials employed diviners not only for bureaucratic tasks, but also for their own personal use. See, for example, the case of

the physiognomer Cui Songyou (not included in Yuan), who became a close adviser and, in effect, a matchmaker, for the district magistrate. *Yihan xianzhi* (Sichuan; 1931), *fangji*, 30: 37b–38a.

62. See, for example, De Groot (1892–1910), 6: 1304–1306. Cf. Sutton (1989), p. 113.

63. See R. J. Smith (1990a).

64. See Elman (1984); cf. Zurndorfer (1988), pp. 64–65.

65. Thomas (1971), pp. 641 ff. For some criticisms of Thomas, see Tambiah (1990), pp. 18–29.

66. *Ibid.*, p. 661. Cf. Nathan Sivin in Ropp, ed. (1990), p. 166.

67. Thomas (1971), pp. 656–662. We should keep in mind, however, that in Song dynasty China, technological development does not seem to have been constrained by the flourishing of the divinatory arts. Furthermore, as Thomas himself admits, even in the West occult practices never disappeared, and in fact periodically experienced revivals in both Europe and America. See *ibid.*, pp. 665–668; also Tambiah (1990), pp. 18–29; Kerr and Crow, eds. (1983), passim.

68. See Elman (1984), esp. pp. xx–xxi, 254–256.

69. See Henderson (1984), pp. 256–257; also Henderson (1986) on the "nativist" reaction of the nineteenth century.

70. John Henderson cited in Elman (1984), p. xx, note 2.

71. See Porter (1982), esp. pp. 543–544.

72. Metzger (1977), pp. 211–215.

73. Chang (1987), pp. 5–7, 99–100, 181 ff., esp. pp. 184–187.

74. *Ibid.*, p. 6.

75. Chiang (1947), pp. 40–41.

76. See Hsiao (1975), pp. 26–28.

77. See chapter 2. The term *mixin* for "superstition" gained currency only during the early twentieth century. QBLC, *mixin*, p. 1, defines it as a blind, indiscriminate belief in something.

78. Sanlian shudian, ed. (1984), 1: 275 and 297. See also Chen's "Resistence" in *Xinnian zazhi* (New Youth Miscellany) 1.3 (November 15, 1915), pp. 1–5, and Chen Daqi's "Happy New Year" in *Xin qingnian* (New Youth), 6.1 (January 15, 1918), pp. 5–9; etc. For brief summaries of the New Culture Movement in the light of these themes, see R. J. Smith (1983), pp. 255–258 and Unschuld (1985), pp. 242–252.

79. Doré (1914–1933), 4: xviii. Cf. C. T. Hsia's assertions cited in Henderson (1984), p. 197.

80. R. J. Smith (1986), pp. 178–179. See also Xu (1941); Rong (1969); Chang (1940); also Graham (1928), pp. 32 ff; Kulp (1925), pp. 171 ff.; Hsu (1967), pp. 84–85 and 156–157; Burkhardt (1955), passim; etc.

81. Cf. Thomas (1971), pp. 663 ff., esp. p. 666.

82. The British Library has one such calendar issued by the Hunan provincial government in 1912. R. J. Smith (1988), p. 133.

83. *Ibid.*, p. 133.

84. R. J. Smith (1986), p. 179, citing *Liben sishiqi zhong*; cf. Chang (1940); Burkhardt (1955), 2: 1 ff.

85. I am presently working on a book on traditional Chinese almanacs, past and present, for the Oxford University Press.

86. See R. J. Smith (1986), pp. 179–180; also R. J. Smith (1988), p. 133.

87. See R. J. Smith (1988), p. 133.

88. See Burkhardt (1955), 2: 1–15.

89. See Guangdong renmin chuban she, ed. (1966), esp. pp. 62–65. For an overview of the effort to suppress "feudal superstition," see MacInnis (1989), pp. 385 ff., esp. pp.

403–404. Cf. R. J. Smith (1983), pp. 261–263 and Pas, ed. (1989), passim. Ironically, Mao Zedong himself is widely believed to have practiced divination, at least on occasion.

90. See, for example, Guangdong kezhi chuban she, ed. (1985).

91. For those who wish to consult a more complete traditional-style almanac, smuggled-in copies from Hong Kong are available, at least in South China. See R. J. Smith (1986), p. 180.

92. MacInnis (1989), p. 403, slightly modified. See also Pas, ed. (1989), passim.

93. MacInnis (1989), p. 404, slightly modified. Cf. Li (1984).

94. *Ibid.*, pp. 387 ff., esp. 412–415. See also Pas (1989), pasim. On the *Yijing* in particular, consult, for example, the relevant articles in the *Renmin ribao* (Overseas Edition), October 12, 1989 and the *Dagong bao*, November 8, 1990.

95. *Xiantian bagua tu* (The Illustrated Former Heaven Eight Trigrams; 1989), pp. 20–21; purchased in Beijing in June of 1989. Among other similar books in my possession are those dealing with conventional physiognomy, *Yijing*-related divinatory techniques, fate calculation, and so forth.

96. See R. J. Smith (1983), p. 263.

97. According to his estimate, only about five percent of Chinese fortune-tellers (not counting shamans) in Taiwan are women—a percentage probably not far off the mark for Hong Kong as well. Compared to the Qing period, relatively few diviners are blind. Private communication from Wang Mingxiong. On the other hand, Paper (1990), p. 165, indicates a great surge in the number of female mediums in Taiwan.

98. Cf. the sociological survey of the San Francisco Bay Area in 1973 by Robert Wuthnow, which found no correlation between belief in astrology and rejection of science. "There was, in fact, a nearly equal representation of strongly positive and strongly negative attitudes toward science among those who believe in astrology or who are strongly interested in it." See Robert Galbreath in Kerr and Crow, eds. (1983), p. 29.

99. For some especially useful studies, consult Ahern (1973 and 1978); Baity (1975); Burkhardt (1955); Eberhard (1965, 1968, 1970); Feuchtwang (1974); Freedman (1966); Gallin (1966); Hayes (1983); Jordan (1972); Jordan and Overmyer (1986); Kleinman, *et al.*, eds. (1975 and 1978); Kleinman and Lin (1981); Lebra, ed. (1976); Morgan (1987); Osgood (1975); Pas, ed. (1989); Sangren (1987); Sutton (1989, 1989a, 1990 and 1990a); Thompson (1988); Topley, ed. (1967); Weller (1987); Wolf, ed. (1974); etc. See esp. the convenient overview by F. I. Tseung in Topley, ed. (1967); also Sydney Greenblatt in Wilson, *et al.*, eds. (1979).

100. Sydney Greenblatt in Wilson, *et al.*, eds. (1979), pp. 94–95. Cf. Sutton (1990a), pp. 549–552.

101. Jordan and Overmyer (1986), p. 276. Cf. the remarks of Bernard Gallin with respect to Chinese medicine in Kleinman, *et al.*, eds. (1979). Not surprisingly, "anti-superstition" ordinances designed to limit profit-taking on the part of fortune-tellers in places like Hong Kong have never been successful. See David Faure in Pas, ed. (1989), p. 266.

102. For a few relevant studies, some explicitly comparative, see Caquot and Leibovici, eds. (1968); Vernant, *et al.*, eds. (1974); Bouché-Leclerq (1963); Park (1963); Fortes (1966); Lessa and Vogt (1979), pp. 332–392; Loewe and Blacker (1981); R. J. Smith (1987 and 1989); and Eliade, ed. (1987) 4: 375–382. See also the more narrowly focused but stimulating works by Colby (1973), Colby and Lore (1981); Mendosa (1982); etc.

103. For some useful leads, see the works cited in note 102 above.

104. Caquot and Leibovici, eds. (1968), 2: 557–559.

105. Evan Zuesse in Eliade, ed. (1988), 4: 376.

106. *Ibid.*, 4: 378.

107. *Ibid.*, 4: 375; see also Park (1963), p. 205.

108. Cited in Thomas (1971), p. 667.

109. "News and Comment," *The Skeptical Inquirer*, 13 (Spring, 1989), pp. 244–245. According to the 1988 poll, sixty percent of teenagers 13–15 believed in astrology, as against fifty-six percent of those between 16–17. Females led males sixty-four percent to fifty-three percent. In the spring of 1988, I might add, news broke of Ronald Reagan's use of astrology in the White House. For details and commentary on this revelation and its background, consult Gardner (1988).

110. Culver and Ianna (1988), p. 2; cf. Kerr and Crow, eds. (1983), p. 20. See also Aphek and Tobin (1989), pp. 1 ff., esp. p. 7.

111. Kerr and Crow, eds. (1983), pp. 23–24.

112. Leahey and Leahey (1983), esp. p. 242.

113. See Vogt and Lessa, eds., (1979), pp. 333–334.

114. See Tambiah (1990), pp. 18–21, 115.

115. Tambiah (1990), pp. 84 ff.

116. LePan (1989), pp. 11–15.

117. Black (1989), pp. 3–47, 55, 108–109, and 164; see also Taylor (1990), esp. pp. 44–47.

118. Tambiah (1990), pp. 106–107.

119. *Ibid.*, pp. 92 ff.; cf. David Johnson in Johnson, *et al.*, eds. (1985), p. 49.

120. For interesting and relevant observations on the problem of rational skepticism in traditional Chinese religion, consult Jordan and Overmyer (1986), pp. 267 ff.; see also Kidder Smith (1989) on the simultaneous use of rational and intuitive modes of thought in early Chinese divination.

121. Tambiah (1990), pp. 72 and 80. See also note 39 above.

122. *Ibid.*, p. 81.

123. See the provocative discussion by John Lagerway in Naundorf, *et al.*, eds. (1985); also note 39 above.

124. See Arthur Kleinman in Kleinman, *et al.*, eds. (1978), pp. 247–248, citing studies by D. Aberle, A. Young and others.

125. Mendosa (1982), p. 1.

126. From Turner's *The Drums of Affliction*, excerpted in Lessa and Vogt, eds. (1979), p. 373.

127. Park (1963), p. 195.

128. *Ibid.*

129. *Ibid.*, pp. 207–208.

130. *Ibid.*, pp. 195–197.

131. Cited in Hayes (1983), p. 147; cf. Park (1963), pp. 200 ff.

132. Evan Zuesse in Eliade, ed. (1988), 4: 378–379. For reflections on issues of religion, divination, and marginality with respect to women, see Kerr and Crow, eds. (1983), pp. 8, 24–25; Thomas (1971), pp. 138–139; also the introductory essay by Carolyn Walker Bynum in Bynum, *et al.*, eds. (1986), and the sources cited in *ibid.*, pp. 17–18, notes 7, 8, 9, and 11. Edward Tiryakian in Tiryakian, ed. (1974), p. 3 sees countercultural "occult" beliefs as providing "a seedbed of innovations and inspirations in religion, science, politics, and other domains (such as art and literature)."

133. See Robert Galbreath in Kerr and Crow, eds. (1983), p. 24, citing an influential sociological survey of the San Francisco Bay Area in 1973 which concluded that astrology was most appealing to the "traditionally marginal": the poorly educated, the unemployed,

people of color, females, the unmarried, the overweight, the ill, and the lonely. See also the discussion in Jordan and Overmyer (1986), pp. 274 ff., esp. p. 277.

134. Field (1887), pp. 124–125.

135. See the articles by Ernest Isaacs and Mary Farrell Bednarowski in Kerr and Crow, eds. (1983); cf. Cf. Paper (1990), p. 165.

136. Cited in R. J. Smith (1987), p. 8; see also R. J. Smith (1989).

Bibliography of
Asian-Language Works

Characters for the authors' names can be found in Glossary C. Characters for titles can be found in Glossary D.

Abbreviations

CSJC	Wang Yunwu, ed. *Congshu jicheng.*
CSJCXB	Xinwenfeng guban gongsi bianji bu, ed. *Congshu jicheng xinbian.*
DQHD	*Da Qing huidian.*
ESLS	Chengwen chuban she youxian gongsi bianji bu, ed. *Ershiliu shi.*
JSWB	He Changling, ed. *Huangchao jingshi wenbian.*
JSWBXB	Sheng Kang, ed. *Huangchao jingshi wenbian xubian.*
JSWXB	Ge Shijun, ed. *Huangchao jingshi wenxubian.*
QBLC	Xu Ke, ed. *Qingbai leichao.*
QS	Qingshi bianzuan weiyuanhui, ed. *Qingshi.*
SBBY	*Sibu beiyao.*
SKQSZB	*Siku quanshu zhenben.*
SKQSZM	Ji Yun, ed. *Qinding siku quanshu zongmu.*
SMTH	Wan Mingying. *Sanming tonghui.*
TSJC	Jiang Tingxi, ed. *Qinding gujin tushu jicheng.*
XBZZJC	Shijie shuju bianji bu, ed. *Xinbian zhuzi jicheng.*
XJBFS	Yun Lu, ed. *Qinding xieji bianfang shu.*
XLKY	*Qinding xingli kaoyuan.*
XSCL	Mingli yanjiu weiyuanhui, ed. *Xingxiang xueshu conglun.*
YJJC	Yan Lingfeng, ed. *Yijing jicheng.*
ZDLZ	Xi Yufu, ed. *Huangchao zhengdian leizuan.*
ZWDCD	Zhang Qiyun, ed. *Zhongwen dacidian.*
ZYJJ	Li Daoping, ed. *Zhouyi jije zuanshu.*
ZZJC	*Zhuzi jicheng.*

Chaizi yi (1801).
Changle xianzhi (Shandong, 1944).
Changsha xianzhi (Hunan, 1810).
Chen Gaoyong (1939). *Zhongguo lidai tianzai renguo biao* (Shanghai).
Chen Guofu (1962). *Daocang yuanliu kao* (Beijing).
Chen Sanmo (1595). *Suixu zongkao quanji.*
Cheng Mingsheng (1842). *Jiali tieshi jicheng.*
Cheng Sile (1833). *Dili sanzi jing.*
Chengwen chuban she youxian gongsi bianji bu, ed. (1971). *Ershiliu shi* (Taibei).

Chongming xianzhi (Jiangsu, 1924).
Chongxiu Xiangshan xianzhi (Guangdong, 1879).
Chuxiong xianzhi (Yunnan, 1909).
Da Qing huidian (1899).
Da Qing lichao shilu (Taibei, 1964).
Da Qing lüli huitong xinzuan (1873).
Da Qing shichao shengxun (1980).
Da Qing tongli (1759).
Daquan tongshu (1819).
Daquan qizheng tongshu (1858).
Dengfeng xianzhi (Henan, n.d.).
Dong Fangyuan (1988). Taiwan min menmei bagua pai shouhu gongyong di yanjiu (Taibei).
Dong Xun (1892). Huandu woshu shi laoren ziding nianpu, reprinted in Nianpu congshu
    (Taibei, 1971).
Dongfang zazhi she, ed. (1923). Mixin yu kexue (Shanghai).
Dongwan xianzhi (Guangdong, 1921).
Enxian xianzhi (Hubei, 1864).
Fan Fanshan (1933). Fanshan pandu (Shanghai).
Fei Yun (1984). Doushu jinghua (Taibei).
Fu Yunsen (1972). Shier chen kao (Hong Kong).
Fuping xianzhi (Shaanxi, 1890).
Fuyang xianzhi (Zhejiang, 1906).
Gan Minzhong, et al., eds. (1981). Rixia jiuwen kao (Taibei).
Gao Heng (1983). Zhouyi gujing tongshuo (Hong Kong).
Gao Huaimin (1970). Liang Han Yixue shi (Taibei).
Gao Zhan (1979). Bushi bianzheng zitong hebian (Taibei).
Ge Shijun, ed. (1888). Huangchao jingshi wenxubian.
Guan shengdi lingqian (Macao, c. 1985).
Guan shengdijun wanying lingqian (1793).
Guangdong kezhi chuban she, ed. (1985). Xin tongshu (Guangzhou).
Guangdong renmin chuban she, ed. (1966). Xin tongshu (Guangzhou).
Guangxian tang daquan tongshu (1819).
Guanshang kuailan (1903, 1908).
Guanyin qian (c. 1800).
Guidong xianzhi (Hunan, 1867).
Guo Licheng (1984). Zhongguo minsu shihua (Taibei).
Guo Yuqing (1864). Da liuren daquan.
Hanyang fuzhi (Hubei, 1747).
He Changling (1826). Huangchao jingshi wenbian.
Hexian xianzhi (Anhui, 1720).
Hu Puan (1968). Zhongguo quanguo fengsu zhi (Taibei).
Huangpo xianzhi (Hubei, 1871).
Huang Yinong (Huang Yi-long; 1990). Yesuhui shi dui Zhongguo chuantong xingzhan
    shushu di taidu (unpublished manuscript, December 17, 1990).
Huang Youpian (1883). Poxie xiangbian.
Ji Yun (1970). Qinding siku quanshu zongmu (Taibei).
Jiang Pingjie (1813). Dili bianzheng.
Jiang Tingxi, ed. (1977). Qinding gujin tushu jicheng (Taibei).
Jiang Yong (n.d.). Lishu gangmu.
_____ (1936). Tuibu fajie (Shanghai).

Jiqing tang xingzong qizheng (1820).
Kangxi qiju zhu (Beijing, 1984).
Lai Zhide (1971). *Yijing Laizhu tujie* (Taibei).
Li Chuanming (1984). *Fengjian mixin shi zenma huishi?* (Jinan).
Li Daoping, ed. (1936). *Zhouyi jijie zuanshu,* in Wang Wuyun (1936).
Li Fang (1960). *Taiping yulan* (Beijing).
Li Guangdi (1702). *Lixue yiwen.*
———— (1715). *Zhouyi zhezhong.*
Li Jingchi (1978). *Zhouyi tanyuan* (Beijing).
———— (1980). *Zhouyi tongyi* (Beijing).
Li Qingzhi (1829). *Wenzhen gong nianpu.*
Li Tianjing (n.d.). *Xinfa suanshu.*
Li Xueqin (1983). "Lun Shuihudi Qinjian Mawangdui baishu zhong di shushu shu." Paper
    for the ACLS Workshop on Divination and Portent Interpretation in Ancient China,
    June 20–July 2, 1983, University of California, Berkeley.
Li Xuzhong (1975). *Li Xuzhong mingshu* (Taibei).
Li Yiyuan and Yang Guoshu, eds. (1972). *Zhongguoren di xingge: keji zonghexing di taolun*
    (Taibei).
Liang Jie (1895). *Jiali quanshu.*
Liang Xiangrun, ed. (1980). *Shenxiang quanbian* (Taibei).
————, ed. (1982). *Kanyu cidian* (Taibei).
Liaoyang xianzhi (Liaoning, 1918).
Liben sishiqi zhong (East Asiatic Library; U. C. Berkeley).
Linyi xianzhi (Shandong, 1917).
Liwen tang zouji tongshu (1876).
Liu Jinzao, ed. (1921). *Huangchao xu wenxian tongkao.*
Liu Tan (1957). *Zhongguo gudai zhi xingsui jinian* (Beijing).
Liu Xunsheng (1966). *Yinyang xue* (Taibei).
Liu Zhiwan (1974). *Zhongguo minjian xinyang lunji* (Taibei).
Longling xianzhi (Yunnan, 1917).
Luquan xianzhi (Yunnan, 1925).
Lü Zizhen (1975). *Jiali dacheng* (Taibei).
Luo Guang (1981). *Zhongguo zhexue sixiang shi: Qingdai* (Taibei).
Luo Guicheng (1982). *Tang Song yinyang wuxing lunji* (Hong Kong).
Ma Xulun (1941). "Shuoming," *Xuelin,* 9.
Maguan xianzhi (Yunnan, 1932).
Mei Wending (1723). *Mei Wuan lisuan quanshu.*
Mingli yanjiu weiyuanhui, ed. (1976–77). *Xingxiang xueshu conglun* (Taibei).
Nan Huairen (Ferdinand Verbiest) (1669). *Wangtui jixiong bian.*
———— (1669a). *Wangze bian.*
Nanle xianzhi (Hebei, 1903).
Naxi xianzhi (Sichuan, 1813).
Neixiang xianzhi (Henan, 1693).
Ning'an (Songjiang) xianzhi (Jilin, 1924).
Ouyang Chun (1814). *Fengshui yishu.*
———— (1831). *Fengshui ershu xingqi leize.*
Peng Duo (1985), ed. *Qianfu lun jian jiaozheng* (Beijing).
Pingyuan xianzhi (Shandong, 1748).
Qian Mu (1935). *Zhongguo jin sanbai nian xueshu shi* (Shanghai).
Qianjiang xianzhi (Hubei, 1880).
Qin Huitian (1880). *Wuli tongkao.*
Qinding Libu zeli (1844; SKQSZB edit.).

Qinding xingli kaoyuan (1713; SKQSZB edit.).
Qinding xuanze lishu (1685; SKQSZB edit.).
Qingshi bianzuan weiyuanhui, ed. (1961). *Qingshi* (Taibei).
Qiu Jun, ed. (1701). *Zhuzi jiali.*
Qixian zhi (Henan, 1788).
Qu Wanli (1984). *Xian Qin Han Wei Yili shuping* (Taibei).
Rao Zongyi (1981). *Yunmeng Qinjian rishu* (Beijing).
Rao Zongyi and Zeng Xiantong (1982). *Yunmeng Qinjian rishu yanjiu* (Hong Kong).
Ren Duanshu (1748). *Xuanze tianjing.*
Riyong jifu tongshu (1757).
Rong Zhaozu (1969). "Zhanbu di yuanliu" reprinted in *Mixin yu chuanshuo* (Taibei).
Ruan Yuan, et al., eds. (1965). *Chouren zhuan* (Taibei).
Sakai, Tadao (1972), *Dokyo Kenkyu bunken mokuroku* (Tokyo).
Sanlian shudian, ed. (1984). *Chen Duxiu wenzhang xuanbian* (Beijing).
Shang Binghe (1966). *Lidai shehui fengsu shiwu kao* (Taibei).
Shanghai guoyi xueshe, ed. (1961). *Bu xing xiang shu bairi tong* (Taibei).
Shen Zhanru (1976). *Mixin wu guo erqian nian* (Houston).
Shen Zhureng (1983). *Shenshi Dili bianzheng jueyao* (Taibei).
────── (1969). *Jiaozeng Zhouyi yijue* (Taibei).
Sheng Kang, ed. (1897). *Huangchao jingshi wenbian xubian.*
Shijie shuju bianji bu, ed. (1974). *Xinbian zhuzi jicheng* (Taipei).
Shui Zhonglong (n.d.). *Xingping huihai* (18th century).
Sihui xianzhi (Guangdong, 1841).
Siku quanshu zhenben.
Suichang xianzhi (Zhejiang, 1896).
Suzhou fuzhi (Jiangsu, 1883).
Taiping tianguo genghao [sic] sannian xinli.
Tang Mingbang et al., eds. (1986). *Zhouyi zongheng lu* (Hubei).
Tang Ruowang (Adam Schall von Bell) (1662). *Minli buzhu jieshuo.*
────── (n.d.). *Xinfa biaoyi.*
Taoyuan xianzhi (Hunan, 1892).
Toda Toyosaburo (1963). "Shincho ekigaku Kanken," *Hiroshima daigaku bungakubu kiyo,* 22.1 (March).
Tuibei tu (Undated and unpaginated handwritten edition in the London School of Oriental and African Studies).
Wang Chi (1986). *Yan Fu ji* (Beijing).
Wang Ermin (1976). *Zhongguo jindai sixiang shilun* (Taibei).
Wang Hongxu (1711). *Yongning tongshu* (Shanghai).
Wang Mingxiong (1988). *Tan Tian shuoming* (Taibei).
Wang Minxin (1972). *Nianpu congshu: Zhongguo lidai mingren nianpu leizuan pian diyi ji lilue* (Taibei).
Wan Minying (1735). *Sanming tonghui.* (SKQSZB edit).
Wang Weide (1709). *Bushi zhengzong.*
────── (1961). *Zengbu bushi zhengzong.*
Wang Yunwu, ed. (1936). *Congshu jicheng* (Shanghai).
Wang Xianqian (1884). *Huang Qing jingjie xubian.*
Wang Xishan (1936). *Xiao'an xinfa* (Shanghai).
Wang Zhaoyuan (n.d. Qing). *Mengshu.*
Wang Zongyi (n.d., Qing dynasty). *Yunqi zhanhou.*
Wei Jian (1967). *Xiangji beiyao* (Taibei).
Wei Liaoweng (1936). *Zhengshuo kao* (Shanghai).

Wei Mingyuan (1721). *Xinzeng xiangji beiyao tongshu.*
Wei Zhengtong (1974). *Zhongguo di zhihui* (Taibei).
———— (1981). *Zhongguo wenhua gailun* (Taibei).
Weng Tonghe (1970). *Weng Tonghe riji paiyinben* (Taibei).
Wenxiang (1971). *Wen Wenzhong gong ziting nianpu* (Taibei).
Wu Mingxiu (1984). *Yijing bushi quanshu* (Taibei).
Wu Rongguang (1832). *Wuxue lu.*
Wuhe xianzhi (Anhui, 1894).
Xi Yufu, ed. (1903). *Huangchao zhengdian leizuan.*
Xian Tian bagua tu (Hong Kong, 1989).
Xiang Da, et al., eds. (1952). *Taiping tianguo* (Beijing).
Xiangmeng Yuxia ji (Taiwan, 1950).
Xiangshan xianzhi (Guangdong, 1750).
Xiangxiang Zengshi wenxian (Taibei, 1965).
Xiao Ji (1925). *Wuxing dayi* in *Yicun congshu* (Shanghai).
Xie Xingyao (1934). "Taiping tianguo lifa kao," *Shixue nianbao*, 2.1.
———— (1936). "Guanyu Taiping tianguo di lifa," *Dagongbao shidi zhoukan*, 30 (April 12).
Xin qingnian.
Xingping yaojue bainian jing (1811).
Xingxiang xueshu conglun.
Xinwenfeng guban gongsi bianji bu, ed. (1986). *Congshu jicheng xinbian* (Taibei).
Xinzeng xiangji beiyao tongshu (1721).
Xu Dishan (1941). *Fuji mixin di yanjiu* (Changsha).
Xuxiu Shunning fuzhi gao (Yunnan, 1904).
Xu Ke (1916). *Qingbai leichao* (Shanghai).
Xu Lewu (1975). *Gujin mingren mingjian* (Taibei).
Xu Qinting (1970). *Yijing yanjiu* (Taibei).
Xu Shaolong (1986). *Qimen dunjia* (Taibei).
———— (1975a). *Liang Han shiliu jia Yizhu zhanwei* (Hong Kong).
Xue Fengzuo (n.d.). *Tianbu zhenyuan* (Kangxi period).
Yan Lingfeng, ed. (1975) *Yijing jicheng* (Taibei).
Yicheng xianzhi (Hubei, 1866).
Yihan xianzhi (Sichuan, 1931).
Yisi nian Yangxuezhai fenlei guanshang bianlan qibai zhong (1905).
Yixin (1867). *Ledao tang wenchao.*
Yongnian xianzhi (Hebei, 1877).
Yongxin xianzhi (Jiangxi, 1874).
Yoshioka Hidenori (1980). *Kigaku hoijutsu* (Tokyo).
Yuxia ji guangji (c. 1700).
Yu Pingbo, ed. (1958). *Honglou meng bashi hui jiaoben* (Beijing).
Yuan Shushan (1919). *Mingli tanyuan.*
———— (1926). *Shu bushi xingxiang xue.*
———— (1947). *Mingpu.*
———— (1948). *Zhongguo lidai buren zhuan* (Shanghai).
———— (1948a). *Zhong Xi xiangren tanyuan* (Shanghai).
———— (1961). *Xin mingli tanyuan* (Hong Kong).
Yuan Zhongche (1797). *Shenxiang quanbian.*
Yun Lu, ed. (1724). *Qinding xieji bianfang shu.*
Zeng Kunzhang (1982). *Zhongguo mingxiang zheli xueshu jiangyi* (Taibei).
Zeng Guofan (1974). *Zeng Wenzheng gong quanji* (Taibei).
Zengbu qimeng tianji duan Yi daquan (1825).

Zhang Ciqi (1934). *Zhongguo shiji fengtu congshu.*
Zhang Dechang (1970). *Qingji yige jingguan di shenghuo* (Hong Kong).
Zhang Qiyun (1968). *Zhongwen dacidian* (Taibei).
Zhang Rucheng (1723). *Jiali huitong* (Changzhou).
Zhang Yaowen (n.d.). *Wushu zhanbu quanshu* (Taibei).
Zhang Zichen (1990). *Zhongguo wushu* (Shanghai).
Zhili yuanqi (18th century).
Zhiming shu Hanxue (British Library, Oriental Division handwritten manuscript; 1876).
Zhougong jiemeng (Taiwan, 1965).
Zhou Liang (1911). *Liyi bianlan.*
Zhu Xi (1979). *Zhouyi benyi.* (Taibei)
Zhu Wenxin (1934). *Lifa tongzhi* (Shanghai).
Zhu Yizun (1968). *Qinding rixia jiuwen kao* (Taibei).
Zhuzi jicheng (1938) (Shanghai)
Zouji tongshu (1876).

Bibliography of
Western-Language Works

Abbreviations

CC   Legge, James. *The Chinese Classics.*

CHC   Twitchett, Denis and John K. Fairbank, general eds. *The Cambridge History of China.*

SCC   Needham, Joseph, *et al. Science and Civilisation in China.*

Ahern, Emily (1973). *The Cult of the Dead in a Chinese Village* (Stanford).

———— (1978). *Chinese Ritual and Politics* (Cambridge, England).

Allan, C. Wilfred (1926). *A Collection of Chinese Proverbs* (Shanghai).

Allan, Sarah, and Alvin Cohen, eds. (1979). *Legend, Lore, and Religion in China: Essays in Honor of Wolfram Eberhard on His Seventieth Birthday* (San Francisco).

Allison, Robert, ed. (1989). *Understanding the Chinese Mind* (Hong Kong).

Anonymous (1868). "Imperial Denunciation of Fung Shui Superstition," *Notes and Queries on China and Japan.*

Aphek, Edna and Yishai Tobin (1989). *The Semiotics of Fortune-telling* (Amsterdam and Philadelphia).

Arlington, L. C. (1928). "Chinese versus Western Chiromancy," *The China Journal,* 7–8.

Baity, Philip (1975). *Religion in a Chinese Town* (Taipei).

Banck, Werner (1976). *Das Chinesische Tempelorakel* (Taipei).

———— (1985). *Das Chinesische Tempelorakel, 2* (Wiesbaden).

Barnes, Andrew and Peter Stearns, eds. (1989). *Social History and Issues in Human Consciousness* (New York and London).

Bennett, Steven (1978). "Patterns of Sky and Earth: A Chinese Science of Applied Cosmology," *Chinese Science,* 3.

Bergeron, Marie-Ina (1986). *Wang Pi, Philosophe du non-avoir* (Taipei and Paris).

Bharati, Agehananda, ed. (1976). *The Realm of the Extra-Human: Agents and Audiences* (The Hague).

Birdwhistell, Anne (1989). *Transition to Neo-Confucianism: Shao Yung on Knowledge and Symbols of Reality* (Stanford).

Birnbaum, Raoul (1980). "Introduction to the Study of T'ang Buddhist Astrology: Research Notes on Primary Sources and Basic Principles," *Bulletin of the Society for the Study of Chinese Religions,* 8 (Fall).

Black, Alison (1989). *Man and Nature in the Philosophical Thought of Wang Fu-chih* (Seattle and London).

Bloom, Alfred (1981). *The Linguistic Shaping of Thought: A Study in the Impact of Language on Thinking in China and the West* (New Jersey).

Bloom, Irene, ed. (1987). *Knowledge Painfully Acquired: The K'un-chih chi by Lo Ch'in-shun* (New York).

Bodde, Derk (1981). *Essays on Chinese Civilization* (Princeton).

Bokenkamp, Stephen (1983). "Taoist Millenarian Prophecies and the Founding of the T'ang Dynasty." Paper for the ACLS Workshop on Divination and Portent Interpretation in Ancient China, June 20–July 2, 1983, University of California, Berkeley.

Boltz, Judith (1987). *A Survey of Taoist Literature, Tenth to Seventeenth Centuries* (Berkeley).

Bond, Michael H., ed. (1986). *The Psychology of the Chinese People* (Hong Kong and New York).

Bouché-Leclercq, Auguste (1963). *Histoire de la divination dans l'antiquité* (Brussels).

Boulais, Guy (1924). *Manuel du code chinois* (Shanghai).

Brown, Carolyn, ed. (1988). *Psycho-Sinology: The Universe of Dreams in Chinese Culture* (Lanham, Md. and London).

Bruner, Katherine, *et al.*, eds. (1986). *Entering China's Service: Robert Hart's Journals, 1854–1863* (Cambridge., Mass.).

Burkhardt, V.R. (1955). *Chinese Creeds and Customs* (Hong Kong).

Buss, Andreas E. ed. (1985). *Max Weber in Asian Studies* (Leiden).

Buswell, Robert E., ed. (1990). *Chinese Buddhist Apocrypha* (Honolulu).

Bynum, Carolyn, *et al.*, eds. (1986). *Gender and Religion: On the Complexity of Symbols* (Boston).

Caldarola, Carlo, ed. (1982). *Religions and Societies: Asia and the Middle East* (Berlin).

Capp, Bernard (1979). *English Almanacs, 1500–1800: Astrology and the Popular Press* (New York).

Caquot, André and Marcel Leibovici, eds. (1968). *La Divination* (Paris).

Carus, Paul (1974). *Chinese Astrology* (La Salle, Illinois).

Chai, Ch'u and Winberg Chai, eds. (1967). *Li Chi: Book of Rites* (New Hyde Park, New York).

Chan, Wing-tsit, ed. (1963). *A Source Book in Chinese Philosophy* (Princeton).

————, ed. (1967) *Reflections on Things at Hand* (New York, 1967).

————, ed. (1986). *Chu Hsi and Neo-Confucianism* (Honolulu).

————, ed. (1986a). *Neo-Confucian Terms Explained* (New York).

———— (1989). *Chu Hsi: New Studies* (Honolulu).

Chang Cheng-lang (1980–1981). "An Inscription of the Divinatory Inscriptions on Early Chou Bronzes," *Early China*, 6.

Chang, Hao (1987). *Chinese Intellectuals in Crisis: Search for Order and Meaning (1890–1911)* (Berkeley).

Chang Hsueh-yen (1940). "The Lunar Calendar as a Social Control Mechanism in Chinese Rural Life" (Ph.D. dissertation in Sociology, Cornell University).

Chang, Kwang-chih (1976). *Early Chinese Civilization: Anthropological Perspectives* (Cambridge, Mass. and London).

———— (1980). *Shang Civilization* (New Haven and London).

Chang, Kwang-chih, ed. (1982). *Studies of Shang Archaeology* (New Haven and London).

Chang, Tung-sun (1939). "A Chinese Philosopher's Theory of Knowledge," *The Yenching Journal of Social Studies*, 1.2 (January).

Chao Wei-pang (1946). "The Chinese Science of Fate-Calculation," *Folklore Studies*, 5.

Chard, Robert L. (1982). "Divination and Dream Interpretation in the Ch'ien-fu Lun" (University of California, Berkeley, M.A. thesis).

Chatley, Herbert (1919). "Chinese Psychology," *The New China Review*, 1.

Chen Chi-yún (1968). "A Confucian Magnate's Idea of Political Violence: Hsün Shuang's (128–190) Interpretation of the *Book of Changes*," *T'oung Pao*, 54.

Cheng Chung-ying (1987). "Logic and Language in Chinese Philosophy," *Journal of Chinese Philosophy*, 14.

Chiang Monglin (1947). *Tides from the West, a Chinese Autobiography* (New Haven).

Chu, W. K. and W. A. Sherrill (1976). *The Astrology of I Ching* (New York).

Ch'ü T'ung-tsu (1972). *Han Social Structure* (Seattle and London).

Cleary, Thomas (1986). *The Taoist I Ching* (Boston and London).

_____ (1987). *The Buddhist I Ching* (Boston and London).

Cohen, Paul A. and John E. Schrecker, eds. (1976). *Reform in Nineteenth-Century China* (Cambridge, Mass. and London).

Colby, Benjamin (1973). *Divination and Narrative Problem Solving* (Cambridge, Mass. and London).

Colby, Benjamin N. and Lore M. Colby (1981). *The Daykeeper: The Life and Discourse of an Ixl Diviner* (Cambridge, Mass. and London).

Culver, Roger and Philip Ianna (1988). *Astrology: True or False? A Scientific Evaluation* (Buffalo).

Cummins, J. S. (1962). *The Travels and Controversies of Friar Domingo Navarrete 1618–1686* (Cambridge).

Day, Clarence (1969). *Chinese Peasant Cults* (Taipei).

De Bary, William T., ed. (1975). *The Unfolding of Neo-Confucianism* (New York and London).

_____ (1981). *Neo-Confucian Orthodoxy and the Learning of the Mind-and-Heart* (New York).

_____ (1989). *The Message of the Mind in Neo-Confucianism* (New York).

De Bary, William T. and Irene Bloom, eds. (1979). *Principle and Practicality: Essays in Neo-Confucian and Practical Learning* (New York).

De Groot, J.J.M. (1890). "On Chinese Divination by Dissecting Written Characters," *T'oung Pao* 1.

_____ (1892–1910). *The Religious System of China* (Leiden).

_____ (1903). *Sectarianism and Religious Persecution in China* (Amsterdam).

De Harlez, Charles (1887). *La religion nationale des tartares orientaux* (Brussels, Belgium).

De Kermadec, Jean-Michel Huon (1983). *The Way to Chinese Astrology: The Four Pillars of Destiny* (London).

De Woskin, Kenneth (1983). *Doctors, Diviners, and Magicians of Ancient China: Biographies of Fang-shih* (New York).

Dennys, N. B. (1876). *The Folk-Lore of China* (London and Hong Kong).

Djang Chu, trans. and ed. (1984). *A Complete Book Concerning Happiness and Benevolence* (Tucson).

Dolezelova-Velingerrova, Milena, ed. (1980). *The Chinese Novel at the Turn of the Century* (Toronto).

Doolittle, Justus (1865). *Social Life of the Chinese* (New York).

_____ (1872). *A Vocabulary and Handbook of the Chinese Language* (London and New York).

Doré, Henri (1914–1933). *Researches into Chinese Superstitions* (Shanghai).

_____ (1970). *Manuel des superstitions des chinois* (Paris and Hong Kong).

Douglas, Robert K. (1882). *China* (London).

Dregè, Jean-Pierre (1981). "Notes d'onirologie chinoise," *Bulletin de l'École Française d'Extrême-Orient*, 70.

DuBose, Hampton C. (1886). *The Dragon, Image, and Demon* (London).

Dunne, George (1962). *Generation of Giants: The Story of the Jesuits in China in the Last Days of the Ming Dynasty* (Notre Dame).

Durand, Gilbert (1965). *Encyclopedie de divination* (Paris).

Eberhard, Wolfram (1965). *Folktales of China* (Chicago and London).
_____ (1968). *The Local Cultures of South and East China* (Leiden).
_____ (1970). *Studies in Chinese Folklore and Related Essays* (Bloomington).
_____ (1970a). *Studies in Taiwanese Folktales* (Taipei).
_____ (1971). *Moral and Social Values of the Chinese* (Taipei).
_____ (1985). *A Dictionary of Chinese Symbols* (New York).
Ebrey, Patricia, ed. (1981). *Chinese Civilization and Society: A Sourcebook* (New York and London).
Edkins, Joseph (1879). *Chinese Buddhism* (London).
Eitel, Ernest J. (1984). *Feng-shui: The Science of Sacred Landscape in Old China* (London).
Eliade, Mircea, ed. (1987). *The Encyclopedia of Religion* (New York and London).
Elliot, Alan J. A. (1955). *Chinese Spirit-Medium Cults in Singapore* (London).
Elman, Benjamin (1984). *From Philosophy to Philology: Intellectual and Social Aspects of Change in Late Imperial China* (Cambridge, Mass. and London).
_____ (1990). *Classicism, Politics, and Kinship: The Ch'ang-chou School of New Text Confucianism in Late Imperial China* (Berkeley, Los Angeles and Oxford).
Feuchtwang, Steven (1974). *An Anthropological Analysis of Chinese Geomancy* (Vithagna).
Forke, Alfred (1925). *The World Conception of the Chinese* (London).
_____ , ed. (1962) *Lun-heng* (New York).
Fortes, M. (1966). "Religious Premises and Logical Technique in Divinatory Ritual," *Philosophical Transactions of the Royal Asiatic Society of London*, series B, 251.
Fraser, J. T., *et al.*, eds. (1986). *Time, Science, and Society in China and the West* (Amherst, Mass.).
Freedman, Maurice (1958). *Lineage Organization in Southeastern China* (New York).
_____ (1966). *Chinese Lineage and Society: Fukien and Kwangtung* (New York).
Fung Yu-lan (1952-1953). *A History of Chinese Philosophy* (Princeton).
Gardner, Martin (1988). "Seeing Stars," *New York Review of Books*, 35.11 (June 30).
Giles, Herbert (1912). *A Chinese-English Dictionary* (Shanghai and London).
_____ (1916). *Strange Stories from a Chinese Studio* (London).
Goldman, Alvin (1986). *Epistemology and Cognition* (Cambridge, Mass. and London).
Goodrich, L. Carrington, ed. (1976). *Dictionary of Ming Biography* (New York).
Graham, A. C. (1958). *Two Chinese Philosophers* (London).
_____ (1989). *Disputers of the Tao* (La Salle, Illinois).
Graham, David C. (1961). *Folk Religion in Southwest China* (Washington, D. C.).
Gray, J. H. (1878) *China: A History of the Laws, Manners and Customs of the People* (London).
Guldin, Gregory (1984). "Seven-Veiled Ethnicity: A Hong Kong Chinese Folk Model," *Journal of Chinese Studies*, 1.2.
Gutzlaff, C. (1856). "Remarks on the Present State of Buddhism in China, *Journal of the Royal Asiatic Society* 16.
Guy, R. Kent (1987). *The Emperor's Four Treasuries: Scholars and the State in the Late Ch'ien-lung Era* (Cambridge, Mass. and London).
Hail, William J. (1927). *Tseng Kuo-fan and the Taiping Rebellion* (New Haven).
Han, Yu-shan (1955). *Elements of Chinese Historiography* (Hollywood).
Hansen, Chad (1983). *Language and Logic in Ancient China* (Ann Arbor).
_____ (1987). "Classical Chinese Philosophy as Linguistic Analysis," *Journal of Chinese Philosophy*, 14.
Hansen, Valerie (1990). *Changing Gods in Medieval China, 1127-1276* (Princeton).
Harper, Donald (1985). "A Chinese Demonography of the Third Century B.C.," *Harvard Journal of Asiatic Studies*, 45.2.
Hawkes, David (1973). *The Story of the Stone* (Harmondsworth, England).

Hayes, James (1983). *The Rural Communities of Hong Kong: Studies and Themes* (Oxford, New York and Melbourne).

Henderson, John (1984). *The Development and Decline of Chinese Cosmology* (New York).

——— (1986). "Ch'ing Scholars' Views of Western Astronomy," *Harvard Journal of Asiatic Studies*, 46.1.

Henry, B.C. (1885). *The Cross and the Dragon* (London).

Ho, Kwok-Man, et al., eds. (1986). *Lines of Destiny* (Boston).

Ho, Peng-Yoke (1966). *The Astronomical Chapters of the Chin Shu* (Paris).

——— (1969). "The Astronomical Bureau in Ming China," *Journal of Asian History*, 3.

——— (1972). "The System of the Book of Changes and Chinese Science," *Japanese Studies in the History of Science*, 11.

——— (1977). *Modern Scholarship on the History of Chinese Astronomy* (Occasional Paper #16; Australian National University, Canberra).

——— (1985). *Li, Qi and Shu: An Introduction to Science and Civilization in China* (Hong Kong).

Ho, Ping-ti (1975). *The Cradle of the East* (Hong Kong and Chicago).

Hoang, Pierre (1904). *A Notice of the Chinese Calendar* (Zi-ka-wei [Shanghai]).

Hodus, Lewis (1929). *Folkways in China* (London).

Hsiao Kung-ch'uan (1967). *Rural China: Imperial Control in the Nineteenth Century* (Seattle and London).

——— (1975). *A Modern China and a New World: K'ang Yu-wei, Reformer and Utopian, 1858–1927* (Seattle and London).

Hsu, Francis L. K. (1967). *Under the Ancestors' Shadow: Kinship, Personality, and Social Mobility in China* (Stanford).

Hsü, Cho-yun (1975). "The Concept of Predetermination and Fate in the Han," *Early China*, 1.

Hsü, Cho-yun and Katheryn M. Linduff (1988). *Western Chou Civilization* (New Haven and London).

Huang, Yi-long (1990). "The Controversy over Selection of Auspicious Dates and Anti-Christian Movements in the K'ang-hsi Reign Period." Paper for the Sixth International Conference on the History of Science in China, August 2–7, 1990, Cambridge University, Cambridge, England.

Hummel, Arthur (1943–1944). *Eminent Chinese of the Ch'ing Period (1644–1912)* (Washington, D.C.).

Itano, Chohachi (1976 and 1978). "The T'u-Ch'en Prophetic Books and the Establishment of Confucianism," *Memoirs of the Research Department of the Toyo Bunko*, 34 and 36.

Jain, Ravindra, ed. (1977). *Text and Context* (Philadelphia).

Jochim, Christian (1988). "'Great' and 'Little', 'Grid' and 'Group': Defining the Poles of the Elite-Popular Continuum in Chinese Religion," *Journal of Chinese Religions*, 16.

Johnson, David, et al., eds. (1985). *Popular Culture in Late Imperial China* (Berkeley, Los Angeles, and London).

Johnston, R.F. (1910). *Lion and Dragon in Northern China* (New York).

——— (1913). *Buddhist China* (London).

Jordan, David (1972). *Gods, Ghosts, and Ancestors: The Folk Religion of a Taiwanese Village* (Berkeley, Los Angeles and London).

Jordan, David, and Daniel Overmyer (1986). *The Flying Phoenix: Aspects of Chinese Sectarianism in Taiwan* (Princeton).

Jou, Tsung Hwa (1984). *The Tao of I Ching* (Taipei).

Kalinowski, Marc (1982). "Cosmologie et gouvernement naturel dans le *Lü Shi Chun Qiu*," *Bulletin de l'École Française d'Extrême-Orient*, 71.

———— (1983). "Les instruments astro-calendriques des Han et la methode *liuren*," *Bulletin de l'École Française d'Extrême-Orient*, 72.

———— (1990). "Scientific Literature in the *Wuxing dayi*. Paper for the Sixth International Conference on the History of Science in China, August 2-7, 1990, Cambridge University, Cambridge, England.

Kao, Henry S.R. and Rumjahn Hoosain, eds. (1986). *Linguistics, Psychology, and the Chinese Language* (Hong Kong).

Katz, Steven, ed. (1978). *Mysticism and Philosophical Analysis* (New York).

Kawakita, Yosio, ed. (1987). *History of Diagnostics: Proceedings of the 9th International Symposium on the Comparative History of Medicine—East and West* (Osaka).

Keightley, David (1978). *Sources of Shang History: The Oracle-Bone Inscriptions of Bronze Age China* (Berkeley).

———— (1978a). "The Religious Commitment: Shang Theology and the Genesis of Chinese Political Culture, *History of Religions*, 17.3-4.

———— (1983). "Royal Shamanism in the Shang: Archaic Vestige or Central Reality?" Paper for the ACLS Workshop on Divination and Portent Interpretation in Ancient China, June 20-July 2, 1983, University of California, Berkeley.

———— (1983a). *The Origins of Chinese Civilization* (Berkeley and Los Angeles).

———— (1987). "Archaeology and Mentality: The Making of China," *Representations*, 18.

Kerr, Howard and Charles L. Crow (1983). *The Occult in America: New Historical Perspectives* (Urbana and Chicago).

Kiang Kang-hu (1925). "The Yi Ching or 'The Book of Changes,'" *China Journal of Science and Art*, 3.

Kleinman, Arthur, et al., eds. (1975). *Medicine in Chinese Cultures: Comparative Studies of Health Care in Chinese and Other Societies* (Washington).

———— (1978). *Culture and Healing in Asian Societies: Anthropological, Psychiatric and Public Health Studies* (Cambridge, Mass.)

Kleinman, Arthur and Tsung-yi Lin, eds. (1981). *Normal and Abnormal Behavior in Chinese Culture* (Dordrecht, Boston, and London).

Knoblock, John (1988). *Xunzi: A Translation and Study of the Complete Works* (Stanford).

Kohn, Livia (1986). "A Textbook of Physiognomy: The Tradition of the *Shenxiang quanbian*," *Asian Folklore Studies*, 45.2.

Konings, Patricia (1990). "Astronomical Reports Offered by Ferdinand Verbiest S. J. to the Chinese Emperor." Paper for the Sixth International Conference on the History of Science in China, August 2-7, 1990, Cambridge University, Cambridge, England.

Kuhnert, Franz (1891). "Der chinesische Kalender," *T'oung-pao*, 2.1.

Kulp, Daniel Harrison (1925). *Country Life in South China: The Sociology of Familism* (New York).

Kunst, Richard A. (1985). "The Original 'Yijing': A Text, Phonetic Transcription, Translation, and Indexes, with Sample Glosses" (Ph.D. dissertation, Oriental Languages, University of California, Berkeley).

Langlois, John D., ed. (1981). *China Under Mongol Rule* (Princeton).

Langlois, John D. and Sun K'o-k'uan (1983). "Three Teaching Syncretism and the Thought of Ming T'ai-tsu," *Harvard Journal of Asiatic Studies*, 43.1.

Leahey, Thomas and Grace Leahey (1983). *Psychology's Occult Doubles: Psychology and the Problem of Pseudoscience* (Chicago).

LeBlanc, Charles and Susan Blader, eds. (1987). *Chinese Ideas about Nature and Society: Studies in Honour of Derk Bodde* (Hong Kong).

Lebra, William, ed. (1976). *Culture-bound Syndromes, Ethnopsychiatry, and Alternative Therapies* (Honolulu).

Legge, James (1882). *The Yi King* (Oxford).

———— (1893–1895). *The Chinese Classics* (London and Oxford).

LePan, Don (1989). *The Cognitive Revolution in Western Culture: The Birth of Expectation* (New York).

Lessa, William (1968). *Chinese Body Divination: Its Forms, Affinities, and Functions* (Los Angeles).

Lessa, William, and Evon Vogt, eds. (1979). *Reader in Comparative Religion* (New York, Philadelphia, etc.).

Li Xueqin (1985). *Eastern Zhou and Qin Civilizations* (New Haven and London).

Li Zehou (1986). "Confucian Cosmology in the Han Dynasty," *Social Sciences in China*, 7.1.

Liebenthal, Walter (1947). "Wang Pi's Interpretation of the *I-ching* and *Lun-yu*," *Harvard Journal of Asiatic Studies*, 10.

Lister, Alfred (1872–1873). "Chinese Almanacs," *China Review*, 1.

Liu Dajun (1986). "A Preliminary Investigation of the Silk Manuscript *Yijing*," *Zhouyi Network*, 1 (January).

Liu, Kwang-Ching, ed. (1990). *Orthodoxy in Late Imperial China* (Berkeley).

Liu, Shu-hsien (1974). "The Use of Analogy and Symbolism in Traditional Chinese Philosophy," *Journal of Chinese Philosophy*, 1.

Liu, Ts'un-yan (1971). "The Penetration of Taoism into the Ming Neo-Confucian Elite," *T'oung Pao*, n.s. 57.

Liu, Yanchi (1988). *The Essential Book of Traditional Chinese Medicine* (New York), vol. 1.

Loewe, Michael (1982). *Chinese Ideas of Life and Death* (London).

———— (1983–1985). "The Term K'an-yü and the Choice of the Moment," *Early China*, 9–10.

Loewe, Michael and Carmen Blacker, eds. (1981). *Oracles and Divination* (Boulder, Colorado).

Lovin, Robin and Frank E. Reynolds (1985). *Cosmogony and Ethical Order: New Studies in Comparative Ethics* (Chicago and London).

Lurhmann, T. M. (1989). *Persuasions of the Witch's Craft: Ritual Magic in Contemporary England* (Cambridge, Mass.).

MacInnis, Donald (1989). *Religion in China Today: Policy and Practice* (Maryknoll, New York).

Macgowan, John (1909). *Lights and Shadows of Chinese Life* (Shanghai).

Major, John (1980). "Astrology in the *Huai-nan-tzu* and Some Related Texts," *Bulletin of the Society for the Study of Chinese Religions*, 8 (Fall).

Marcella, Anthony and Geoffrey White, eds. (1982). *Cultural Conceptions of Mental Health and Therapy* (Dordrecht, Boston, and London).

March, Andrew (1968). "An Appreciation of Chinese Geomancy," *Journal of Asian Studies*, 27.2.

Marcus, George E. and Michael M. J. Fischer (1986). *Anthropology as Cultural Critique: An Experimental Moment in the Human Sciences* (Chicago and London).

Martin, W. A. P. (1897). *A Cycle of Cathay* (Edinburgh and London).

Mather, Richard B. (1976). *A New Account of Tales of the World* (Minneapolis).

McKinstry, John (1990). "Fortunetelling and Divination in Contemporary Japan." Paper for the Annual (Joint) Meeting of the Western and Southwestern Conference(s) of the Association for Asian Studies, October 9–10, 1990, Austin, Texas.

McMahon, Keith (1988). *Causality and Containment in Seventeenth Century Chinese Fiction* (Leiden).

McRae, John, et al. (1989). "The Historical Legacy of Religion in China," *Journal of Chinese Religions*, 17 (Fall).

Mendonsa, Eugene (1982). *The Politics of Divination: A Processual View of Reactions to Illness and Deviance among the Sisala of Northern Ghana* (Berkeley, Los Angeles and London).

Metzger, Thomas (1977). *Escape from Predicament: Neo-Confucianism and China's Evolving Political Culture* (New York).

Meyer, Jeffrey (1976). *Peking as a Sacred City* (Taipei).

───── (1978). "Feng-shui of the Chinese City," *History of Religions*, 18.2.

───── (1987). "The Image of Religion in Taiwan Textbooks," *Journal of Chinese Religions*, 15 (Fall).

Milne, William (1820). *Retrospect of the First Ten Years of the Protestant Mission to China* (Malacca).

───── (1858). *Life in China* (London).

Miyazaki Ichisada (1966). "Le développment de l'idée de divination en Chine," *Mélanges de Sinologie*, 1.

Morgan, Carole (1980). *Le tableau du boeuf du printemps: Étude d'une page de l'almanach chinois* (Paris).

───── (1980a). "A Short Glossary of Geomantic Terms," *Journal of the Hong Kong Branch of the Royal Asiatic Society*, 20.

───── (1983). "De l'authenticité des calendriers Qing," *Journal Asiatique*, 271.3–4.

───── (1987). "A propos des fiches oraculaires de Huang Daxian," *Journal Asiatique*, 275.1–2.

Mortier, F. (1936). "Les animaux dans la divination et la medecine populaire chinoise," *Bulletin de la societe royale belge d'anthropologie, bruxelles*, 51.

Mostaert, Antoine (1969). *Manual of Mongolian Astrology and Divination* (Cambridge, Mass.).

Myers, John T. (1974). *A Chinese Spirit-Medium Temple in Kwun Tong: A Preliminary Report* (Hong Kong).

Nakamura, Hajime (1964). *Ways of Thinking of Eastern Peoples: India-China-Tibet-Japan* (Honolulu).

Nakayama, Shigeru (1966). "Characteristics of Chinese Astrology," *Isis*, 57.4.

Naquin, Susan (1976). *Millenarian Rebellion in China* (New Haven and London).

Naquin, Susan and Evelyn Rawski (1987). *Chinese Society in the Eighteenth Century* (New Haven and London).

Naundorf, Gert, et al., eds. (1985), *Religion und Philosophie in Ostasien* (Würzburg).

Needham, Joseph, et al., (1968–present). *Science and Civilisation in China* (Cambridge, England).

Nevius, John (1869). *China and the Chinese* (New York).

Ng, On-cho (1986). "Toward an Interpretation of Ch'ing Ontology." Paper for the Annual Meeting of the Pacific Coast Branch of the American Historical Association, Honolulu, Hawaii, August 13–17, 1982.

Ng, Vivien (1990). *Madness in Late Imperial China: From Illness to Deviance* (Norman and London).

Ngo, Van Xuyet (1976). *Divination, magie et politique dans la Chine ancienne* (Paris).

Nivison, David (1982). "The 'Question' Question." Paper for the International Conference on Shang Civilization, University of Hawaii, East-West Center, Honolulu, Hawaii, September 7–11, 1982.

Ocko, Jonathan (1983). *Bureaucratic Reform in Provincial China: Ting Jih-ch'ang in Restoration Kiangsu, 1867–1870* (Cambridge, Mass. and London).

Ohlinger, Franklin (1905 and 1906). "Studies in Chinese Dreamlore, *East of Asia*, 4 and 5.

Ong, Roberto (1985). *The Interpretation of Dreams in Ancient China* (Bochum).

Osgood, Cornelius (1975). *The Chinese: A Study of a Hong Kong Community* (Tucson, Arizona).

Overmyer, Daniel (1972). "Folk Buddhist Religion: Creation and Eschatology in Medieval China," *History of Religions*, 12.1.

———— (1976). *Folk Buddhist Religion* (Cambridge, Mass.).

Palmer, Martin, ed. and trans. (1986). *T'ung Shu: The Ancient Chinese Almanac* (Boston).

Pang Pu (1985). "Origins of the Yin-Yang and Five Elements Concepts," *Social Sciences in China*, 6.1.

Paper, Jordan (1985). "Riding on a White Cloud: Aesthetics as Religion in China," *Religion*, 15.

———— (1990). "Notes On Recent Developments Regarding Religion in Taiwan." *Journal of Chinese Religions*, 18 (Fall).

Park, George (1963). "Divination and Its Social Contexts," *Journal of the Royal Anthropological Institute*, 93.2.

Parker, A.P. (1888). "The Chinese Almanac," *Chinese Recorder*, 19.2.

———— (1888a). "Review of the Imperial Guide to Astrology," *Chinese Recorder*, 19.11.

Pas, Julian, ed. (1989). *The Turning of the Tide: Religion in China Today* (Hong Kong, Oxford and New York).

Peterson, Willard (1979). *Bitter Gourd: Fang I-chih and the Impetus for Intellectual Change* (New Haven and London).

———— (1982). "Making Connections: 'Commentary on the Attached Verbalizations' of the Book of Change," *Harvard Journal of Asiatic Studies*, 42.

———— (1986). "Calendar Reform prior to the Arrival of Missionaries at the Ming Court," *Ming Studies*, 21 (Spring).

Plopper, Clifford (1926). *Chinese Religion as Seen through the Proverb* (Shanghai).

Pollard, S. (London, 1921). *In Unknown China* (London).

Porter, Jonathan (1980). "Bureaucracy and Science in Early Modern China: The Imperial Astronomical Bureau in the Ch'ing Period," *Journal of Oriental Studies*, 18.

———— (1982). "The Scientific Community in Early Modern China," *Isis*, 73.

Rao, Tsungyi (1983). "Further Comments on the *Yunmen Ch'in chien Jih shu.*" Paper for the ACLS Workshop on Divination and Portent Interpretation in Ancient China, June 20–July 2, 1983, University of California, Berkeley.

Rawski, Evelyn (1979). *Education and Popular Literacy in Ch'ing China* (Ann Arbor).

Riegel, Jeffrey (1983). "The T'ung-yao: Ancient Chinese Prophetic Arts and Historiography." Paper for the ACLS Workshop on Divination and Portent Interpretation in Ancient China, June 20–July 2, 1983, University of California, Berkeley.

Roe, A. S. (1910). *China as I Saw It* (London).

Ropp, Paul (1981). *Dissent in Early Modern China* (Ann Arbor).

————, ed. (1990). *Heritage of China: Contemporary Perspectives on Chinese Civilization* (Berkeley, Los Angeles and Oxford).

Rosemont, Henry, Jr., ed. (1983). *Explorations in Early Chinese Cosmology* (Chico, Calif.).

Rossi, Ino, ed. (1980). *People in Culture: A Survey of Cultural Anthropology* (New York and Brooklyn).

Rowe, William T. (1989). *Hankow: Conflict and Community in a Chinese City, 1796–1895* (Stanford).

Roy, David and Tsuen-hsuin Tsien, eds. (1978). *Ancient China: Studies in Early Civilization* (Hong Kong).

Rozman, Gilbert (1982). *Population and Marketing Settlements in Ch'ing China* (Cambridge, England).

Sangren, P. Steven (1984). "Great and Little Traditions Reconsidered: The Question of Cultural Integration in China," *Journal of Chinese Studies*, 1.1.

———— (1987). *History and Magical Power in a Chinese Community* (Stanford).

Saso, Michael (1978). "What is the Ho-t'u?," *History of Religions*, 17.3–4.

———— (1978a). *The Teachings of Taoist Master Chuang* (New Haven and London).

Schafer, Edward (1977). *Pacing the Void: T'ang Approaches to the Stars* (Berkeley, Los Angeles, and London).

Schipper, Kristopher (1978). "The Taoist Body," *History of Religions*, 17.3–4 (February–May).

Schneidau, Herbert (1976). *Sacred Discontent* (Baton Rouge).

Schulz, Larry (1982). "Lai Chih-te (1525–1604) and the Phenomenology of the *Classic of Change* (*I-ching*)" (Ph.D. dissertation, Princeton University).

Schwartz, Benjamin (1985). *The World of Thought in Ancient China* (Cambridge, Mass. and London).

Seaman, Gary (1986). "Only Half-Way to Godhead: The Chinese Geomancer as Alchemist and Cosmic Pivot," *Asian Folklore Studies*, 45.

Shaughnessy, Edward (1983). "The Composition of the *Zhouyi*." (Ph.D. dissertation, Stanford University).

———— (1983a). "Divination with the *Zhouyi*." Paper for the ACLS Workshop on Divination and Portent Interpretation in Ancient China, June 20–July 2, 1983, University of California, Berkeley.

Shchutskii, Iulian (1980). *Researches on the I Ching* (London).

Shryock, John (1931). *The Temples of Anking and Their Cults: A Study of Modern Chinese Religion* (Paris).

Shuck, Henrietta (1853). *Scenes in China* (Philadelphia).

Sivin, Nathan (1969). *Cosmos and Computation in Early Chinese Mathematical Astronomy* (Leiden).

———— (1978). "On the Word 'Taoist' As a Source of Perplexity," *History of Religions*, 17.3–4 (February–May).

———— (1982). "Why the Scientific Revolution Did Not Take Place in China—or Didn't It?" *Chinese Science*, 5.

———— (1988). "Science and Medicine in Imperial China—The State of the Field," *Journal of Asian Studies*, 47.1 (February)

Skinner, G. William (1971). "Chinese Peasants and the Closed Community: An Open and Shut Case," *Comparative Studies in Society and History*, 13.

————, ed. (1979). *The Study of Chinese Society* (Stanford).

Smith, Arthur (1894). *Chinese Characteristics* (New York).

———— (1914). *Proverbs and Common Sayings from the Chinese* (Shanghai).

Smith, Kidder (1989). "Zhouyi Divination from Accounts in the *Zuozhuan*," *Harvard Journal of Asiatic Studies*, 49.2.

Smith, Kidder, et al. (1990). *Sung Dynasty Uses of the I Ching* (Princeton).

Smith, Richard J. (1978). "An Approach to the Study of Traditional Chinese Culture," *Chinese Culture*, 19.2

———— (1978a). *Traditional Chinese Culture: An Interpretive Introduction* (Houston).

———— (1978b). *The Ever-Victorious Army in Nineteenth Century China* (Millwood, New York).

_____ (1983). *China's Cultural Heritage: The Ch'ing Dynasty, 1644–1912* (Boulder, Colorado and London).

_____ (1986). "'Knowing Fate:' Divination in Late Imperial China," *Journal of Chinese Studies*, 3.2.

_____ (1987). "China and the West: Some Comparative Possibilities," *Liberal Education*, 73.4 (September-October).

_____ (1988). "A Note on Qing Dynasty Calendars," *Late Imperial China*, 9.1 (June).

_____ (1989). "The Significance of the Yijing in World Culture." *Proceedings of the Sixth International Conference on I-ching Studies*, Shizuoka, Japan, October 18–22, 1989.

_____ (1989a). "The Future of Chinese Culture, *Futures*, (October).

_____ (1990). "Qing Dynasty Yijing Specialists in Yuan Shushan's *Zhongguo lidai burenzhuan*," *Zhouyi Network*, 5.

_____ (1990a). "Divination, Science and Medicine in Qing China." Paper for the Sixth International Conference on the History of Science in China, August 2–7, 1990, Cambridge University, Cambridge, England.

_____ (1990b). "The Languages of the Yijing and the Representation of Reality." Paper for the Third Conference of the International Society for Philosophy and Psychotherapy," October 25–28, 1990, University of Puerto Rico, Mayaguez, Puerto Rico.

Smith, Richard J., et al., eds. (forthcoming). *Robert Hart and China's Early Modernization: His Journals, 1863–1866* (Cambridge, Mass. and London).

Soymié, Michel (1981). "Un calendrier de douze jours par an dans les manuscrits de Touen-houang," *Bulletin de l'École Française d'Extrême-Orient*, 69.

Spence, Jonathan (1975). *Emperor of China: Self-Portrait of K'ang-hsi* (New York).

_____ (1978). *Death of Woman Wang* (New York).

Spence, Jonathan, and John E. Wills, eds. (1979). *From Ming to Ch'ing: Conquest, Region and Continuity in Seventeenth-Century China* (London and New Haven).

Stokes, Gale (1988). "Literacy, Cognition, and the Function of Nationalism." Unpublished paper.

Strickmann, Michel (1983). "Chinese Oracles in Buddhist Vestments." Paper for the ACLS Workshop on Divination and Portent Interpretation in Ancient China, June 20–July 2, 1983, University of California, Berkeley.

_____ (1980). "History, Anthropology, and Chinese Religion," *Harvard Journal of Asiatic Studies*, 40.1 (June).

Struve, Lynn (1988). "Huang Zongxi in Context: A Reappraisal of His Major Writings," *Journal of Asian Studies* 47.3 (August).

Sun, E-tu Zen (1961). *Ch'ing Administrative Terms* (Cambridge, Mass.).

Sutton, Donald (1981). "Pilot Surveys of Chinese Shamans, 1875–1945: A Spatial Approach to Social History," *Journal of Social History*, 15.1.

_____ (1981a). "Ming and Ch'ing Elite Attitudes toward Shamanism." Paper for the ACLS-NEH Conference on Orthodoxy and Heterodoxy in Late Imperial China, August 20–26, 1981. Montecito, California.

_____ (1989). "A Case of Literati Piety: The Ma Yuan Cult from High-Tang to High-Qing," *Chinese Literature: Essays, Articles, Reviews*, 11.

_____ (1990). "Rituals of Self-Mortification: Taiwanese Spirit-Mediums in Comparative Perspective," *Journal of Ritual Studies*, 4:1 (Winter).

_____ (1990a). "Ritual Drama and Moral Order: Interpreting the Gods' Festival Troupes of Southern Taiwan," *Journal of Asian Studies*, 49.3 (August).

Swanson, Gerald (1974). "The Great Treatise: Commentarial Tradition to the Book of Changes" (Ph.D. Dissertation, University of Washington).

Sze, Mai-mai (1959). *The Way of Chinese Painting* (New York).

Tambiah, Stanley J. (1990). *Magic, Science, Religion and the Scope of Rationality* (Cambridge, etc.).

Taylor, Rodney (1990). *The Religious Dimensions of Confucianism* (Albany, New York).

Teboul, Michel (1982). "Les premiers développements de l'astronomie Chinoise des royaumes combattants au début de l'ere chrétianne," *Bulletin de l'École Française d'Extrême-Orient*, 71.

Thomas, Keith (1971). *Religion and the Decline of Magic* (New York).

Thompson, Laurence (1973). *The Chinese Way in Religion* (Encino and Belmont, California).

———— (1982). "The Moving Finger Writes: A Note on Revelation and Renewal in Chinese Religion," *Journal of Chinese Religions*, 10.

———— (1985). *Chinese Religion in Western Languages: A Comprehensive and Classified Bibliography of Publications in English, French, and German through 1980* (Tucson).

———— (1988). "Dream Divination and Chinese Popular Religion," *Journal of Chinese Religions*, 16.

Ting, Nai-tung and Lee-hsia Hsu Ting (1975). *Chinese Folk Narratives: A Bibliographical Guide* (San Francisco).

Tiryakian, Edward, ed. (1974). *On the Margin of the Visible* (New York, London, etc.).

Topley, Marjorie, ed. (1967). *Some Traditional Chinese Ideas and Conceptions in Hong Kong Social Life Today* (Hong Kong).

Traube, Elizabeth (1986). *Cosmology and Social Life: Ritual Exchange among the Mambai of East Timor* (Chicago and London).

Tseng, Wen-Shing and David Y. H. Wu, eds. (1985). *Chinese Culture and Mental Health* (Orlando, San Diego, etc.).

Tung, Gea (1975). "Metaphor and Analogy in the I-ching." (Ph.D. dissertation, Claremont Graduate School).

Turner, Victor (1972). "Religious Specialists," *International Encyclopedia of the Social Sciences* 13.

Twitchett, Denis and John K. Fairbank, general eds. (1978–present). *The Cambridge History of China* (London, New York, etc.)

Unschuld, Paul (1979). *Medical Ethics in Imperial China: A Study in Historical Anthropology* (Berkeley, Los Angeles and London).

———— (1985). *Medicine in China: A History of Ideas* (Berkeley, Los Angeles and London).

Van Straten, N.H. (1983). *Concepts of Health, Disease and Vitality in Traditional Chinese Society: A Psychological Interpretation* (Wiesbaden).

Vandermeerch, Leon. (1983). "The Origin of Milfoil Divination and the Primitive Form of the I-Ching." Paper for the ACLS Workshop on Divination and Portent Interpretation in Ancient China, June 20–July 2, 1983, University of California, Berkeley.

Vernant, J. P. (1948). "La divination: Contexte et sens psychologique des rites et des doctrines," *Journal de psychologie*, 41.

————, et al., eds. (1974). *Divination et rationalité* (Paris).

Von Falkenhausen, Lothar (1986). "International Conference on Shang Civilization: Abstracts of the Papers Presented and a Summary of the Discussions," *Early China*, 9–10.

Wakeman, Frederic, Jr. (1986). *The Great Enterprise* (Berkeley).

Waley, Arthur (1938). *The Analects of Confucius* (London).

———— (1970). *Yuan Mei* (Stanford).

Walshe, W. G. (1906). *Ways That Are Dark* (Shanghai, Hong Kong, etc.).

Walters, Derek (1983). *The T'ai Hsuan Ching* (Wellingborough, Northamptonshire).

———— (1987). *Chinese Astrology* (Wellingborough, Northamptonshire).

Watson, James L. and Evelyn S., eds. (1988). *Death Ritual in Late Imperial China* (Berkeley).

Wechsler, Howard (1985). *Offerings of Jade and Silk: Ritual and Symbol in the Legitimation of the Tang Dynasty* (New Haven and London).

Wei, Henry (1987). *The Authentic I-Ching* (North Hollywood).

Wei, Tat (1970). *An Exposition of the I-ching* (Taipei, 1970).

Welch, Holmes (1967). *The Practice of Chinese Buddhism 1900–1950* (Cambridge, Mass.).

Welch, Holmes, and Anna Sidel, eds. (1979). *Facets of Taoism: Essays in Chinese Religion* (New Haven and London).

Weller, Robert (1987). *Unities and Diversities in Chinese Religion* (Seattle).

Wieger, L. (1913). *Moral Tenets and Customs in China* (Ho-kien Fu).

Wilhelm, Hellmut (1959). "I Ching Oracles in the *Tso-chuan* and *Kuo-yü*," *Journal of the American Oriental Society*, 79.4.

_____ (1960). *Change: Six Lectures on the I Ching* (New York).

_____ (1977). *Heaven, Earth, and Man in the Book of Changes* (Seattle).

Wilhelm, Richard, trans. (1967). *The I Ching or Book of Changes* (New York).

_____ (1979). *Lectures on the I Ching* (Princeton).

Williams, E.T. (1907). "Witchcraft in the Chinese Penal Code," *Journal of the North China Branch of the Royal Asiatic Society*, n.s. 38.

_____ (1923). *China Yesterday and Today* (New York).

Williams, S.W. (1883). *The Middle Kingdom* (New York).

Wilson, Richard, *et al.*, eds. (1979). *Value Change in Chinese Society* (New York).

Wincup, Greg (1986). *Rediscovering the I Ching* (New York).

Wolf, Arthur, ed. (1974). *Religion and Ritual in Chinese Society* (Stanford).

Wong, Chimin and Wu Lien-teh (1936). *History of Chinese Medicine* (Shanghai).

Wright, Arthur, ed. (1964). *Confucianism and Chinese Civilization* (New York).

Wright, Mary (1962). *The Last Stand of Chinese Conservatism* (Stanford).

Wu, Pei-yi (1990). *The Confucian's Progress: Autobiographical Writings in Traditional China* (Princeton).

Wuthnow, Robert (1987). *Meaning and Moral Order* (Berkeley, Los Angeles and London).

Wyatt, Don (1985). "Chu Hsi's Critique of Shao Yung: One Instance of the Stand against Fatalism," *Harvard Journal of Asiatic Studies*, 45.2.

Wylie, Alexander (1897). *Chinese Researches* (Shanghai).

Yan, Pingqiu (1989). "Ceremonies of Milfoil Divination," *Zhouyi Network*, 4 (March).

Yang, C.K. (1961). *Religion in Chinese Society* (Berkeley and Los Angeles).

Yang, Gladys, and Yang Xianyi, eds. (1980). *The Selected Works of Lu Xun* (Beijing).

Yü, Chü-fang (1981). *The Renewal of Buddhism in China* (New York).

Yü, Ying-shih (1981). *Early Chinese History in the People's Republic of China* (Seattle).

Yip, Evelyn (1989). *Feng Shui: A Layman's Guide to Chinese Geomancy* (Union City, California).

Zurndorfer, Harriet (1988). "Comment la science et la technologie se vendaient à la Chine au XVIIIe siècle: Essai d'analyse interne," *Études Chinoises*, 7.2, Autumn.

_____ (1988a). "A Guide to the 'New' Chinese History: Recent Publications Concerning Chinese Social and Economic Development Before 1800," *International Review of Social History*, 33.

Glossary A:
Groups of Ordered Terms

I. The five xing 行. I have generally rendered xing as "agents," "phases" or "elements," according to context. Although many scholars object to the term "elements" on the grounds that xing implies mutual interaction and cyclical movement rather than static "qualities" (see chapter 1), in certain situations the use of "elements" seems appropriate. That is, in some cases, the wuxing act roughly in the fashion of "elements" such as carbon and oxygen, which, under varying circumstances, produce different substances.

The mutual production (xiangsheng 相生) sequence:
1. mu (wood) 木
2. huo (fire) 火
3. tu (earth) 土
4. jin (metal) 金
5. shui (water) 水

The mutual conquest (xiangke 相剋) sequence:
1. mu (wood) 木
2. jin (metal) 金
3. huo (fire) 火
4. shui (water) 水
5. tu (earth) 土

II. The eight gua (卦 trigrams)

The Former Heaven (xiantian 先天 sequence (clockwise from the south):
1. Qian 乾
2. Sun (Xun) 巽

3. Kan 坎
4. Gen 艮
5. Kun 坤
6. Zhen 辰
7. Li 離
8. Dui 兌

The Later Heaven (<u>houtian</u> 後天) sequence (beginning in the east and moving clockwise):

1. Zhen 辰
2. Sun (Xun) 巽
3. Li 離
4. Kun 坤
5. Dui 兌
6. Qian 乾
7. Kan 坎
8. Gen 艮

III. The ten heavenly <u>gan</u> (干 or 幹 stems):

1. jia 甲
2. yi 乙
3. bing 丙
4. ding 丁
5. wu 戊
6. ji 己
7. geng 庚
8. xin 辛
9. ren 壬
10. geng 庚

IV. The twelve earthly <u>zhi</u> (支 or 枝 branches):

1. zi 子
2. chou 丑
3. yin 寅
4. mao 卯

5. chen 辰
6. yi 巳
7. wu 午
8. wei 未
9. shen 申
10. you 酉
11. xu 戌
12. hai 亥

V. The twenty-eight xiu (宿 lodges):

1. Jiao (horn) 角
2. Kang (parched throat) 亢
3. Di (base) 氐
4. Fang (room) 房
5. Xin (heart) 心
6. Wei (tail) 尾
7. Ji (winnower) 箕
8. Dou (dipper) 斗
9. Niu (ox) 牛
10. Nü (woman) 女
11. Xu (void) 虛
12. Wei (roof or danger) 危
13. Abode (shi) 室
14. Bi (wall) 壁
15. Kui (strider) 奎
16. Lou (gatherer) 婁
17. Wei (stomach) 胃
18. Mao (mane) 昴
19. Bi (net) 畢
20. Zi (beak) 觜
21. Can (triad) 參
22. Jing (well) 井
23. Gui (ghost) 鬼
24. Liu (willow) 柳
25. Xing (star) 星

26. Zhang (displayer) 張
27. Yi (wing) 翼
28. Zhen (carriage) 軫

VI. The sixty four gua (卦 hexagrams):
1. Qian 乾
2. Kun 坤
3. Chun 屯
4. Meng 蒙
5. Xu 需
6. Song 訟
7. Shi 師
8. Bi 比
9. Xiaochu 小畜
10. Lü 履
11. Tai 泰
12. Pi 否
13. Tongren 同人
14. Dayou 大有
15. Qian 謙
16. Yu 豫
17. Sui 隨
18. Gu 蠱
19. Lin 臨
20. Guan 觀
21. Shike 噬嗑
22. Bi 賁
23. Po 剝
24. Fu 復
25. Wuwang 无妄
26. Dachu 大畜
27. Yi 頤
28. Daguo 大過
29. Kan 坎
30. Li 離

31. Xian 咸
32. Heng 恆
33. Dun 遯
34. Dazhuang 大壯
35. Jin 晉
36. Mingyi 明夷
37. Jiaren 家人
38. Kui 睽
39. Jian 蹇
40. Jie 解
41. Sun 損
42. Yi 益
43. Guai 夬
44. Gou 姤
45. Cui 萃
46. Sheng 升
47. Kun 困
48. Jing 井
49. Ge 革
50. Ding 鼎
51. Zhen 震
52. Gen 艮
53. Qian 漸
54. Guimei 歸妹
55. Feng 豐
56. Lü 旅
57. Sun (Xun) 巽
58. Dui 兌
59. Huan 渙
60. Jie 節
61. Zhongfu 中孚
62. Xiaoguo 小過
63. Jiji 既濟
64. Weiji 未濟

Glossary B:
Terms, Titles, and Phrases

Note: In the interest of space, this glossary does not include characters for extremely common terms and titles that virtually all readers of Chinese will immediately recognize from the translations that follow the transliterations in the text.

anjian 暗箭
anming 安命
bagong 八宮
bai 敗
bao 報
baojuan 寶卷
baozhang zheng 保章正
bazi 八字
bei 杯
Beidou 北斗
beijiao 杯珓
bengua 本卦
Benji 本紀
benyao 本要
benyuan 本原
bi (azure) 碧
bi (holding together) 比
biangua 變卦
bianhua 變化
bianhua zhi dao 變化之道
biezhuan 別傳
bili 比例
bishen 筆神

bisi xialian 閉肆下簾

bo 博

Boshi 博士

boxue hongci 博學宏詞

boza 駁雜

bu qi zhaizhao er ancuo zhi 卜其宅兆而安厝之

bubi bu zhi yu Tian 不必卜之於天

budi 卜地

bugua 卜卦

bujia 不嘉

bujiang 不將

bujing 卜經

buling 不靈

bushi 卜筮

bushuang 不爽

buxin shu xin qiyun 不信書信氣運

buyi (inauspicious, inappropriate, etc.) 不宜

buyi (permanence) 不易

buyi chuxing 不宜出行

buzhai 卜宅

buzhen 不真

buzhi buzhi you buzhi 不知不知又不知

cai 財

Canshi 蠶室

ceng 層

Ceshen 廁神

cezi 測字

chai 拆

chaizi 拆字

chan 蟾

changong zhegui 蟾宮折桂

changsheng 長生

Chaoyang men 朝陽門

chen (asterisms; divisions of time) 辰

chen (prophecy) 讖

cheng 誠

chenggua zhi zhu 成卦之主

chenwei 讖緯

chi 尺

chidu 尺度

chijiao dixian 赤腳地仙

chong (clash) 沖

chong (attack) 衝

chouchu 丑初

chu (kitchen) 廚

chu (time indicator) 初

chu (to take away) 除

chuai'gu 揣骨

chuan 穿

chuan shui ye tai 川水葉台

chuantu 傳徒

Chunguan 春官

chunniu 春牛

chuxing 出行

ci 次

ciqiu 刺球

cu 粗

cuimian shu 催眠術

cuo (antipode; chaotic) 錯

da baofu 打保福

da guansi 打官司

dabu 大卜

Daguan yuan 大觀園

daji 大吉

daming 大命

dan 單

dao 道

daquan 大全

dashi 打時

Datong li 大統曆

dayi 大義
dayun 大運
de 德
di 地
dili 地理
dipan 地盤
diqi 地氣
dixian 地仙
dixing 地形
dixue 地學
dizhi (earthly branches; see Appendix "A") 地支
dongtu 動土
du 度
duangong 端公
duanpo 端婆
duanyi 斷疑
duidui 對對
duiguan 對關
duiyi 對易
dun 頓
dunjia 遁甲
emeng 噩夢
erming 耳鳴
erre 耳熱
Ershisi xiao 二十四孝
fa 法
fan (invaded; invading) 犯
fan (paradoxical; oppositional) 反
fandui 反對
fangji 方技
fangshi 方士
fanyi 反易
fanyu 泛喻
fei 飛
feifu 飛伏

fen 分
fenfen buyi 紛紛不一
fengjian 風鑑
fengjiao 風角
fengpo 風波
fengsha 風煞
fengshan shu 封禪書
fengshui 風水
fengshui ta 風水塔
fengshui xiansheng 風水先生
fengzhen 縫針
fenshi zhi ya 豶豕之牙
fenye 分野
fu (bat) 蝠
fu (blessings) 福
fu (captive) 孚 (俘)
fu (latent) 伏
fu (man or husband) 夫
fu (rhyme-prose) 賦
fu (to hold) 扶
Fugui tang 富貴堂
fuji 扶乩(扶箕)
fuluan 扶鸞
fuming 釜鳴
fuqi fanmu 父妻反目
gaitian 蓋天
gan (bamboo pole) 竿
gan (stems; see Appendix "A") 干
ganying 感應
ganzhi (dried gristly meat) 乾胏
ganzhi (stems and branches; see Appendix "A") 干支
geju 格局
gengwu 庚午
gewu 格物
geyan 格言

gong 宮
gonggong jingjing 恭 恭 敬 敬
gongguo 功 過
Gu (Orphan Star) 孤
gu (firmness) 固
gu (husband's mother) 姑
gu (poison) 蠱
gu yue 古月
gua (hexagrams or trigrams; see Appendix "A") 卦
guabian 卦變
guaci 卦辭
guade 卦德
guage 卦歌
guagu 卦姑
guai 怪
guaming 卦名
guan (capping) 冠
guan (coffin) 棺
guan (large fish) 鰥
guan (official) 官
guan (pass) 關
guan xingdou 觀星斗
guandai 冠帶
guantong 關童
guaqi 卦氣
guaying 掛影
guazong 卦綜
gui 鬼
guishen 鬼 神
Gujing jingshe 詁 經 精 舍
haizhong jin 海 中 金
He (Conjunction Star) 合
he (conjunction) 合
he (grain) 禾
he (harmonize) 和

Hetu 河圖

Hetu zhi shu 河圖之數

Hong (surname) 洪

hong (vast) 洪

Hongfan 洪範

houqi 候氣

houtian 後天

hugua 互卦

hui 會

huiguan 會館

Huihui li 回回曆

Huihui sitian jian 回回司天監

huiyi 會意

hun 魂

huntian 渾天

huo (calamities) 禍

huo (deceit, deception) 惑

huofu 禍福

huoren zuoluan 惑人作亂

huoyi 火逸

huozhong 惑眾

ji (auspicious, fortunate, etc.) 吉

ji (incipient moment or "trigger" of change) 幾

ji (misfortune; avoid; taboo, etc.) 忌

ji (writing stick) 乩 (箕)

jia (good) 嘉

jia you yingyang zhai fangzi nuoqilai 家有陰陽宅房子挪起來

jiajie 假借

jian 建

jianbi 減筆

jianchu 建除

jianfeng jin 劍鋒金

jiansheng 監生

jiao (divining blocks) 珓

jiao (interlocked) 交

jiao ("x") 交
jiaobei 珓杯
jiaogua 珓卦
jiaoshu 校書
jiaozhu 教主
jiazi 甲子
jibi 乩筆
jidi 吉地
jie (divisions) 節
jie (explanation) 解
jie (plunder) 劫
jie (severed) 截
jing (essence; semen; also earnest [dreams]) 精
jing guishen er yuan zhi 敬鬼神而遠之
Jingbu 經部
Jingji 經籍
Jingshan 景山
jingshen 精神
jingshi zhi xue 經世之學
jingtian 敬天
jinshi 進士
Jinshui 金水
Jinwen 今文
jipan 乩盤
jishu 極數
jishuo 集說
jitan 乩壇
jitong 乩童
jiugong 九宮
jiutian 九天
jiuxing 九星
jixian 乩仙
jixiong 吉凶
Jizi 箕子
juan 卷

juanshou 卷首

jue 絕

jue xianyi 決嫌疑

jueyi 決疑

jumeng 懼夢

Junzi yi ziqiang buxi 君子以自強不息

juren 舉人

kan fengshui 看風水

kang 康

kang Mei yuan Chao 抗美援朝

kanming 看命

kanxiang 看相

kanyu 堪輿

kanzhang 看掌

kaozheng xue 考證學

ke 刻

keyi qianzhi 可以前知

kong 空

kongwang 空亡

latong 拉童 (see also lüetong)

lei (emaciated) 羸

lei (to tie with a rope) 累

leishi fu zhizhu 羸豕孚蹢躅

li (1/3 mile) 里

li (calendrical) 曆

li (discarded) 離

li (principle) 理

li (ritual) 禮

lian (also read nian) 輦

liang 兩

liao ru zhizhang 燎如指掌

Libu 禮部

liezhuan 列傳

liming 立命

ling 靈

lingbian 靈鞭
lingpai 靈牌
lingqian 靈籤
linguan 臨官
lingzhi 靈芝
Lishi 力士
lishu 曆書 (also 歷書)
Liubu 六部
liulian 留連
Liunian shikuan 流年事款
liunian dali 流年大利
liunian yunqi 流年運氣
liupo 六婆
liuren 六壬
long 龍
longfa 龍法
longmai 龍脈
longxue 龍穴
longxue shashui lun 龍穴砂水論
lu (deer) 鹿
lu (emoluments) 祿
lü 律
luanti 巒體
luantou 巒頭
lüetong 掠童
luming 祿命
luojing 羅經
luopan 羅盤
Luoshu 洛書
mai 脈
maibu 賣卜
Man (Manchus; full) 滿
mangshen 芒神
maodun 矛盾
Maqian ke 馬前課

Mayi 麻衣

Meihua shi 梅花詩

meihua yishu 梅花易數

meishen qiufu 媚神求福

meng you zheng ye 夢有徵也

mengzhan 夢占

mianre 面熱

Min li 民曆

min 皿

ming 命

mingci 命辭

mingjiao 名教

mingnian xinli 明年新曆

minsheng 民生

miyun buyu 密雲不雨

mo 沒

mogu 摸骨

mu (1/6 acre; also mou) 畝

mu (big toe) 拇

mumin 牧民

muyu 沐浴

na 納

nacai 納采

najia 納甲

nayin 納音

nazheng 納徵

neigua 內卦

ni (go against the flow) 逆

ni (muddy) 泥

nian 拈 (or 捻)

Nianguo Yijing hui suangua 念過易經會算卦

nianshen fangwei zhi tu 年神方位之圖

nüwu 女巫

pangtong 旁通

pei 配

pi 否

pi ji ze tai 否極則泰

pian 偏

pingji 平吉

po 魄

pomiao 破廟

qi (breath, material force, ether, etc.) 氣

qi (chess piece, wood radical) 棋

qi (chess piece, stone radical) 碁

qi (implements) 器

qian (cash) 錢

qian (divining sticks) 籤

qianbu 錢卜

qiangpei 強配

qianpo 虔婆

Qianqing men 乾清門

qianxu 乾戌

qianzhi 前知

qiaosao 鵲噪

qicai 奇才

qigai 氣概

qimen dunjia 奇門遁甲

qimeng 祈夢

qinding 欽定

Qinglong 青龍

qingtan 清談

qingwu shu 青烏術

Qintian jian 欽天監

Qintian jian yinzao li 欽天監印造曆

qinying 親迎

qise 氣色

qisha 七殺 (or 煞)

qishier long 七十二龍

qiu 囚

qizheng 七政

Qizheng li 七政曆

quanfei 犬吠

ren (cutting edge) 刃

ren (humaneness) 仁

ren you renyuan di you diyuan 人有人緣地有地緣

rendun 壬遁

rensheng fugui ben yu Tian ding 人生福貴本於天定

rishu 日書

rizhe 日者

rongmao yanyu 容貌言語

rouchan 肉顫

ru 乳

sancai 三才

sangang 三綱

sangu 三姑

sanjia 三家

sanjiao heyi 三教合一

sanjie 三界

sanshi 三世

sanyuan 三元

sha (evil or baleful spirit) 煞

sha (pebbles; alluvial formations, etc.) 砂

shan (mountain; compass point) 山

shangji 上吉

shangshang 上上

Shangwei li 上位曆

shangzhong 上中

shanshang 善上

shanshu 善書

shantou huo 山頭火

shaobing 燒餅

shaqi 煞氣

she 舍

shefou 射覆

shen (spirit; deity) 神

shen (deep) 深

sheng (holy) 聖

sheng (life, birth, alive, etc.) 生

sheng (pint) 升

sheng (victorious) 勝

sheng tou si zu 生頭死足

shengjiang 升降

shengqi 生氣

shengsheng 生生

shengyi 聖意

shenming 神明

shenshi 紳士

shentong (divine herdsman; male shaman) 神童

shi (divining board) 式

shi (divisions of time; seasonal [dreams]) 時

shi (food) 食

shi (loss) 失

shi (milfoil or "yarrow sticks") 蓍

shi (real, true, substantial, etc.) 實

shi (situation; esp. "strength" of a location) 勢

shigong 師公

shili butong feng 十里不同風

shiling 時令

shipo 師婆

shiqin 事親

shishi qiushi 實事求是

Shixian li 時憲曆

Shixian shu 時憲書

Shixian zhi 時憲志

shiyi (explication of meaning) 釋義

shiyi (milfoil etiquette) 筮儀

shou (tetragrams) 首

shou (collected) 收

shouming (longevity fate) 壽命

shouming (received fate) 受命

shouqi 受氣
shoushi 授時
shouxiang 手相
shu (classified as) 屬
shu (coiled up) 縮
shu (numbers; calculations; fate) 數
shu yue zhu 水月主
shuai 衰
shuang 雙
shufang 書坊
Shuide ting 水德亭
shuixing 水星
shun (compliant; to go with the flow) 順
shun (pure and simple) 純
shuohe di 說合的
shushu 數術
shuxue 數學
Siji huangdi 四季皇帝
sili 私曆
simeng 思夢
siqi 死氣
sizhu 四柱
Suide 歲德
suiming 隨命
suming 宿命
sunshan qianxiang 巽山乾向
suxi 速喜
tai (good) 泰
tai (womb) 胎
Taibu 太卜
Taihe dian 太和殿
Taiji 太極
Taiji tu 太極圖
Taiyi (star; numerological system) 太乙
tan (altar) 壇

tang 堂

ti 體

tian (to take the field) 田

tianbi 添筆

tiancao xianli 天曹仙吏

Tianchi 天池

Tiandao 天道

Tiande 天德

tiangan (heavenly stems; see Appendix "A") 天干

Tianhuang dadi 天皇大帝

tianli 天理

tianpan 天盤

tianqi 天氣

Tianshi yuan 天市垣

Tianwen guan 天文官

tianwen xue 天文學

tianxiang 天象

Tianxing 天星

Tianyuan 天元

Tianyun 天運

tiaoshen 跳神

tingsheng 聽聲

tipen 嚏噴

tong 筒

tongji 童乩

tonglei 同類

tongsheng 通勝 (or 通聖)

tongshu 通書

tongshu xuanze 通書選擇

tongyao 童謠

tuan 彖

tuchen 圖讖

tui 推

tui luming 推祿命

tuibu 推步

tuiming 推命
tuiyi 推易
tuxing 土星
wa 蛙
waigua 外卦
waimen han 外門漢
wan wu yi shi 萬無一失
wang (demise) 亡
wang (flourishing) 旺
wangqi 望氣
wangyan 妄言
wangyi 尪姨
Wannian li 萬年曆
Wannian shu 萬年書
wanshi zu wuyi 萬事足無疑
wei (guards; garrison) 衛
wei (position) 位
weiqi 圍棋
weiyou jixiang 微有吉象
wenfeng 文風
weng 翁
wenmi po 問米婆
wenming 問名
Wenwang ke 文王課
wo 窩
wu (shamans) 巫
wu (things) 物
wu bu gou zhi 無不購之
wuben 務本
wuguan 五官
wuguan zheng 五官正
Wumen 午門
wumeng 寤夢
wupo 巫婆
wushuang 無爽

wuxing 五行 (five agents, etc.; see Appendix "A")

wuyong 勿用

xi (accumulation) 息

xi (binding) 係

xi (refinement) 細

xi ti ruo li 夕惕若厲

xiaji 下吉

xian 賢

xiang (images; symbolic [dreams]) 象

xiang (mutual; assisting; direct observation or analysis) 相

xiang (orientation) 向

xiang (pensive or longing [dreams]) 想

xiangdeng 香燈

xianghua 相化

xiangke 相剋

xiangmian 相面

xiangmu 相墓

xiangqi 象棋

xiangren 相人

xiangsheng 相生

xiangshu (images and numbers) 象數

xiangshu (physiognomy) 相數

xiangyi 祥異

xiangxing 象 (or 像) 形

xiangying 相應

xiangyu 相雨

xiangzhai 相宅

xiangzhi 相制

xiangzi 相字

Xianjue guaguan 先覺卦館

Xianmen dong 仙門洞

xianpo 仙婆

xiantian (Former Heaven; see Appendix "A") 先天

xiao (dispersal) 消

xiao (imitate) 效

xiaochen 爻辰
xiaodao 道小
xiaoren 小人
xiaoyun 小運
xiaping 下平
xiaxia 下下
xici 繫辭
xie (heretical) 邪
xie (shoe) 鞋
xiegui 邪鬼
xieqi 邪氣
xieshen 邪神
xiesheng 諧聲
xieshu (heretical arts) 邪術
xieshu (heretical books) 邪書
xieshuo 邪說
ximeng 喜夢
xin 信
xin tongshu 新通書
xing (nature; affective [dreams]) 性
xing (forms; formations) 形
xing (punishments) 刑
xing (stars; heavenly bodies) 星
xing er shang 形而上
xing er xia 形而下
xingbu 星卜
xingfa 形法
xingjia 形家
xingming 星命
xingshen 星神
xingsheng 形聲
xingshi 形勢
xingtu 星土
xingxiang 星相
xingxuan 星算

xingxue 星學

xinjing 心驚

xinli 新曆

xiong 凶

xiongsha 凶煞

xipo 覡婆

Xishen 喜神

xisong 息訟

xiu (cultivate) 修

xiu (lunar lodges; see Appendix "A") 宿

xiu (retiring) 休

Xizhi men 西直門

xizi ta 惜字塔

Xu (star) 虛

xu (empty, false, void, etc.) 虛

xuanxiang 玄象

xuanxue 玄學

xuanye 宣夜

xuanze 選擇

xue 穴

yamen bazi kai wuqian wushi lai 衙門八字開無錢無使來

Yan (state; swallow) 燕

yan (verify or fulfill) 驗

yan qu er zhong 言曲而中

yanci 驗辭

yang (cosmic force; and correlative designation for light, odd, left, round, circle, etc.) 陽

yang (nourishment) 養

yangyu 仰盂

yantiao 眼跳 (also mutiao 目跳)

Yanwang 閻王

yao 爻

yao busheng de 妖不勝德

yaoci 爻辭

yaoshu 妖書

yaoyan 妖魔

ye (also) 也

ye (repression) 厭

yeguan wuji 夜觀無忌

Yi wei junzi mou buwei xiaoren mou 易為君子謀不為小人謀

yi (change) 易

yi (disperses) 泄

yi (medicine) 醫

yi (should; appropriate; etc.) 宜

yicheng mouwang 意稱謀望

yiduan 異端

yili 義理

yiliu 衣留

yin (cosmic force and correlative designation for dark, even, right, flat, square, etc.) 陰

yin (seal) 印

yin (hidden) 隱

yindang 淫蕩

yinfang 陰方

ying (camps) 營

ying (parrot) 鸚

yingchun 迎春

yingbi 影壁

yingong 隱功

yingshen saihui 迎神賽會

yinshou 印綬

yinsi 淫祀

yinxiang 印相

yinyang jiayan 陰陽家言

yinyang shushi 陰陽術士

yiren 異人

Yishu 藝術

yitu 易圖

yiwen 藝文

Yiwen zhi 藝文志

yiwu liangti 一物兩體
yiyi 一義
yiyong 宜用
yong 用
yongshen 用神
you shiqing qiuqian 有事情求籤
yu shui cao tou 雨水草頭
yuan 元
yuan heng li zhen 元亨利貞
yuanfen 緣分
yuanguang 圓光
yue 月
Yuehe 月合
Yueling li 月令曆
Yuesha 月煞
Yueye 月厭
yumin 愚民
yumin huo yu fengshui 愚民惑於風水
yun 運
yunhui 運會
Yunming 運命
yushen yuling 於神於靈
yuyong 御用
zai 災
zaiyi 災異
zaizhong 栽種
zan 贊
zang 葬
zangjing 葬經
zangshu 葬書
zaoming 早命
zaoyun 遭運
zaozuo dongliang 造作棟梁
ze zhi zhengdao 擇之正道
zedi 擇地

zeri 擇日

zhan 占

zhanci 占辭

zhang 璋

zhangxiang 掌相

zhanhou 占候

Zhanmeng (Interpreter of Dreams) 占夢

zhanmeng (dream divination) 占夢

zhanmu 占墓

zhanren 占人

zhanxing 占星

zhanyun 占運

zhanzhai 占宅

zhao 兆

zhaohun 招魂

zhen (to examine [a patient, pulse, dream, etc.]) 診

zhen (firm correctness) 貞

zhen (stabilizing) 鎮

zhenci 針刺

zheng (correct; time indicator) 正

zheng (verify) 徵

zheng renxin 正人心

zhengguan 正官

zhengmeng 正夢

zhengming 正命

zhengying 正應

zhengzhen 正針

zhenmo 診脈

zhenwu 鎮物

Zhenzai 真宰

zhequ 摘取

zhi (branches; see Appendix "A") 支

zhi (character) 質

zhi (control) 制

zhi (high rank) 秩

zhi (straightforward [dreams]) 直

zhi (to govern; to control) 治

zhi (walk) 蹢

zhigua 之卦

zhijing 致敬

zhili 治曆

zhiming 知命

zhishi 指事

zhizhu 蹢躅

zhongji 中吉

Zhongli 中曆

zhongping 中平

zhongxia 中下

zhongyao 中爻

zhongyun 中運

zhongzhong 中中

zhu (commentary) 注

zhu (to limp or amble) 躅

zhugua zhi zhu 主卦之主

zhui 綴

zhuo 濁

zhupi 硃批

zhuyi 主意

zichu 子初

ziran zhi li 自然之理

Ziwei doushu 紫薇斗數

zizheng 子正

zong 綜

zongjiao 宗教

Zongzi fangfa 種子方法

zouma kanhua 走馬看花

Zoushu 奏書

zouyi 奏議

zuixin guishen 最信鬼神

zuo 坐

Glossary C:
Names of Individuals

Note: In the interest of space, this glossary excludes extremely well-known historical figures, as well as prominent Qing personalities for whom Chinese characters are provided in Hummel (1943-1944), unless they are listed as authors in the Asian-language bibliography. It also does not provide characters for individuals mentioned in the notes if their names are cited only to facilitate identification in the QBLC, Yuan (1948) and other such sources.

Ba Jianlong 巴見龍
Bei Zao 神灶
Bi Wan 畢萬
Bi Xian 碧仙
Boniu 伯牛
Bu Yan 卜偃
Cai Mao 蔡茂
Cao Yuanbi 曹元弼
Chen 陳
Chen Chun 陳淳
Chen Gaoyong 陳高傭
Chen Guofu 陳國符
Chen Hansheng 陳翰升
Chen Mingsheng 陳鳴盛
Chen Que 陳確
Chen Sanmo 陳三謨
Chen Shirong 陳世鎔
Chen Shiyuan 陳士元
Chen Shou 陳壽
Chen Wen 陳雯

Chen Xitai 陳喜泰
Chen Yiyun 陳翊運
Chen Yuan 陳元
Chen Zhibing 陳志炳
Cheng Sile 程思樂
Chunqiu bizhe 春秋筆者
Dai Shangwen 戴尚文
Dian Daoshi 顛道士
Ding Huan 丁煥
Ding Ruipu 丁芮樸
Ding Shoucun 丁守存
Ding Yan 丁晏
Dong Fangyuan 董芳苑
Dong Xun 董恂
Dong Yi 董懿
Dongfang Shuo 東方朔
Dou Diangao 竇甸膏
Fan Fanshan 樊樊山
Fan Lai 范睞
Fan Lei 藩耒

Fan Shixing 范時行
Fang Dongshu 方東樹
Fang Xiushui 方秀水
Fang Zhengming 方正明
Fei Chun 費淳
Fei Yun 飛雲
Feng Dengfu 馮登府
Feng Hou 風后
Feng Jing 馮景
Feng Wenyao 馮文耀
Fu Sheng 富生
Fu Xian 傅咸
Fu Yunsen 傅運森
Gan De 甘德
Gan Minzhong 干敏中
Gao Heng (modern author) 高亨
Gao Heng (Qing official) 高珩
Gao Huaimin 高懷民
Gao Jiyang 高激揚
Gao Mingde 高明德
Gao Qizhuo 高其倬
Gao Renjian 高人鑑
Gao Zhan 高瞻
Gao Zhaoxiang 高兆祥
Ge Shijun 葛士濬
Ge Tianmin 葛天民
Gong Bu 龔布
Gongbo Liao 公伯寮
Gu Fengwei 顧鳳威
Gu Heming 顧鶴鳴
Guan Lu 管輅
Guan Wenkui 管文奎
Guan Zhining 管志寧
Guandi 關帝
Guanyin 觀音

Guiguzi 鬼谷子
Gui Jipan 桂繼攀
Guo Licheng 郭立誠
Guo Pu 郭璞
Guo Yan 郭偃
Guo Yuqing 郭御青
Hao Jibao 郝繼堡
Hatori Unokichi 服部宇之吉
He (doctor) 和
He Changling 賀長齡
He Futang 何馥堂
Hong Chaohe 洪潮和
Hu Puan 胡樸安
Hu Yuanjing 胡元靜
Hua Tuo 華陀
Huai Zhenxi 懷振熙
Huang Daxian 黃大仙
Huang Mingzhuang 黃明莊
Huang Shi 黃奭
Huang Yinong 黃一農
Huang Yizhi 黃宜之
Huang Yupian 黃育楩
Huang Zhucheng 黃卓誠
Huang Zifa 黃子發
Hui (Duke) 惠公
Ji Yun 紀昀
Jia Yanling 賈延齡
Jia Yucun 賈雨村
Jian Yaopo 簡堯坡
Jiang Dahong 蔣大鴻
Jiang Pingjie 蔣平階
Jiang Tingxi 蔣廷錫
Jiang Yinglong 姜應隴
Jiang Yitang 蔣一鐙
Jiang Yong 江永

Jiao Yanshou 焦廷壽
Jie Dashen 解大紳
Jin Daoren 金道人
Jin Dayu 金大煜
Jin Guang 金光
Jin Ma 金馬
Jing Fang 京房
Jizi 箕子
Kang Wenduo 康文鐸
Kang Zhengji 康正吉
Kong Jilian 孔繼廉
Kong Richang 孔日昌
Kong Yingda 孔穎達
Kulena 庫勒納
Lai Dayou 賴大有
Lai Zhide 來知德
Le Zhixian 樂治賢
Li Benshan 李本善
Li Chuanming 李傳明
Li Chunfeng 李淳風
Li Daoming 李道明
Li Daoping 李道平
Li Dingzuo 李鼎祚
Li Fang 李芳
Li Fangchun 李芳春
Li Fuyao 李輔燿
Li Genchang 李根暢
Li Guangdi 李光地
Li Jingchi 李鏡池
Li Haonian 李浩年
Li Keqi 李克岐
Li Kui 李逵
Li Liuming 李六名
Li Mengqun 李孟群
Li Mi 李泌

Li Mu 力牧
Li Qingzhi 李清植
Li Qingxi 李清溪
Li Sanyang 李三陽
Li Suiqiu 黎遂球
Li Suzhen 李素貞
Li Taichu 李太初
Li Tianjing 李天經
Li Weixin 李維新
Li Xingyu 李興禹
Li Xuan 李璇
Li Xueqin 李學勤
Li Xuzhong 李虛中
Li Yiqing 李一清
Li Yiyuan 李亦園
Li Youlong 李友龍
Li Yuhong 李玉鋐
Li Zhixian 李治賢
Li Zonghui 李宗匯
Liang Jie 梁傑
Liang Tianlai 梁天來
Liang Xiangrun 梁湘潤
Liao Chunshan 廖春山
Lin Lan 林瀾
Lin Qingping 林慶炳
Lin Sen 林森
Lin Shihe 林士者
Ling Guixing 凌貴興
Ling Kun 凌坤
Liu Bingzhong 劉秉忠
Liu Bowen 劉伯文
Liu Erhuan 柳爾煥
Liu Heng 劉恆
Liu Ji (Song) 劉攽
Liu Ji (Ming) 劉基

Liu Jinzao 劉錦藻
Liu Longguang 劉龍光
Liu Lu 劉璐
Liu Lu 劉禄
Liu Mouji 劉茂吉
Liu Shijun 劉世駿
Liu Tan 劉坦
Liu Tang 劉唐
Liu Wanchong 劉萬崇
Liu Xiandi 劉詵迪
Liu Xianjia 劉先甲
Liu Xie 劉勰
Liu Xunsheng 劉訓昇
Liu Yiming 劉一明
Liu Yusong 劉毓菘
Liu Zhiwan 劉枝萬
Liu Zhong 劉鐘
Lu Deming 陸德明
Lu Han 盧翰
Lu Jun 陸鈞
Lu Qimeng 陸其蒙
Lu Yixian 魯繹先
Luo 羅
Luo Guang 羅光
Luo Guicheng 羅桂成
Luo Hao 羅浩
Luo Shijing 駱師璟
Luo Xizhu 羅席珠
Lü Cai 呂才
Lü Dongbin 呂洞賓
Lü Zizhen 呂子振
Ma Bailiang 馬百良
Ma Jinzhi 馬進之
Ma Rong 馬融
Ma Shan 馬善

Ma Wenzhi 馬文植
Ma Xulun 馬敍倫
Mei Wending 梅文鼎
Meng Hao 孟浩
Meng Xi 孟喜
Miu Xiyong 繆希雍
Mu (Duke) 穆公
Nagao Ryuzo 永尾龍造
Nan Huairen 南懷仁
Ni Yuanlu 倪元鷺
Nie Ting 聶庭
Ouyang Chun 歐陽純
Peng Duo 彭鐸
Peng Tianlun 彭天綸
Pi Xirui 皮錫瑞
Ping Zhang 平章
Qian Lucan 錢陸燦
Qian Mu 錢穆
Qian Tang 錢塘
Qian Wenmin 錢文敏
Qin Huitian 秦惠田
Qin Luhai 秦陸海
Qin Zhongyuan 秦仲原
Qing Wu 青烏
Qiu Jun 丘濬
Qu Donghai 瞿東海
Qu Fuhou 曲福厚
Qu Wanli 屈萬里
Rao Zongyi 饒宗頤
Ren Duanshu 任端書
Rong (prince) 榮親王
Rong Bangda 榮邦達
Rong Zhaozu 容肇祖
Ruan Yuan 阮元
Sakai Tadao 酒井忠夫

Shang Binghe 尚秉和

Shen Gua 沈括

Shen Hao 沈鎬

Shen Hengzhang 沈衡章

Shen Zhanru 沈展如

Shen Zhureng 沈竹仍

Sheng Kang 盛康

Shi (diviner) 史

Shi Hulian 施瑚璉

Shi Kuang 師曠

Shi Kui 史夔

Shi Shen 石申

Shi Su 史蘇

Shizeng 師曾

Shui Zhonglong 水中龍

Sima Jizhu 司馬季主

Song 宋

Song Jiang 宋江

Song Xiance 宋獻策

Song Yishi 宋一士

Sun Buyun 孫步雲

Sun Derun 孫德潤

Sun Pafang 孫爬房

Sun Wukong 孫晤空

Sun Yiyan 孫衣言

Tang Ju 唐舉

Tang Mingbang 唐明邦

Tang Ruowang 湯若望

Tao Luzi 韜廬子

Teng Yunlong 騰雲龍

Tian He 天何

Tianhou 天后

Toda Toyosaburo 戶田豐三郎

Tong Ershu 童二樹

Tong Guoxiang 佟國相

Tu Fu 徒父

Wan Guoning 萬國寧

Wan Minying 萬民英

Wan Shouqi 萬壽祺

Wang Baile 王佰樂

Wang Chenglie 汪承烈

Wang Chi 王杕

Wang Chun 汪椿

Wang Ermin 王爾敏

Wang Fu 王符

Wang Hongxu 王洪緒

Wang Huaguo 王華國

Wang Ji (Tang) 王伋

Wang Ji (Ming) 王基

Wang Jihong 王績宏

Wang Kui 王逵

Wang Laosan 王老三

Wang Ming-hsiung

(see Wang Mingxiong)

Wang Mingxiong 王明雄

Wang Minxin 王民信

Wang Qi 王岐

Wang Wei (Ming) 王褘

Wang Weide 王維德

Wang Weixiong 王渭熊

Wang Xianqian 王先謙

Wang Xingzhen 王星軫

Wang Xishan 王錫闡

Wang Yinzhi 王引之

Wang Yunwu 王雲五

Wang Zhaoyuan 王朝元

Wang Zongyi 王宗沂

Wei Boyang 魏佰陽

Wei Guangtao 魏光燾

Wei Jian 魏鑑

Wei Liaoweng 魏了翁

Wei Mingyuan 魏明遠

Wei Zhengtong 韋政通

Wen Tong 文通

Wei Wuzhuang 魏午莊

Wenchang 文昌

Weng Tonghe 翁同龢

Wenxiang 文祥

Wong Tai Sin (see Wang Daxian)

Wu Ding 武丁

Wu Ge 吳哥

Wu Mingxiu 吳明修

Wu Rongguang 吳榮光

Wu Tianhong 吳天洪

Wu Wanggang 吳望崗

Wu Xian 巫咸

Wu Yi 武億

Wu Yuan 五員

Wu Yuanyin 吳元音

Wu Zhenchuan 吳鎮川

Wu Ziying 吳子纓

Xi (Duke) 僖公

Xi Yufu 席裕福

Xia Bingnan 夏炳南

Xia Sheng 夏聲

Xian (Prince) 諴親王

Xiang Da 向達

Xiao 蕭

Xiao Gonghui 蕭功悔

Xiao Ji 蕭吉

Xie Hong 謝鴻

Xie Lanjie 謝蘭階

Xie Shi 謝石

Xie Tian'ao 謝天翶

Xie Xianting 謝獻庭

Xie Xingyao 謝興堯

Xie Xinzhi 謝心治

Xie Ziyi 謝子逸

Xing Congyang 邢崇陽

Xiong Deqian 熊德謙

Xiong Deqing 熊德卿

Xiong Liukui 熊六夔

Xiong Yingxiong 熊應雄

Xu Dachun 許大椿

Xu Dishan 許地山

Xu Fu 許負

Xu Guangdi 徐光第

Xu Guifen 許桂芬

Xu Honggao 徐洪高

Xu Ke 徐珂

Xu Lewu 徐樂吾

Xu Qinting 徐芹庭

Xu Shaolong 許紹龍

Xu Shen 許慎

Xu Wenjing 徐文靖

Xu Xigong 徐習功

Xu Ziping 徐子平

Xue Fengzuo 薛鳳祚

Xun Shuang 荀爽

Yan Junping 嚴君平

Yan Lingfeng 嚴靈峰

Yang Fengting 楊鳳庭

Yang Guoshu 楊國樞

Yang Jisheng 楊繼盛

Yang Pang 楊龐

Yang Shutai 楊書臺

Yang Xiong 楊雄

Yang Yunsong 楊筠松

Yansheng (Duke) 衍聖公

Yao Dian 姚典

Ye Fang'ai 葉方藹
Ye Tai 葉泰
Yelü Chucai 耶律楚材
Ying Shan 英善
Yingnian 英年
Yin Kehai 尹克海
Yixin 奕訢
Yixing 一行
Yoshioka Hidenori 吉岡秀憲
Yu Chuntan 虞春潭
Yu Fan 虞翻
Yu Mingsheng 余明陞
Yu Pingbo 俞平伯
Yu Rongkuan 俞榮寬
Yuan Chengyu 袁承裕
Yuan Shushan 袁樹珊
Yuan Tiangang 袁天綱
Yuan Zhongche 袁忠徹
Yue Baohe 岳保和
Yun Lu 允祿
Zeng Guofan 曾國藩
Zeng Kunzhang 曾坤章
Zeng Wendi 曾文迪
Zeng Xiantong 曾憲通
Zhai Junlian 翟均廉
Zhang 張
Zhang Ciqi 張次溪
Zhang Dechang 張德昌
Zhang Fengming 張鳳鳴
Zhang Fengyi 張鳳翼
Zhang Guo 張果
Zhang Heng 張衡
Zhang Hongru 張鴻儒
Zhang Huaide 張懷德
Zhang Jiuxiao 張九霄

Zhang Liusun 張留孫
Zhang Lun 張輪
Zhang Panggui 章攀桂
Zhang Qiyun 張其昀
Zhang Rucheng 張如誠
Zhang Shao 張韶
Zhang Tun 張屯
Zhang Xingwu 張星五
Zhang Xinheng 張心恆
Zhang Yanyi 張延已
Zhang Yaowen 張耀文
Zhang Ying 張英
Zhang Yue 張說
Zhang Yushu 張玉書
Zhang Zichen 張紫晨
Zhang Zongyan 張宗演
Zhao Caidong 趙采董
Zhao Dongzhou 趙東周
Zhao Houan 趙厚安
Zhao Meng 趙孟
Zhao Qi 趙岐
Zhao Tingdong 趙廷棟
Zhao Yan 趙衍
Zhao Yanhua 趙延華
Zhen Shiyin 甄士隱
Zheng Xianfu 鄭獻甫
Zheng Xuan 鄭玄
Zhi Tianbao 智天豹
Zhixu Ouyi 智旭藕益
Zhou Cang 周倉
Zhou Jiaxiang 周家相
Zhou Liang 周良
Zhou Lianggong 周亮工
Zhou Lüjing 周履靖
Zhou Meiliang 周梅梁

Zhou Xuan 周宣

Zhou Yingji 周應驥

Zhu (diviner) 朱

Zhu Cheng 朱誠

Zhu Chou 祝疇

Zhu Mouxiang 諸梅香

Zhu Wenxin 朱文鑫

Zhu Xi 朱熹

Zhu Ying 朱英

Zhu Yizun 朱彝尊

Zhuang Zhongyu 莊忠域

Zi Shen 梓慎

Zigu 紫姑

Zilu 子路

Zi Wei 子韋

Zou Shijin 鄒式金

Glossary D:
Titles of Articles, Books,
Collections, and Other Documents

Note: In the interest of space, this glossary does not include characters for extremely well known sources--the dynastic histories and the Confucian classics, for instance.

Baihu tong 白虎通
Beixi ziyi 北溪字義
Bianmin tongshu 便民通書
Bowu zhi 博物志
Bu xing xiang shu bairi tong 卜星術百日通
Bushi bianzheng zitong hebian 卜筮辨正自通合編
Bushi zhengzong 卜筮正宗
Bushi zhengzong quanshu 卜筮正宗全書
Caibaixing jun qian 財帛星君籤
Cantong qi 參同契
Ceze mizhi 測字祕旨
Cezi midie 測字祕牒
Chaizi shu 拆字書
Chaizi yi 拆字意
Changle xianzhi 昌樂縣志
Changsha xianzhi 長沙縣志
Chen Duxiu wenzhang xuanbian 陳獨秀文章選編
Chongming xianzhi 崇明縣志
Chongxiu Xiangshan xianzhi 重修香山縣志
Chouren zhuan 疇人傳
Chunqiu fanlu 春秋繁露
Chunqiu zhanshi shu 春秋占筮書
Chuxiong xianzhi 楚雄縣志

409

Congshu jicheng 叢書集成
Congshu jicheng xinbian 叢書集成新編
Da liuren daquan 大六壬大全
Da Ming huidian 大明會典
Da Qing huidian 大清會典
Da Qing lüli huitong xinzuan 大清律例會通新纂
Da Qing lichao shilu 大清歷朝實錄
Da Qing shichao shengxun 大清十朝聖訓
Da Qing tongli 大清通禮
Dagongbao shidi zhoukan 大公報史地周刊
Daocang yuanliu kao 道藏源流考
Daquan qizheng tongshu 大全七政通書
Daquan tongshu 大全通書
Dazhuan 大傳
Dengfeng xianzhi 登封縣志
Dili beiyao 地理備要
Dili bianzheng 地理辨正
Dili dacheng 地理大成
Dili renxiao bidu 地理仁孝必讀
Dili sanzi jing 地理三字經
Dili wujue 地理五訣
Dili zhengzong 地理正宗
Dixue 地學
Dokyo Kenkyu bunken mokuroku 道教研究文獻目錄
Dongwan xianzhi 東莞縣志
Dongyue qian 東嶽籤
Doushu jinghua 斗數精華
Duli congchao 讀禮叢鈔
Duyi lu 讀易錄
Duyi zashuo 讀易雜說
Enshi xianzhi 恩施縣志
Ershiliu shi 二十六史
Fanshan pandu 樊山判牘
Fayan 法言
Fengjian mixin shi zenma huishi 封建迷信是怎麼回事

Fengshui ershu xingqi leize 風水二書形氣類則

Fengshui quhuo 風水袪惑

Fengshui yishu 風水一書

Fuji mixin di yanjiu 扶箕 (乩) 迷信底研究

Fuping xianzhi 富平縣志

Fuyang xianzhi 富陽縣志

Fuzhou quanshu 符咒全書

Gongyuan yijiubaba nian wuchen lishu 公元一九八八年戊辰曆書

Guan shengdi jun lingqian 關聖帝君靈籤

Guan shengdi jun wanying lingqian 關聖帝君萬應靈籤

Guandi qian 關帝籤

Guanding jing 灌頂經

Guangxian tang daquan tongshu 廣賢堂大全通書

Guanshang kuailan 官商快覽

Guanyin qian 觀音籤

Guanyu Taiping tianguo di lifa 關於太平天國的曆法

Guidong xianzhi 桂東縣志

Gujin mingren mingjian 古今名人命鑑

Gujin tushu jicheng (See Qinding gujin tushu jicheng)

Hanlong jing 撼龍經

Hanyang fuzhi 漢陽府志

Hexian xianzhi 賀縣縣志

Hiroshima daigaku bungakubu kiyo 広島大學文學部紀要

Honglou meng 紅樓夢

Honglou meng bashi hui jiaoben 紅樓夢八十回校本

Huan Tian tushuo xubian 圜天圖說續編

Huandu woshu shi laoren ziding nianpu 還讀我書室老人手訂年譜

Huang Daxian lingqian 黃大仙靈籤

Huang Qing jingjie xubian 皇清經解續編

Huangchao jingshi wenbian 皇朝經世文編

Huangchao jingshi wenbian xubian 皇朝經世文編續編

Huangchao jingshi wenxubian 皇朝經世文續編

Huangchao xu wenxian tongkao 皇朝續文獻通考

Huangchao zhengdian leizuan 皇朝政典類纂

Huangdi changliu zhanmeng 黃帝長柳占夢

Huangdi neijing 黃帝內經
Huangdi neijing taisu 黃帝內經太素宅經
Huangdi zhaijing 黃帝宅經
Huangji jingshi shu 皇極經世書
Huangpo xianzhi 黃陂縣志
Huato qian 華陀籤
Jiali dacheng 家禮大成
Jiali huitong 家禮會通
Jiali quanshu 家禮全書
Jiali tieshi jicheng 家禮帖式集成
Jiaozeng Zhouyi yijie 校增周易易解
Jieziyuan huazhuan 芥子園畫傳
Jin Ping Mei 金瓶梅
Jing Fang Yi zazhan tiaoli fa 京房易雜占條例法
Jingdian shiwen 經典釋文
Jinghua yuan 鏡花緣
Jinshan xianzhi 金山縣志
Jinsi lu 近思錄
Jiqing tang xingzong qizheng 吉慶堂星宗七政
Jiuming qiyuan 九命奇冤
Jixiang ruyi tongshu 吉祥如意通書
Kangxi qiju zhu 康熙起居注
Kanyu cidian 堪輿辭典
Kanyu zhinan 堪輿指南
Ledao tang wenchao 樂道堂文鈔
Li Xuzhong mingshu 李虛中命書
Liang Han shiliu jia Yizhu chanwei 兩漢十六家易注闡微
Liang Han Yixue shi 兩漢易學史
Liaoyang xianzhi 遼陽縣志
Liben sishiqi zhong 曆本四十七種
Lidai shehui fengsu shiwu kao 歷代社會風俗事物考
Lifa tongzhi 曆法通志
Lingqi jing 靈棋經
Lingshu jing 靈樞經
Linyi xianzhi 臨沂縣志

Lishu gangmu 禮書綱目

Liuren daquan 六壬大全

Liwen tang zouji tongshu 利文堂諏吉通書

Lixue huitong 曆學會通

Lixue yiwen 曆學疑問

Liyi bianlan 禮儀便覽

Longling xianzhi 龍陵縣志

Lun Shuihudi Qinjian Mawangdui baishu zhong di shushu shu 論睡虎地秦簡與馬王堆帛書中的數術書

Lunheng 論衡

Luojing jie 羅經解

Luquan xianzhi 祿勸縣志

Maguan xianzhi 馬關縣志

Mei Wuan lisuan quanshu 梅勿庵曆算全書

Meihua shi 梅花詩

Mengshu 夢書

Mengzhan leikao 夢占類考

Mengzhan yizhi 夢占逸旨

Mingli tanyuan 命理探原

Mingpu 命譜

Mingshu (see Li Xuzhong mingshu)

Minli buzhu jieshuo 民曆補註解說

Mixin wu guo erqian nian 迷信誤國二千年

Mixin yu chuanshuo 迷信與傳說

Mixin yu kexue 迷信與科學

Mizhuan shuilong jing 祕傳水龍經

Nanjing 難經

Nanle xianzhi 南樂縣志

Naxi xianzhi 納溪縣志

Neixiang xianzhi 內鄉縣志

Nianpu congshu 年譜叢書

Ning'an (Songjiang) xianzhi 寧安 (松江) 縣志

Pingyuan xianzhi 平原縣志

Poxie xiangbian 破邪詳辨

Qianfu lun 潛夫論

Qianfu lun jian jiaozheng 潛夫論箋校正
Qianjiang xianzhi 潛江縣志
Qiankun wannian ge 乾坤萬年歌
Qianyi 籤易
Qimen dunjia 奇門遁甲
Qinding gujin tushu jicheng 欽定古今圖書集成
Qinding Libu zeli 欽定禮部則例
Qinding rixia jiuwen kao 欽定日下舊聞考
Qinding siku quanshu 欽定四庫全書
Qinding siku quanshu zongmu 欽定四庫全書總目
Qinding xieji bianfang shu 欽定協紀辨方書
Qinding xingli kaoyuan 欽定星歷考原
Qinding xuanze lishu 欽定選擇曆書
Qingbai leichao 清稗類鈔
Qingji yige jingguan di shenghuo 清季一個京官的生活史
Qixian zhi 杞縣志
Qiyao rang zai jue 七曜攘災訣
Quancheng jiyao 勸懲輯要
Renwu fengsu zhidu congtan 人物風俗制度叢談
Rixia jiuwen kao (See Qinding rixia jiuwen kao)
Riyong bianlan 日用便覽
Riyong jifu tongshu 日用集福通書
Rulin waishi 儒林外史
San Fo yingjie tongguan tongshu 三佛應劫統觀通書
Sancai fami 三才發秘
Sancai tuhui 三才圖會
Sanming tonghui 三命通會
Shaobing ge 燒餅歌
Shengdi lingqian 聖帝靈籤
Shengyu guangxun 聖諭廣訓
Shenshi Dili bianzheng jueyao 沈氏地理辨正抉要
Shenxiang quanbian 神相全編
Shier chen kao 十二辰考
Shier zhang fa 十二杖法
Shilu (See Da Qing lichao shilu)

Shina minzoku shi 支那民俗志

Shincho Ekigaku kanken 清朝易學管見

Shishuo xinyu 世說新語

Shixian li 時憲曆

Shixian shu 時憲書

Shixue nianbao 史學年報

Shu bushi xingxiang xue 述卜筮星相學

Shuihu zhuan 水滸傳

Shuilu zongguan lingqian 水陸總管靈籤

Shunning xianzhi 順寧縣志

Shuoming 說命

Shuowen jiezi 說文解字

Sihui xianzhi 四會縣志

Siku quanshu (See Qinding siku quanshu)

Siku quanshu zhenben 四庫全書珍本

Siku quanshu zongmu (See Qinding siku quanshu zongmu)

Siku quanshu zongmu tiyao 四庫全書總目提要

Soushen ji 搜神記

Suanming jue 算命訣

Suichang xianzhi 遂昌縣志

Suichu tang Yilun 遂初堂易論

Suixu zongkao quanji 歲序總考全集

Suzhou fuzhi 蘇州府志

Taiping tianguo 太平天國

Taiping tianguo genghao [sic] sannian xinli 太平天國庚好三年新曆

Taiping tianguo lifa kao 太平天國曆法考

Taiping yulan 太平御覽

Taisu mofa 太素脈法

Taiwan min menmei bagua pai shouhu gongyong di yanjiu 臺灣民宅門楣八卦牌守護功用的研究

Taixuan jing 太玄經

Tan Tian shuoming 談天說命

Tang Song yinyang wuxing lunji 唐宋陰陽五行論集

Taoyuan xianzhi 桃源縣志

Tianbu zhenyuan 天步真原

Tianhou qian 天后籤

Tianwen zhanyan 天文占驗

Tongyi tang wenji 通義堂文集

Tudi qian 土地籤

Tui Yi shimo 推易始末

Tuibei tu 推背圖

Tuibu fajie 推步法解

Tushu jicheng (see Qinding gujin tushu jicheng)

Wanbao quanshu 萬寶全書

Wangtui jixiong bian 妄推吉凶辯

Wangze bian 妄擇辯

Wannian li 萬年曆

Wannian shu 萬年書

Wen Wenzhong gong ziting nianpu 文文忠公自訂年譜

Weng Tonghe riji paiyinben 翁同龢日記排印本

Wenxin diaolong 文心雕龍

Wenzhen gong nianpu 文貞公年譜

Wuchang xianzhi 武昌縣志

Wuhe xianzhi 五河縣志

Wuli tongkao 五禮通考

Wusheng Guandi lingqian 武聖關帝靈籤

Wushu zhanbu quanshu 五術占卜全書

Wuxing dayi 五行大義

Wuxue lu 吾學錄

Xian Qin Han Wei Yili shuping 先秦漢魏易例述評

Xiang'er jing 相兒經

Xiangji beiyao (see Xinzeng xiangji beiyao tongshu)

Xiangmeng Yuxia ji 詳夢玉匣記

Xiangshan xianzhi 香山縣志

Xiangxiang Zengshi wenxian 湘鄉曾氏文獻

Xiangyu shu 相雨書

Xiantian bagua tu 先天八卦圖

Xiao'an xinfa 曉庵新法

Xieji bianfang shu (see Qinding xieji bianfang shu)

Xin mingli tanyuan 新命理探原

Xin qingnian 新青年

Xin tongshu 新通書

Xinbian zhuzi jicheng 新編諸子集成

Xinding zhi mingxin fa 新訂指明心法

Xinfa biaoyi 新法表異

Xinfa suanshu 新法算書

Xingli kaoyuan (see Qinding xingli kaoyuan)

Xingli ziyi 性理字義

Xingping huihai 星平會海

Xingping yaojue bainian jing 星平要訣百年經

Xingshen xiangfa 形神相法

Xingxiang xueshu conglun 星相學術叢論

Xingzong 星宗

Xinzeng xiangji beiyao tongshu 新增象吉備要通書

Xiuyao jing 宿曜經

Xiyou ji 西游記

Xuanze tianjing 選擇天鏡

Xuanze tongshu 選擇通書

Xuanze zhengzong 選擇正宗

Xueli 學禮

Xuelin 學林

Xuxiu Shunning fuzhi gao 續修順寧府志稿

Yan Fu ji 嚴復集

Yangzhai 陽宅

Yangzhai cuoyao 陽宅撮要

Yangzhai jing 陽宅經

Yangzhai sanyao 陽宅三要

Yangzhai shishu 陽宅十書

Yanshi jiaxun 顏氏家訓

Yesuhui shi dui Zhongguo chuantong xingzhan shushu di taidu 耶穌會士對中國傳統星占術數的態度

Yi Hanxue 易漢學

Yicheng xianzhi 宜城縣志

Yidao rumen 易道入門

Yidu kaoyi 易讀考異

Yihan xianzhi 宜漢縣志
Yijing bushi quanshu 易經卜筮全書
Yijing dawen 易經答問
Yijing jicheng 易經集成
Yijing Laizhu tujie 易經來注圖解
Yijing yanjiu 易經研究
Yilin 易林
Yinyang xue 陰陽學
Yisi nian Yingxue zhai fenlei guanshang bianlan qibai zhong 乙巳年映雪齋
分類官商便覽七百種
Yitu mingbian 易圖明辨
Yiwei Qianzuodu 易緯乾鑿度
Yixue qimeng 易學啟蒙
Yongnian xianzhi 永年縣志
Yongning tongshu 永寧通書
Yongxin xianzhi 永新縣志
Yunmeng Qinjian rishu 雲夢秦簡日書
Yunmeng Qinjian rishu yanjiu 雲夢秦簡日書研究
Yunqi zhanhou 運氣占候
Yuxia ji guangji 玉匣記廣記
Zangjing 葬經
Zangjing yi 葬經翼
Zangshu 葬書
Zangtu 葬圖
Zaoming qieyao 造命挈要
Zeng Wenzheng gong quanji 曾文正公全集
Zengbu bushi zhengzong 增補卜筮正宗
Zengbu qimeng tianji duan Yi daquan 增補啟蒙天機斷易大全
Zengbu xiangji beiyao tongshu 增補象吉備要通書
Zhanbu di yuanliu 占卜的源流
Zhancha shano yebao jing 占察善惡業報經
Zhanyan lu 占驗錄
Zhengshuo kao 正朔考
Zhili yuanqi 治曆緣起
Zhiming shu Hanxue 知命術漢學

Zhong Xi xiangren tanyuan 中西相人探源
Zhongguo di zhihui 中國的智慧
Zhongguo gudai zhi xingsui jinian 中國古代之星歲紀年
Zhongguo jin sanbai nian xueshu shi 中國近三百年學術史
Zhongguo jindai sixiang shilun 中國近代思想史論
Zhongguo lidai buren zhuan 中國歷代卜人傳
Zhongguo lidai tianzai renhuo biao 中國歷代天災人禍表
Zhongguo mingxiang zheli xueshu jiangyi 中國命相哲理學術講義
Zhongguo minjian xinyang lunji 中國民間信仰論集
Zhongguo minsu shihua 中國民俗史話
Zhongguo quanguo fengsu zhi 中國全國風俗志
Zhongguo shiji fengtu congshu 中國史蹟風土叢書
Zhongguo wenhua gailun 中國文化概論
Zhongguo wushu 中國巫術
Zhongguo zhexue sixiang shi: Qingdai pian 中國哲學思想史：清代篇
Zhongguoren di xingge: keji zonghexing di taolun 中國人的性格科際綜
合性的討論
Zhongshi Yi 仲氏易
Zhongwen dacidian 中文大辭典
Zhougong jiemeng 周公解夢
Zhougong jiemeng quanshu 周公解夢全書
Zhouyi benyi 周易本義
Zhouyi bianlan 周易便覽
Zhouyi cantong qi 周易參同契
Zhouyi dawen 周易答問
Zhouyi daxiang jie 周易大象解
Zhouyi gujing tongshuo 周易古經通說
Zhouyi jiegu 周易解故
Zhouyi jijie 周易集解
Zhouyi jijie bujian 周易集解補箋
Zhouyi jijie bushi 周易集解補釋
Zhouyi jijie zuanshu 周易集解纂疏
Zhouyi kao 周易考
Zhouyi lueli 周易略例
Zhouyi neizhuan fali 周易內傳發例

Zhouyi shiyi 周易拾遺
Zhouyi shu 周易述
Zhouyi shubu 周易述補
Zhouyi shuwen 周易述聞
Zhouyi tanyuan 周易探源
Zhouyi tongyi 周易通義
Zhouyi xue 周易學
Zhouyi yaowu dangming 周易爻物當名
Zhouyi yijie 周易易解
Zhouyi zhangju zhengyi 周易章句證異
Zhouyi zhengyi 周易正義
Zhouyi zhezhong 周易折中
Zhouyi zongheng lu 周易縱橫錄
Zhuzi jiali 朱子家禮
Zhuzi jicheng 朱子集成
Zi hanyan 子罕言
Zichu 字觸
Zongzheng buyi 宗正卜易
Zouji bianlan 諏吉便覽
Zouji tongshu 諏吉通書

About the Book and Author

Fortune-tellers and Philosophers is the first scholarly book that provides a comprehensive analysis of Chinese divination as a means of organizing and interpreting "reality." Richard Smith examines a wide variety of mantic techniques—from the use of the hallowed *Yijing* (Classic of Changes) to such popular practices as siting (geomancy), astrology, numerology, physiognomy, the analysis of written characters, meteorological divination, mediumistic prognostication (including spirit-writing), and dream interpretation. As he explains the pervasiveness and tenacity of divination in China, the author explores not only the connections between various mantic techniques but also the relationship between divination and other facets of Chinese culture, including philosophy, science, and medicine. He discusses the symbolism of divination, its aesthetics, its ritual aspects, and its psychological and social significance, pointing out that in traditional China divination helped order the future, just as history helped order the past and rituals helped order the present. The book concludes with a discussion of divination in twentieth-century China and offers comparative reflections and suggestions for further cross-cultural research.

Richard J. Smith is professor of history at Rice University and adjunct professor at the Center for Asian Studies at the University of Texas–Austin.

Index

Li, Gong, 70, 71
Li, Guangdi, 98, 112, 114–115, 246, 251,
    341(n185)
Li, Hongzhang, 70, 112, 211, 213, 215,
    312(n88)
Li, Keqi, 71
Li, Liuming, 200
Li Mengqun, 215
Li, Mi, 251
Li, Mu, 40
Li, Qingzhi, 154
Li, Sanyang, 138
Li, Shixu, 212
Li, Suzhen, 215
Li, Taichu, 215
Li, Wei, 214
Li, Weixin, 212
Li, Wentian, 148, 188
Li, Xingyu, 153
Li, Xuan, 39, 200
Li, Xupin, 227
Li, Xuzhong, 40, 177–178, 209
Li, Yanshi, 56
Li, Yiqing, 155
Li, Youlong, 154
Li, Yuanhong, 217
Li, Yuhong, 229
Li, Zicheng, 49, 216, 332(n170)
Li, Zonghui, 157
Liang, Qichao, 97, 273
Liang, Tianlai, 169
Liao, Chunshan, 201
Libu. *See* Board of Ritual
Liezi, 247
Lin, Lan, 205
Lin, Qing, 87, 215
Lin, Sen, 202
Lin, Xiangru, 236
Ling, Guixing, 169
Ling, Kun, 216
Lingqian. *See* Spiritual sticks
Literati networks, 260, 342(n3)
Litigation, 166–169, 212–213, 215, 216,
    231. *See also* Geomancy,
    disruptiveness of; Law
Liu, An, 33
Liu, Bingzhong, 44
Liu, Bowen. *See* Liu Ji
Liu, Erhuan, 214
Liu, Heng, 208
Liu, Ji, 217

Liu, Kunyi, 218
Liu, Longguang, 116–117
Liu, Lu, 200
Liu, Lü, 211, 213
Liu, Mingchuan, 213
Liu, Mouji, 174
Liu, Shaoqi, 276
Liu, Shijun, 153
Liu, Songnian, 121
Liu, Wanchong, 232
Liu, Xiandi, 157
Liu, Xianjia, 154
Liu, Xie, 123
Liu, Yiming, 121
Liu, Yusong, 182
Liu, Zhong, 215
Lodges, 34, 63 ff., 135–136, 175, 219,
    235, 300(n58)
    listed in sequence, 373–374.
    See also Asterisms; Astrology;
    Cosmology; Stars
Logic, xi, 10, 24–25, 26–27, 41, 51, 105–
    106, 121–122, 126–127, 188, 203,
    235, 251 ff., 255, 257, 265, 283–285,
    313(n127), 319(n95), 328(n65),
    348(n120). *See also* Language; Word
    analysis
Lou, Yu, 153
Lu, Deming, 97
Lu, Jun, 210
Lu, Longji, 248
Lu, Qimeng, 216
Lu, Shiyi, 72, 186
Lu, Yixian, 250
Lu, Zuqian, 41
Lü, Cai, 40, 72, 73, 88
Lü, Dongbin, 228, 239
Lü, Gong, 116
Lü, Kun, 46
Lunar lodges. *See* Lodges
Luo, Hao, 209
Luo, Shijing, 115
Luo, Xizhu, 212
Luopan. *See* Compass
Luoshu, 31, 59–62, 79, 96, 125, 133, 135,
    302(n99)
Lu Xun, 259, 267

Ma, Bailiang, 154
Ma, Jinzhi, 116
Ma, Rong, 33